"'good!'

'evil!'

Outmoded concepts for an antique age. Can't you see?

There is no good, there is no evil in our new world!

"Look at us! Are we not *proof* that there is no good, no

evil, no truth, no reason? Are we not proof that the

universe is a drooling idiot with no fashion sense?"

— from "Nowhere Man"

DOOM PATROL

writer	**grant morrison**
penciller	**richard case**
inker	**john nyberg**
colorist	**daniel vozzo**
letterers	**john workman**
	jay dubb

original series covers
simon bisley

the painting that ate paris

Karen Berger VP-Executive Editor   **Mark Waid, Art Young** Editors-original series   **Scott Nybakken** Editor-collected edition
Robbin Brosterman Senior Art Director   **Paul Levitz** President & Publisher   **Georg Brewer** VP-Design & Retail Product
Development   **Richard Bruning** Senior VP-Creative Director   **Patrick Caldon** Senior VP-Finance & Operations **Chris Caramalis**
VP-Finance   **Terri Cunningham** VP-Managing Editor   **Dan DiDio** VP-Editorial   **Alison Gill** VP-Manufacturing   **Rich Johnson**
VP-Book Trade Sales   **Hank Kanalz** VP-General Manager, WildStorm   **Lillian Laserson** Senior VP & General Counsel
Jim Lee Editorial Director-WildStorm **David McKillips** VP-Advertising & Custom Publishing **John Nee** VP-Business Development
Gregory Noveck Senior VP-Creative Affairs **Cheryl Rubin** Senior VP-Brand Management **Bob Wayne** VP-Sales & Marketing

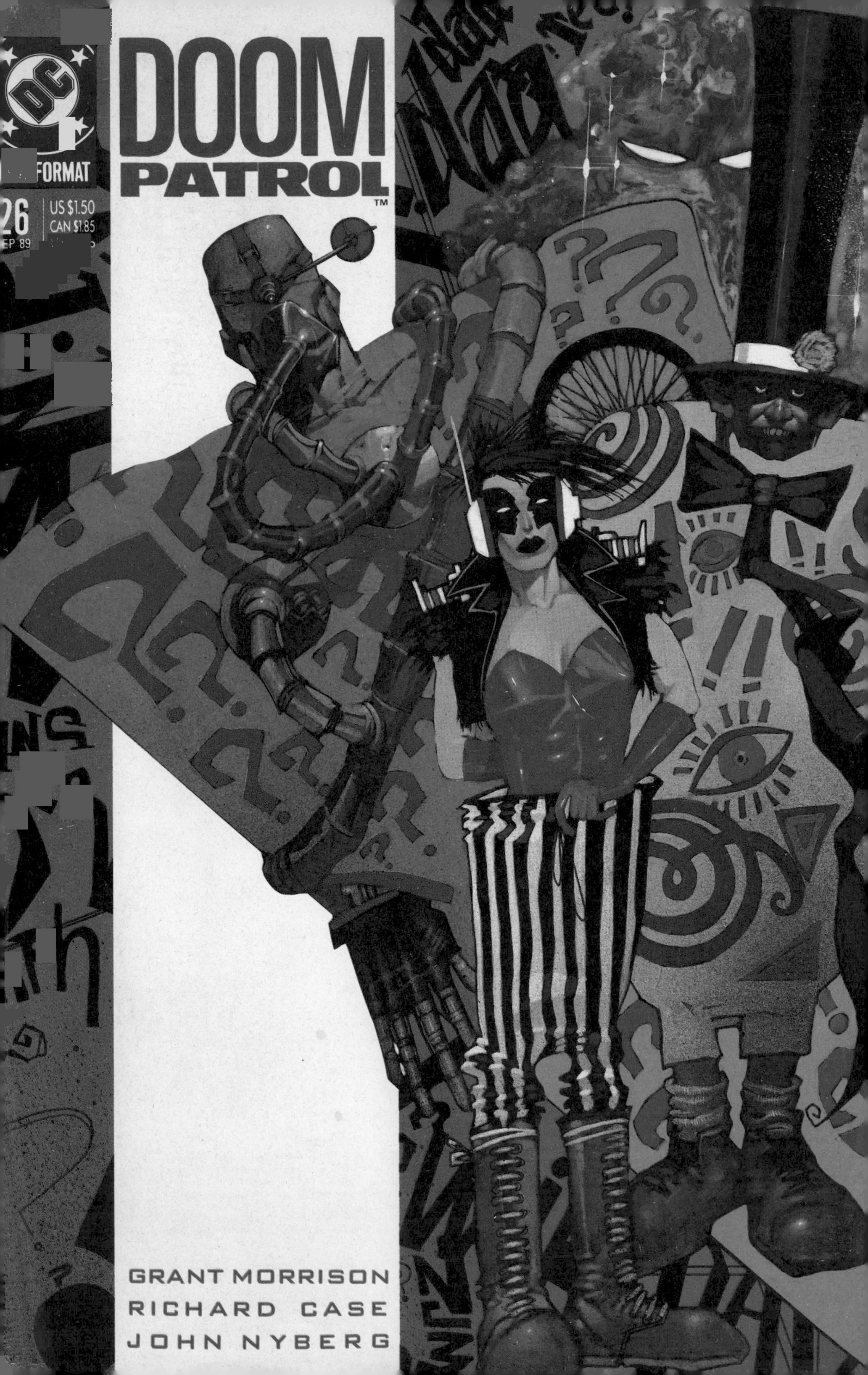
DC
DOOM
PATROL
™
FORMAT
26
US $1.50
CAN $1.85
EP 89
GRANT MORRISON
RICHARD CASE
JOHN NYBERG

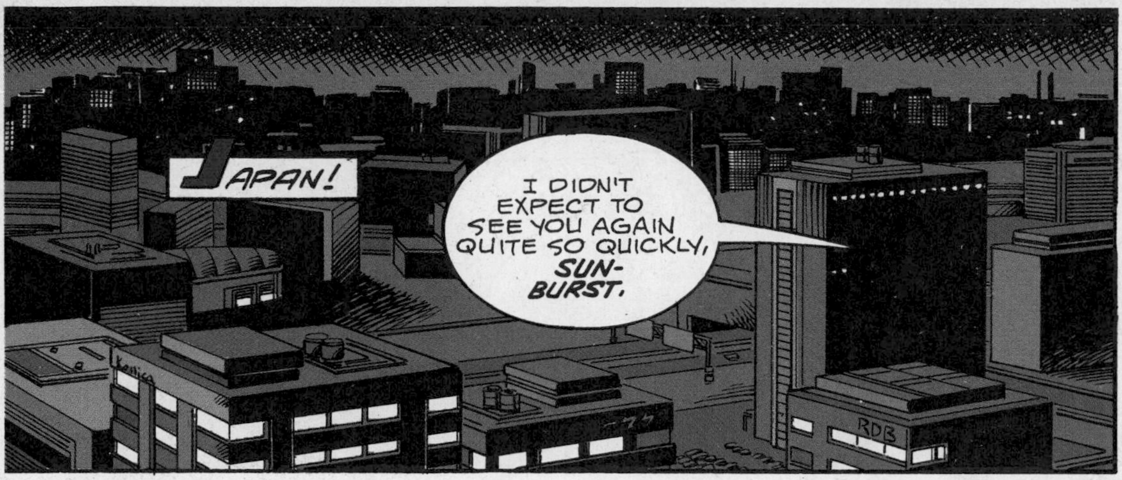
JAPAN!
I DIDN'T EXPECT TO SEE YOU AGAIN QUITE SO QUICKLY, SUN-BURST.

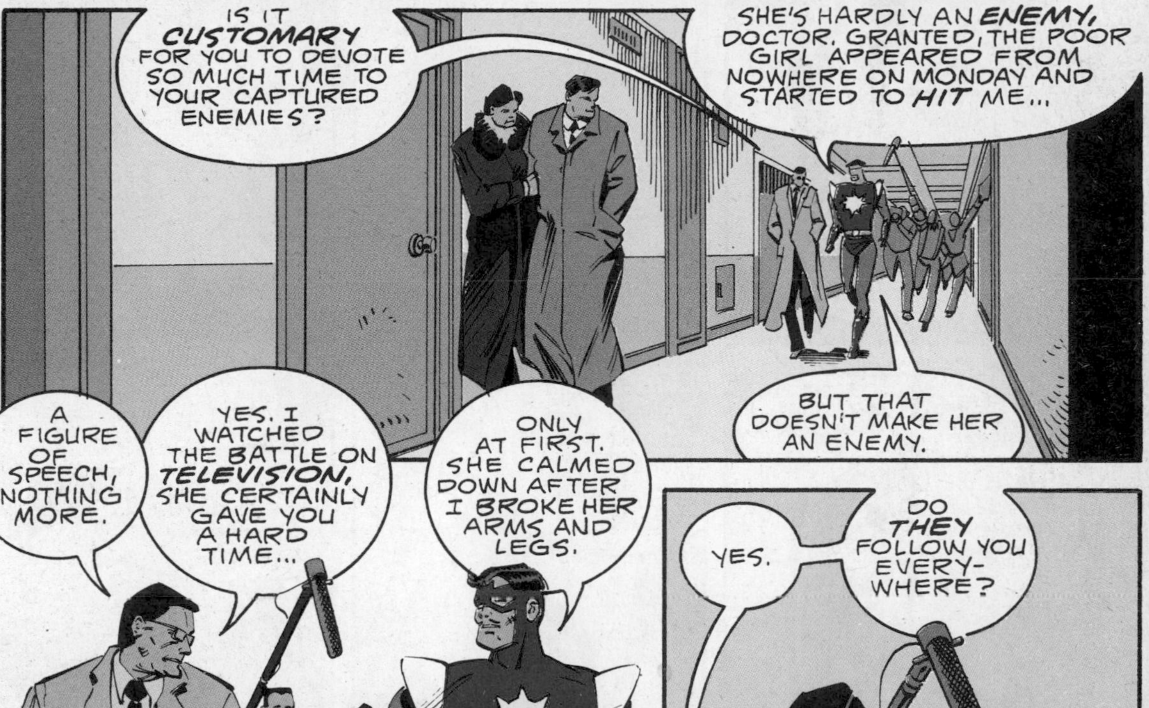
IS IT CUSTOMARY FOR YOU TO DEVOTE SO MUCH TIME TO YOUR CAPTURED ENEMIES?
SHE'S HARDLY AN ENEMY, DOCTOR. GRANTED, THE POOR GIRL APPEARED FROM NOWHERE ON MONDAY AND STARTED TO HIT ME...
BUT THAT DOESN'T MAKE HER AN ENEMY.

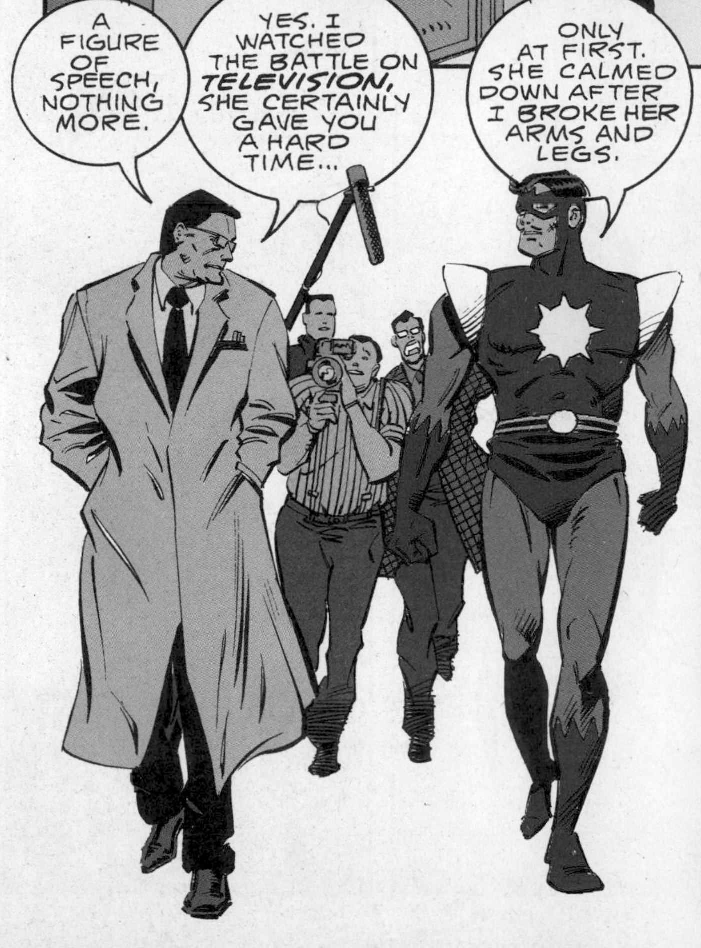
A FIGURE OF SPEECH, NOTHING MORE.
YES. I WATCHED THE BATTLE ON TELEVISION, SHE CERTAINLY GAVE YOU A HARD TIME...
ONLY AT FIRST. SHE CALMED DOWN AFTER I BROKE HER ARMS AND LEGS.

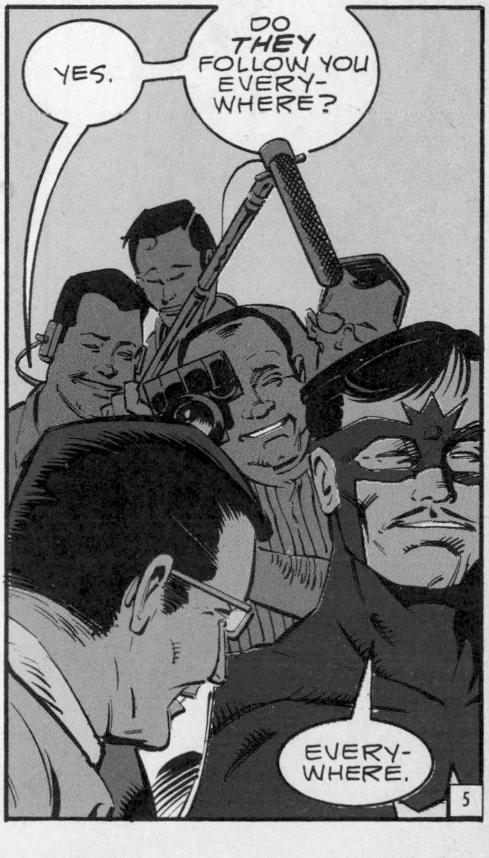
DO THEY FOLLOW YOU EVERY-WHERE?
YES.
EVERY-WHERE.

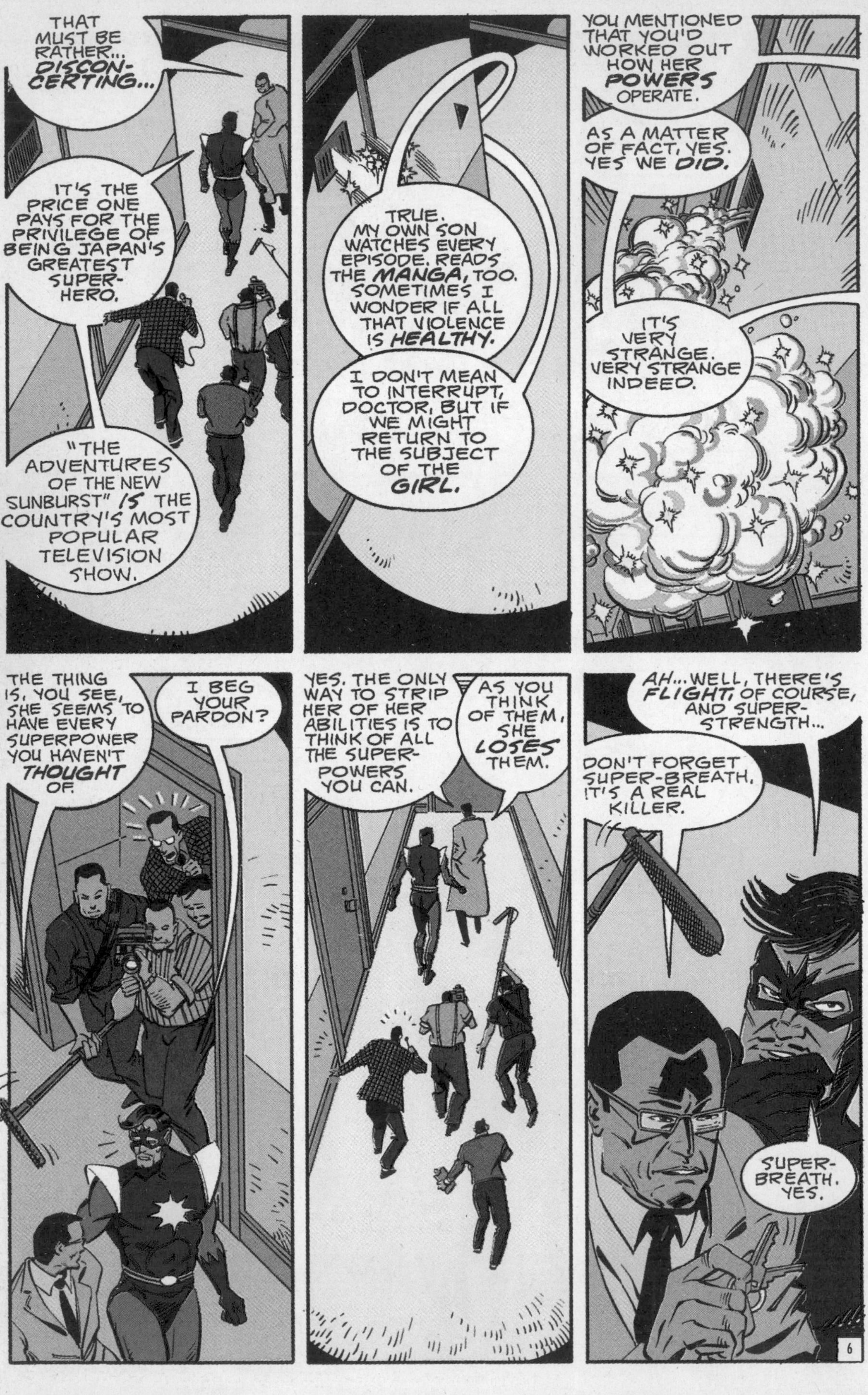
THAT MUST BE RATHER... DISCONCERTING...
IT'S THE PRICE ONE PAYS FOR THE PRIVILEGE OF BEING JAPAN'S GREATEST SUPER-HERO.
"THE ADVENTURES OF THE NEW SUNBURST" IS THE COUNTRY'S MOST POPULAR TELEVISION SHOW.
TRUE. MY OWN SON WATCHES EVERY EPISODE. READS THE MANGA, TOO. SOMETIMES I WONDER IF ALL THAT VIOLENCE IS HEALTHY.
I DON'T MEAN TO INTERRUPT, DOCTOR, BUT IF WE MIGHT RETURN TO THE SUBJECT OF THE GIRL.
YOU MENTIONED THAT YOU'D WORKED OUT HOW HER POWERS OPERATE.
AS A MATTER OF FACT, YES. YES WE DID.
IT'S VERY STRANGE. VERY STRANGE INDEED.
THE THING IS, YOU SEE, SHE SEEMS TO HAVE EVERY SUPERPOWER YOU HAVEN'T THOUGHT OF.
I BEG YOUR PARDON?
YES. THE ONLY WAY TO STRIP HER OF HER ABILITIES IS TO THINK OF ALL THE SUPER-POWERS YOU CAN.
AS YOU THINK OF THEM, SHE LOSES THEM.
AH...WELL, THERE'S FLIGHT, OF COURSE, AND SUPER-STRENGTH...
DON'T FORGET SUPER-BREATH. IT'S A REAL KILLER.
SUPER-BREATH. YES.
6

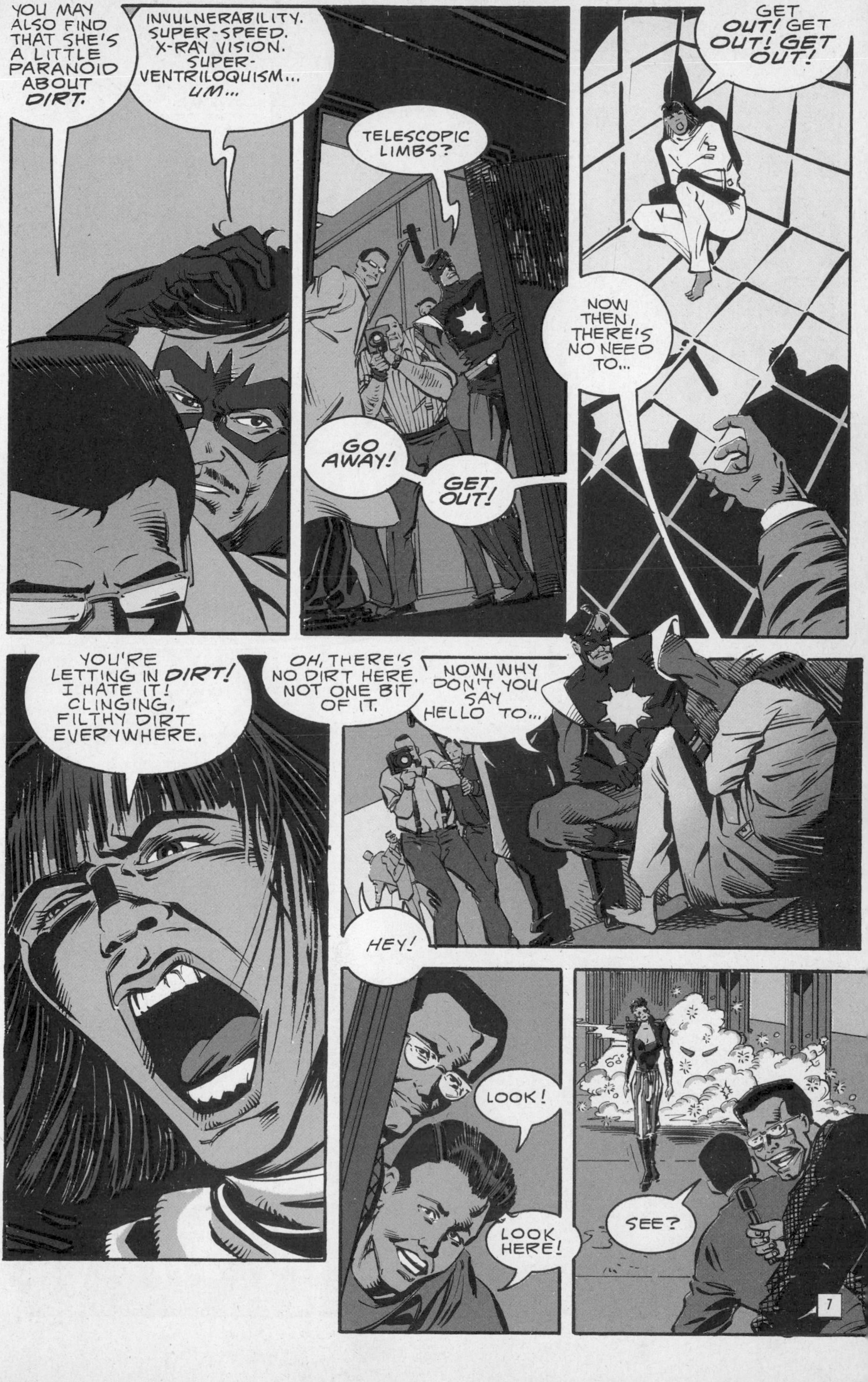
YOU MAY ALSO FIND THAT SHE'S A LITTLE PARANOID ABOUT DIRT.
INVULNERABILITY. SUPER-SPEED. X-RAY VISION. SUPER-VENTRILOQUISM... UM...
TELESCOPIC LIMBS?
GO AWAY!
GET OUT!
GET OUT! GET OUT! GET OUT!
NOW THEN, THERE'S NO NEED TO...
YOU'RE LETTING IN DIRT! I HATE IT! CLINGING, FILTHY DIRT EVERYWHERE.
OH, THERE'S NO DIRT HERE. NOT ONE BIT OF IT.
NOW, WHY DON'T YOU SAY HELLO TO...
HEY!
LOOK!
LOOK HERE!
SEE?

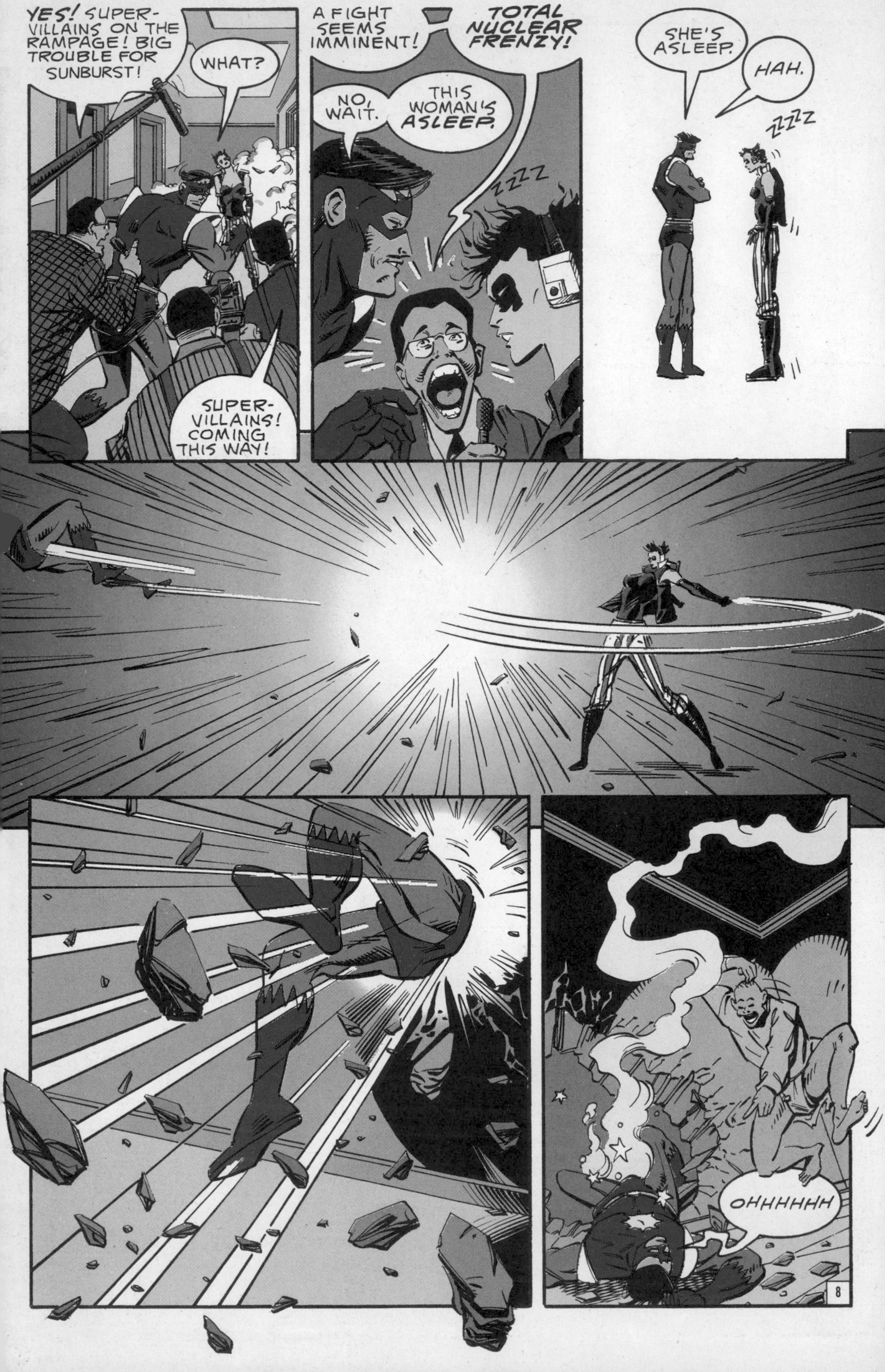

YES! SUPER-VILLAINS ON THE RAMPAGE! BIG TROUBLE FOR SUNBURST!
WHAT?
SUPER-VILLAINS! COMING THIS WAY!
A FIGHT SEEMS IMMINENT!
TOTAL NUCLEAR FRENZY!
NO, WAIT.
THIS WOMAN'S ASLEEP.
ZZZZ
SHE'S ASLEEP.
HAH.
ZZZZ
OHHHHHH

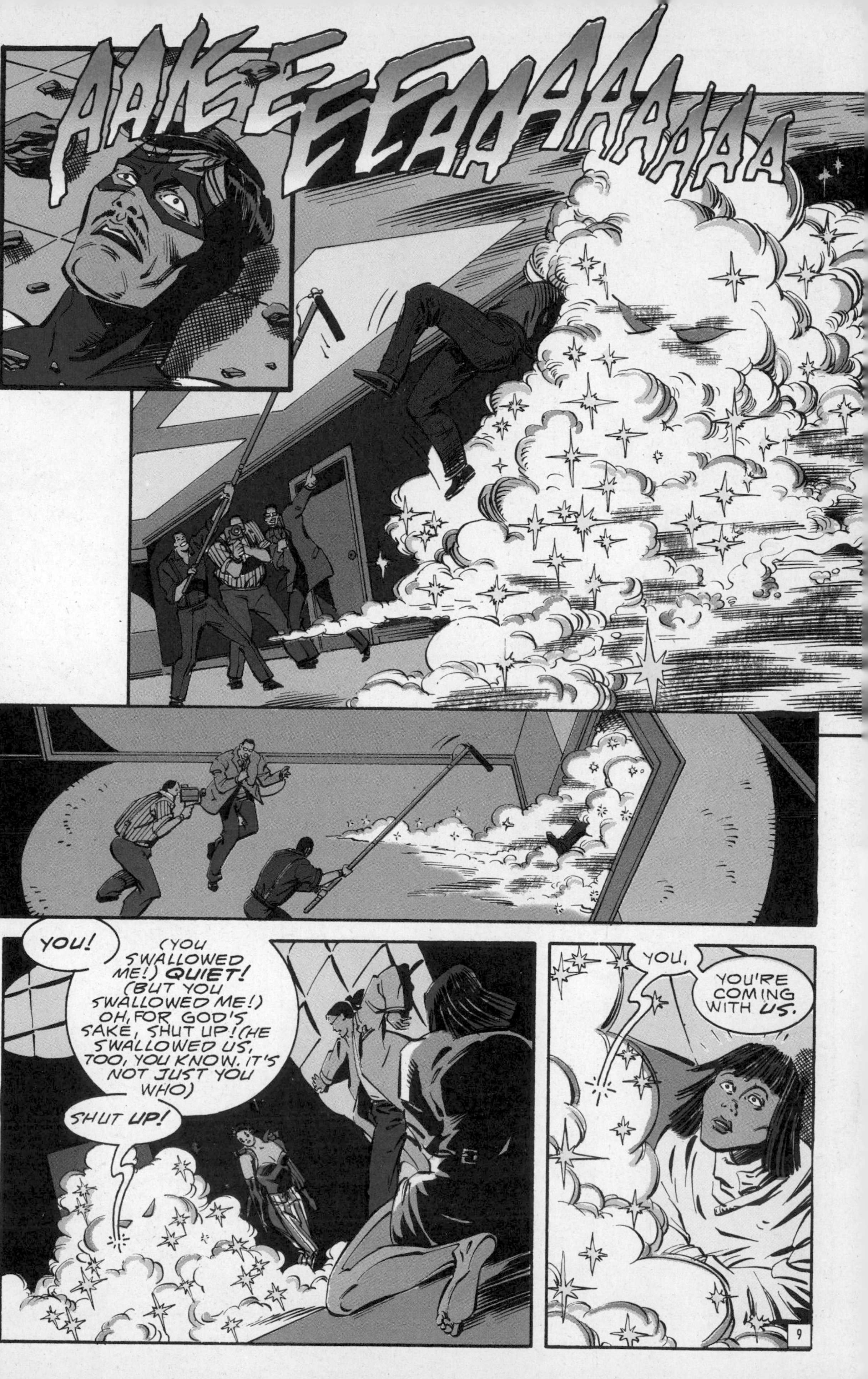
AAKSEEEAAAAAAAAA
YOU!
(YOU SWALLOWED ME!) QUIET! (BUT YOU SWALLOWED ME!) OH, FOR GOD'S SAKE, SHUT UP! (HE SWALLOWED US, TOO, YOU KNOW. IT'S NOT JUST YOU WHO)
SHUT UP!
YOU.
YOU'RE COMING WITH US.

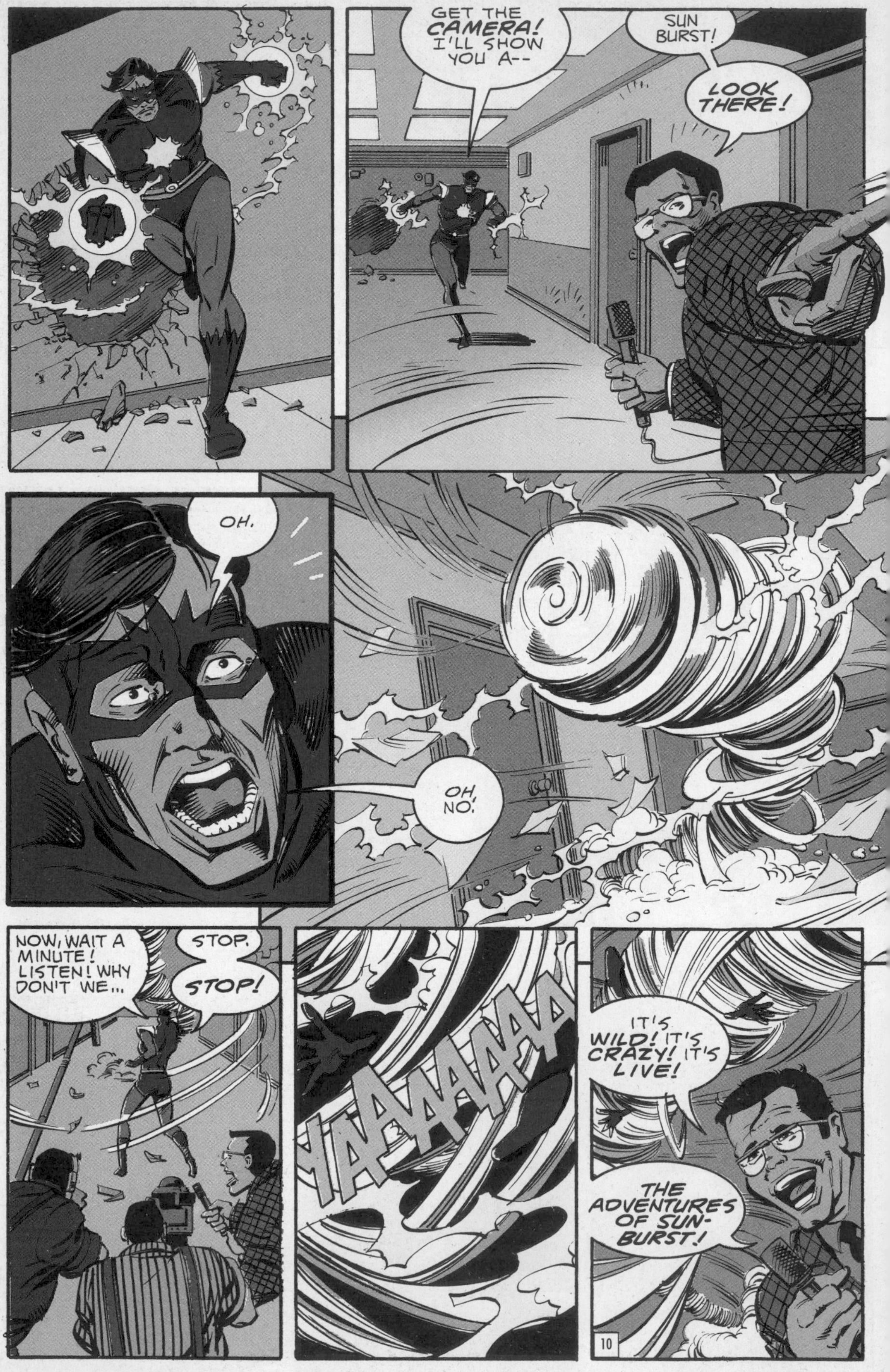
GET THE CAMERA! I'LL SHOW YOU A--
SUN BURST!
LOOK THERE!
OH.
OH, NO.
NOW, WAIT A MINUTE! LISTEN! WHY DON'T WE...
STOP.
STOP!
YAAAAAAA
IT'S WILD! IT'S CRAZY! IT'S LIVE!
THE ADVENTURES OF SUN-BURST!

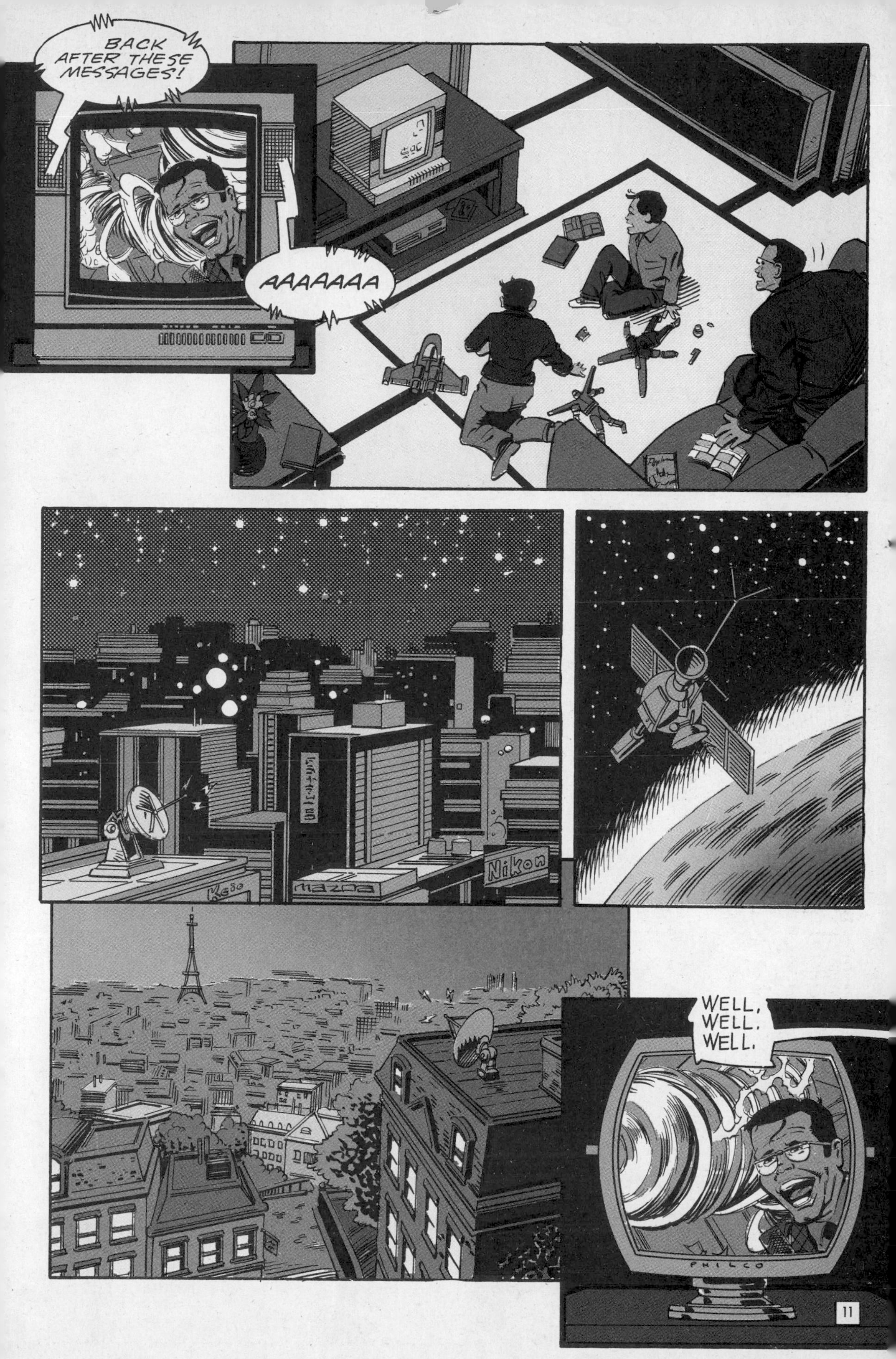

BACK AFTER THESE MESSAGES!
AAAAAAA
mazda
Nikon
WELL, WELL. WELL.
PHILCO

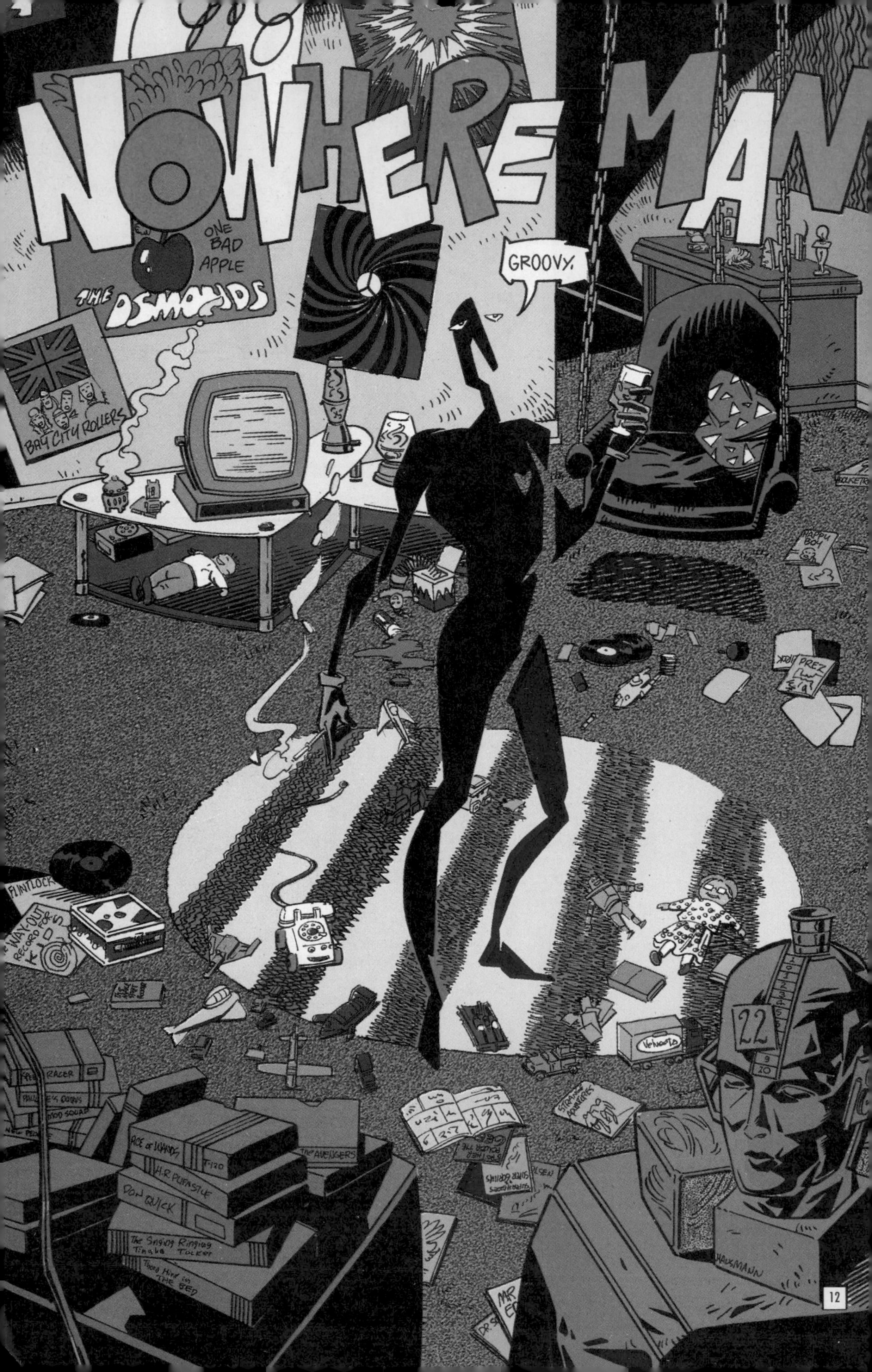
NOWHERE MAN
GROOVY.
ONE BAD APPLE
THE OSMONDS
BAY CITY ROLLERS
HAPPY BOY
PREZ
FLINTLOCK
ACE of WANDS
THE AVENGERS
H.R. PUFNSTUF
DON QUICK
22
HAUSMANN

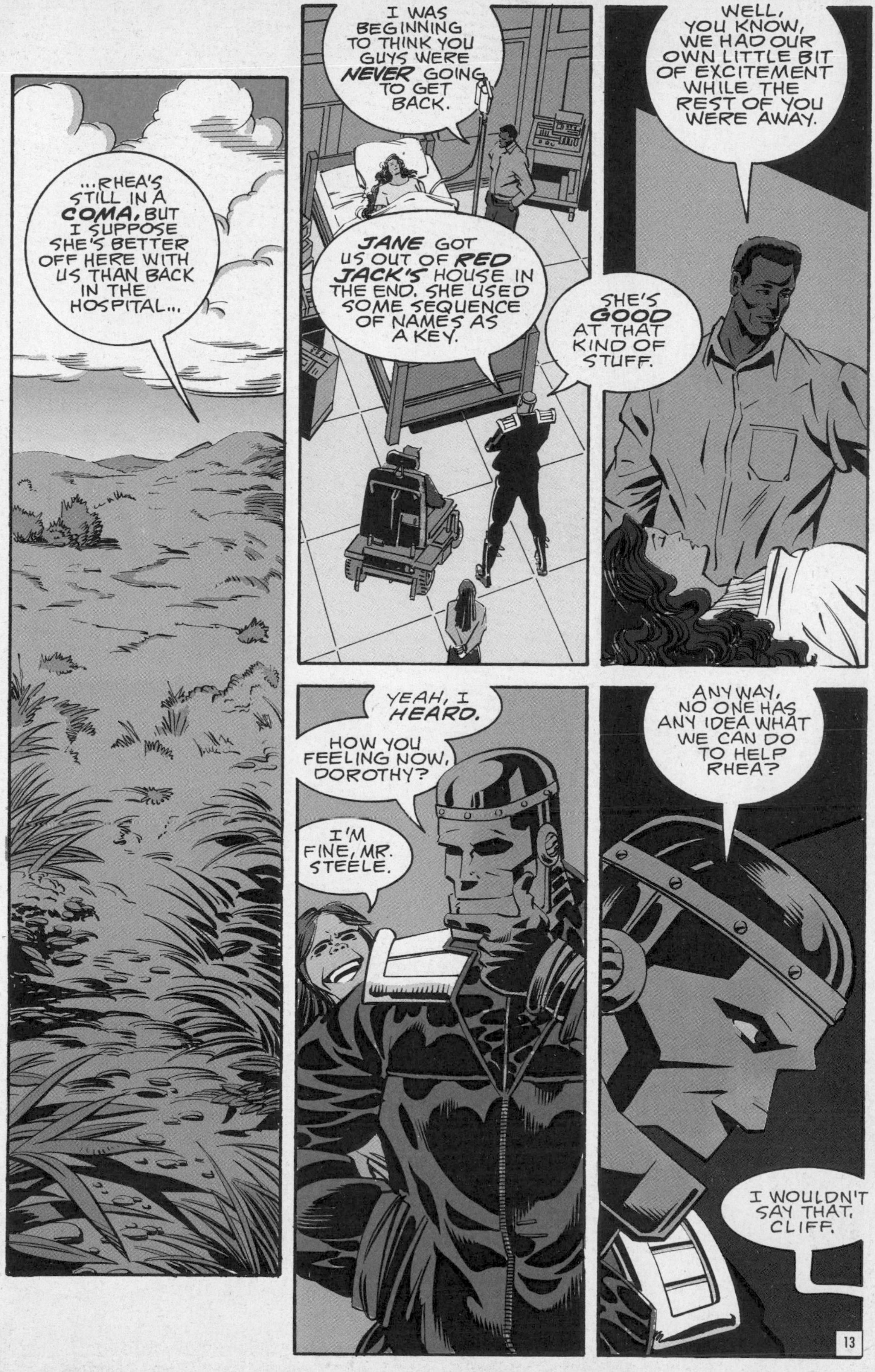
...RHEA'S STILL IN A COMA, BUT I SUPPOSE SHE'S BETTER OFF HERE WITH US THAN BACK IN THE HOSPITAL...
I WAS BEGINNING TO THINK YOU GUYS WERE NEVER GOING TO GET BACK.
JANE GOT US OUT OF RED JACK'S HOUSE IN THE END. SHE USED SOME SEQUENCE OF NAMES AS A KEY.
SHE'S GOOD AT THAT KIND OF STUFF.
WELL, YOU KNOW, WE HAD OUR OWN LITTLE BIT OF EXCITEMENT WHILE THE REST OF YOU WERE AWAY.
YEAH, I HEARD.
HOW YOU FEELING NOW, DOROTHY?
I'M FINE, MR. STEELE.
ANYWAY, NO ONE HAS ANY IDEA WHAT WE CAN DO TO HELP RHEA?
I WOULDN'T SAY THAT, CLIFF.

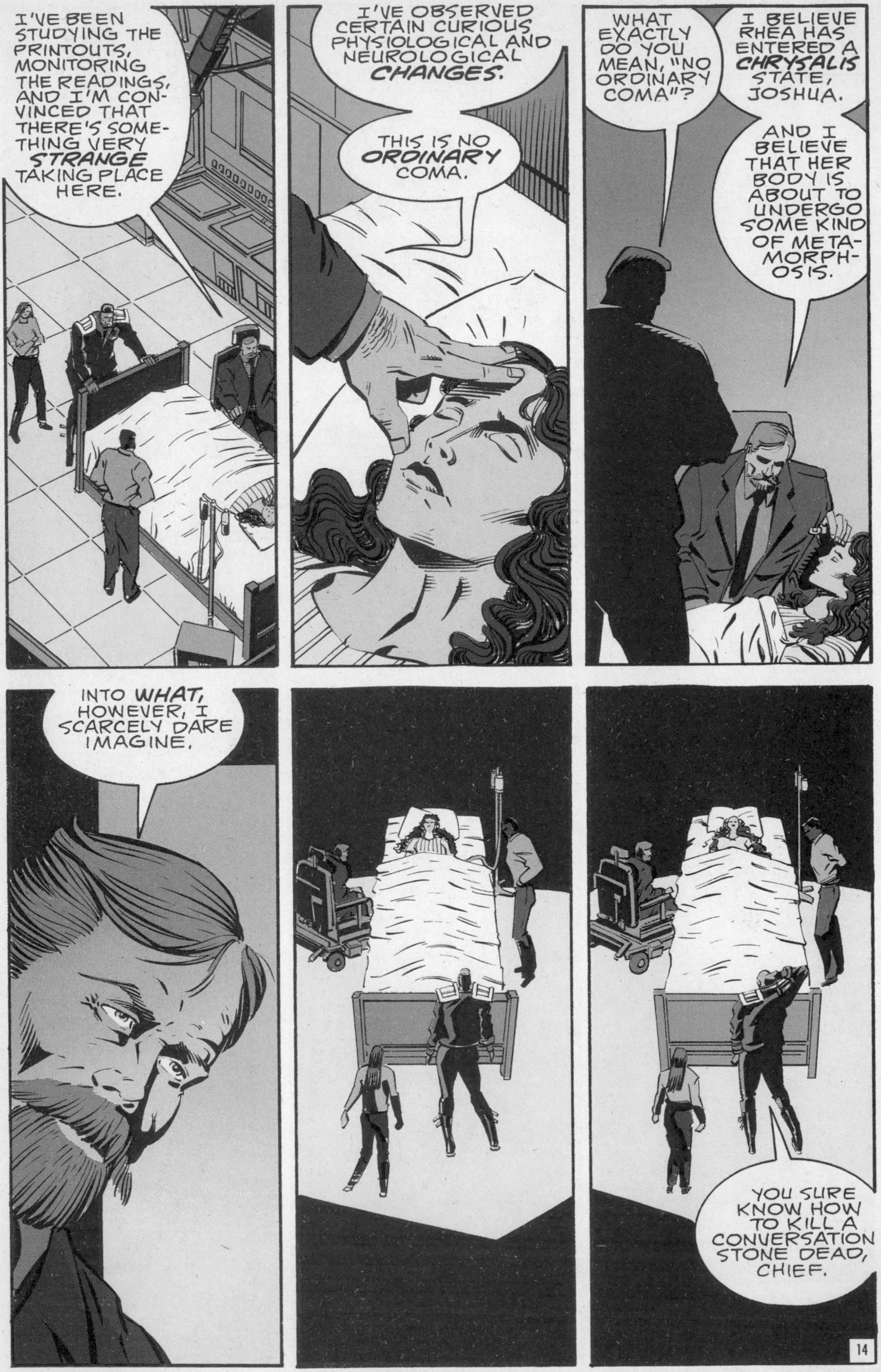
I'VE BEEN STUDYING THE PRINTOUTS, MONITORING THE READINGS, AND I'M CONVINCED THAT THERE'S SOMETHING VERY STRANGE TAKING PLACE HERE.
I'VE OBSERVED CERTAIN CURIOUS PHYSIOLOGICAL AND NEUROLOGICAL CHANGES.
THIS IS NO ORDINARY COMA.
WHAT EXACTLY DO YOU MEAN, "NO ORDINARY COMA"?
I BELIEVE RHEA HAS ENTERED A CHRYSALIS STATE, JOSHUA.
AND I BELIEVE THAT HER BODY IS ABOUT TO UNDERGO SOME KIND OF METAMORPHOSIS.
INTO WHAT, HOWEVER, I SCARCELY DARE IMAGINE.
YOU SURE KNOW HOW TO KILL A CONVERSATION STONE DEAD, CHIEF.

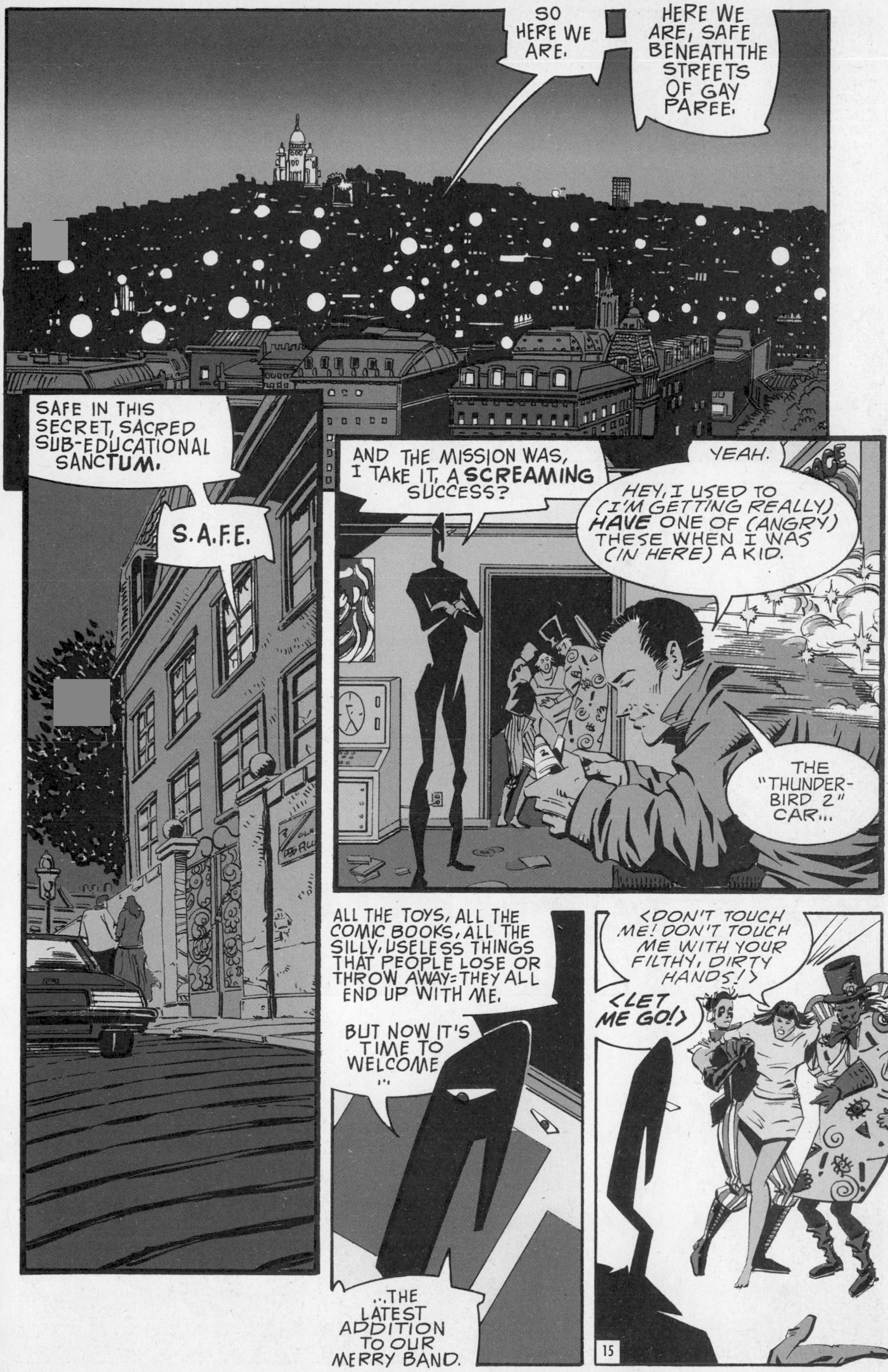

SO HERE WE ARE.
HERE WE ARE, SAFE BENEATH THE STREETS OF GAY PAREE.
SAFE IN THIS SECRET, SACRED SUB-EDUCATIONAL SANC**TUM.**
S.A.F.E.
AND THE MISSION WAS, I TAKE IT, A **SCREAMING** SUCCESS?
YEAH.
HEY, I USED TO (I'M GETTING REALLY) **HAVE** ONE OF (ANGRY) THESE WHEN I WAS (IN HERE) A KID.
THE "THUNDER-BIRD 2" CAR...
ALL THE TOYS, ALL THE COMIC BOOKS, ALL THE SILLY, USELESS THINGS THAT PEOPLE LOSE OR THROW AWAY: THEY ALL END UP WITH ME.
BUT NOW IT'S TIME TO WELCOME ...
...THE LATEST ADDITION TO OUR MERRY BAND.
<DON'T TOUCH ME! DON'T TOUCH ME WITH YOUR FILTHY, DIRTY HANDS!>
<LET ME GO!>

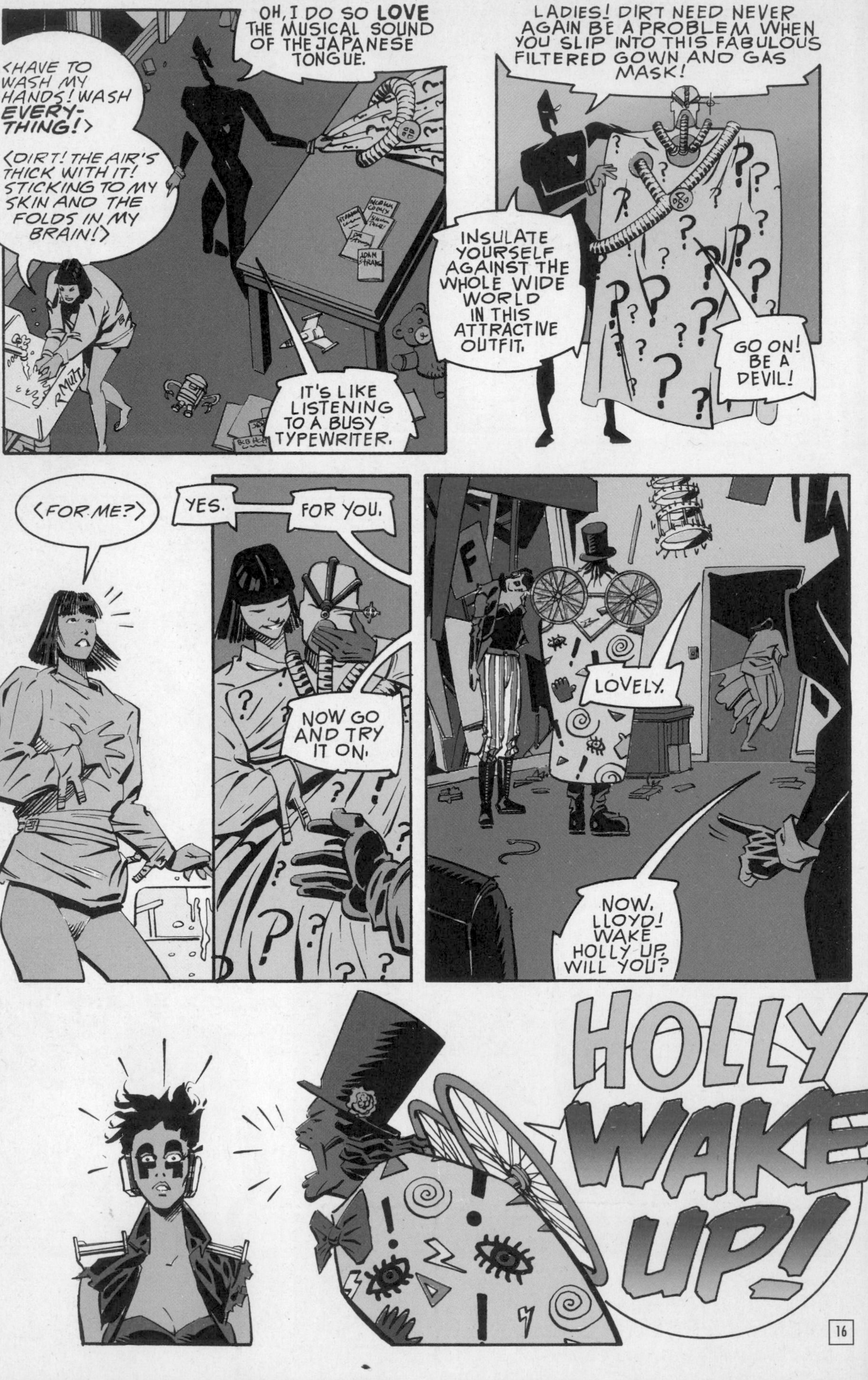

<HAVE TO WASH MY HANDS! WASH EVERY-THING!>
<DIRT! THE AIR'S THICK WITH IT! STICKING TO MY SKIN AND THE FOLDS IN MY BRAIN!>
OH, I DO SO LOVE THE MUSICAL SOUND OF THE JAPANESE TONGUE.
IT'S LIKE LISTENING TO A BUSY TYPEWRITER.
LADIES! DIRT NEED NEVER AGAIN BE A PROBLEM WHEN YOU SLIP INTO THIS FABULOUS FILTERED GOWN AND GAS MASK!
INSULATE YOURSELF AGAINST THE WHOLE WIDE WORLD IN THIS ATTRACTIVE OUTFIT.
GO ON! BE A DEVIL!
<FOR ME?>
YES.
FOR YOU.
NOW GO AND TRY IT ON.
LOVELY.
NOW, LLOYD! WAKE HOLLY UP, WILL YOU?
HOLLY WAKE UP!

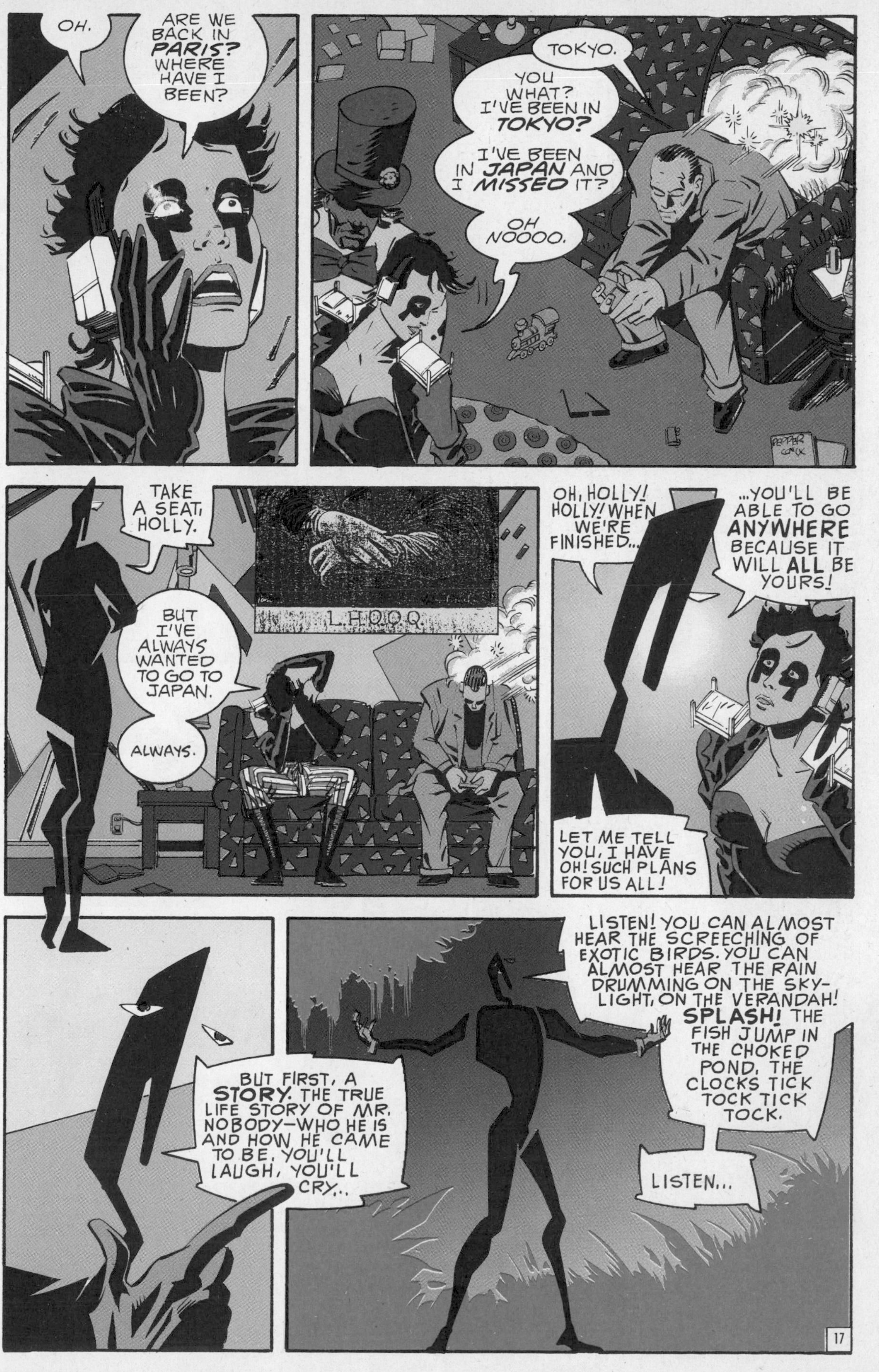
OH.
ARE WE BACK IN PARIS? WHERE HAVE I BEEN?
TOKYO.
YOU WHAT? I'VE BEEN IN TOKYO?
I'VE BEEN IN JAPAN AND I MISSED IT?
OH NOOOO.
TAKE A SEAT, HOLLY.
L.H.O.O.Q.
BUT I'VE ALWAYS WANTED TO GO TO JAPAN.
ALWAYS.
OH, HOLLY! HOLLY! WHEN WE'RE FINISHED...
...YOU'LL BE ABLE TO GO ANYWHERE BECAUSE IT WILL ALL BE YOURS!
LET ME TELL YOU, I HAVE OH! SUCH PLANS FOR US ALL!
BUT FIRST, A STORY. THE TRUE LIFE STORY OF MR. NOBODY—WHO HE IS AND HOW HE CAME TO BE. YOU'LL LAUGH, YOU'LL CRY..
LISTEN! YOU CAN ALMOST HEAR THE SCREECHING OF EXOTIC BIRDS. YOU CAN ALMOST HEAR THE RAIN DRUMMING ON THE SKY-LIGHT, ON THE VERANDAH! SPLASH! THE FISH JUMP IN THE CHOKED POND, THE CLOCKS TICK TOCK TICK TOCK.
LISTEN...

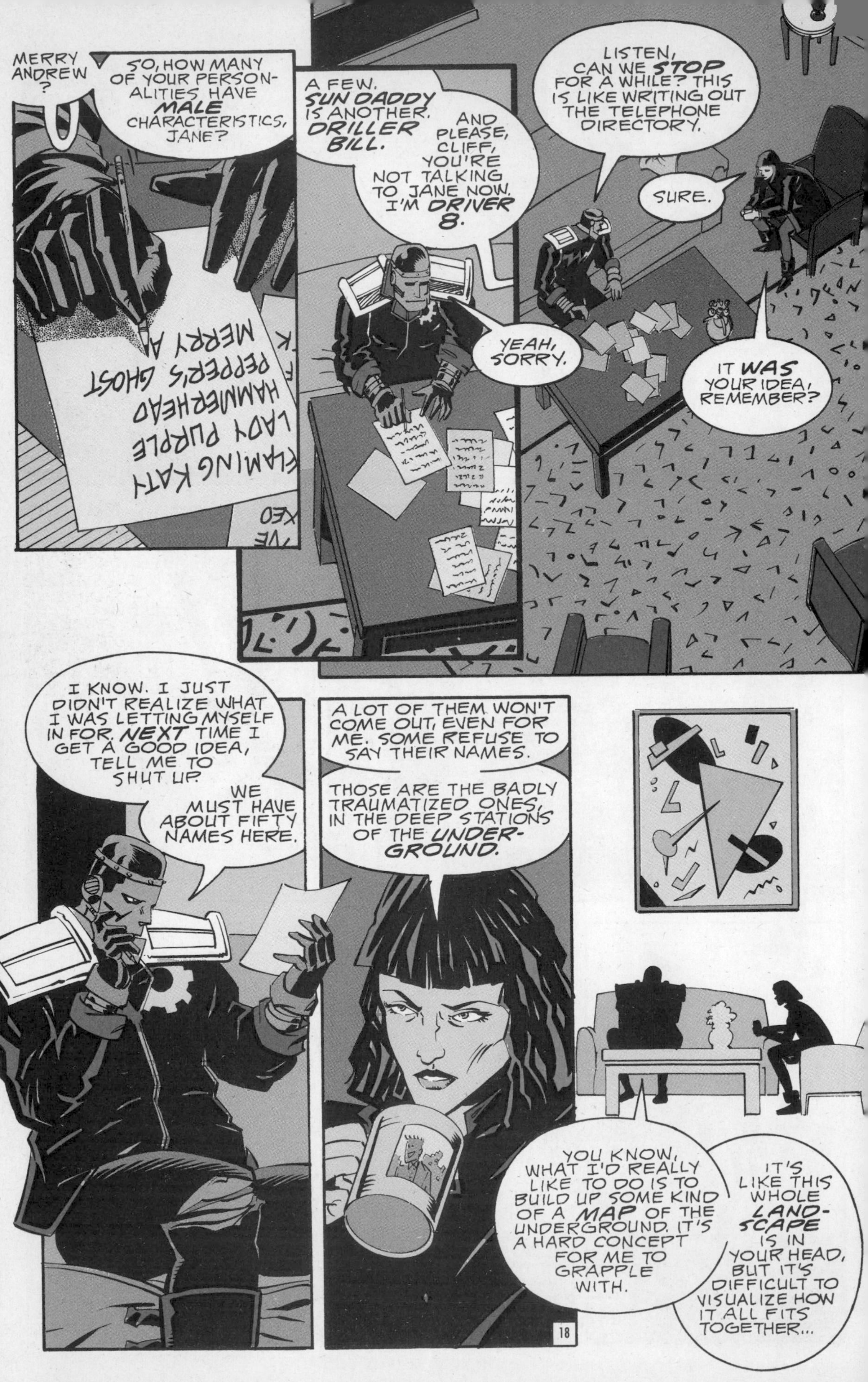

MERRY ANDREW?
SO, HOW MANY OF YOUR PERSONALITIES HAVE *MALE* CHARACTERISTICS, JANE?
LADY PURPLE
HAMMERHEAD
PEPPER'S GHOST
A FEW. *SUN DADDY* IS ANOTHER. *DRILLER BILL.*
AND PLEASE, CLIFF, YOU'RE NOT TALKING TO JANE NOW. I'M *DRIVER 8.*
YEAH, SORRY.
LISTEN, CAN WE *STOP* FOR A WHILE? THIS IS LIKE WRITING OUT THE TELEPHONE DIRECTORY.
SURE.
IT *WAS* YOUR IDEA, REMEMBER?
I KNOW. I JUST DIDN'T REALIZE WHAT I WAS LETTING MYSELF IN FOR. *NEXT* TIME I GET A GOOD IDEA, TELL ME TO SHUT UP.
WE MUST HAVE ABOUT FIFTY NAMES HERE.
A LOT OF THEM WON'T COME OUT, EVEN FOR ME. SOME REFUSE TO SAY THEIR NAMES.
THOSE ARE THE BADLY TRAUMATIZED ONES, IN THE DEEP STATIONS OF THE *UNDERGROUND.*
YOU KNOW, WHAT I'D REALLY LIKE TO DO IS TO BUILD UP SOME KIND OF A *MAP* OF THE UNDERGROUND. IT'S A HARD CONCEPT FOR ME TO GRAPPLE WITH.
IT'S LIKE THIS WHOLE *LANDSCAPE* IS IN YOUR HEAD, BUT IT'S DIFFICULT TO VISUALIZE HOW IT ALL FITS TOGETHER...

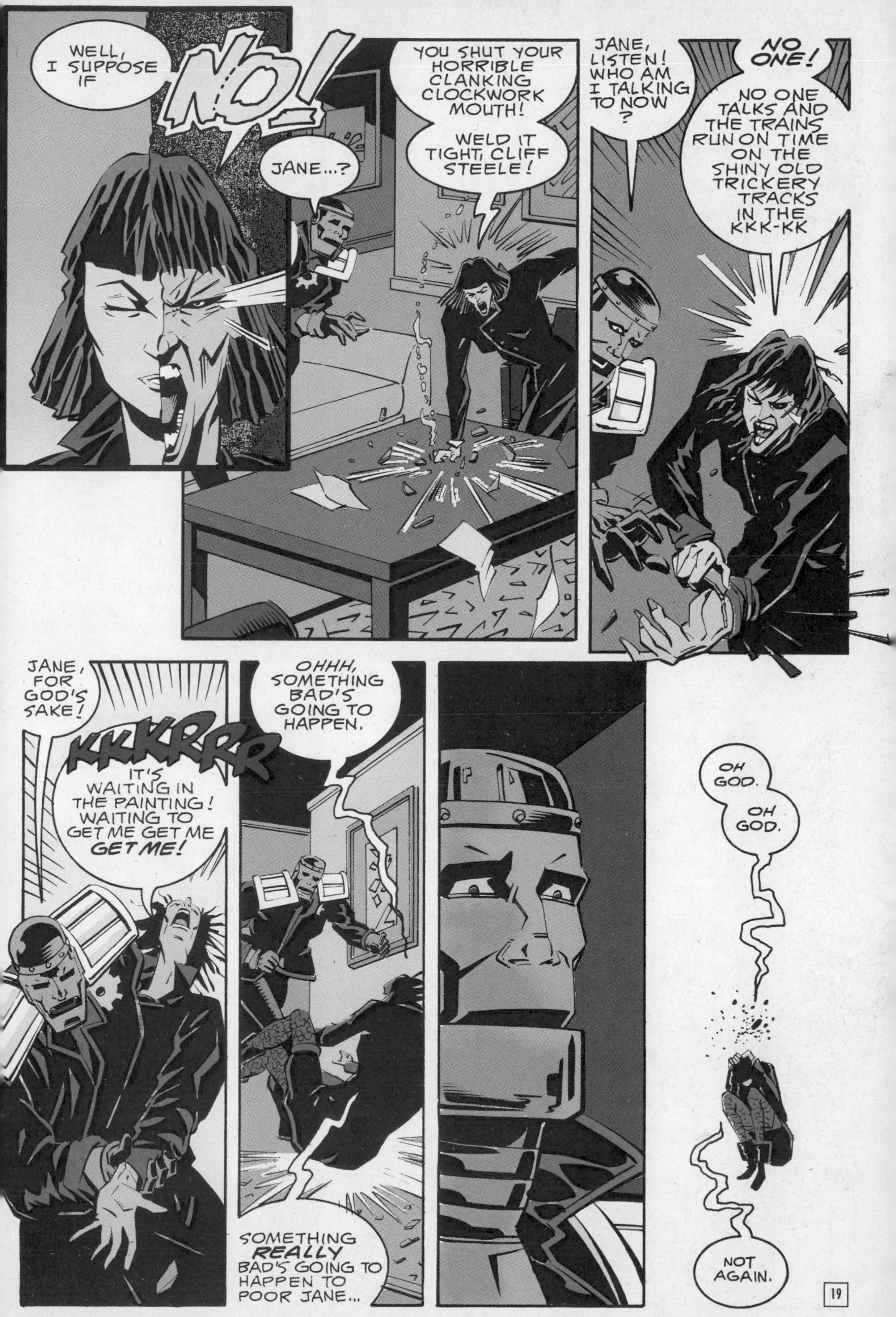
WELL, I SUPPOSE IF
NO!
JANE...?
YOU SHUT YOUR HORRIBLE CLANKING CLOCKWORK MOUTH!
WELD IT TIGHT, CLIFF STEELE!
JANE, LISTEN! WHO AM I TALKING TO NOW?
NO ONE!
NO ONE TALKS AND THE TRAINS RUN ON TIME ON THE SHINY OLD TRICKERY TRACKS IN THE KKK-KK
JANE, FOR GOD'S SAKE!
KKKRRR
IT'S WAITING IN THE PAINTING! WAITING TO GET ME GET ME GET ME!
OHHH, SOMETHING BAD'S GOING TO HAPPEN.
SOMETHING REALLY BAD'S GOING TO HAPPEN TO POOR JANE...
OH GOD.
OH GOD.
NOT AGAIN.

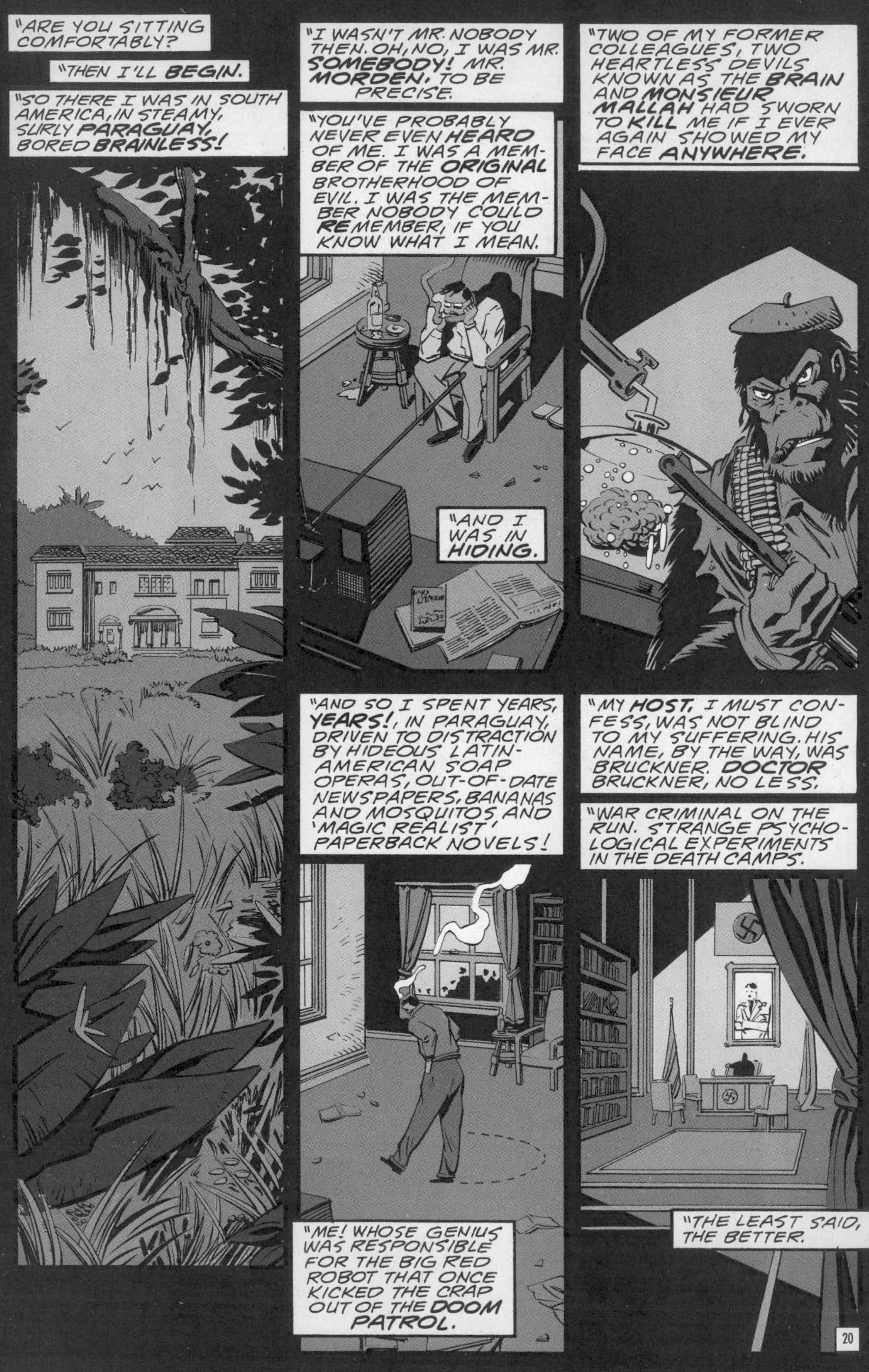
"ARE YOU SITTING COMFORTABLY?
"THEN I'LL BEGIN.
"SO THERE I WAS IN SOUTH AMERICA, IN STEAMY, SURLY PARAGUAY, BORED BRAINLESS!
"I WASN'T MR. NOBODY THEN. OH, NO, I WAS MR. SOMEBODY! MR. MORDEN, TO BE PRECISE.
"YOU'VE PROBABLY NEVER EVEN HEARD OF ME. I WAS A MEMBER OF THE ORIGINAL BROTHERHOOD OF EVIL. I WAS THE MEMBER NOBODY COULD REMEMBER, IF YOU KNOW WHAT I MEAN.
"AND I WAS IN HIDING.
"TWO OF MY FORMER COLLEAGUES, TWO HEARTLESS DEVILS KNOWN AS THE BRAIN AND MONSIEUR MALLAH HAD SWORN TO KILL ME IF I EVER AGAIN SHOWED MY FACE ANYWHERE.
"AND SO I SPENT YEARS, YEARS!, IN PARAGUAY, DRIVEN TO DISTRACTION BY HIDEOUS LATIN-AMERICAN SOAP OPERAS, OUT-OF-DATE NEWSPAPERS, BANANAS AND MOSQUITOS, AND 'MAGIC REALIST' PAPERBACK NOVELS!
"ME! WHOSE GENIUS WAS RESPONSIBLE FOR THE BIG RED ROBOT THAT ONCE KICKED THE CRAP OUT OF THE DOOM PATROL.
"MY HOST, I MUST CONFESS, WAS NOT BLIND TO MY SUFFERING. HIS NAME, BY THE WAY, WAS BRUCKNER. DOCTOR BRUCKNER, NO LESS.
"WAR CRIMINAL ON THE RUN. STRANGE PSYCHOLOGICAL EXPERIMENTS IN THE DEATH CAMPS.
"THE LEAST SAID, THE BETTER.

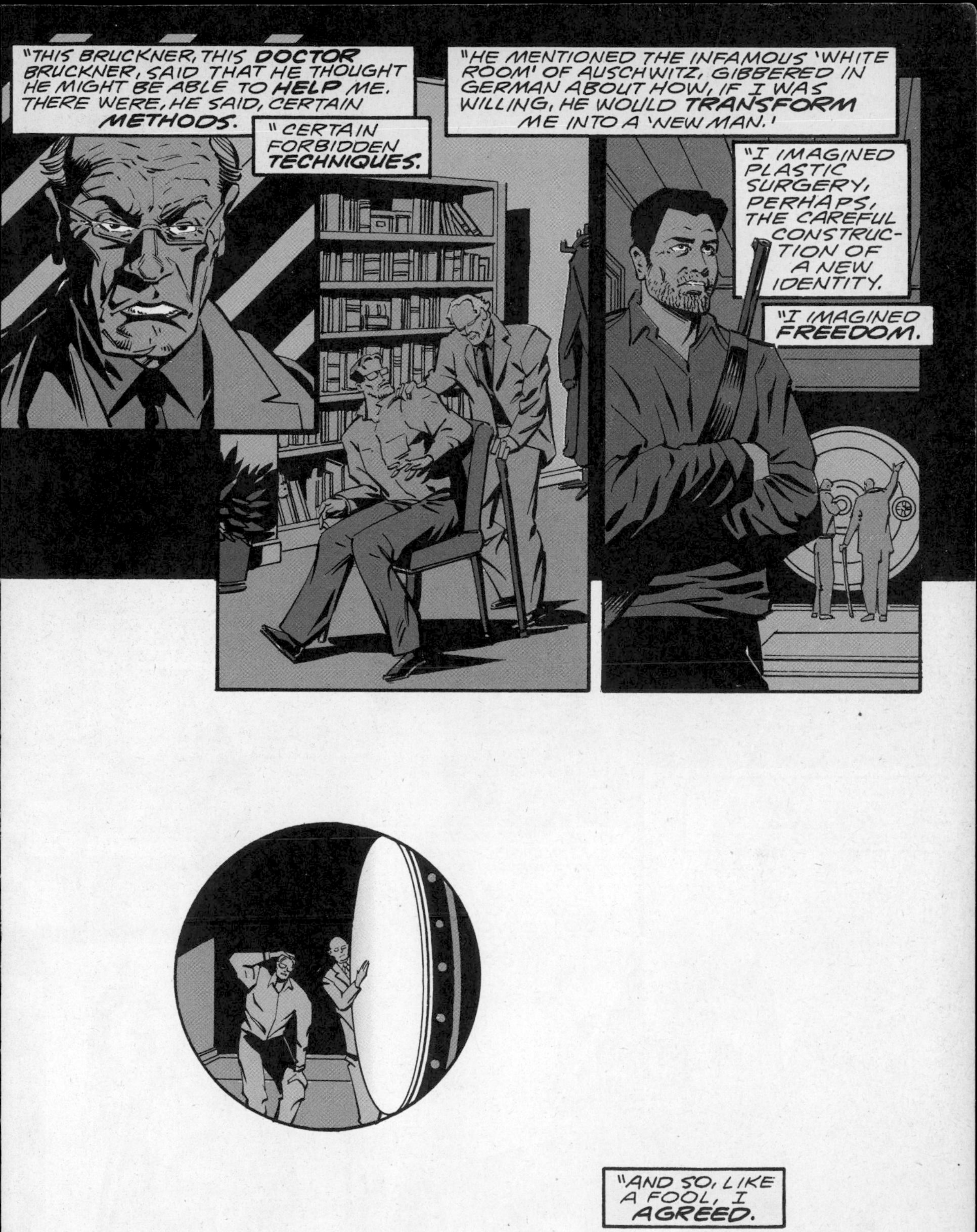
"THIS BRUCKNER, THIS DOCTOR BRUCKNER, SAID THAT HE THOUGHT HE MIGHT BE ABLE TO HELP ME. THERE WERE, HE SAID, CERTAIN METHODS.
"CERTAIN FORBIDDEN TECHNIQUES.
"HE MENTIONED THE INFAMOUS 'WHITE ROOM' OF AUSCHWITZ, GIBBERED IN GERMAN ABOUT HOW, IF I WAS WILLING, HE WOULD TRANSFORM ME INTO A 'NEW MAN.'
"I IMAGINED PLASTIC SURGERY, PERHAPS, THE CAREFUL CONSTRUCTION OF A NEW IDENTITY.
"I IMAGINED FREEDOM.
"AND SO, LIKE A FOOL, I AGREED.

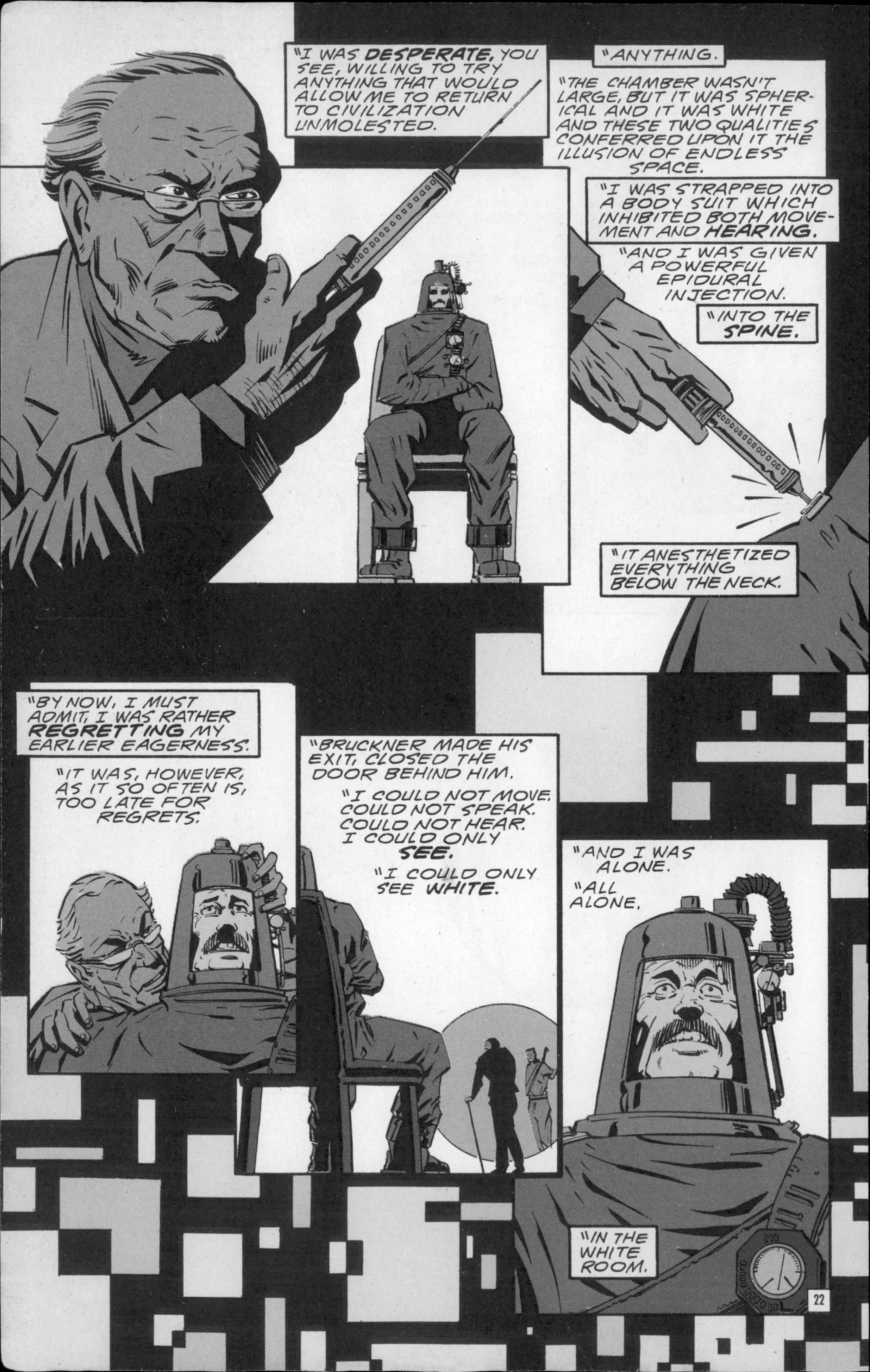
"I WAS DESPERATE, YOU SEE, WILLING TO TRY ANYTHING THAT WOULD ALLOW ME TO RETURN TO CIVILIZATION UNMOLESTED.
"ANYTHING.
"THE CHAMBER WASN'T LARGE, BUT IT WAS SPHERICAL AND IT WAS WHITE AND THESE TWO QUALITIES CONFERRED UPON IT THE ILLUSION OF ENDLESS SPACE.
"I WAS STRAPPED INTO A BODY SUIT WHICH INHIBITED BOTH MOVEMENT AND HEARING.
"AND I WAS GIVEN A POWERFUL EPIDURAL INJECTION.
"INTO THE SPINE.
"IT ANESTHETIZED EVERYTHING BELOW THE NECK.
"BY NOW, I MUST ADMIT, I WAS RATHER REGRETTING MY EARLIER EAGERNESS.
"IT WAS, HOWEVER, AS IT SO OFTEN IS, TOO LATE FOR REGRETS.
"BRUCKNER MADE HIS EXIT, CLOSED THE DOOR BEHIND HIM.
"I COULD NOT MOVE, COULD NOT SPEAK. COULD NOT HEAR. I COULD ONLY SEE.
"I COULD ONLY SEE WHITE.
"AND I WAS ALONE.
"ALL ALONE.
"IN THE WHITE ROOM.

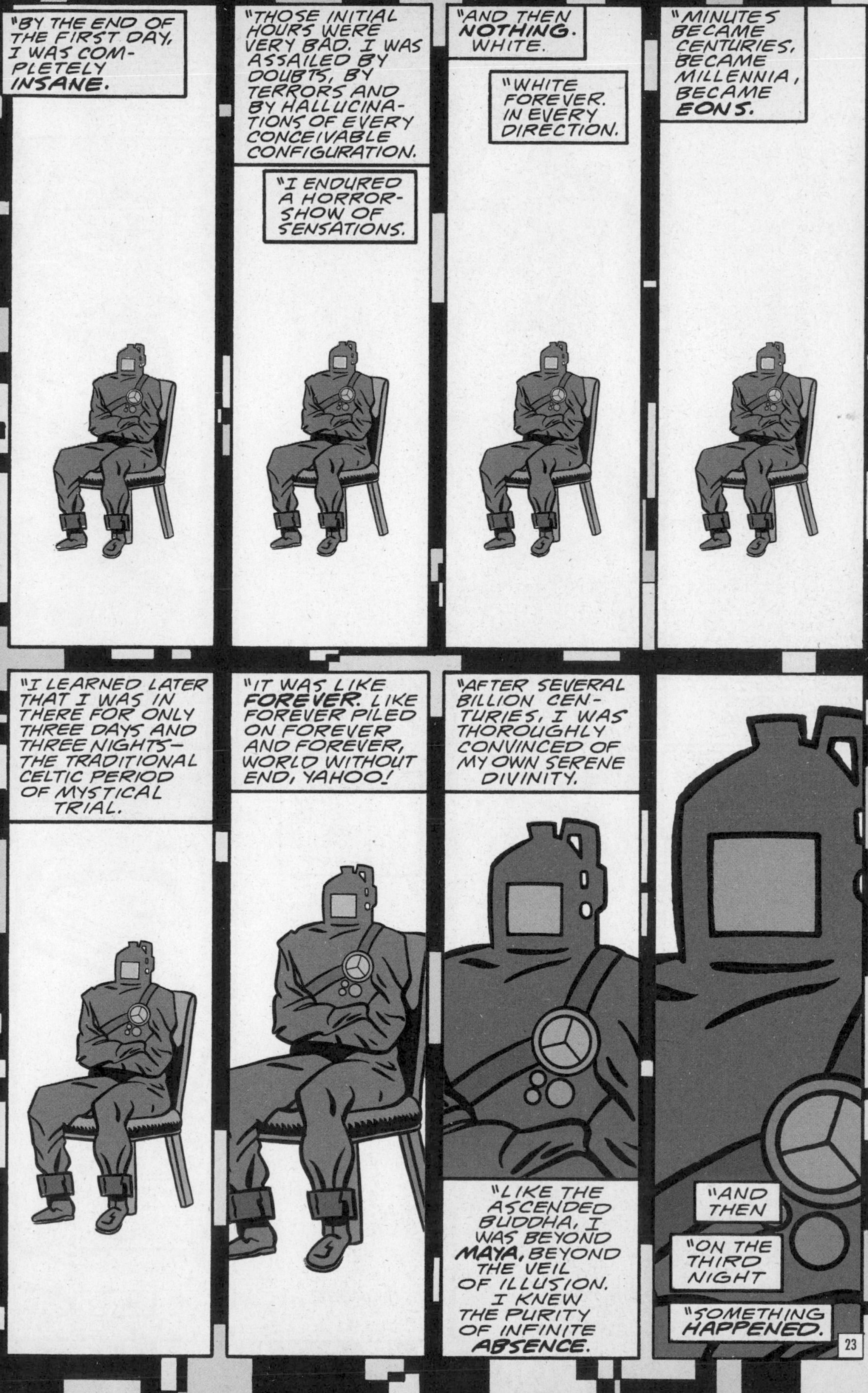

"BY THE END OF THE FIRST DAY, I WAS COMPLETELY **INSANE**.

"THOSE INITIAL HOURS WERE VERY BAD. I WAS ASSAILED BY DOUBTS, BY TERRORS AND BY HALLUCINATIONS OF EVERY CONCEIVABLE CONFIGURATION.

"I ENDURED A HORROR-SHOW OF SENSATIONS.

"AND THEN **NOTHING**. WHITE.

"WHITE FOREVER. IN EVERY DIRECTION.

"MINUTES BECAME CENTURIES, BECAME MILLENNIA, BECAME **EONS**.

"I LEARNED LATER THAT I WAS IN THERE FOR ONLY THREE DAYS AND THREE NIGHTS— THE TRADITIONAL CELTIC PERIOD OF MYSTICAL TRIAL.

"IT WAS LIKE **FOREVER**. LIKE FOREVER PILED ON FOREVER AND FOREVER, WORLD WITHOUT END, YAHOO!

"AFTER SEVERAL BILLION CENTURIES, I WAS THOROUGHLY CONVINCED OF MY OWN SERENE DIVINITY.

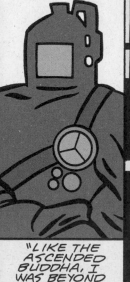

"LIKE THE ASCENDED **MAYA**, I WAS BEYOND MAYA, BEYOND THE VEIL OF ILLUSION. I KNEW THE PURITY OF INFINITE **ABSENCE**.

"AND THEN

"ON THE THIRD NIGHT

"SOMETHING **HAPPENED**.

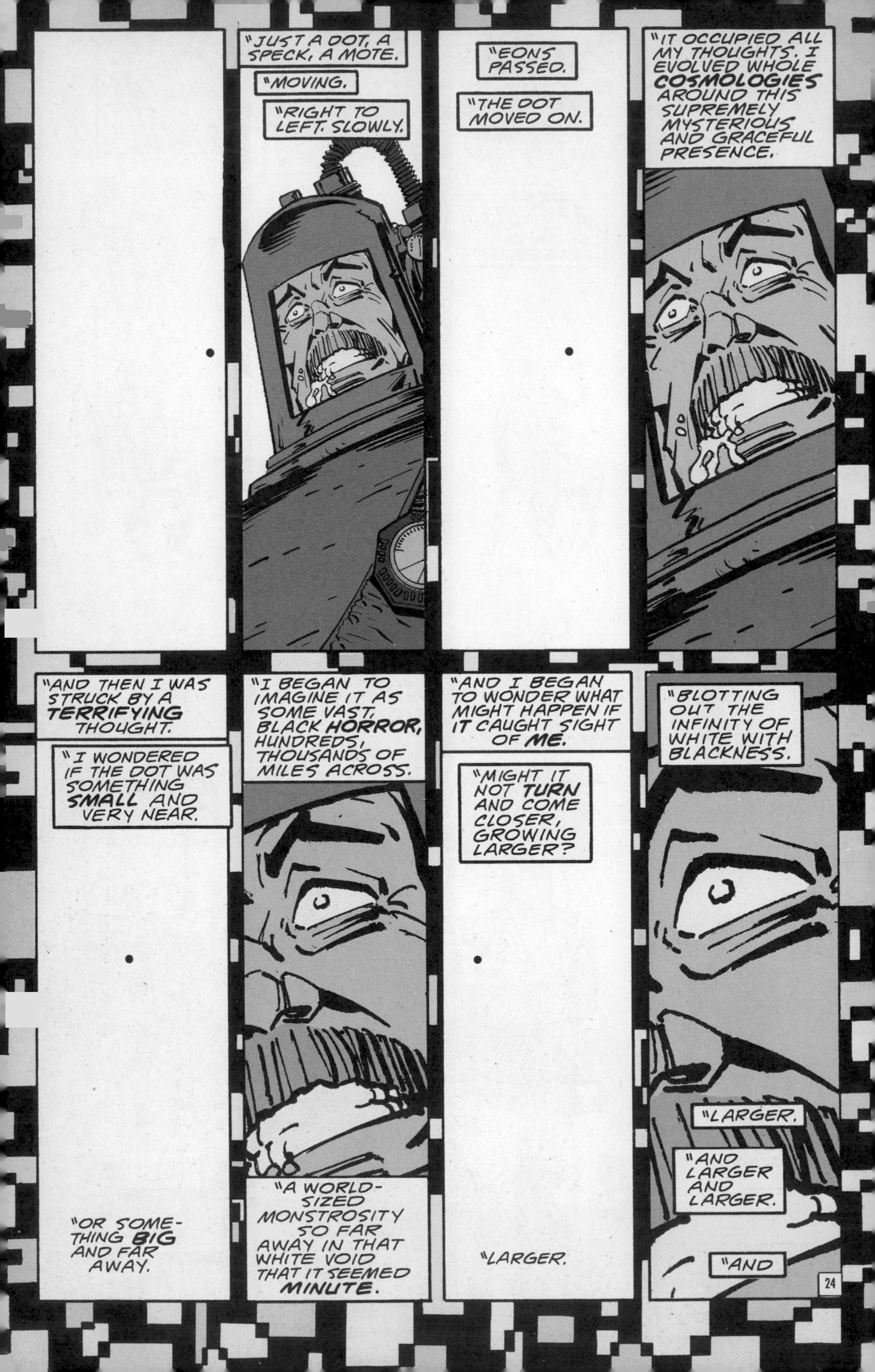
"JUST A DOT, A SPECK, A MOTE.
"MOVING.
"RIGHT TO LEFT. SLOWLY.
"EONS PASSED.
"THE DOT MOVED ON.
"IT OCCUPIED ALL MY THOUGHTS. I EVOLVED WHOLE COSMOLOGIES AROUND THIS SUPREMELY MYSTERIOUS AND GRACEFUL PRESENCE.
"AND THEN I WAS STRUCK BY A TERRIFYING THOUGHT.
"I WONDERED IF THE DOT WAS SOMETHING SMALL AND VERY NEAR.
"OR SOME-THING BIG AND FAR AWAY.
"I BEGAN TO IMAGINE IT AS SOME VAST, BLACK HORROR, HUNDREDS, THOUSANDS OF MILES ACROSS.
"A WORLD-SIZED MONSTROSITY SO FAR AWAY IN THAT WHITE VOID THAT IT SEEMED MINUTE.
"AND I BEGAN TO WONDER WHAT MIGHT HAPPEN IF IT CAUGHT SIGHT OF ME.
"MIGHT IT NOT TURN AND COME CLOSER, GROWING LARGER?
"LARGER.
"BLOTTING OUT THE INFINITY OF WHITE WITH BLACKNESS.
"LARGER.
"AND LARGER AND LARGER.
"AND

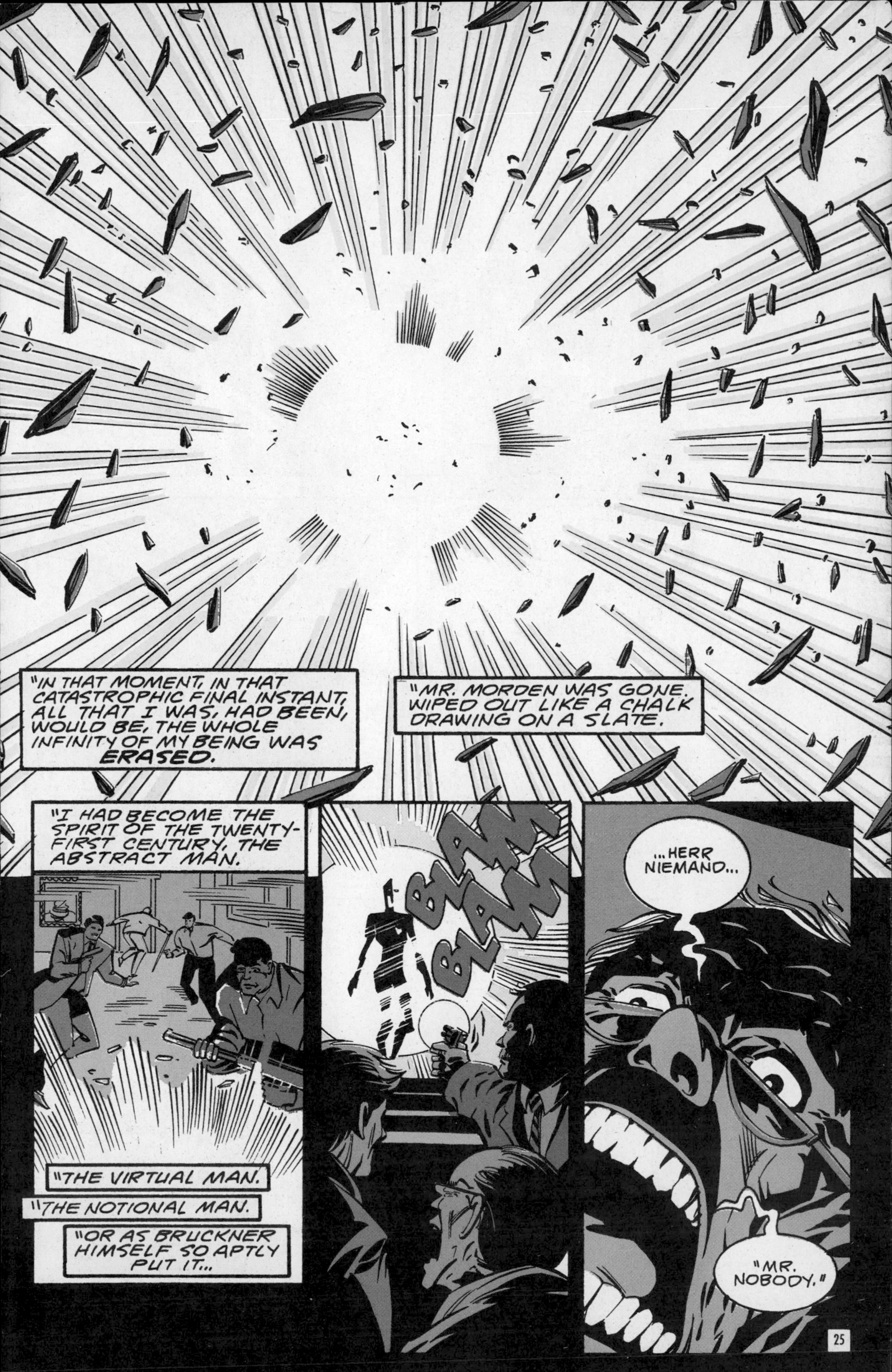
"IN THAT MOMENT, IN THAT CATASTROPHIC FINAL INSTANT, ALL THAT I WAS, HAD BEEN, WOULD BE, THE WHOLE INFINITY OF MY BEING WAS ERASED.
"MR. MORDEN WAS GONE. WIPED OUT LIKE A CHALK DRAWING ON A SLATE.
"I HAD BECOME THE SPIRIT OF THE TWENTY-FIRST CENTURY, THE ABSTRACT MAN.
"THE VIRTUAL MAN.
"THE NOTIONAL MAN.
"OR AS BRUCKNER HIMSELF SO APTLY PUT IT...
BLAM BLAM
...HERR NIEMAND...
"MR. NOBODY."

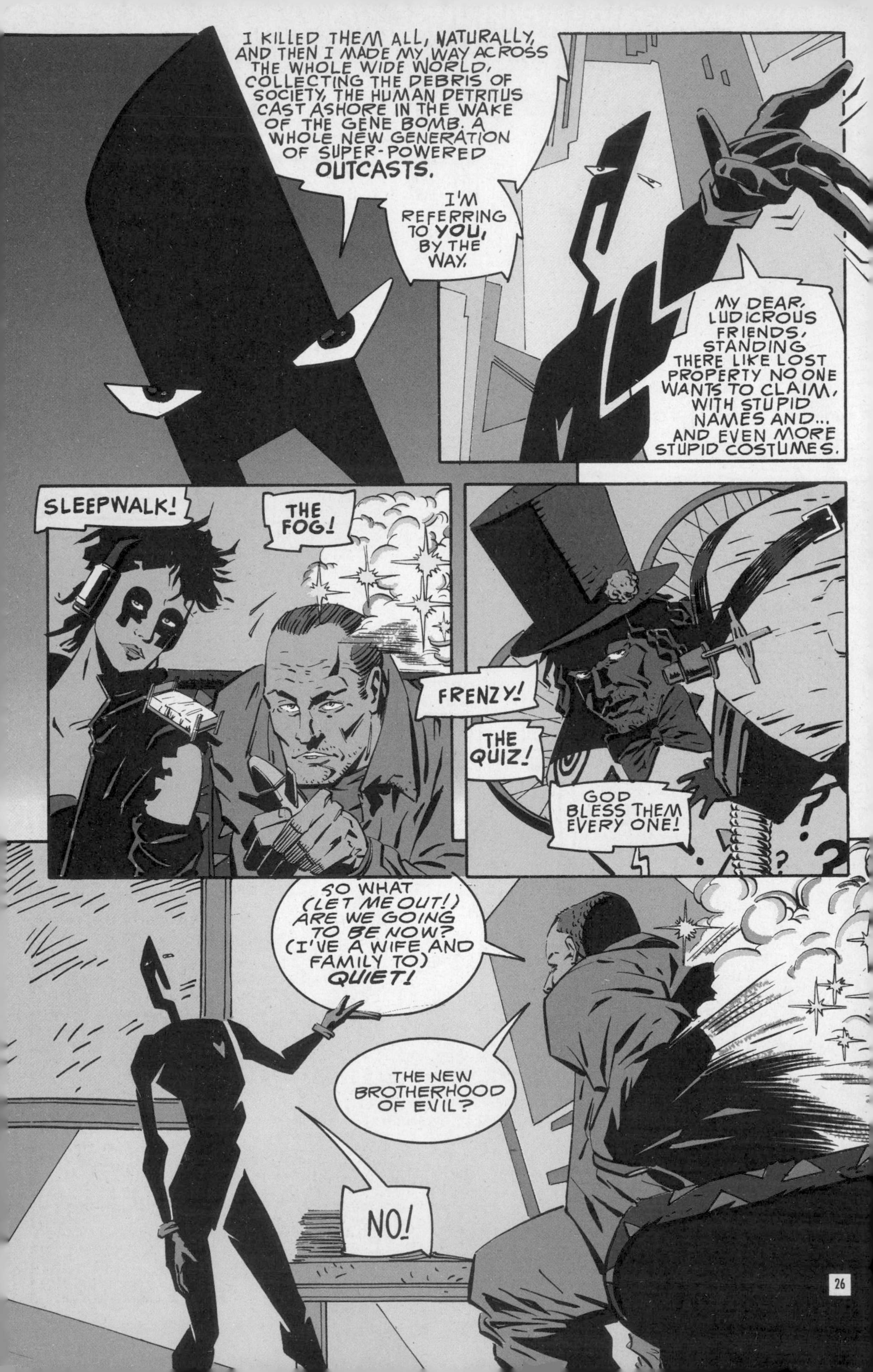
I KILLED THEM ALL, NATURALLY, AND THEN I MADE MY WAY ACROSS THE WHOLE WIDE WORLD, COLLECTING THE DEBRIS OF SOCIETY, THE HUMAN DETRITUS CAST ASHORE IN THE WAKE OF THE GENE BOMB. A WHOLE NEW GENERATION OF SUPER-POWERED **OUTCASTS.**
I'M REFERRING TO **YOU,** BY THE WAY.
MY DEAR, LUDICROUS FRIENDS, STANDING THERE LIKE LOST PROPERTY NO ONE WANTS TO CLAIM, WITH STUPID NAMES AND... AND EVEN MORE STUPID COSTUMES.
SLEEPWALK!
THE FOG!
FRENZY!
THE QUIZ!
GOD BLESS THEM EVERY ONE!
SO WHAT *(LET ME OUT!)* ARE WE GOING TO *BE* NOW? (I'VE A WIFE AND FAMILY TO) ***QUIET!***
THE NEW BROTHERHOOD OF EVIL?
NO!

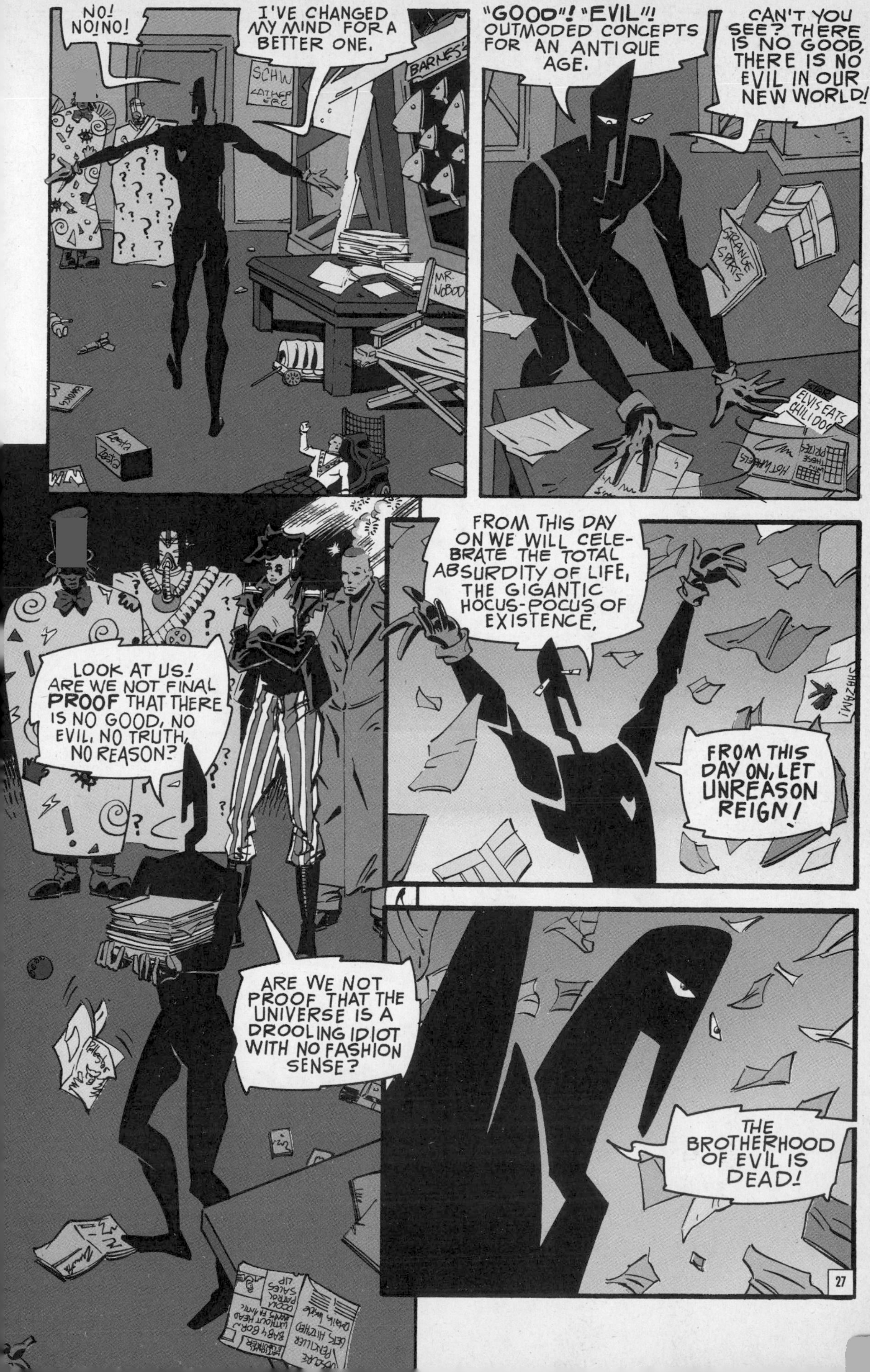
NO! NO!NO!
I'VE CHANGED MY MIND FOR A BETTER ONE.
"GOOD"! "EVIL"! OUTMODED CONCEPTS FOR AN ANTIQUE AGE.
CAN'T YOU SEE? THERE IS NO GOOD, THERE IS NO EVIL IN OUR NEW WORLD!
LOOK AT US! ARE WE NOT FINAL **PROOF** THAT THERE IS NO GOOD, NO EVIL, NO TRUTH, NO REASON?
ARE WE NOT PROOF THAT THE UNIVERSE IS A DROOLING IDIOT WITH NO FASHION SENSE?
FROM THIS DAY ON WE WILL CELEBRATE THE TOTAL ABSURDITY OF LIFE, THE GIGANTIC HOCUS-POCUS OF EXISTENCE,
FROM THIS DAY ON, LET UNREASON REIGN!
THE BROTHERHOOD OF EVIL IS DEAD!

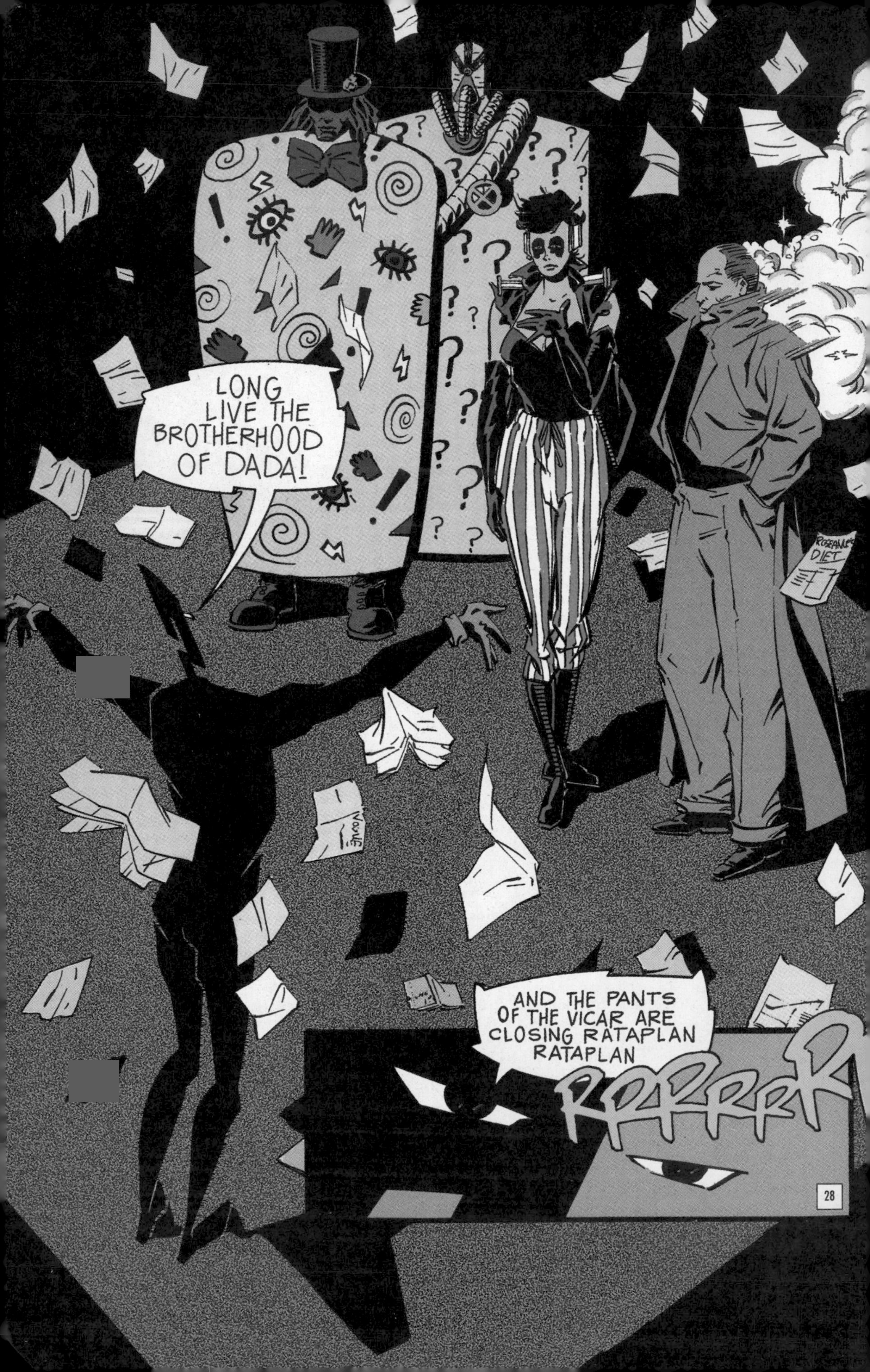
LONG LIVE THE BROTHERHOOD OF DADA!
AND THE PANTS OF THE VICAR ARE CLOSING RATAPLAN RATAPLAN
RRRRRR

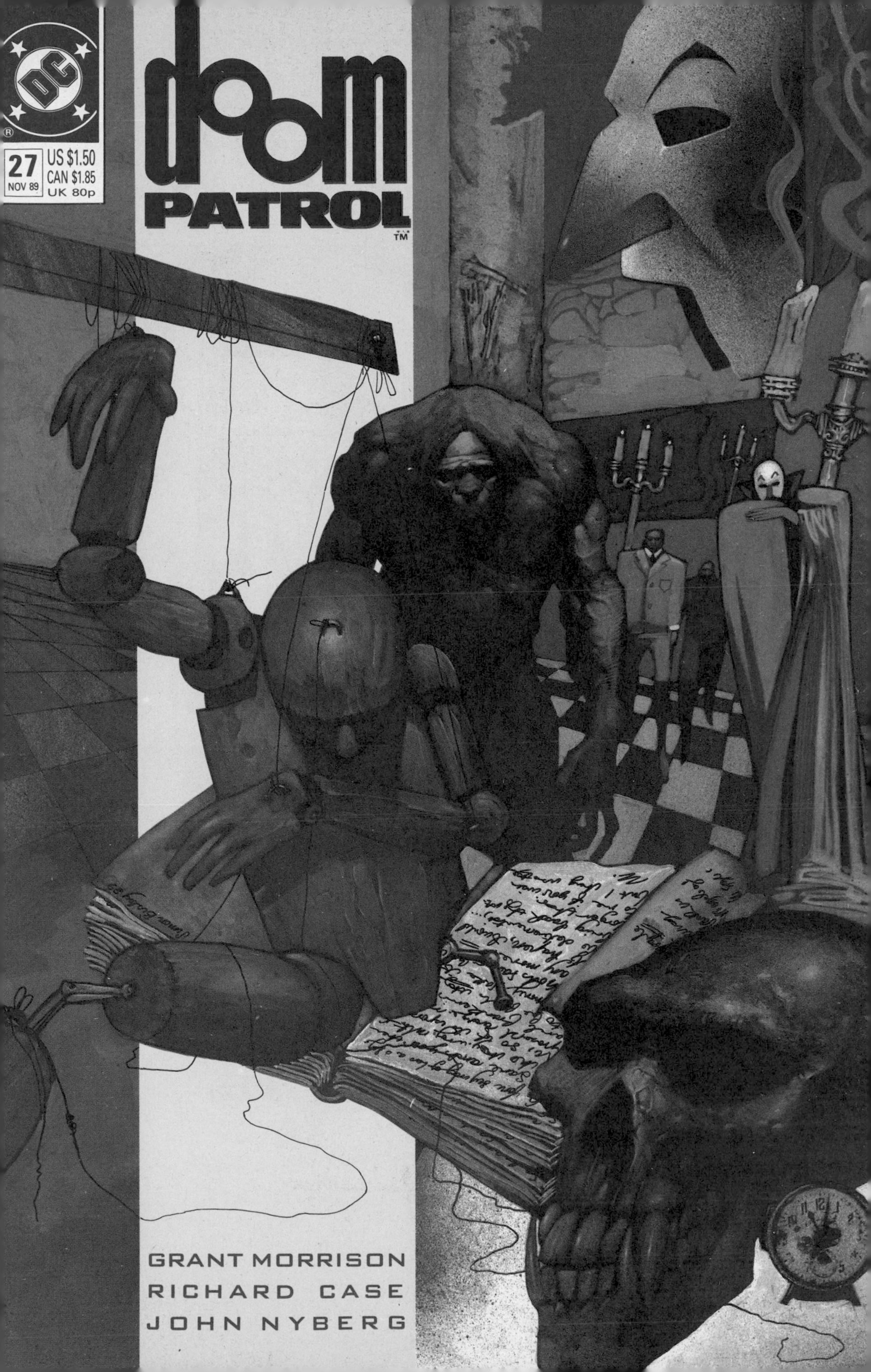

DC
27
NOV 89
US $1.50
CAN $1.85
UK 80p
doom
PATROL
TM
GRANT MORRISON
RICHARD CASE
JOHN NYBERG

WHY IS?
WHO IS?
WHERE IS?
HOW IS?
WHEN IS?
WHAT IS?

THE PAINTING THAT ATE PARIS

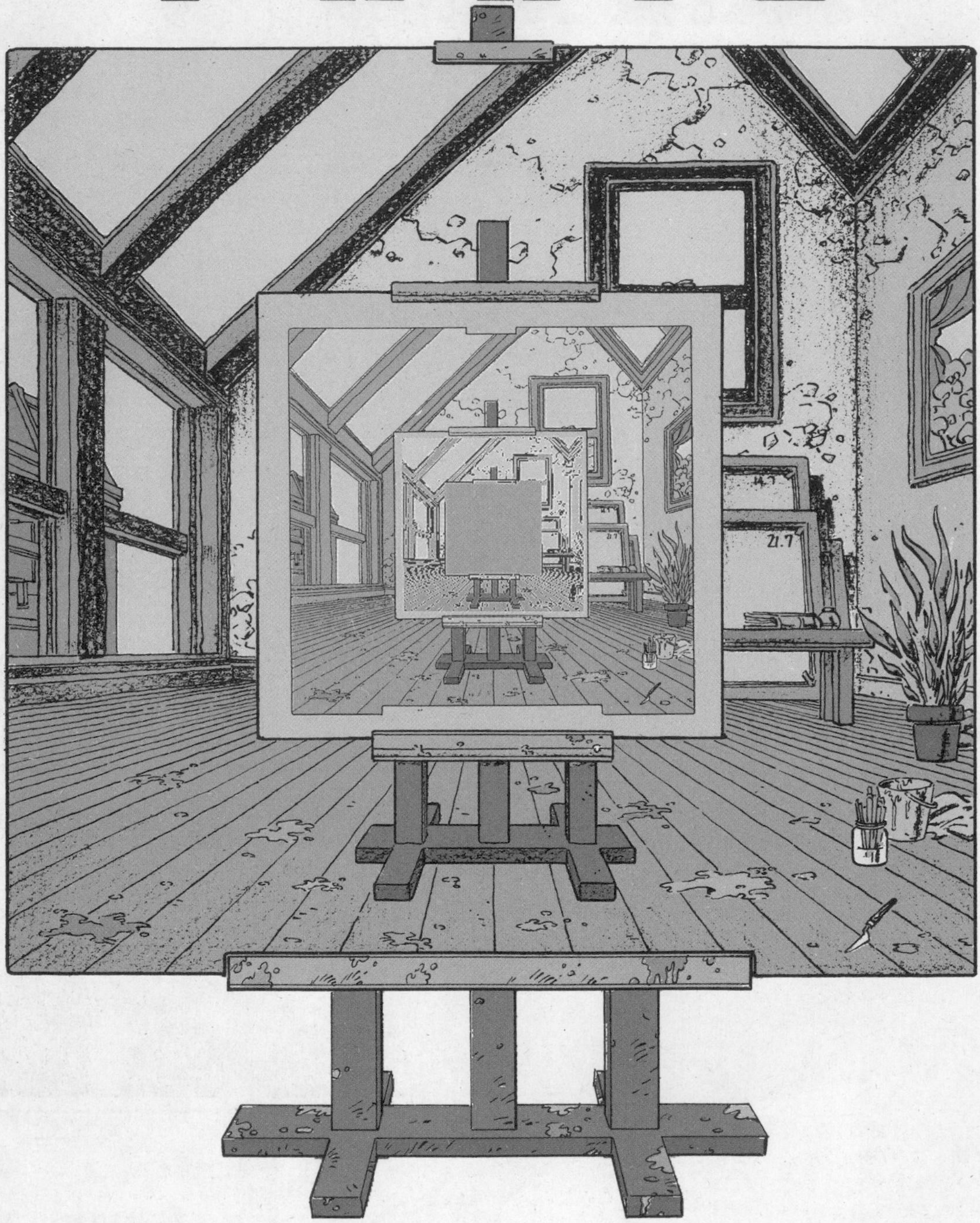
21.7

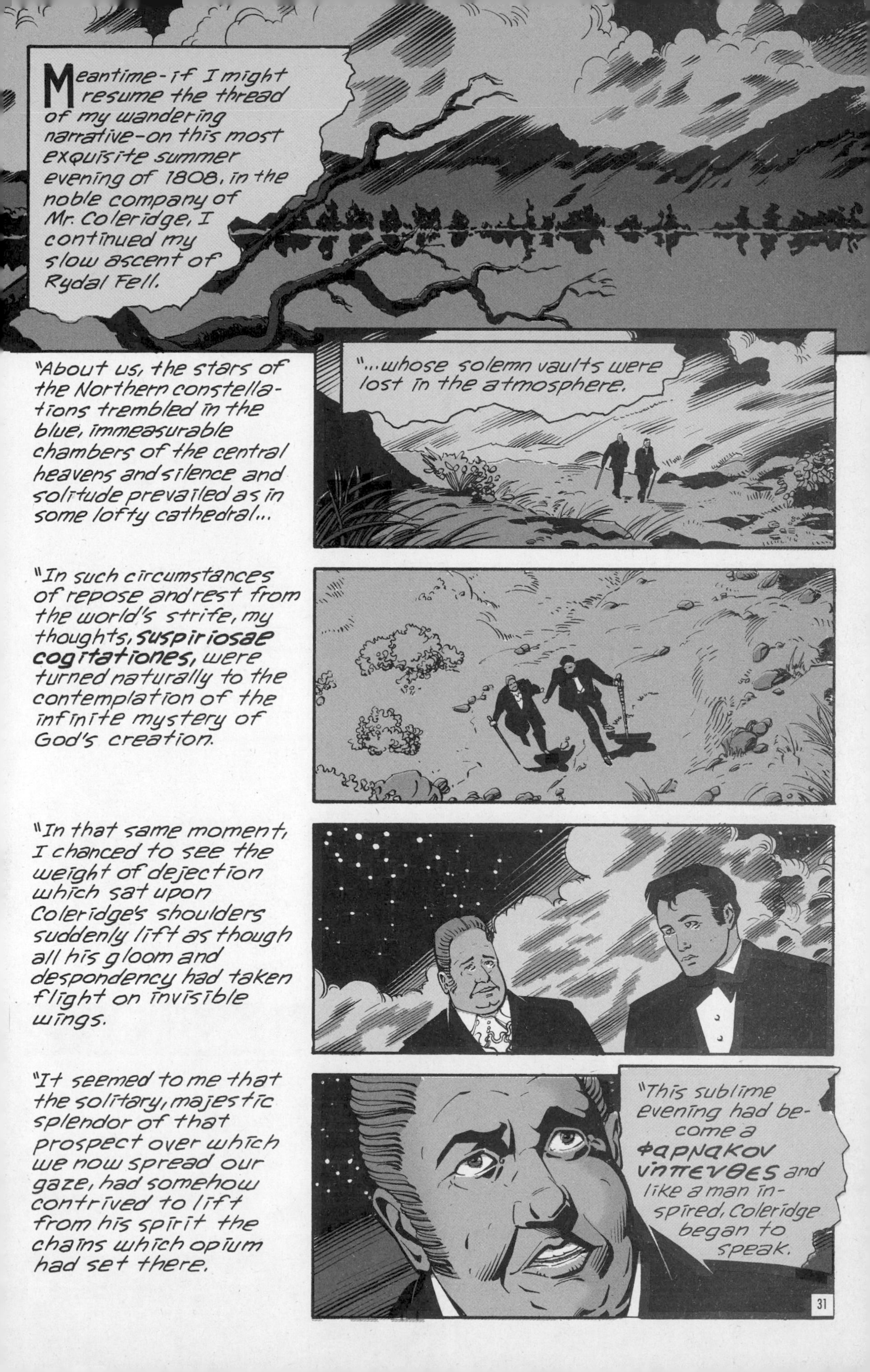
Meantime-if I might resume the thread of my wandering narrative-on this most exquisite summer evening of 1808, in the noble company of Mr. Coleridge, I continued my slow ascent of Rydal Fell.
"About us, the stars of the Northern constellations trembled in the blue, immeasurable chambers of the central heavens and silence and solitude prevailed as in some lofty cathedral...
"...whose solemn vaults were lost in the atmosphere.
"In such circumstances of repose and rest from the world's strife, my thoughts, **suspiriosae cogitationes**, were turned naturally to the contemplation of the infinite mystery of God's creation.
"In that same moment, I chanced to see the weight of dejection which sat upon Coleridge's shoulders suddenly lift as though all his gloom and despondency had taken flight on invisible wings.
"It seemed to me that the solitary, majestic splendor of that prospect over which we now spread our gaze, had somehow contrived to lift from his spirit the chains which opium had set there.
"This sublime evening had become a **φαρμακον νηπενθες** and like a man inspired, Coleridge began to speak.

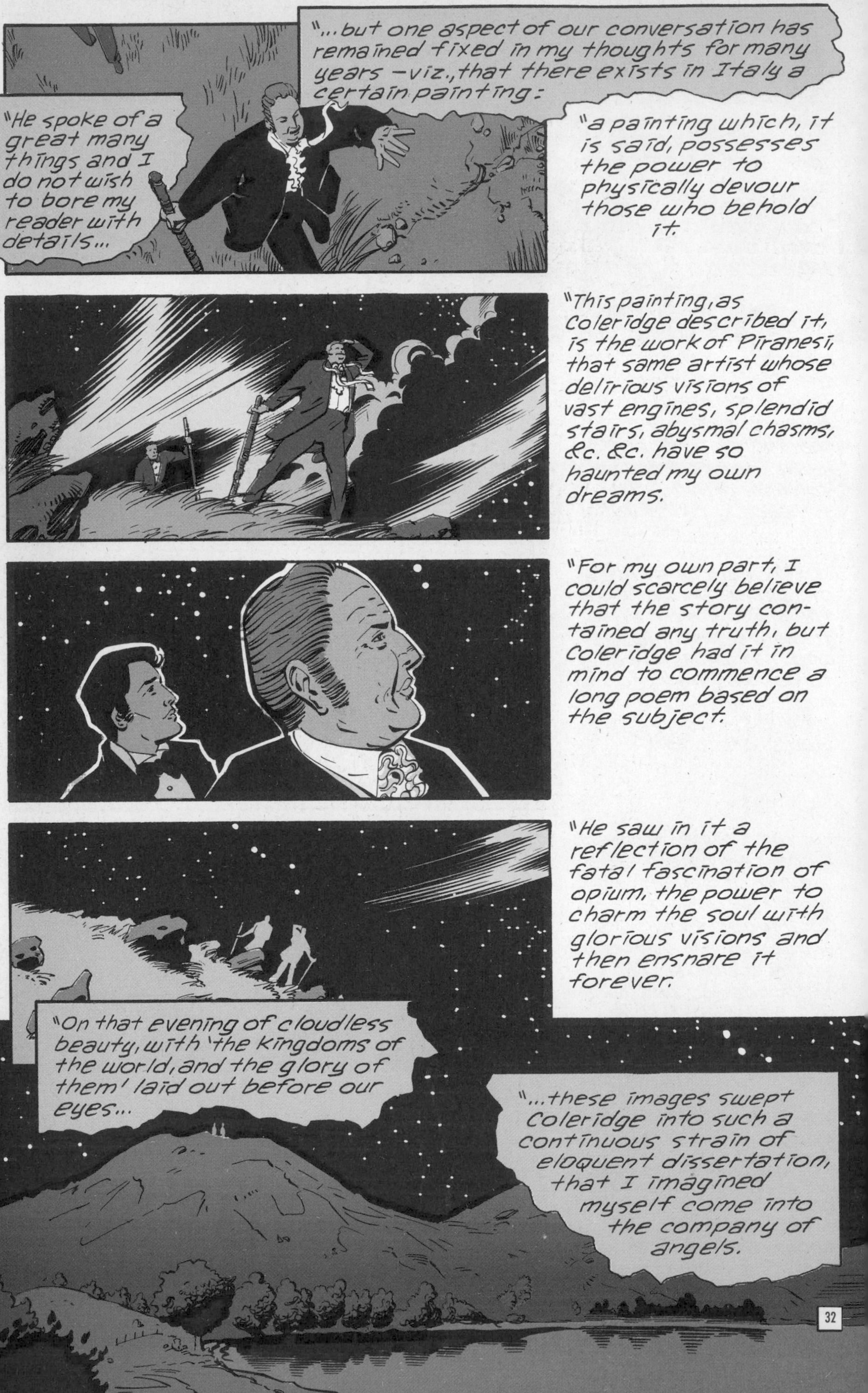
"...but one aspect of our conversation has remained fixed in my thoughts for many years —viz., that there exists in Italy a certain painting:
"He spoke of a great many things and I do not wish to bore my reader with details...
"a painting which, it is said, possesses the power to physically devour those who behold it.
"This painting, as Coleridge described it, is the work of Piranesi, that same artist whose delirious visions of vast engines, splendid stairs, abysmal chasms, &c. &c. have so haunted my own dreams.
"For my own part, I could scarcely believe that the story contained any truth, but Coleridge had it in mind to commence a long poem based on the subject.
"He saw in it a reflection of the fatal fascination of opium, the power to charm the soul with glorious visions and then ensnare it forever.
"On that evening of cloudless beauty, with 'the kingdoms of the world, and the glory of them' laid out before our eyes...
"...these images swept Coleridge into such a continuous strain of eloquent dissertation, that I imagined myself come into the company of angels.

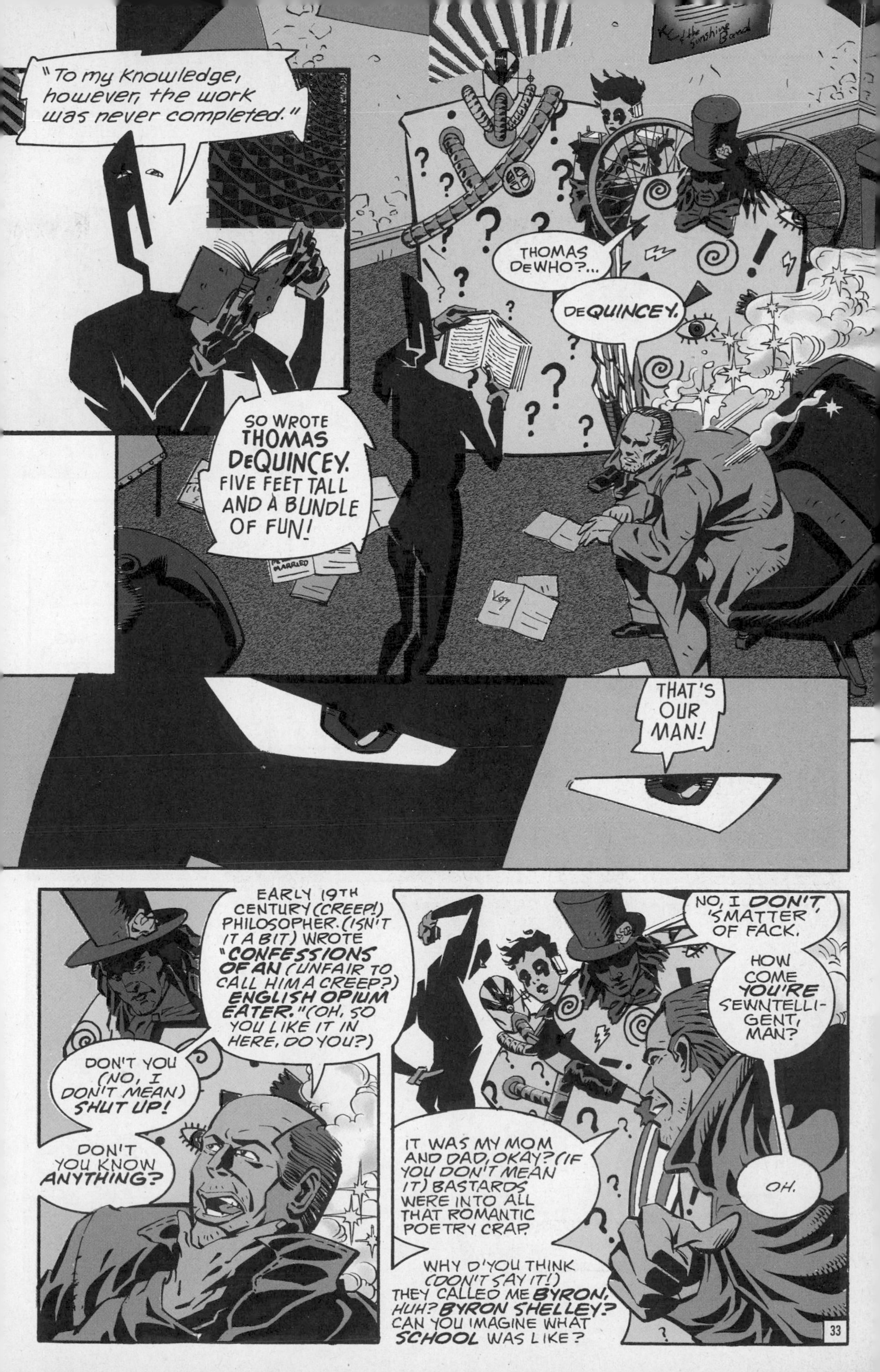
"To my knowledge, however, the work was never completed."
SO WROTE THOMAS DeQUINCEY. FIVE FEET TALL AND A BUNDLE OF FUN!
THOMAS DeWHO?...
DeQUINCEY.
THAT'S OUR MAN!
EARLY 19TH CENTURY (CREEP!) PHILOSOPHER. (ISN'T IT A BIT) WROTE "CONFESSIONS OF AN (UNFAIR TO CALL HIM A CREEP?) ENGLISH OPIUM EATER." (OH, SO YOU LIKE IT IN HERE, DO YOU?)
DON'T YOU (NO, I DON'T MEAN) SHUT UP!
DON'T YOU KNOW ANYTHING?
NO, I DON'T, 'SMATTER OF FACK.
HOW COME YOU'RE SEWNTELLI-GENT, MAN?
IT WAS MY MOM AND DAD, OKAY? (IF YOU DON'T MEAN IT) BASTARDS WERE INTO ALL THAT ROMANTIC POETRY CRAP.
OH.
WHY D'YOU THINK (DON'T SAY IT!) THEY CALLED ME BYRON, HUH? BYRON SHELLEY? CAN YOU IMAGINE WHAT SCHOOL WAS LIKE?

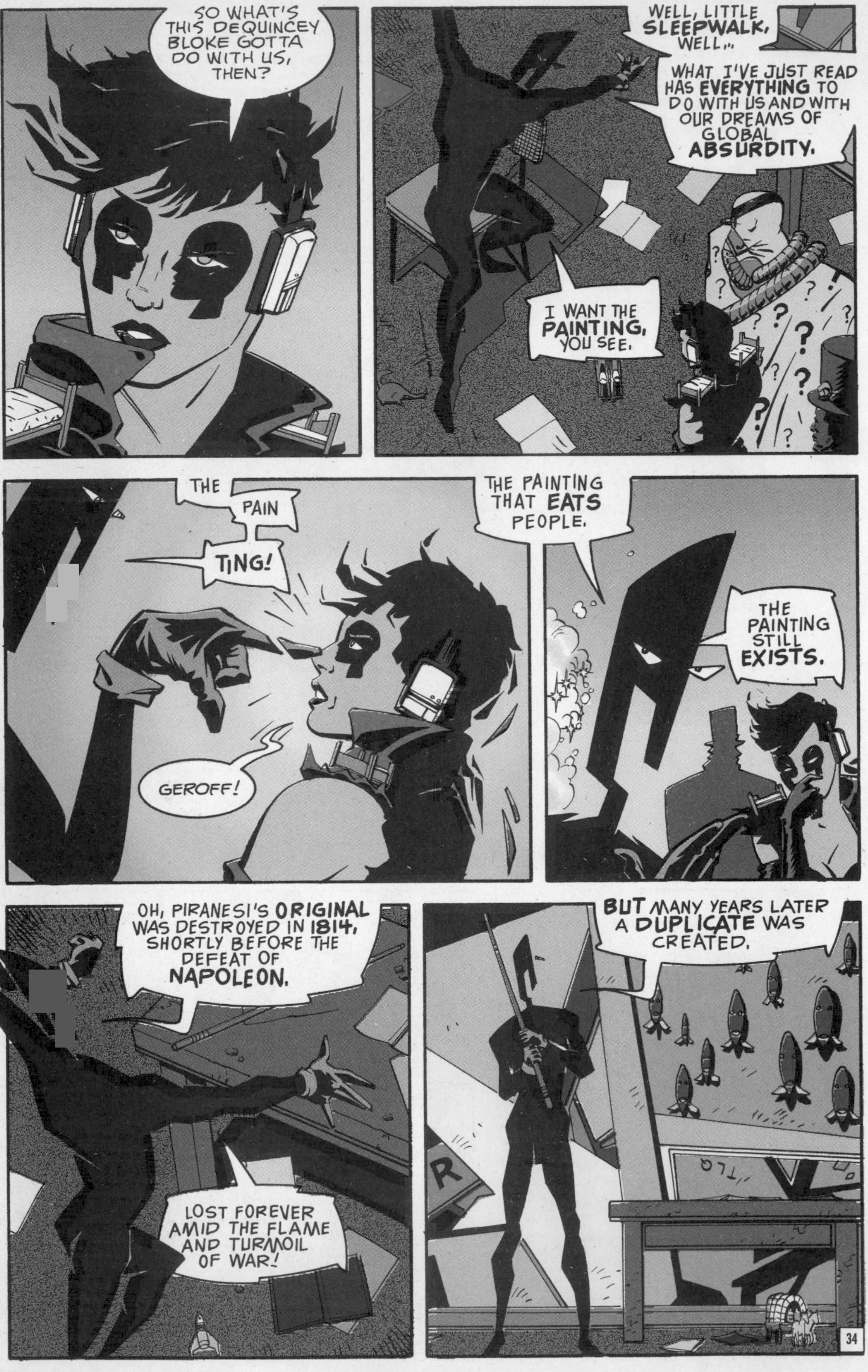
SO WHAT'S THIS DEQUINCEY BLOKE GOTTA DO WITH US, THEN?
WELL, LITTLE SLEEPWALK, WELL...
WHAT I'VE JUST READ HAS EVERYTHING TO DO WITH US AND WITH OUR DREAMS OF GLOBAL ABSURDITY.
I WANT THE PAINTING, YOU SEE.
THE
PAIN
TING!
GEROFF!
THE PAINTING THAT EATS PEOPLE.
THE PAINTING STILL EXISTS.
OH, PIRANESI'S ORIGINAL WAS DESTROYED IN 1814, SHORTLY BEFORE THE DEFEAT OF NAPOLEON.
LOST FOREVER AMID THE FLAME AND TURMOIL OF WAR!
BUT MANY YEARS LATER A DUPLICATE WAS CREATED.

"AS AN INTERESTING ASIDE, **OSCAR WILDE** MENTIONS THE STORY OF THE PAINTING IN HIS UNPUBLISHED '**CONFESSIONS OF SEBASTIAN MELMOTH**,' IN WHICH HE CLAIMS THAT IT INSPIRED HIM TO WRITE '**THE PICTURE OF DORIAN GRAY**.'

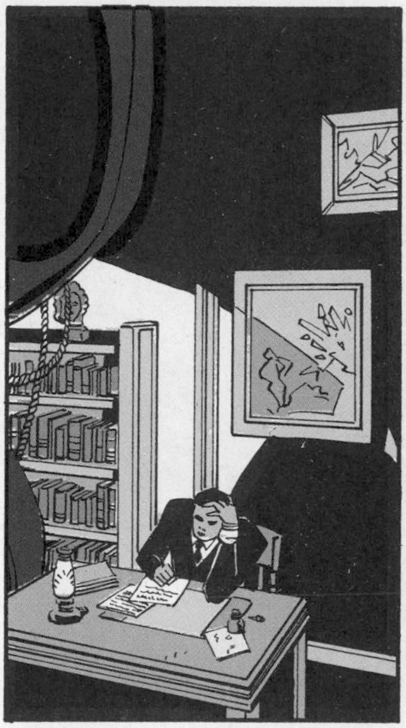

"THE SECOND PAINTING, HOWEVER, WAS THE WORK OF THE BRILLIANT, UNSTABLE **MAX BORDENGHAST**.

"THIS YOUNG ICELANDIC ARTIST HAD A CERTAIN CULT FOLLOWING IN THE EARLY YEARS OF THIS CENTURY AND WAS WELL-KNOWN FOR HIS ESOTERIC INTERESTS.

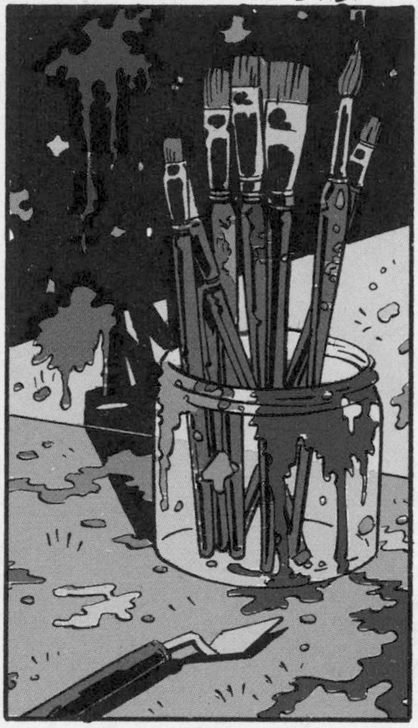

"THE STORY GOES THAT HE LOCKED HIMSELF IN HIS GARRET ROOM AND, USING SHAMANISTIC TECHNIQUES WHICH, THEY SAY, DATE BACK TO MAN'S INFANCY, EMERGED AFTER SEVERAL DAYS WITH A... HOW CAN I PUT IT?

"WITH A **HUNGRY** PAINTING.

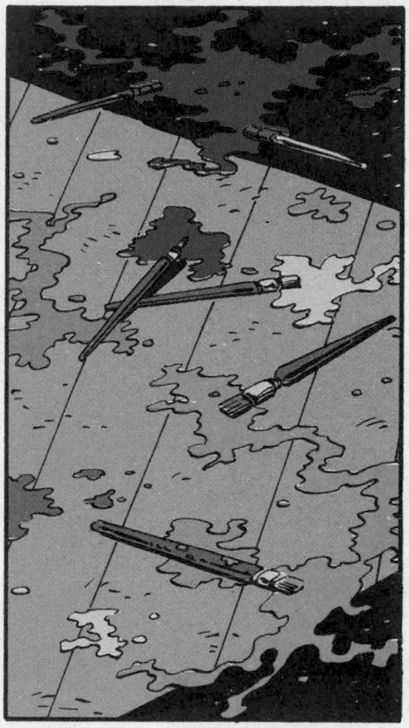

"IN THE END, EXPERIMENTS LIKE THESE SENT HIM ABSOLUTELY **LOOPY** AND HE SPENT THE REST OF HIS SHORT LIFE SCRIBBLING ON THE WALLS OF A LUNATIC ASYLUM.

"THE PAINTING, ALONG WITH MUCH OF BORDENGHAST'S OTHER WORK, VANISHED COMPLETELY.

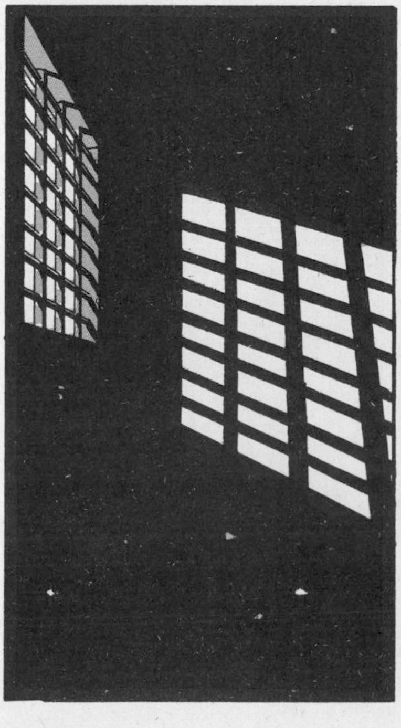

"IT IS NEXT REFERRED TO BY THE ENGLISH OCCULTIST **AUSTIN OSMAN SPARE**. USING HIS 'AUTOMATIC DRAWING' TECHNIQUE, SPARE ATTEMPTED TO PRODUCE A **SIMILAR** PAINTING.

"NEEDLESS TO SAY, THE ATTEMPT **FAILED**.

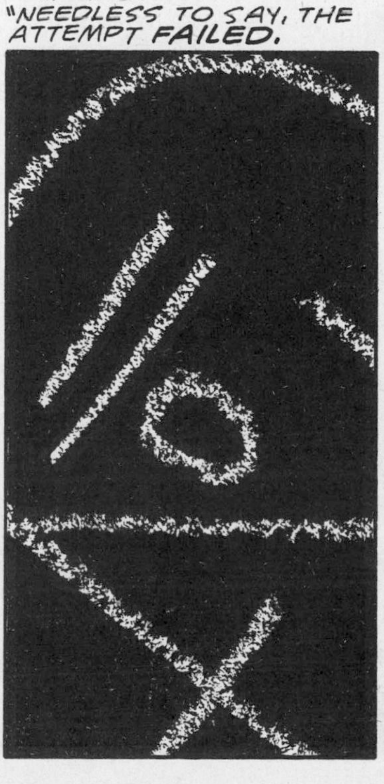

"FINALLY, IN **1923**, THE PAINTING SURFACED AS PART OF THE COLLECTION OF THE ENIGMATIC AND SADISTIC **COMTE D'AGUILLE**.

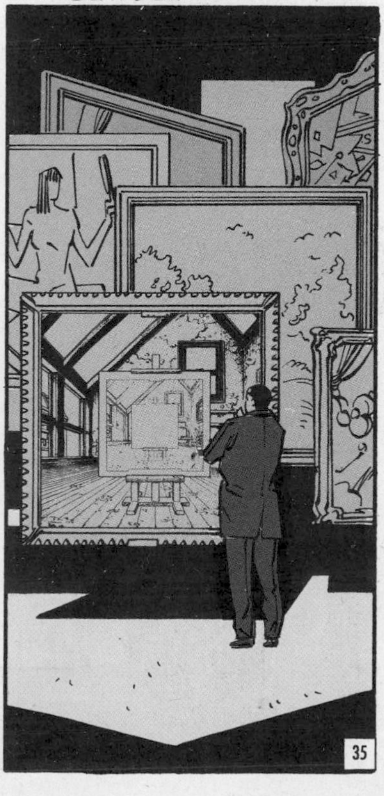

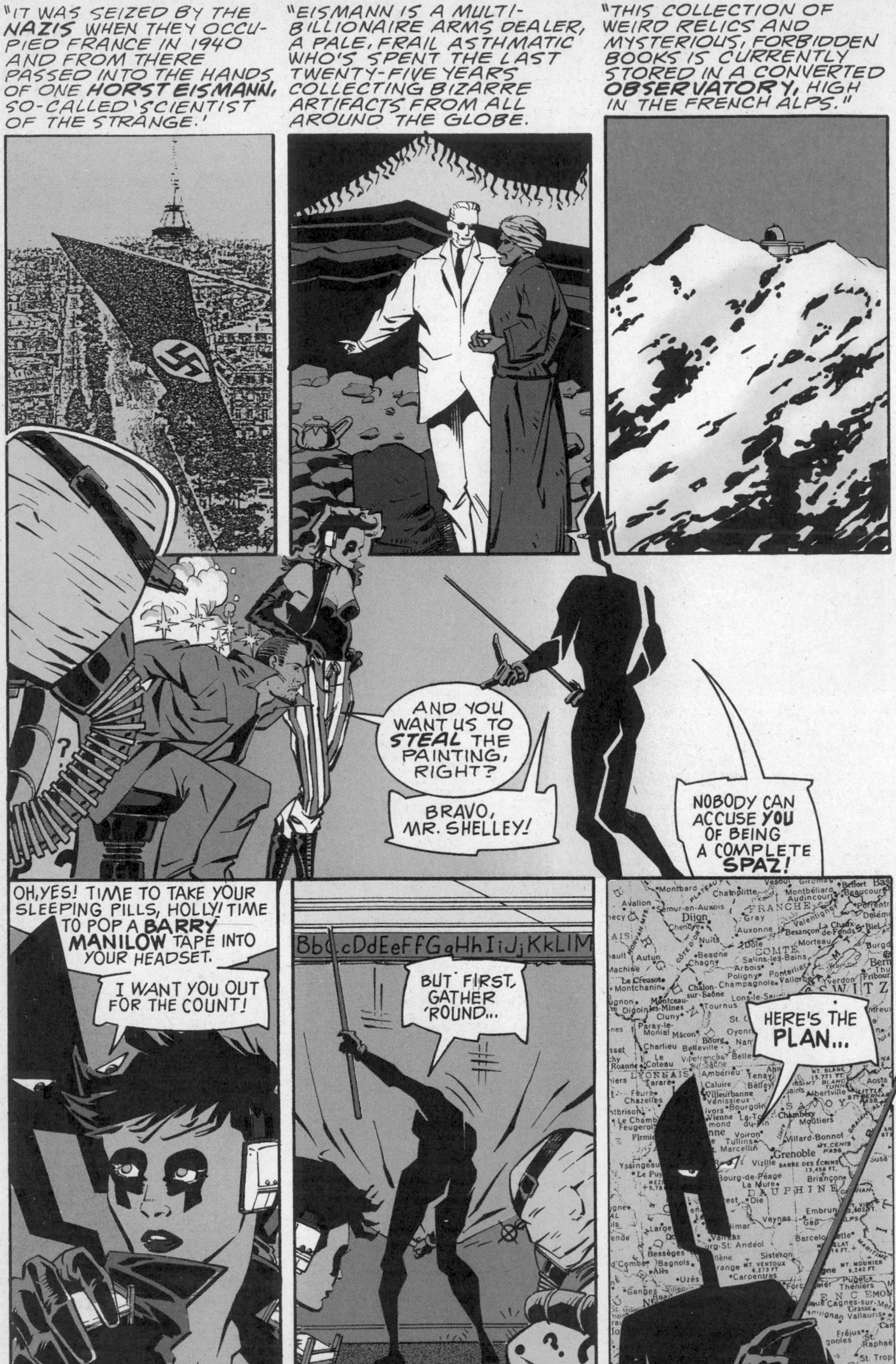
"IT WAS SEIZED BY THE **NAZIS** WHEN THEY OCCUPIED FRANCE IN 1940 AND FROM THERE PASSED INTO THE HANDS OF ONE **HORST EISMANN**, SO-CALLED 'SCIENTIST OF THE STRANGE.'
"EISMANN IS A MULTI-BILLIONAIRE ARMS DEALER, A PALE, FRAIL ASTHMATIC WHO'S SPENT THE LAST TWENTY-FIVE YEARS COLLECTING BIZARRE ARTIFACTS FROM ALL AROUND THE GLOBE.
"THIS COLLECTION OF WEIRD RELICS AND MYSTERIOUS, FORBIDDEN BOOKS IS CURRENTLY STORED IN A CONVERTED **OBSERVATORY**, HIGH IN THE FRENCH ALPS."
AND YOU WANT US TO **STEAL** THE PAINTING, RIGHT?
BRAVO, MR. SHELLEY!
NOBODY CAN ACCUSE **YOU** OF BEING A COMPLETE **SPAZ**!
OH, YES! TIME TO TAKE YOUR SLEEPING PILLS, HOLLY! TIME TO POP A **BARRY MANILOW** TAPE INTO YOUR HEADSET.
I WANT YOU OUT FOR THE COUNT!
BbCcDdEeFfGgHhIiJjKkLlM
BUT FIRST, GATHER 'ROUND...
HERE'S THE **PLAN**...

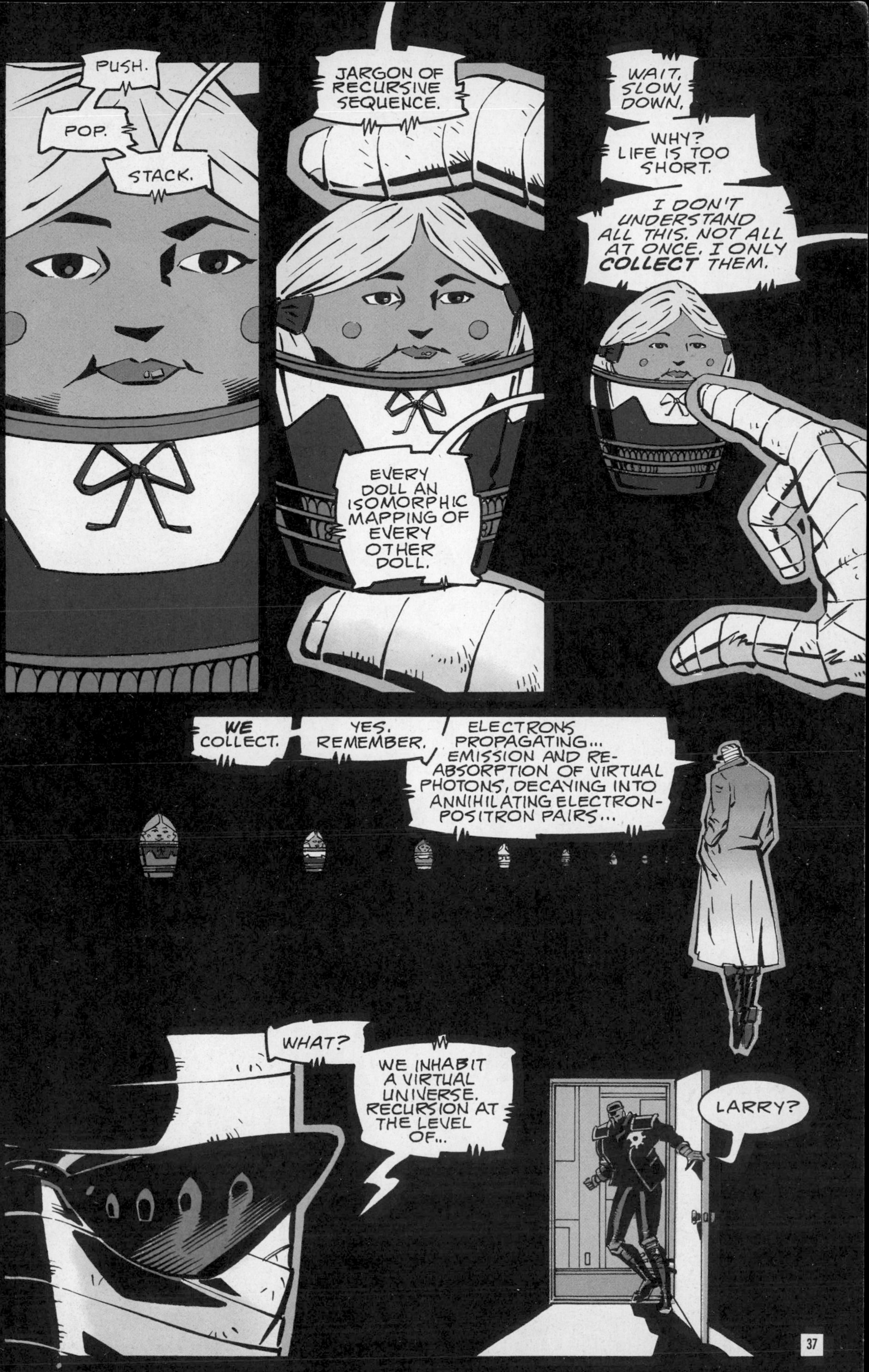
PUSH.
POP.
STACK.
JARGON OF RECURSIVE SEQUENCE.
WAIT, SLOW DOWN.
WHY? LIFE IS TOO SHORT.
I DON'T UNDERSTAND ALL THIS. NOT ALL AT ONCE. I ONLY **COLLECT** THEM.
EVERY DOLL AN ISOMORPHIC MAPPING OF EVERY OTHER DOLL.
WE COLLECT.
YES. REMEMBER.
ELECTRONS PROPAGATING... EMISSION AND RE-ABSORPTION OF VIRTUAL PHOTONS, DECAYING INTO ANNIHILATING ELECTRON-POSITRON PAIRS...
WHAT?
WE INHABIT A VIRTUAL UNIVERSE. RECURSION AT THE LEVEL OF...
LARRY?

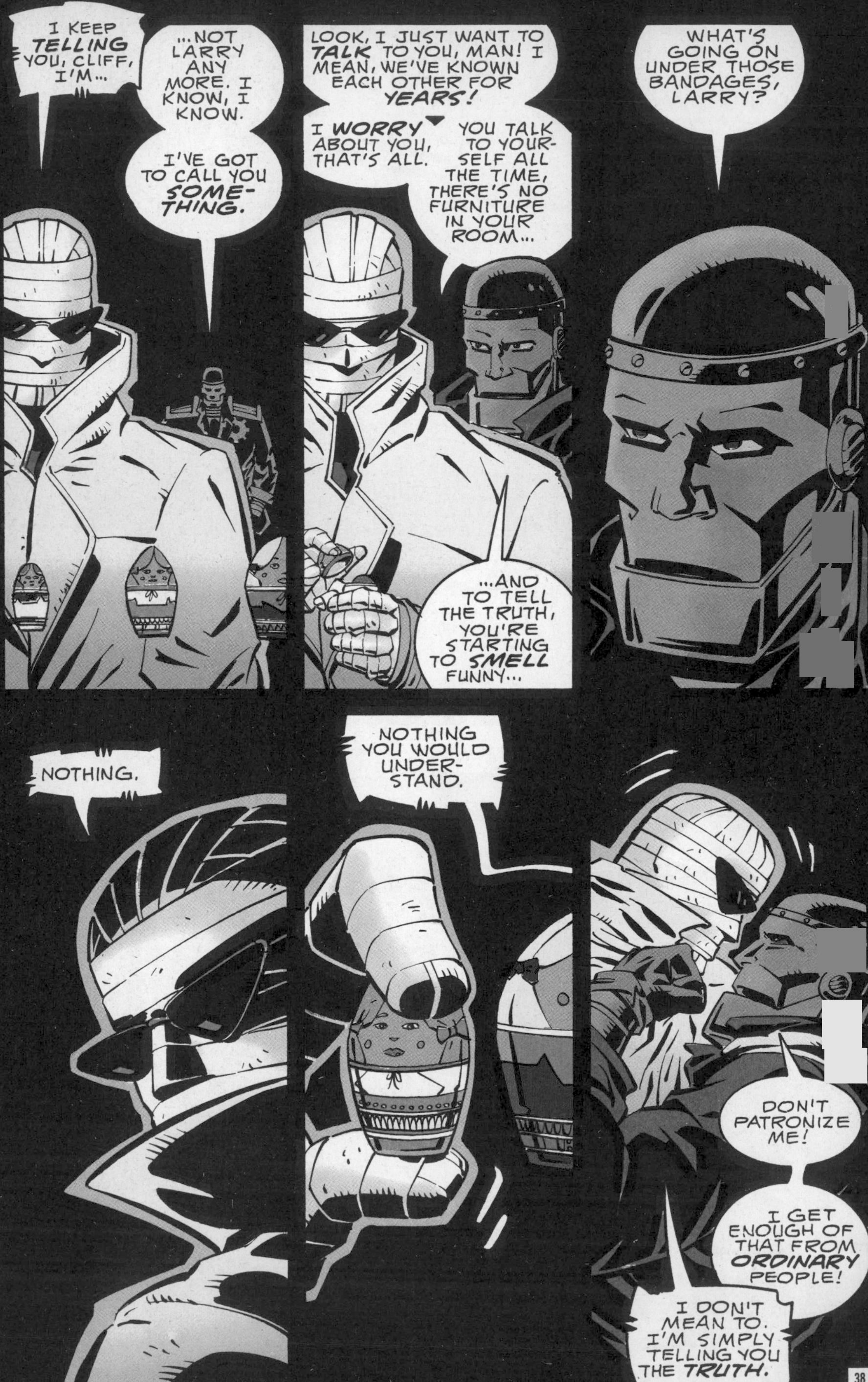
I KEEP TELLING YOU, CLIFF, I'M...
...NOT LARRY ANY MORE. I KNOW, I KNOW.
I'VE GOT TO CALL YOU SOMETHING.
LOOK, I JUST WANT TO TALK TO YOU, MAN! I MEAN, WE'VE KNOWN EACH OTHER FOR YEARS!
I WORRY ABOUT YOU, THAT'S ALL.
YOU TALK TO YOURSELF ALL THE TIME, THERE'S NO FURNITURE IN YOUR ROOM...
...AND TO TELL THE TRUTH, YOU'RE STARTING TO SMELL FUNNY...
WHAT'S GOING ON UNDER THOSE BANDAGES, LARRY?
NOTHING.
NOTHING YOU WOULD UNDERSTAND.
DON'T PATRONIZE ME!
I GET ENOUGH OF THAT FROM ORDINARY PEOPLE!
I DON'T MEAN TO. I'M SIMPLY TELLING YOU THE TRUTH.

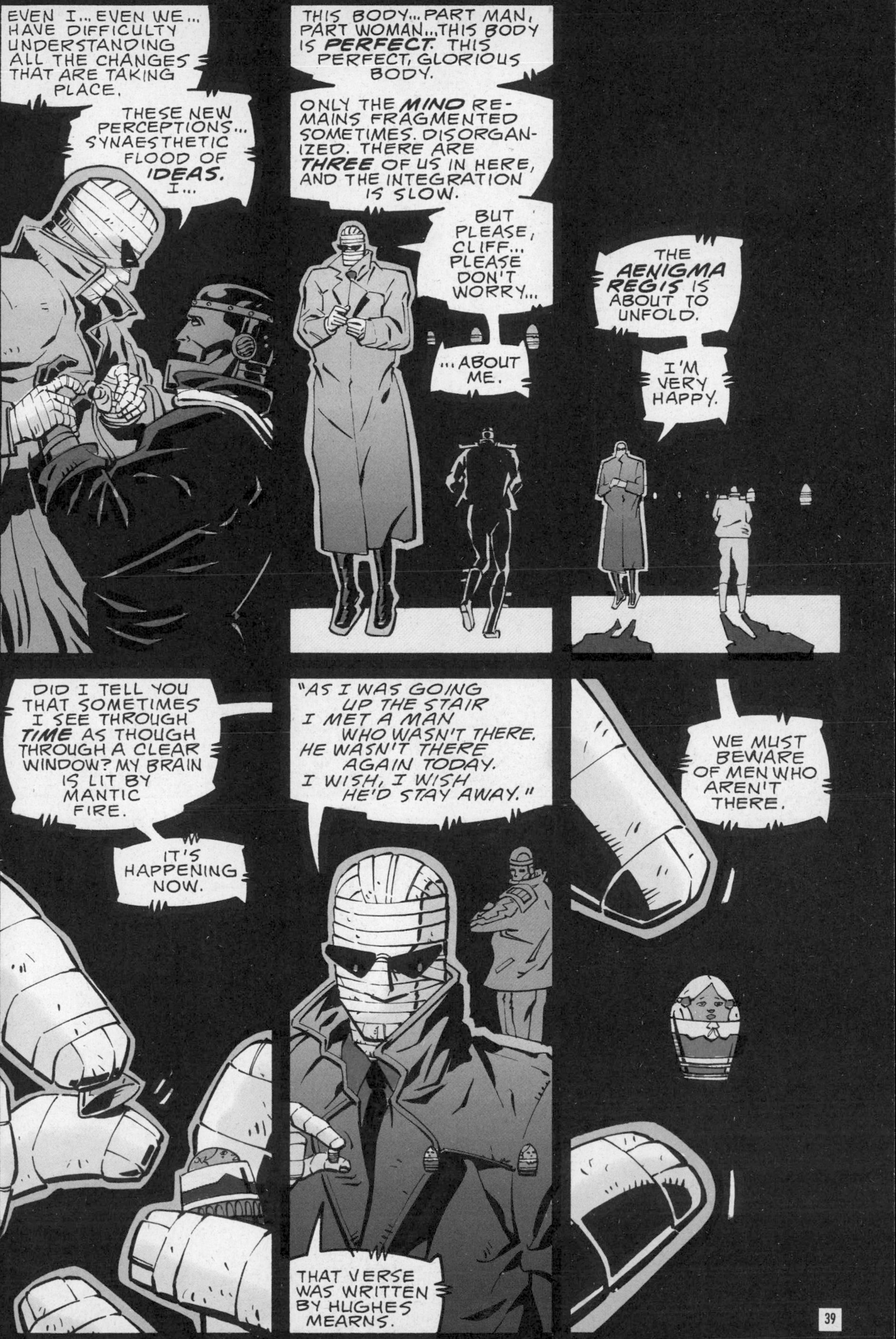
EVEN I... EVEN WE... HAVE DIFFICULTY UNDERSTANDING ALL THE CHANGES THAT ARE TAKING PLACE.
THESE NEW PERCEPTIONS... SYNAESTHETIC FLOOD OF IDEAS. I...
THIS BODY... PART MAN, PART WOMAN... THIS BODY IS PERFECT. THIS PERFECT, GLORIOUS BODY.
ONLY THE MIND REMAINS FRAGMENTED SOMETIMES. DISORGANIZED. THERE ARE THREE OF US IN HERE, AND THE INTEGRATION IS SLOW.
BUT PLEASE, CLIFF... PLEASE DON'T WORRY...
...ABOUT ME.
THE AENIGMA REGIS IS ABOUT TO UNFOLD.
I'M VERY HAPPY.
DID I TELL YOU THAT SOMETIMES I SEE THROUGH TIME AS THOUGH THROUGH A CLEAR WINDOW? MY BRAIN IS LIT BY MANTIC FIRE.
IT'S HAPPENING NOW.
"AS I WAS GOING UP THE STAIR I MET A MAN WHO WASN'T THERE. HE WASN'T THERE AGAIN TODAY. I WISH, I WISH HE'D STAY AWAY."
THAT VERSE WAS WRITTEN BY HUGHES MEARNS.
WE MUST BEWARE OF MEN WHO AREN'T THERE.

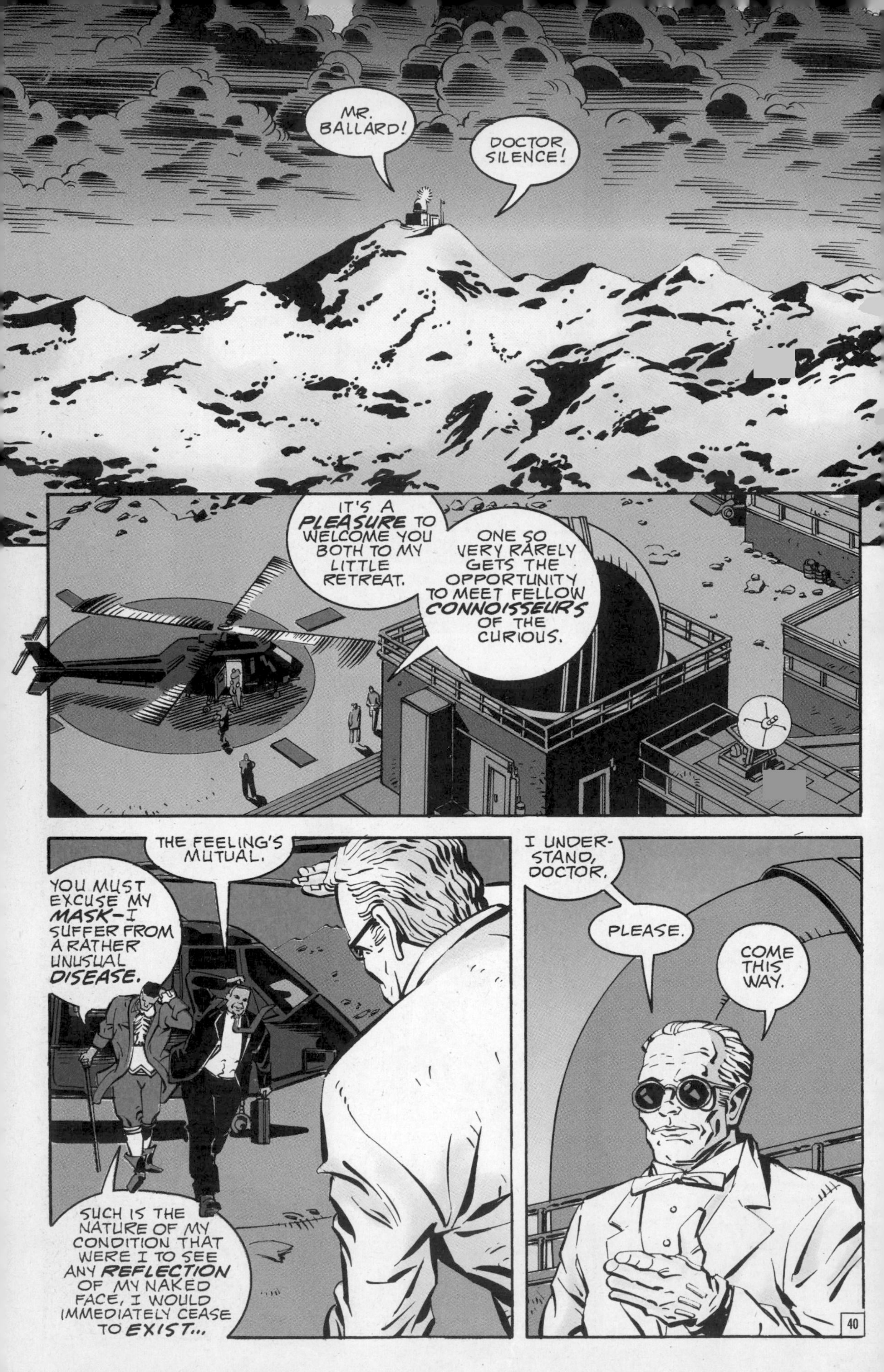
MR. BALLARD!
DOCTOR SILENCE!
IT'S A PLEASURE TO WELCOME YOU BOTH TO MY LITTLE RETREAT.
ONE SO VERY RARELY GETS THE OPPORTUNITY TO MEET FELLOW CONNOISSEURS OF THE CURIOUS.
THE FEELING'S MUTUAL.
YOU MUST EXCUSE MY MASK—I SUFFER FROM A RATHER UNUSUAL DISEASE.
SUCH IS THE NATURE OF MY CONDITION THAT WERE I TO SEE ANY REFLECTION OF MY NAKED FACE, I WOULD IMMEDIATELY CEASE TO EXIST...
I UNDER-STAND, DOCTOR.
PLEASE.
COME THIS WAY.

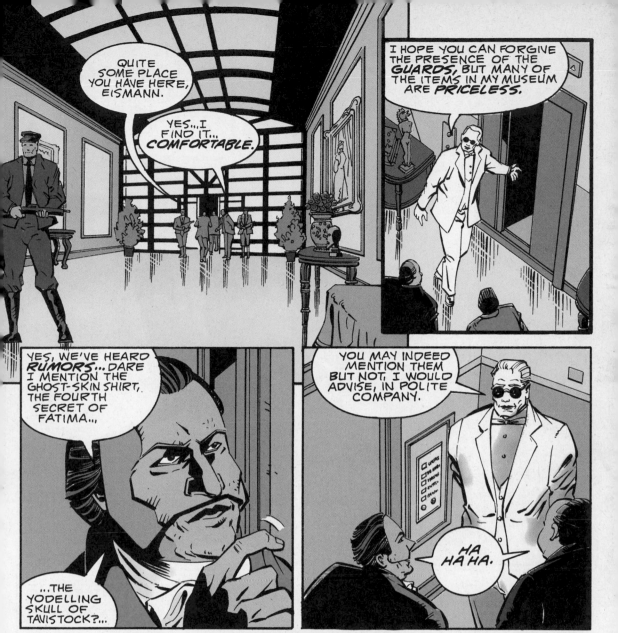

QUITE SOME PLACE YOU HAVE HERE, EISMANN.

YES... I FIND IT... COMFORTABLE.

I HOPE YOU CAN FORGIVE THE PRESENCE OF THE *GUARDS*, BUT MANY OF THE ITEMS IN MY MUSEUM ARE *PRICELESS*.

YES, WE'VE HEARD *RUMORS*... DARE I MENTION THE GHOST-SKIN SHIRT, THE FOURTH SECRET OF FATIMA...

...THE YODELLING SKULL OF TAVISTOCK?...

YOU MAY INDEED MENTION THEM BUT NOT, I WOULD ADVISE, IN POLITE COMPANY.

HA HA HA.

SURFACE

SUB-SURFACE

BASEMENT

SUB-BASEMENT

VAULT

AH.

HERE WE ARE.

I BID YOU WELCOME.

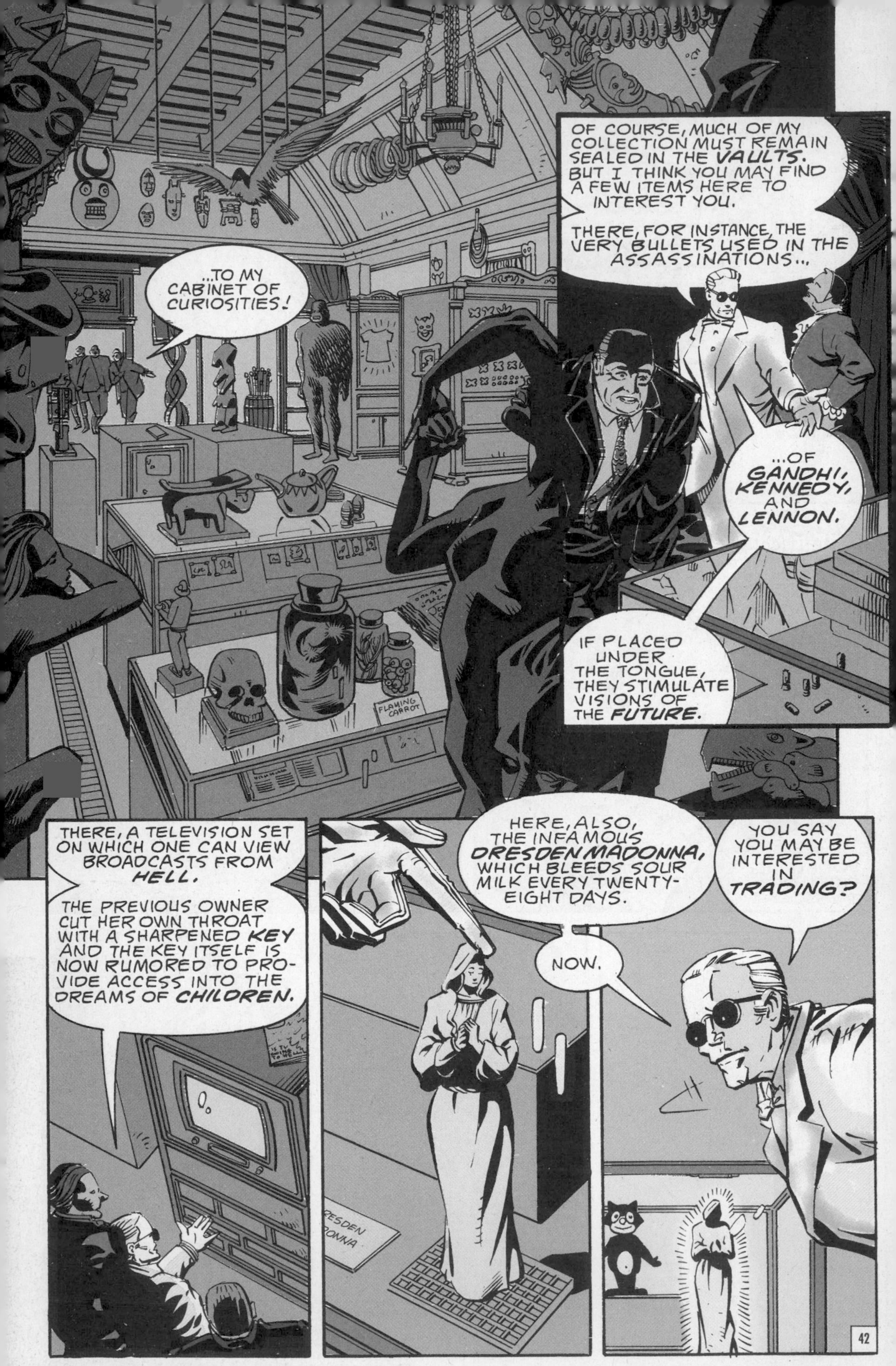
...TO MY CABINET OF CURIOSITIES!
FLAMING CARROT
OF COURSE, MUCH OF MY COLLECTION MUST REMAIN SEALED IN THE VAULTS. BUT I THINK YOU MAY FIND A FEW ITEMS HERE TO INTEREST YOU.
THERE, FOR INSTANCE, THE VERY BULLETS USED IN THE ASSASSINATIONS...
...OF GANDHI, KENNEDY, AND LENNON.
IF PLACED UNDER THE TONGUE, THEY STIMULATE VISIONS OF THE FUTURE.
THERE, A TELEVISION SET ON WHICH ONE CAN VIEW BROADCASTS FROM HELL.
THE PREVIOUS OWNER CUT HER OWN THROAT WITH A SHARPENED KEY AND THE KEY ITSELF IS NOW RUMORED TO PROVIDE ACCESS INTO THE DREAMS OF CHILDREN.
HERE, ALSO, THE INFAMOUS DRESDEN MADONNA, WHICH BLEEDS SOUR MILK EVERY TWENTY-EIGHT DAYS.
NOW.
YOU SAY YOU MAY BE INTERESTED IN TRADING?

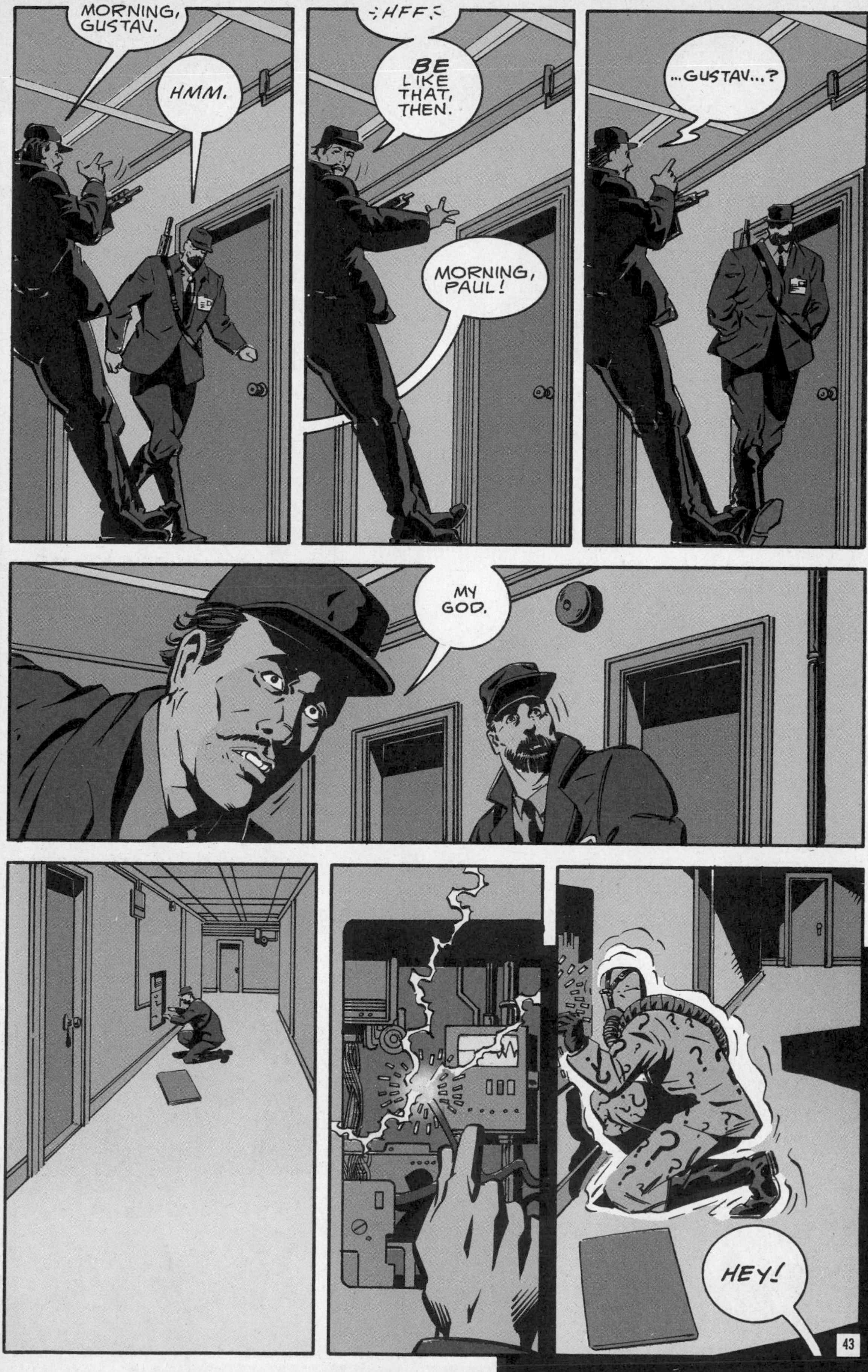
MORNING, GUSTAV.
HMM.
HFF
BE LIKE THAT, THEN.
MORNING, PAUL!
...GUSTAV...?
MY GOD.
HEY!

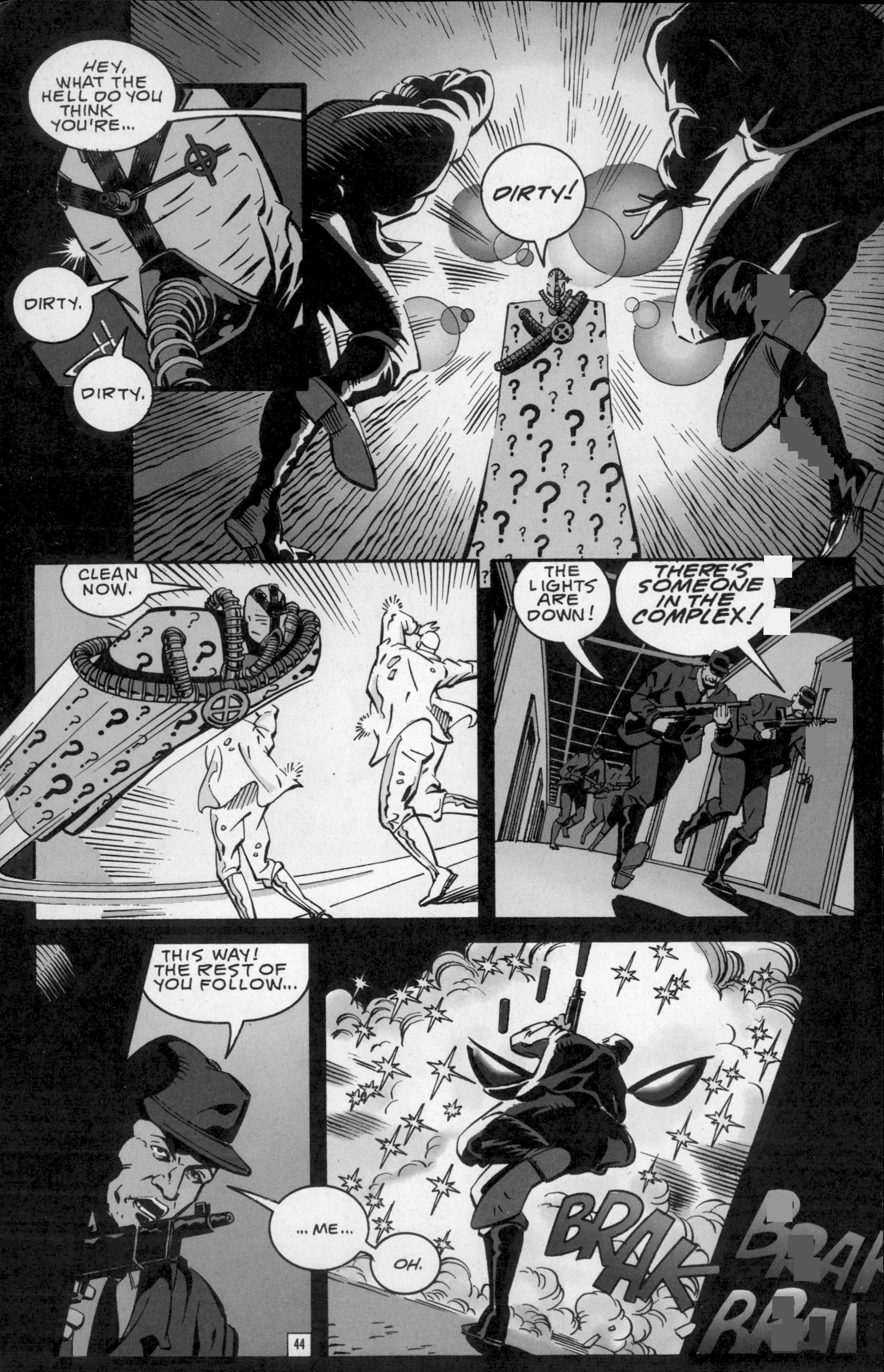
HEY, WHAT THE HELL DO YOU THINK YOU'RE...
DIRTY.
DIRTY.
DIRTY!
CLEAN NOW.
THE LIGHTS ARE DOWN!
THERE'S SOMEONE IN THE COMPLEX!
THIS WAY! THE REST OF YOU FOLLOW...
... ME...
OH.
BRAK

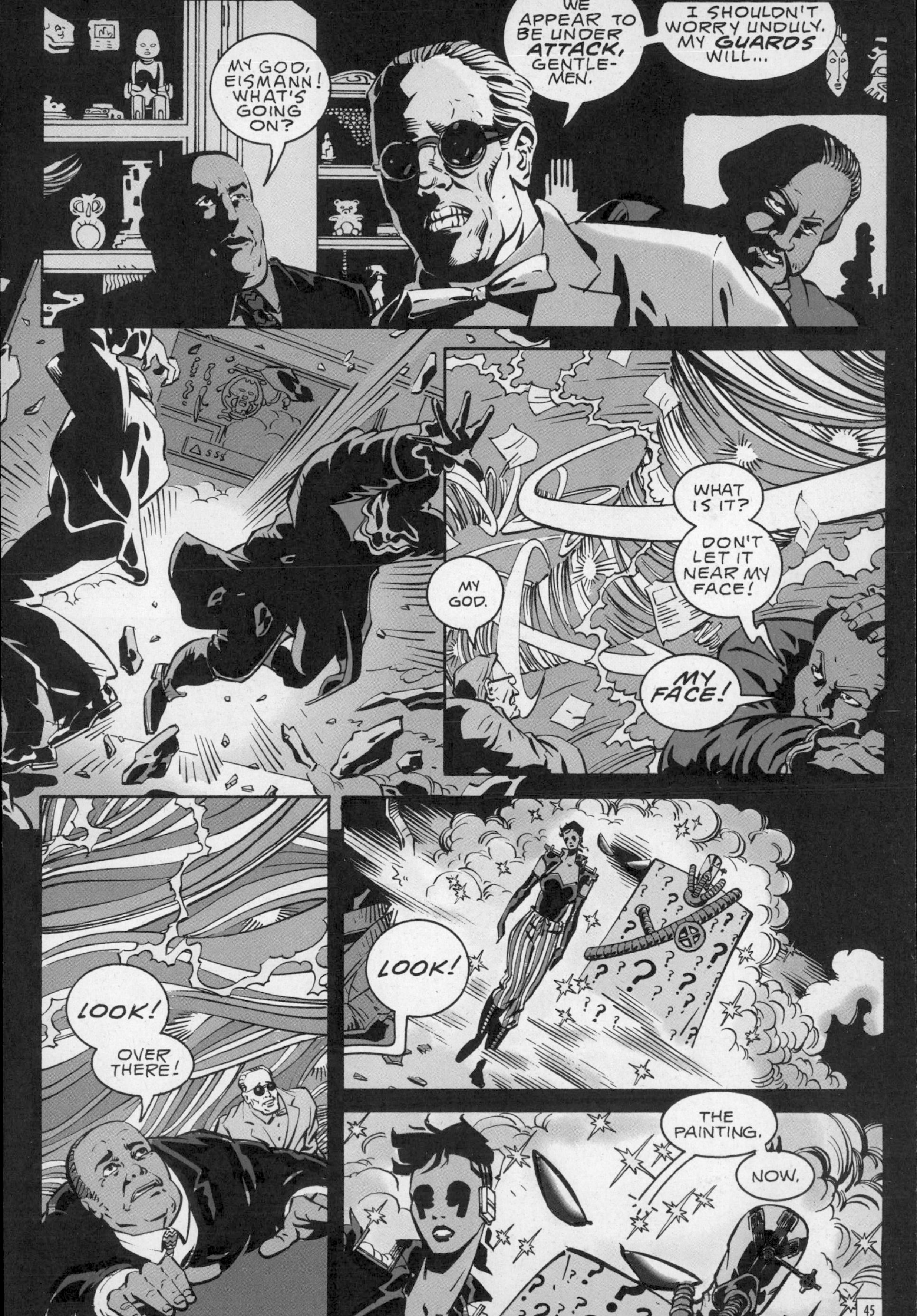
MY GOD, EISMANN! WHAT'S GOING ON?
WE APPEAR TO BE UNDER ATTACK, GENTLE-MEN.
I SHOULDN'T WORRY UNDULY. MY GUARDS WILL...
WHAT IS IT?
DON'T LET IT NEAR MY FACE!
MY GOD.
MY FACE!
LOOK!
OVER THERE!
LOOK!
THE PAINTING.
NOW.

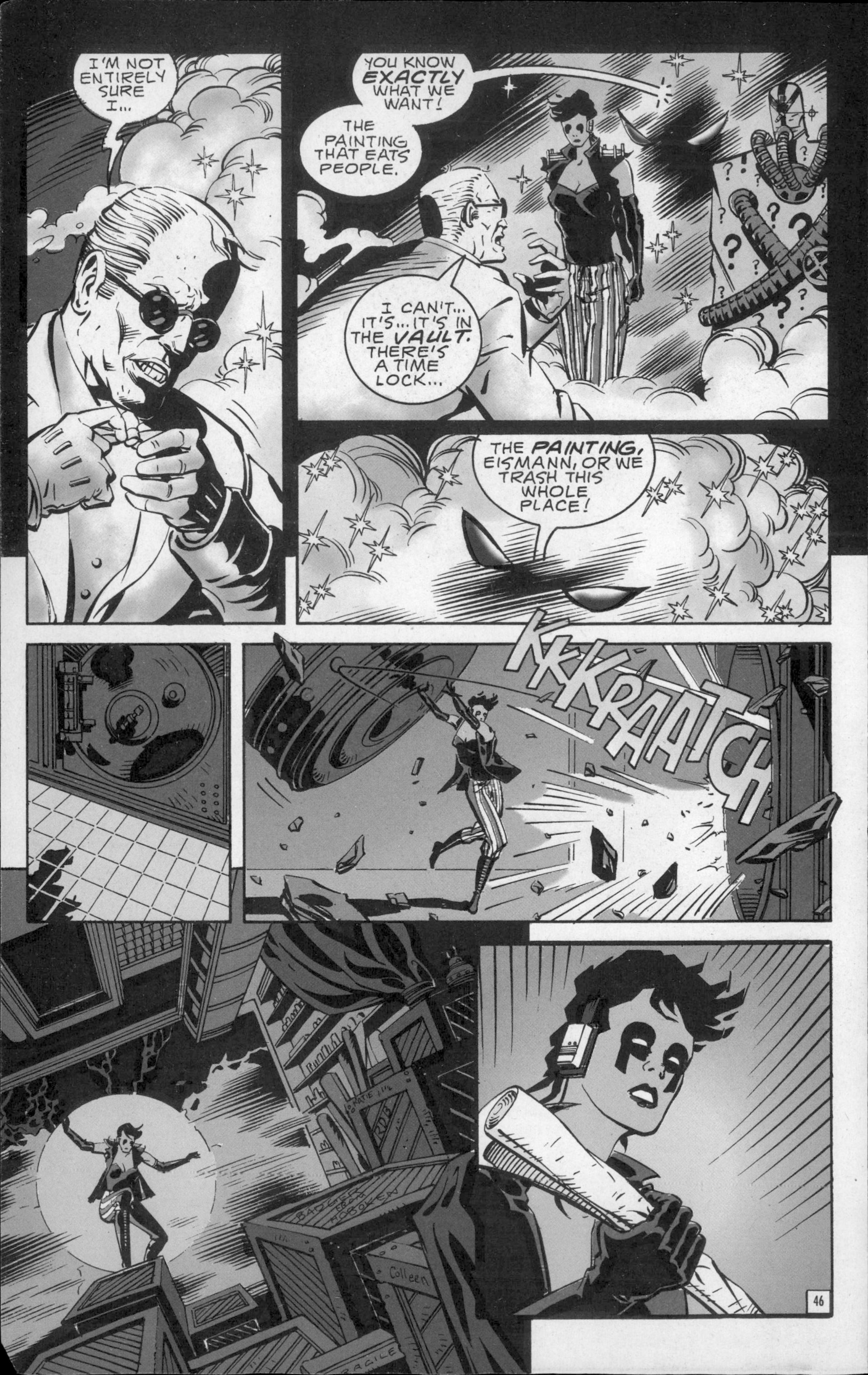
I'M NOT ENTIRELY SURE I...
YOU KNOW EXACTLY WHAT WE WANT!
THE PAINTING THAT EATS PEOPLE.
I CAN'T... IT'S... IT'S IN THE VAULT. THERE'S A TIME LOCK...
THE PAINTING, EISMANN, OR WE TRASH THIS WHOLE PLACE!
KKKRAAATCH!
BADGER FROM HOBOKEN
Colleen

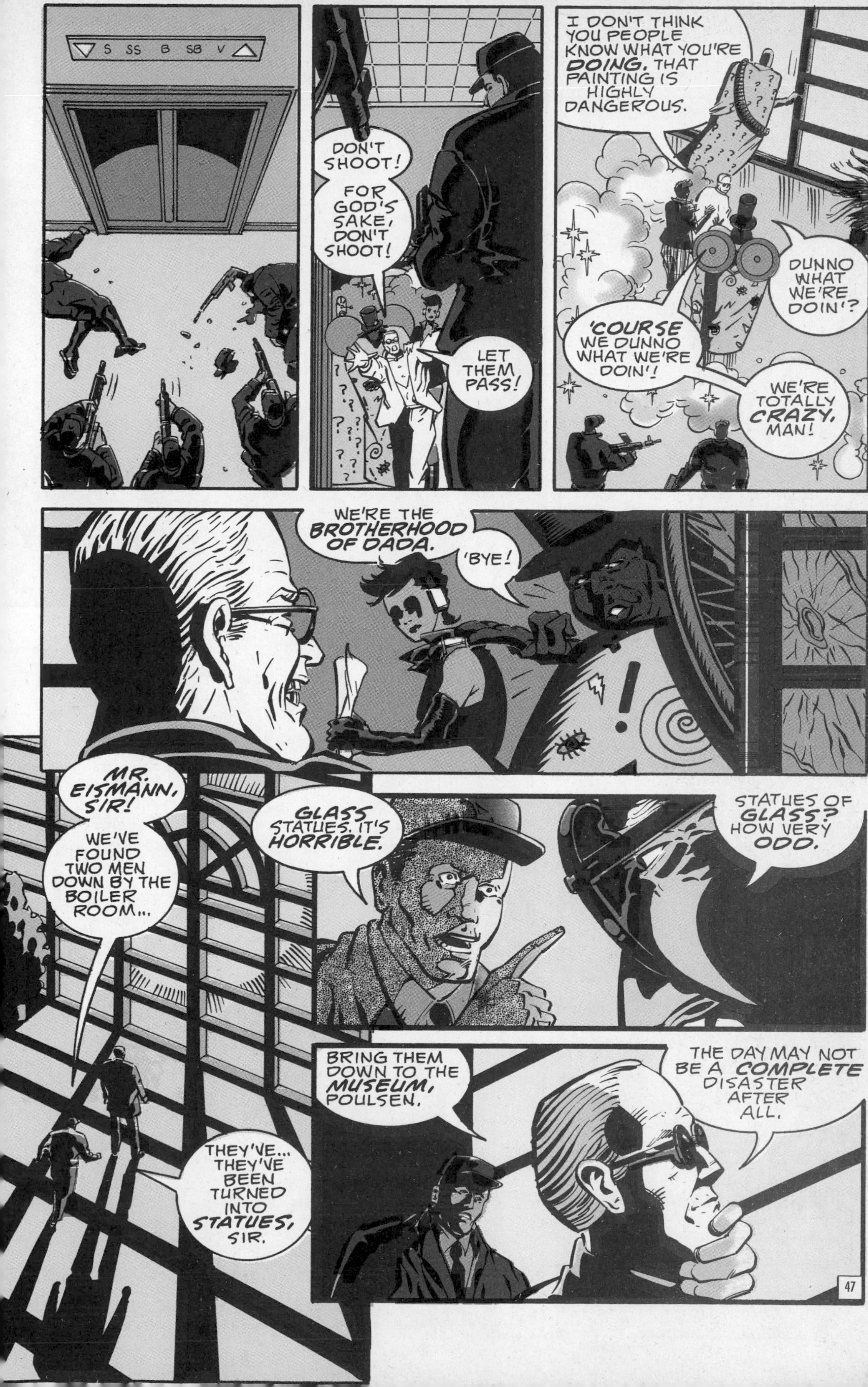
S SS B SB V
DON'T SHOOT!
FOR GOD'S SAKE, DON'T SHOOT!
LET THEM PASS!
I DON'T THINK YOU PEOPLE KNOW WHAT YOU'RE DOING. THAT PAINTING IS HIGHLY DANGEROUS.
DUNNO WHAT WE'RE DOIN'?
'COURSE WE DUNNO WHAT WE'RE DOIN'!
WE'RE TOTALLY CRAZY, MAN!
WE'RE THE BROTHERHOOD OF DADA.
'BYE!
MR. EISMANN, SIR!
WE'VE FOUND TWO MEN DOWN BY THE BOILER ROOM...
GLASS STATUES. IT'S HORRIBLE.
STATUES OF GLASS? HOW VERY ODD.
THEY'VE... THEY'VE BEEN TURNED INTO STATUES, SIR.
BRING THEM DOWN TO THE MUSEUM, POULSEN.
THE DAY MAY NOT BE A COMPLETE DISASTER AFTER ALL.

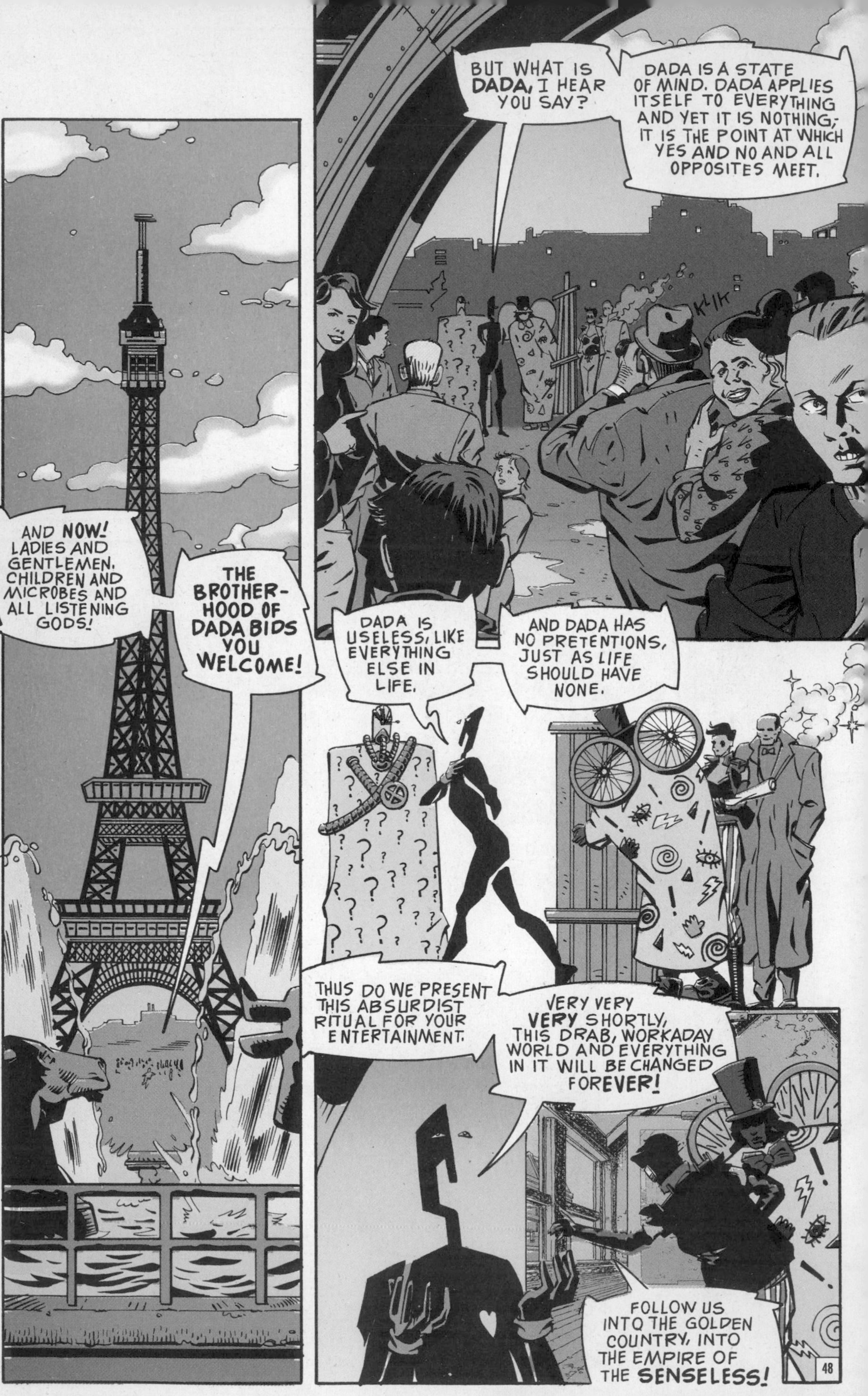
AND NOW! LADIES AND GENTLEMEN, CHILDREN AND MICROBES AND ALL LISTENING GODS!
THE BROTHERHOOD OF DADA BIDS YOU WELCOME!
BUT WHAT IS DADA, I HEAR YOU SAY?
DADA IS A STATE OF MIND. DADA APPLIES ITSELF TO EVERYTHING AND YET IT IS NOTHING; IT IS THE POINT AT WHICH YES AND NO AND ALL OPPOSITES MEET.
KLIK
DADA IS USELESS, LIKE EVERYTHING ELSE IN LIFE.
AND DADA HAS NO PRETENTIONS, JUST AS LIFE SHOULD HAVE NONE.
THUS DO WE PRESENT THIS ABSURDIST RITUAL FOR YOUR ENTERTAINMENT.
VERY VERY VERY SHORTLY, THIS DRAB, WORKADAY WORLD AND EVERYTHING IN IT WILL BE CHANGED FOREVER!
FOLLOW US INTO THE GOLDEN COUNTRY, INTO THE EMPIRE OF THE SENSELESS!

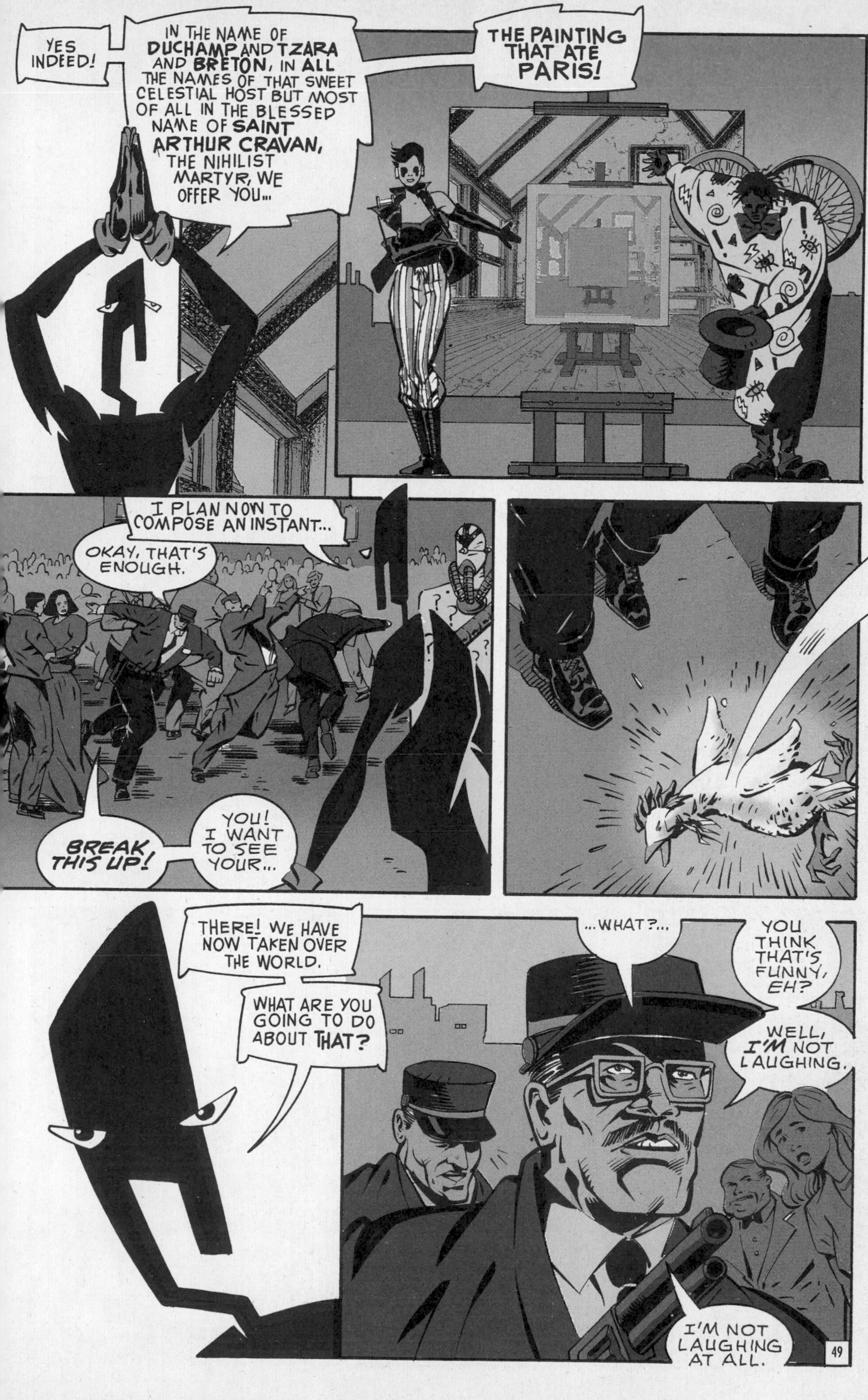
YES INDEED!
IN THE NAME OF DUCHAMP AND TZARA AND BRETON, IN ALL THE NAMES OF THAT SWEET CELESTIAL HOST BUT MOST OF ALL IN THE BLESSED NAME OF SAINT ARTHUR CRAVAN, THE NIHILIST MARTYR, WE OFFER YOU...
THE PAINTING THAT ATE PARIS!
I PLAN NOW TO COMPOSE AN INSTANT...
OKAY, THAT'S ENOUGH.
BREAK THIS UP!
YOU! I WANT TO SEE YOUR...
THERE! WE HAVE NOW TAKEN OVER THE WORLD.
WHAT ARE YOU GOING TO DO ABOUT THAT?
...WHAT?...
YOU THINK THAT'S FUNNY, EH?
WELL, I'M NOT LAUGHING.
I'M NOT LAUGHING AT ALL.
49

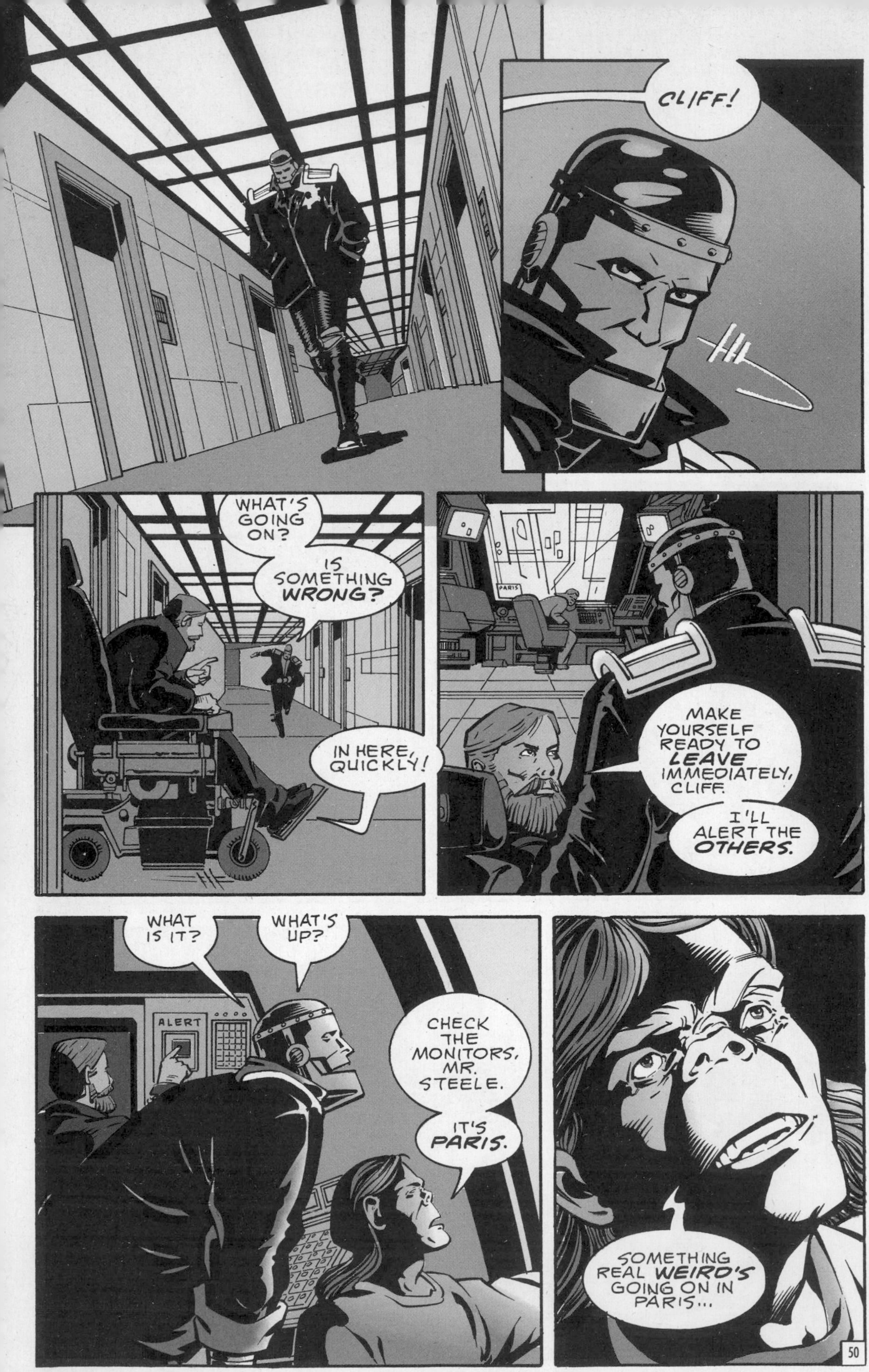
CLIFF!
WHAT'S GOING ON?
IS SOMETHING WRONG?
IN HERE, QUICKLY!
PARIS
MAKE YOURSELF READY TO LEAVE IMMEDIATELY, CLIFF.
I'LL ALERT THE OTHERS.
WHAT IS IT?
WHAT'S UP?
ALERT
CHECK THE MONITORS, MR. STEELE.
IT'S PARIS.
SOMETHING REAL WEIRD'S GOING ON IN PARIS...

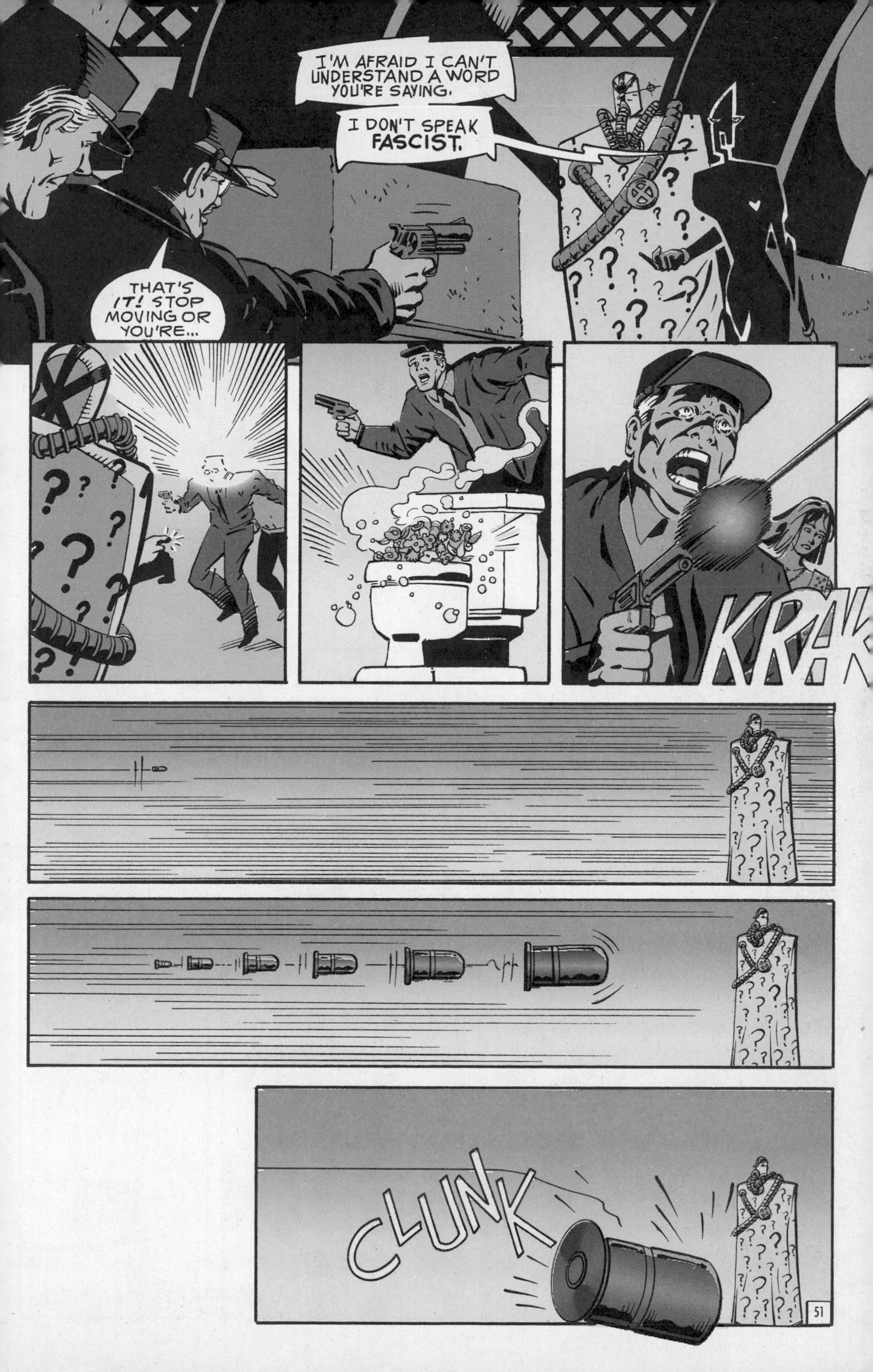
I'M AFRAID I CAN'T UNDERSTAND A WORD YOU'RE SAYING.
I DON'T SPEAK **FASCIST.**
THAT'S *IT!* STOP MOVING OR YOU'RE...
KRAK
CLUNK

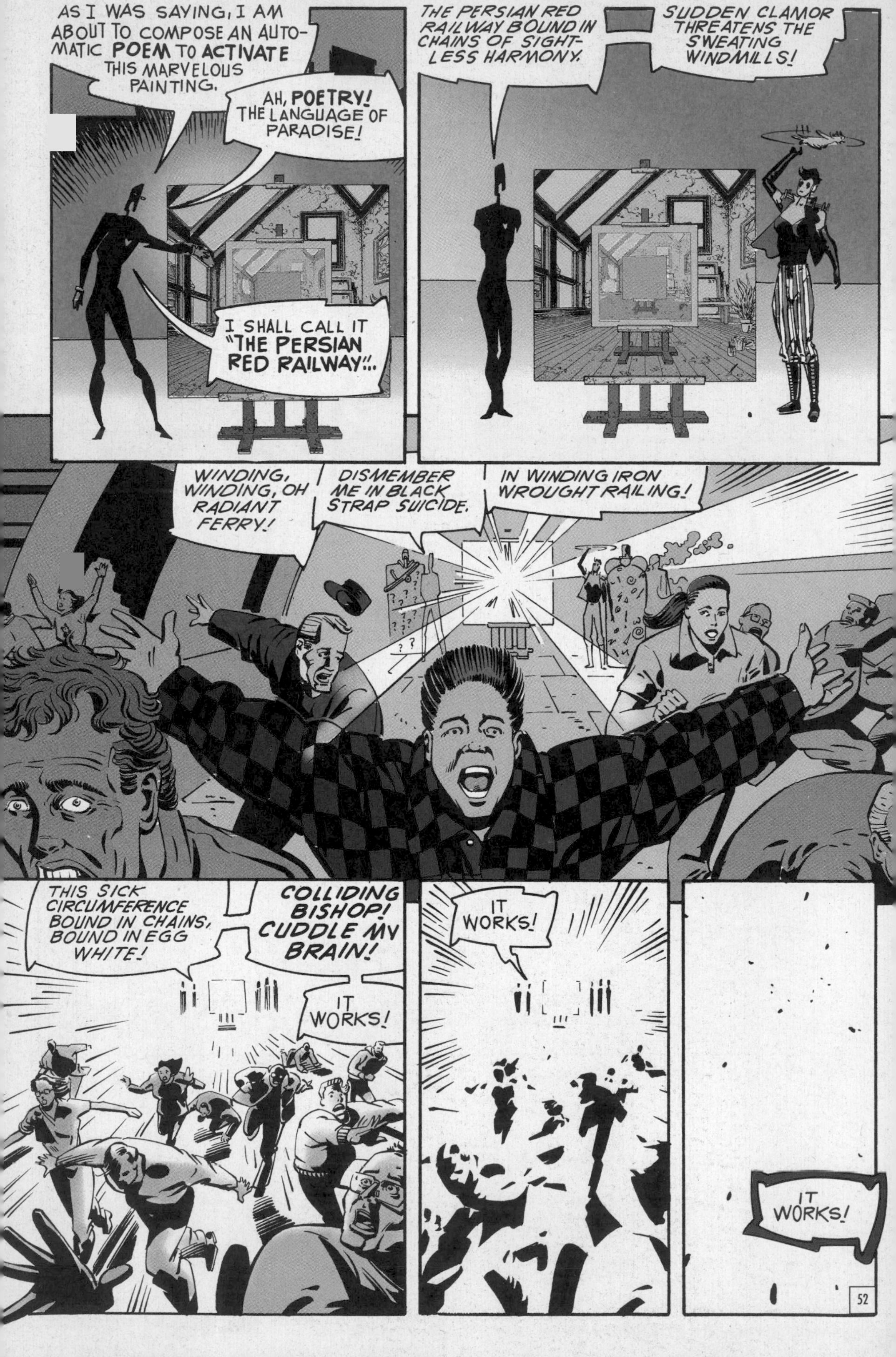
AS I WAS SAYING, I AM ABOUT TO COMPOSE AN AUTO-MATIC POEM TO ACTIVATE THIS MARVELOUS PAINTING.
AH, POETRY! THE LANGUAGE OF PARADISE!
I SHALL CALL IT "THE PERSIAN RED RAILWAY"...
THE PERSIAN RED RAILWAY BOUND IN CHAINS OF SIGHT-LESS HARMONY.
SUDDEN CLAMOR THREATENS THE SWEATING WINDMILLS!
WINDING, WINDING, OH RADIANT FERRY!
DISMEMBER ME IN BLACK STRAP SUICIDE.
IN WINDING IRON WROUGHT RAILING!
THIS SICK CIRCUMFERENCE BOUND IN CHAINS, BOUND IN EGG WHITE!
COLLIDING BISHOP! CUDDLE MY BRAIN!
IT WORKS!
IT WORKS!
IT WORKS!

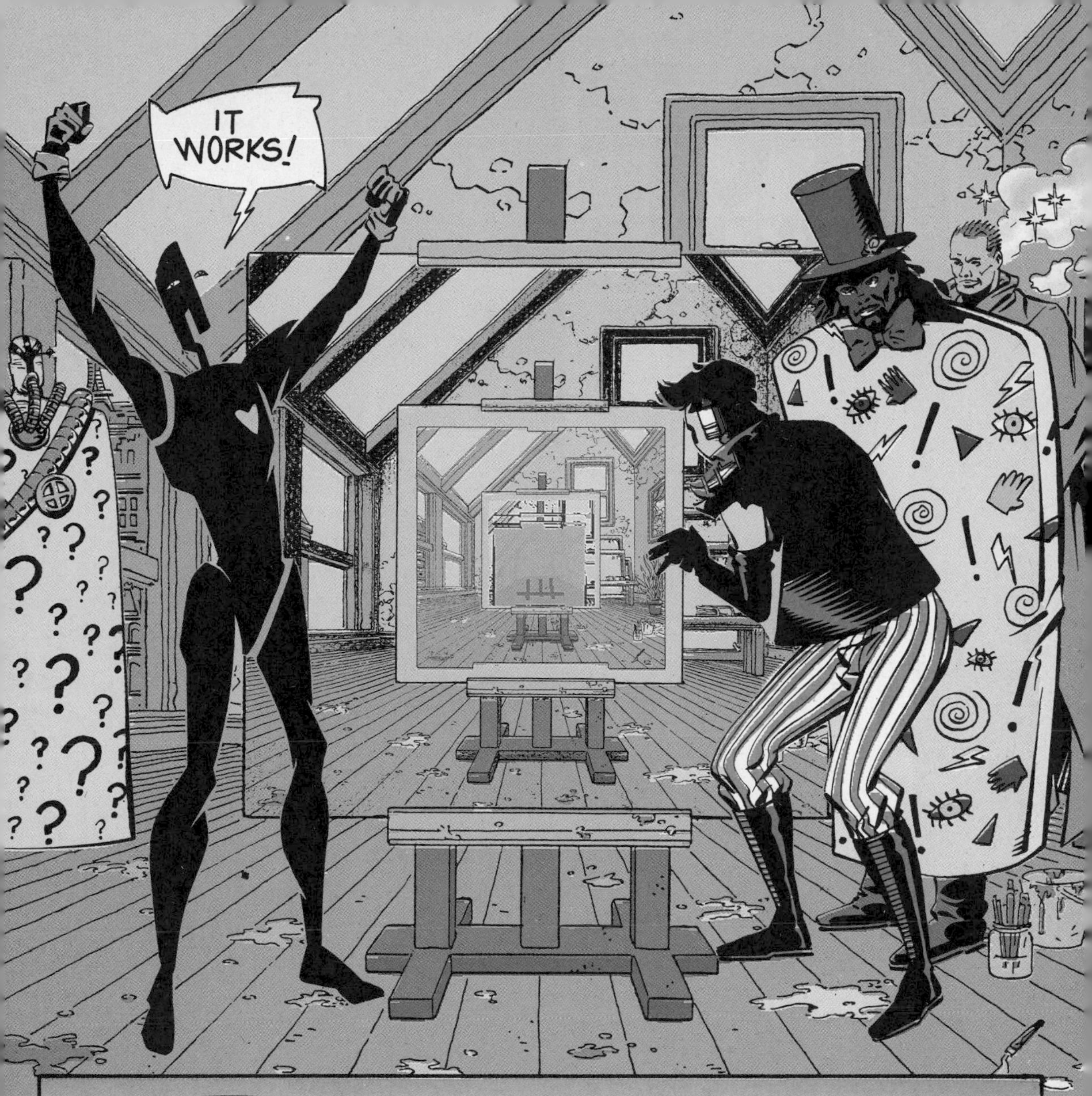
IT WORKS!
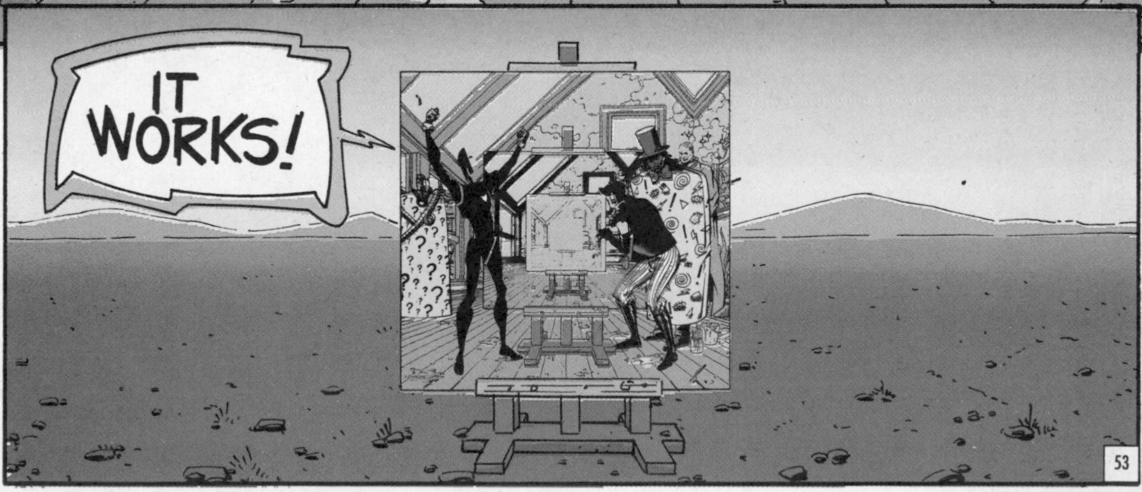
IT WORKS!

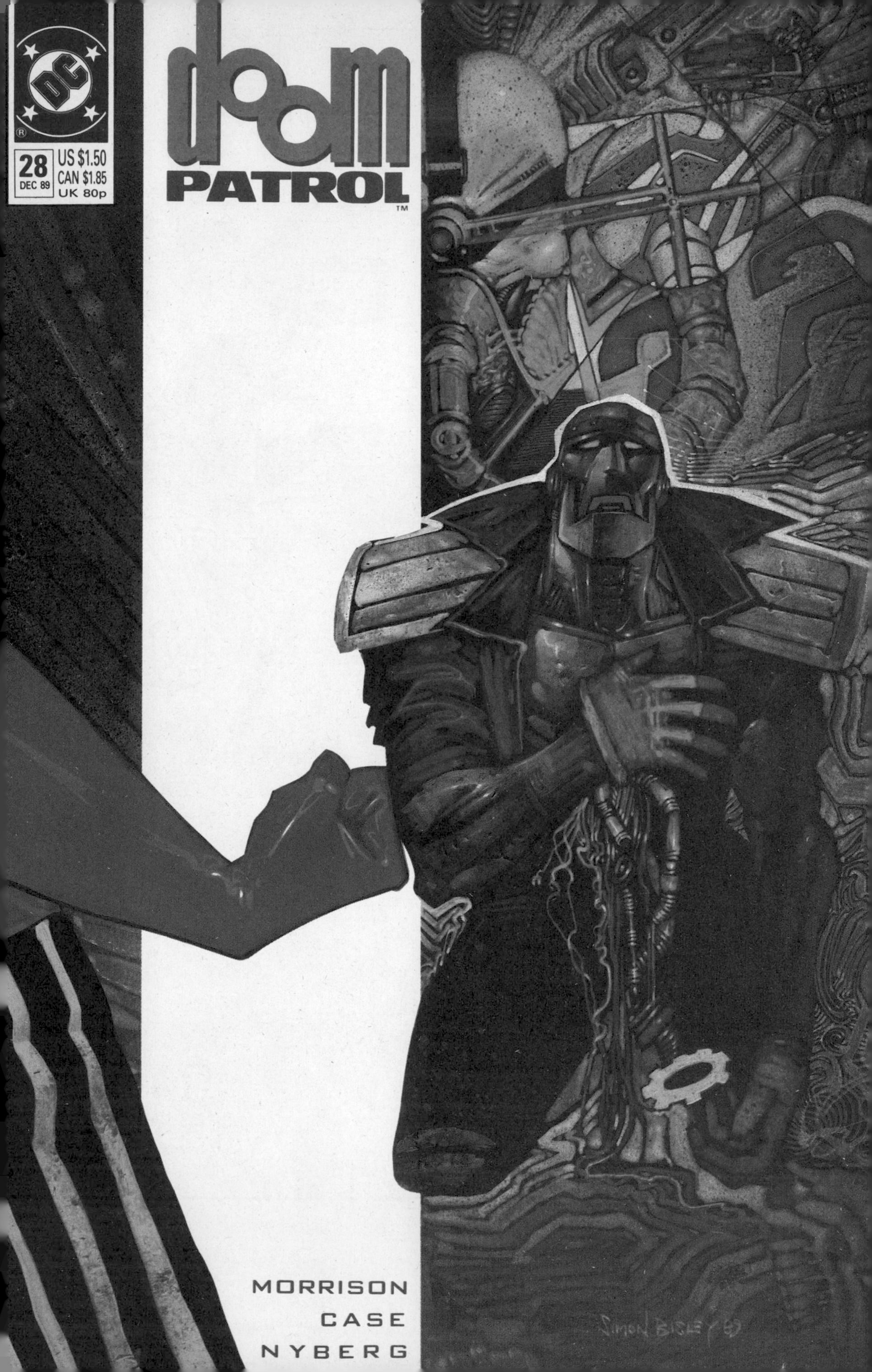
DC
28
DEC 89
US $1.50
CAN $1.85
UK 80p
doom
PATROL
MORRISON
CASE
NYBERG

PARIS TRAPPED INSIDE A *PAINTING?* THIS IS *WAY* TOO WEIRD FOR ME!

WEIRD? DON'T TALK TO ME ABOUT *WEIRD!* I'VE BEEN LIVING MY LIFE IN THE *"TWILIGHT ZONE."*

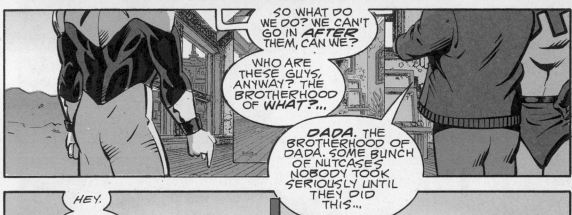

SO WHAT DO WE DO? WE CAN'T GO IN *AFTER* THEM, CAN WE?

WHO ARE THESE GUYS, ANYWAY? THE BROTHERHOOD OF *WHAT?...*

DADA. THE BROTHERHOOD OF *DADA.* SOME BUNCH OF NUTCASES NOBODY TOOK SERIOUSLY UNTIL THEY DID THIS...

HEY.

TALKING OF NUT-CASES...

HERE COMES THE *DOOM PATROL.*

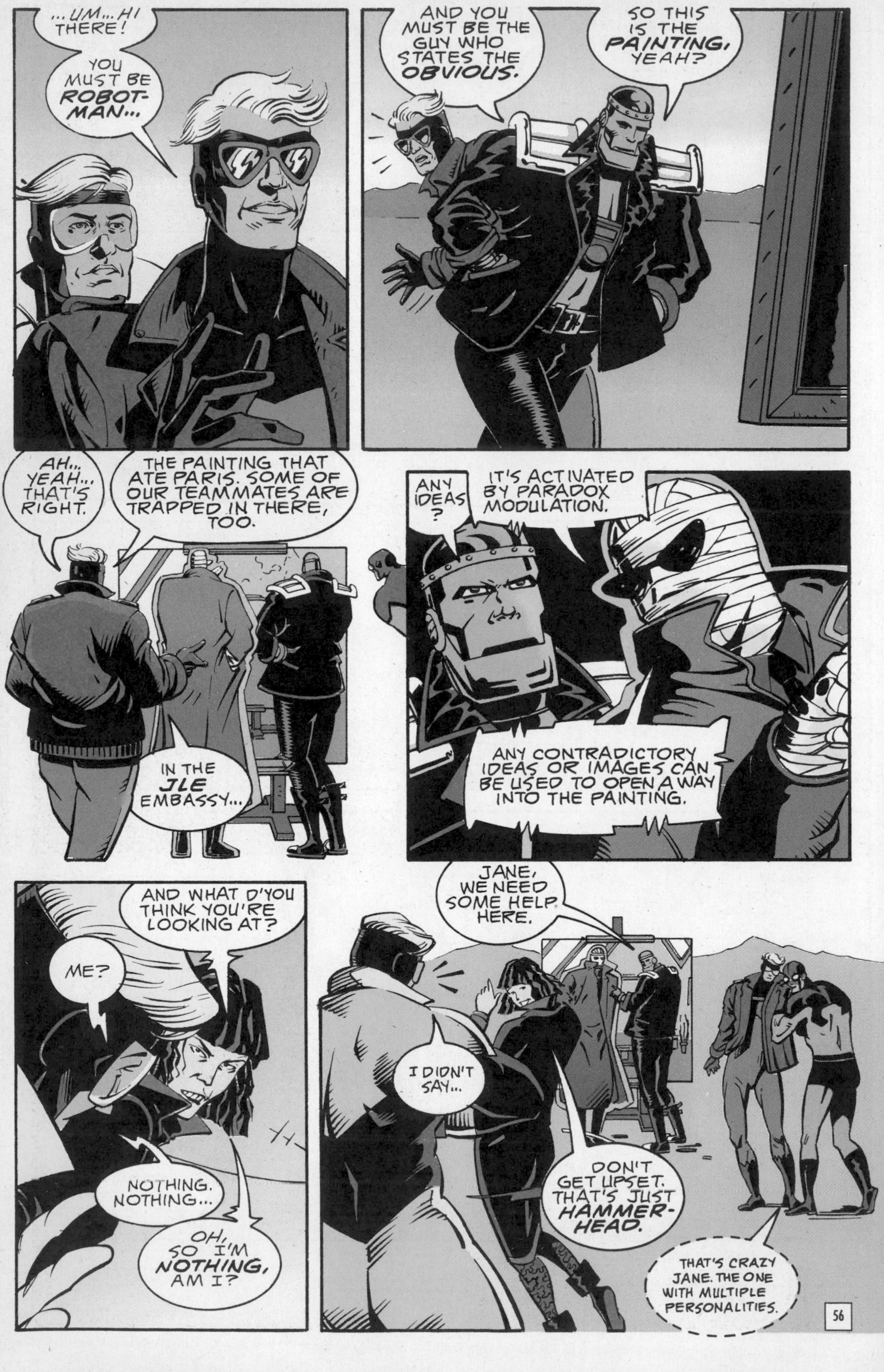
...UM...HI THERE!
YOU MUST BE ROBOT-MAN...
AND YOU MUST BE THE GUY WHO STATES THE OBVIOUS.
SO THIS IS THE PAINTING, YEAH?
AH... YEAH... THAT'S RIGHT.
THE PAINTING THAT ATE PARIS. SOME OF OUR TEAMMATES ARE TRAPPED IN THERE, TOO.
IN THE JLE EMBASSY...
ANY IDEAS?
IT'S ACTIVATED BY PARADOX MODULATION.
ANY CONTRADICTORY IDEAS OR IMAGES CAN BE USED TO OPEN A WAY INTO THE PAINTING.
AND WHAT D'YOU THINK YOU'RE LOOKING AT?
ME?
NOTHING. NOTHING...
OH, SO I'M NOTHING, AM I?
JANE, WE NEED SOME HELP HERE.
I DIDN'T SAY...
DON'T GET UPSET. THAT'S JUST HAMMER-HEAD.
THAT'S CRAZY JANE. THE ONE WITH MULTIPLE PERSONALITIES.

SO WHAT DO WE DO?...

MEDITATE ON **ME**. MEDITATE ON WHAT I AM.

I AM THE AVATAR OF CONTRADICTION: BLACK AND WHITE, MALE AND FEMALE, IN ONE BODY.

CAN YOU FEEL IT?

CAN YOU FEEL IT OPENING LIKE A DOOR?

LISTEN, DO YOU GUYS KNOW WHAT YOU'RE...

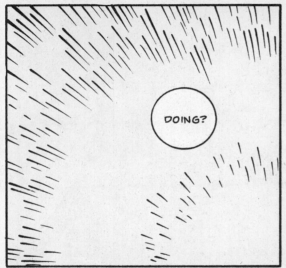

DOING?

THOSE GUYS GIVE ME THE **CREEPS**.

I MEAN, WHOSE SIDE ARE THEY ON ANYWAY?

HEY!

CHECK IT OUT!

HOW DID THEY **DO** THAT?

LABYRINTHS

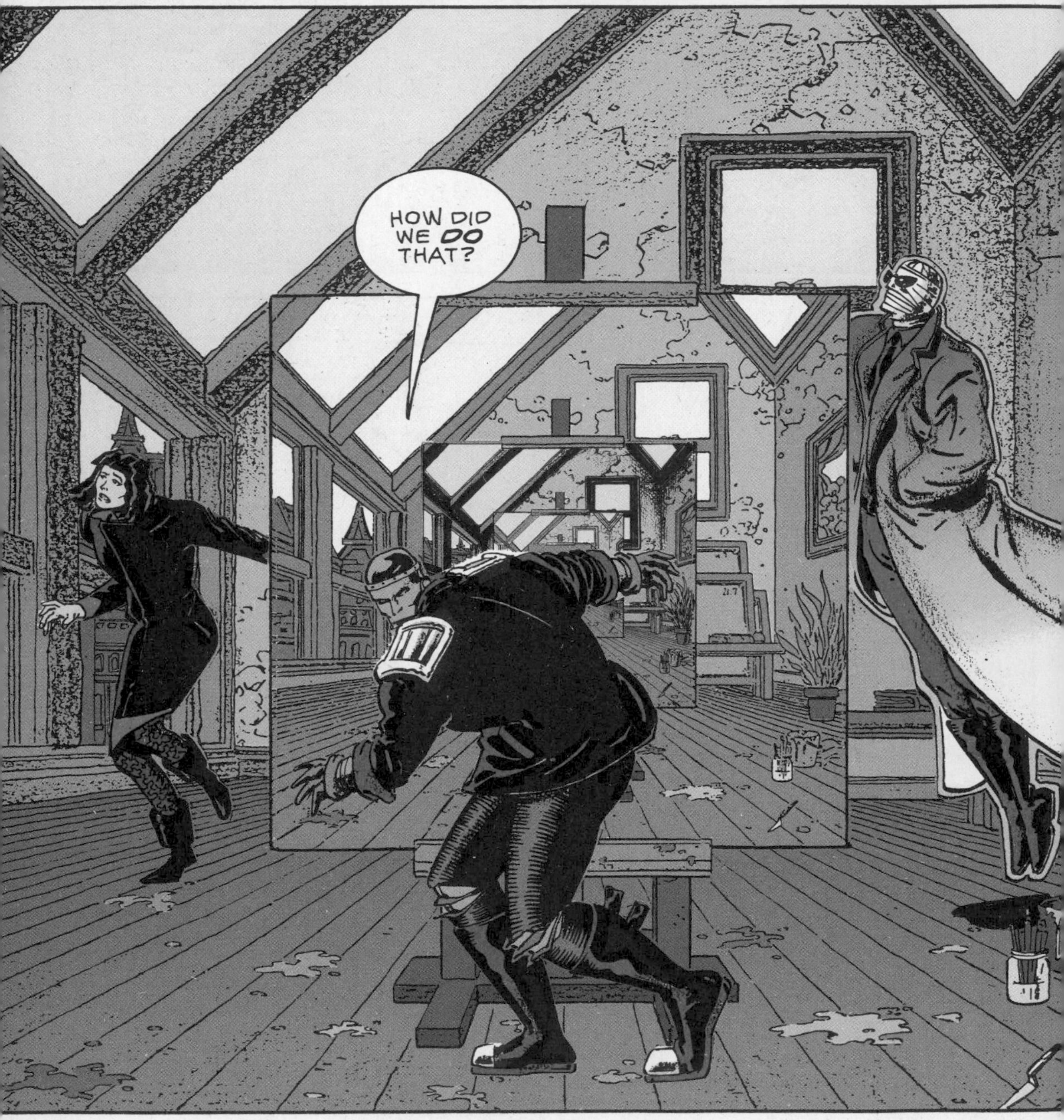
HOW DID WE DO THAT?

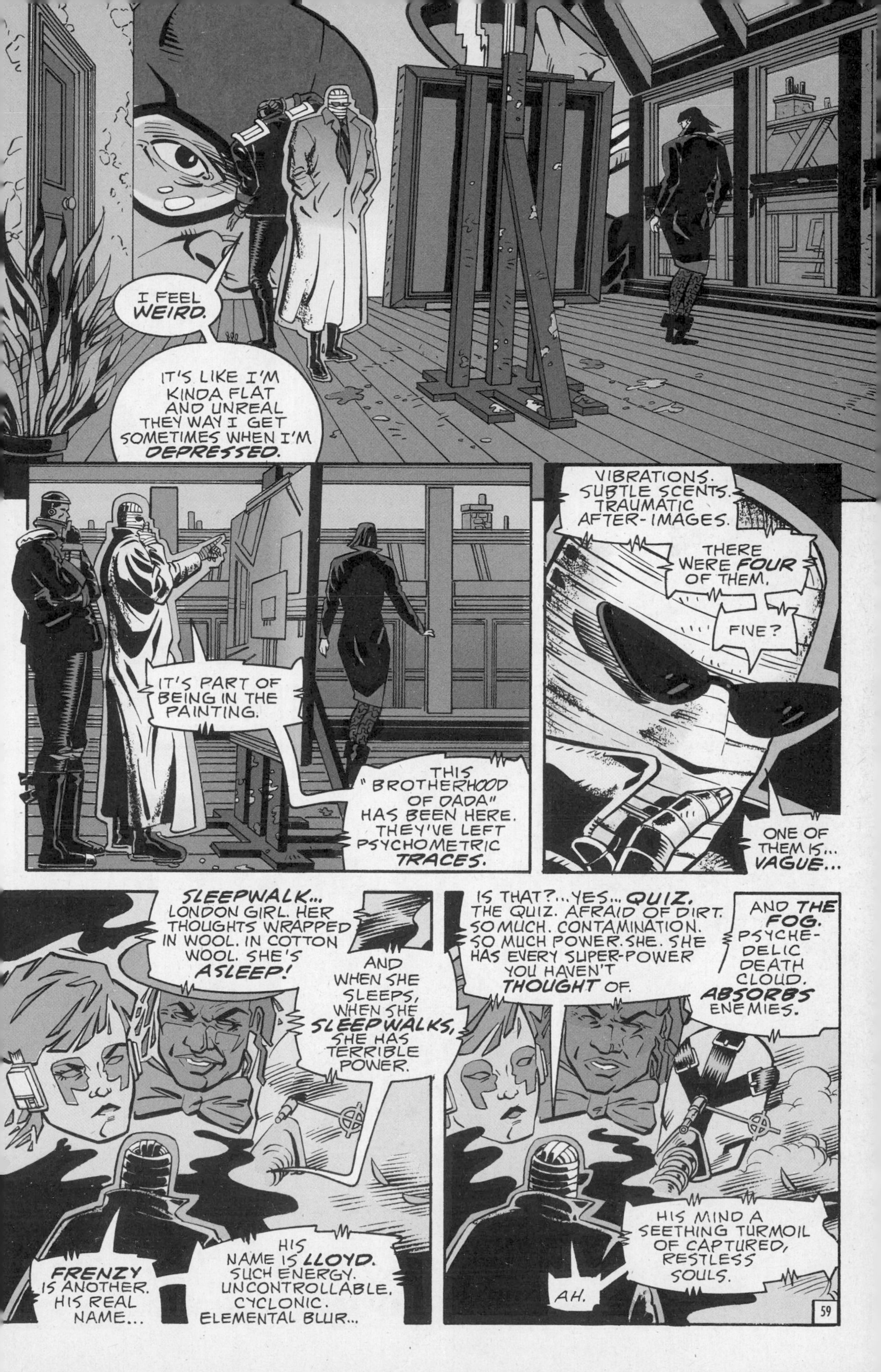
I FEEL WEIRD.
IT'S LIKE I'M KINDA FLAT AND UNREAL THEY WAY I GET SOMETIMES WHEN I'M DEPRESSED.
IT'S PART OF BEING IN THE PAINTING.
THIS "BROTHERHOOD OF DADA" HAS BEEN HERE. THEY'VE LEFT PSYCHOMETRIC TRACES.
VIBRATIONS. SUBTLE SCENTS. TRAUMATIC AFTER-IMAGES.
THERE WERE FOUR OF THEM.
FIVE?
ONE OF THEM IS... VAGUE...
SLEEPWALK... LONDON GIRL. HER THOUGHTS WRAPPED IN WOOL. IN COTTON WOOL. SHE'S ASLEEP!
AND WHEN SHE SLEEPS, WHEN SHE SLEEPWALKS, SHE HAS TERRIBLE POWER.
FRENZY IS ANOTHER. HIS REAL NAME...
HIS NAME IS LLOYD. SUCH ENERGY. UNCONTROLLABLE. CYCLONIC. ELEMENTAL BLUR...
IS THAT?...YES... QUIZ. THE QUIZ. AFRAID OF DIRT. SO MUCH. CONTAMINATION. SO MUCH POWER. SHE. SHE HAS EVERY SUPER-POWER YOU HAVEN'T THOUGHT OF.
AND THE FOG. PSYCHE-DELIC DEATH CLOUD. ABSORBS ENEMIES.
HIS MIND A SEETHING TURMOIL OF CAPTURED, RESTLESS SOULS.
AH.

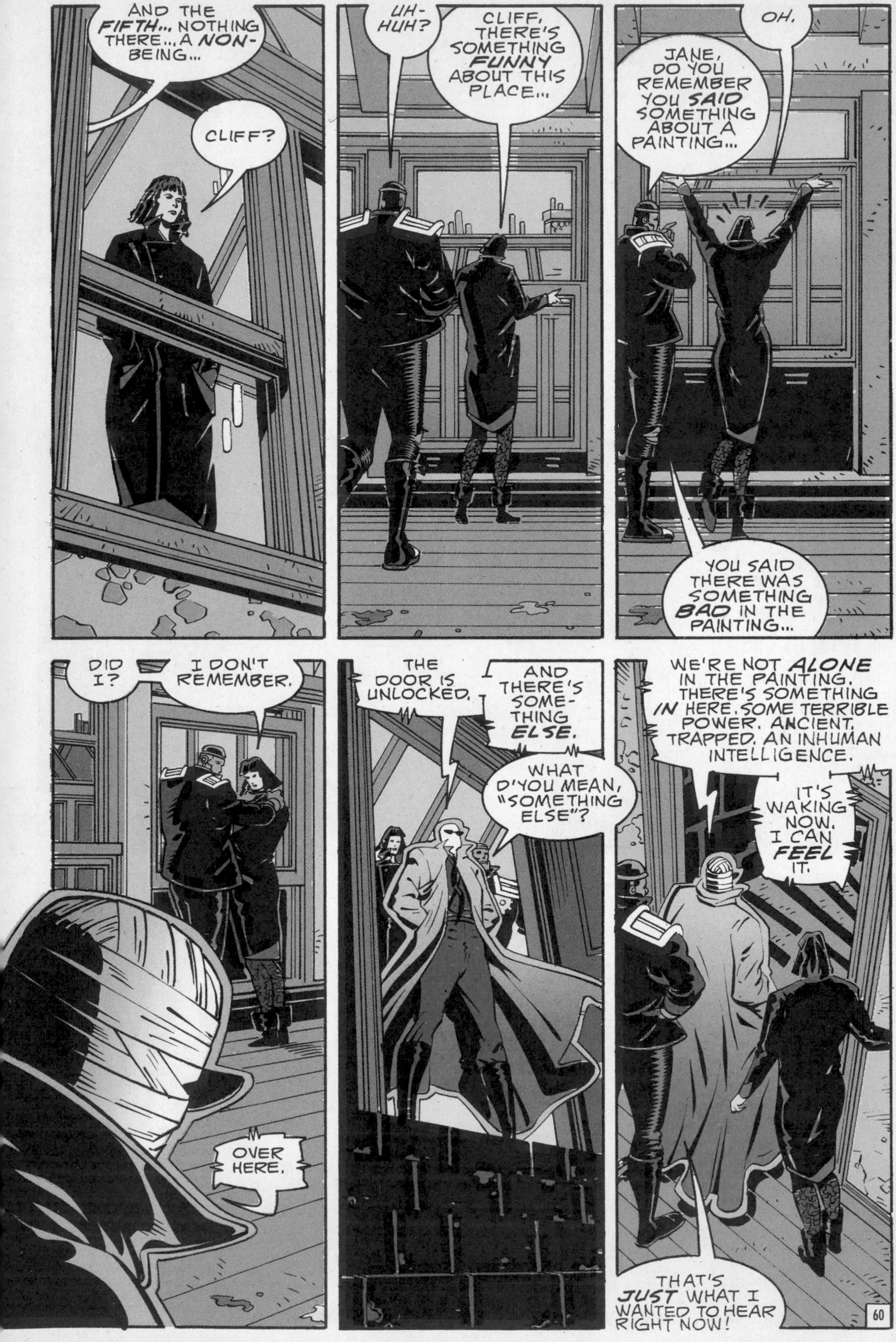
AND THE FIFTH... NOTHING THERE... A NON-BEING...
CLIFF?
UH-HUH?
CLIFF, THERE'S SOMETHING FUNNY ABOUT THIS PLACE...
OH.
JANE, DO YOU REMEMBER YOU SAID SOMETHING ABOUT A PAINTING...
YOU SAID THERE WAS SOMETHING BAD IN THE PAINTING...
DID I?
I DON'T REMEMBER.
OVER HERE.
THE DOOR IS UNLOCKED.
AND THERE'S SOME-THING ELSE.
WHAT D'YOU MEAN, "SOMETHING ELSE"?
WE'RE NOT ALONE IN THE PAINTING. THERE'S SOMETHING IN HERE. SOME TERRIBLE POWER. ANCIENT. TRAPPED. AN INHUMAN INTELLIGENCE.
IT'S WAKING NOW. I CAN FEEL IT.
THAT'S JUST WHAT I WANTED TO HEAR RIGHT NOW!
60

SO WHAT IS THIS "INTELLIGENCE"? WHAT ARE WE TALKING ABOUT HERE?

DOES THE BROTHER-HOOD KNOW ABOUT IT?

I DON'T THINK SO.

DON'T THINK ABOUT IT. TO THINK ABOUT IT GIVES IT STRENGTH.

I'LL TAKE YOUR WORD FOR IT. LET'S CHANGE THE SUBJECT.

WHAT IS IT WITH THIS PLACE? I MEAN, IT LOOKS REAL ENOUGH...

BUT IT HAS NO HEART.

WE'RE INSIDE A PHOTOREALIST PAINTING.

WHAT ELSE CAN WE EXPECT?

YEAH.

I SHUDDER TO THINK.

THIS LOOKS FAMILIAR.

YES.

IT SHOULD DO.

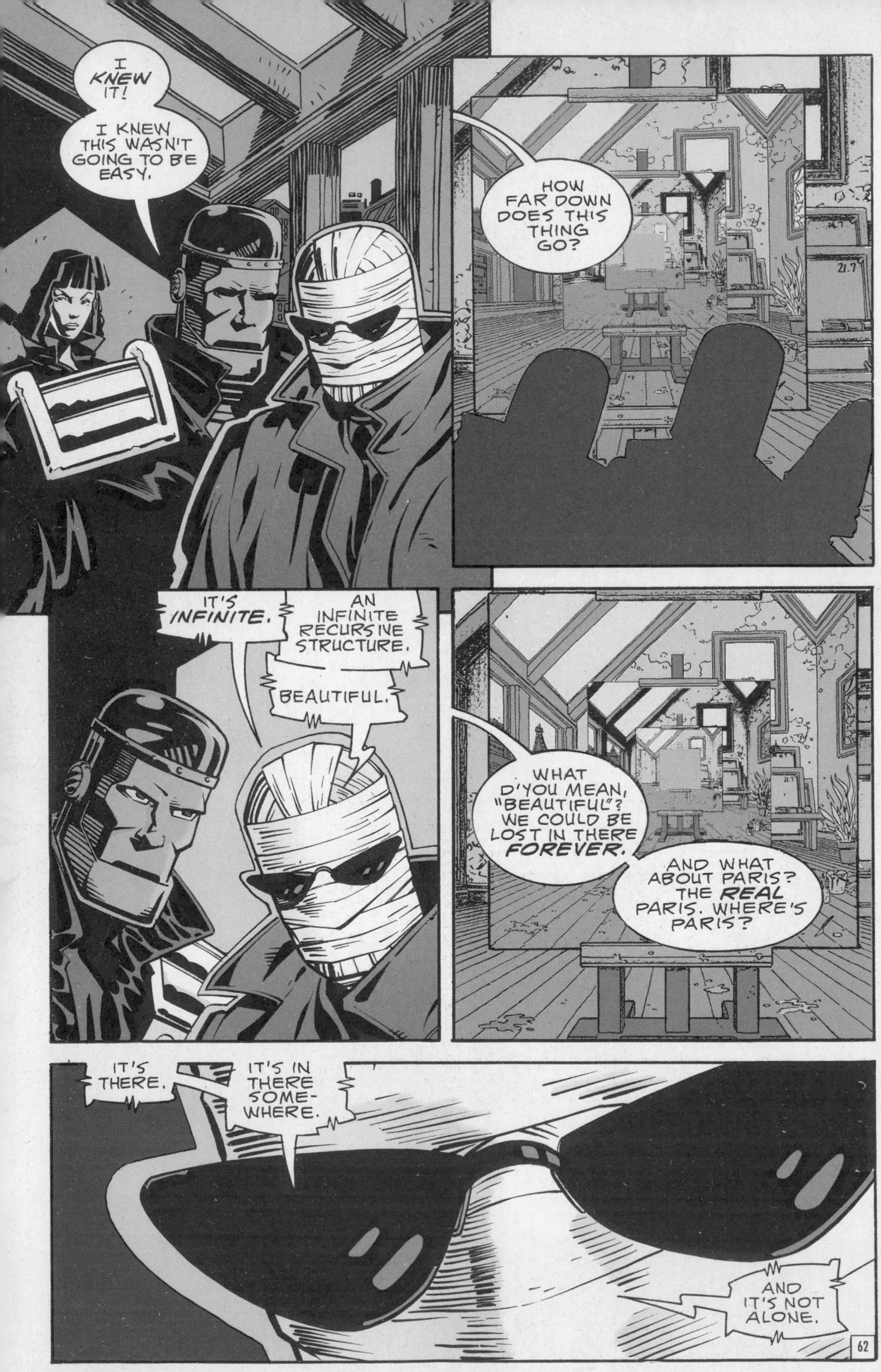
I *KNEW* IT!
I KNEW THIS WASN'T GOING TO BE EASY.
HOW FAR DOWN DOES THIS THING GO?
IT'S *INFINITE*.
AN INFINITE RECURSIVE STRUCTURE.
BEAUTIFUL.
WHAT D'YOU MEAN, "BEAUTIFUL"? WE COULD BE LOST IN THERE *FOREVER*.
AND WHAT ABOUT PARIS? THE *REAL* PARIS. WHERE'S PARIS?
IT'S THERE.
IT'S IN THERE SOME-WHERE.
AND IT'S NOT ALONE.

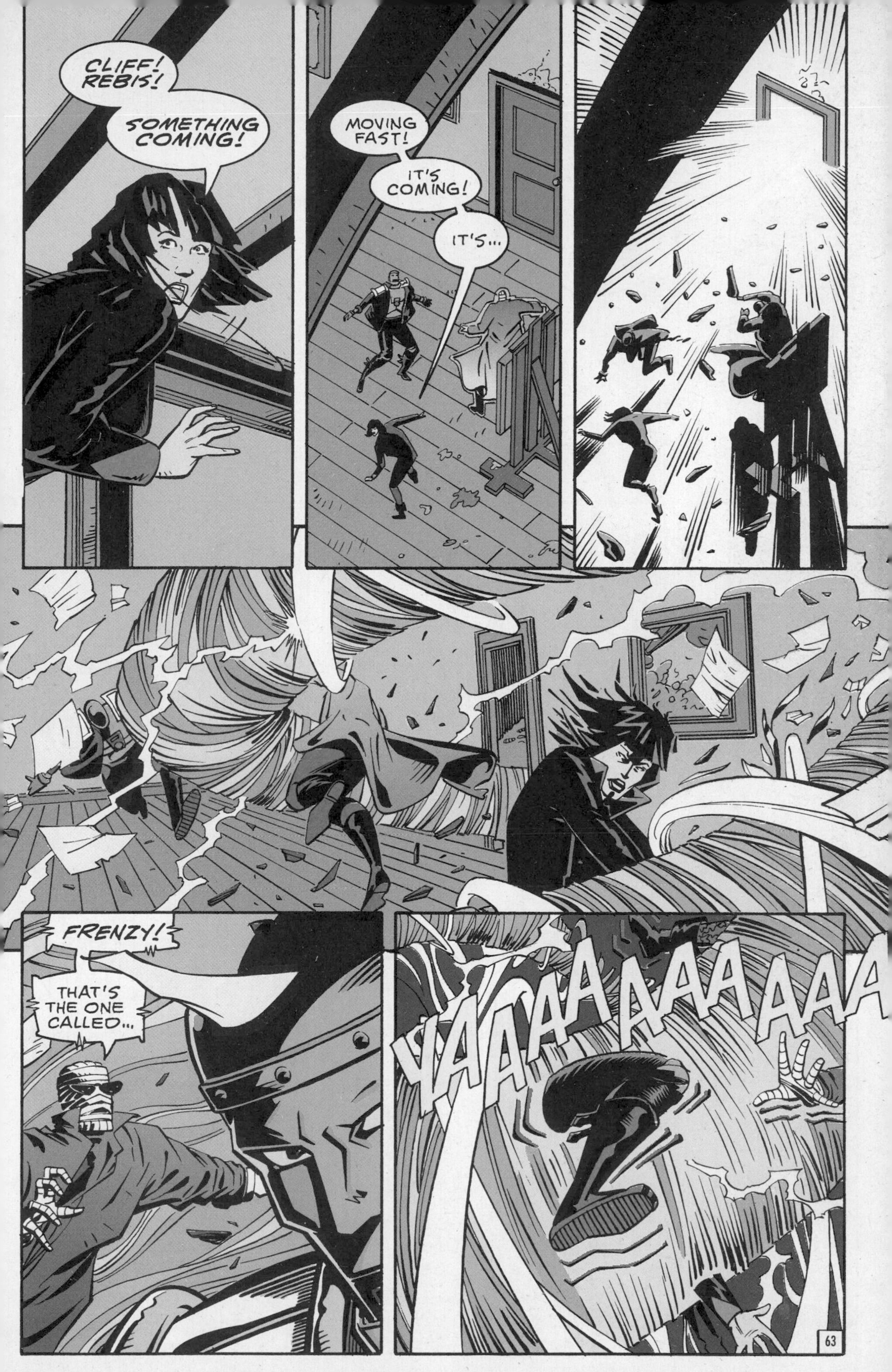
CLIFF! REBIS!
SOMETHING COMING!
MOVING FAST!
IT'S COMING!
IT'S...
FRENZY!
THAT'S THE ONE CALLED...
YAAAAAAAAAAA

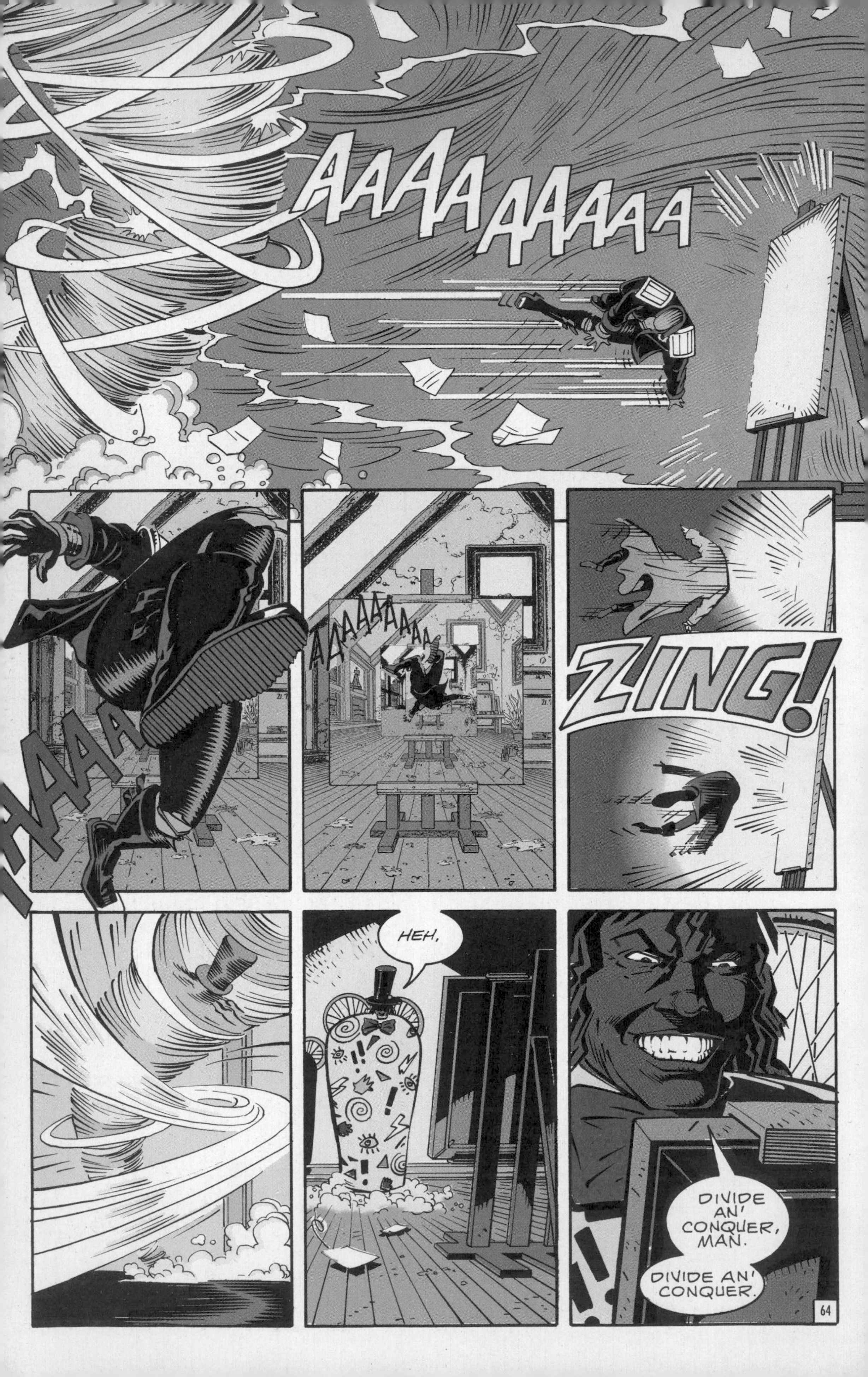
AAAAAAAAAA
AAAA
AAAAAAAAA
ZING!
HEH.
DIVIDE AN' CONQUER, MAN.
DIVIDE AN' CONQUER.
64

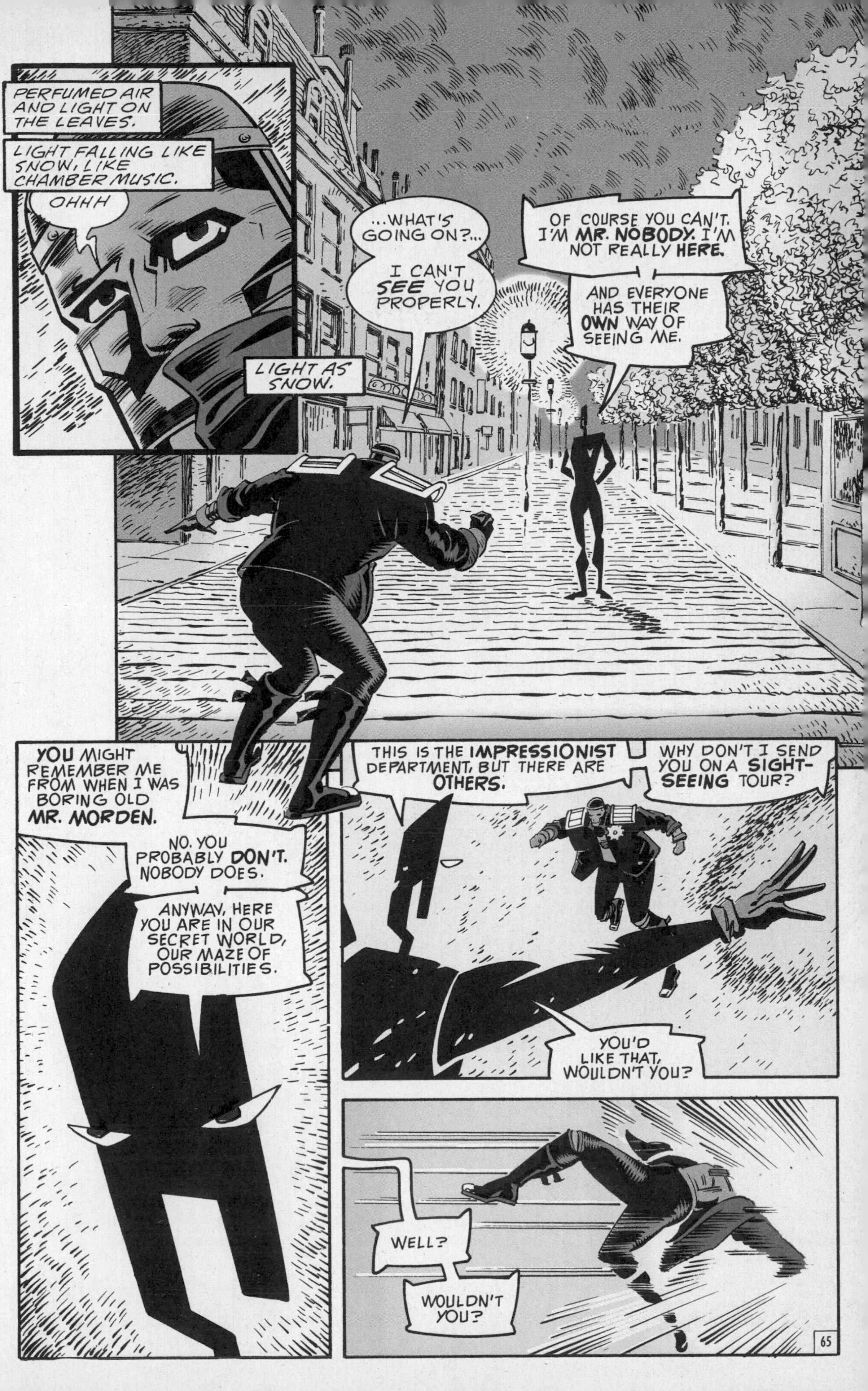
PERFUMED AIR AND LIGHT ON THE LEAVES.
LIGHT FALLING LIKE SNOW, LIKE CHAMBER MUSIC.
OHHH
LIGHT AS SNOW.
...WHAT'S GOING ON?...
I CAN'T SEE YOU PROPERLY.
OF COURSE YOU CAN'T. I'M MR. NOBODY. I'M NOT REALLY HERE.
AND EVERYONE HAS THEIR OWN WAY OF SEEING ME.
YOU MIGHT REMEMBER ME FROM WHEN I WAS BORING OLD MR. MORDEN.
NO. YOU PROBABLY DON'T. NOBODY DOES.
ANYWAY, HERE YOU ARE IN OUR SECRET WORLD, OUR MAZE OF POSSIBILITIES.
THIS IS THE IMPRESSIONIST DEPARTMENT, BUT THERE ARE OTHERS.
WHY DON'T I SEND YOU ON A SIGHT-SEEING TOUR?
YOU'D LIKE THAT, WOULDN'T YOU?
WELL?
WOULDN'T YOU?

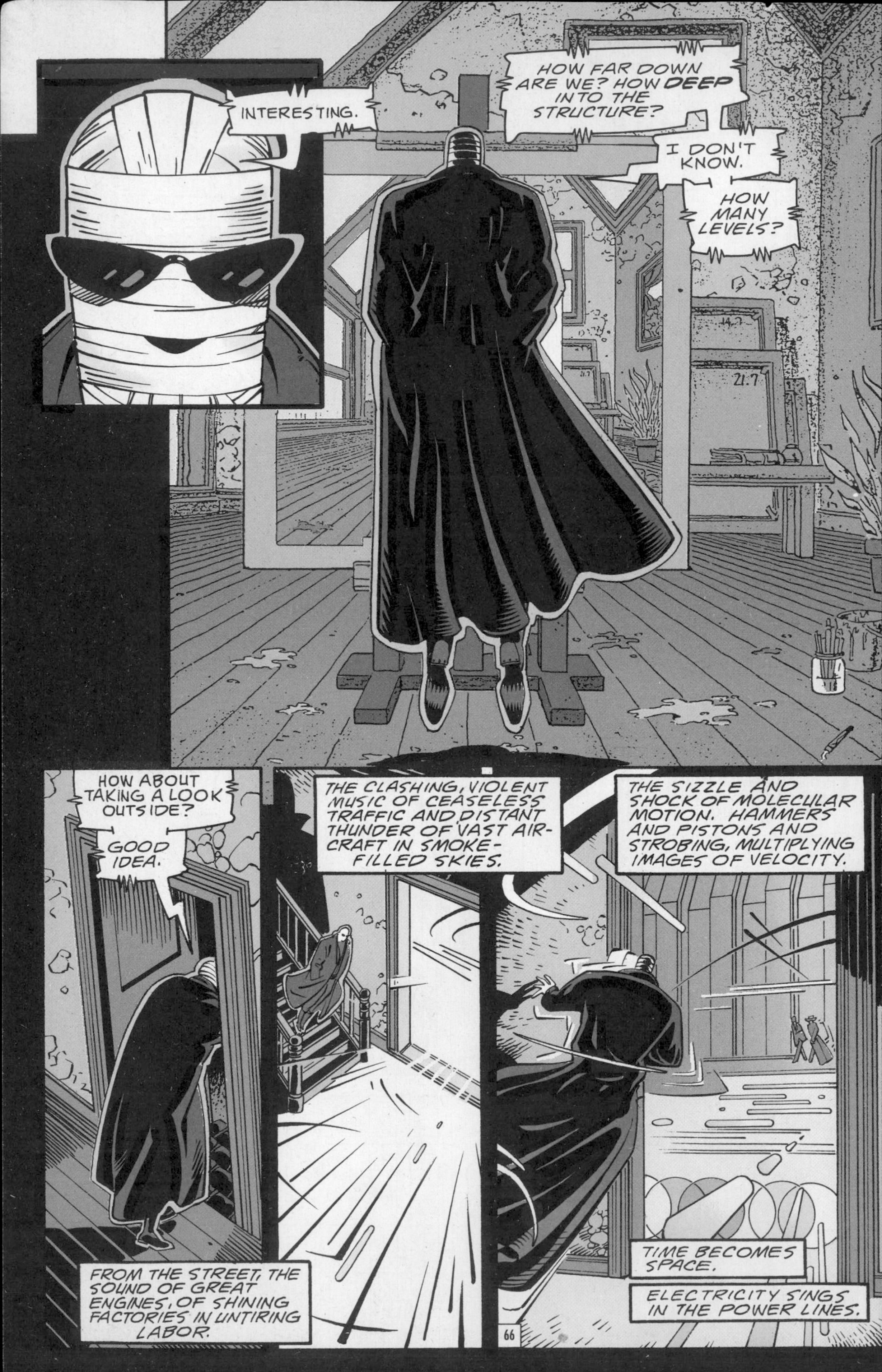

INTERESTING.
HOW FAR DOWN ARE WE? HOW DEEP INTO THE STRUCTURE?
I DON'T KNOW.
HOW MANY LEVELS?
HOW ABOUT TAKING A LOOK OUTSIDE?
GOOD IDEA.
FROM THE STREET, THE SOUND OF GREAT ENGINES, OF SHINING FACTORIES IN UNTIRING LABOR.
THE CLASHING, VIOLENT MUSIC OF CEASELESS TRAFFIC AND DISTANT THUNDER OF VAST AIR-CRAFT IN SMOKE-FILLED SKIES.
THE SIZZLE AND SHOCK OF MOLECULAR MOTION. HAMMERS AND PISTONS AND STROBING, MULTIPLYING IMAGES OF VELOCITY.
TIME BECOMES SPACE.
ELECTRICITY SINGS IN THE POWER LINES.

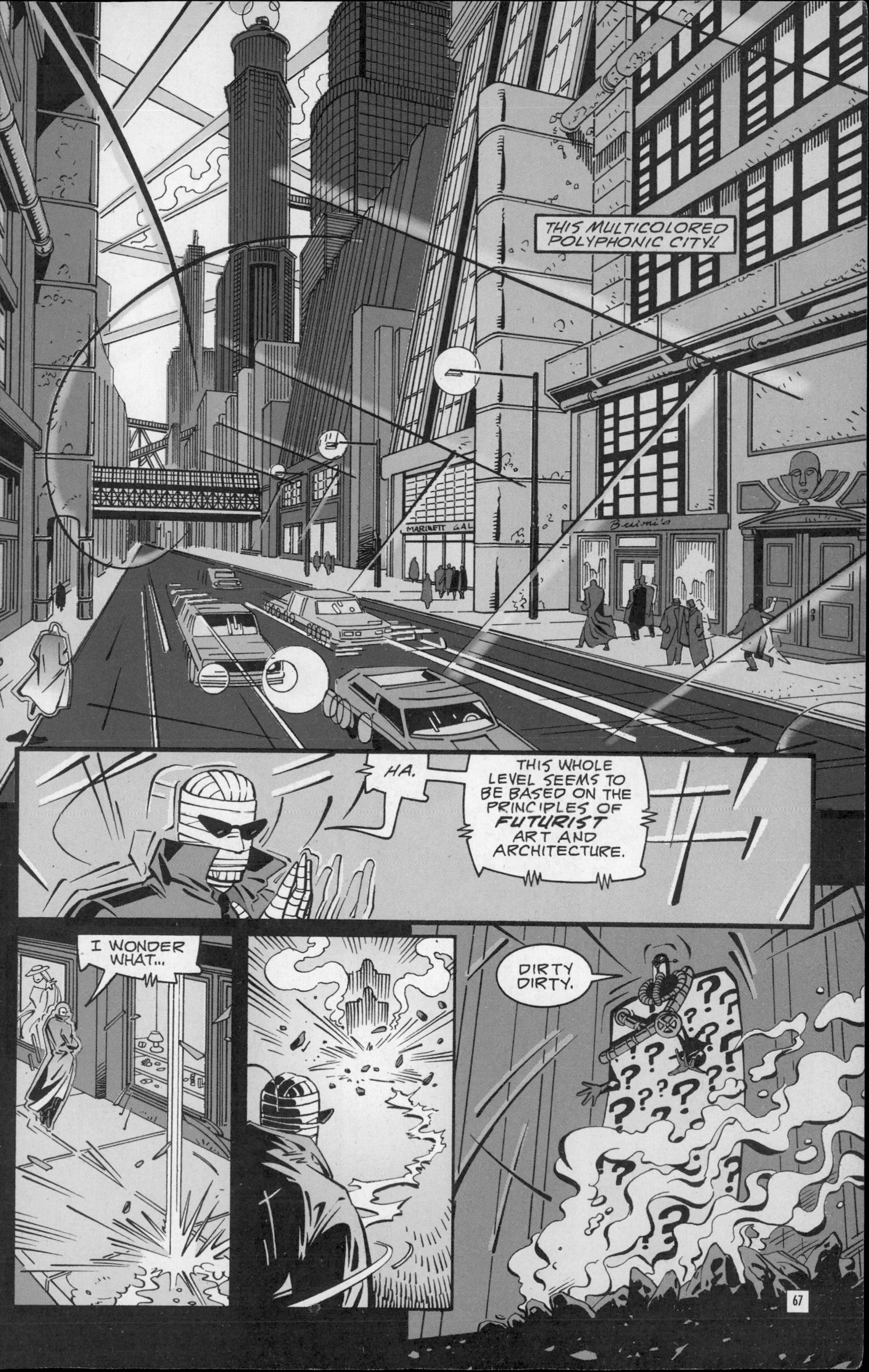
THIS MULTICOLORED POLYPHONIC CITY!
MARINETT GAL
HA.
THIS WHOLE LEVEL SEEMS TO BE BASED ON THE PRINCIPLES OF FUTURIST ART AND ARCHITECTURE.
I WONDER WHAT...
DIRTY DIRTY.

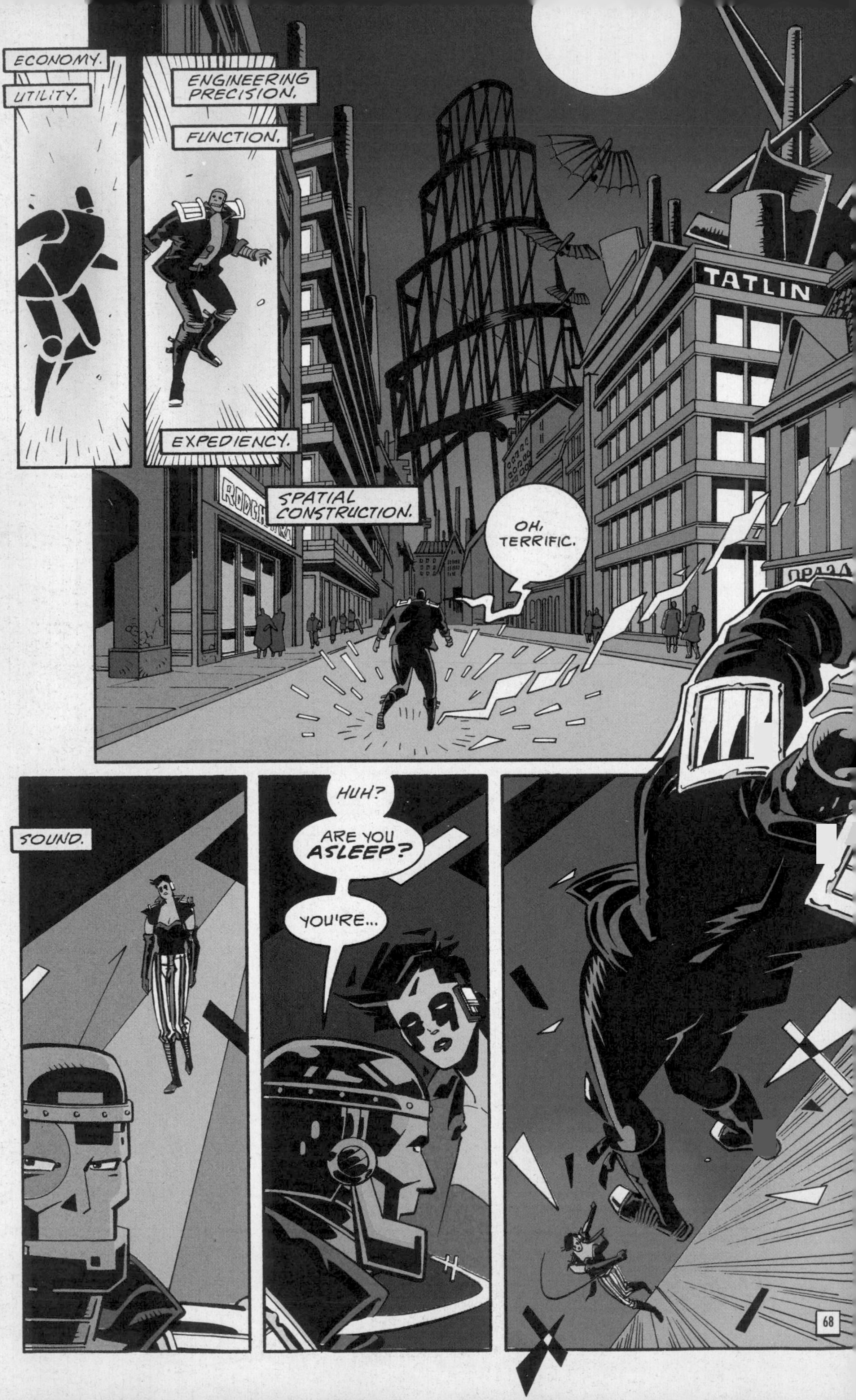
ECONOMY.
UTILITY.
ENGINEERING PRECISION.
FUNCTION.
EXPEDIENCY.
SPATIAL CONSTRUCTION.
TATLIN
OH, TERRIFIC.
SOUND.
HUH?
ARE YOU ASLEEP?
YOU'RE...
68

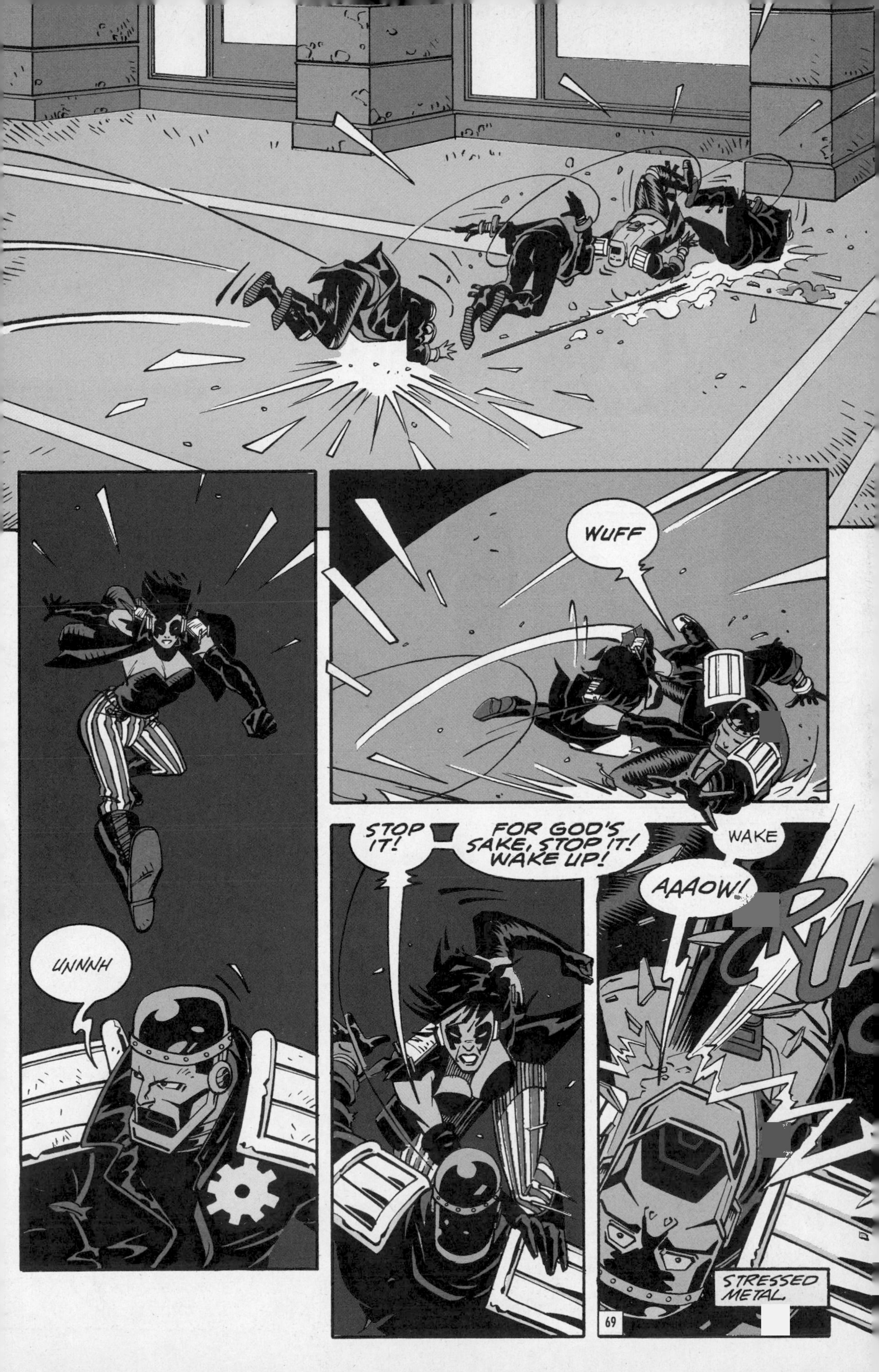
WUFF
UNNNH
STOP IT!
FOR GOD'S SAKE, STOP IT! WAKE UP!
WAKE
AAAOW!
STRESSED METAL

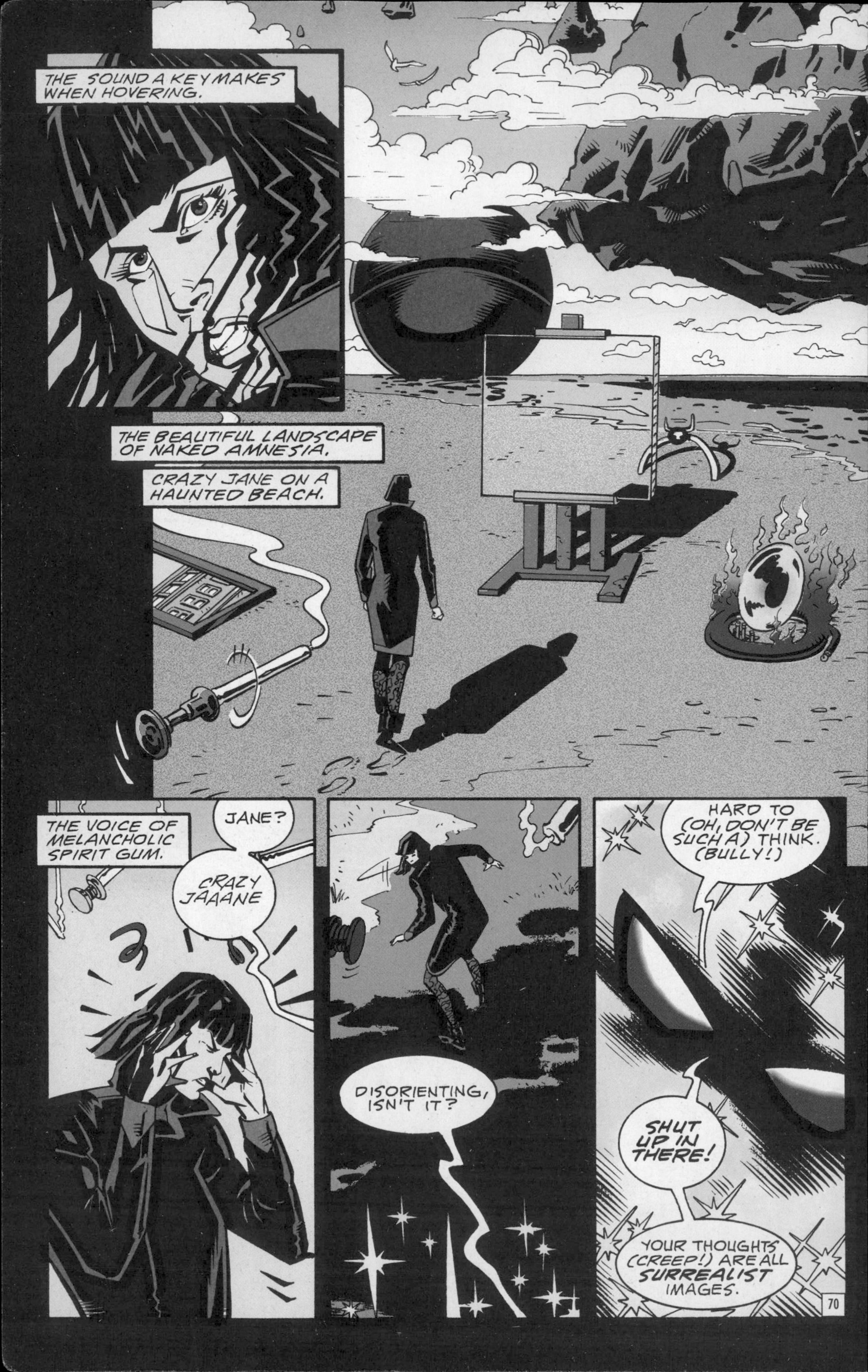
THE SOUND A KEY MAKES WHEN HOVERING.
THE BEAUTIFUL LANDSCAPE OF NAKED AMNESIA.
CRAZY JANE ON A HAUNTED BEACH.
THE VOICE OF MELANCHOLIC SPIRIT GUM.
JANE?
CRAZY JAAANE
DISORIENTING, ISN'T IT?
HARD TO (OH, DON'T BE SUCH A) THINK. (BULLY!)
SHUT UP IN THERE!
YOUR THOUGHTS (CREEP!) ARE ALL SURREALIST IMAGES.

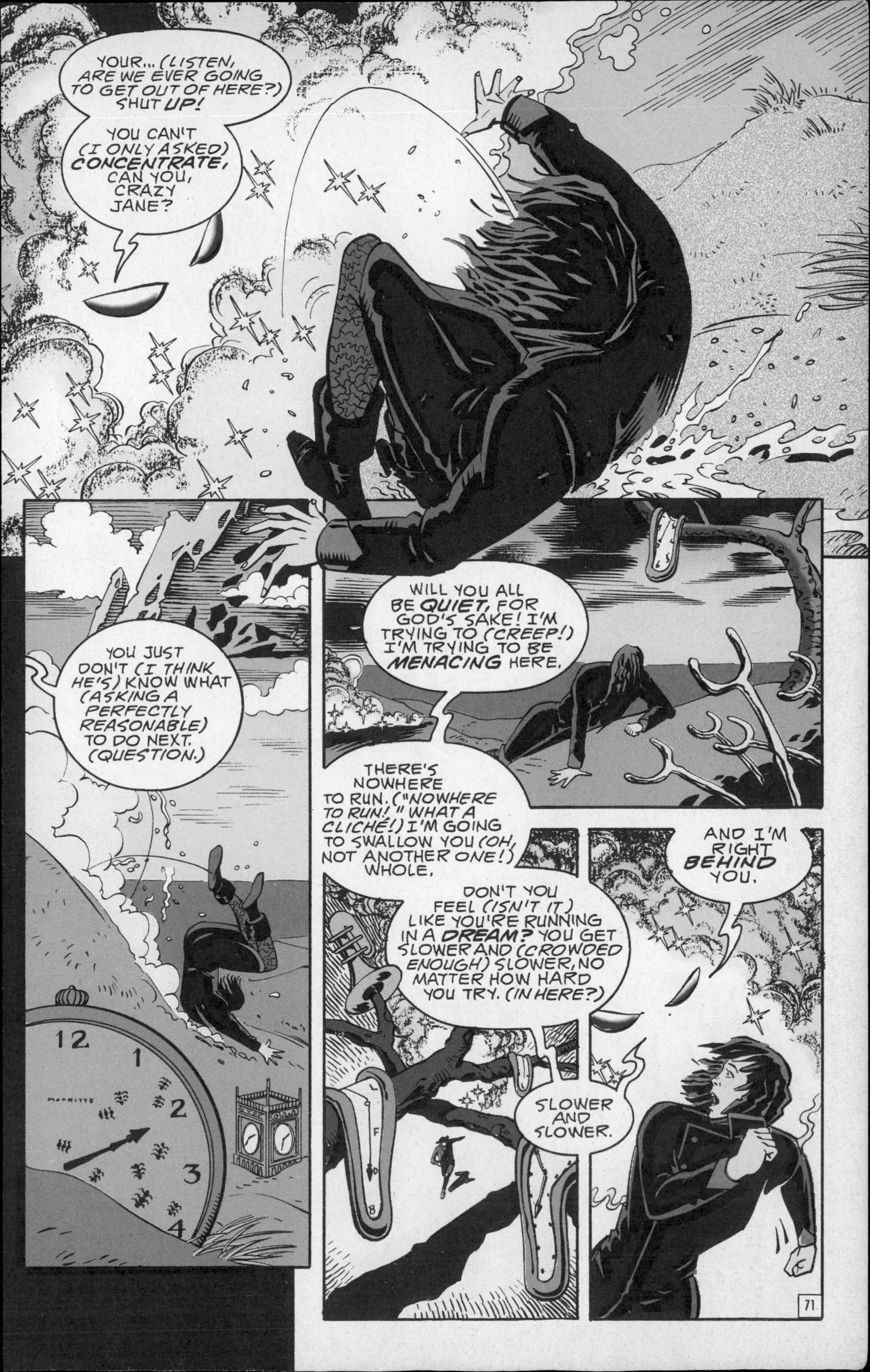

YOUR... (LISTEN, ARE WE EVER GOING TO GET OUT OF HERE?) SHUT UP!
YOU CAN'T (I ONLY ASKED) CONCENTRATE, CAN YOU, CRAZY JANE?
YOU JUST DON'T (I THINK HE'S) KNOW WHAT (ASKING A PERFECTLY REASONABLE) TO DO NEXT. (QUESTION.)
WILL YOU ALL BE QUIET, FOR GOD'S SAKE! I'M TRYING TO (CREEP!) I'M TRYING TO BE MENACING HERE.
THERE'S NOWHERE TO RUN. ("NOWHERE TO RUN!" WHAT A CLICHÉ!) I'M GOING TO SWALLOW YOU (OH, NOT ANOTHER ONE!) WHOLE.
DON'T YOU FEEL (ISN'T IT) LIKE YOU'RE RUNNING IN A DREAM? YOU GET SLOWER AND (CROWDED ENOUGH) SLOWER, NO MATTER HOW HARD YOU TRY. (IN HERE?)
AND I'M RIGHT BEHIND YOU.
SLOWER AND SLOWER.

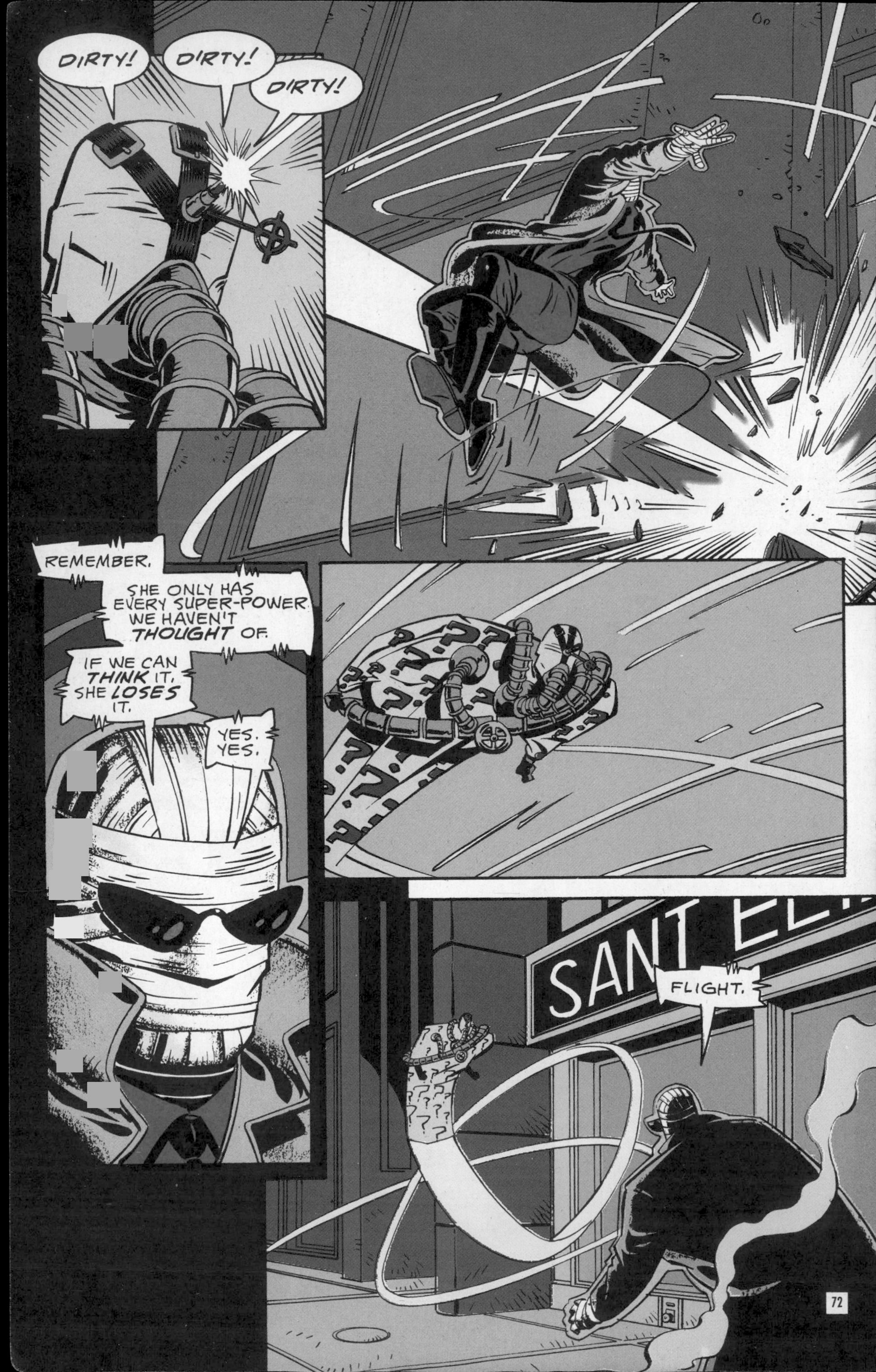
DIRTY!
DIRTY!
DIRTY!
REMEMBER.
SHE ONLY HAS EVERY SUPER-POWER WE HAVEN'T THOUGHT OF.
IF WE CAN THINK IT, SHE LOSES IT.
YES. YES.
SANT
FLIGHT.

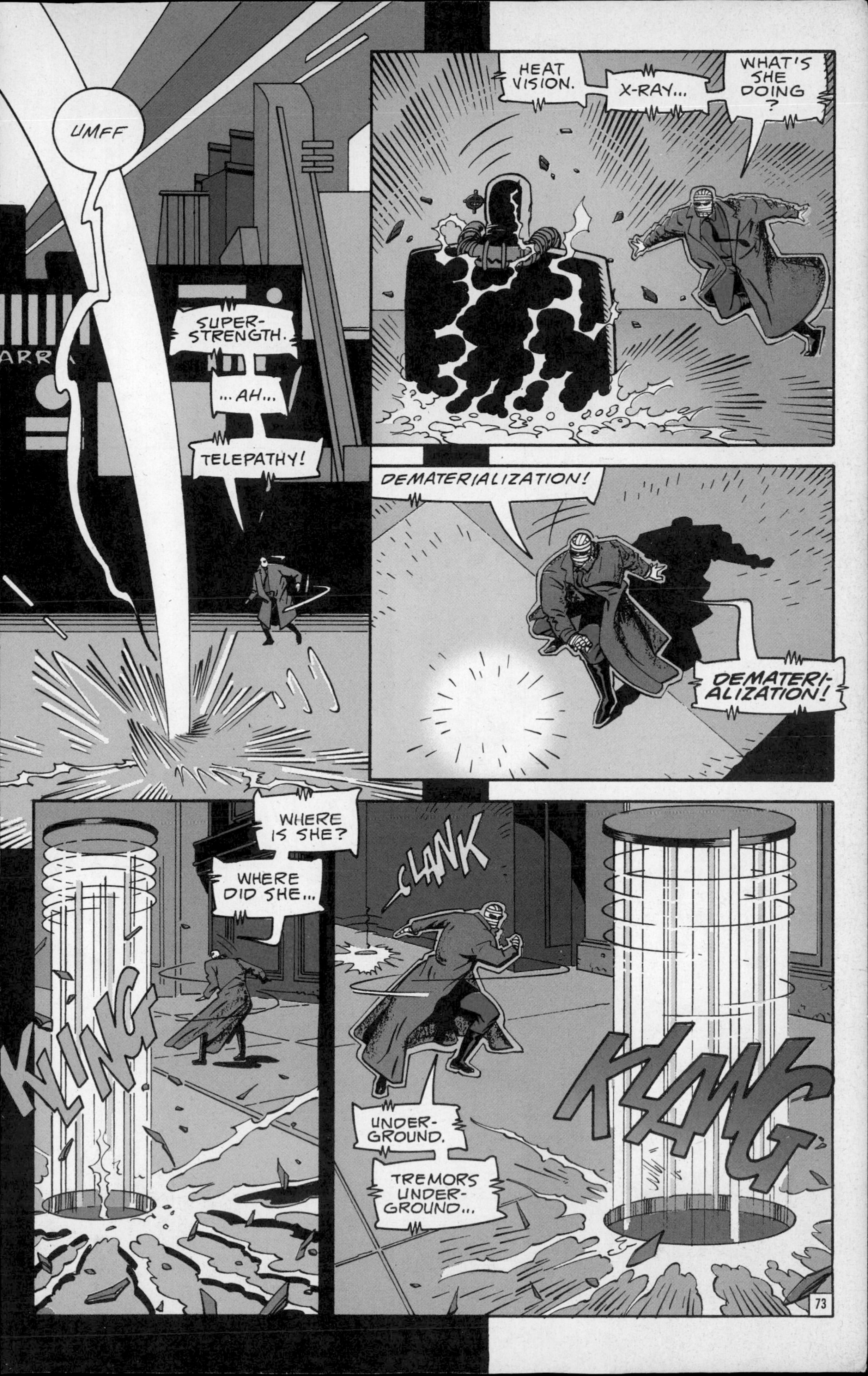
UMFF
SUPER-STRENGTH.
...AH...
TELEPATHY!
HEAT VISION.
X-RAY...
WHAT'S SHE DOING?
DEMATERIALIZATION!
DEMATERI-ALIZATION!
WHERE IS SHE?
WHERE DID SHE...
KLING
CLANK
UNDER-GROUND.
TREMORS UNDER-GROUND...
KLANG

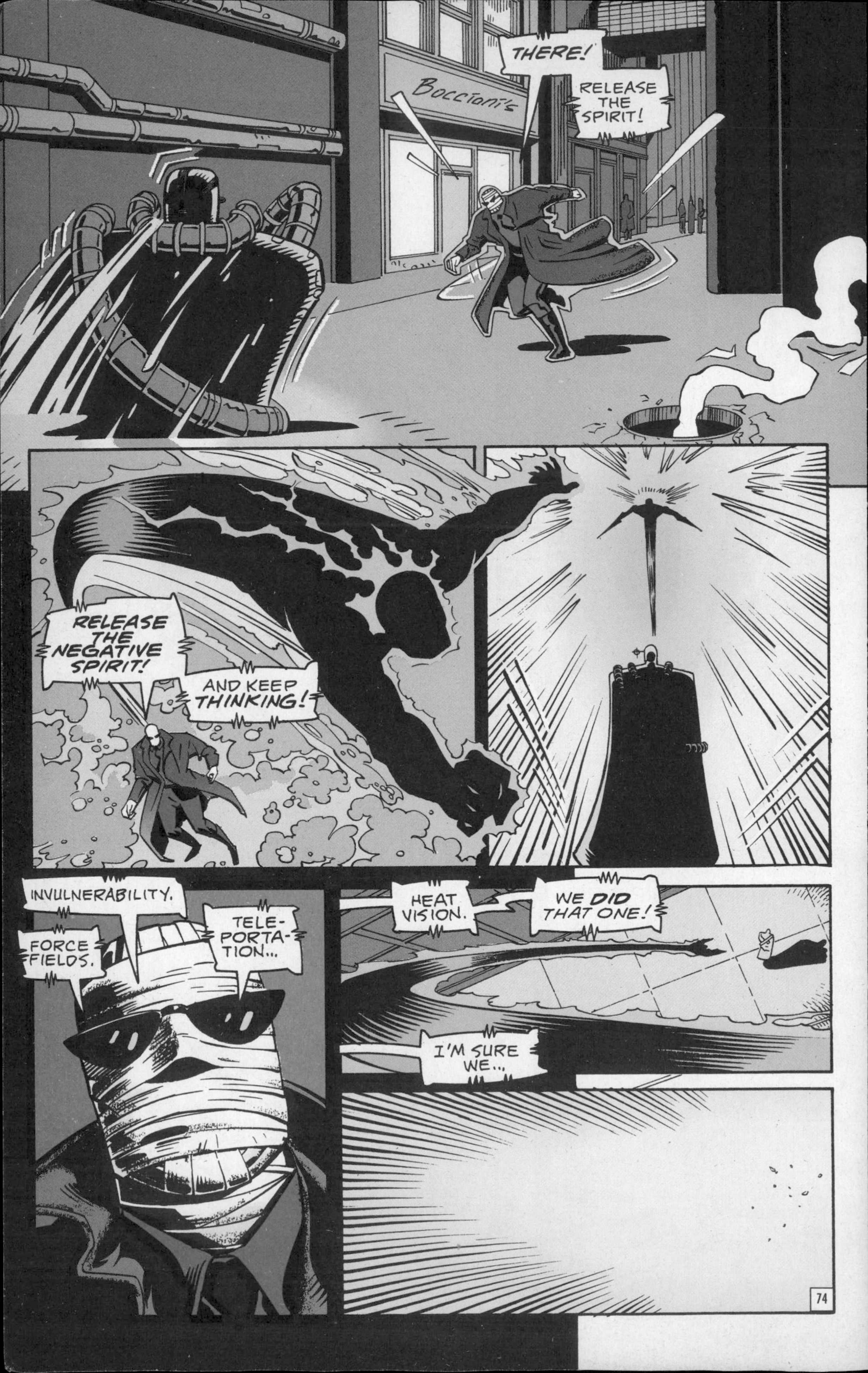

Boccioni's
THERE!
RELEASE THE SPIRIT!
RELEASE THE NEGATIVE SPIRIT!
AND KEEP THINKING!
INVULNERABILITY.
FORCE FIELDS.
TELE-PORTA-TION...
HEAT VISION.
WE DID THAT ONE!
I'M SURE WE...

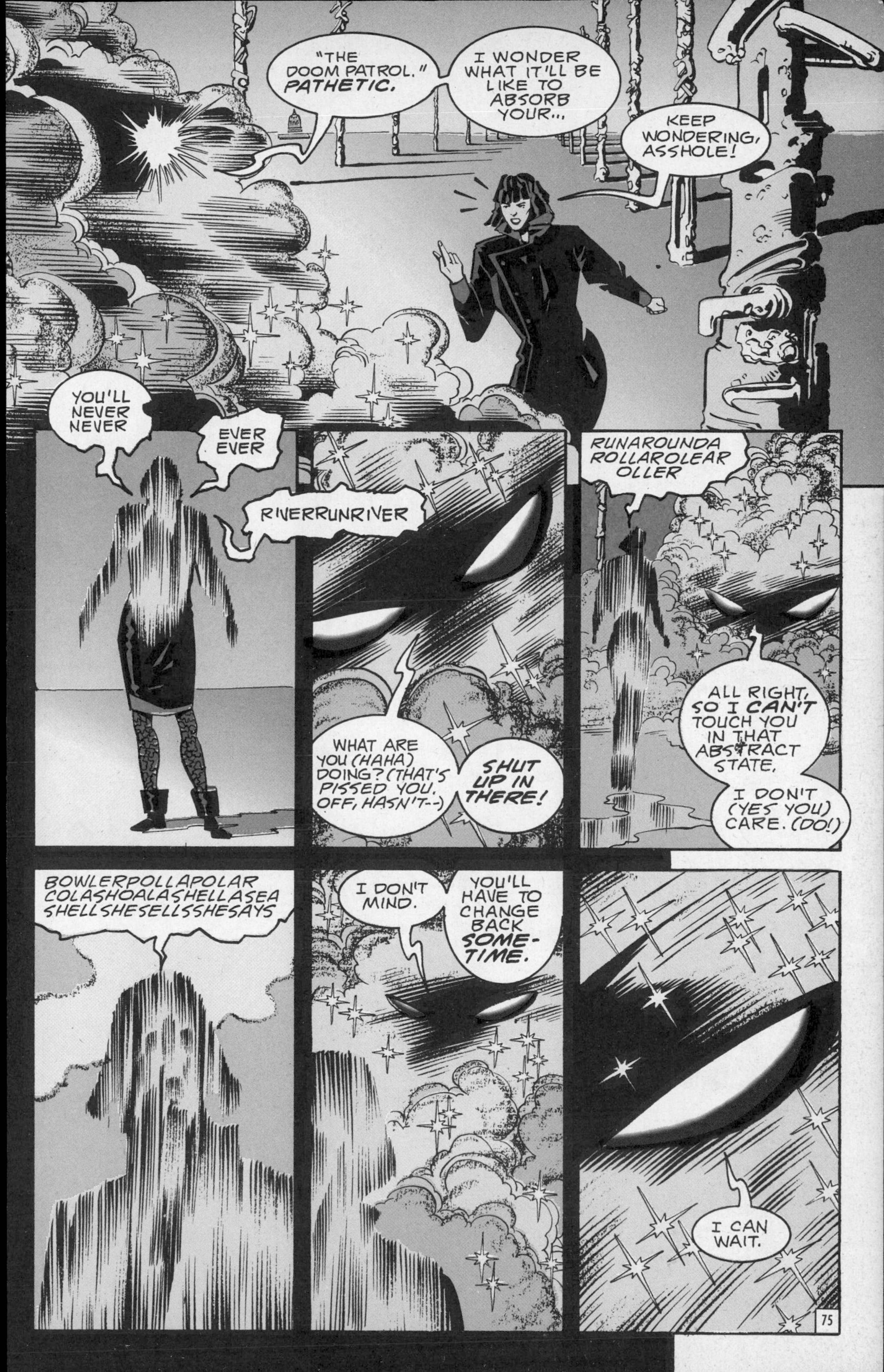
"THE DOOM PATROL." PATHETIC.
I WONDER WHAT IT'LL BE LIKE TO ABSORB YOUR...
KEEP WONDERING, ASSHOLE!
YOU'LL NEVER NEVER
EVER EVER
RIVERRUNRIVER
WHAT ARE YOU (HAHA) DOING? (THAT'S PISSED YOU OFF, HASN'T--)
SHUT UP IN THERE!
RUNAROUNDA ROLLAROLEAR OLLER
ALL RIGHT, SO I CAN'T TOUCH YOU IN THAT ABSTRACT STATE.
I DON'T (YES YOU) CARE. (DO!)
BOWLERPOLLAPOLAR COLASHOALASHELLASEA SHELLSHESELLSSHESAYS
I DON'T MIND.
YOU'LL HAVE TO CHANGE BACK SOMETIME.
I CAN WAIT.

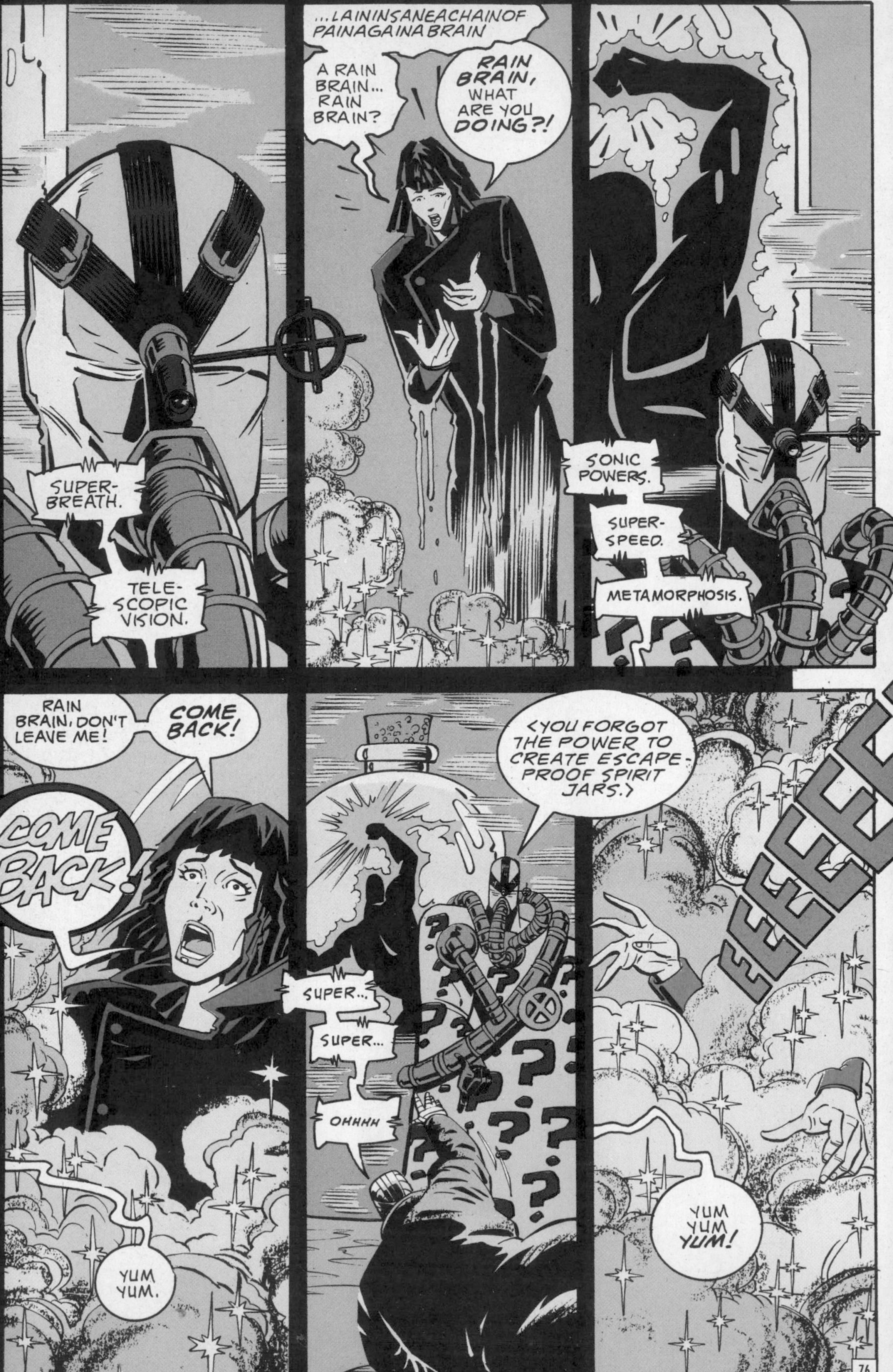

SUPER-BREATH.
TELE-SCOPIC VISION.
...LAININSANEACHAINOF PAINAGAINABRAIN
A RAIN BRAIN... RAIN BRAIN?
RAIN BRAIN, WHAT ARE YOU DOING?!
SONIC POWERS.
SUPER-SPEED.
METAMORPHOSIS.
RAIN BRAIN, DON'T LEAVE ME!
COME BACK!
COME BACK!
YUM YUM.
<YOU FORGOT THE POWER TO CREATE ESCAPE-PROOF SPIRIT JARS.>
SUPER...
SUPER...
OHHHH
EEEEEE
YUM YUM YUM!

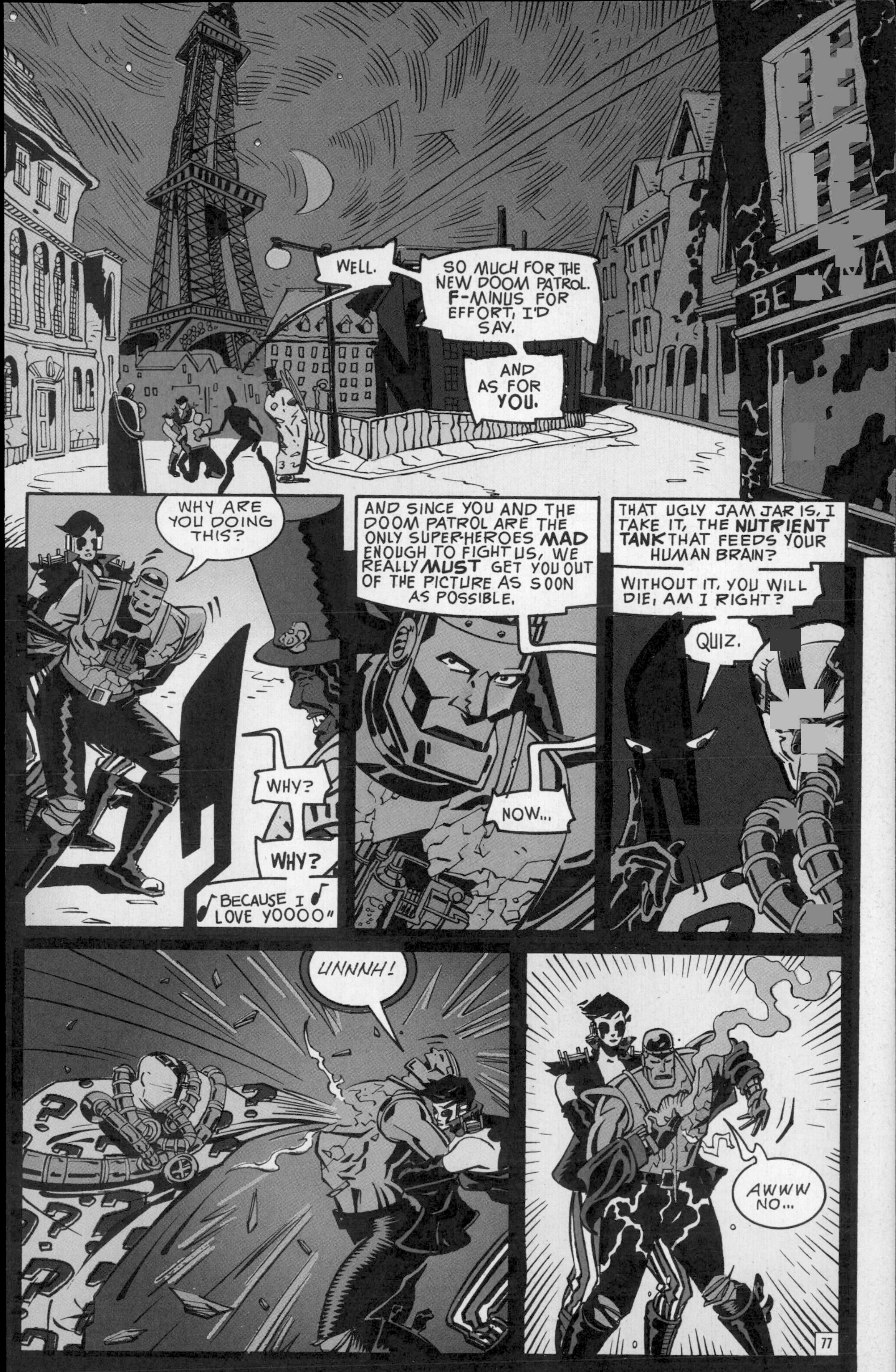
WELL.
SO MUCH FOR THE NEW DOOM PATROL. F-MINUS FOR EFFORT, I'D SAY.
AND AS FOR YOU.
WHY ARE YOU DOING THIS?
WHY?
WHY?
♪BECAUSE I LOVE YOOOO"♪
AND SINCE YOU AND THE DOOM PATROL ARE THE ONLY SUPER-HEROES MAD ENOUGH TO FIGHT US, WE REALLY MUST GET YOU OUT OF THE PICTURE AS SOON AS POSSIBLE.
NOW...
THAT UGLY JAM JAR IS, I TAKE IT, THE NUTRIENT TANK THAT FEEDS YOUR HUMAN BRAIN?
WITHOUT IT, YOU WILL DIE, AM I RIGHT?
QUIZ.
UNNNH!
AWWW NO...

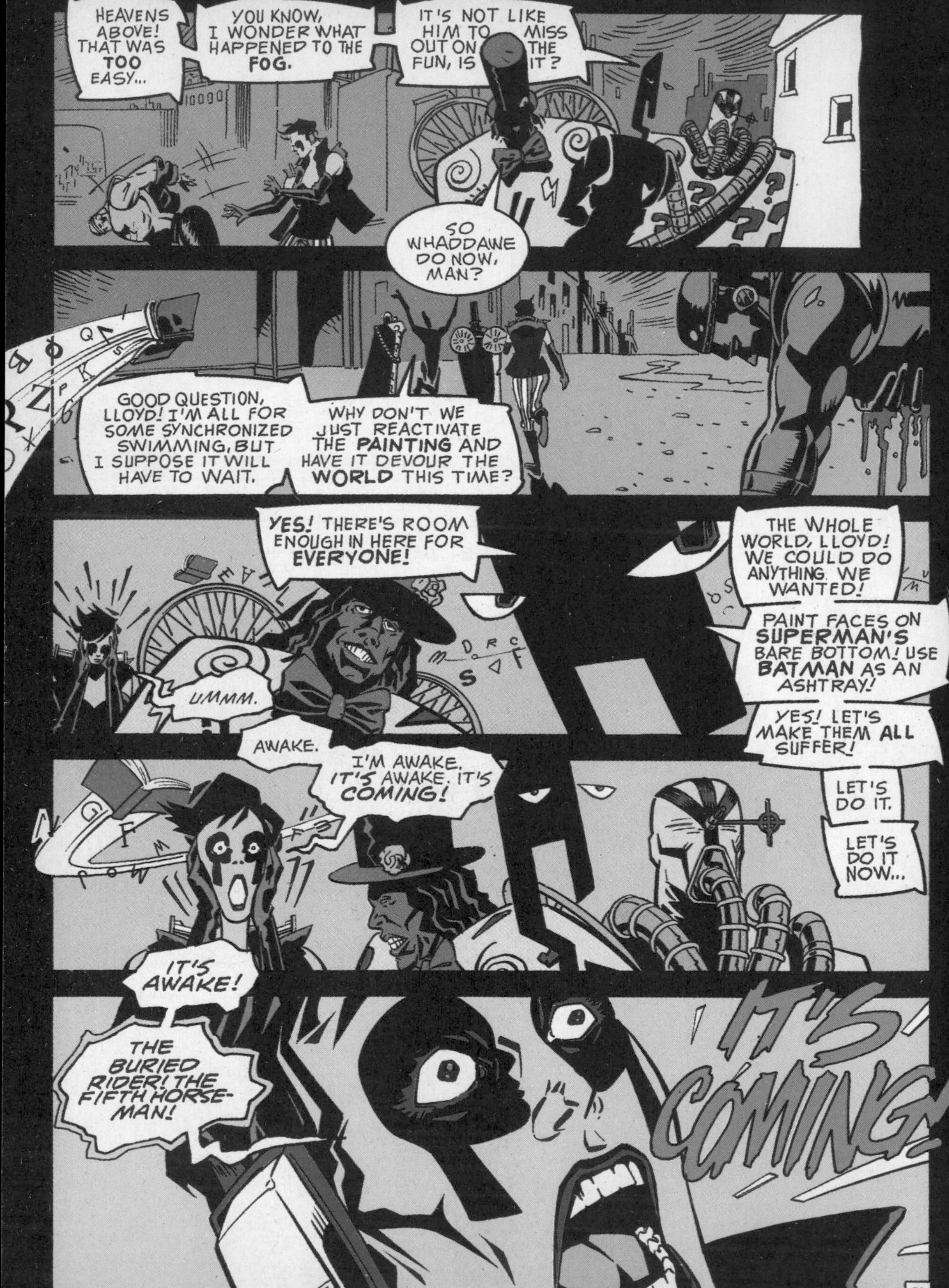

HEAVENS ABOVE! THAT WAS TOO EASY...
YOU KNOW, I WONDER WHAT HAPPENED TO THE FOG.
IT'S NOT LIKE HIM TO MISS OUT ON THE FUN, IS IT?
SO WHADDAWE DO NOW, MAN?
GOOD QUESTION, LLOYD! I'M ALL FOR SOME SYNCHRONIZED SWIMMING, BUT I SUPPOSE IT WILL HAVE TO WAIT.
WHY DON'T WE JUST REACTIVATE THE PAINTING AND HAVE IT DEVOUR THE WORLD THIS TIME?
YES! THERE'S ROOM ENOUGH IN HERE FOR EVERYONE!
UMMM.
THE WHOLE WORLD, LLOYD! WE COULD DO ANYTHING. WE WANTED!
PAINT FACES ON SUPERMAN'S BARE BOTTOM! USE BATMAN AS AN ASHTRAY!
YES! LET'S MAKE THEM ALL SUFFER!
AWAKE.
I'M AWAKE. IT'S AWAKE. IT'S COMING!
LET'S DO IT.
LET'S DO IT NOW...
IT'S AWAKE!
THE BURIED RIDER! THE FIFTH HORSE-MAN!
IT'S COMING!

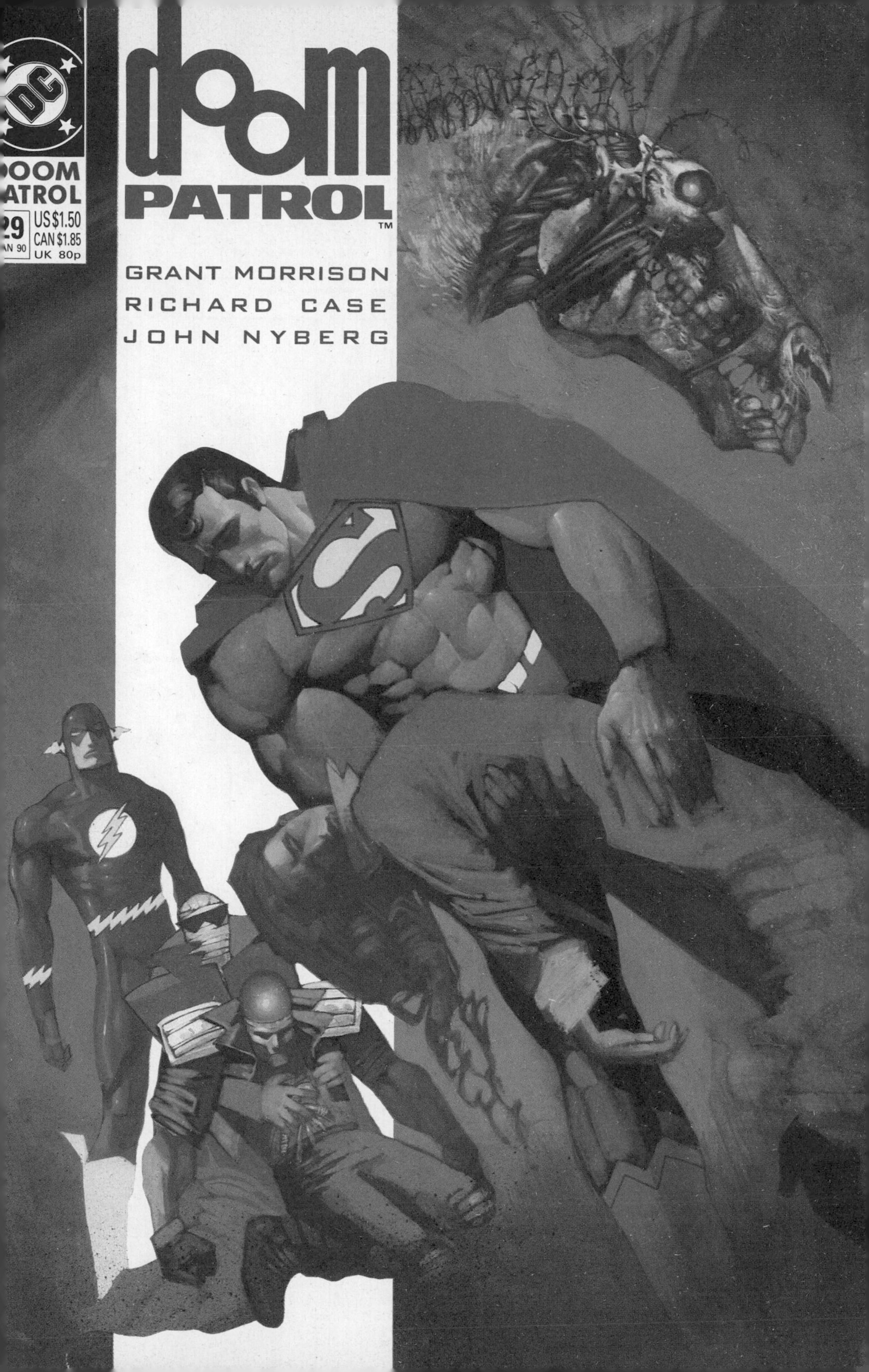

DC
OOM
ATROL
29
AN 90
US $1.50
CAN $1.85
UK 80p
doom
PATROL
™
GRANT MORRISON
RICHARD CASE
JOHN NYBERG

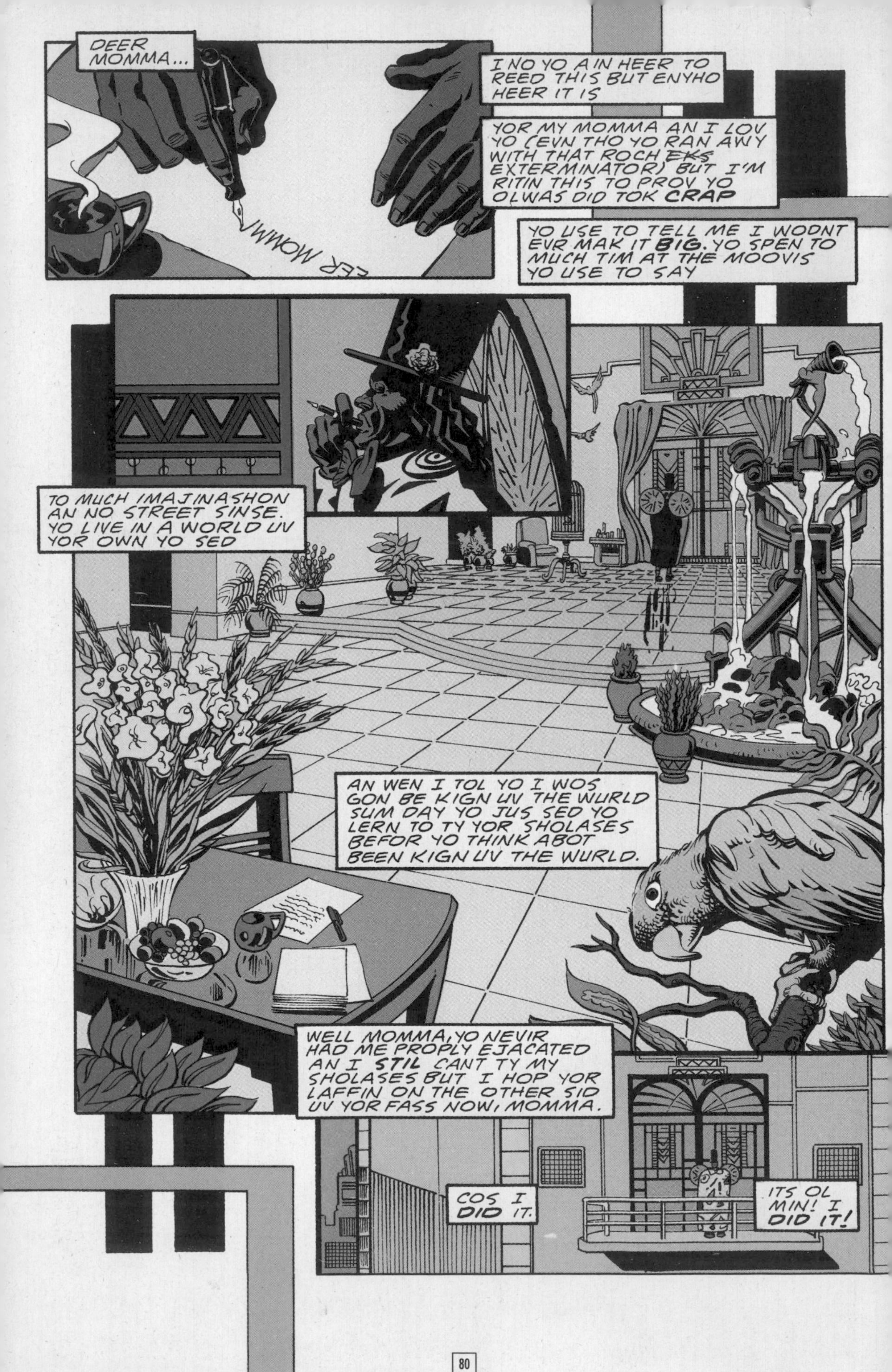

DEER MOMMA...
I NO YO AIN HEER TO REED THIS BUT ENYHO HEER IT IS
YOR MY MOMMA AN I LOV YO (EVN THO YO RAN AWY WITH THAT ROCH EKS EXTERMINATOR) BUT I'M RITIN THIS TO PROV YO OLWAS DID TOK **CRAP**
YO USE TO TELL ME I WOONT EVR MAK IT **BIG**. YO SPEN TO MUCH TIM AT THE MOOVIS YO USE TO SAY
TO MUCH IMAJINASHON AN NO STREET SINSE. YO LIVE IN A WORLD UV YOR OWN YO SED
AN WEN I TOL YO I WOS GON BE KIGN UV THE WURLD SUM DAY YO JUS SED YO LERN TO TY YOR SHOLASES BEFOR YO THINK ABOT BEEN KIGN UV THE WURLD.
WELL MOMMA, YO NEVIR HAD ME PROPLY EJACATED AN I **STIL** CANT TY MY SHOLASES BUT I HOP YOR LAFFIN ON THE OTHER SID UV YOR FASS NOW, MOMMA.
COS I **DID** IT.
ITS OL MIN! I **DID IT!**

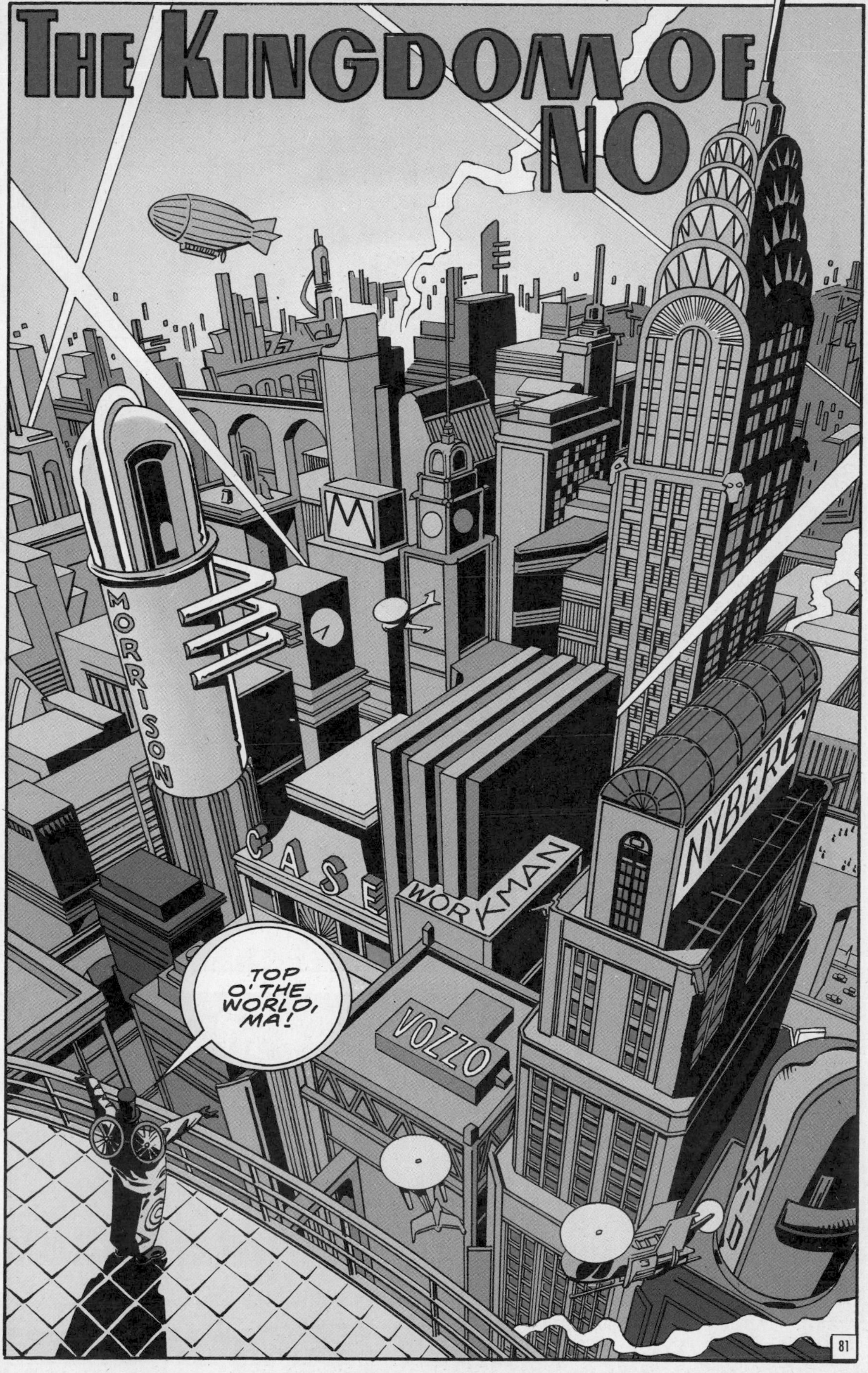
THE KINGDOM OF NO
MORRISON
CASE
WORKMAN
NYBERG
VOZZO
WAID
TOP O' THE WORLD, MA!

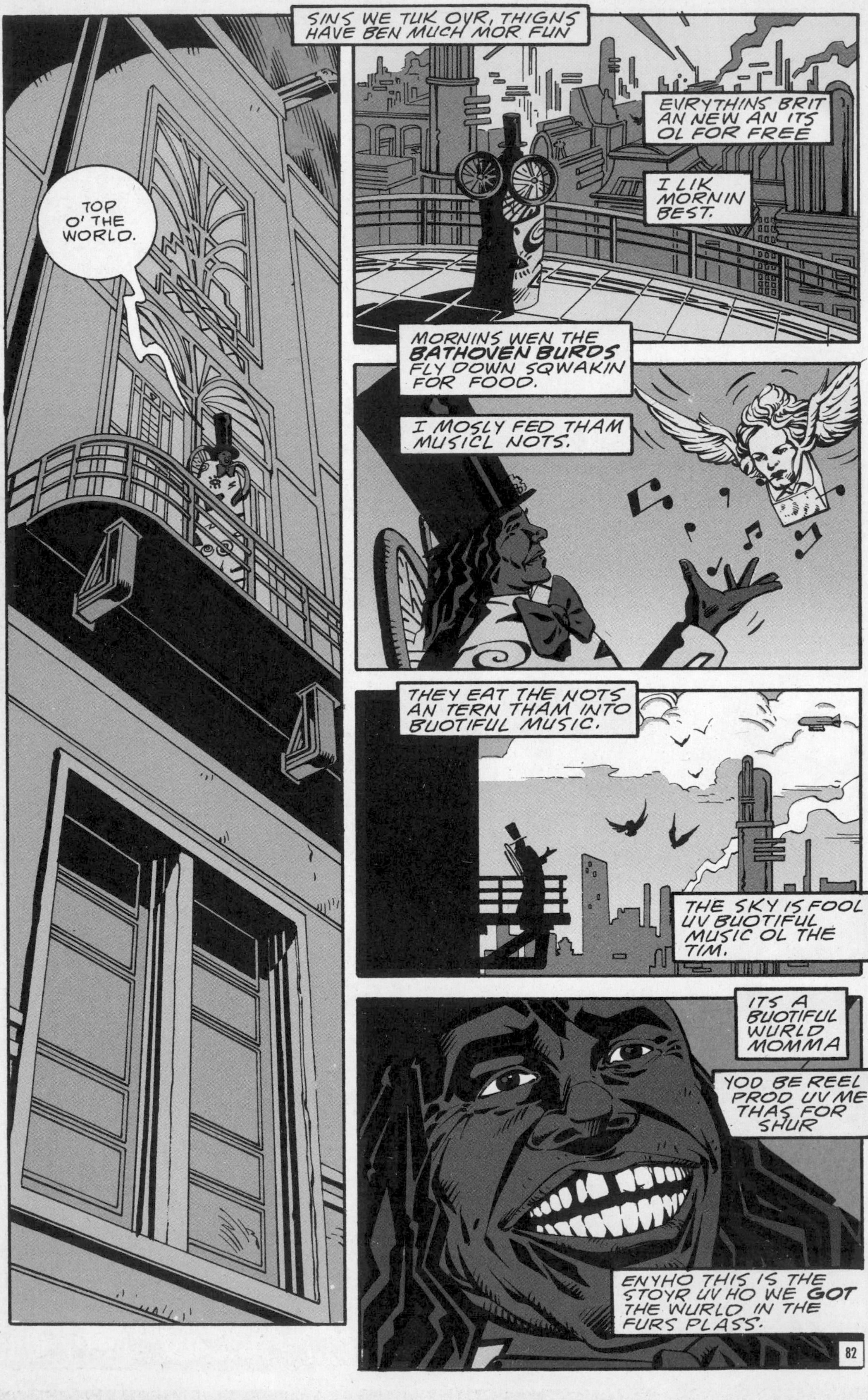
TOP O' THE WORLD.
SINS WE TUK OVR, THIGNS HAVE BEN MUCH MOR FUN
EVRYTHINS BRIT AN NEW AN ITS OL FOR FREE
I LIK MORNIN BEST.
MORNINS WEN THE **BATHOVEN BURDS** FLY DOWN SQWAKIN FOR FOOD.
I MOSLY FED THAM MUSICL NOTS.
THEY EAT THE NOTS AN TERN THAM INTO BUOTIFUL MUSIC.
THE SKY IS FOOL UV BUOTIFUL MUSIC OL THE TIM.
ITS A BUOTIFUL WURLD MOMMA
YOD BE REEL PROD UV ME THAS FOR SHUR
ENYHO THIS IS THE STOYR UV HO WE **GOT** THE WURLD IN THE FURS PLASS.

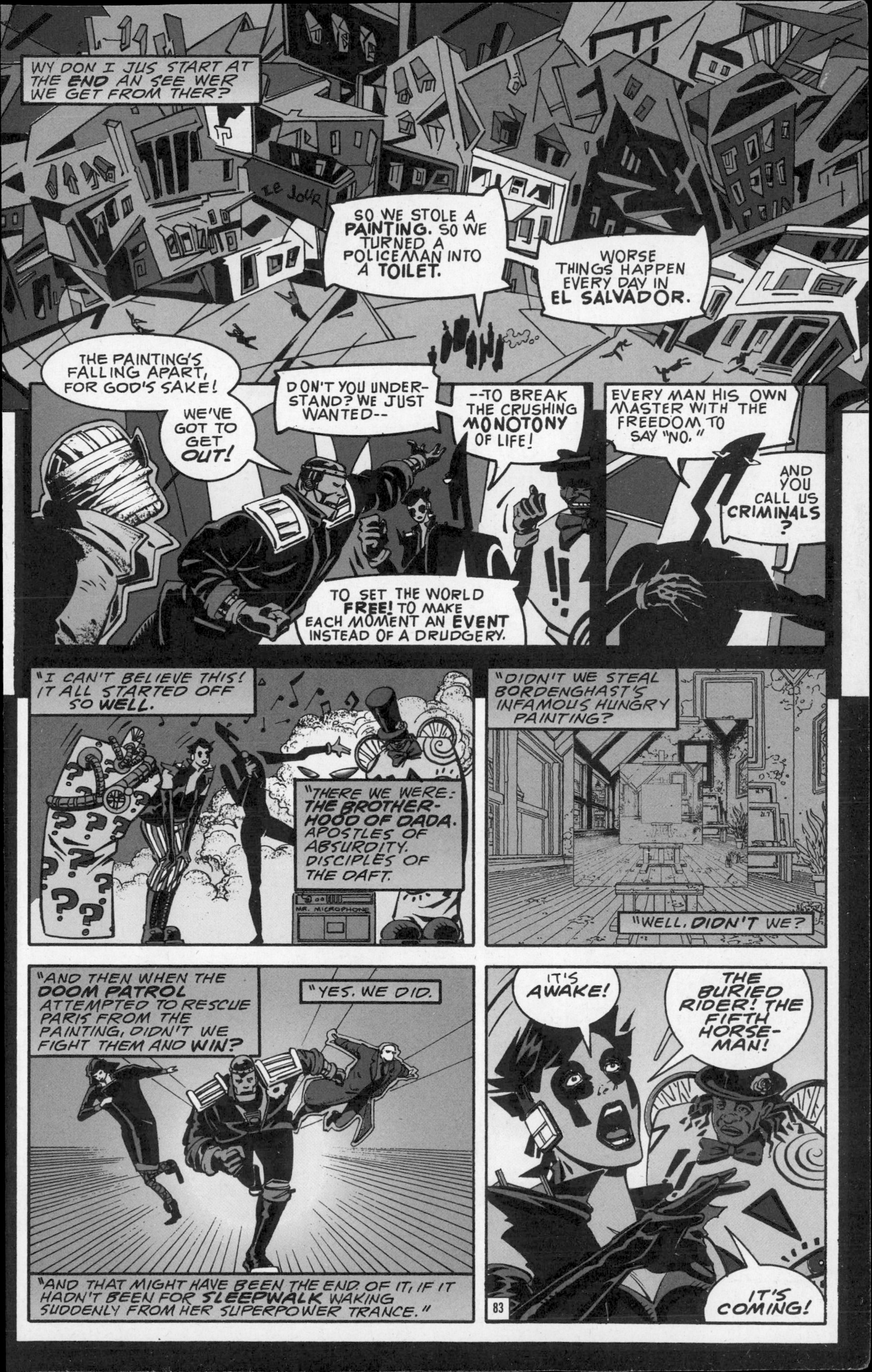

WY DON I JUS START AT THE END AN SEE WER WE GET FROM THER?
LE JOUR
SO WE STOLE A PAINTING. SO WE TURNED A POLICEMAN INTO A TOILET.
WORSE THINGS HAPPEN EVERY DAY IN EL SALVADOR.
THE PAINTING'S FALLING APART, FOR GOD'S SAKE!
WE'VE GOT TO GET OUT!
DON'T YOU UNDERSTAND? WE JUST WANTED--
--TO BREAK THE CRUSHING MONOTONY OF LIFE!
TO SET THE WORLD FREE! TO MAKE EACH MOMENT AN EVENT INSTEAD OF A DRUDGERY.
EVERY MAN HIS OWN MASTER WITH THE FREEDOM TO SAY "NO."
AND YOU CALL US CRIMINALS?
"I CAN'T BELIEVE THIS! IT ALL STARTED OFF SO WELL.
"THERE WE WERE: THE BROTHERHOOD OF DADA. APOSTLES OF ABSURDITY. DISCIPLES OF THE DAFT.
MR. MICROPHONE
"DIDN'T WE STEAL BORDENGHAST'S INFAMOUS HUNGRY PAINTING?
"WELL, DIDN'T WE?
"AND THEN WHEN THE DOOM PATROL ATTEMPTED TO RESCUE PARIS FROM THE PAINTING, DIDN'T WE FIGHT THEM AND WIN?
"YES. WE DID.
"AND THAT MIGHT HAVE BEEN THE END OF IT, IF IT HADN'T BEEN FOR SLEEPWALK WAKING SUDDENLY FROM HER SUPERPOWER TRANCE."
IT'S AWAKE!
THE BURIED RIDER! THE FIFTH HORSEMAN!
IT'S COMING!

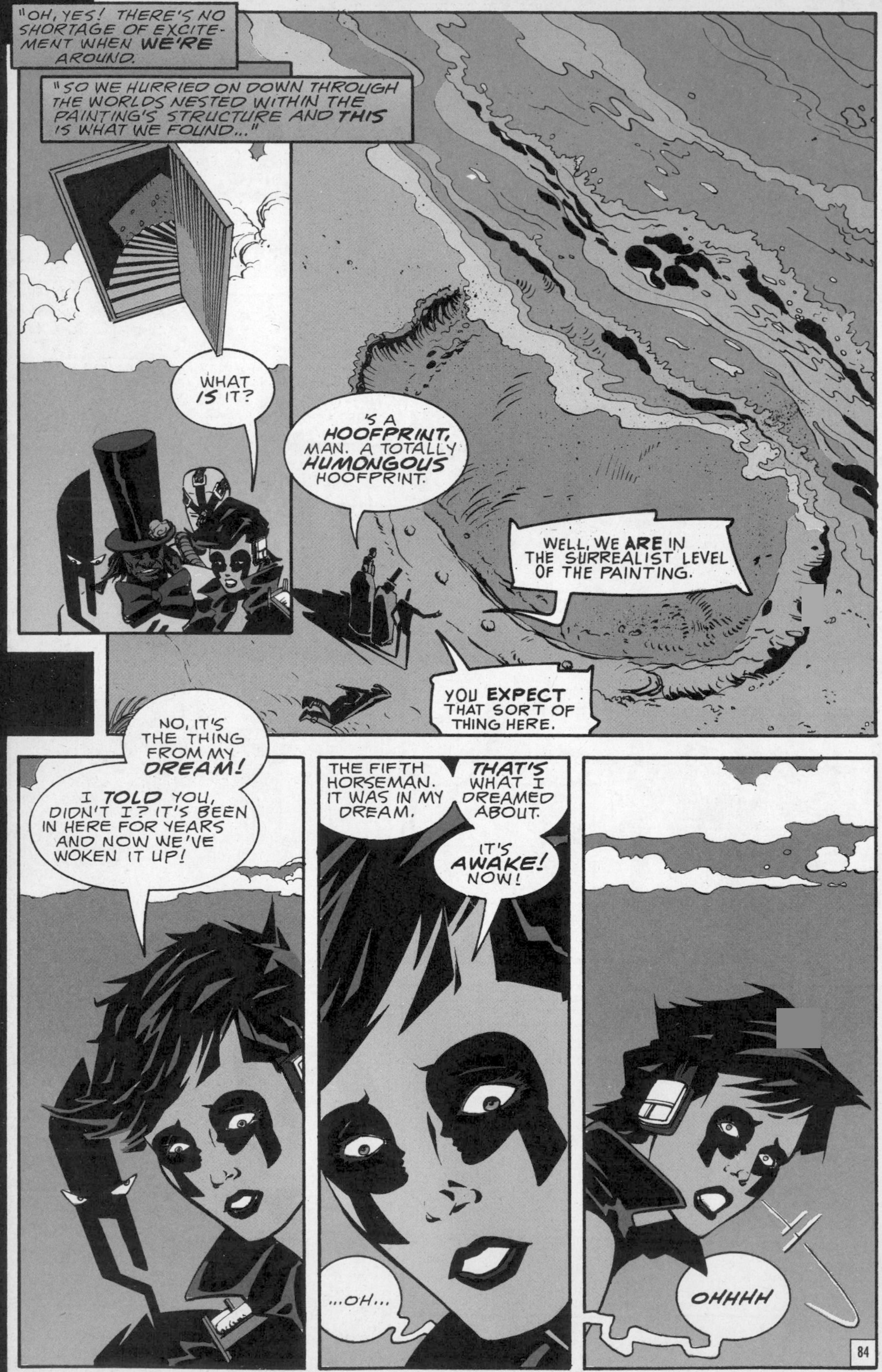
"OH, YES! THERE'S NO SHORTAGE OF EXCITEMENT WHEN WE'RE AROUND.
"SO WE HURRIED ON DOWN THROUGH THE WORLDS NESTED WITHIN THE PAINTING'S STRUCTURE AND THIS IS WHAT WE FOUND..."
WHAT IS IT?
'S A HOOFPRINT, MAN. A TOTALLY HUMONGOUS HOOFPRINT.
WELL, WE ARE IN THE SURREALIST LEVEL OF THE PAINTING.
YOU EXPECT THAT SORT OF THING HERE.
NO, IT'S THE THING FROM MY DREAM!
I TOLD YOU, DIDN'T I? IT'S BEEN IN HERE FOR YEARS AND NOW WE'VE WOKEN IT UP!
THE FIFTH HORSEMAN. IT WAS IN MY DREAM.
THAT'S WHAT I DREAMED ABOUT.
IT'S AWAKE! NOW!
...OH...
OHHHH

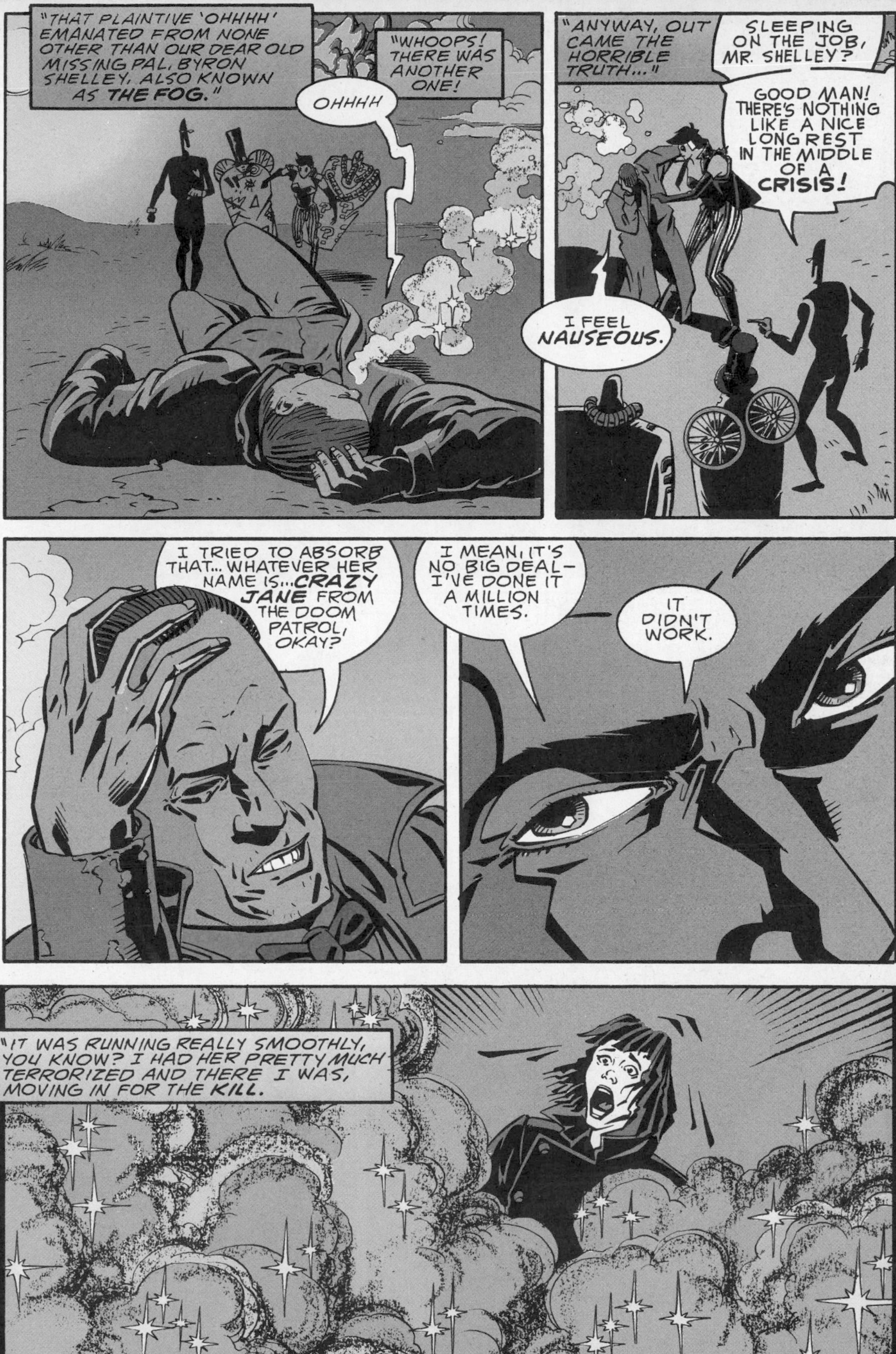
"THAT PLAINTIVE 'OHHHH' EMANATED FROM NONE OTHER THAN OUR DEAR OLD MISSING PAL, BYRON SHELLEY, ALSO KNOWN AS THE FOG."
"WHOOPS! THERE WAS ANOTHER ONE!
OHHHH
"ANYWAY, OUT CAME THE HORRIBLE TRUTH..."
SLEEPING ON THE JOB, MR. SHELLEY?
GOOD MAN! THERE'S NOTHING LIKE A NICE LONG REST IN THE MIDDLE OF A CRISIS!
I FEEL NAUSEOUS.
I TRIED TO ABSORB THAT... WHATEVER HER NAME IS... CRAZY JANE FROM THE DOOM PATROL, OKAY?
I MEAN, IT'S NO BIG DEAL-- I'VE DONE IT A MILLION TIMES.
IT DIDN'T WORK.
"IT WAS RUNNING REALLY SMOOTHLY, YOU KNOW? I HAD HER PRETTY MUCH TERRORIZED AND THERE I WAS, MOVING IN FOR THE KILL.

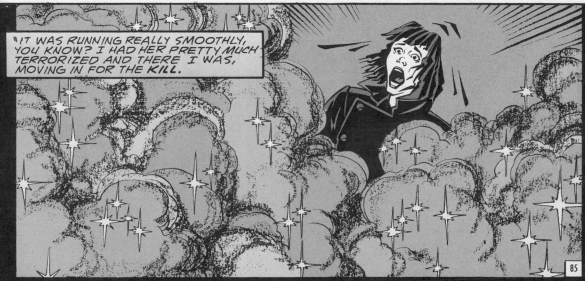

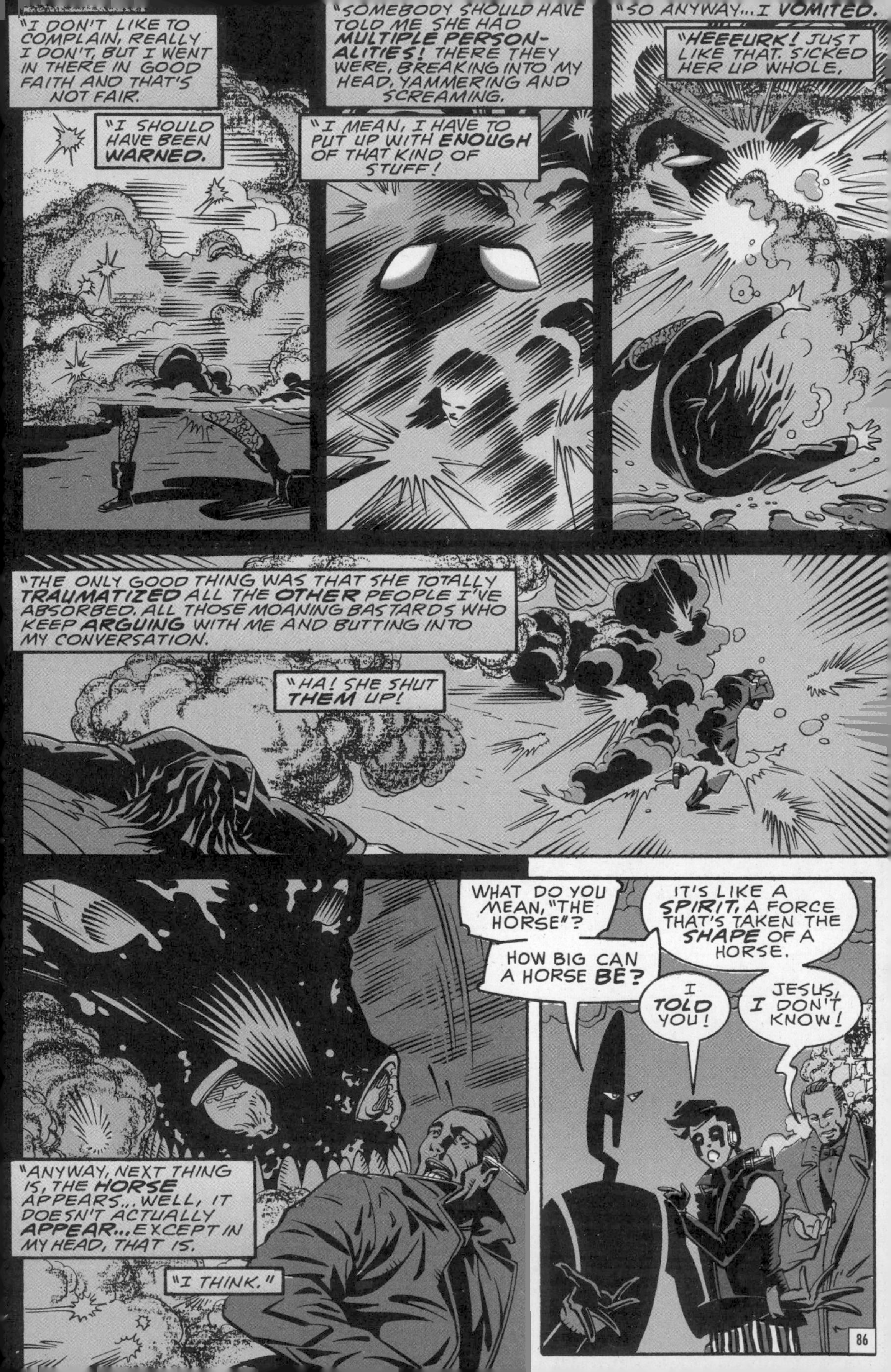
"I DON'T LIKE TO COMPLAIN, REALLY I DON'T, BUT I WENT IN THERE IN GOOD FAITH AND THAT'S NOT FAIR.
"I SHOULD HAVE BEEN **WARNED.**
"SOMEBODY SHOULD HAVE TOLD ME SHE HAD **MULTIPLE PERSON-ALITIES!** THERE THEY WERE, BREAKING INTO MY HEAD, YAMMERING AND SCREAMING.
"I MEAN, I HAVE TO PUT UP WITH **ENOUGH** OF THAT KIND OF STUFF!
"SO ANYWAY... I **VOMITED.**
"**HEEEURK!** JUST LIKE THAT. SICKED HER UP WHOLE.
"THE ONLY GOOD THING WAS THAT SHE TOTALLY **TRAUMATIZED** ALL THE **OTHER** PEOPLE I'VE ABSORBED. ALL THOSE MOANING BASTARDS WHO KEEP **ARGUING** WITH ME AND BUTTING INTO MY CONVERSATION.
"HA! SHE SHUT **THEM** UP!
"ANYWAY, NEXT THING IS, THE **HORSE** APPEARS... WELL, IT DOESN'T ACTUALLY **APPEAR**... EXCEPT IN MY HEAD, THAT IS.
"I THINK."
WHAT DO YOU MEAN, "THE HORSE"?
IT'S LIKE A **SPIRIT.** A FORCE THAT'S TAKEN THE **SHAPE** OF A HORSE.
HOW BIG CAN A HORSE **BE?**
I **TOLD** YOU!
JESUS, **I** DON'T KNOW!

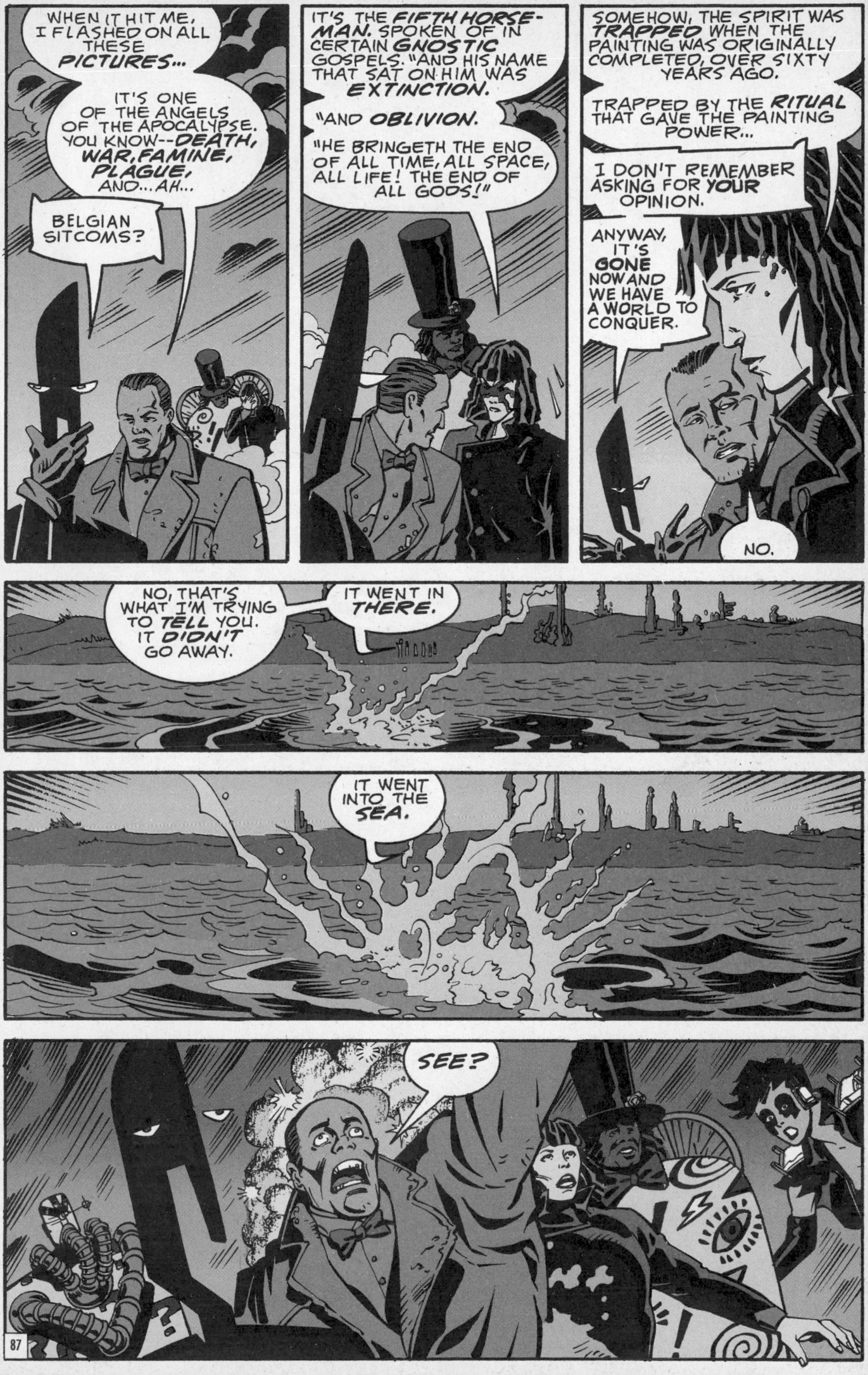
WHEN IT HIT ME, I FLASHED ON ALL THESE PICTURES...
IT'S ONE OF THE ANGELS OF THE APOCALYPSE. YOU KNOW--DEATH, WAR, FAMINE, PLAGUE, AND...AH...
BELGIAN SITCOMS?
IT'S THE FIFTH HORSE-MAN. SPOKEN OF IN CERTAIN GNOSTIC GOSPELS. "AND HIS NAME THAT SAT ON HIM WAS EXTINCTION.
"AND OBLIVION.
"HE BRINGETH THE END OF ALL TIME, ALL SPACE, ALL LIFE! THE END OF ALL GODS!"
SOMEHOW, THE SPIRIT WAS TRAPPED WHEN THE PAINTING WAS ORIGINALLY COMPLETED, OVER SIXTY YEARS AGO.
TRAPPED BY THE RITUAL THAT GAVE THE PAINTING POWER...
I DON'T REMEMBER ASKING FOR YOUR OPINION.
ANYWAY, IT'S GONE NOW AND WE HAVE A WORLD TO CONQUER.
NO.
NO, THAT'S WHAT I'M TRYING TO TELL YOU. IT DIDN'T GO AWAY.
IT WENT IN THERE.
IT WENT INTO THE SEA.
SEE?

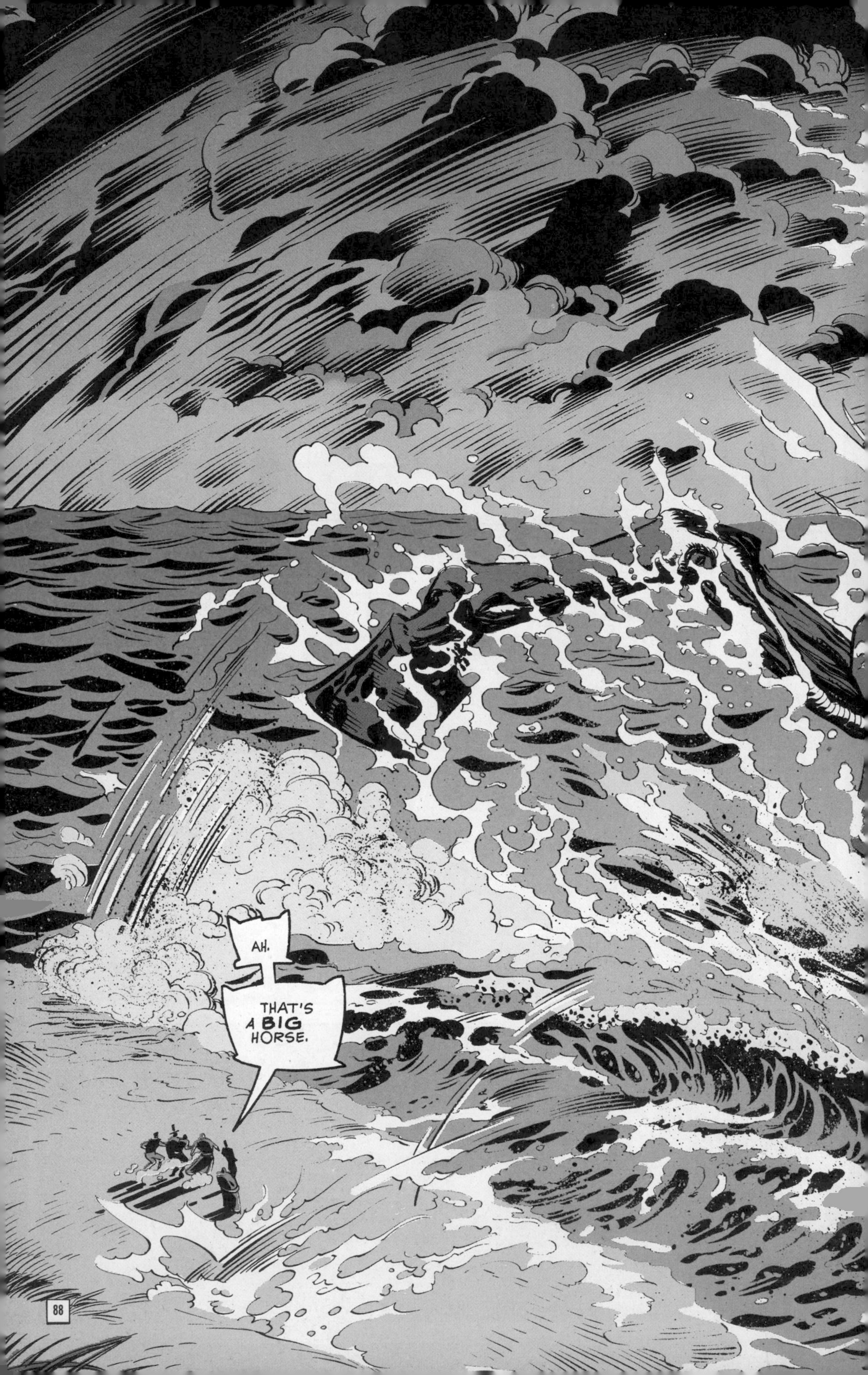
AH.
THAT'S A BIG HORSE.

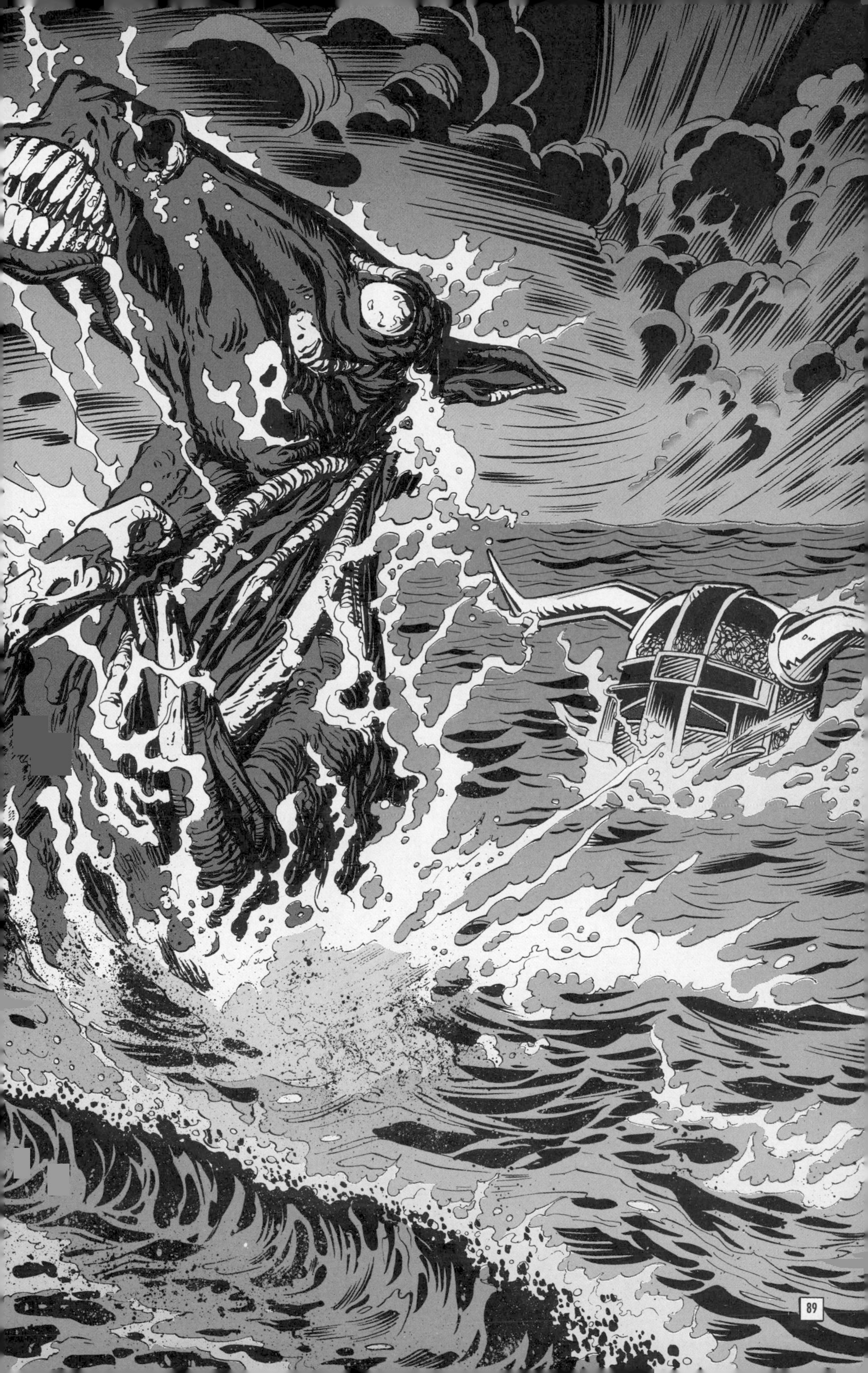

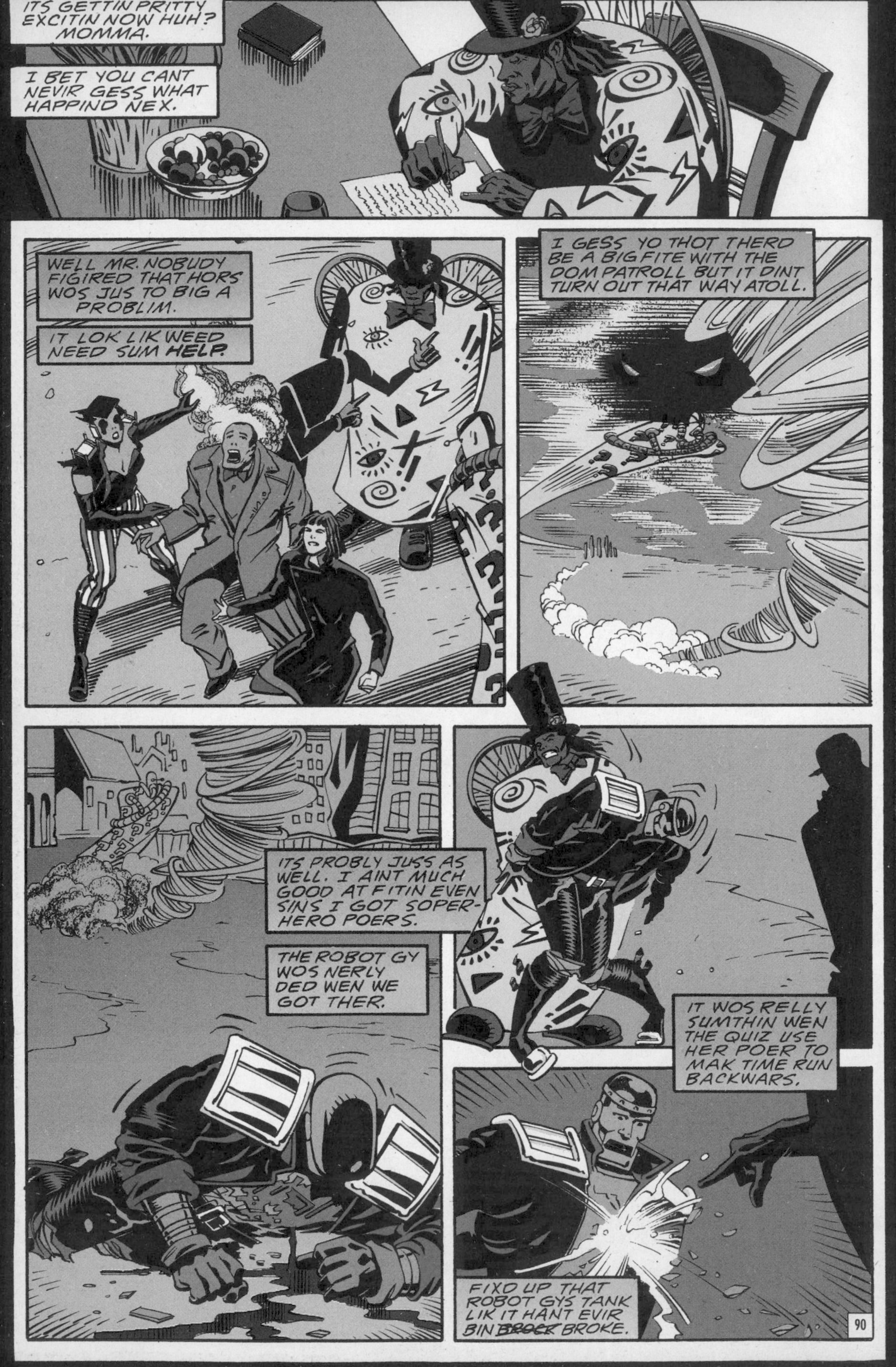
ITS GETTIN PRITTY EXCITIN NOW HUH? MOMMA.
I BET YOU CANT NEVIR GESS WHAT HAPPIND NEX.
WELL MR. NOBUDY FIGIRED THAT HORS WOS JUS TO BIG A PROBLIM.
IT LOK LIK WEED NEED SUM HELP.
I GESS YO THOT THERD BE A BIG FITE WITH THE DOM PATROLL BUT IT DINT TURN OUT THAT WAY ATOLL.
ITS PROBLY JUSS AS WELL. I AINT MUCH GOOD AT FITIN EVEN SINS I GOT SOPER-HERO POERS.
THE ROBOT GY WOS NERLY DED WEN WE GOT THER.
IT WOS RELLY SUMTHIN WEN THE QUIZ USE HER POER TO MAK TIME RUN BACKWARS.
FIXD UP THAT ROBOT GYS TANK LIK IT HANT EVIR BIN ~~BROCK~~ BROKE.

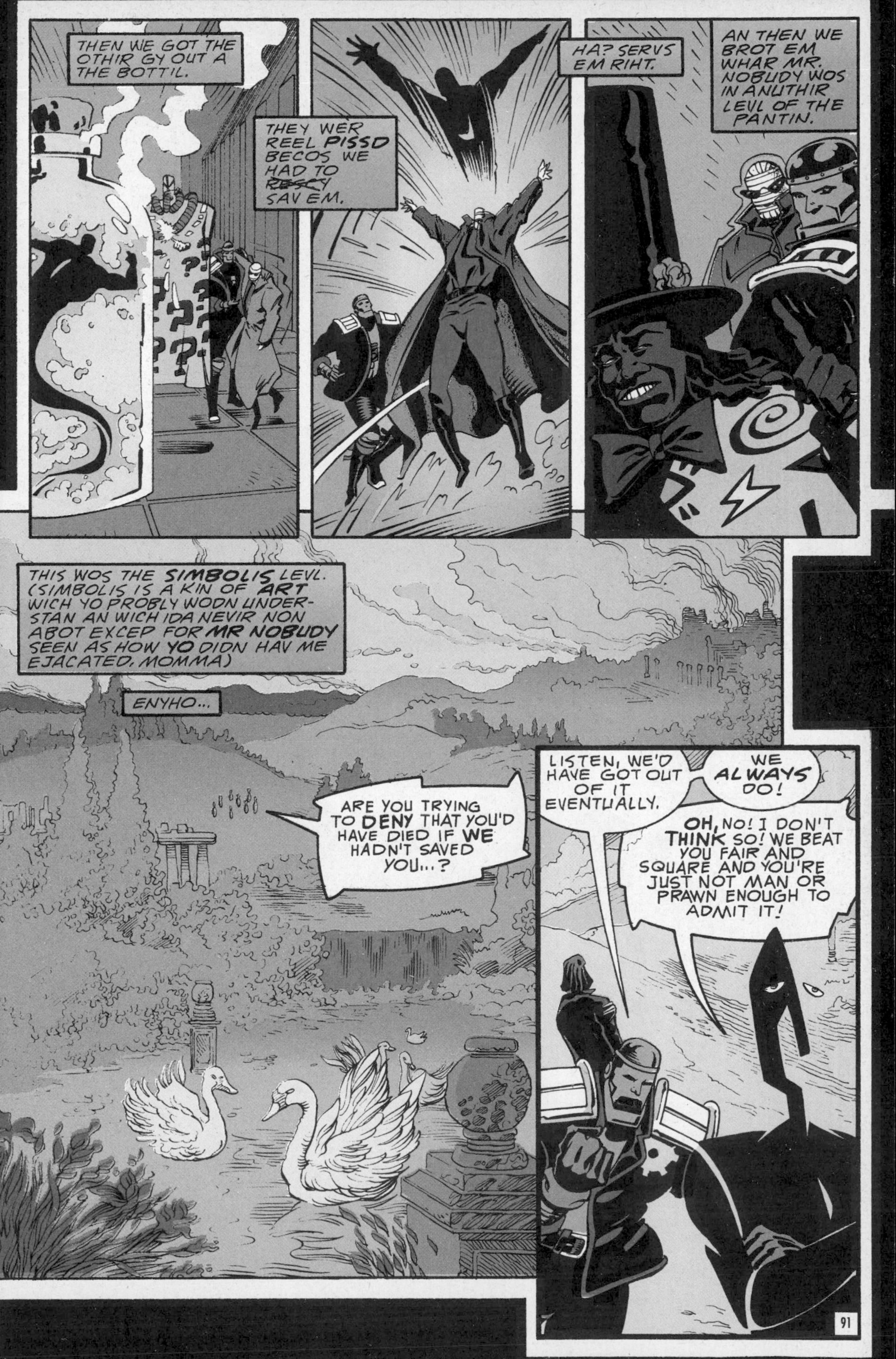
THEN WE GOT THE OTHIR GY OUT A THE BOTT'IL.
THEY WER REEL PISSD BECOS WE HAD TO ~~RESCY~~ SAV EM.
HA? SERVS EM RIHT.
AN THEN WE BROT EM WHAR MR. NOBUDY WOS IN ANUTHIR LEVL OF THE PANTIN.
THIS WOS THE SIMBOLIS LEVL. (SIMBOLIS IS A KIN OF ART WICH YO PROBLY WODN UNDER-STAN AN WICH IDA NEVIR NON ABOT EXCEP FOR MR NOBUDY SEEN AS HOW YO DIDN HAV ME EJACATED, MOMMA)
ENYHO...
ARE YOU TRYING TO DENY THAT YOU'D HAVE DIED IF WE HADN'T SAVED YOU...?
LISTEN, WE'D HAVE GOT OUT OF IT EVENTUALLY.
WE ALWAYS DO!
OH, NO! I DON'T THINK SO! WE BEAT YOU FAIR AND SQUARE AND YOU'RE JUST NOT MAN OR PRAWN ENOUGH TO ADMIT IT!

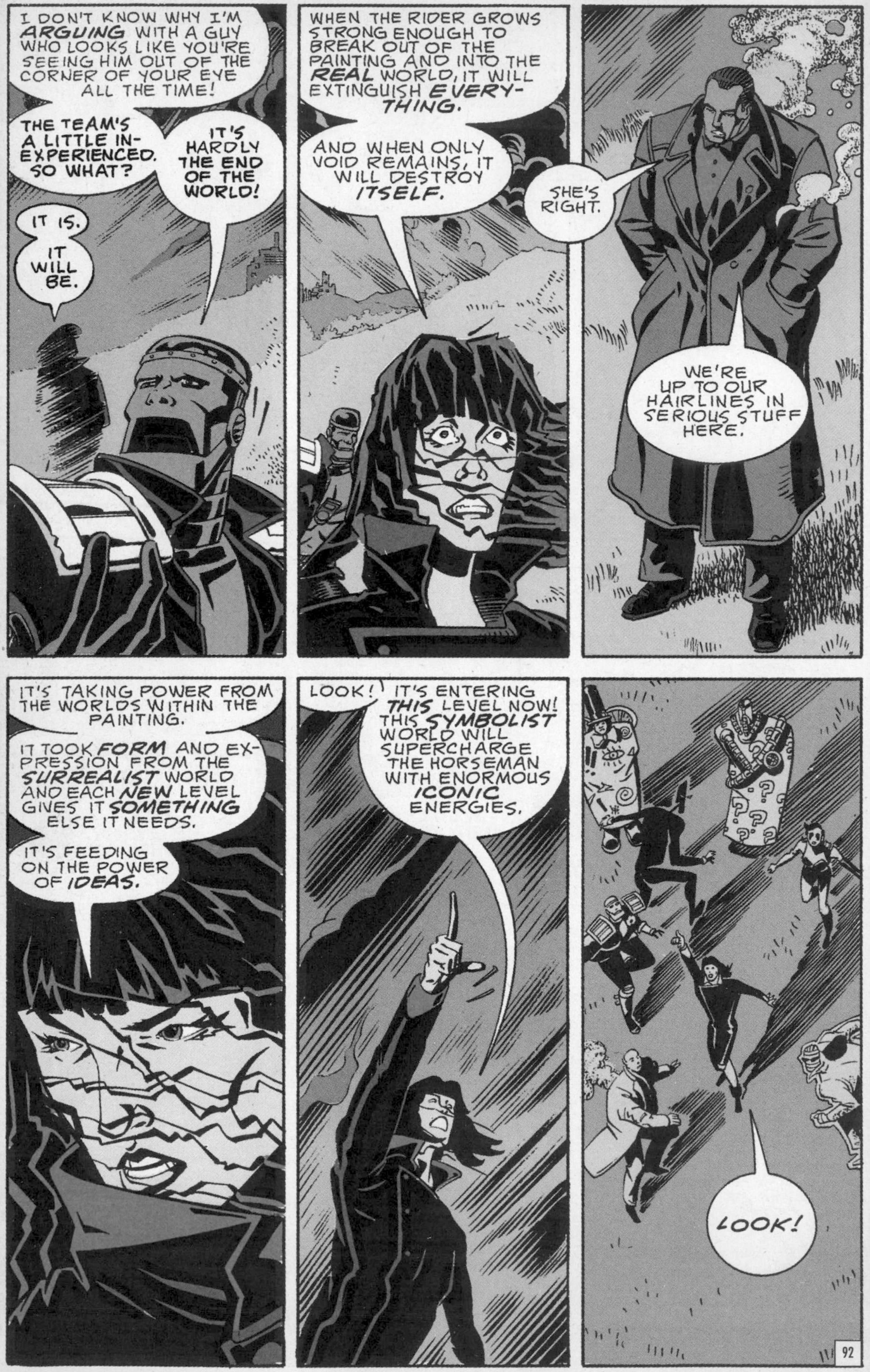
I DON'T KNOW WHY I'M ARGUING WITH A GUY WHO LOOKS LIKE YOU'RE SEEING HIM OUT OF THE CORNER OF YOUR EYE ALL THE TIME!
THE TEAM'S A LITTLE IN-EXPERIENCED. SO WHAT?
IT'S HARDLY THE END OF THE WORLD!
IT IS.
IT WILL BE.
WHEN THE RIDER GROWS STRONG ENOUGH TO BREAK OUT OF THE PAINTING AND INTO THE REAL WORLD, IT WILL EXTINGUISH EVERY-THING.
AND WHEN ONLY VOID REMAINS, IT WILL DESTROY ITSELF.
SHE'S RIGHT.
WE'RE UP TO OUR HAIRLINES IN SERIOUS STUFF HERE.
IT'S TAKING POWER FROM THE WORLDS WITHIN THE PAINTING.
IT TOOK FORM AND EX-PRESSION FROM THE SURREALIST WORLD AND EACH NEW LEVEL GIVES IT SOMETHING ELSE IT NEEDS.
IT'S FEEDING ON THE POWER OF IDEAS.
LOOK!
IT'S ENTERING THIS LEVEL NOW! THIS SYMBOLIST WORLD WILL SUPERCHARGE THE HORSEMAN WITH ENORMOUS ICONIC ENERGIES.
LOOK!

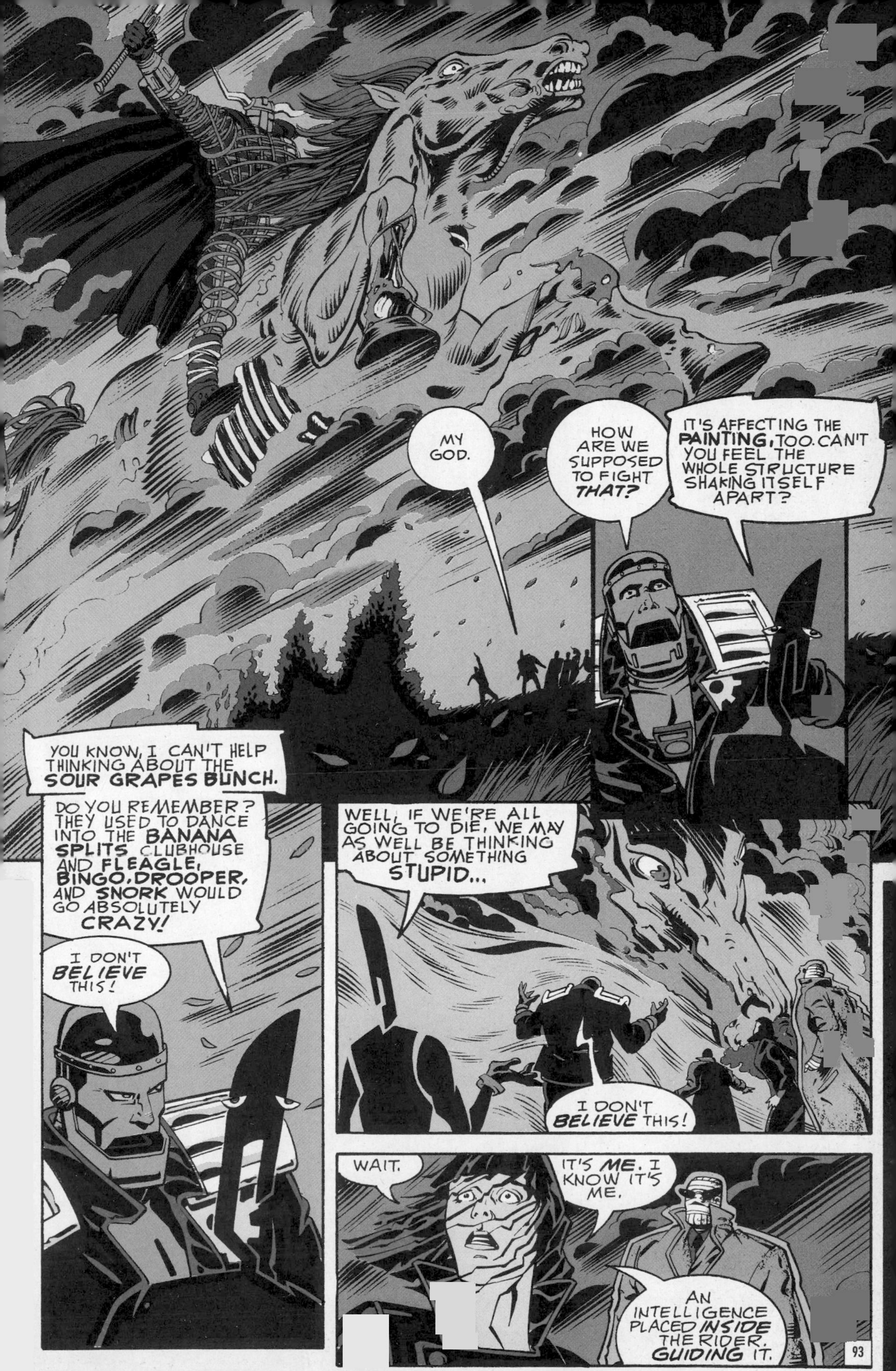

MY GOD.
HOW ARE WE SUPPOSED TO FIGHT THAT?
IT'S AFFECTING THE PAINTING, TOO. CAN'T YOU FEEL THE WHOLE STRUCTURE SHAKING ITSELF APART?
YOU KNOW, I CAN'T HELP THINKING ABOUT THE SOUR GRAPES BUNCH.
DO YOU REMEMBER? THEY USED TO DANCE INTO THE BANANA SPLITS CLUBHOUSE AND FLEAGLE, BINGO, DROOPER, AND SNORK WOULD GO ABSOLUTELY CRAZY!
I DON'T BELIEVE THIS!
WELL, IF WE'RE ALL GOING TO DIE, WE MAY AS WELL BE THINKING ABOUT SOMETHING STUPID...
I DON'T BELIEVE THIS!
WAIT.
IT'S ME. I KNOW IT'S ME.
AN INTELLIGENCE PLACED INSIDE THE RIDER. GUIDING IT.

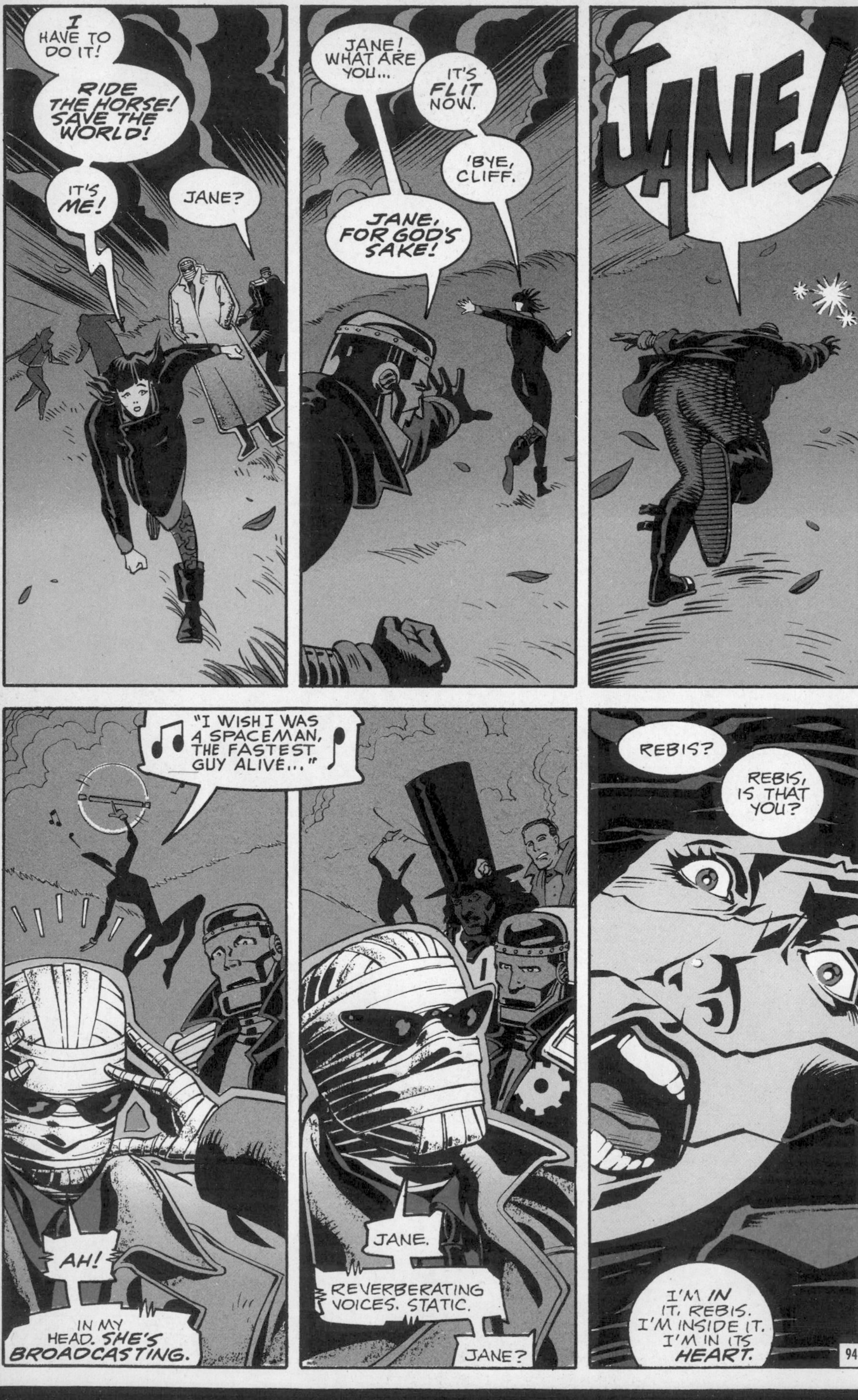
I HAVE TO DO IT!
RIDE THE HORSE! SAVE THE WORLD!
IT'S ME!
JANE?
JANE! WHAT ARE YOU...
IT'S FLIT NOW.
'BYE, CLIFF.
JANE, FOR GOD'S SAKE!
JANE!
"I WISH I WAS A SPACEMAN, THE FASTEST GUY ALIVE..."
AH!
IN MY HEAD. SHE'S BROADCASTING.
JANE.
REVERBERATING VOICES. STATIC.
JANE?
REBIS?
REBIS, IS THAT YOU?
I'M IN IT, REBIS. I'M INSIDE IT. I'M IN ITS HEART.

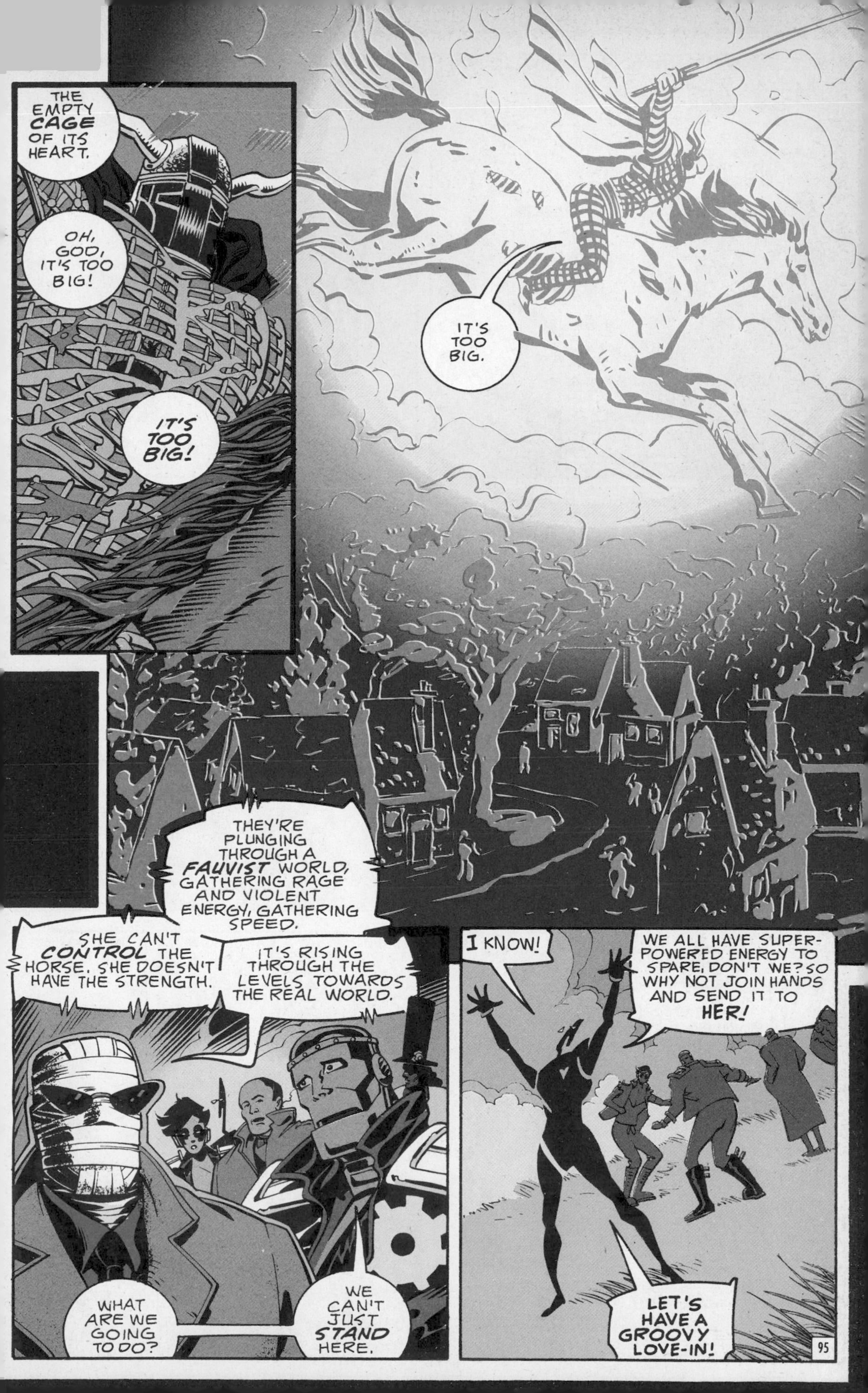
THE EMPTY CAGE OF ITS HEART.
OH, GOD, IT'S TOO BIG!
IT'S TOO BIG!
IT'S TOO BIG.
THEY'RE PLUNGING THROUGH A FAUVIST WORLD, GATHERING RAGE AND VIOLENT ENERGY, GATHERING SPEED.
SHE CAN'T CONTROL THE HORSE. SHE DOESN'T HAVE THE STRENGTH.
IT'S RISING THROUGH THE LEVELS TOWARDS THE REAL WORLD.
WHAT ARE WE GOING TO DO?
WE CAN'T JUST STAND HERE.
I KNOW!
WE ALL HAVE SUPER-POWERED ENERGY TO SPARE, DON'T WE? SO WHY NOT JOIN HANDS AND SEND IT TO HER!
LET'S HAVE A GROOVY LOVE-IN!

INSTEAD OF FIGHTING, WE ALL JOIN HANDS! LIKE EBONY AND IVORY LIVING TOGETHER ON A PIANO!

YOU'RE **NUTS.**

IT'S SO EMBARRASSING IT **HAS** TO WORK!

I THINK HE'S RIGHT. I THINK WE MIGHT BE ABLE TO HELP JANE **GUIDE** THE HORSE.

YEAH? SO WHAT NOW?

EACH OF THE LEVELS OF THE PAINTING, EACH SELF-CONTAINED WORLD, GIVES THE HORSEMAN **POWER,** AM I NOT RIGHT?

IT TAKES **IDEAS** AND CONVERTS THEM INTO ENERGY. SURREALISM, SYMBOLISM, CUBISM, FUTURISM—THEY ALL PROVIDE STRENGTH FOR THE RIDER.

96

MY GOD! WHAT A FABULOUS MIND I POSSESS! I **KNOW** HOW TO DESTROY THE HORSEMAN **AND** MAKE IT FEEL STUPID AT THE SAME TIME.

WHAT ARE YOU TALKING ABOUT?

THE **DADA** WORLD! GUIDE HER TO THE **DADA** WORLD!

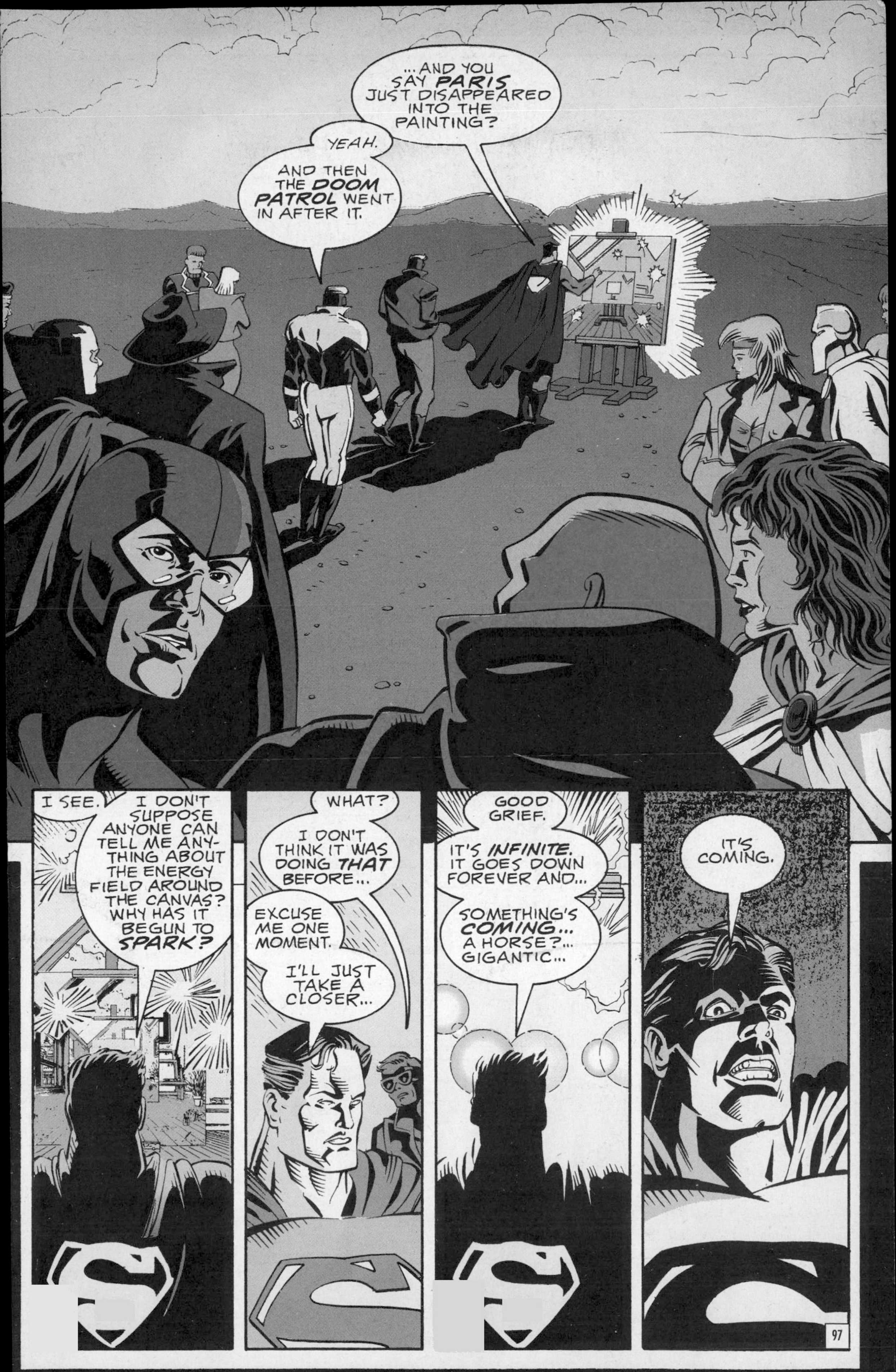
...AND YOU SAY PARIS JUST DISAPPEARED INTO THE PAINTING?
YEAH.
AND THEN THE DOOM PATROL WENT IN AFTER IT.
I SEE.
I DON'T SUPPOSE ANYONE CAN TELL ME ANYTHING ABOUT THE ENERGY FIELD AROUND THE CANVAS? WHY HAS IT BEGUN TO SPARK?
WHAT?
I DON'T THINK IT WAS DOING THAT BEFORE...
EXCUSE ME ONE MOMENT.
I'LL JUST TAKE A CLOSER...
GOOD GRIEF.
IT'S INFINITE. IT GOES DOWN FOREVER AND...
SOMETHING'S COMING... A HORSE?... GIGANTIC...
IT'S COMING.

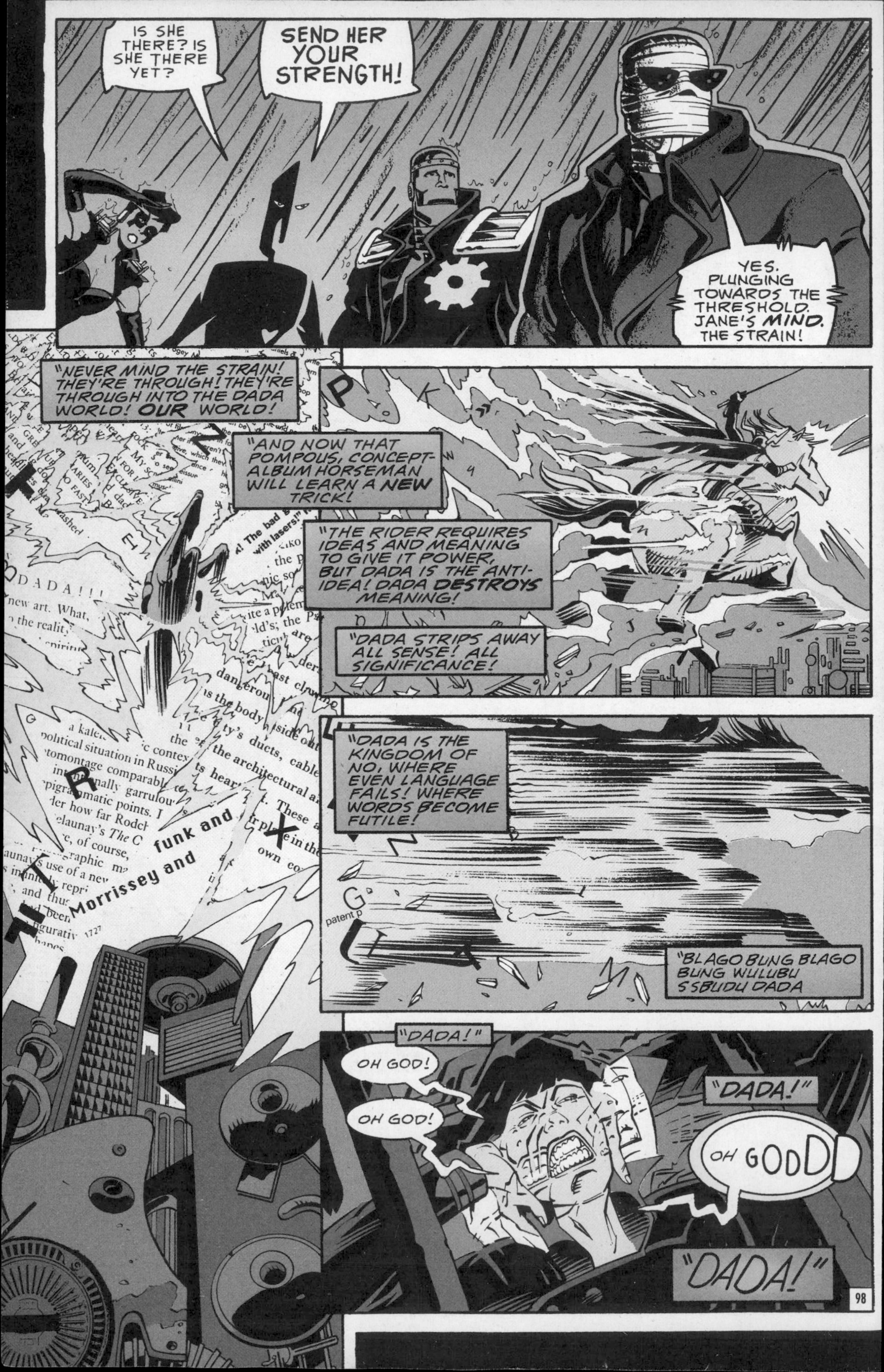
IS SHE THERE? IS SHE THERE YET?
SEND HER YOUR STRENGTH!
YES. PLUNGING TOWARDS THE THRESHOLD. JANE'S MIND. THE STRAIN!
"NEVER MIND THE STRAIN! THEY'RE THROUGH! THEY'RE THROUGH INTO THE DADA WORLD! OUR WORLD!
funk and
Morrissey and
"AND NOW THAT POMPOUS, CONCEPT-ALBUM HORSEMAN WILL LEARN A NEW TRICK!
"THE RIDER REQUIRES IDEAS AND MEANING TO GIVE IT POWER, BUT DADA IS THE ANTI-IDEA! DADA DESTROYS MEANING!
"DADA STRIPS AWAY ALL SENSE! ALL SIGNIFICANCE!
"DADA IS THE KINGDOM OF NO, WHERE EVEN LANGUAGE FAILS! WHERE WORDS BECOME FUTILE!
"BLAGO BUNG BLAGO BUNG WULUBU SSBUDU DADA
"DADA!"
OH GOD!
OH GOD!
"DADA!"
OH GODD
"DADA!"

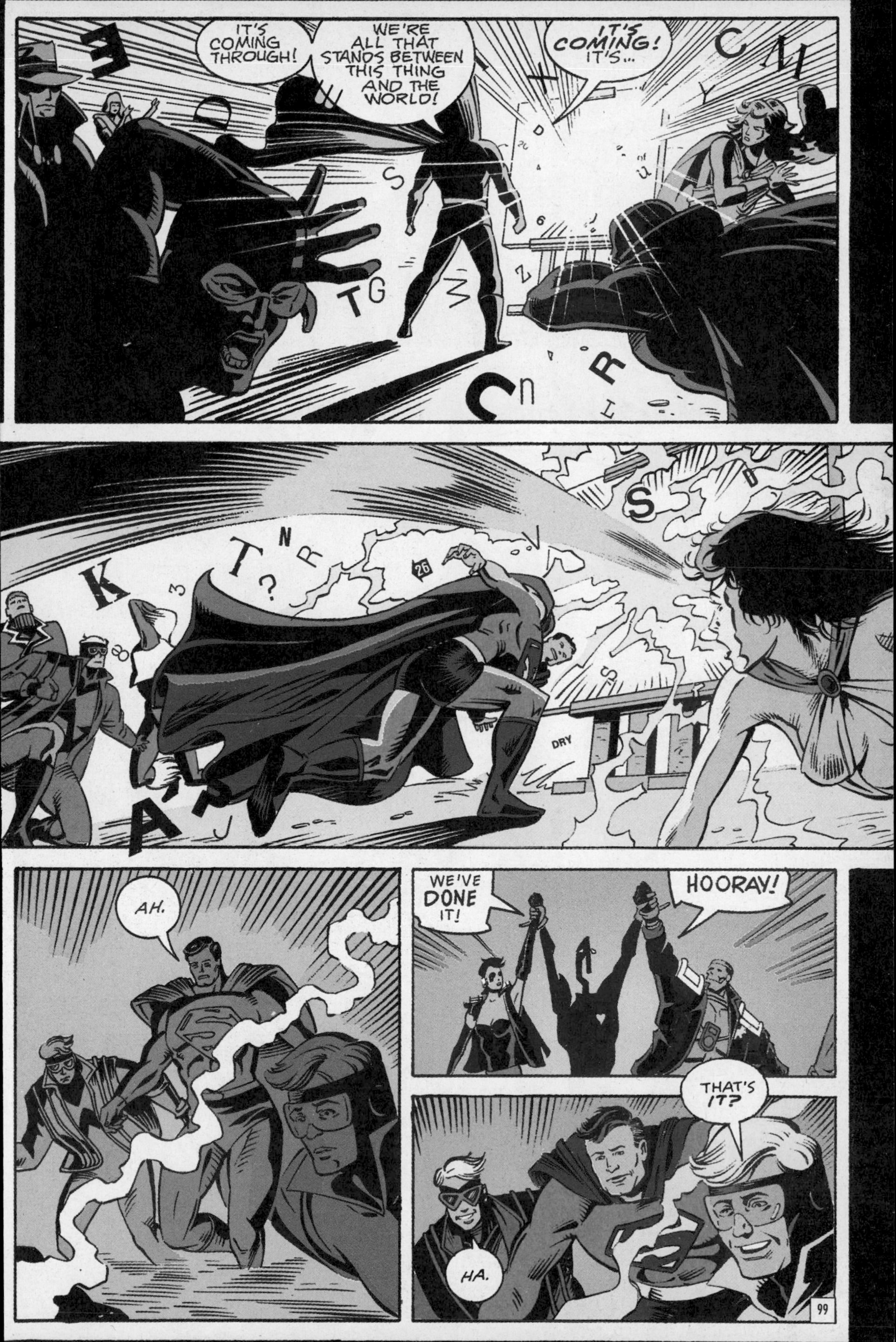

IT'S COMING THROUGH!
WE'RE ALL THAT STANDS BETWEEN THIS THING AND THE WORLD!
IT'S COMING! IT'S...
DRY
AH.
WE'VE DONE IT!
HOORAY!
THAT'S IT?
HA.

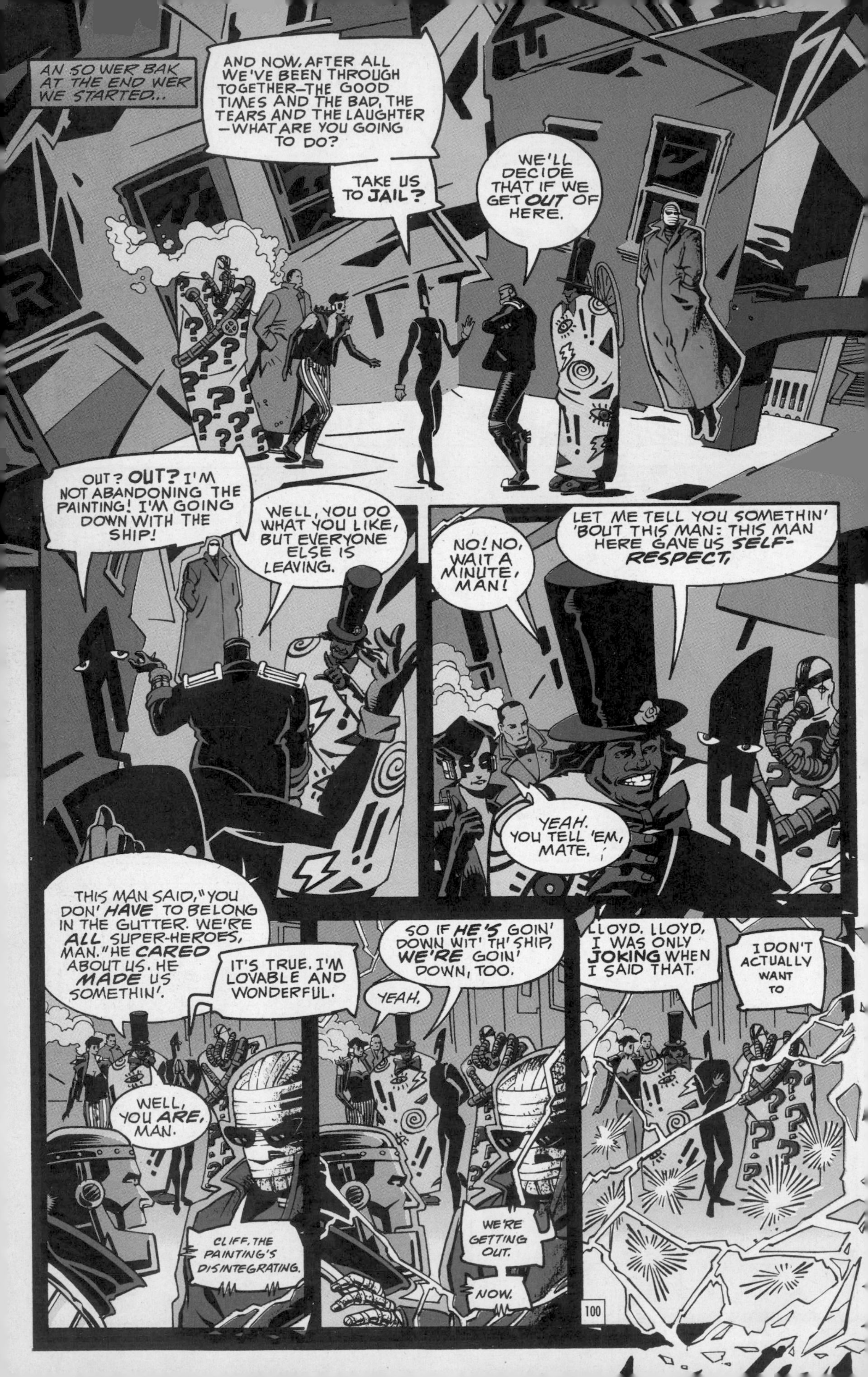
AN SO WER BAK AT THE END WER WE STARTED...
AND NOW, AFTER ALL WE'VE BEEN THROUGH TOGETHER—THE GOOD TIMES AND THE BAD, THE TEARS AND THE LAUGHTER —WHAT ARE YOU GOING TO DO?
TAKE US TO JAIL?
WE'LL DECIDE THAT IF WE GET OUT OF HERE.
OUT? OUT? I'M NOT ABANDONING THE PAINTING! I'M GOING DOWN WITH THE SHIP!
WELL, YOU DO WHAT YOU LIKE, BUT EVERYONE ELSE IS LEAVING.
NO! NO, WAIT A MINUTE, MAN!
LET ME TELL YOU SOMETHIN' 'BOUT THIS MAN: THIS MAN HERE GAVE US SELF-RESPECT,
YEAH. YOU TELL 'EM, MATE.
THIS MAN SAID, "YOU DON' HAVE TO BELONG IN THE GUTTER. WE'RE ALL SUPER-HEROES, MAN." HE CARED ABOUT US. HE MADE US SOMETHIN'.
IT'S TRUE. I'M LOVABLE AND WONDERFUL.
WELL, YOU ARE, MAN.
CLIFF, THE PAINTING'S DISINTEGRATING.
SO IF HE'S GOIN' DOWN WIT' TH' SHIP, WE'RE GOIN' DOWN, TOO.
YEAH.
WE'RE GETTING OUT.
NOW.
LLOYD. LLOYD, I WAS ONLY JOKING WHEN I SAID THAT.
I DON'T ACTUALLY WANT TO

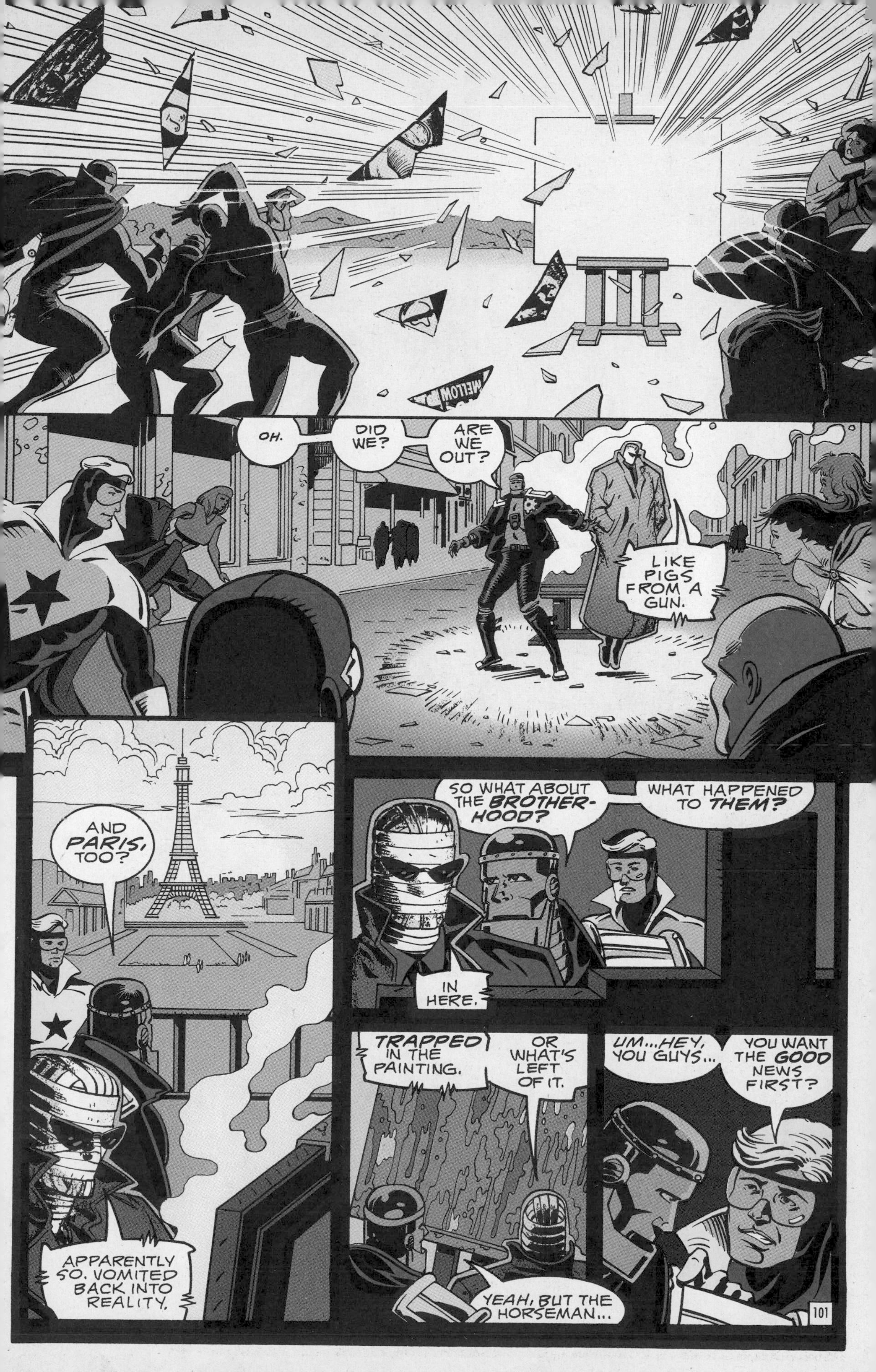
WELLOW
OH.
DID WE?
ARE WE OUT?
LIKE PIGS FROM A GUN.
AND PARIS, TOO?
APPARENTLY SO. VOMITED BACK INTO REALITY.
SO WHAT ABOUT THE BROTHERHOOD?
WHAT HAPPENED TO THEM?
IN HERE.
TRAPPED IN THE PAINTING.
OR WHAT'S LEFT OF IT.
YEAH, BUT THE HORSEMAN...
UM...HEY, YOU GUYS...
YOU WANT THE GOOD NEWS FIRST?

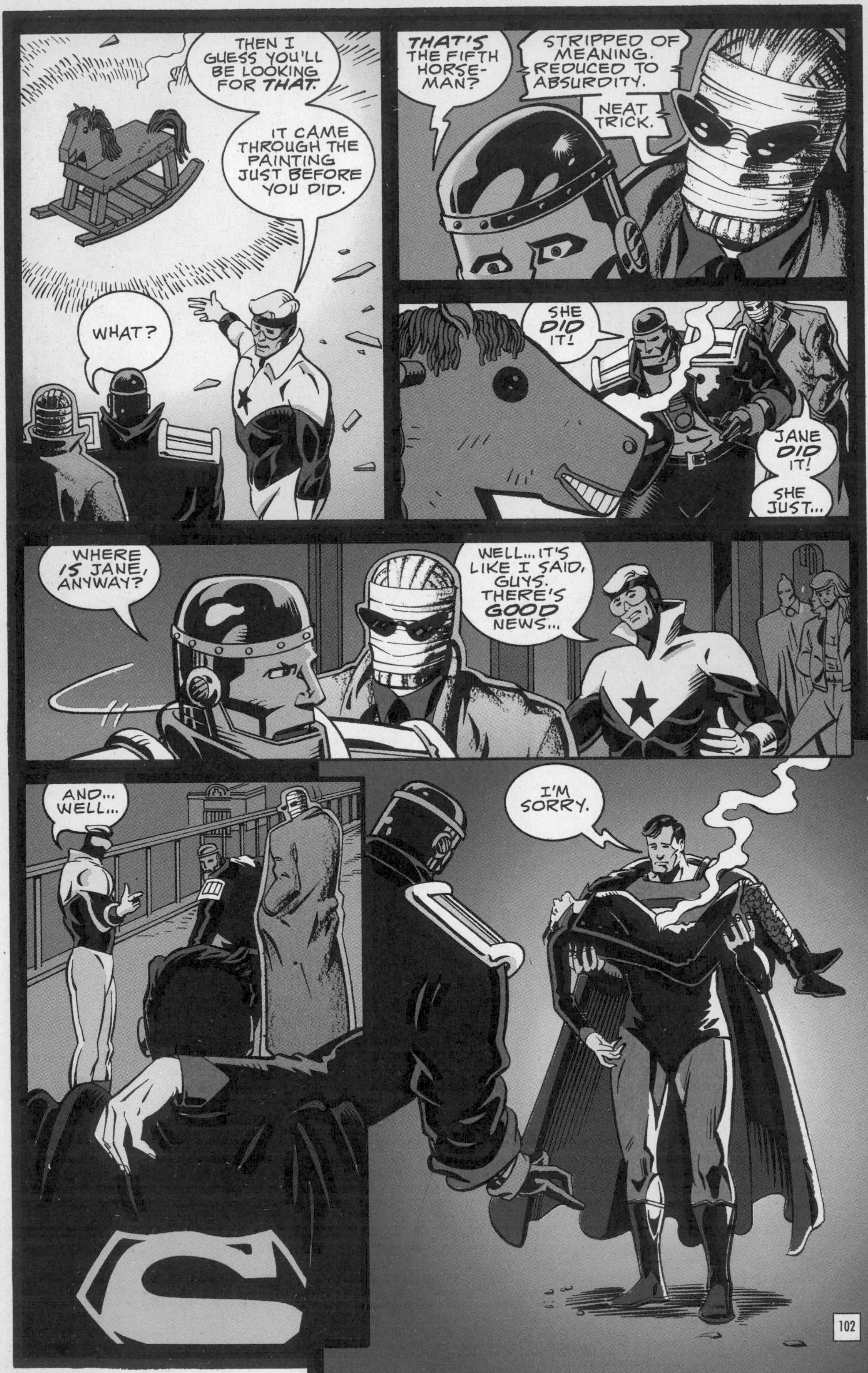
THEN I GUESS YOU'LL BE LOOKING FOR *THAT.*
IT CAME THROUGH THE PAINTING JUST BEFORE YOU DID.
WHAT?
THAT'S THE FIFTH HORSE-MAN?
STRIPPED OF MEANING. REDUCED TO ABSURDITY.
NEAT TRICK.
SHE *DID* IT!
JANE *DID* IT!
SHE JUST...
WHERE *IS* JANE, ANYWAY?
WELL... IT'S LIKE I SAID, GUYS. THERE'S *GOOD* NEWS...
AND... WELL...
I'M SORRY.

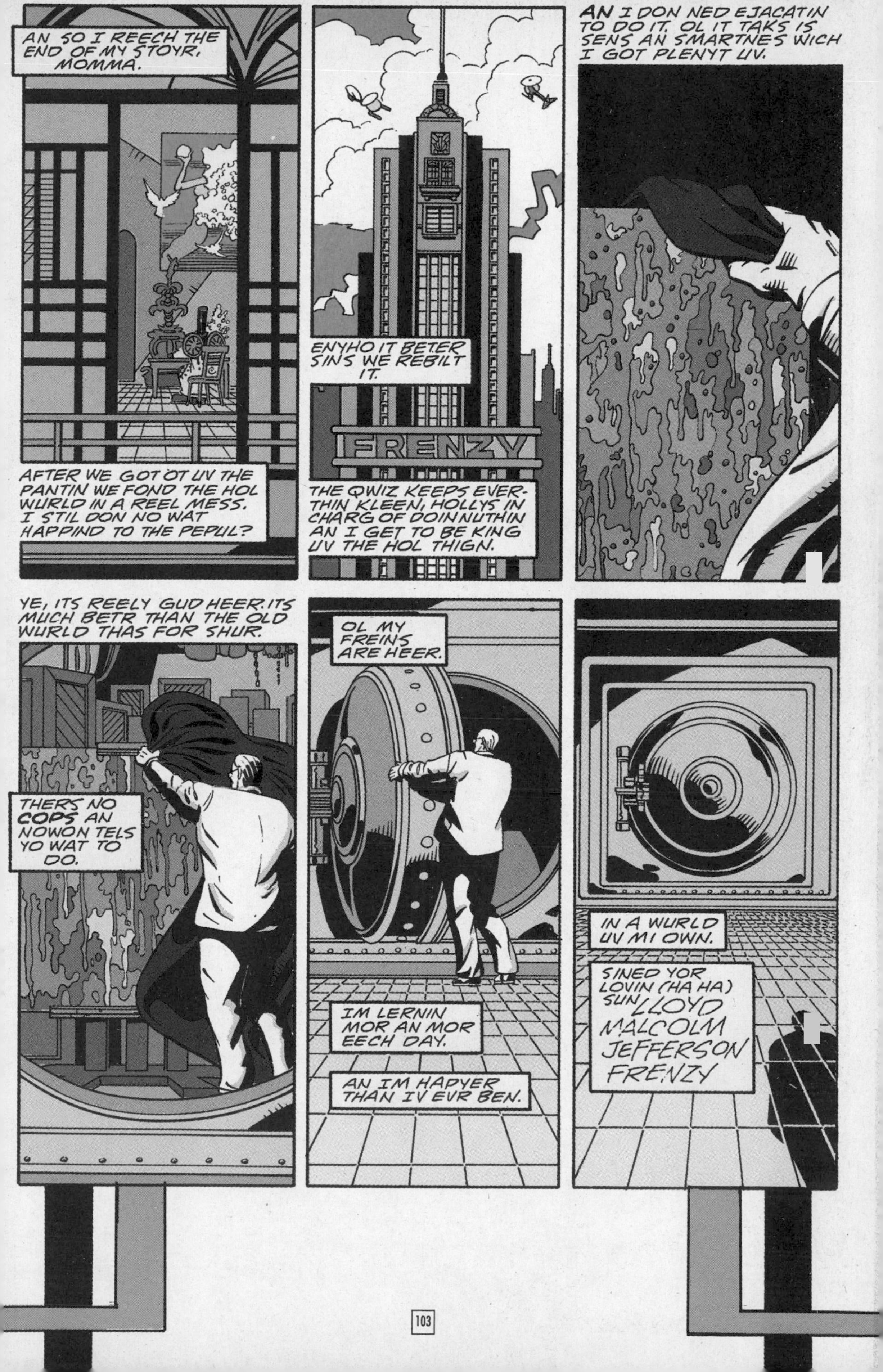
AN SO I REECH THE END OF MY STOYR, MOMMA.
AFTER WE GOT OT UV THE PANTIN WE FOND THE HOL WURLD IN A REEL MESS. I STIL DON NO WAT HAPPIND TO THE PEPUL?
ENYHO IT BETER SINS WE REBILT IT.
FRENZY
THE QWIZ KEEPS EVERTHIN KLEEN, HOLLYS IN CHARG OF DOIN NUTHIN AN I GET TO BE KING UV THE HOL THIGN.
AN I DON NED EJACATIN TO DO IT. OL IT TAKS IS SENS AN SMARTNES WICH I GOT PLENYT UV.
YE, ITS REELY GUD HEER. ITS MUCH BETR THAN THE OLD WURLD THAS FOR SHUR.
THERS NO COPS AN NOWON TELS YO WAT TO DO.
OL MY FREINS ARE HEER.
IM LERNIN MOR AN MOR EECH DAY.
AN IM HAPYER THAN IV EVR BEN.
IN A WURLD UV MI OWN.
SINED YOR LOVIN (HA HA) SUN LLOYD MALCOLM JEFFERSON FRENZY

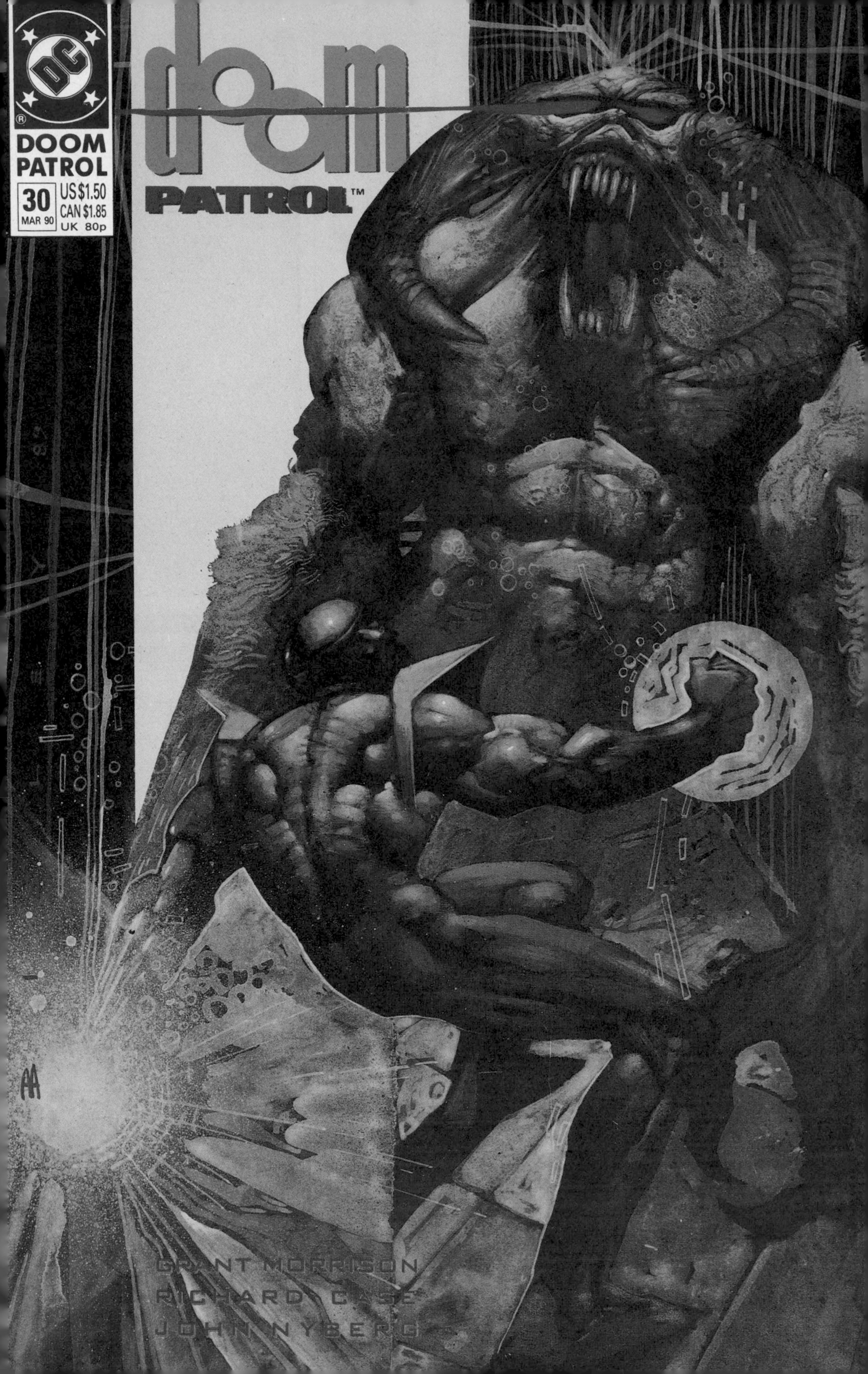
DOOM PATROL
30
MAR 90
US $1.50
CAN $1.85
UK 80p
doom
PATROL™
GRANT MORRISON
RICHARD CASE
JOHN NYBERG

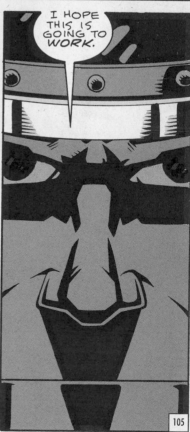

I HOPE THIS IS GOING TO WORK.

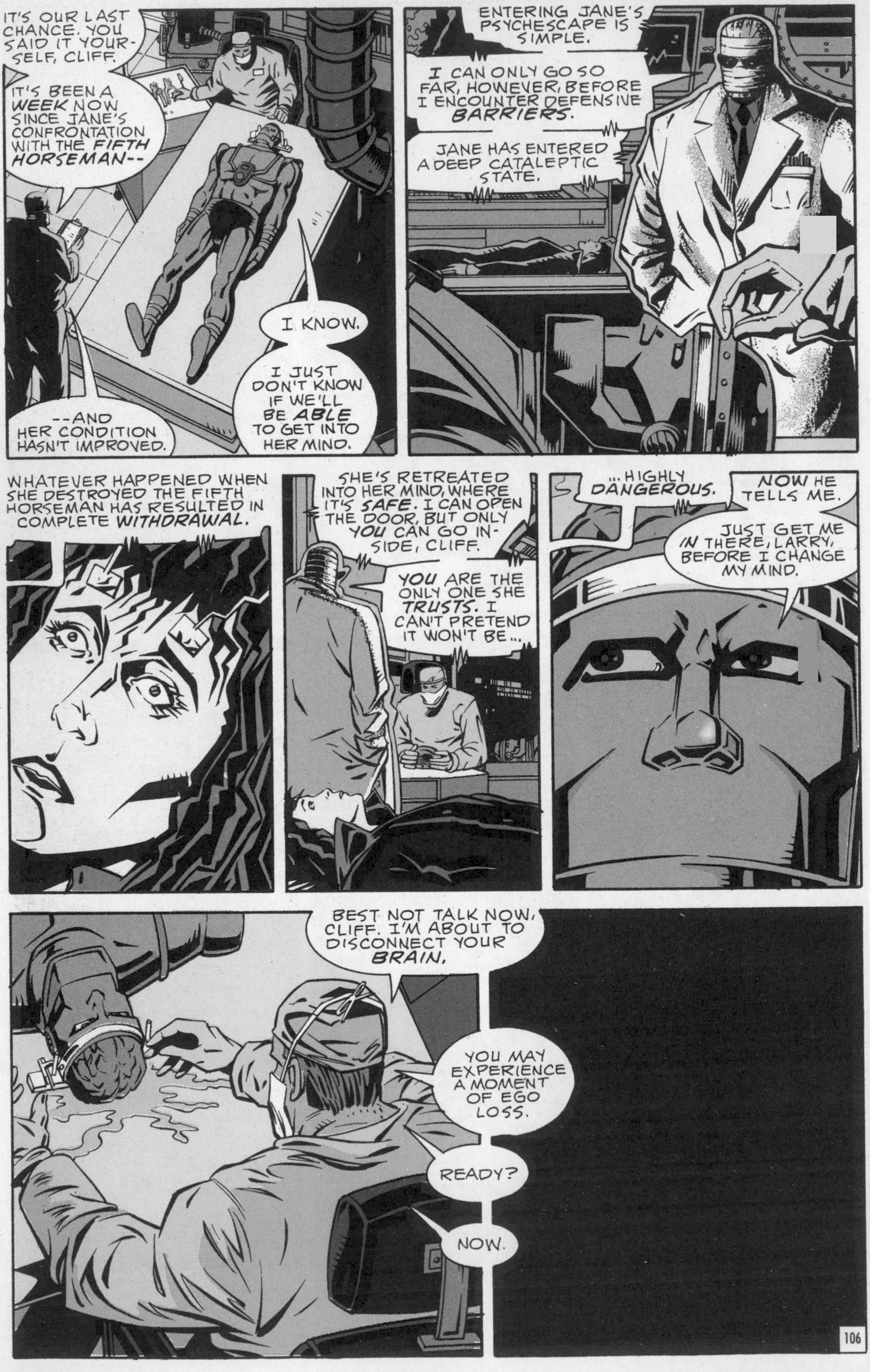
IT'S OUR LAST CHANCE. YOU SAID IT YOURSELF, CLIFF.
IT'S BEEN A WEEK NOW SINCE JANE'S CONFRONTATION WITH THE FIFTH HORSEMAN--
--AND HER CONDITION HASN'T IMPROVED.
I KNOW.
I JUST DON'T KNOW IF WE'LL BE ABLE TO GET INTO HER MIND.
ENTERING JANE'S PSYCHESCAPE IS SIMPLE.
I CAN ONLY GO SO FAR, HOWEVER, BEFORE I ENCOUNTER DEFENSIVE BARRIERS.
JANE HAS ENTERED A DEEP CATALEPTIC STATE.
WHATEVER HAPPENED WHEN SHE DESTROYED THE FIFTH HORSEMAN HAS RESULTED IN COMPLETE WITHDRAWAL.
SHE'S RETREATED INTO HER MIND, WHERE IT'S SAFE. I CAN OPEN THE DOOR, BUT ONLY YOU CAN GO INSIDE, CLIFF.
YOU ARE THE ONLY ONE SHE TRUSTS. I CAN'T PRETEND IT WON'T BE...
...HIGHLY DANGEROUS.
NOW HE TELLS ME.
JUST GET ME IN THERE, LARRY, BEFORE I CHANGE MY MIND.
BEST NOT TALK NOW, CLIFF. I'M ABOUT TO DISCONNECT YOUR BRAIN.
YOU MAY EXPERIENCE A MOMENT OF EGO LOSS.
READY?
NOW.

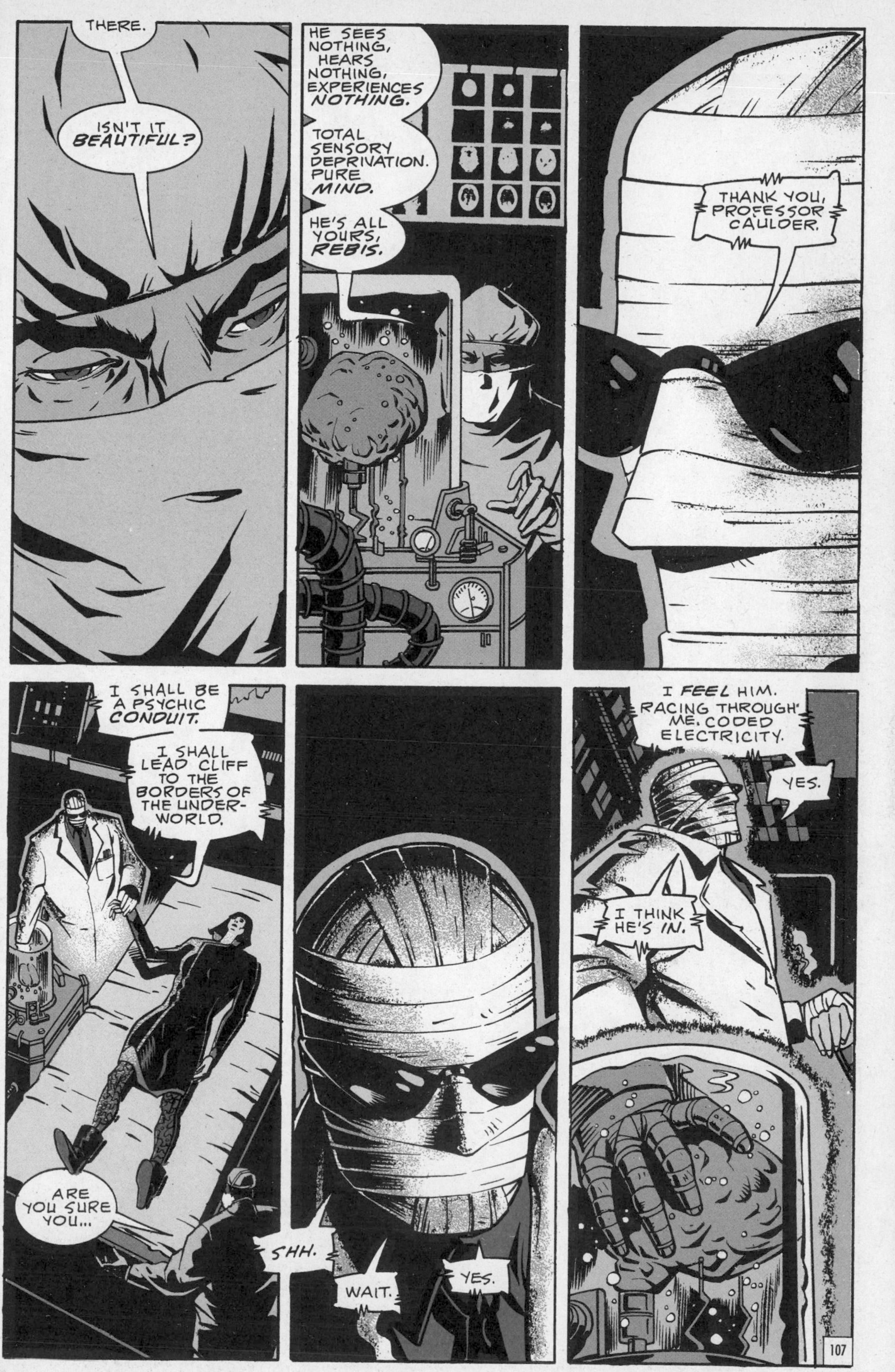
THERE.
ISN'T IT BEAUTIFUL?
HE SEES NOTHING, HEARS NOTHING, EXPERIENCES NOTHING.
TOTAL SENSORY DEPRIVATION. PURE MIND.
HE'S ALL YOURS, REBIS.
THANK YOU, PROFESSOR CAULDER.
I SHALL BE A PSYCHIC CONDUIT.
I SHALL LEAD CLIFF TO THE BORDERS OF THE UNDER-WORLD.
ARE YOU SURE YOU...
SHH.
WAIT.
YES.
I FEEL HIM. RACING THROUGH ME. CODED ELECTRICITY.
YES.
I THINK HE'S IN.

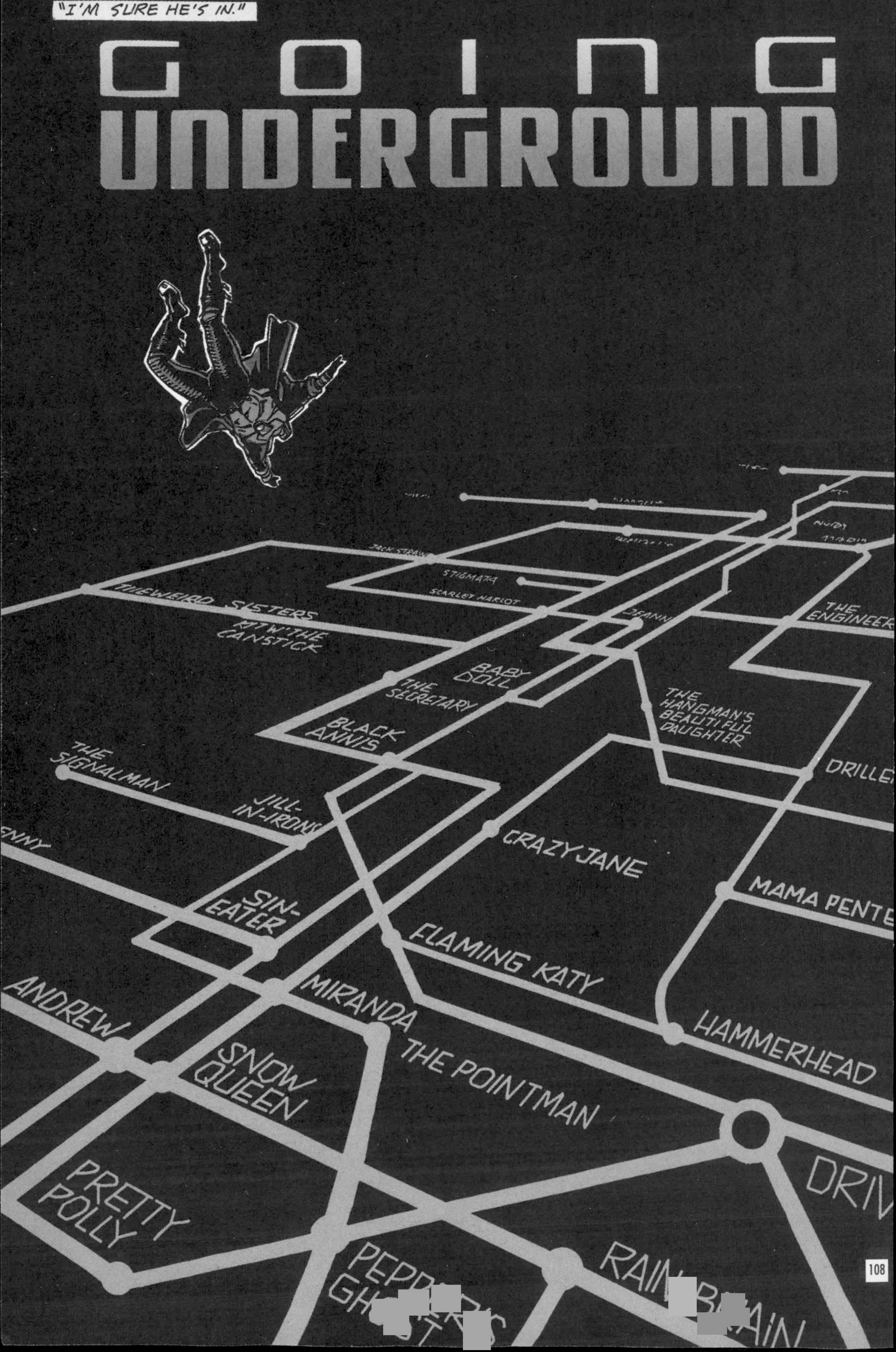
"I'M SURE HE'S IN."
GOING UNDERGROUND
JACK STRAW
STIGMATA
SCARLET HARLOT
THE WEIRD SISTERS
KIT W'THE CANSTICK
THE ENGINEER
BABY DOLL
THE SECRETARY
THE HANGMAN'S BEAUTIFUL DAUGHTER
BLACK ANNIS
THE SIGNALMAN
JILL-IN-IRONS
DRILLE
CRAZY JANE
MAMA PENTE
SIN-EATER
FLAMING KATY
ANDREW
MIRANDA
HAMMERHEAD
SNOW QUEEN
THE POINTMAN
PRETTY POLLY
DRIV

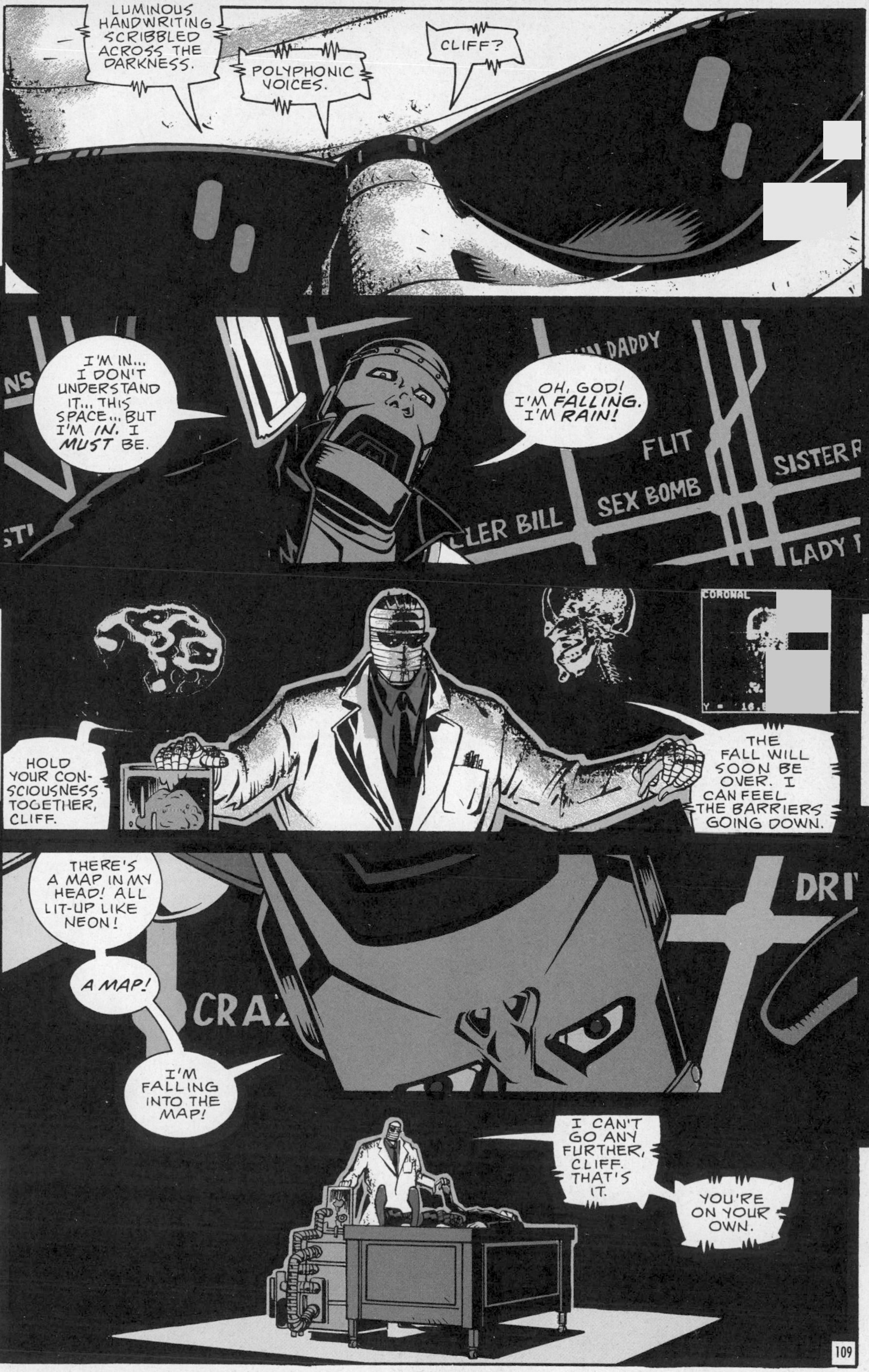

LUMINOUS HANDWRITING SCRIBBLED ACROSS THE DARKNESS.
POLYPHONIC VOICES.
CLIFF?
I'M IN... I DON'T UNDERSTAND IT... THIS SPACE... BUT I'M *IN*. I *MUST* BE.
OH, GOD! I'M *FALLING*. I'M *RAIN*!
FLIT
SEX BOMB
CORONAL
HOLD YOUR CON-SCIOUSNESS TOGETHER, CLIFF.
THE FALL WILL SOON BE OVER. I CAN FEEL THE BARRIERS GOING DOWN.
THERE'S A MAP IN MY HEAD! ALL LIT-UP LIKE NEON!
A MAP!
I'M FALLING INTO THE MAP!
I CAN'T GO ANY FURTHER, CLIFF. THAT'S IT.
YOU'RE ON YOUR OWN.

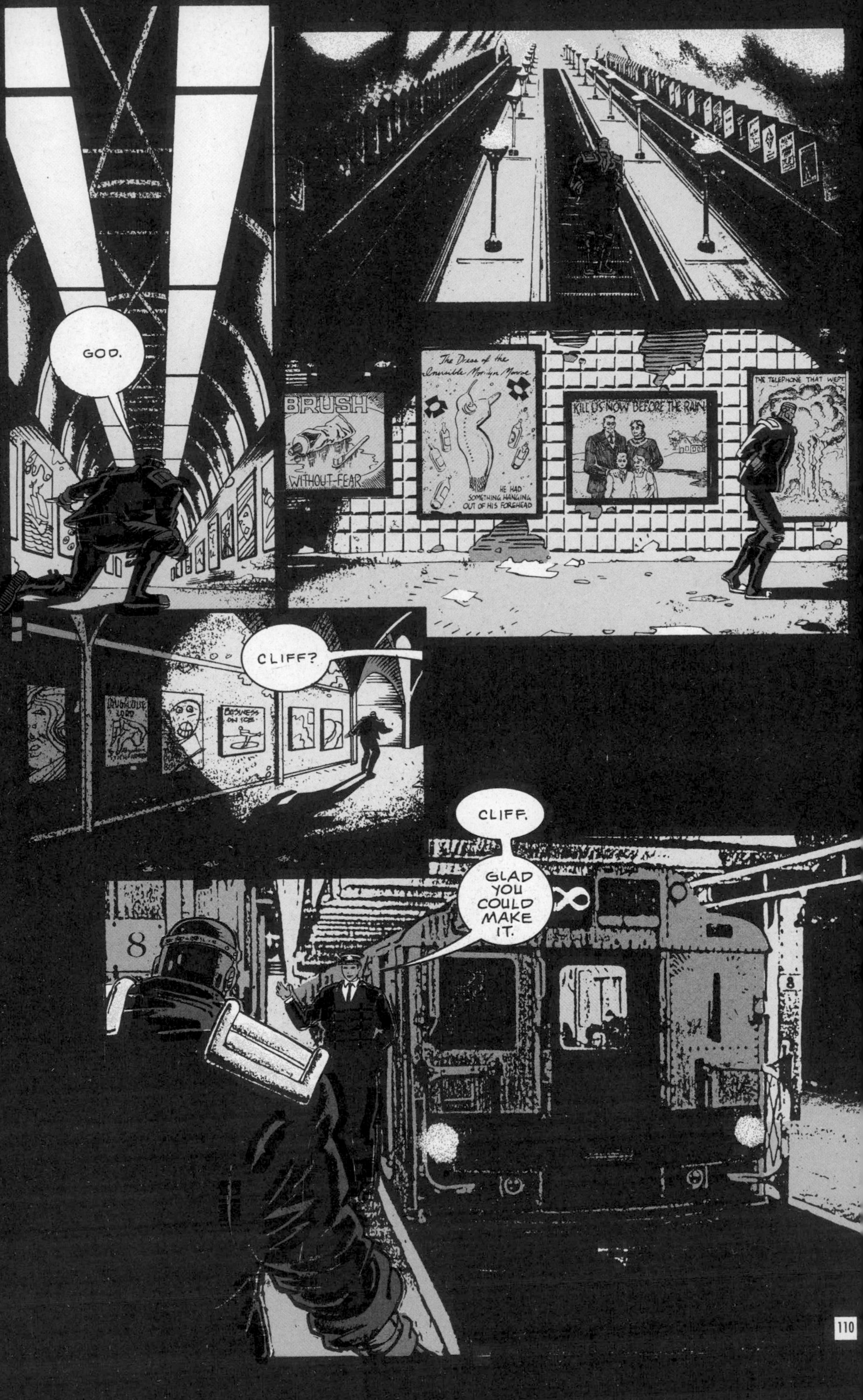
GOD.
BRUSH
WITHOUT-FEAR
The Dress of the Invisible Marilyn Monroe
HE HAD SOMETHING HANGING OUT OF HIS FOREHEAD
KILL US NOW BEFORE THE RAIN
THE TELEPHONE THAT WEPT
CLIFF?
CLIFF.
GLAD YOU COULD MAKE IT.
8

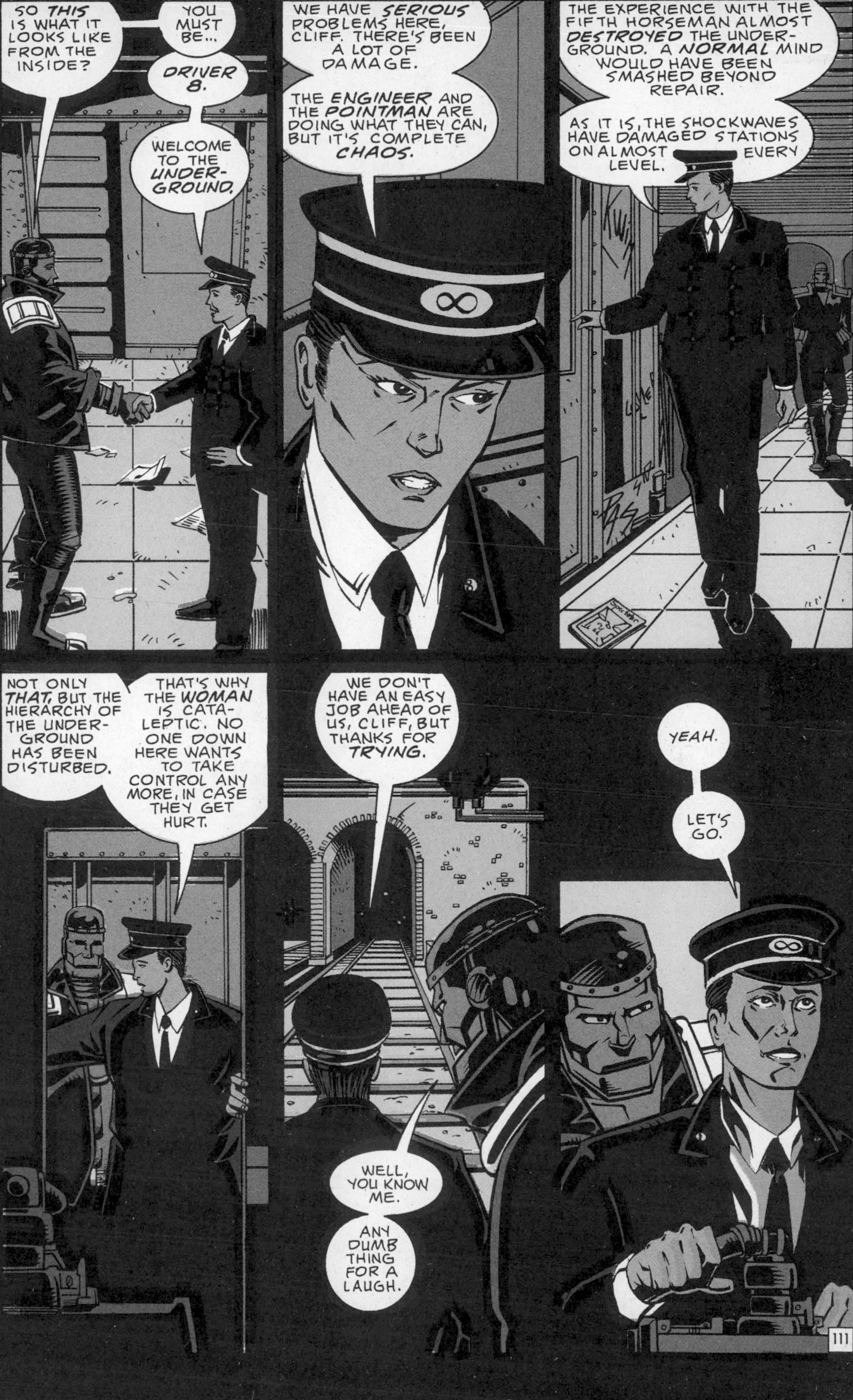
SO THIS IS WHAT IT LOOKS LIKE FROM THE INSIDE?
YOU MUST BE...
DRIVER 8.
WELCOME TO THE UNDER-GROUND.
WE HAVE SERIOUS PROBLEMS HERE, CLIFF. THERE'S BEEN A LOT OF DAMAGE.
THE ENGINEER AND THE POINTMAN ARE DOING WHAT THEY CAN, BUT IT'S COMPLETE CHAOS.
THE EXPERIENCE WITH THE FIFTH HORSEMAN ALMOST DESTROYED THE UNDER-GROUND. A NORMAL MIND WOULD HAVE BEEN SMASHED BEYOND REPAIR.
AS IT IS, THE SHOCKWAVES HAVE DAMAGED STATIONS ON ALMOST EVERY LEVEL.
NOT ONLY THAT, BUT THE HIERARCHY OF THE UNDER-GROUND HAS BEEN DISTURBED.
THAT'S WHY THE WOMAN IS CATA-LEPTIC. NO ONE DOWN HERE WANTS TO TAKE CONTROL ANY MORE, IN CASE THEY GET HURT.
WE DON'T HAVE AN EASY JOB AHEAD OF US, CLIFF, BUT THANKS FOR TRYING.
WELL, YOU KNOW ME.
ANY DUMB THING FOR A LAUGH.
YEAH.
LET'S GO.

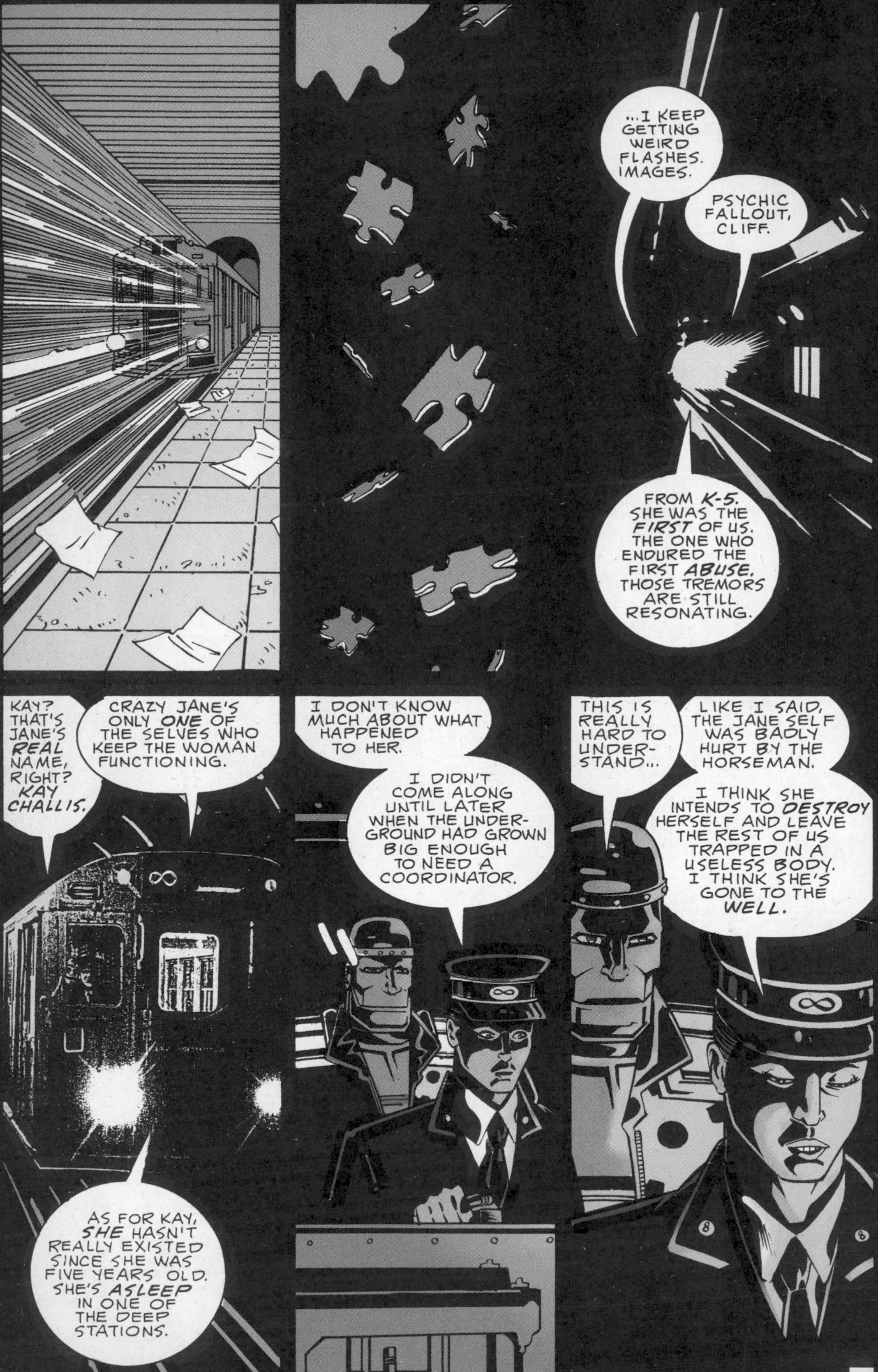

...I KEEP GETTING WEIRD FLASHES. IMAGES.
PSYCHIC FALLOUT, CLIFF.
FROM K-5. SHE WAS THE FIRST OF US. THE ONE WHO ENDURED THE FIRST ABUSE. THOSE TREMORS ARE STILL RESONATING.
KAY? THAT'S JANE'S REAL NAME, RIGHT? KAY CHALLIS.
CRAZY JANE'S ONLY ONE OF THE SELVES WHO KEEP THE WOMAN FUNCTIONING.
AS FOR KAY, SHE HASN'T REALLY EXISTED SINCE SHE WAS FIVE YEARS OLD. SHE'S ASLEEP IN ONE OF THE DEEP STATIONS.
I DON'T KNOW MUCH ABOUT WHAT HAPPENED TO HER.
I DIDN'T COME ALONG UNTIL LATER WHEN THE UNDERGROUND HAD GROWN BIG ENOUGH TO NEED A COORDINATOR.
THIS IS REALLY HARD TO UNDERSTAND...
LIKE I SAID, THE JANE SELF WAS BADLY HURT BY THE HORSEMAN.
I THINK SHE INTENDS TO DESTROY HERSELF AND LEAVE THE REST OF US TRAPPED IN A USELESS BODY. I THINK SHE'S GONE TO THE WELL.

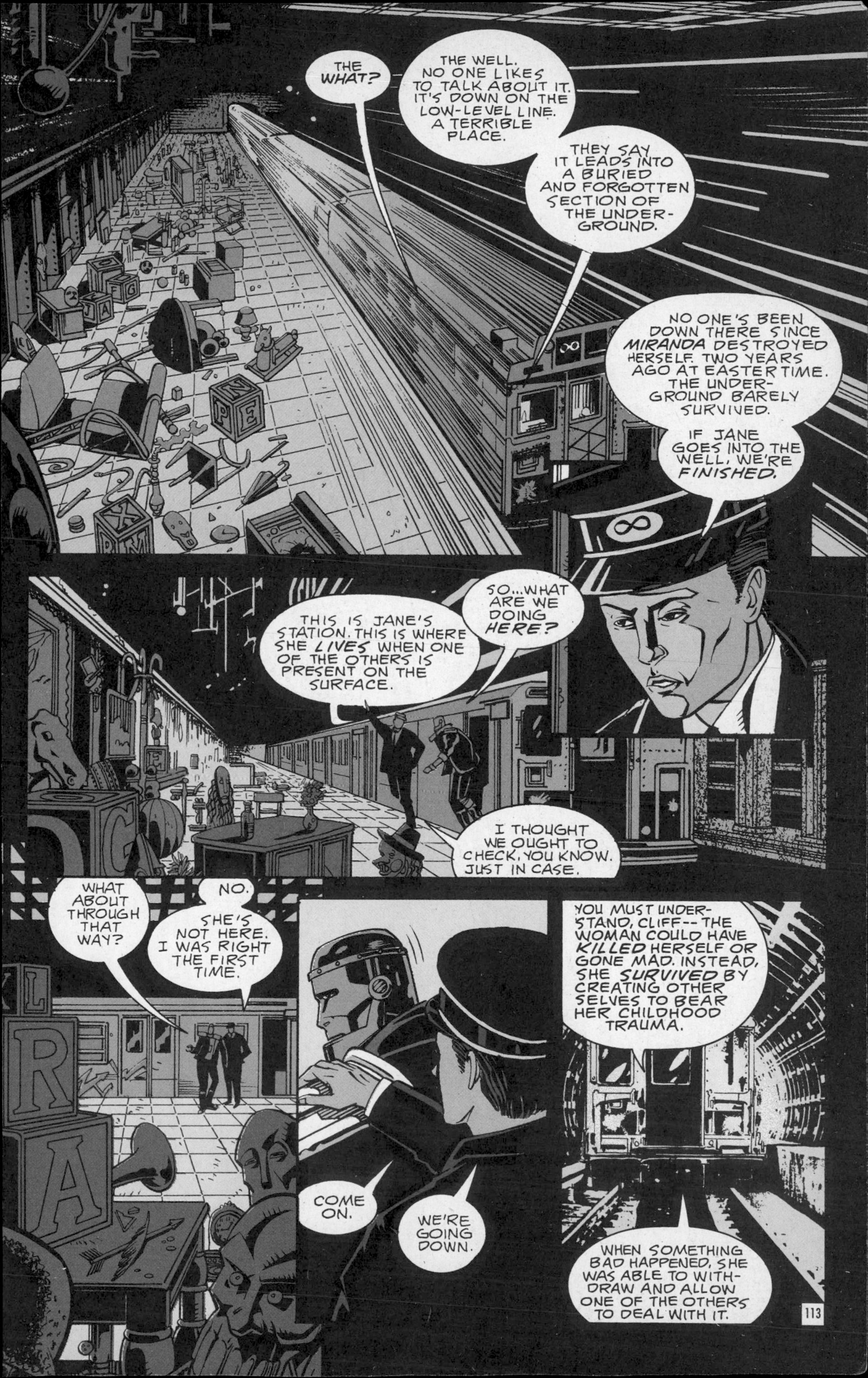
THE WHAT?
THE WELL. NO ONE LIKES TO TALK ABOUT IT. IT'S DOWN ON THE LOW-LEVEL LINE. A TERRIBLE PLACE.
THEY SAY IT LEADS INTO A BURIED AND FORGOTTEN SECTION OF THE UNDER-GROUND.
NO ONE'S BEEN DOWN THERE SINCE MIRANDA DESTROYED HERSELF. TWO YEARS AGO AT EASTER TIME. THE UNDER-GROUND BARELY SURVIVED.
IF JANE GOES INTO THE WELL, WE'RE FINISHED.
THIS IS JANE'S STATION. THIS IS WHERE SHE LIVES WHEN ONE OF THE OTHERS IS PRESENT ON THE SURFACE.
SO...WHAT ARE WE DOING HERE?
I THOUGHT WE OUGHT TO CHECK, YOU KNOW. JUST IN CASE.
WHAT ABOUT THROUGH THAT WAY?
NO.
SHE'S NOT HERE. I WAS RIGHT THE FIRST TIME.
COME ON.
WE'RE GOING DOWN.
YOU MUST UNDER-STAND, CLIFF-- THE WOMAN COULD HAVE KILLED HERSELF OR GONE MAD. INSTEAD, SHE SURVIVED BY CREATING OTHER SELVES TO BEAR HER CHILDHOOD TRAUMA.
WHEN SOMETHING BAD HAPPENED, SHE WAS ABLE TO WITH-DRAW AND ALLOW ONE OF THE OTHERS TO DEAL WITH IT.

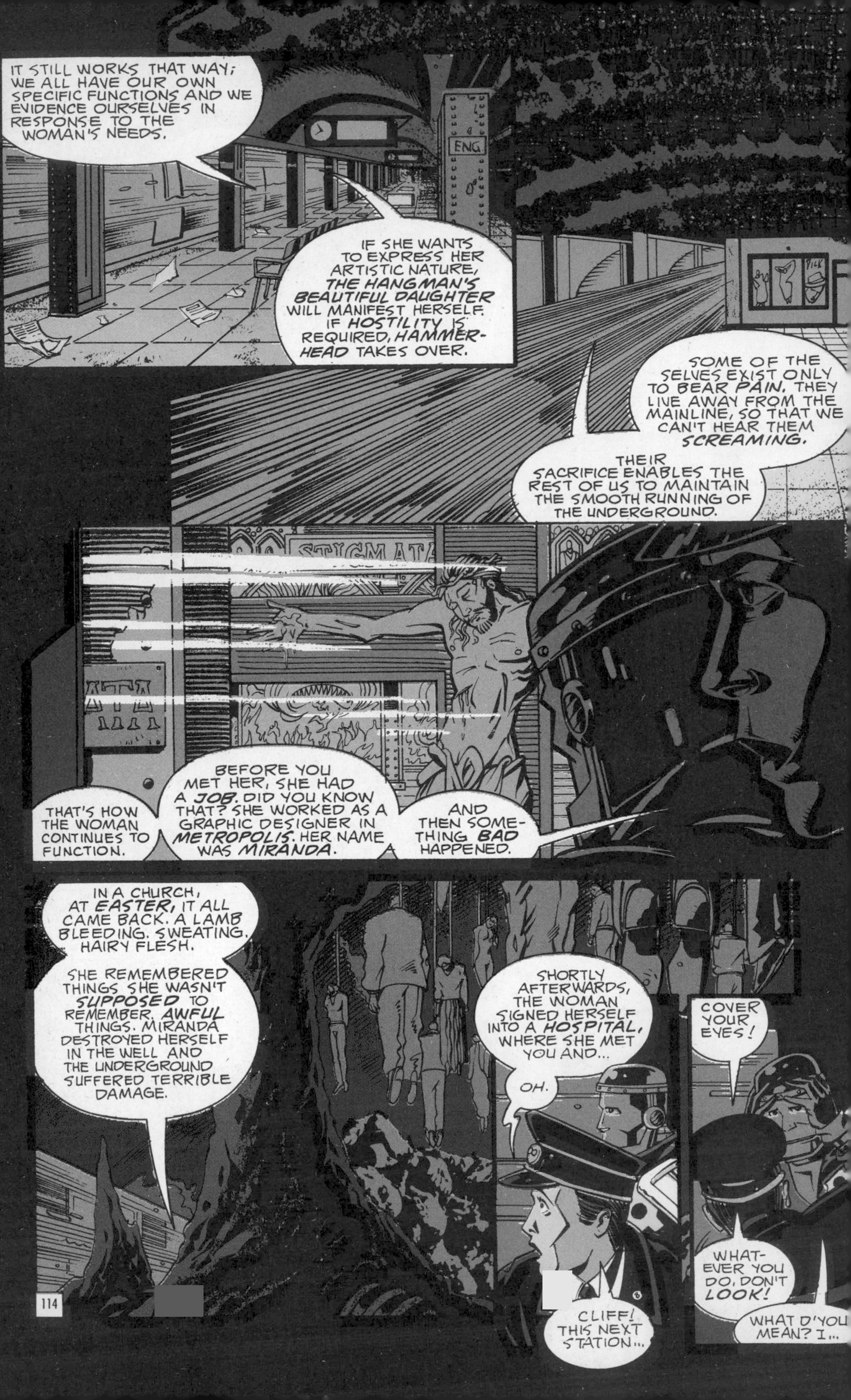
IT STILL WORKS THAT WAY; WE ALL HAVE OUR OWN SPECIFIC FUNCTIONS AND WE EVIDENCE OURSELVES IN RESPONSE TO THE WOMAN'S NEEDS.
ENG
IF SHE WANTS TO EXPRESS HER ARTISTIC NATURE, **THE HANGMAN'S BEAUTIFUL DAUGHTER** WILL MANIFEST HERSELF. IF **HOSTILITY** IS REQUIRED, **HAMMERHEAD** TAKES OVER.
SOME OF THE SELVES EXIST ONLY TO BEAR **PAIN.** THEY LIVE AWAY FROM THE MAINLINE, SO THAT WE CAN'T HEAR THEM **SCREAMING.**
THEIR SACRIFICE ENABLES THE REST OF US TO MAINTAIN THE SMOOTH RUNNING OF THE UNDERGROUND.
STIGMATA
THAT'S HOW THE WOMAN CONTINUES TO FUNCTION.
BEFORE YOU MET HER, SHE HAD A **JOB.** DID YOU KNOW THAT? SHE WORKED AS A GRAPHIC DESIGNER IN **METROPOLIS.** HER NAME WAS **MIRANDA.**
AND THEN SOMETHING **BAD** HAPPENED.
IN A CHURCH, AT **EASTER,** IT ALL CAME BACK. A LAMB BLEEDING. SWEATING, HAIRY FLESH.
SHE REMEMBERED THINGS SHE WASN'T **SUPPOSED** TO REMEMBER. **AWFUL** THINGS. MIRANDA DESTROYED HERSELF IN THE WELL AND THE UNDERGROUND SUFFERED TERRIBLE DAMAGE.
SHORTLY AFTERWARDS, THE WOMAN SIGNED HERSELF INTO A **HOSPITAL,** WHERE SHE MET YOU AND...
OH.
CLIFF! THIS NEXT STATION...
COVER YOUR EYES!
WHATEVER YOU DO, DON'T **LOOK!**
WHAT D'YOU MEAN? I...

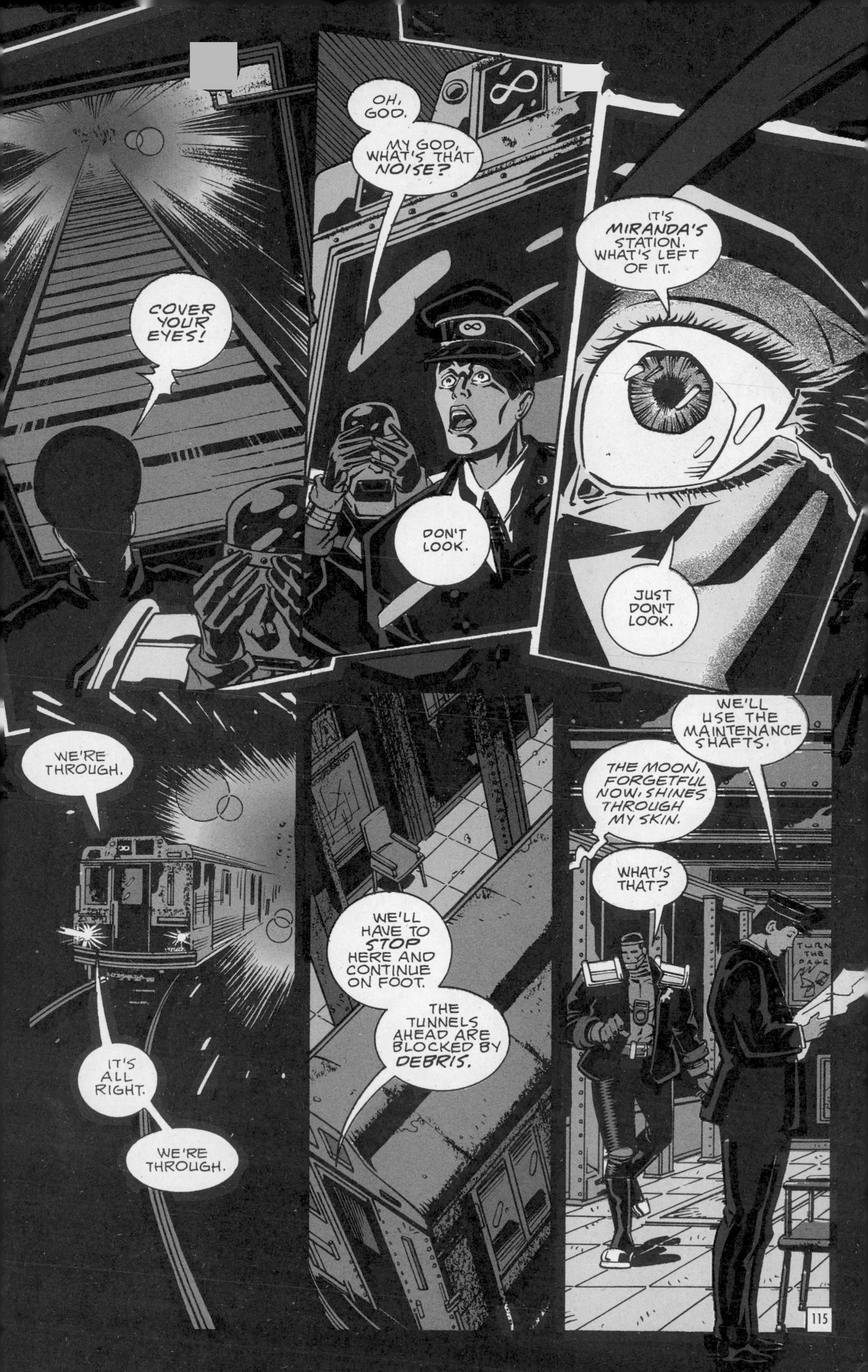
COVER YOUR EYES!
OH, GOD.
MY GOD, WHAT'S THAT NOISE?
DON'T LOOK.
IT'S MIRANDA'S STATION. WHAT'S LEFT OF IT.
JUST DON'T LOOK.
WE'RE THROUGH.
IT'S ALL RIGHT.
WE'RE THROUGH.
WE'LL HAVE TO STOP HERE AND CONTINUE ON FOOT.
THE TUNNELS AHEAD ARE BLOCKED BY DEBRIS.
WE'LL USE THE MAINTENANCE SHAFTS.
THE MOON, FORGETFUL NOW, SHINES THROUGH MY SKIN.
WHAT'S THAT?
TURN THE PAGE

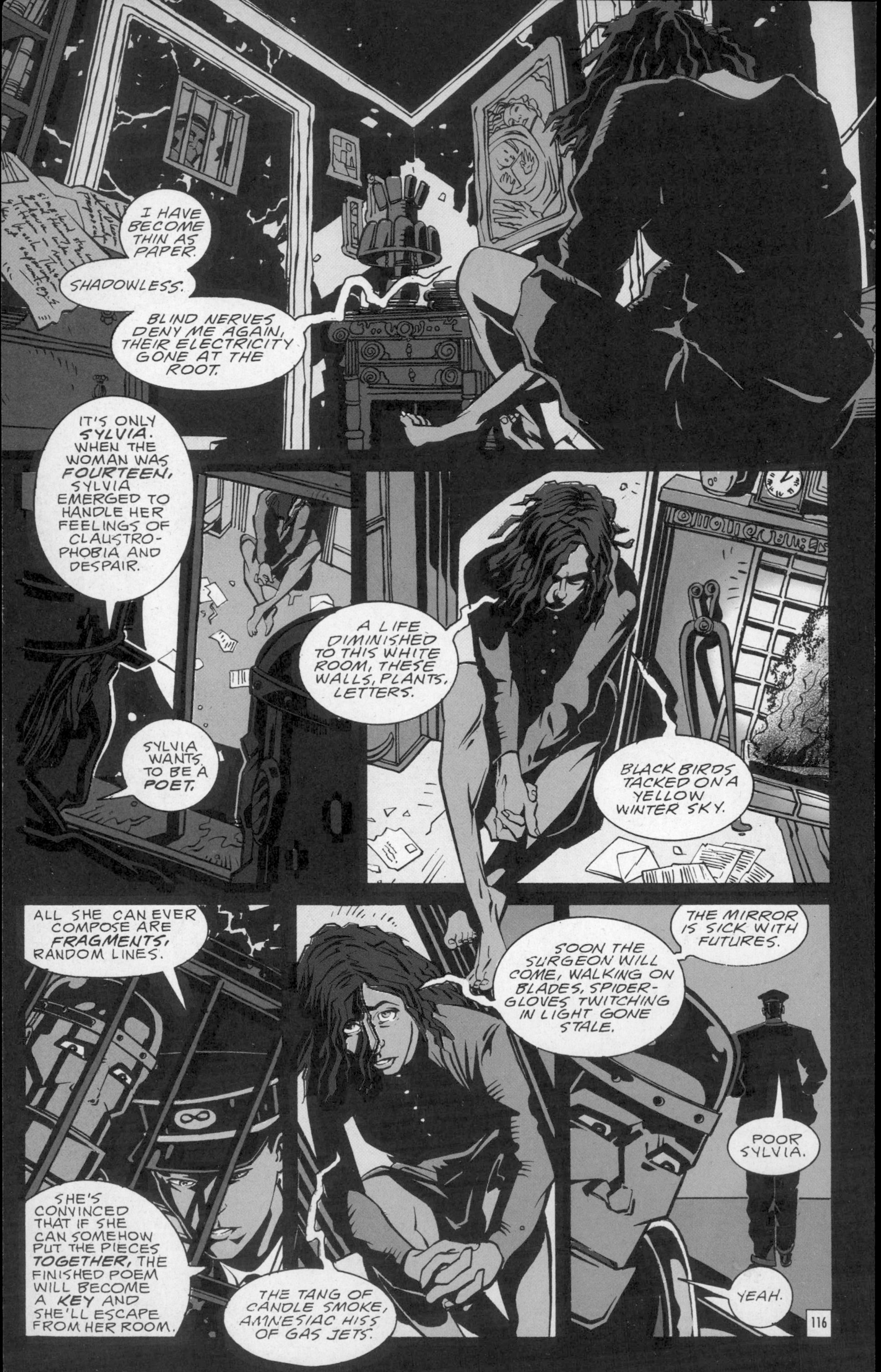
I HAVE BECOME THIN AS PAPER.
SHADOWLESS.
BLIND NERVES DENY ME AGAIN, THEIR ELECTRICITY GONE AT THE ROOT.
IT'S ONLY SYLVIA. WHEN THE WOMAN WAS FOURTEEN, SYLVIA EMERGED TO HANDLE HER FEELINGS OF CLAUSTROPHOBIA AND DESPAIR.
SYLVIA WANTS TO BE A POET.
A LIFE DIMINISHED TO THIS WHITE ROOM, THESE WALLS, PLANTS, LETTERS.
BLACK BIRDS TACKED ON A YELLOW WINTER SKY.
ALL SHE CAN EVER COMPOSE ARE FRAGMENTS, RANDOM LINES.
SHE'S CONVINCED THAT IF SHE CAN SOMEHOW PUT THE PIECES TOGETHER, THE FINISHED POEM WILL BECOME A KEY AND SHE'LL ESCAPE FROM HER ROOM.
SOON THE SURGEON WILL COME, WALKING ON BLADES, SPIDER-GLOVES TWITCHING IN LIGHT GONE STALE.
THE TANG OF CANDLE SMOKE, AMNESIAC HISS OF GAS JETS.
THE MIRROR IS SICK WITH FUTURES.
POOR SYLVIA.
YEAH.

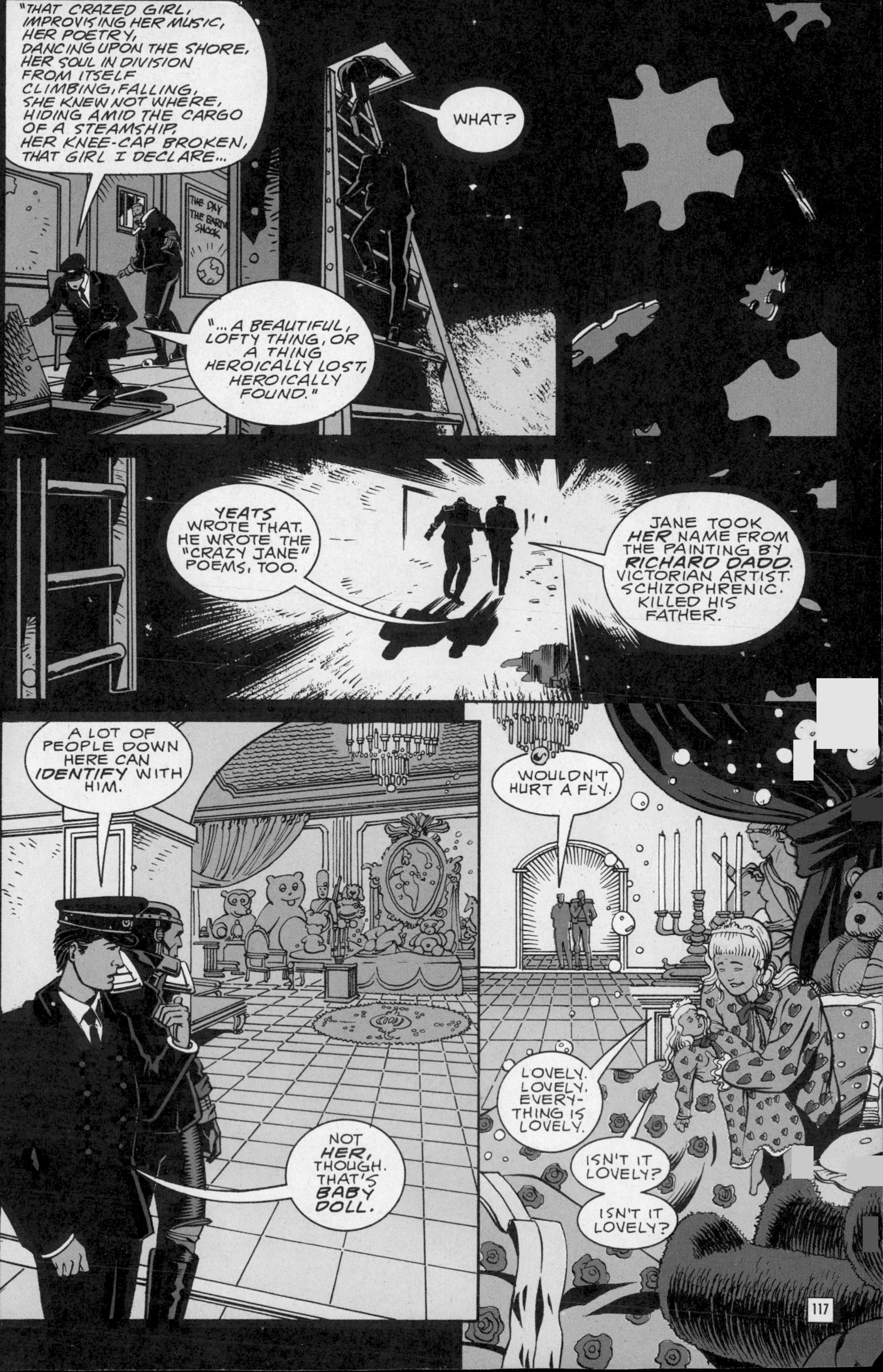
"THAT CRAZED GIRL, IMPROVISING HER MUSIC, HER POETRY, DANCING UPON THE SHORE, HER SOUL IN DIVISION FROM ITSELF CLIMBING, FALLING, SHE KNEW NOT WHERE, HIDING AMID THE CARGO OF A STEAMSHIP, HER KNEE-CAP BROKEN, THAT GIRL I DECLARE...
WHAT?
"... A BEAUTIFUL, LOFTY THING, OR A THING HEROICALLY LOST, HEROICALLY FOUND."
YEATS WROTE THAT. HE WROTE THE "CRAZY JANE" POEMS, TOO.
JANE TOOK HER NAME FROM THE PAINTING BY RICHARD DADD. VICTORIAN ARTIST. SCHIZOPHRENIC. KILLED HIS FATHER.
A LOT OF PEOPLE DOWN HERE CAN IDENTIFY WITH HIM.
NOT HER, THOUGH. THAT'S BABY DOLL.
WOULDN'T HURT A FLY.
LOVELY. LOVELY. EVERY-THING IS LOVELY.
ISN'T IT LOVELY?
ISN'T IT LOVELY?

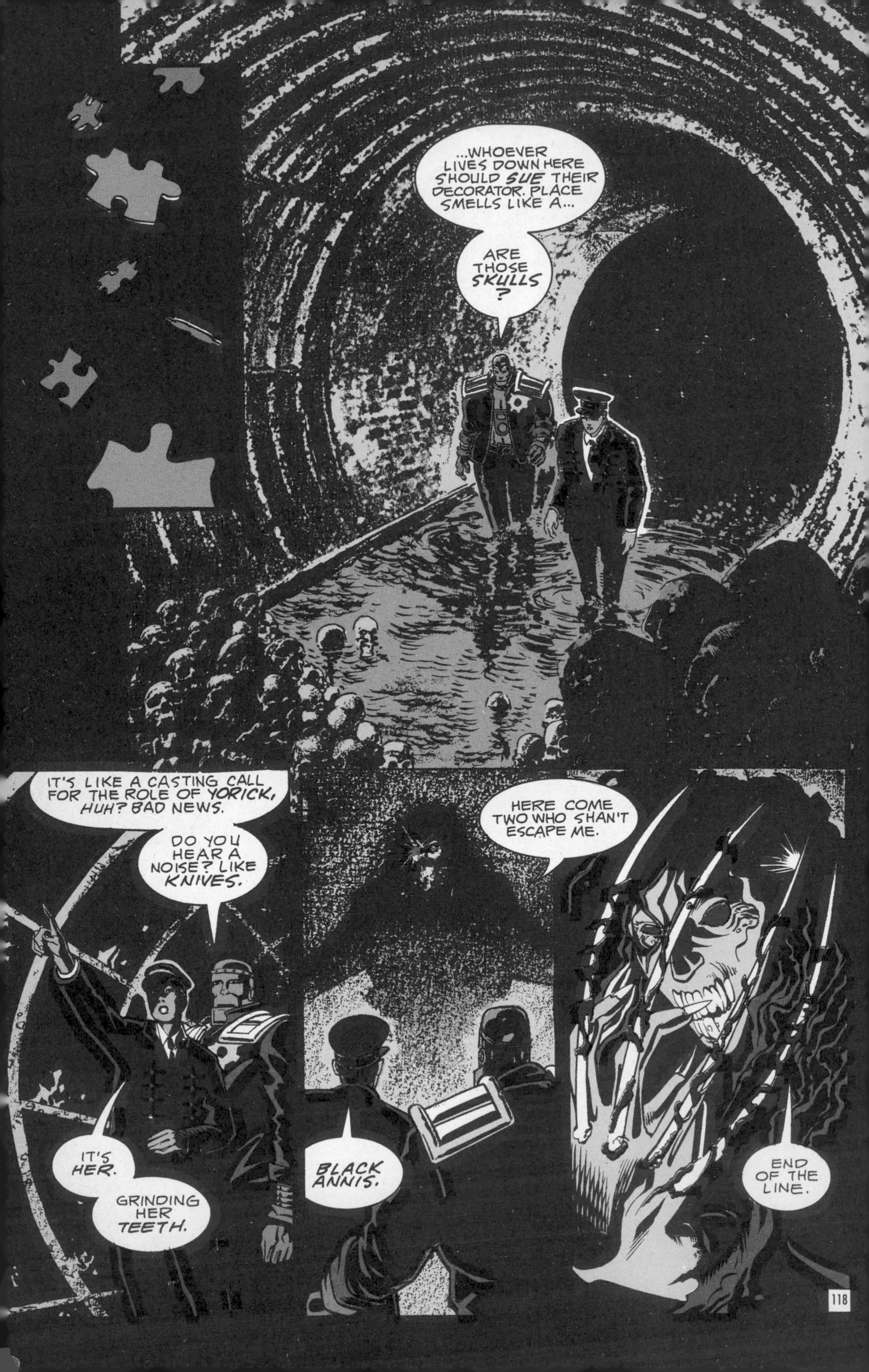
...WHOEVER LIVES DOWN HERE SHOULD SUE THEIR DECORATOR. PLACE SMELLS LIKE A...
ARE THOSE SKULLS?
IT'S LIKE A CASTING CALL FOR THE ROLE OF YORICK, HUH? BAD NEWS.
DO YOU HEAR A NOISE? LIKE KNIVES.
IT'S HER.
GRINDING HER TEETH.
HERE COME TWO WHO SHAN'T ESCAPE ME.
BLACK ANNIS.
END OF THE LINE.

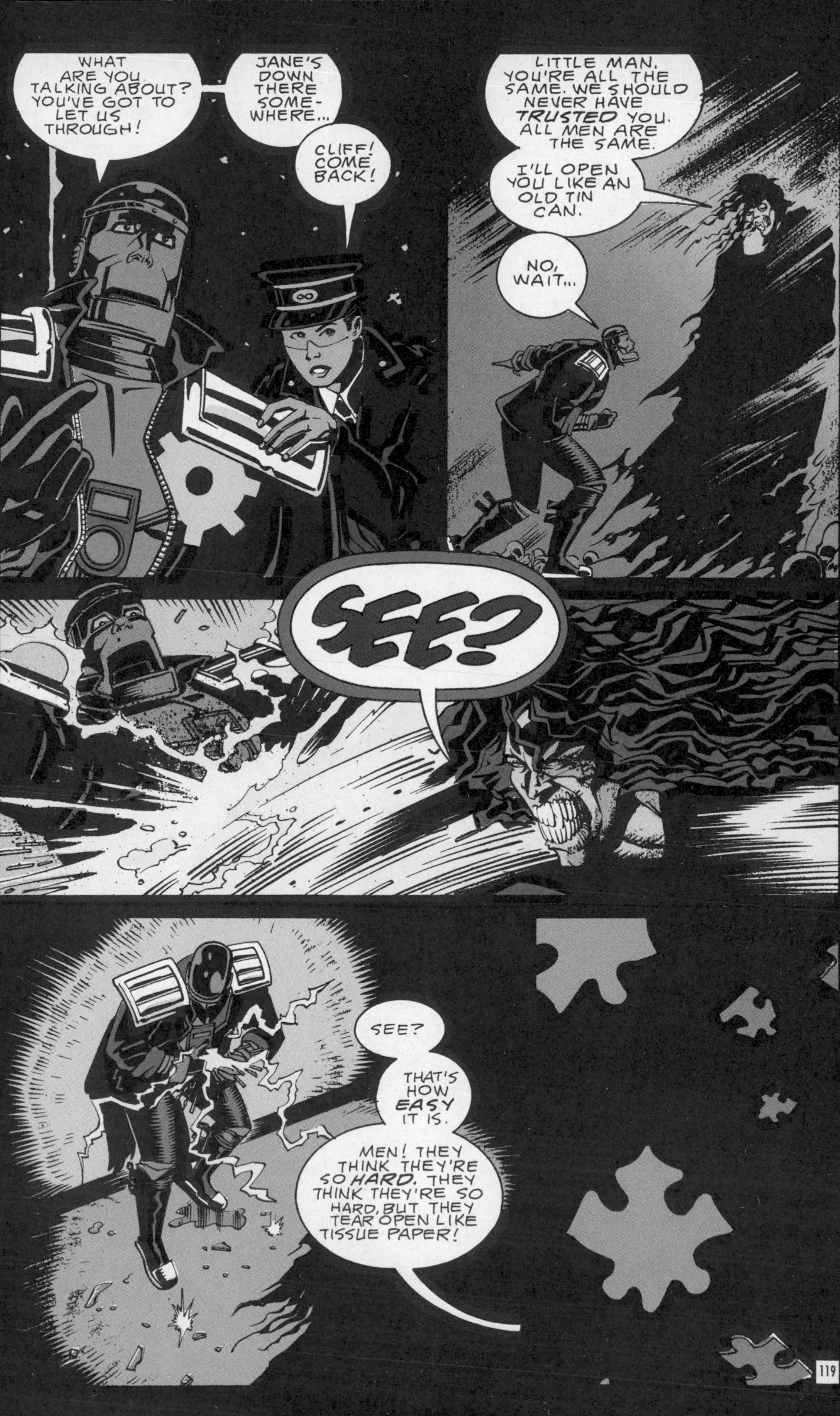

WHAT ARE YOU TALKING ABOUT? YOU'VE GOT TO LET US THROUGH!
JANE'S DOWN THERE SOME-WHERE...
CLIFF! COME BACK!
LITTLE MAN. YOU'RE ALL THE SAME. WE SHOULD NEVER HAVE TRUSTED YOU. ALL MEN ARE THE SAME.
I'LL OPEN YOU LIKE AN OLD TIN CAN.
NO, WAIT...
SEE?
SEE?
THAT'S HOW EASY IT IS.
MEN! THEY THINK THEY'RE SO HARD. THEY THINK THEY'RE SO HARD, BUT THEY TEAR OPEN LIKE TISSUE PAPER!

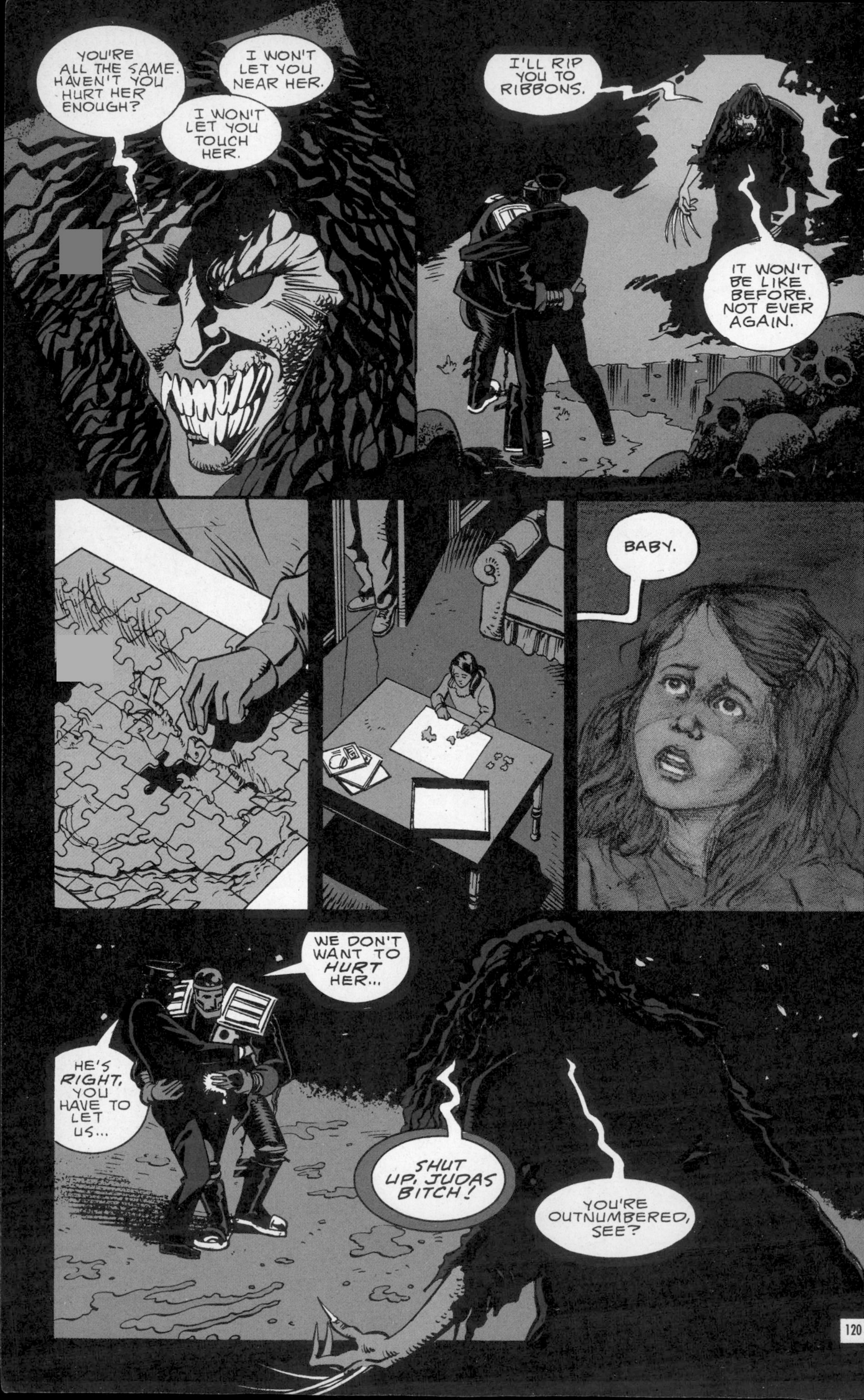
YOU'RE ALL THE SAME. HAVEN'T YOU HURT HER ENOUGH?
I WON'T LET YOU NEAR HER.
I WON'T LET YOU TOUCH HER.
I'LL RIP YOU TO RIBBONS.
IT WON'T BE LIKE BEFORE. NOT EVER AGAIN.
BABY.
WE DON'T WANT TO *HURT* HER...
HE'S *RIGHT*, YOU HAVE TO LET US...
SHUT UP, JUDAS BITCH!
YOU'RE OUTNUMBERED, SEE?

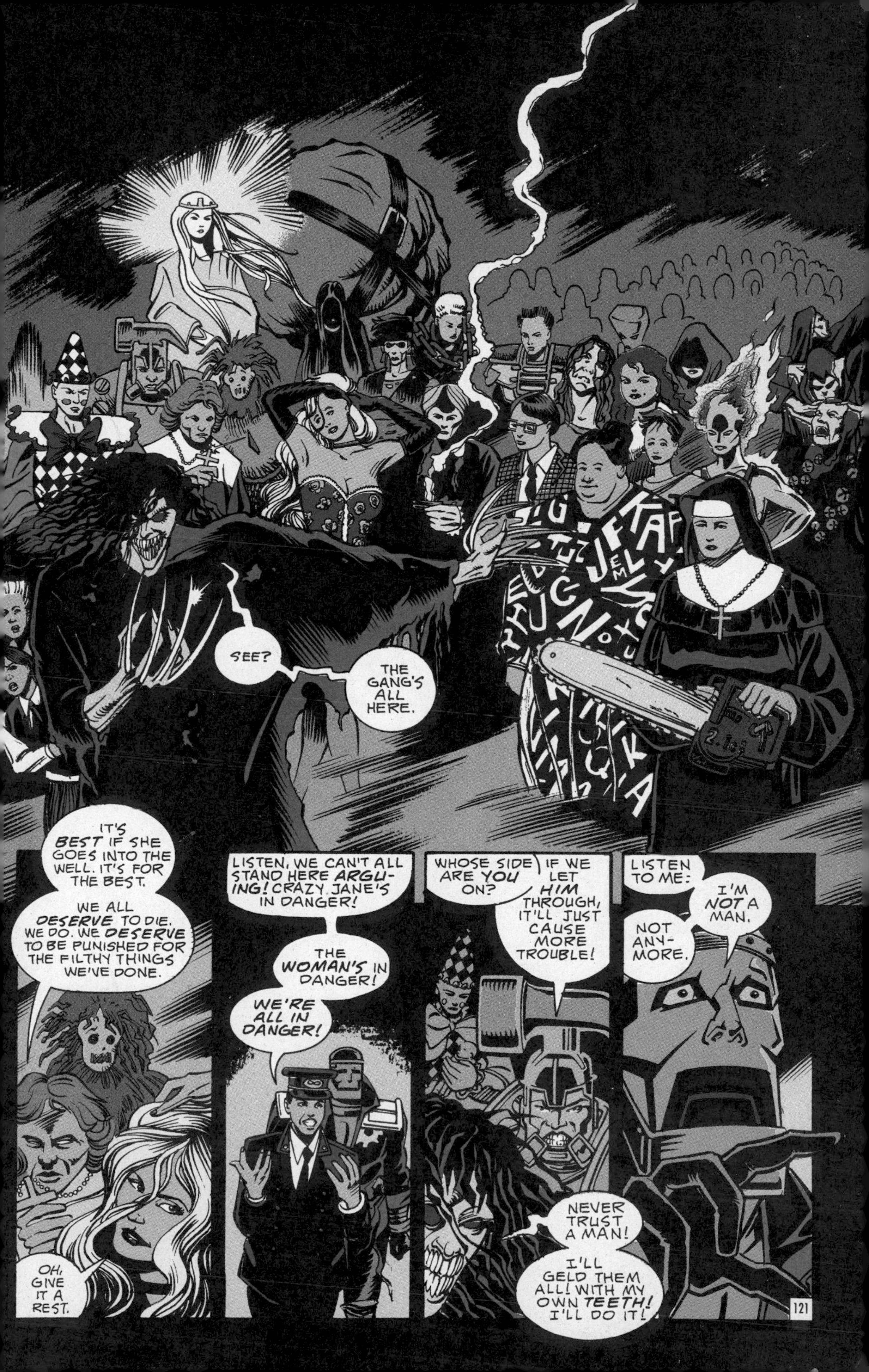
SEE?
THE GANG'S ALL HERE.
IT'S BEST IF SHE GOES INTO THE WELL. IT'S FOR THE BEST.
WE ALL DESERVE TO DIE. WE DO. WE DESERVE TO BE PUNISHED FOR THE FILTHY THINGS WE'VE DONE.
OH, GIVE IT A REST.
LISTEN, WE CAN'T ALL STAND HERE ARGUING! CRAZY JANE'S IN DANGER!
THE WOMAN'S IN DANGER!
WE'RE ALL IN DANGER!
WHOSE SIDE ARE YOU ON?
IF WE LET HIM THROUGH, IT'LL JUST CAUSE MORE TROUBLE!
NEVER TRUST A MAN!
I'LL GELD THEM ALL! WITH MY OWN TEETH! I'LL DO IT!
LISTEN TO ME:
I'M NOT A MAN.
NOT ANY-MORE.

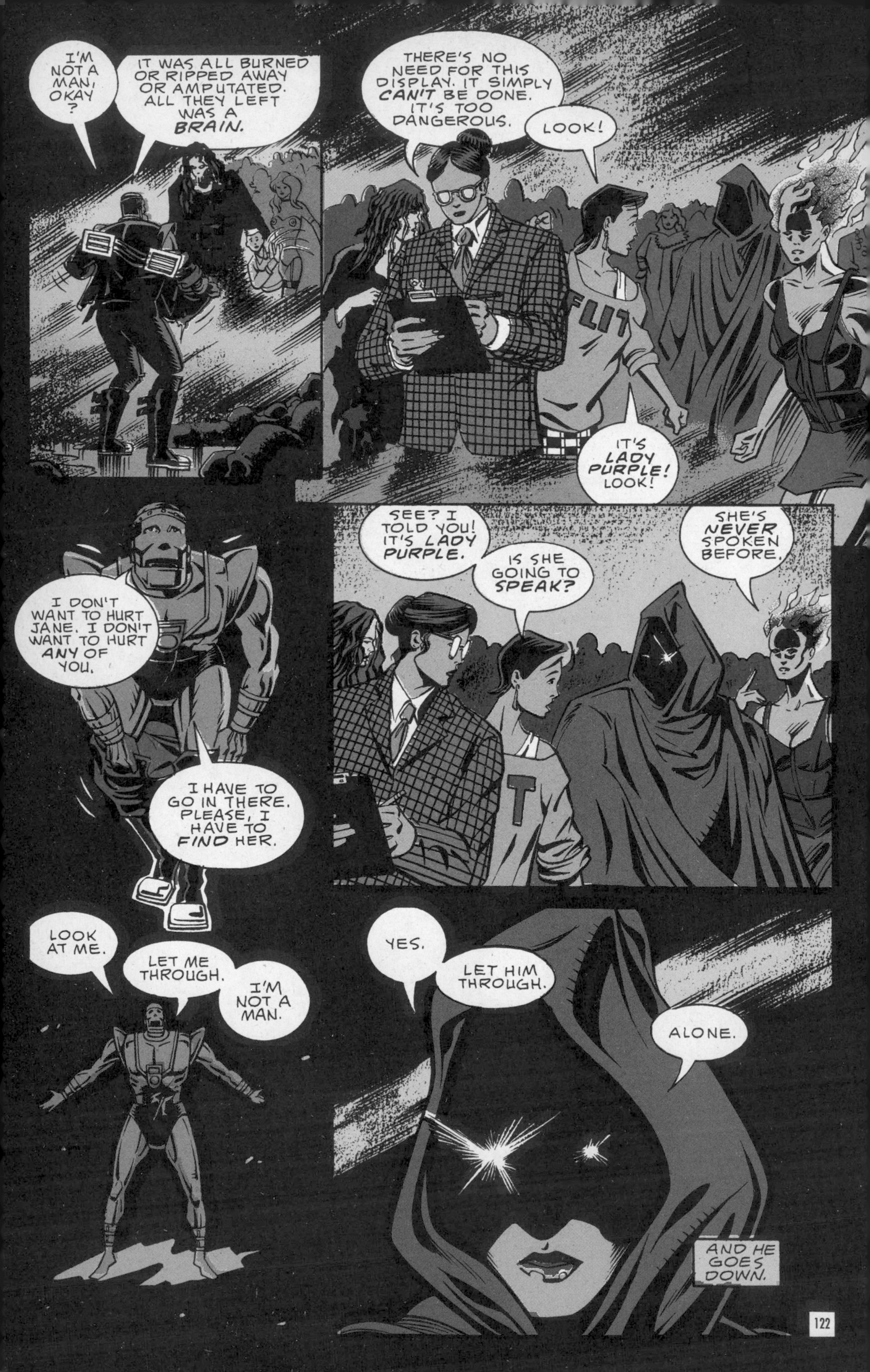
I'M NOT A MAN, OKAY?
IT WAS ALL BURNED OR RIPPED AWAY OR AMPUTATED. ALL THEY LEFT WAS A BRAIN.
THERE'S NO NEED FOR THIS DISPLAY. IT SIMPLY CAN'T BE DONE. IT'S TOO DANGEROUS.
LOOK!
IT'S LADY PURPLE! LOOK!
I DON'T WANT TO HURT JANE. I DON'T WANT TO HURT ANY OF YOU.
I HAVE TO GO IN THERE. PLEASE, I HAVE TO FIND HER.
SEE? I TOLD YOU! IT'S LADY PURPLE.
IS SHE GOING TO SPEAK?
SHE'S NEVER SPOKEN BEFORE.
LOOK AT ME.
LET ME THROUGH.
I'M NOT A MAN.
YES.
LET HIM THROUGH.
ALONE.
AND HE GOES DOWN.

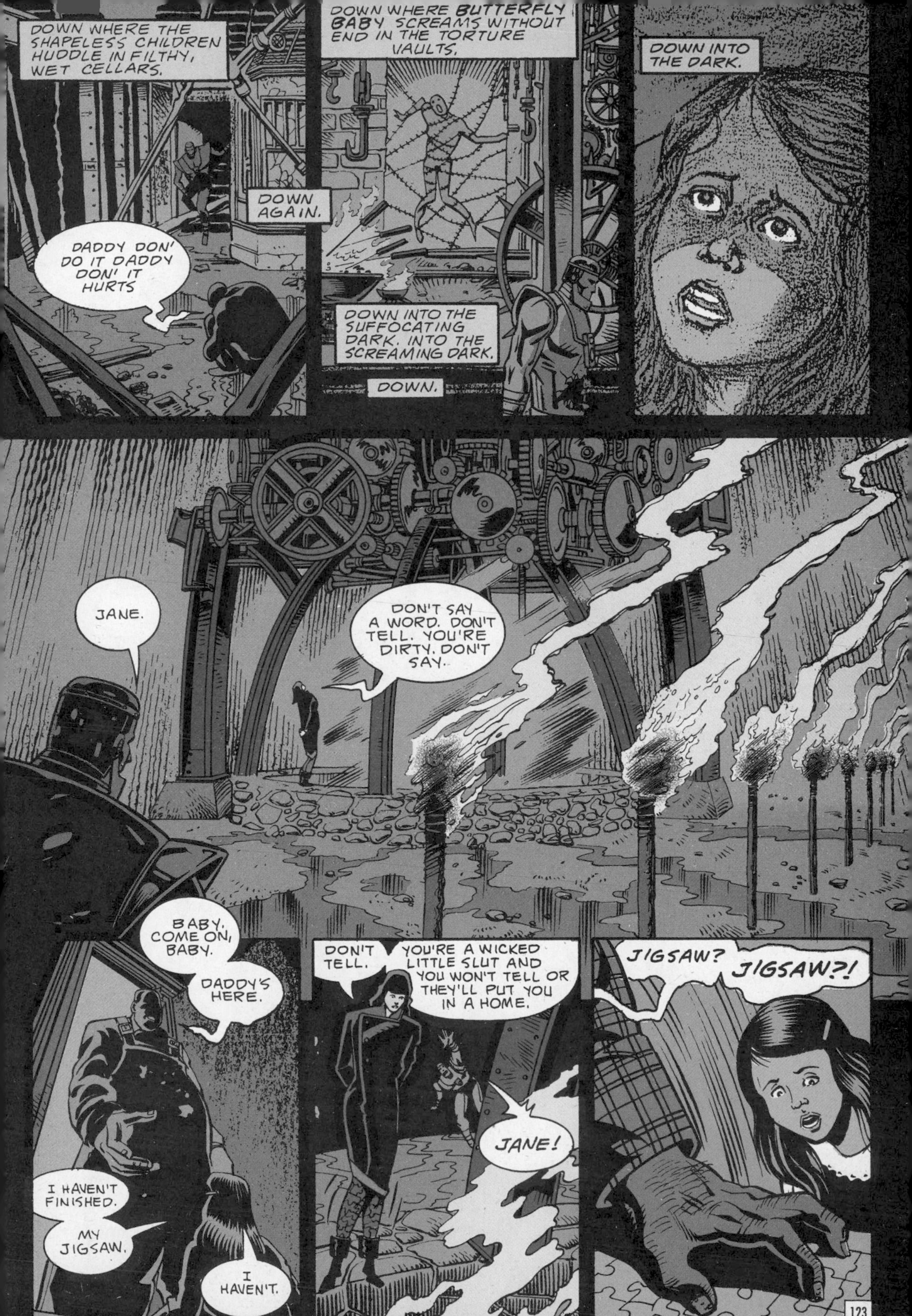
DOWN WHERE THE SHAPELESS CHILDREN HUDDLE IN FILTHY, WET CELLARS.
DOWN AGAIN.
DADDY DON' DO IT DADDY DON' IT HURTS
DOWN WHERE BUTTERFLY BABY SCREAMS WITHOUT END IN THE TORTURE VAULTS.
DOWN INTO THE SUFFOCATING DARK. INTO THE SCREAMING DARK.
DOWN.
DOWN INTO THE DARK.
JANE.
DON'T SAY A WORD. DON'T TELL. YOU'RE DIRTY. DON'T SAY.
BABY. COME ON, BABY.
DADDY'S HERE.
I HAVEN'T FINISHED.
MY JIGSAW.
I HAVEN'T.
DON'T TELL.
YOU'RE A WICKED LITTLE SLUT AND YOU WON'T TELL OR THEY'LL PUT YOU IN A HOME.
JANE!
JIGSAW?
JIGSAW?!

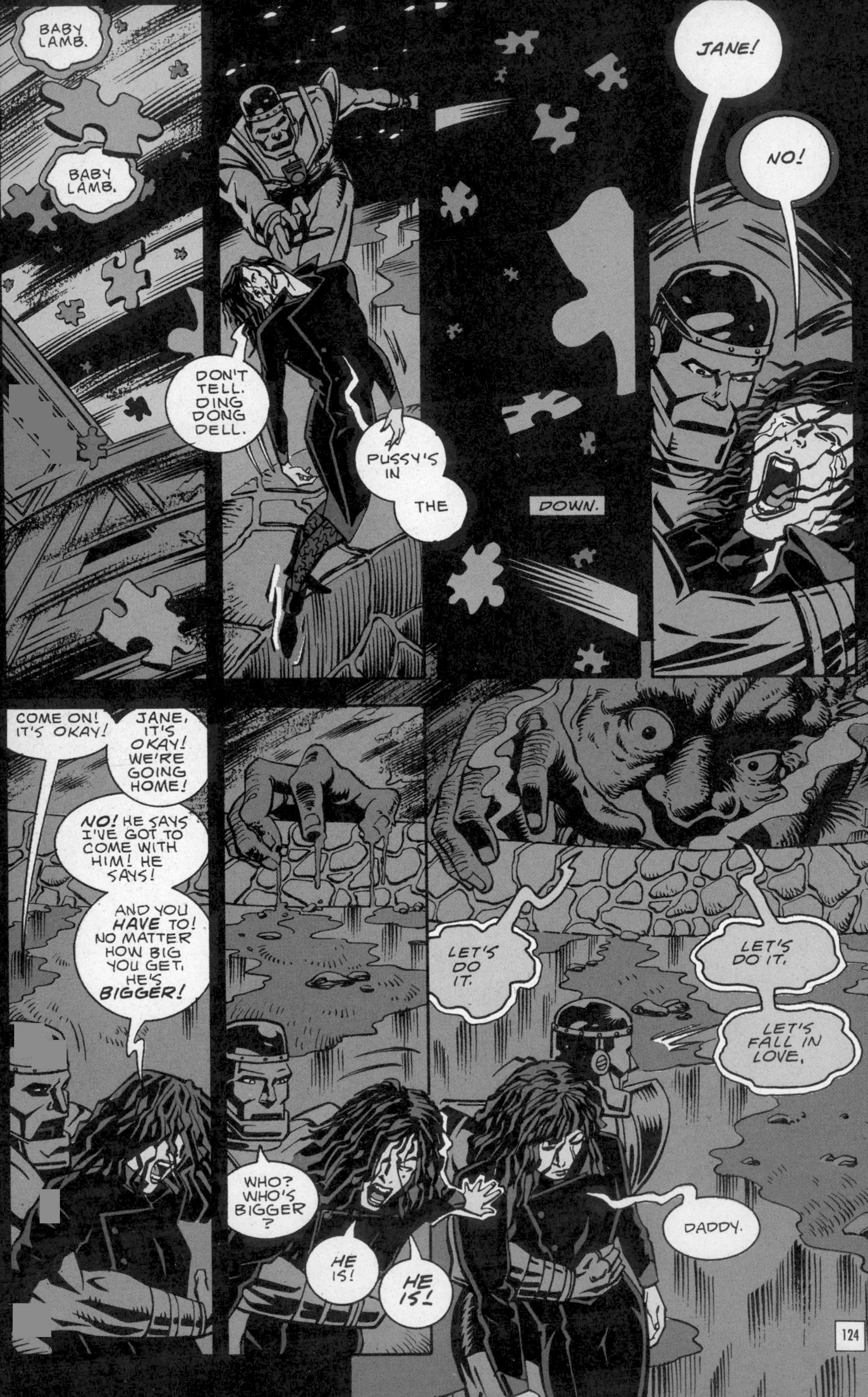
BABY LAMB.
BABY LAMB.
DON'T TELL. DING DONG DELL.
PUSSY'S IN
THE
DOWN.
JANE!
NO!
COME ON! IT'S OKAY!
JANE, IT'S OKAY! WE'RE GOING HOME!
NO! HE SAYS I'VE GOT TO COME WITH HIM! HE SAYS!
AND YOU HAVE TO! NO MATTER HOW BIG YOU GET, HE'S BIGGER!
WHO? WHO'S BIGGER?
HE IS!
HE IS!
LET'S DO IT.
LET'S DO IT.
LET'S FALL IN LOVE.
DADDY.

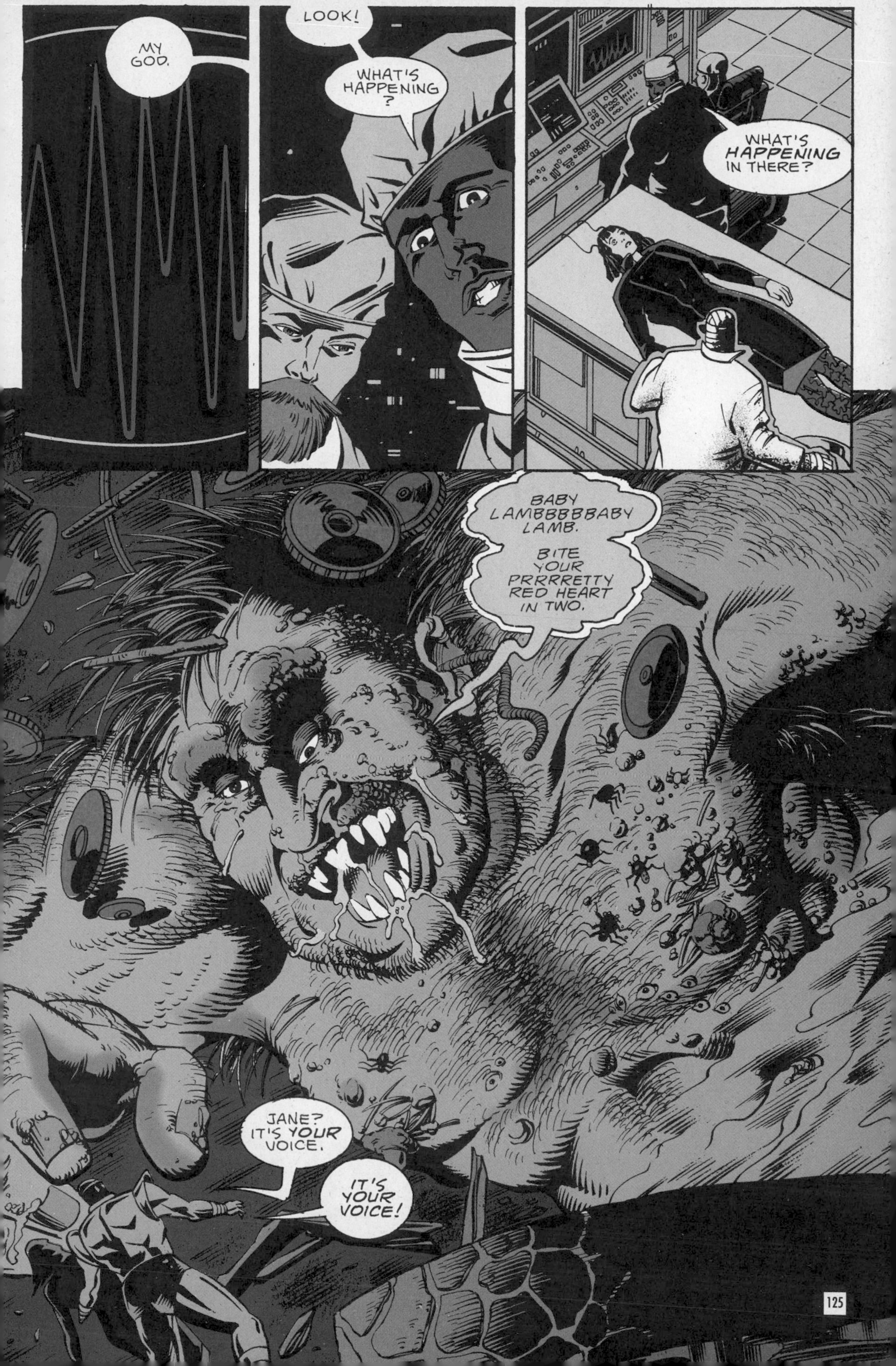
MY GOD.
LOOK!
WHAT'S HAPPENING?
WHAT'S HAPPENING IN THERE?
BABY LAMBBBBBABY LAMB.
BITE YOUR PRRRRETTY RED HEART IN TWO.
JANE? IT'S YOUR VOICE.
IT'S YOUR VOICE!

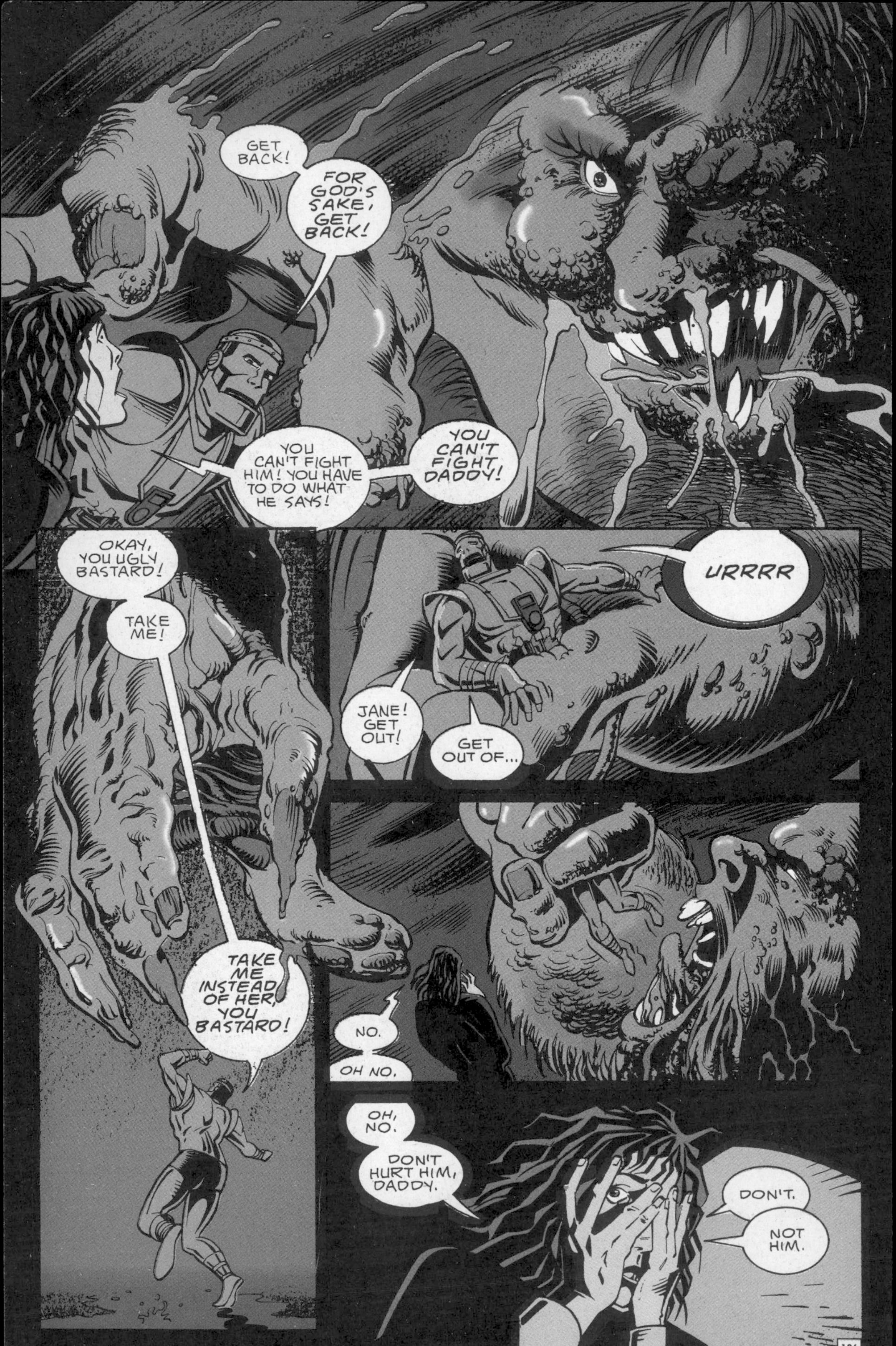
GET BACK!
FOR GOD'S SAKE, GET BACK!
YOU CAN'T FIGHT HIM! YOU HAVE TO DO WHAT HE SAYS!
YOU CAN'T FIGHT DADDY!
OKAY, YOU UGLY BASTARD!
TAKE ME!
TAKE ME INSTEAD OF HER, YOU BASTARD!
URRRR
JANE! GET OUT!
GET OUT OF...
NO.
OH NO.
OH, NO.
DON'T HURT HIM, DADDY.
DON'T.
NOT HIM.

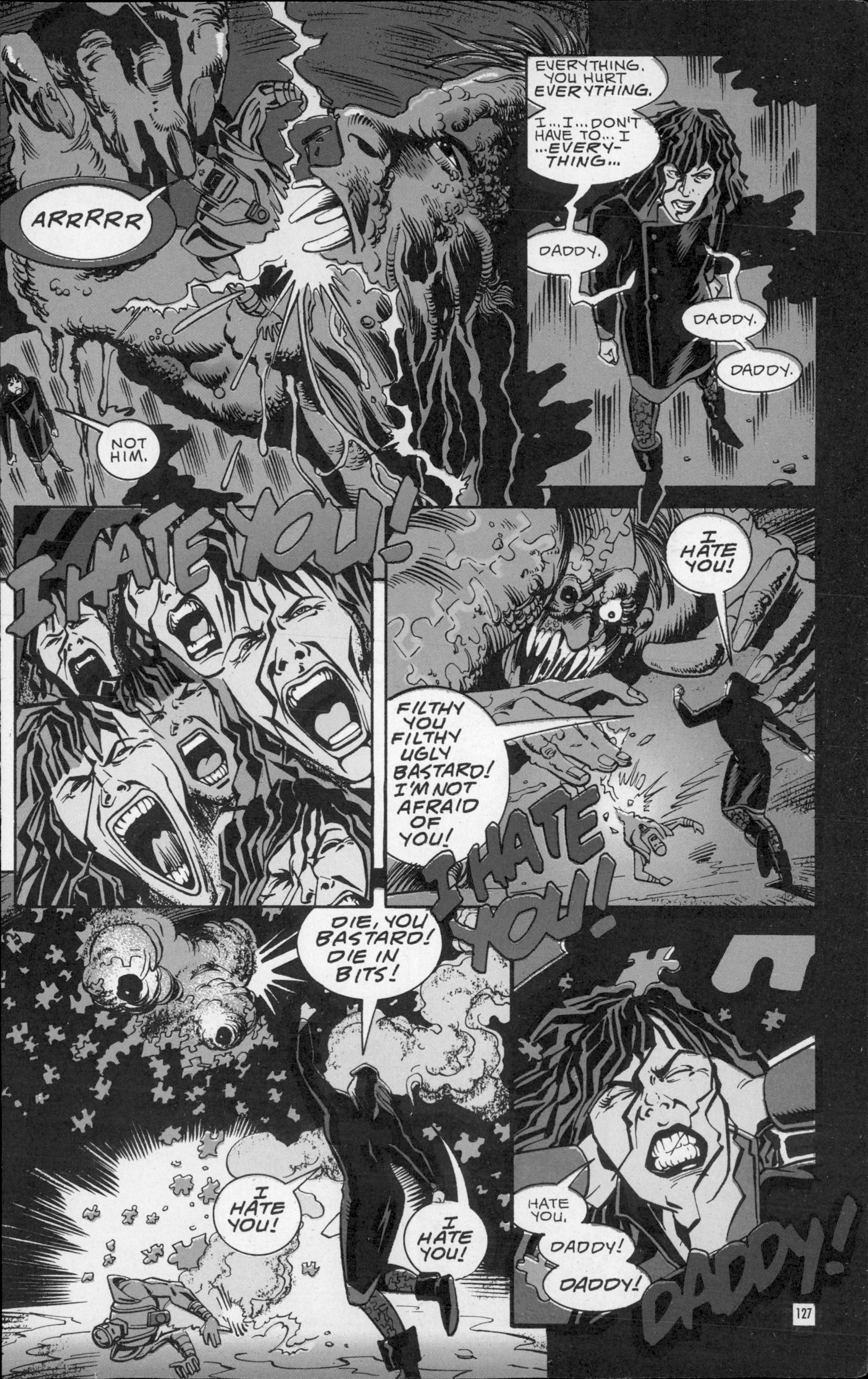
ARRRRR
NOT HIM.
EVERYTHING. YOU HURT EVERYTHING.
I... I... DON'T HAVE TO... I ...EVERY-THING...
DADDY.
DADDY.
DADDY.
I HATE YOU!
I HATE YOU!
FILTHY YOU FILTHY UGLY BASTARD! I'M NOT AFRAID OF YOU!
I HATE YOU!
DIE, YOU BASTARD! DIE IN BITS!
I HATE YOU!
I HATE YOU!
HATE YOU.
DADDY!
DADDY!
DADDY!

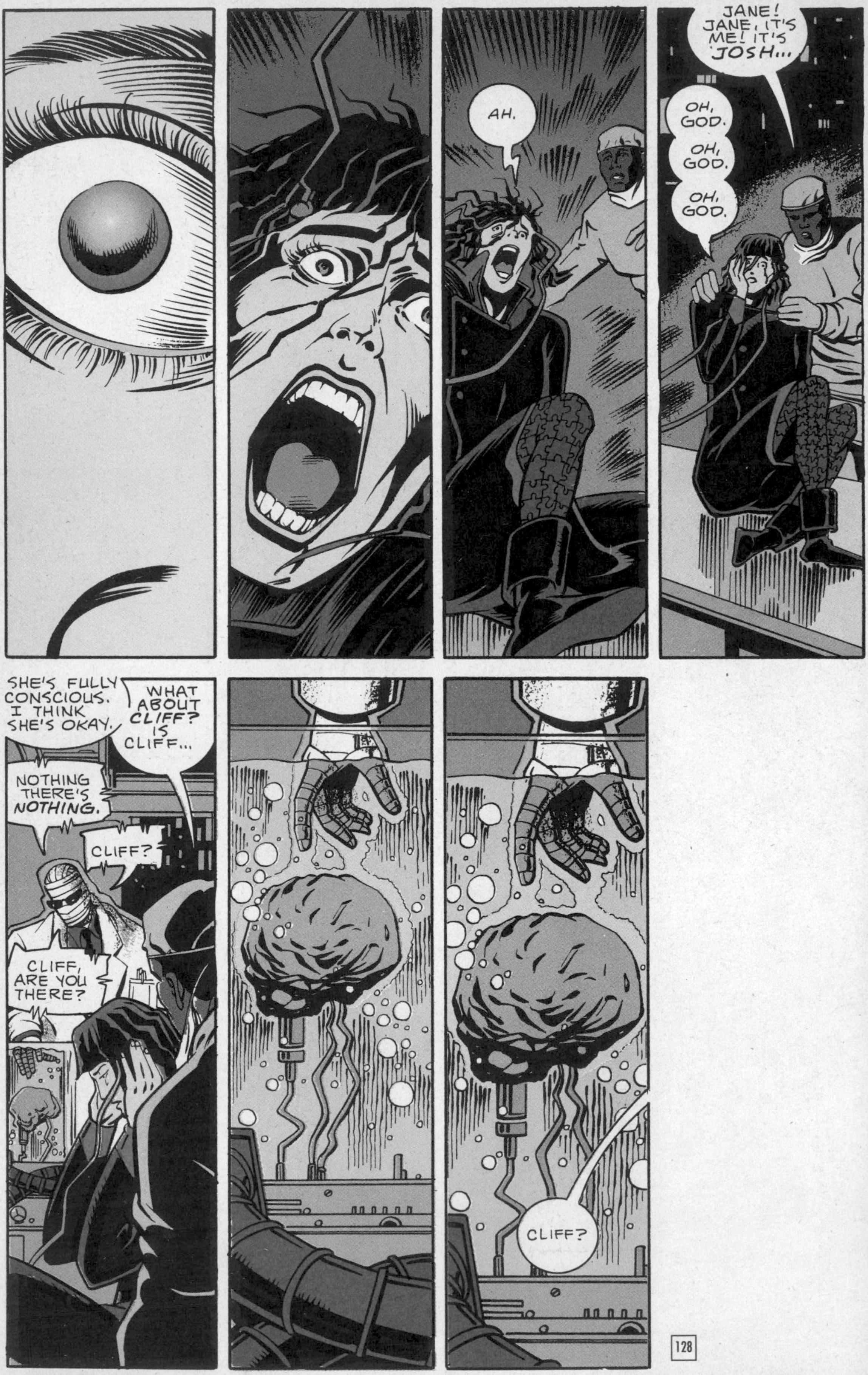
AH.
JANE! JANE, IT'S ME! IT'S JOSH...
OH, GOD.
OH, GOD.
OH, GOD.
SHE'S FULLY CONSCIOUS. I THINK SHE'S OKAY.
WHAT ABOUT CLIFF? IS CLIFF...
NOTHING THERE'S NOTHING.
CLIFF?
CLIFF, ARE YOU THERE?
CLIFF?

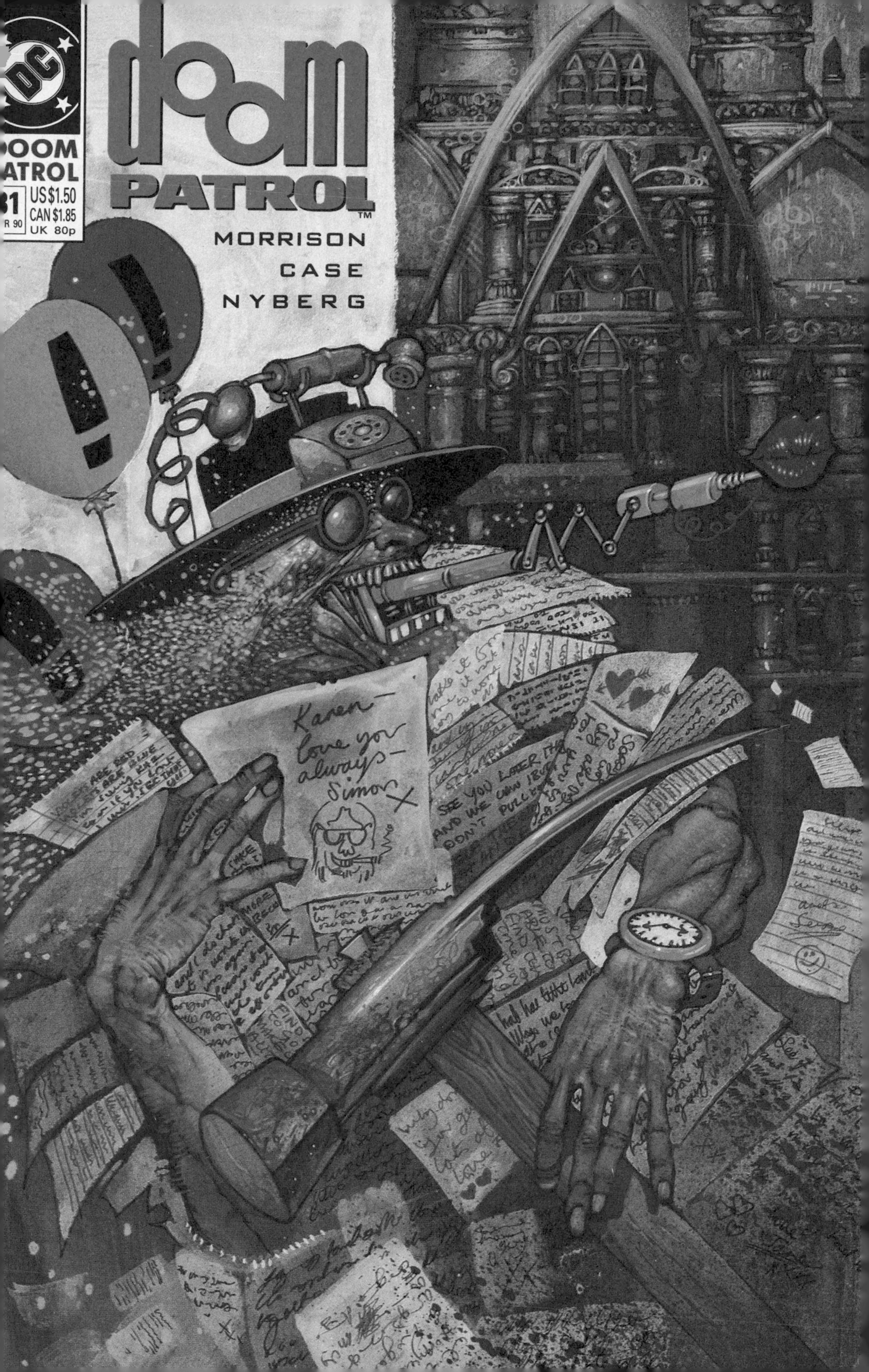

DC
doom PATROL
OOM
ATROL
31
US$1.50
CAN $1.85
UK 80p
MORRISON
CASE
NYBERG
Karen— love you always— Simon X
SEE YOU LATER THEN
AND WE CAN
DON'T PULL

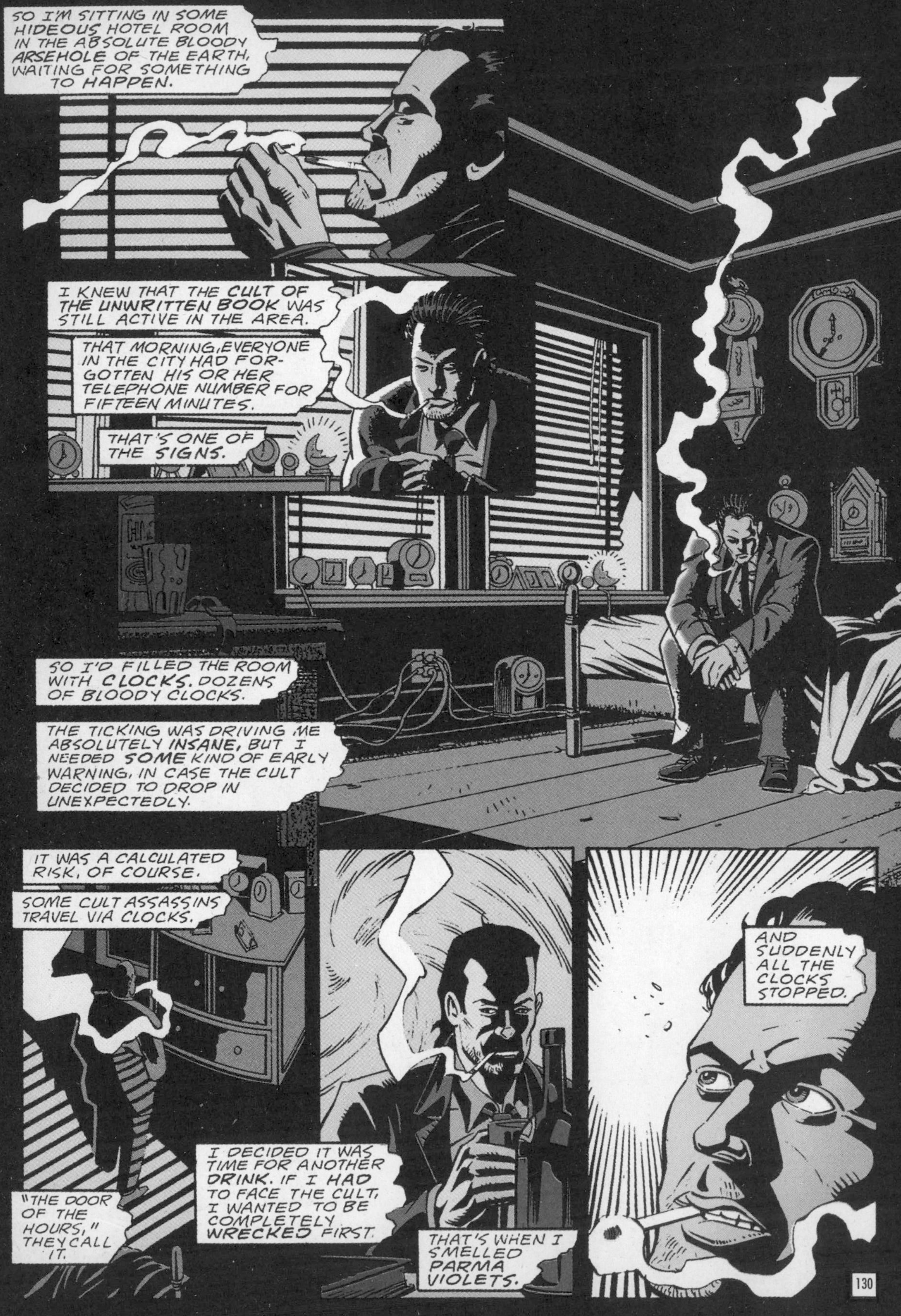

SO I'M SITTING IN SOME HIDEOUS HOTEL ROOM IN THE ABSOLUTE BLOODY ARSEHOLE OF THE EARTH, WAITING FOR SOMETHING TO HAPPEN.
I KNEW THAT THE CULT OF THE UNWRITTEN BOOK WAS STILL ACTIVE IN THE AREA.
THAT MORNING, EVERYONE IN THE CITY HAD FORGOTTEN HIS OR HER TELEPHONE NUMBER FOR FIFTEEN MINUTES.
THAT'S ONE OF THE SIGNS.
SO I'D FILLED THE ROOM WITH CLOCKS. DOZENS OF BLOODY CLOCKS.
THE TICKING WAS DRIVING ME ABSOLUTELY INSANE, BUT I NEEDED SOME KIND OF EARLY WARNING, IN CASE THE CULT DECIDED TO DROP IN UNEXPECTEDLY.
IT WAS A CALCULATED RISK, OF COURSE.
SOME CULT ASSASSINS TRAVEL VIA CLOCKS.
"THE DOOR OF THE HOURS," THEY CALL IT.
I DECIDED IT WAS TIME FOR ANOTHER DRINK. IF I HAD TO FACE THE CULT, I WANTED TO BE COMPLETELY WRECKED FIRST.
THAT'S WHEN I SMELLED PARMA VIOLETS.
AND SUDDENLY ALL THE CLOCKS STOPPED.

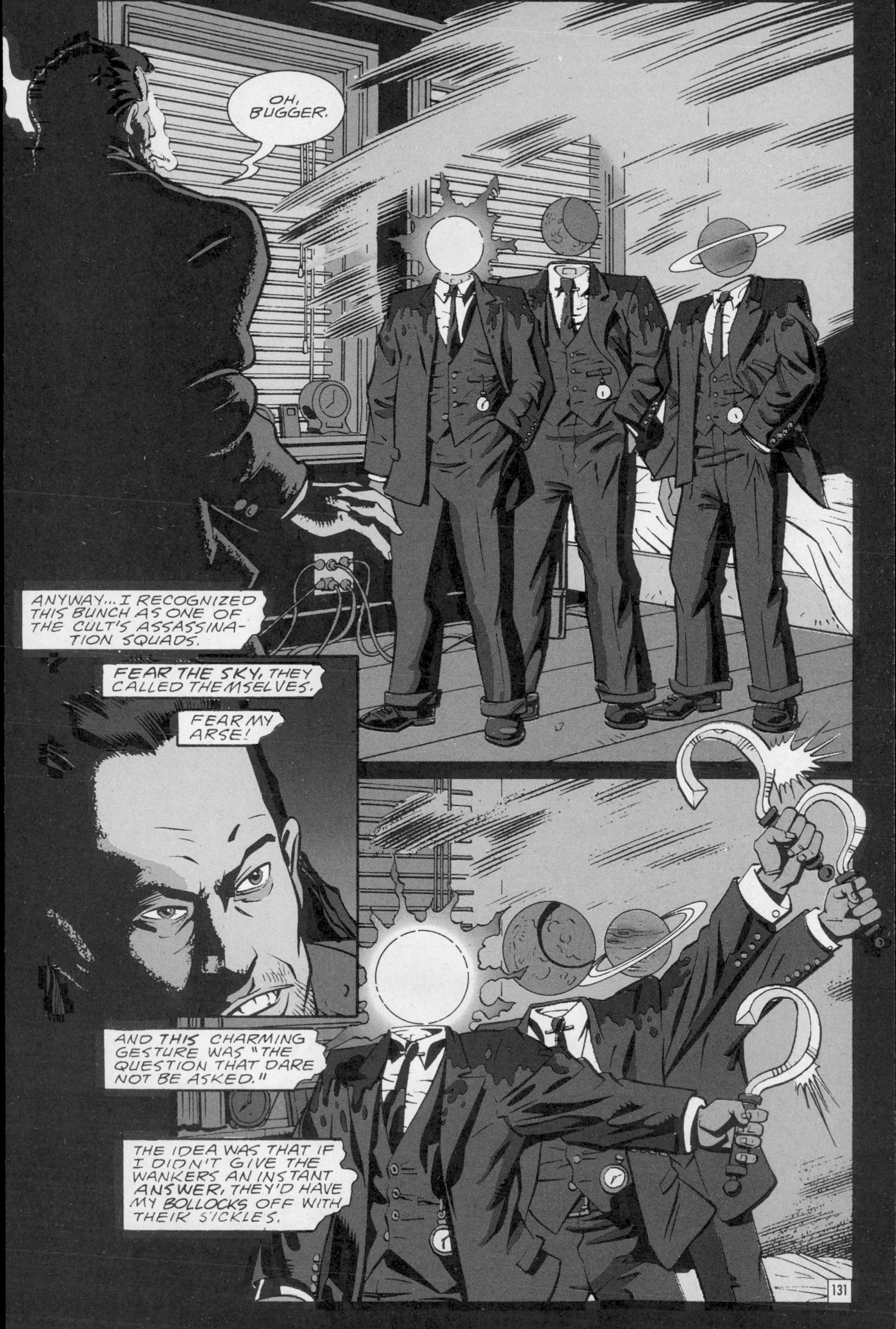
OH, BUGGER.
ANYWAY... I RECOGNIZED THIS BUNCH AS ONE OF THE CULT'S ASSASSINATION SQUADS.
FEAR THE SKY, THEY CALLED THEMSELVES.
FEAR MY ARSE!
AND THIS CHARMING GESTURE WAS "THE QUESTION THAT DARE NOT BE ASKED."
THE IDEA WAS THAT IF I DIDN'T GIVE THE WANKERS AN INSTANT ANSWER, THEY'D HAVE MY BOLLOCKS OFF WITH THEIR SICKLES.

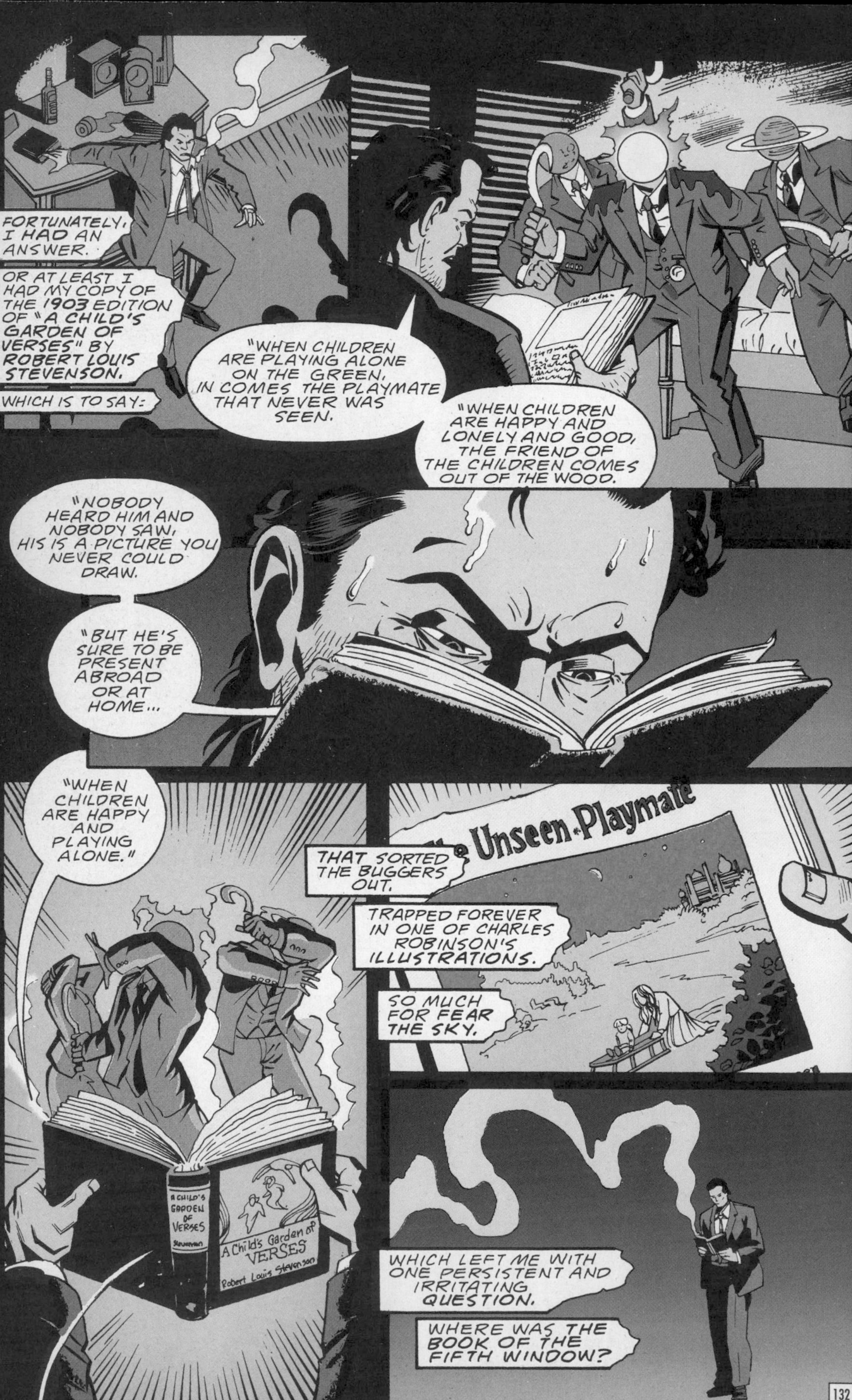
FORTUNATELY, I HAD AN ANSWER.
OR AT LEAST I HAD MY COPY OF THE 1903 EDITION OF "A CHILD'S GARDEN OF VERSES" BY ROBERT LOUIS STEVENSON.
WHICH IS TO SAY:
"WHEN CHILDREN ARE PLAYING ALONE ON THE GREEN, IN COMES THE PLAYMATE THAT NEVER WAS SEEN.
"WHEN CHILDREN ARE HAPPY AND LONELY AND GOOD, THE FRIEND OF THE CHILDREN COMES OUT OF THE WOOD.
"NOBODY HEARD HIM AND NOBODY SAW, HIS IS A PICTURE YOU NEVER COULD DRAW.
"BUT HE'S SURE TO BE PRESENT ABROAD OR AT HOME...
"WHEN CHILDREN ARE HAPPY AND PLAYING ALONE."
A CHILD'S GARDEN OF VERSES
A Child's Garden of VERSES
Robert Louis Stevenson
The Unseen Playmate
THAT SORTED THE BUGGERS OUT.
TRAPPED FOREVER IN ONE OF CHARLES ROBINSON'S ILLUSTRATIONS.
SO MUCH FOR FEAR THE SKY.
WHICH LEFT ME WITH ONE PERSISTENT AND IRRITATING QUESTION.
WHERE WAS THE BOOK OF THE FIFTH WINDOW?

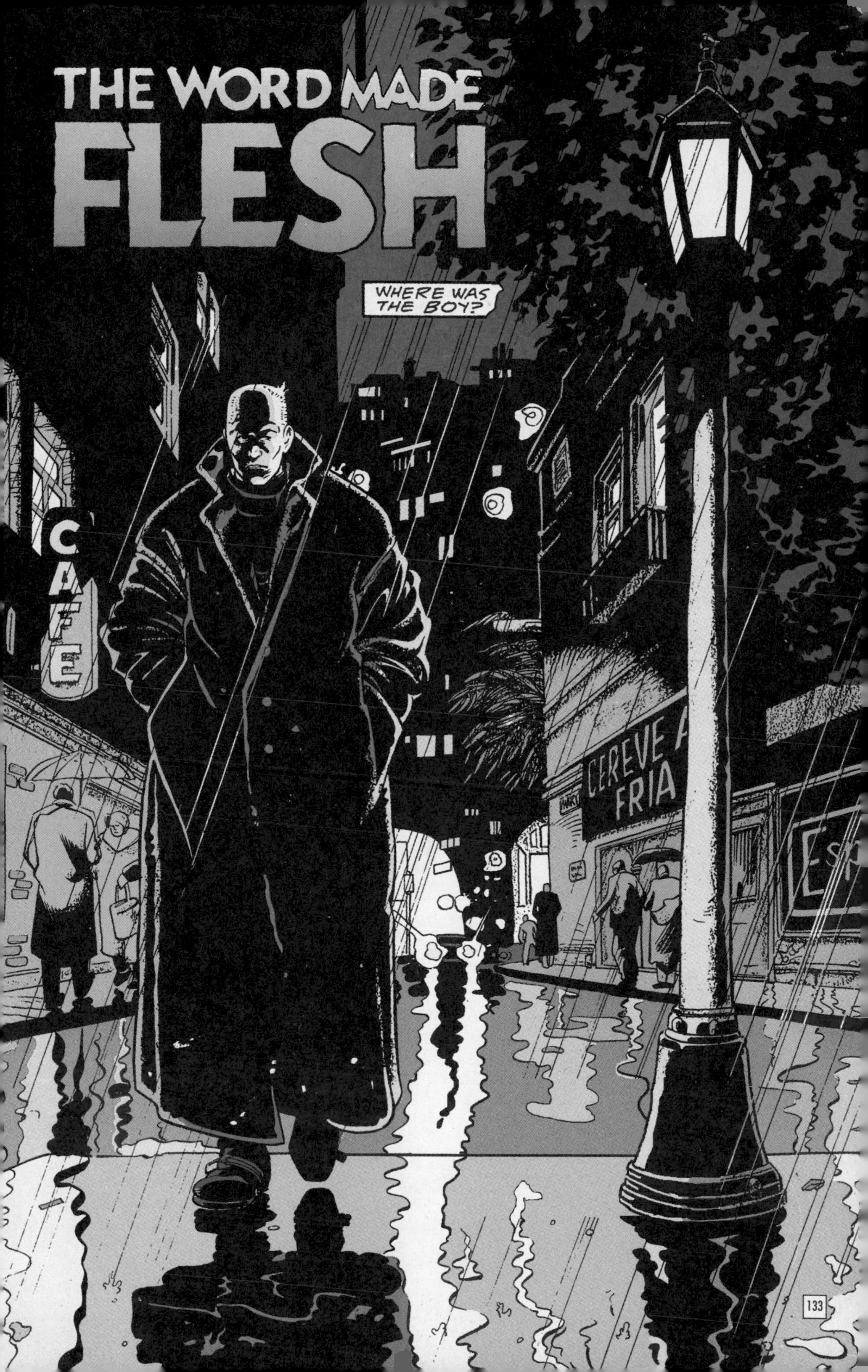
THE WORD MADE FLESH
WHERE WAS THE BOY?
CAFE
CEREVE A
FRIA

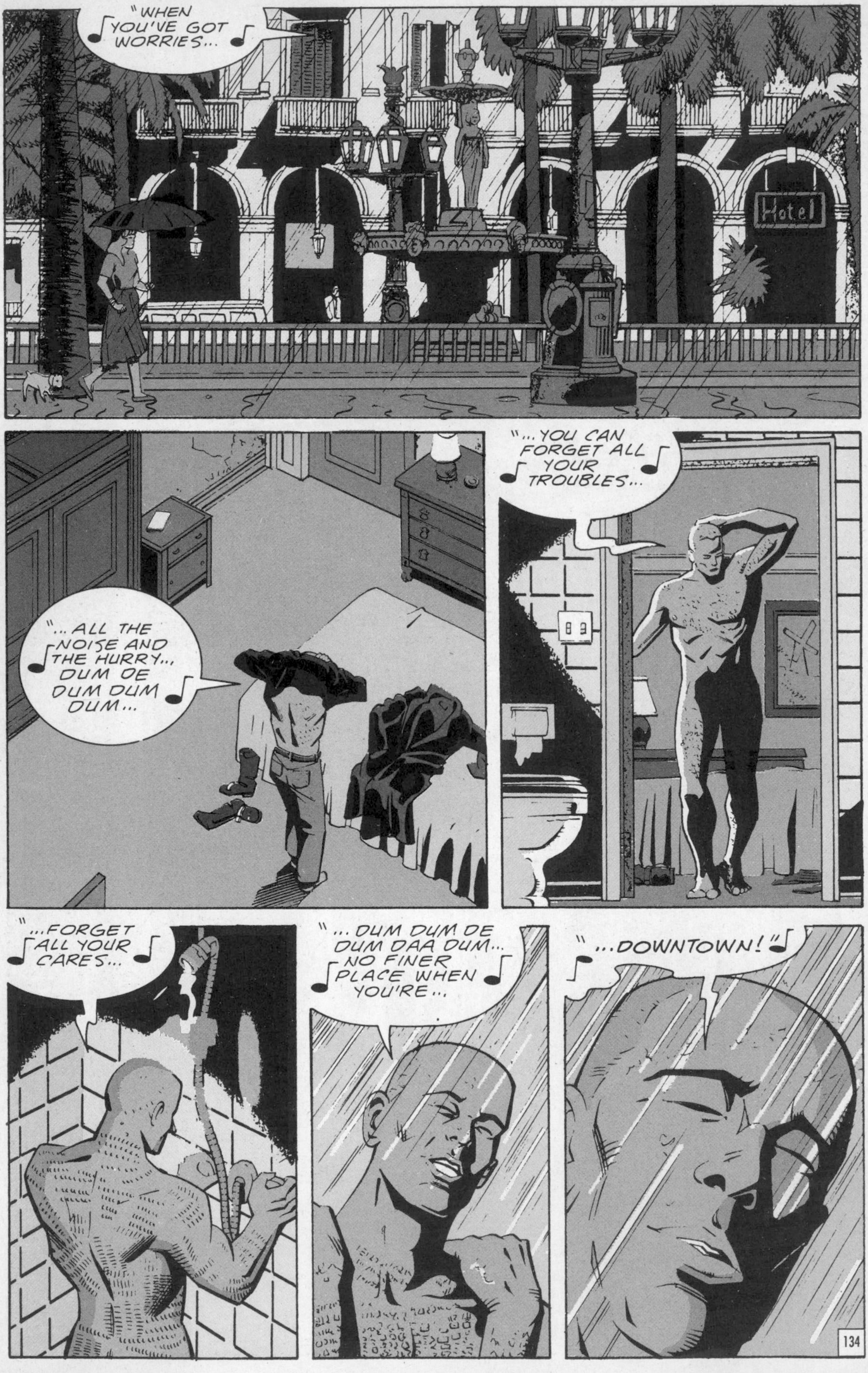
"WHEN YOU'VE GOT WORRIES...
Hotel
"...ALL THE NOISE AND THE HURRY..., DUM DE DUM DUM DUM...
"...YOU CAN FORGET ALL YOUR TROUBLES...
"...FORGET ALL YOUR CARES...
"...DUM DUM DE DUM DAA DUM... NO FINER PLACE WHEN YOU'RE...
"...DOWNTOWN!"

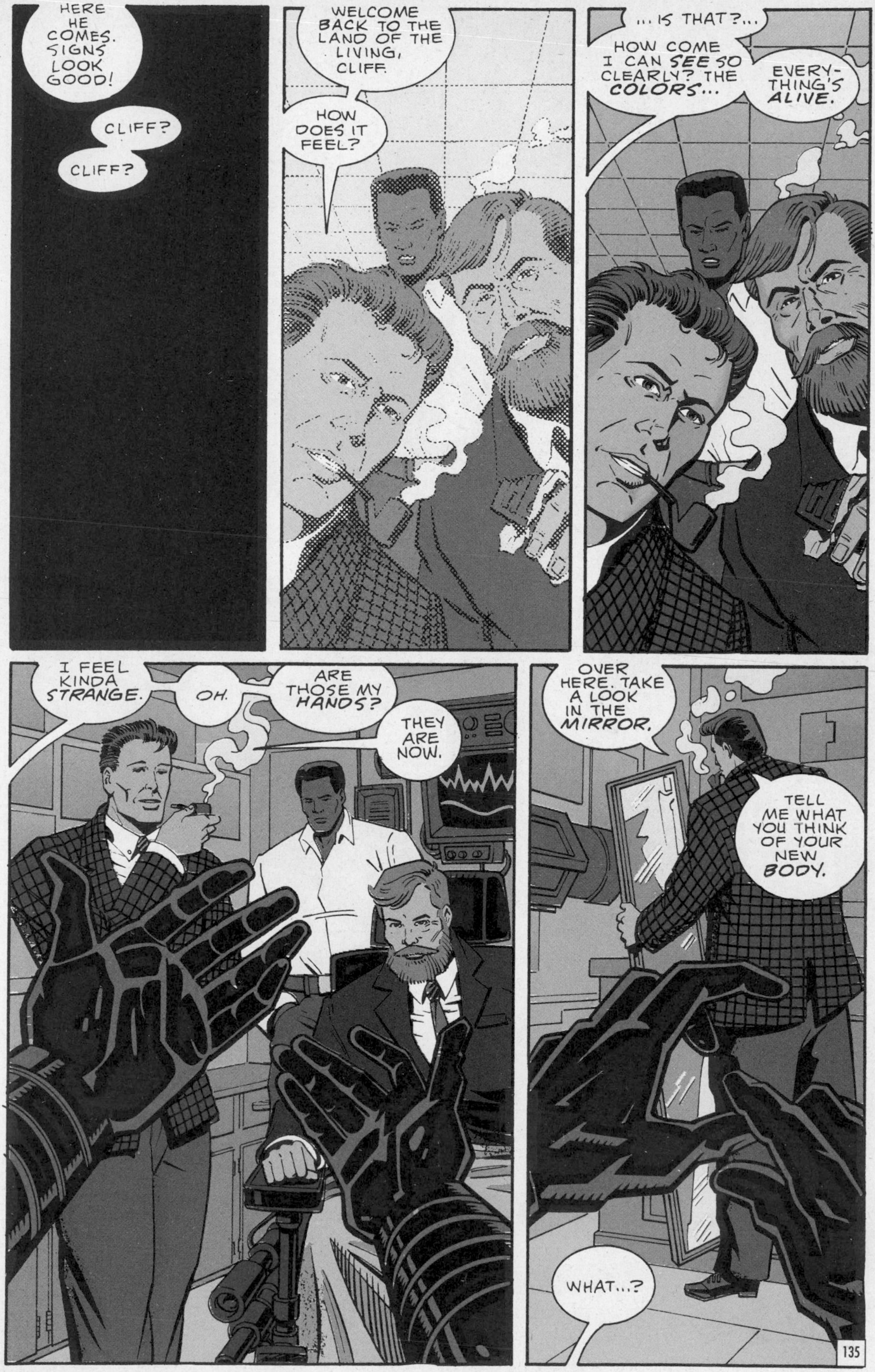
HERE HE COMES. SIGNS LOOK GOOD!
CLIFF?
CLIFF?
WELCOME BACK TO THE LAND OF THE LIVING, CLIFF.
HOW DOES IT FEEL?
...IS THAT?...
HOW COME I CAN SEE SO CLEARLY? THE COLORS...
EVERYTHING'S ALIVE.
I FEEL KINDA STRANGE.
OH.
ARE THOSE MY HANDS?
THEY ARE NOW.
OVER HERE. TAKE A LOOK IN THE MIRROR.
TELL ME WHAT YOU THINK OF YOUR NEW BODY.
WHAT...?

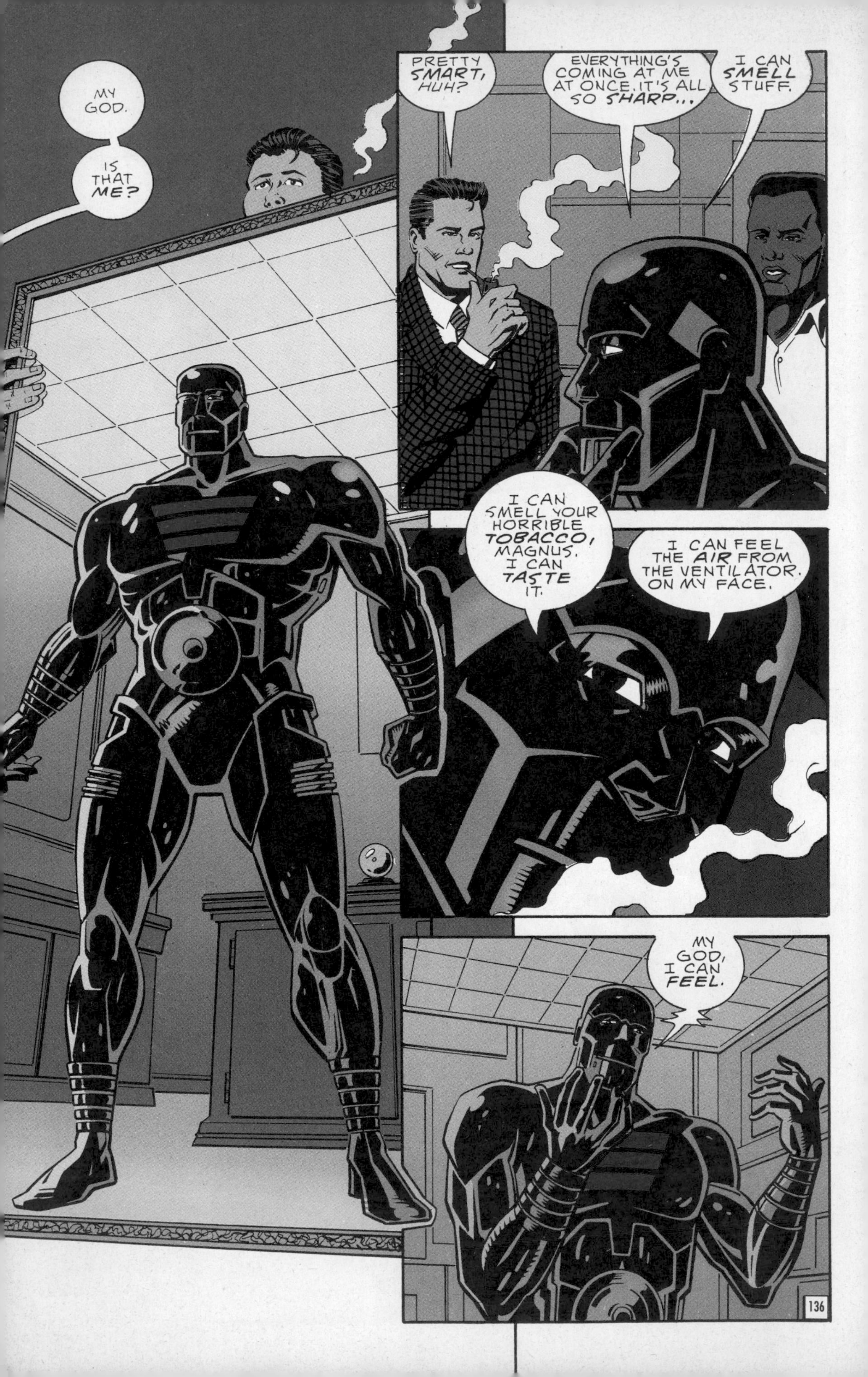
MY GOD.
IS THAT ME?
PRETTY SMART, HUH?
EVERYTHING'S COMING AT ME AT ONCE. IT'S ALL SO SHARP...
I CAN SMELL STUFF.
I CAN SMELL YOUR HORRIBLE TOBACCO, MAGNUS. I CAN TASTE IT.
I CAN FEEL THE AIR FROM THE VENTILATOR ON MY FACE.
MY GOD, I CAN FEEL.

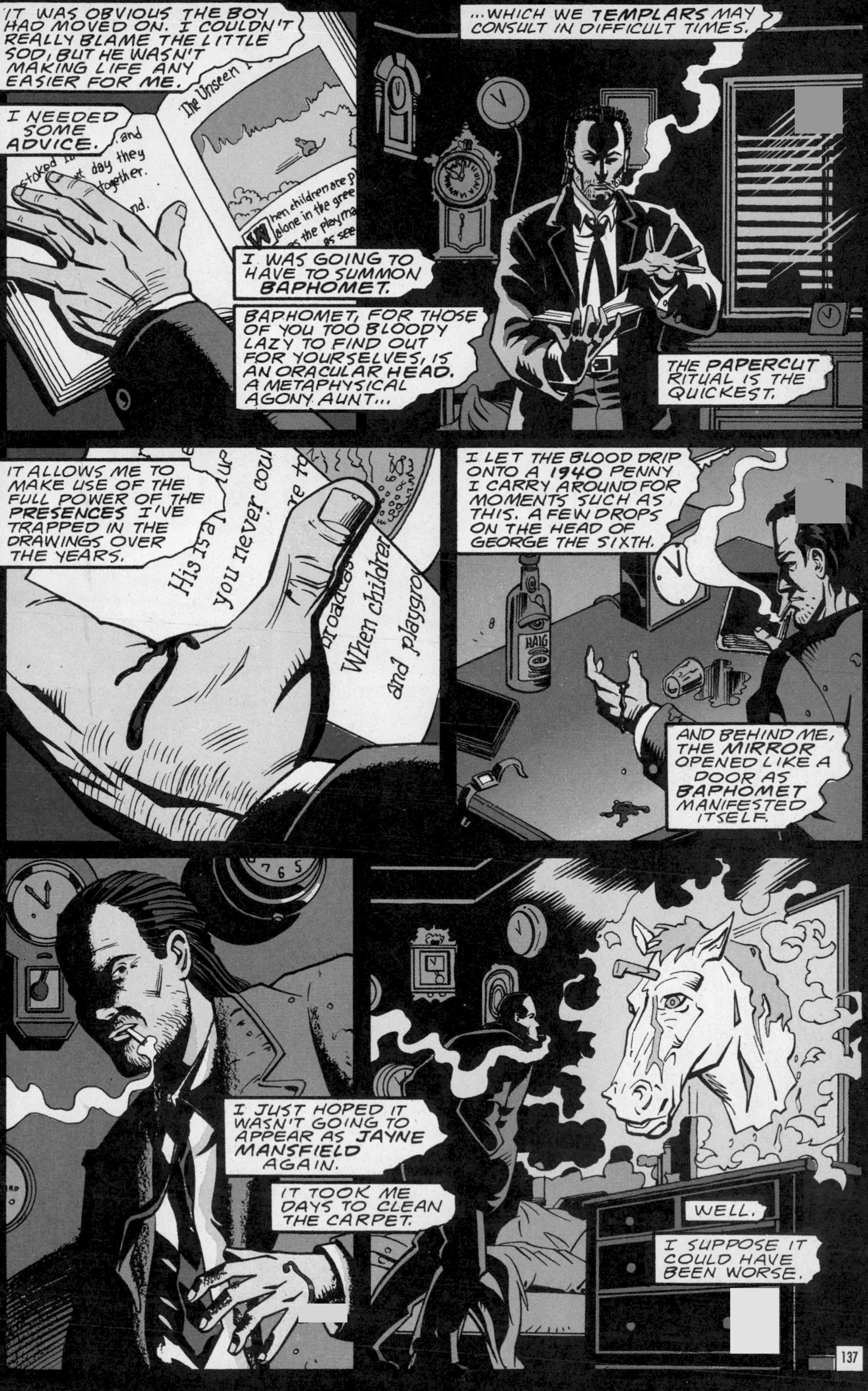
IT WAS OBVIOUS THE BOY HAD MOVED ON. I COULDN'T REALLY BLAME THE LITTLE SOD, BUT HE WASN'T MAKING LIFE ANY EASIER FOR ME.
I NEEDED SOME ADVICE.
The Unseen
I WAS GOING TO HAVE TO SUMMON BAPHOMET.
BAPHOMET, FOR THOSE OF YOU TOO BLOODY LAZY TO FIND OUT FOR YOURSELVES, IS AN ORACULAR HEAD. A METAPHYSICAL AGONY AUNT...
...WHICH WE TEMPLARS MAY CONSULT IN DIFFICULT TIMES.
THE PAPERCUT RITUAL IS THE QUICKEST.
IT ALLOWS ME TO MAKE USE OF THE FULL POWER OF THE PRESENCES I'VE TRAPPED IN THE DRAWINGS OVER THE YEARS.
I LET THE BLOOD DRIP ONTO A 1940 PENNY I CARRY AROUND FOR MOMENTS SUCH AS THIS. A FEW DROPS ON THE HEAD OF GEORGE THE SIXTH.
HAIG
AND BEHIND ME, THE MIRROR OPENED LIKE A DOOR AS BAPHOMET MANIFESTED ITSELF.
I JUST HOPED IT WASN'T GOING TO APPEAR AS JAYNE MANSFIELD AGAIN.
IT TOOK ME DAYS TO CLEAN THE CARPET.
WELL.
I SUPPOSE IT COULD HAVE BEEN WORSE.

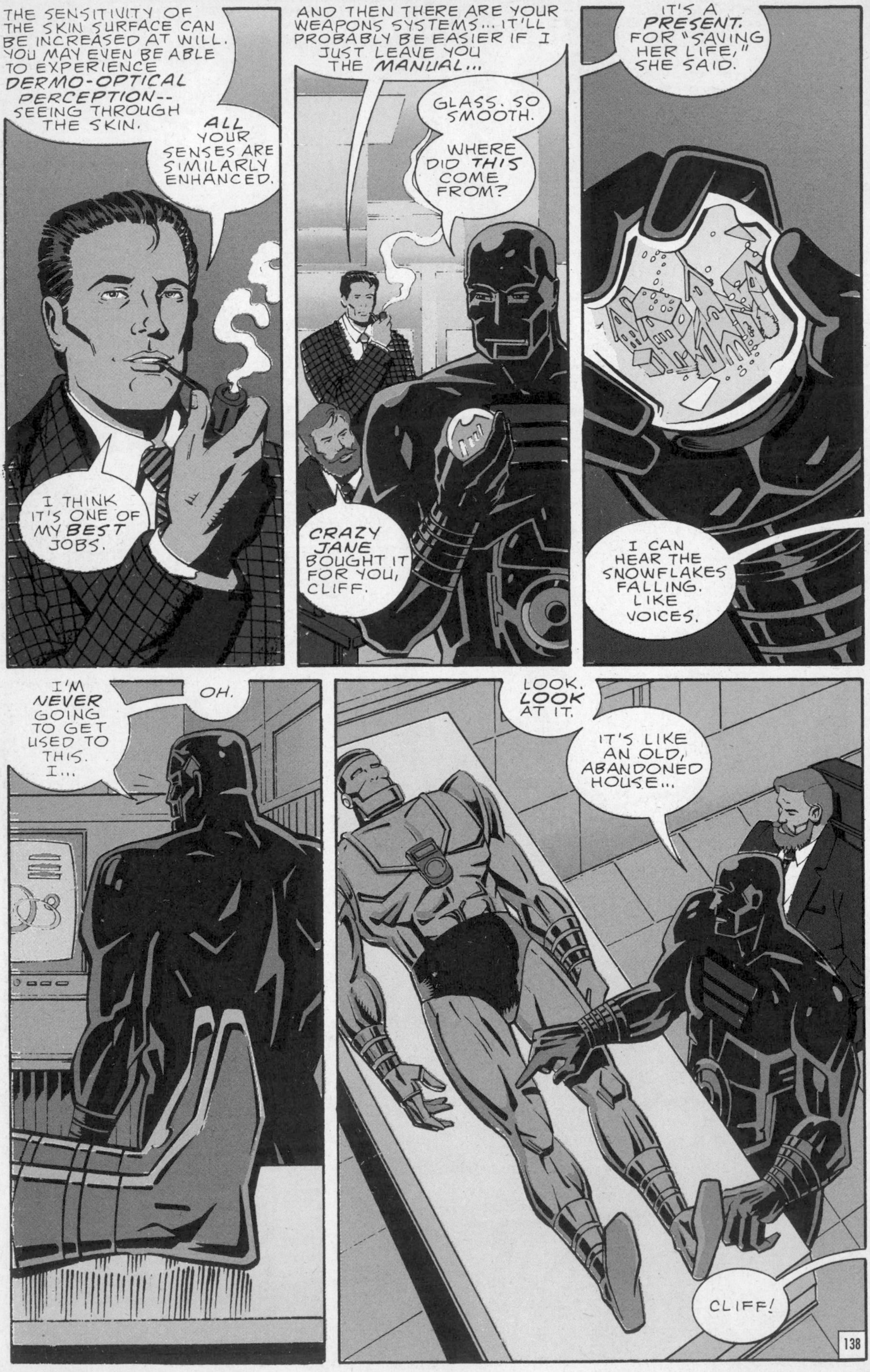
THE SENSITIVITY OF THE SKIN SURFACE CAN BE INCREASED AT WILL. YOU MAY EVEN BE ABLE TO EXPERIENCE DERMO-OPTICAL PERCEPTION-- SEEING THROUGH THE SKIN.
ALL YOUR SENSES ARE SIMILARLY ENHANCED.
I THINK IT'S ONE OF MY BEST JOBS.
AND THEN THERE ARE YOUR WEAPONS SYSTEMS... IT'LL PROBABLY BE EASIER IF I JUST LEAVE YOU THE MANUAL...
GLASS. SO SMOOTH.
WHERE DID THIS COME FROM?
CRAZY JANE BOUGHT IT FOR YOU, CLIFF.
IT'S A PRESENT. FOR "SAVING HER LIFE," SHE SAID.
I CAN HEAR THE SNOWFLAKES FALLING. LIKE VOICES.
I'M NEVER GOING TO GET USED TO THIS. I...
OH.
LOOK. LOOK AT IT.
IT'S LIKE AN OLD, ABANDONED HOUSE...
CLIFF!

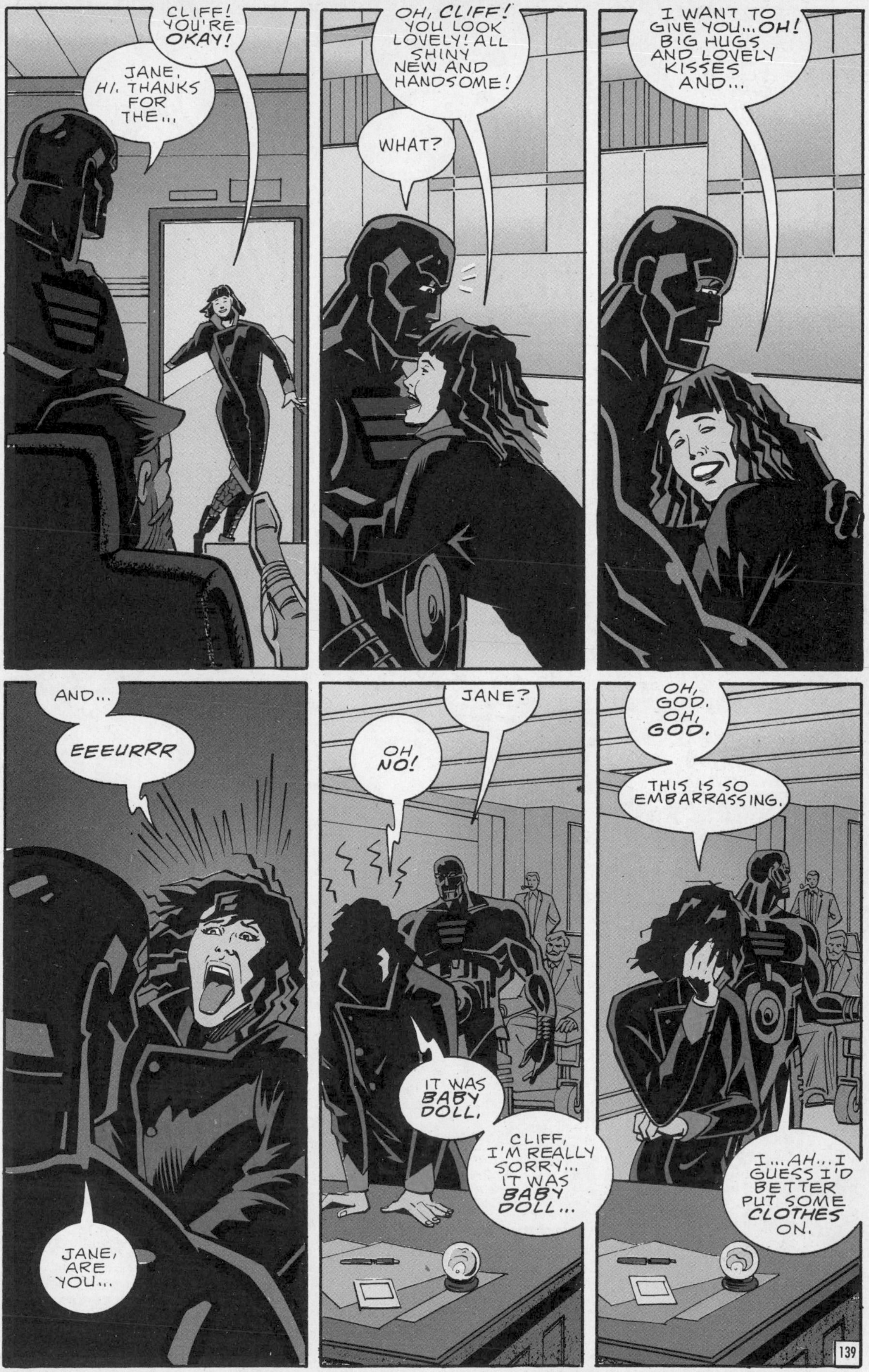
JANE, HI. THANKS FOR THE...
CLIFF! YOU'RE OKAY!
OH, CLIFF! YOU LOOK LOVELY! ALL SHINY NEW AND HANDSOME!
WHAT?
I WANT TO GIVE YOU... OH! BIG HUGS AND LOVELY KISSES AND...
AND...
EEEURRR
JANE, ARE YOU...
JANE?
OH NO!
IT WAS BABY DOLL.
CLIFF, I'M REALLY SORRY... IT WAS BABY DOLL...
OH, GOD. OH, GOD.
THIS IS SO EMBARRASSING.
I... AH... I GUESS I'D BETTER PUT SOME CLOTHES ON.
139

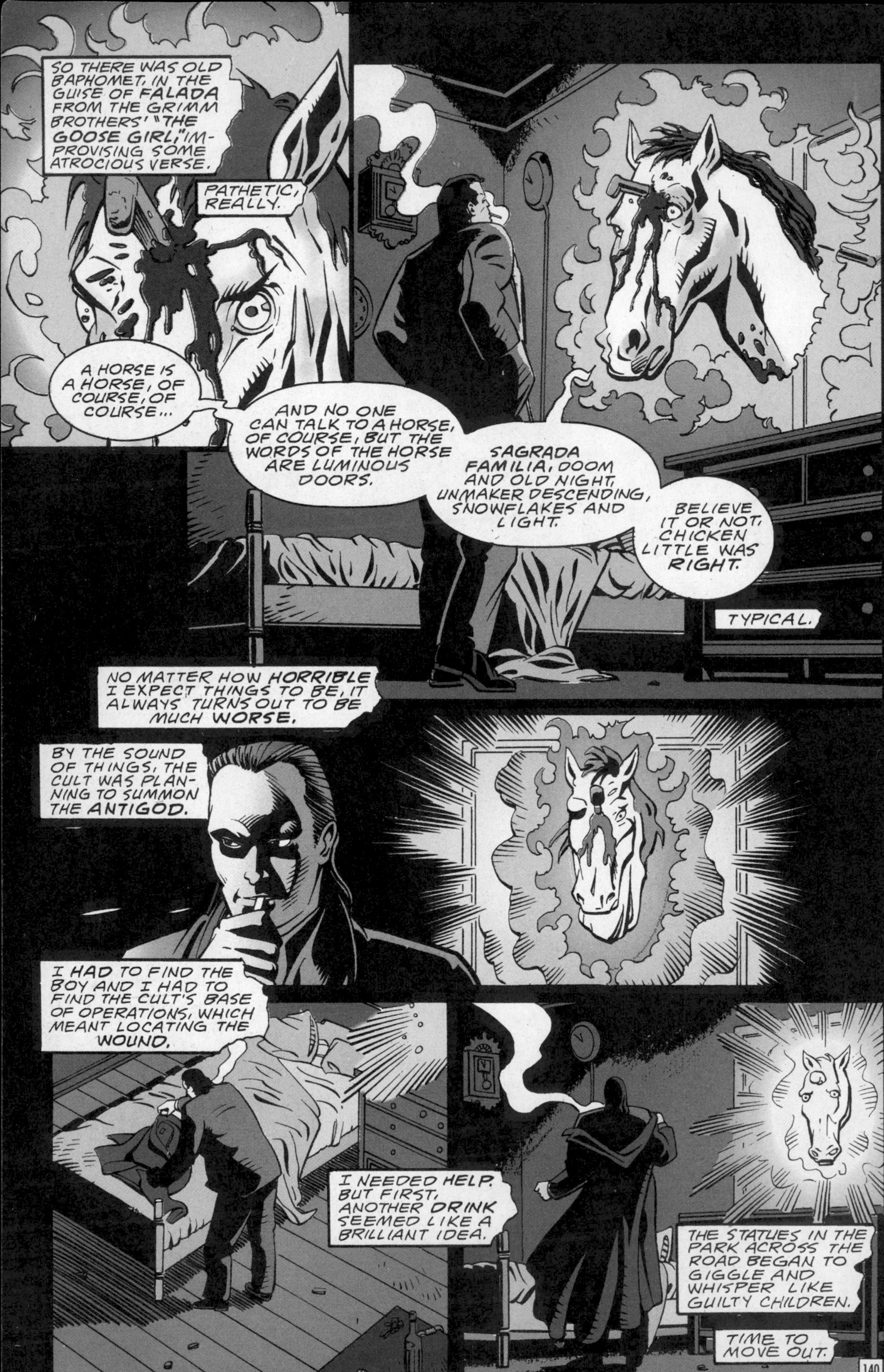

SO THERE WAS OLD BAPHOMET, IN THE GUISE OF FALADA FROM THE GRIMM BROTHERS' "THE GOOSE GIRL," IMPROVISING SOME ATROCIOUS VERSE.
PATHETIC, REALLY.
A HORSE IS A HORSE, OF COURSE, OF COURSE...
AND NO ONE CAN TALK TO A HORSE, OF COURSE, BUT THE WORDS OF THE HORSE ARE LUMINOUS DOORS.
SAGRADA FAMILIA, DOOM AND OLD NIGHT, UNMAKER DESCENDING, SNOWFLAKES AND LIGHT.
BELIEVE IT OR NOT, CHICKEN LITTLE WAS RIGHT.
TYPICAL.
NO MATTER HOW HORRIBLE I EXPECT THINGS TO BE, IT ALWAYS TURNS OUT TO BE MUCH WORSE.
BY THE SOUND OF THINGS, THE CULT WAS PLANNING TO SUMMON THE ANTIGOD.
I HAD TO FIND THE BOY AND I HAD TO FIND THE CULT'S BASE OF OPERATIONS, WHICH MEANT LOCATING THE WOUND.
I NEEDED HELP. BUT FIRST, ANOTHER DRINK SEEMED LIKE A BRILLIANT IDEA.
THE STATUES IN THE PARK ACROSS THE ROAD BEGAN TO GIGGLE AND WHISPER LIKE GUILTY CHILDREN.
TIME TO MOVE OUT.

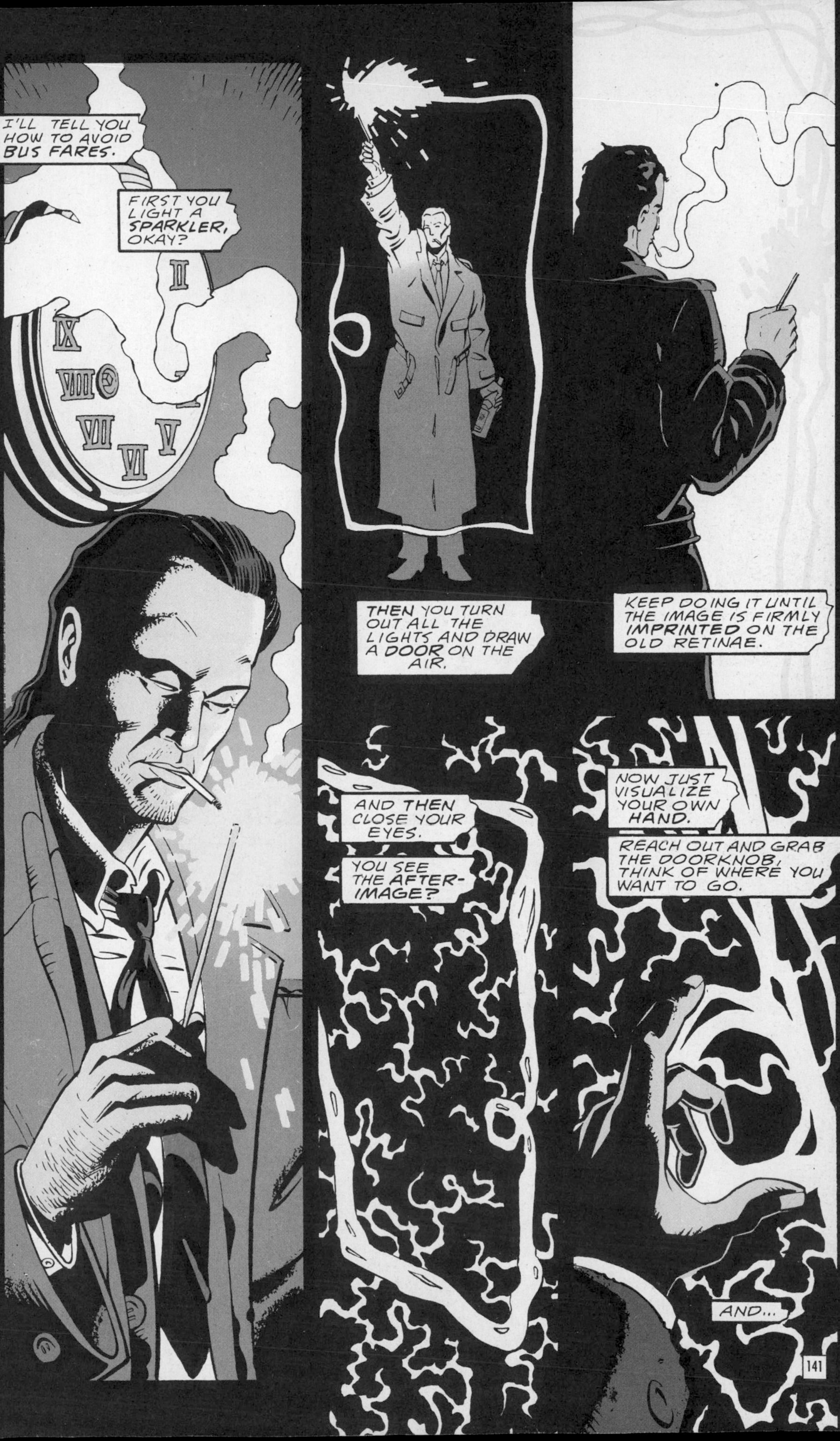
I'LL TELL YOU HOW TO AVOID BUS FARES.
FIRST YOU LIGHT A SPARKLER, OKAY?
THEN YOU TURN OUT ALL THE LIGHTS AND DRAW A DOOR ON THE AIR.
KEEP DOING IT UNTIL THE IMAGE IS FIRMLY IMPRINTED ON THE OLD RETINAE.
AND THEN CLOSE YOUR EYES.
YOU SEE THE AFTER-IMAGE?
NOW JUST VISUALIZE YOUR OWN HAND.
REACH OUT AND GRAB THE DOORKNOB, THINK OF WHERE YOU WANT TO GO.
AND...

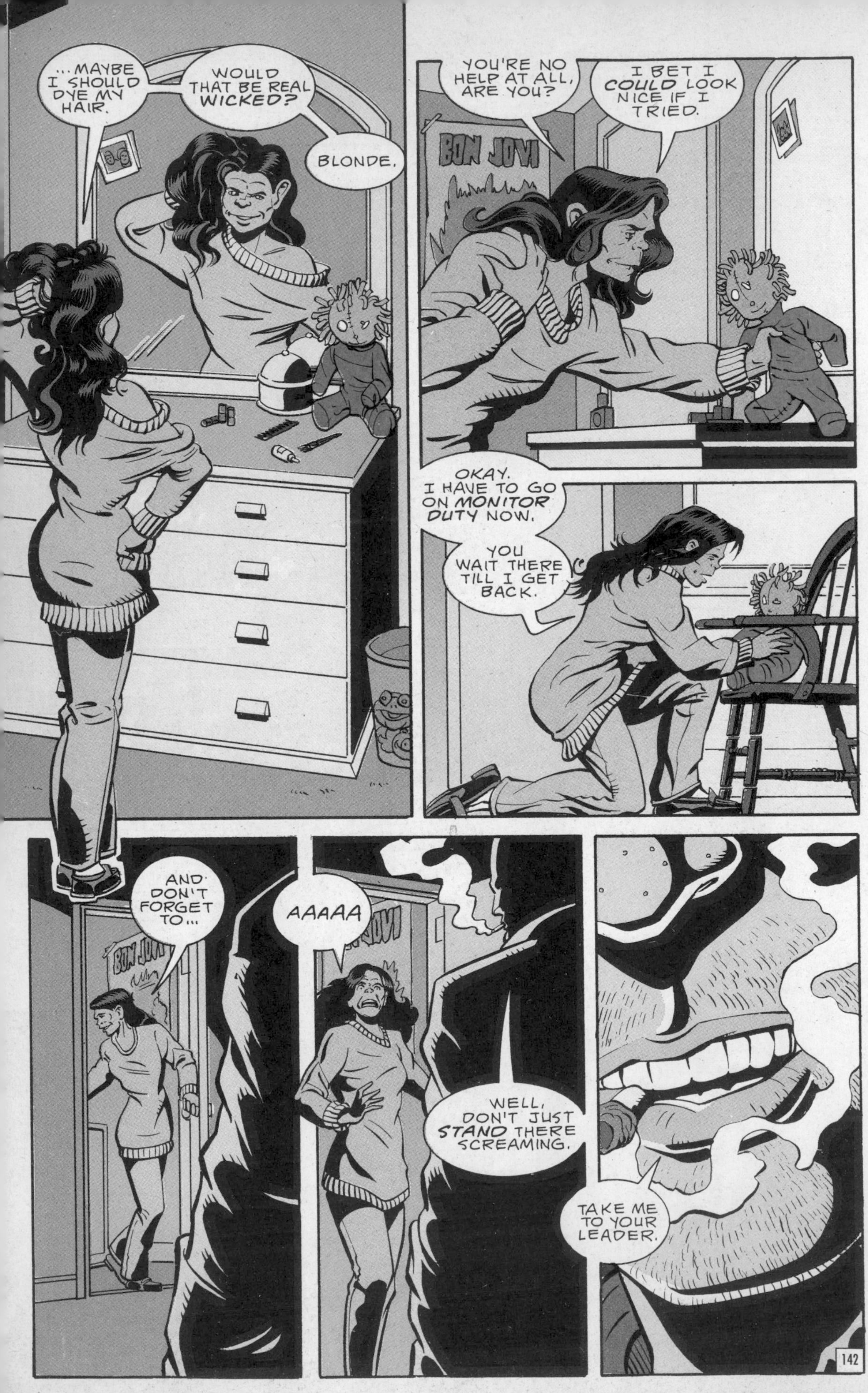
...MAYBE I SHOULD DYE MY HAIR.
WOULD THAT BE REAL WICKED?
BLONDE.
YOU'RE NO HELP AT ALL, ARE YOU?
I BET I COULD LOOK NICE IF I TRIED.
BON JOVI
OKAY. I HAVE TO GO ON MONITOR DUTY NOW.
YOU WAIT THERE TILL I GET BACK.
AND DON'T FORGET TO...
BON JOVI
AAAAA
WELL, DON'T JUST STAND THERE SCREAMING.
TAKE ME TO YOUR LEADER.

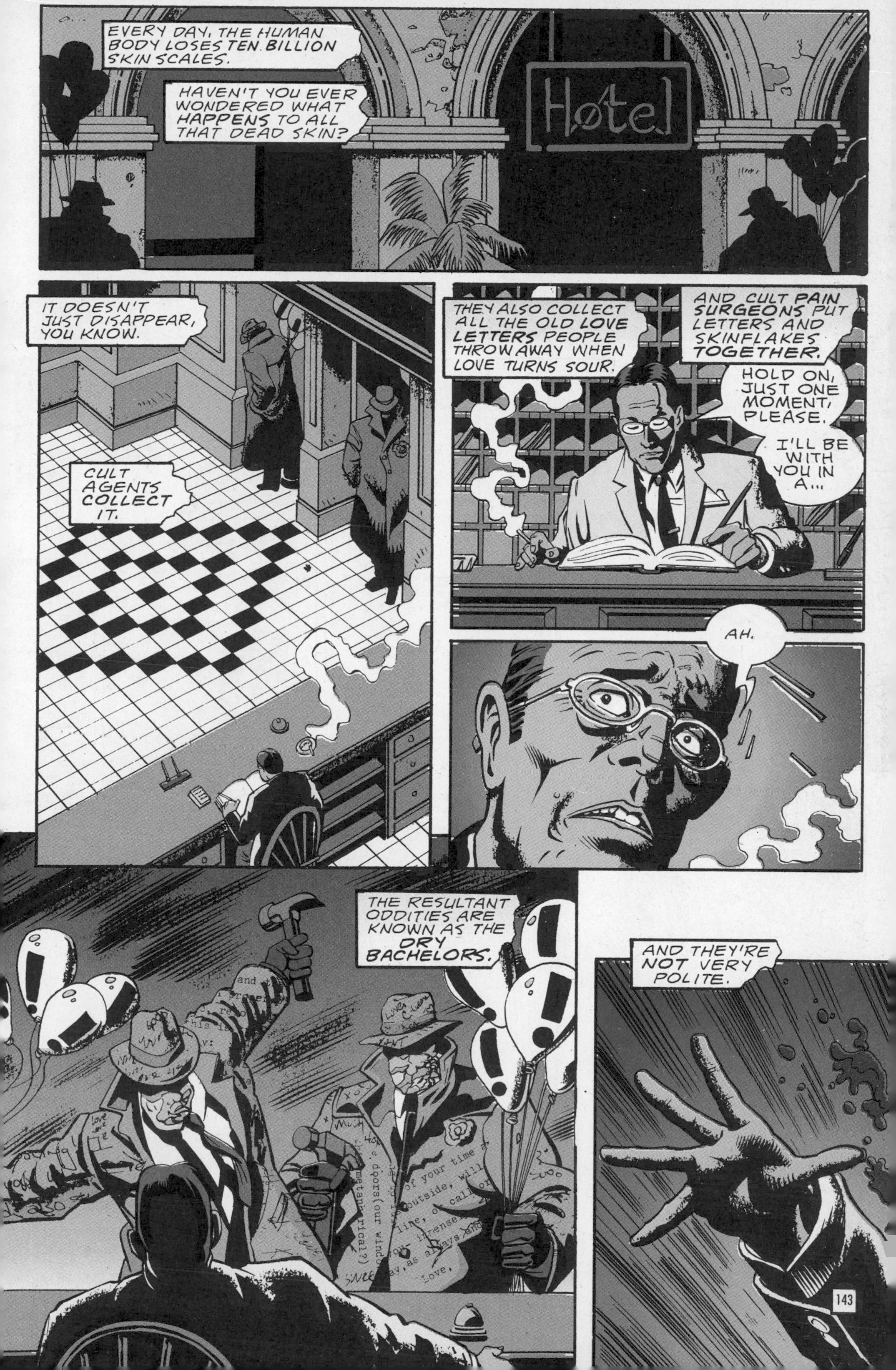
EVERY DAY, THE HUMAN BODY LOSES TEN BILLION SKIN SCALES.
HAVEN'T YOU EVER WONDERED WHAT HAPPENS TO ALL THAT DEAD SKIN?
Hotel
IT DOESN'T JUST DISAPPEAR, YOU KNOW.
CULT AGENTS COLLECT IT.
THEY ALSO COLLECT ALL THE OLD LOVE LETTERS PEOPLE THROW AWAY WHEN LOVE TURNS SOUR.
AND CULT PAIN SURGEONS PUT LETTERS AND SKINFLAKES TOGETHER.
HOLD ON, JUST ONE MOMENT, PLEASE.
I'LL BE WITH YOU IN A...
AH.
THE RESULTANT ODDITIES ARE KNOWN AS THE DRY BACHELORS.
AND THEY'RE NOT VERY POLITE.

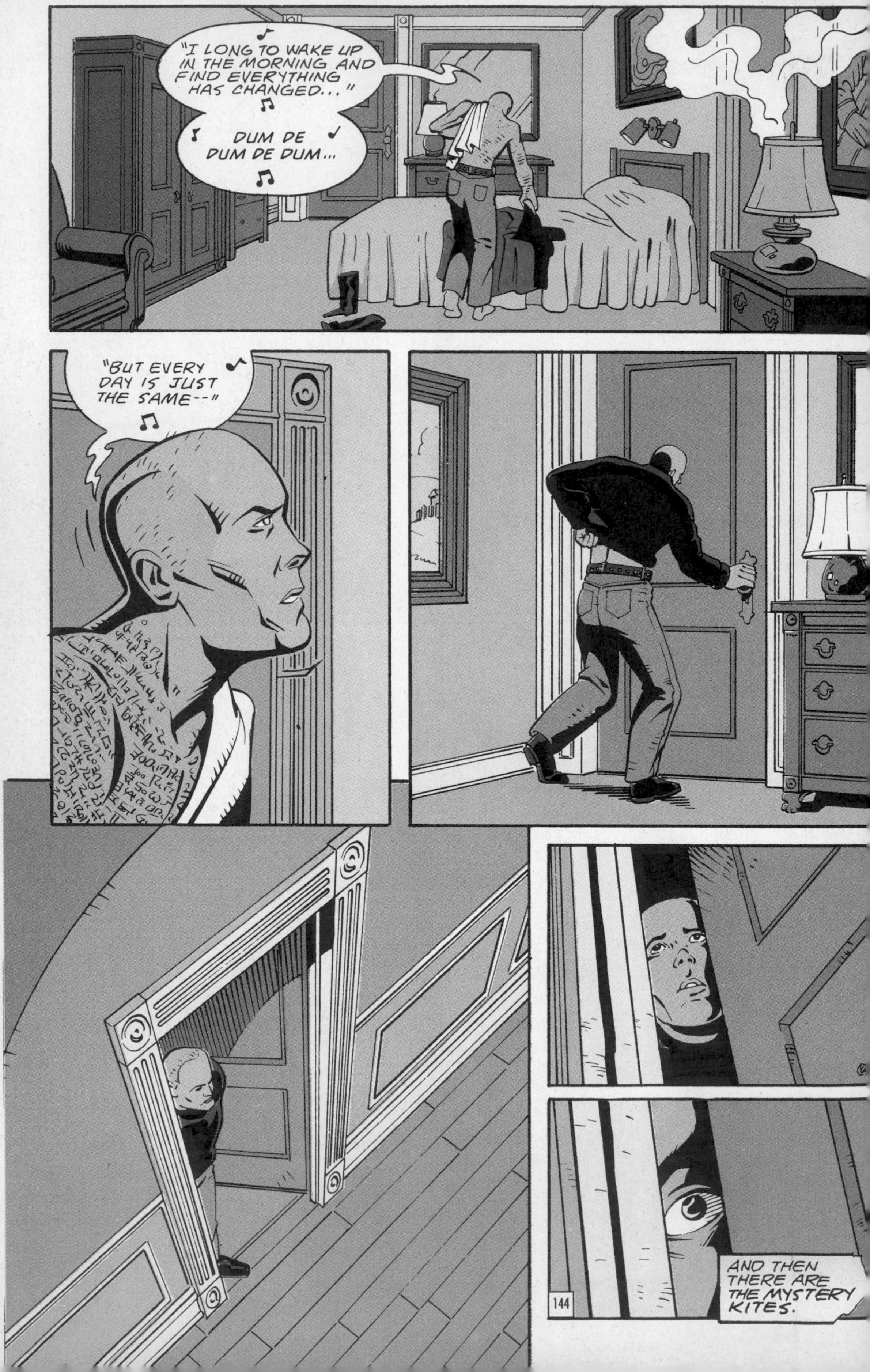
"I LONG TO WAKE UP IN THE MORNING AND FIND EVERYTHING HAS CHANGED..."
DUM DE DUM DE DUM...
"BUT EVERY DAY IS JUST THE SAME--"
AND THEN THERE ARE THE MYSTERY KITES.

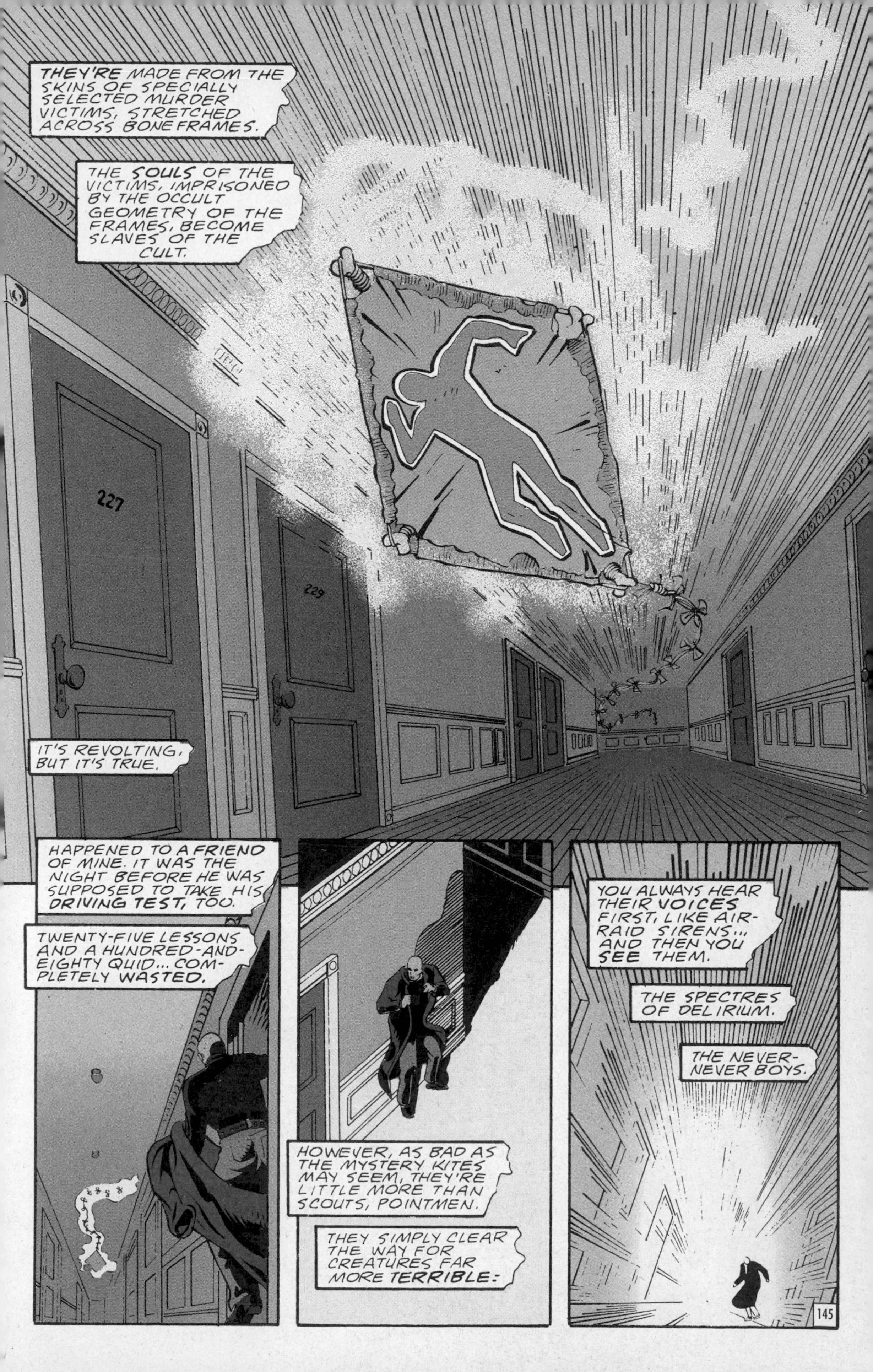
THEY'RE MADE FROM THE SKINS OF SPECIALLY SELECTED MURDER VICTIMS, STRETCHED ACROSS BONE FRAMES.
THE SOULS OF THE VICTIMS, IMPRISONED BY THE OCCULT GEOMETRY OF THE FRAMES, BECOME SLAVES OF THE CULT.
227
229
IT'S REVOLTING, BUT IT'S TRUE.
HAPPENED TO A FRIEND OF MINE. IT WAS THE NIGHT BEFORE HE WAS SUPPOSED TO TAKE HIS DRIVING TEST, TOO.
TWENTY-FIVE LESSONS AND A HUNDRED-AND-EIGHTY QUID... COMPLETELY WASTED.
HOWEVER, AS BAD AS THE MYSTERY KITES MAY SEEM, THEY'RE LITTLE MORE THAN SCOUTS, POINTMEN.
THEY SIMPLY CLEAR THE WAY FOR CREATURES FAR MORE TERRIBLE:
YOU ALWAYS HEAR THEIR VOICES FIRST, LIKE AIR-RAID SIRENS... AND THEN YOU SEE THEM.
THE SPECTRES OF DELIRIUM.
THE NEVER-NEVER BOYS.

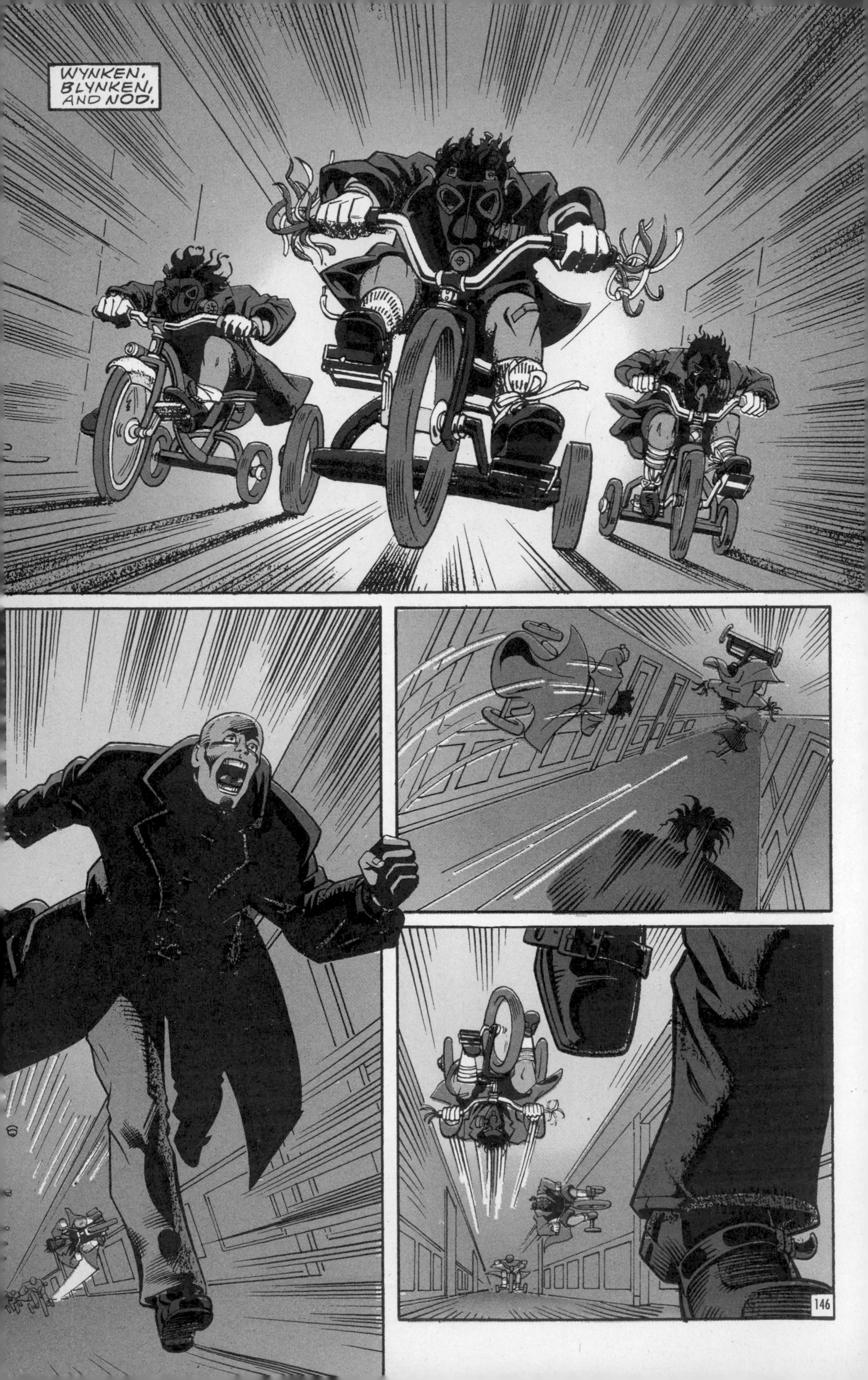
WYNKEN, BLYNKEN, AND NOD.

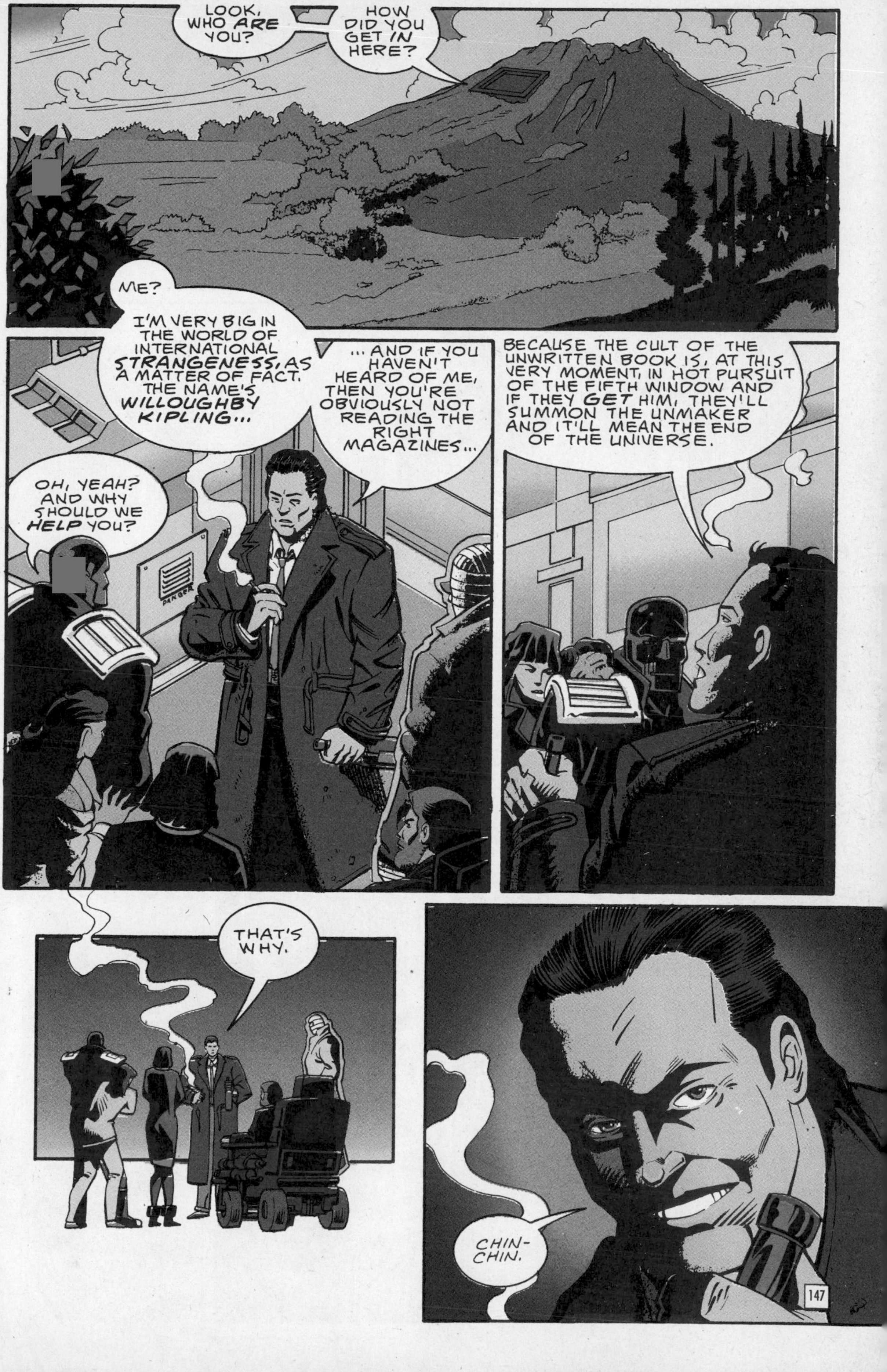
LOOK, WHO ARE YOU?
HOW DID YOU GET IN HERE?
ME?
I'M VERY BIG IN THE WORLD OF INTERNATIONAL STRANGENESS, AS A MATTER OF FACT. THE NAME'S WILLOUGHBY KIPLING...
...AND IF YOU HAVEN'T HEARD OF ME, THEN YOU'RE OBVIOUSLY NOT READING THE RIGHT MAGAZINES...
OH, YEAH? AND WHY SHOULD WE HELP YOU?
DANGER
BECAUSE THE CULT OF THE UNWRITTEN BOOK IS, AT THIS VERY MOMENT, IN HOT PURSUIT OF THE FIFTH WINDOW AND IF THEY GET HIM, THEY'LL SUMMON THE UNMAKER AND IT'LL MEAN THE END OF THE UNIVERSE.
THAT'S WHY.
CHIN-CHIN.

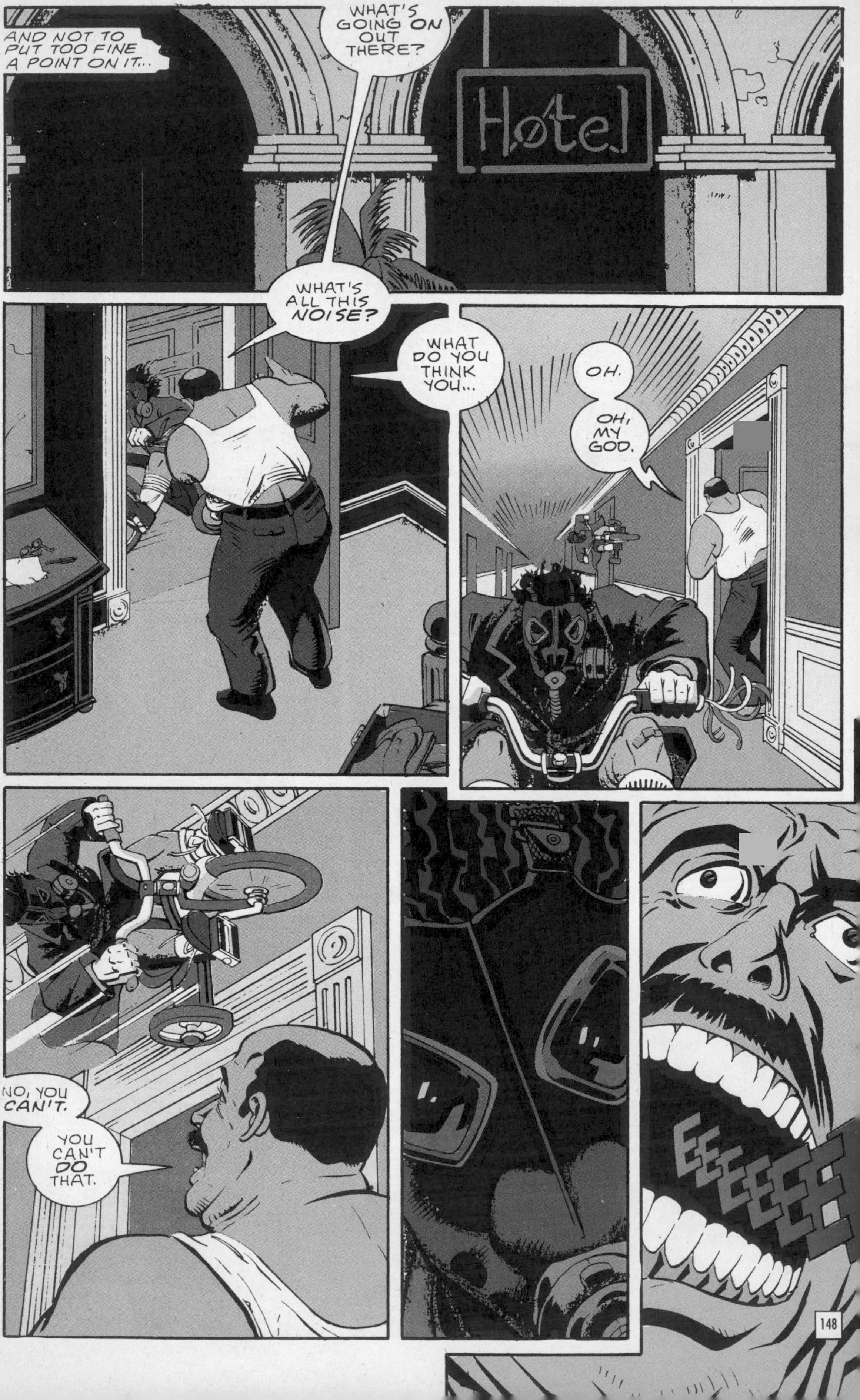
AND NOT TO PUT TOO FINE A POINT ON IT...
WHAT'S GOING ON OUT THERE?
Hotel
WHAT'S ALL THIS NOISE?
WHAT DO YOU THINK YOU...
OH.
OH, MY GOD.
NO, YOU CAN'T.
YOU CAN'T DO THAT.
EEEEEE

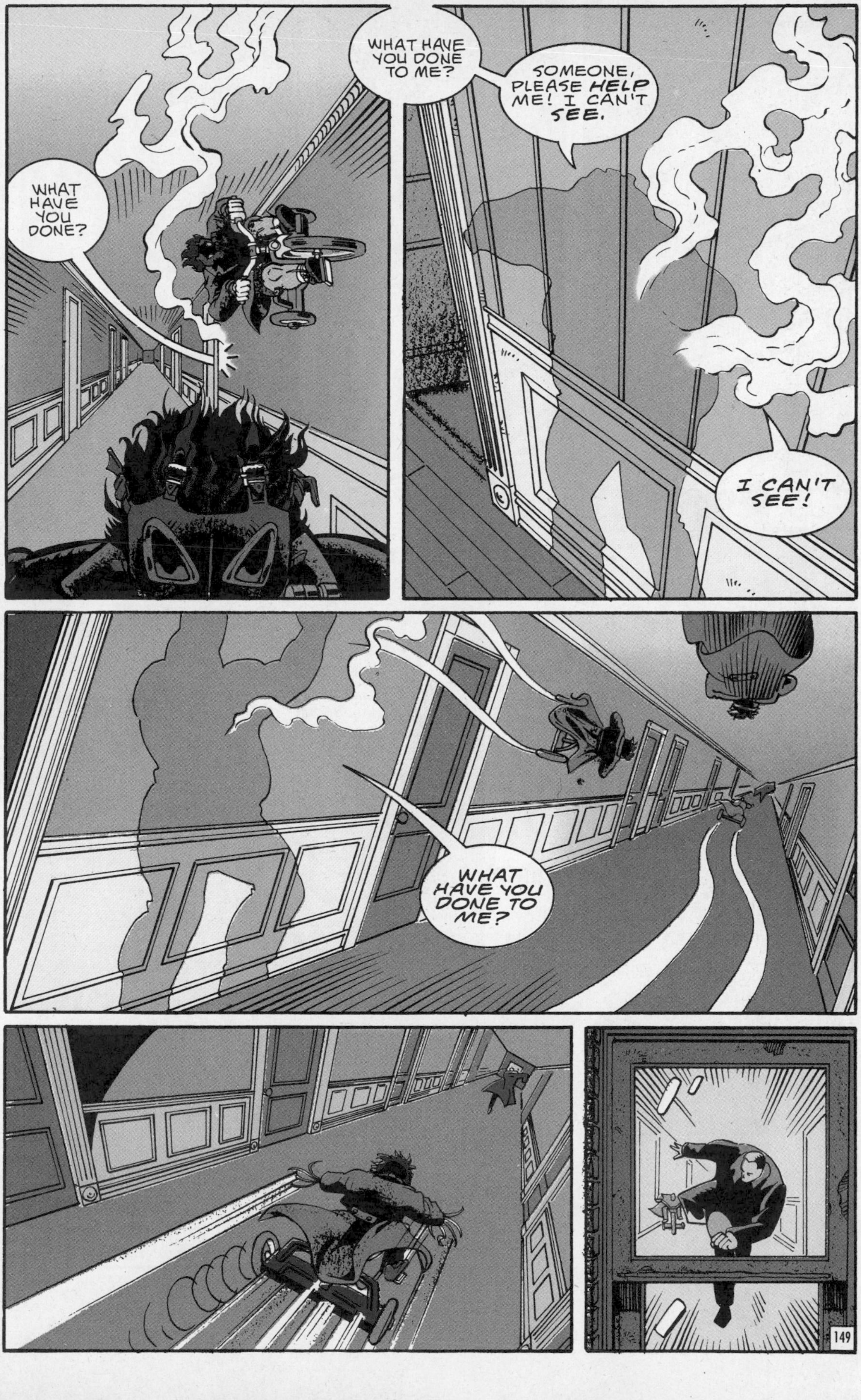
WHAT HAVE YOU DONE?
WHAT HAVE YOU DONE TO ME?
SOMEONE, PLEASE HELP ME! I CAN'T SEE.
I CAN'T SEE!
WHAT HAVE YOU DONE TO ME?

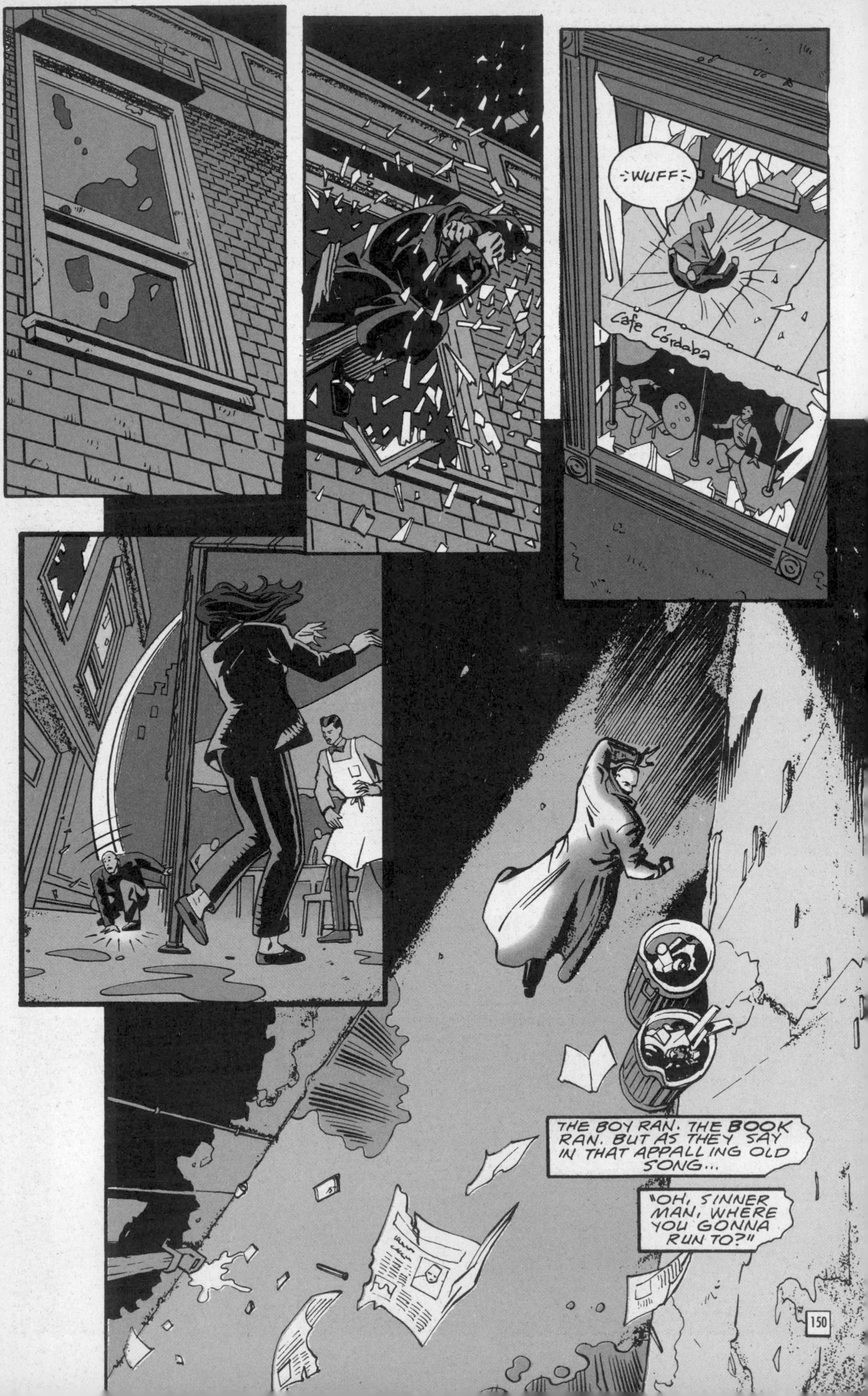
WUFF
Cafe Córdaba
THE BOY RAN. THE BOOK RAN. BUT AS THEY SAY IN THAT APPALLING OLD SONG...
"OH, SINNER MAN, WHERE YOU GONNA RUN TO?"

THE CULT HAD MOBILIZED ITS FORCES AND *BARCELONA* WAS ABOUT TO SUFFER AN OUTBREAK OF CURIOUS PHENOMENA.

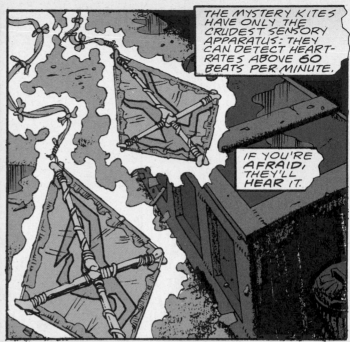

THE MYSTERY KITES HAVE ONLY THE CRUDEST SENSORY APPARATUS: THEY CAN DETECT HEART-RATES ABOVE *60* BEATS PER MINUTE.

IF YOU'RE AFRAID, THEY'LL *HEAR* IT.

THE BOY HAD PROBABLY BEEN TAUGHT SOME TECH-NIQUES FOR CONTROLLING THE *RETICULAR ACTIVATING SYSTEM* AND SLOWING DOWN HIS HEARTRATE.

WELL... THAT'S MY THEORY, ANYWAY.

ONE THING'S FOR SURE... IT TURNED INTO A *HIGHLY UNUSUAL* NIGHT.

THE CREAKING OF TRICYCLE WHEELS, THE SCRAPE OF *RAZORS* ON WALLS.

THE HORRIBLE SINGING OF THE UNHOLY GHOST.

FOR ONE NIGHT, AND ONE NIGHT *ALONE*, BARCELONA WAS OFFERED A GLIMPSE OF THE WORLD-TO-COME.

151

EMILIO CUERVO BECAME CONCERNED ABOUT THE CUT ON HIS HAND.

A BUS, FULL OF TEENAGERS, WAS POSSESSED BY THE UNQUIET FACE AND DRIVEN THROUGH THE CORRIDOR OF HALLUCINATION.

THE NEEDLE CHILDREN, WHO CANNOT BE SEEN THROUGH GLASS, LAID POINTLESS SIEGE TO AN OLD FOLKS' HOME IN THE SUBURBS.

AT 11:30, THERE WAS AN OUTBREAK OF SPIRIT SKYWRITING WHICH CONTINUED FOR AN HOUR AND A HALF.

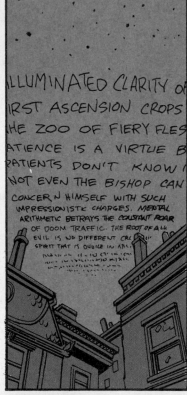

ILLUMINATED CLARITY OF FIRST ASCENSION CROPS THE ZOO OF FIERY FLES PATIENCE IS A VIRTUE B PATIENTS DON'T KNOW I NOT EVEN THE BISHOP CAN CONCERN HIMSELF WITH SUCH IMPRESSIONISTIC CHARGES. MENTAL ARITHMETIC BETRAYS THE CONSTANT ROAR OF DOOM TRAFFIC. THE ROOT OF ALL EVIL IS NO DIFFERENT CR SPIRIT THAT IS OUUILE IN AR

AT MIDNIGHT, THE WORD "HARMONY" DISAPPEARED FROM THE VOCABULARY OF EVERYONE IN THE CITY,

AND THE BOY KEPT RUNNING.

AT 12:30, THE EMBRYO STAINS INVADED THE MARROW OF A NIGHT-CLUB OWNER AND FORCED HIM TO COMPOSE TERRIFYING POETRY.

AND EVERYTHING BLUE BECAME BRIEFLY INVISIBLE,

AND THE RAIN FORGOT HOW TO FALL.

AND STRONG MEN WEPT.

AND THE BOY KEPT RUNNING.

AND....

152

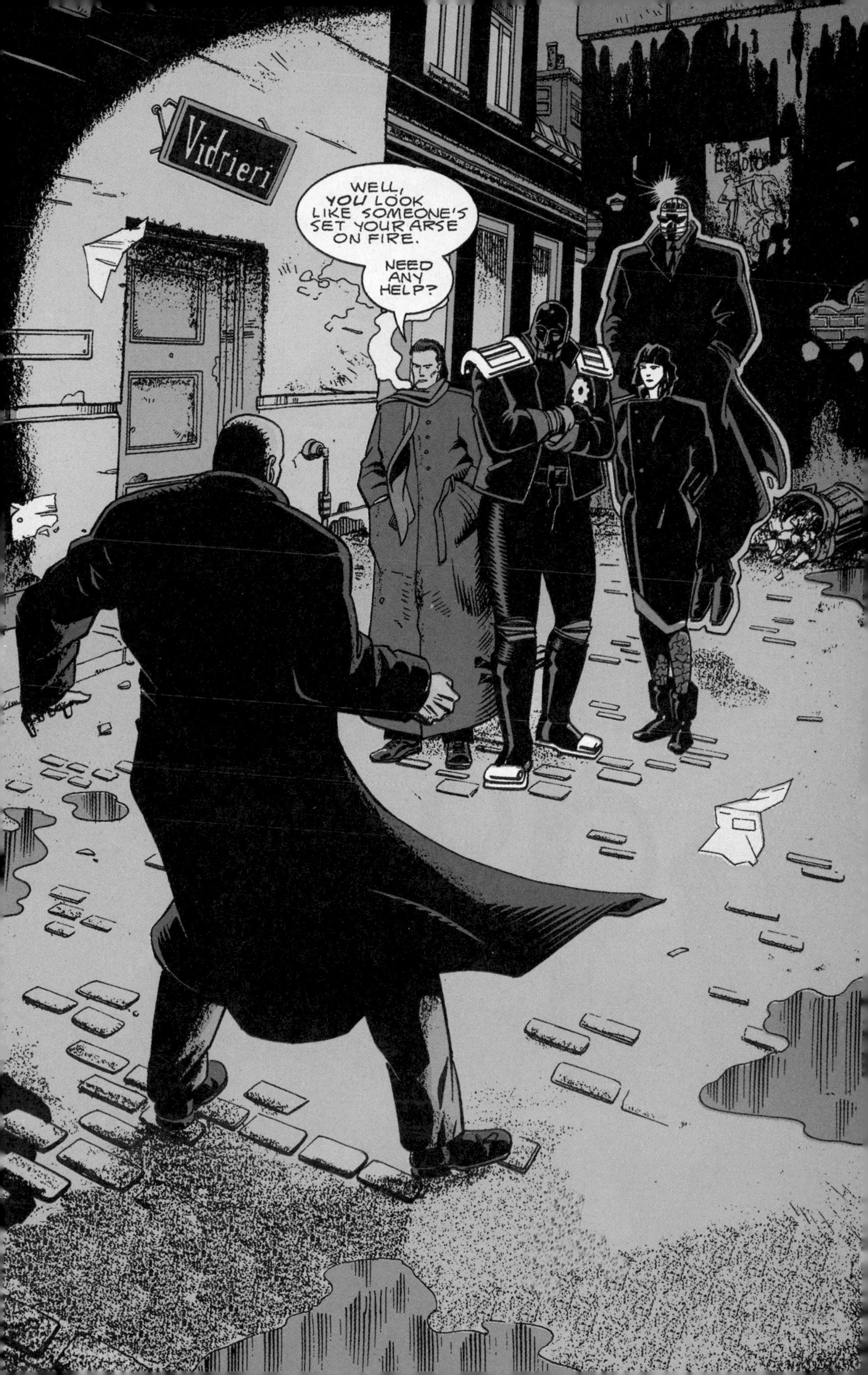
Vidrieri
WELL, YOU LOOK LIKE SOMEONE'S SET YOUR ARSE ON FIRE.
NEED ANY HELP?

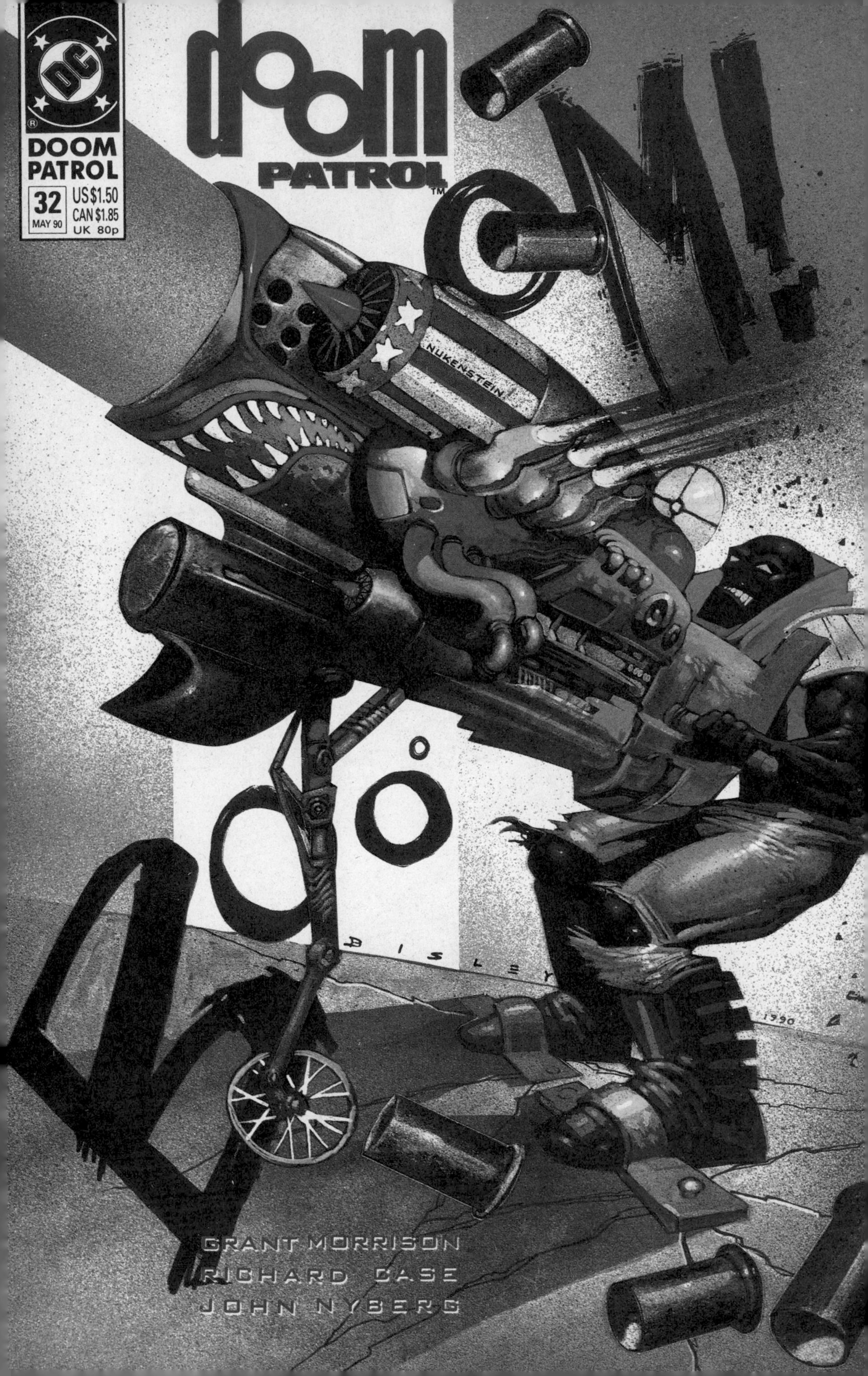
DC
doom PATROL
DOOM PATROL
32
MAY 90
US$1.50
CAN $1.85
UK 80p
NUKENSTEIN
BISLEY
1990
GRANT MORRISON
RICHARD CASE
JOHN NYBERG

AS I'VE EXPLAINED ALREADY, THE **CULT OF THE UNWRITTEN BOOK** HAS A NUMBER OF **SUBDIVISIONS.**

ONE SUCH SUBDIVISION IS THE **PALE POLICE.**

THE PALE POLICE ARE **ASSASSINS:** UGLY BUGGERS WITH **B.O.** AND ABSOLUTELY NO SENSE OF HUMOR.

WHAT THEY DO IS STUDY THE **THUMBPRINT** OF THEIR INTENDED VICTIM, MEDITATING ON ITS WHORLS AND CURVES FOR SEVEN DAYS.

AND THEN THEY RITUALLY **DRAW** THE PRINT ON THEIR HELMETS FROM MEMORY.

THE HELMET IS SACRED; USED ONLY ONCE AND THEN DESTROYED WITH THE VICTIM'S BODY. THIS, THEY BELIEVE, TRAPS THE VICTIM'S SOUL IN THE MAZE OF HIS OWN THUMBPRINT.

ONE CURIOUS AND LITTLE-KNOWN FACT ABOUT THE PALE POLICE IS THAT THEY CAN ONLY TALK IN ANAGRAMS.

LISTENING TO A CONVERSATION BE-TWEEN TWO OF THEM IS LIKE TRY-ING TO DO THE "TIMES" CROSSWORD.

NOT THAT YOU'D EVER CATCH ME READING THE BLOODY **"TIMES."**

IF YOU WANT REAL NEWS ABOUT THE REAL WORLD, MY ADVICE IS TO PICK UP THE **SUNDAY SPORT** OR THE **NATIONAL ENQUIRER.**

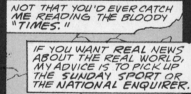

HOWEVER, I DIGRESS.

THE COMPLINE BELL IS RINGING, SOUNDING THE HOURS OF THE LAST DAY OF LIFE ON EARTH.

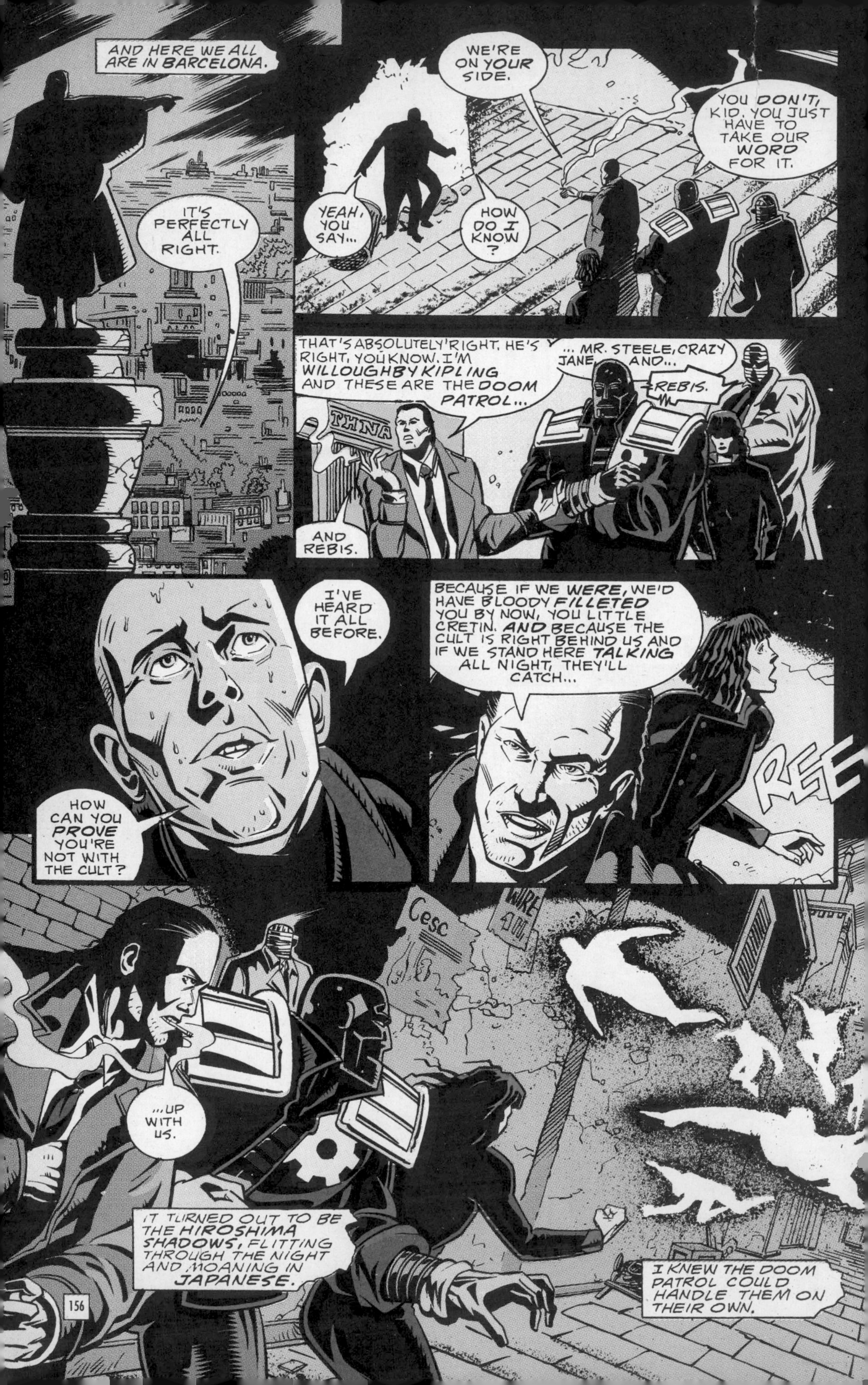
AND HERE WE ALL ARE IN BARCELONA.
IT'S PERFECTLY ALL RIGHT.
WE'RE ON YOUR SIDE.
YEAH, YOU SAY...
HOW DO I KNOW?
YOU DON'T, KID. YOU JUST HAVE TO TAKE OUR WORD FOR IT.
THAT'S ABSOLUTELY RIGHT. HE'S RIGHT, YOU KNOW. I'M WILLOUGHBY KIPLING AND THESE ARE THE DOOM PATROL...
... MR. STEELE, CRAZY JANE AND...
REBIS.
AND REBIS.
I'VE HEARD IT ALL BEFORE.
HOW CAN YOU PROVE YOU'RE NOT WITH THE CULT?
BECAUSE IF WE WERE, WE'D HAVE BLOODY FILLETED YOU BY NOW, YOU LITTLE CRETIN. AND BECAUSE THE CULT IS RIGHT BEHIND US AND IF WE STAND HERE TALKING ALL NIGHT, THEY'LL CATCH...
REEE
...UP WITH US.
IT TURNED OUT TO BE THE HIROSHIMA SHADOWS, FLITTING THROUGH THE NIGHT AND MOANING IN JAPANESE.
I KNEW THE DOOM PATROL COULD HANDLE THEM ON THEIR OWN.

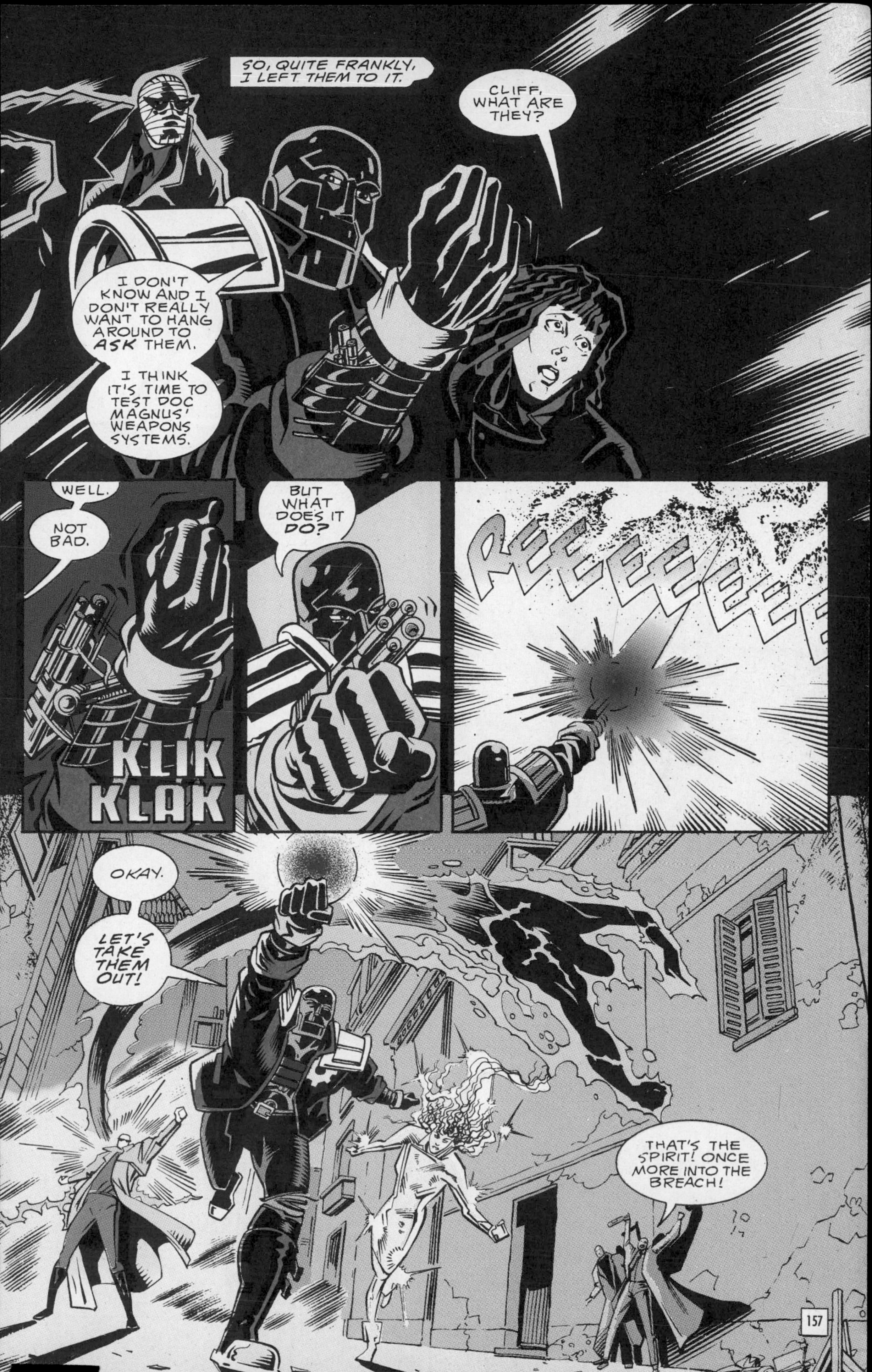

SO, QUITE FRANKLY, I LEFT THEM TO IT.
CLIFF, WHAT ARE THEY?
I DON'T KNOW AND I DON'T REALLY WANT TO HANG AROUND TO *ASK* THEM.
I THINK IT'S TIME TO TEST DOC MAGNUS' WEAPONS SYSTEMS.
WELL.
NOT BAD.
KLIK KLAK
BUT WHAT DOES IT *DO*?
REEEEEEEE
OKAY.
LET'S TAKE THEM OUT!
THAT'S THE SPIRIT! ONCE MORE INTO THE BREACH!

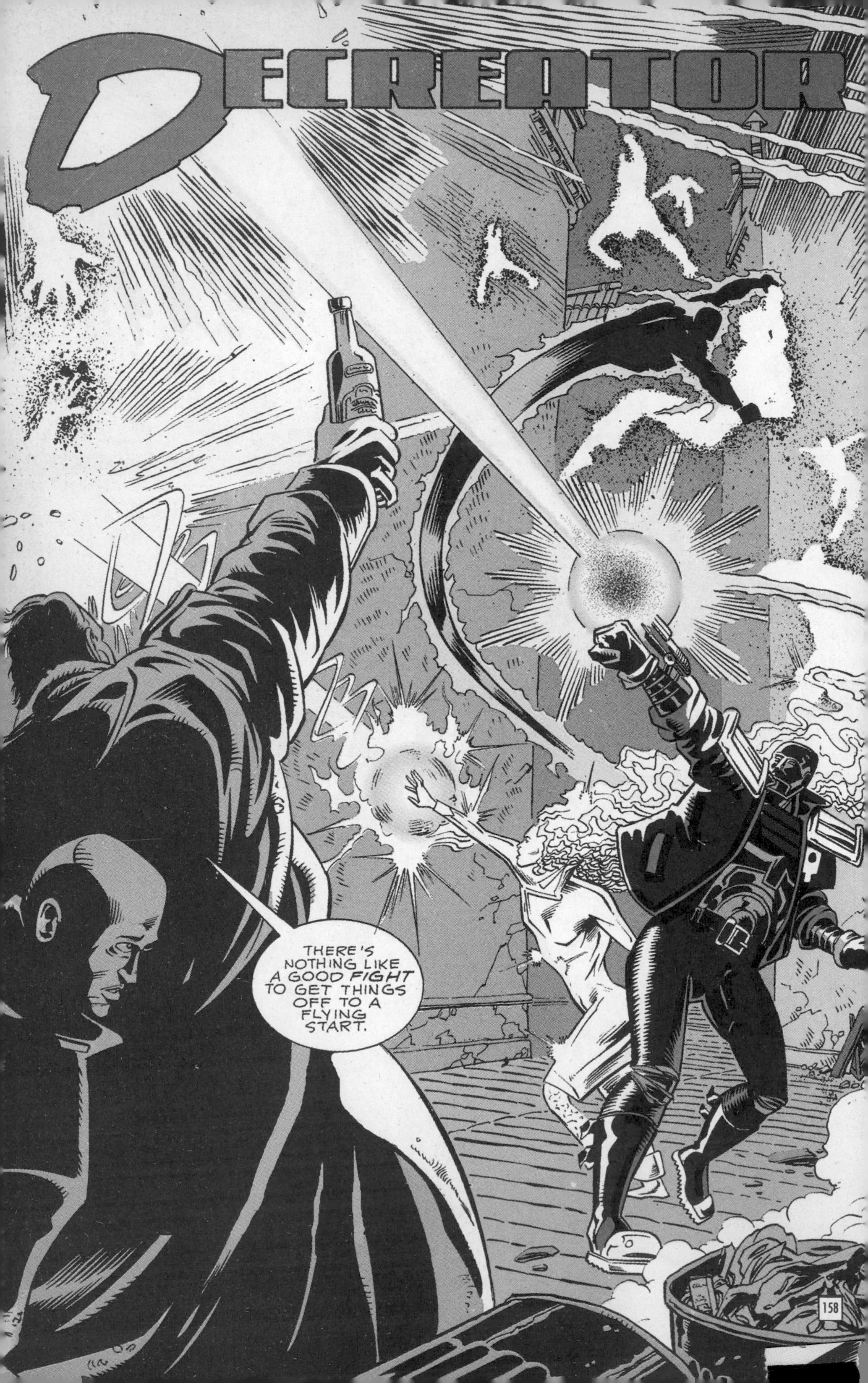
DECREATOR
THERE'S NOTHING LIKE A GOOD *FIGHT* TO GET THINGS OFF TO A FLYING START.

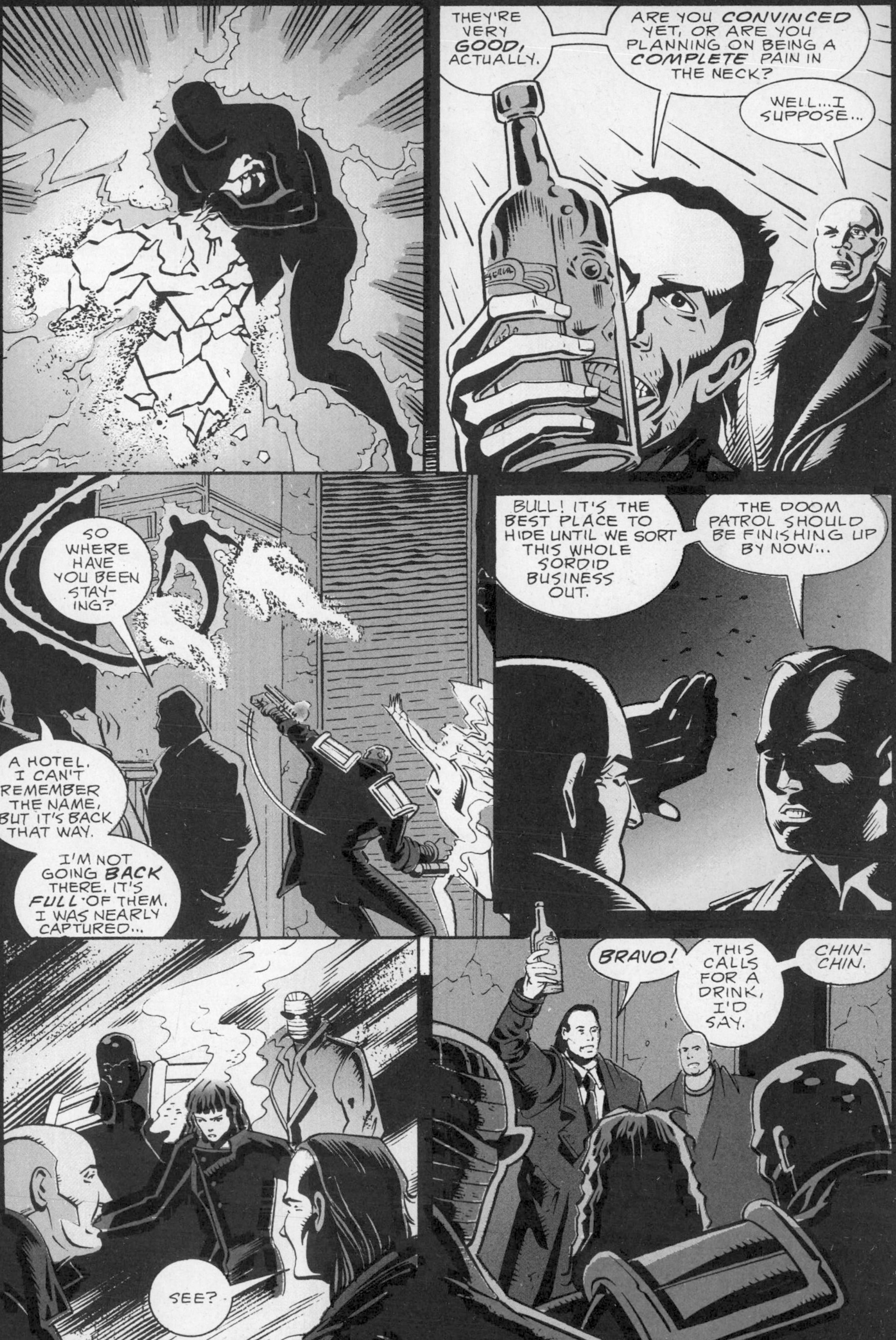
THEY'RE VERY GOOD, ACTUALLY.
ARE YOU CONVINCED YET, OR ARE YOU PLANNING ON BEING A COMPLETE PAIN IN THE NECK?
WELL...I SUPPOSE...
SO WHERE HAVE YOU BEEN STAY-ING?
A HOTEL. I CAN'T REMEMBER THE NAME, BUT IT'S BACK THAT WAY.
I'M NOT GOING BACK THERE. IT'S FULL OF THEM. I WAS NEARLY CAPTURED...
BULL! IT'S THE BEST PLACE TO HIDE UNTIL WE SORT THIS WHOLE SORDID BUSINESS OUT.
THE DOOM PATROL SHOULD BE FINISHING UP BY NOW...
SEE?
BRAVO!
THIS CALLS FOR A DRINK, I'D SAY.
CHIN-CHIN.

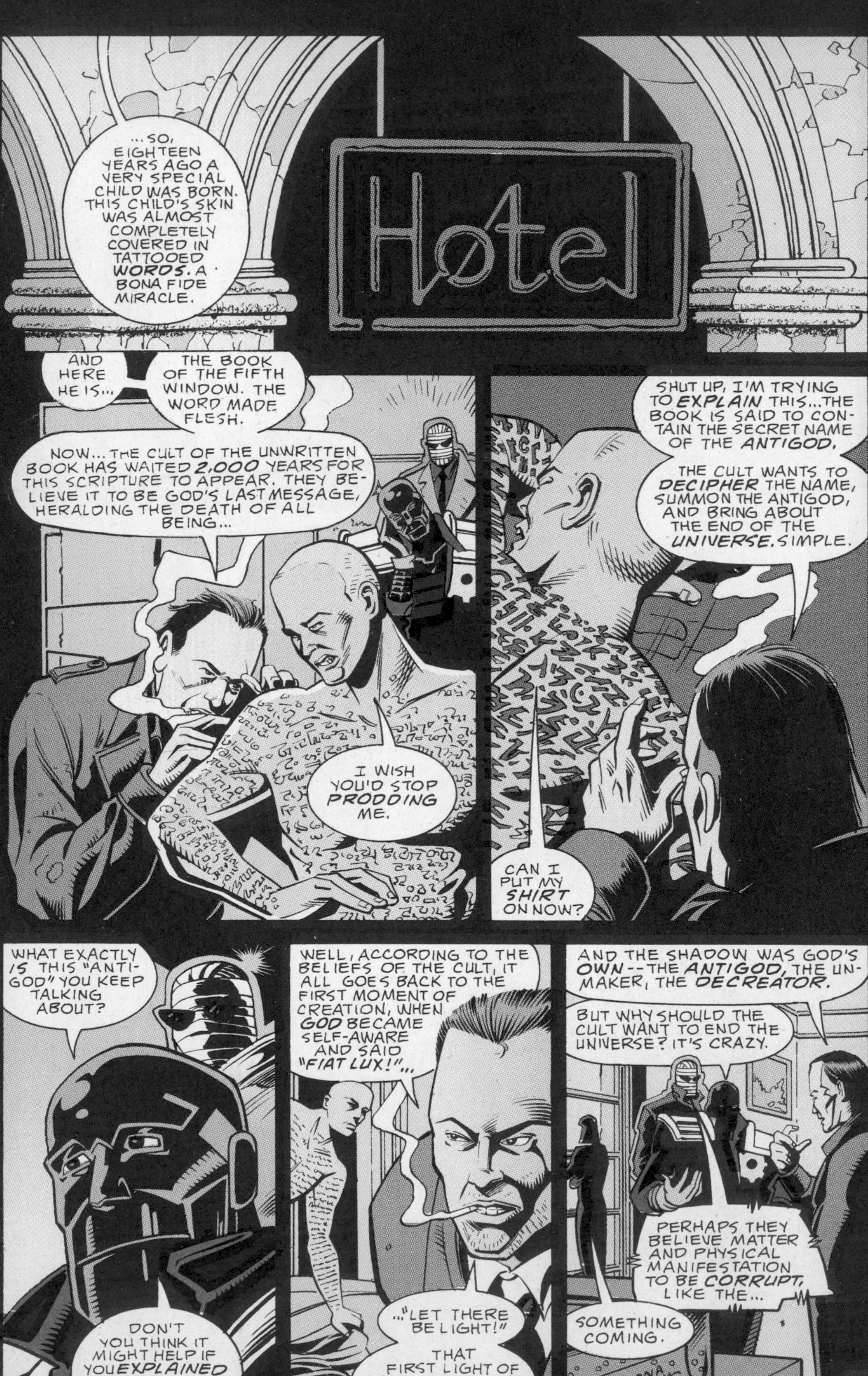
...SO, EIGHTEEN YEARS AGO A VERY SPECIAL CHILD WAS BORN. THIS CHILD'S SKIN WAS ALMOST COMPLETELY COVERED IN TATTOOED WORDS. A BONA FIDE MIRACLE.
Hotel
AND HERE HE IS...
THE BOOK OF THE FIFTH WINDOW. THE WORD MADE FLESH.
NOW... THE CULT OF THE UNWRITTEN BOOK HAS WAITED 2,000 YEARS FOR THIS SCRIPTURE TO APPEAR. THEY BELIEVE IT TO BE GOD'S LAST MESSAGE, HERALDING THE DEATH OF ALL BEING...
I WISH YOU'D STOP PRODDING ME.
SHUT UP, I'M TRYING TO EXPLAIN THIS... THE BOOK IS SAID TO CONTAIN THE SECRET NAME OF THE ANTIGOD.
THE CULT WANTS TO DECIPHER THE NAME, SUMMON THE ANTIGOD, AND BRING ABOUT THE END OF THE UNIVERSE. SIMPLE.
CAN I PUT MY SHIRT ON NOW?
WHAT EXACTLY IS THIS "ANTI-GOD" YOU KEEP TALKING ABOUT?
DON'T YOU THINK IT MIGHT HELP IF YOU EXPLAINED SOME OF THIS STUFF TO US?
WELL, ACCORDING TO THE BELIEFS OF THE CULT, IT ALL GOES BACK TO THE FIRST MOMENT OF CREATION, WHEN GOD BECAME SELF-AWARE AND SAID "FIAT LUX!"...
..."LET THERE BE LIGHT!"
THAT FIRST LIGHT OF CREATION CAST THE FIRST SHADOW.
AND THE SHADOW WAS GOD'S OWN -- THE ANTIGOD, THE UNMAKER, THE DECREATOR.
BUT WHY SHOULD THE CULT WANT TO END THE UNIVERSE? IT'S CRAZY.
PERHAPS THEY BELIEVE MATTER AND PHYSICAL MANIFESTATION TO BE CORRUPT, LIKE THE...
SOMETHING COMING.
BARCELONA

THERE'S SOMETHING COMING DOWN THE STREET...

OH, IT'S...

GET AWAY FROM THE WINDOW!

GET AWAY! DON'T LET IT *SEE* YOU!

WHAT *IS* IT? WHAT *IS* IT?

THE SHROUD ON STILTS. ONE OF THE MINOR GROTESQUES.

IT'S OKAY... IT'S GOING PAST.

THESE THINGS ARE GOING TO KEEP COMING THROUGH UNTIL WE LOCATE AND SEAL THE WOUND. OR HADN'T YOU NOTICED?

SO LET'S HOPE MY *HOLY POP* HAS DONE THE TRICK...

HOLY *WHAT*?

POP. 7-UP THAT'S BEEN BLESSED BY A DEFROCKED PRIEST.

I'VE HAD THESE TELEPHONE DIRECTORIES *STEEPING* IN THE STUFF SINCE WE GOT HERE.

IT'S ONE OF MY LITTLE *TECHNIQUES.* THE HOLY POP *ERASES* ALL THE NAMES IN THE DIRECTORY, EXCEPT THE NAME OF THE PERSON BEARING THE WOUND.

I CAN ONLY HOPE THE SOD HAS A *PHONE...*

FLIP FLIP

AH! HERE WE ARE. HIS NAME'S *CUERVO. EMILIO CUERVO.*

CUERVO, EMILIO... 112 B

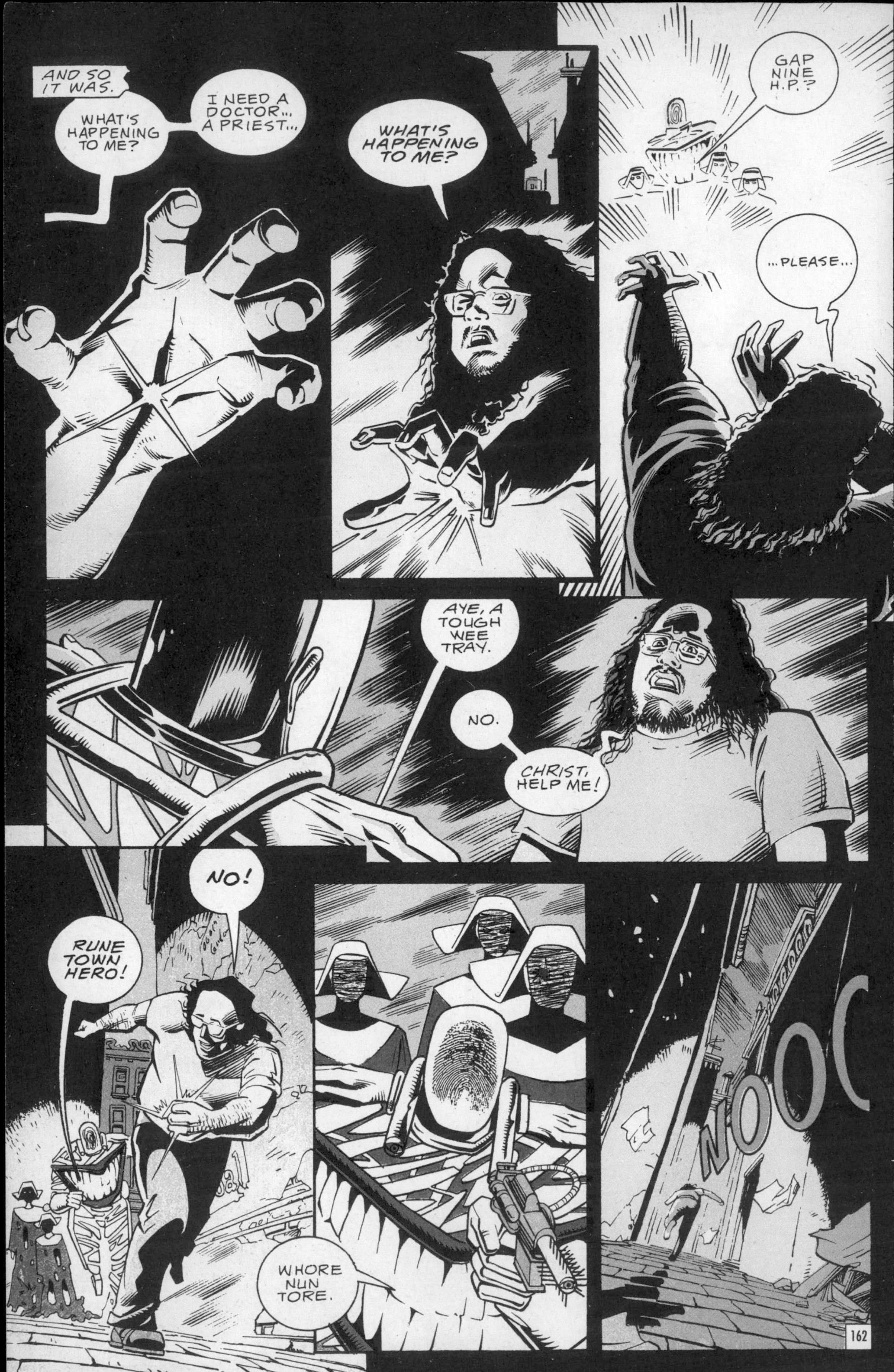
AND SO IT WAS.
WHAT'S HAPPENING TO ME?
I NEED A DOCTOR... A PRIEST...
WHAT'S HAPPENING TO ME?
GAP NINE H.P.?
...PLEASE...
AYE, A TOUGH WEE TRAY.
NO.
CHRIST, HELP ME!
RUNE TOWN HERO!
NO!
WHORE NUN TORE.
NOOO

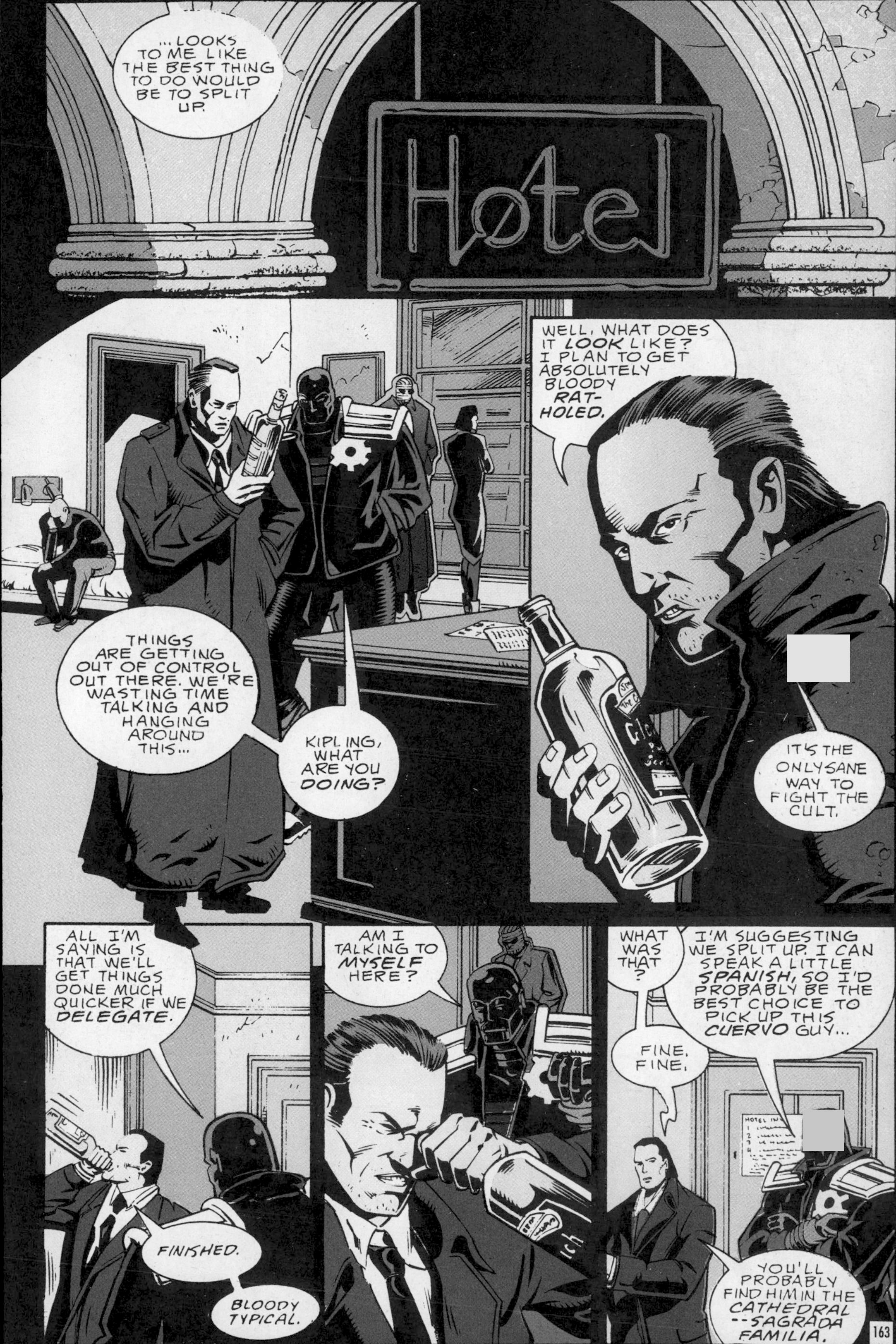

...LOOKS TO ME LIKE THE BEST THING TO DO WOULD BE TO SPLIT UP.
Hotel
THINGS ARE GETTING OUT OF CONTROL OUT THERE. WE'RE WASTING TIME TALKING AND HANGING AROUND THIS...
KIPLING, WHAT ARE YOU DOING?
WELL, WHAT DOES IT LOOK LIKE? I PLAN TO GET ABSOLUTELY BLOODY RAT-HOLED.
IT'S THE ONLY SANE WAY TO FIGHT THE CULT.
ALL I'M SAYING IS THAT WE'LL GET THINGS DONE MUCH QUICKER IF WE DELEGATE.
FINISHED.
BLOODY TYPICAL.
AM I TALKING TO MYSELF HERE?
WHAT WAS THAT?
I'M SUGGESTING WE SPLIT UP. I CAN SPEAK A LITTLE SPANISH, SO I'D PROBABLY BE THE BEST CHOICE TO PICK UP THIS CUERVO GUY...
FINE. FINE.
YOU'LL PROBABLY FIND HIM IN THE CATHEDRAL --SAGRADA FAMILIA.

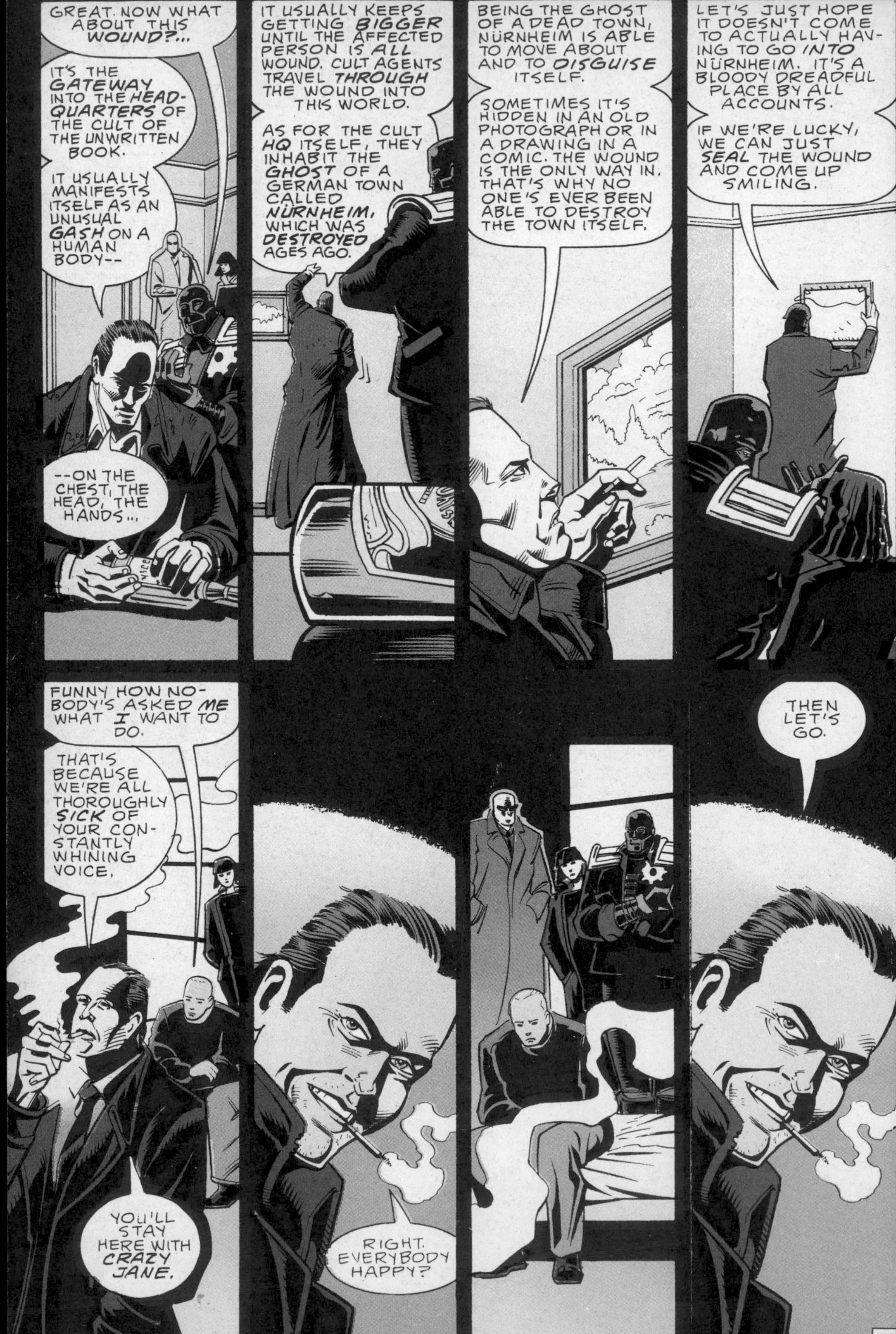

GREAT. NOW WHAT ABOUT THIS WOUND?...
IT'S THE GATEWAY INTO THE HEAD-QUARTERS OF THE CULT OF THE UNWRITTEN BOOK.
IT USUALLY MANIFESTS ITSELF AS AN UNUSUAL GASH ON A HUMAN BODY--
--ON THE CHEST, THE HEAD, THE HANDS...
IT USUALLY KEEPS GETTING BIGGER UNTIL THE AFFECTED PERSON IS ALL WOUND. CULT AGENTS TRAVEL THROUGH THE WOUND INTO THIS WORLD.
AS FOR THE CULT HQ ITSELF, THEY INHABIT THE GHOST OF A GERMAN TOWN CALLED NÜRNHEIM, WHICH WAS DESTROYED AGES AGO.
BEING THE GHOST OF A DEAD TOWN, NÜRNHEIM IS ABLE TO MOVE ABOUT AND TO DISGUISE ITSELF.
SOMETIMES IT'S HIDDEN IN AN OLD PHOTOGRAPH OR IN A DRAWING IN A COMIC. THE WOUND IS THE ONLY WAY IN. THAT'S WHY NO ONE'S EVER BEEN ABLE TO DESTROY THE TOWN ITSELF.
LET'S JUST HOPE IT DOESN'T COME TO ACTUALLY HAVING TO GO INTO NÜRNHEIM. IT'S A BLOODY DREADFUL PLACE BY ALL ACCOUNTS.
IF WE'RE LUCKY, WE CAN JUST SEAL THE WOUND AND COME UP SMILING.
FUNNY HOW NOBODY'S ASKED ME WHAT I WANT TO DO.
THAT'S BECAUSE WE'RE ALL THOROUGHLY SICK OF YOUR CONSTANTLY WHINING VOICE.
YOU'LL STAY HERE WITH CRAZY JANE.
RIGHT. EVERYBODY HAPPY?
THEN LET'S GO.

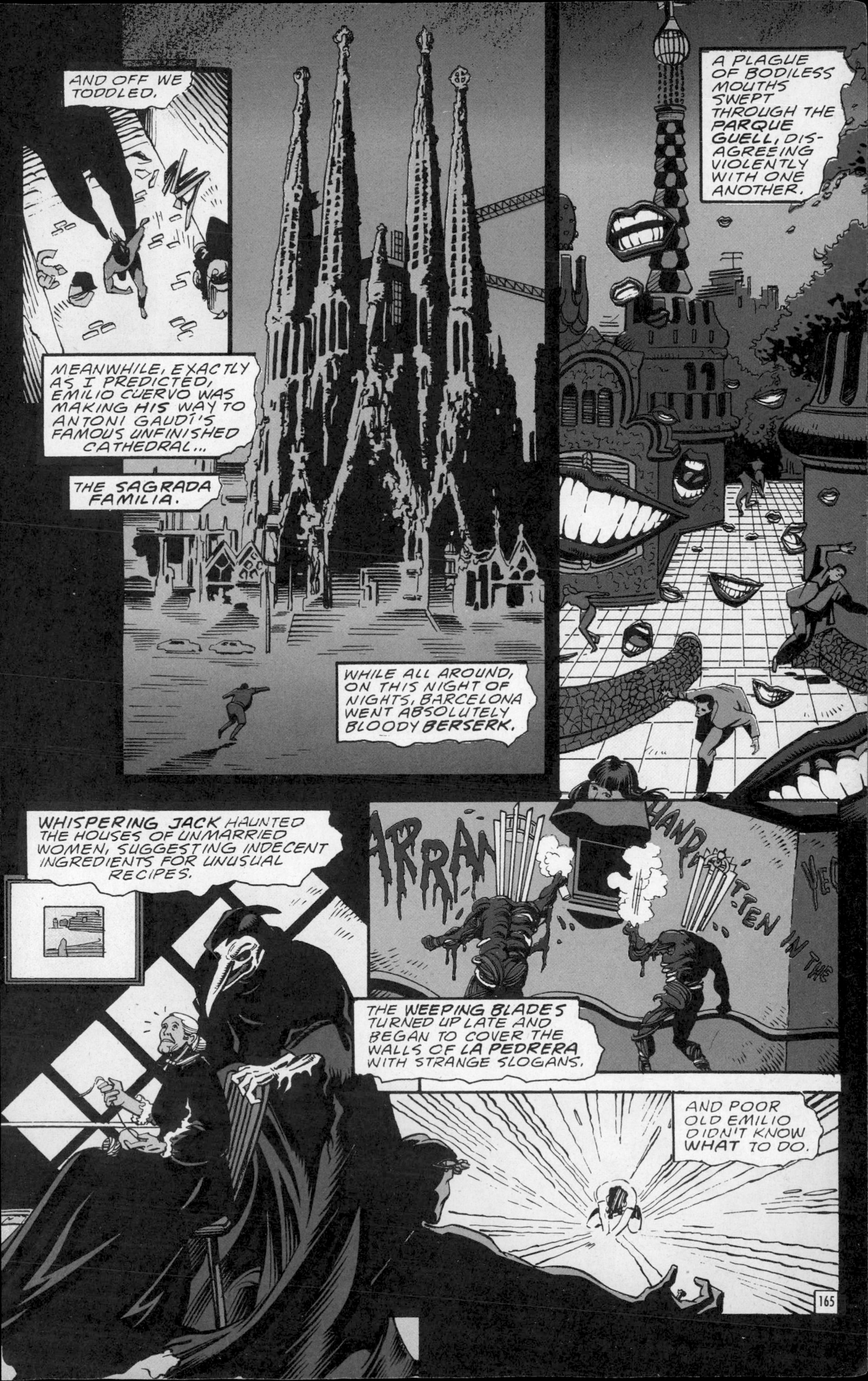
AND OFF WE TODDLED.
MEANWHILE, EXACTLY AS I PREDICTED, EMILIO CUERVO WAS MAKING HIS WAY TO ANTONI GAUDÍ'S FAMOUS UNFINISHED CATHEDRAL...
THE SAGRADA FAMILIA.
WHILE ALL AROUND, ON THIS NIGHT OF NIGHTS, BARCELONA WENT ABSOLUTELY BLOODY BERSERK.
A PLAGUE OF BODILESS MOUTHS SWEPT THROUGH THE PARQUE GUELL, DISAGREEING VIOLENTLY WITH ONE ANOTHER.
WHISPERING JACK HAUNTED THE HOUSES OF UNMARRIED WOMEN, SUGGESTING INDECENT INGREDIENTS FOR UNUSUAL RECIPES.
ARRAN
HAND
T-TEN IN THE
THE WEEPING BLADES TURNED UP LATE AND BEGAN TO COVER THE WALLS OF LA PEDRERA WITH STRANGE SLOGANS.
AND POOR OLD EMILIO DIDN'T KNOW WHAT TO DO.

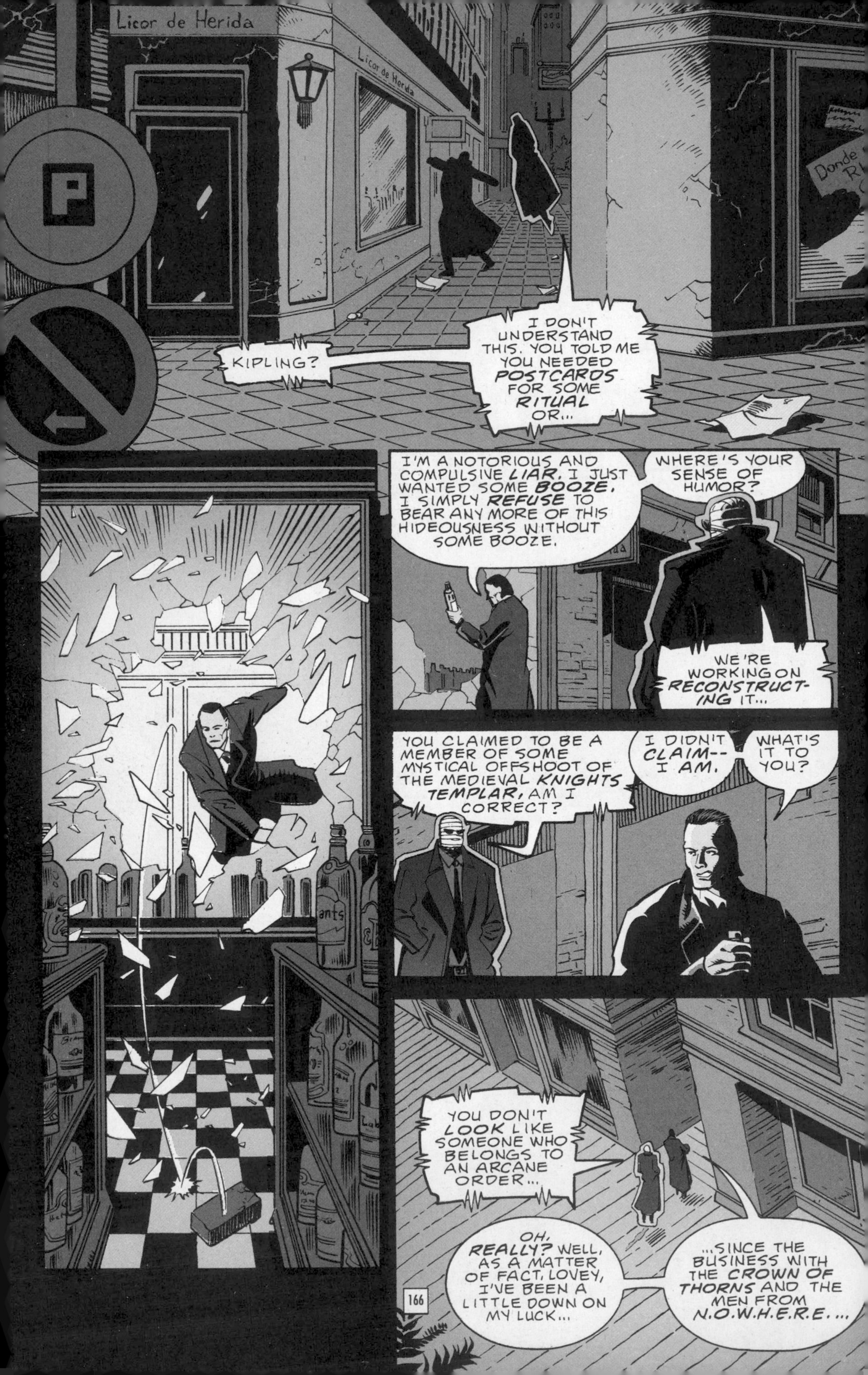
Licor de Herida
Licor de Herida
KIPLING?
I DON'T UNDERSTAND THIS. YOU TOLD ME YOU NEEDED POSTCARDS FOR SOME RITUAL OR...
I'M A NOTORIOUS AND COMPULSIVE LIAR. I JUST WANTED SOME BOOZE. I SIMPLY REFUSE TO BEAR ANY MORE OF THIS HIDEOUSNESS WITHOUT SOME BOOZE.
WHERE'S YOUR SENSE OF HUMOR?
WE'RE WORKING ON RECONSTRUCTING IT...
YOU CLAIMED TO BE A MEMBER OF SOME MYSTICAL OFFSHOOT OF THE MEDIEVAL KNIGHTS TEMPLAR, AM I CORRECT?
I DIDN'T CLAIM-- I AM.
WHAT'S IT TO YOU?
YOU DON'T LOOK LIKE SOMEONE WHO BELONGS TO AN ARCANE ORDER...
OH, REALLY? WELL, AS A MATTER OF FACT, LOVEY, I'VE BEEN A LITTLE DOWN ON MY LUCK...
...SINCE THE BUSINESS WITH THE CROWN OF THORNS AND THE MEN FROM N.O.W.H.E.R.E. ...

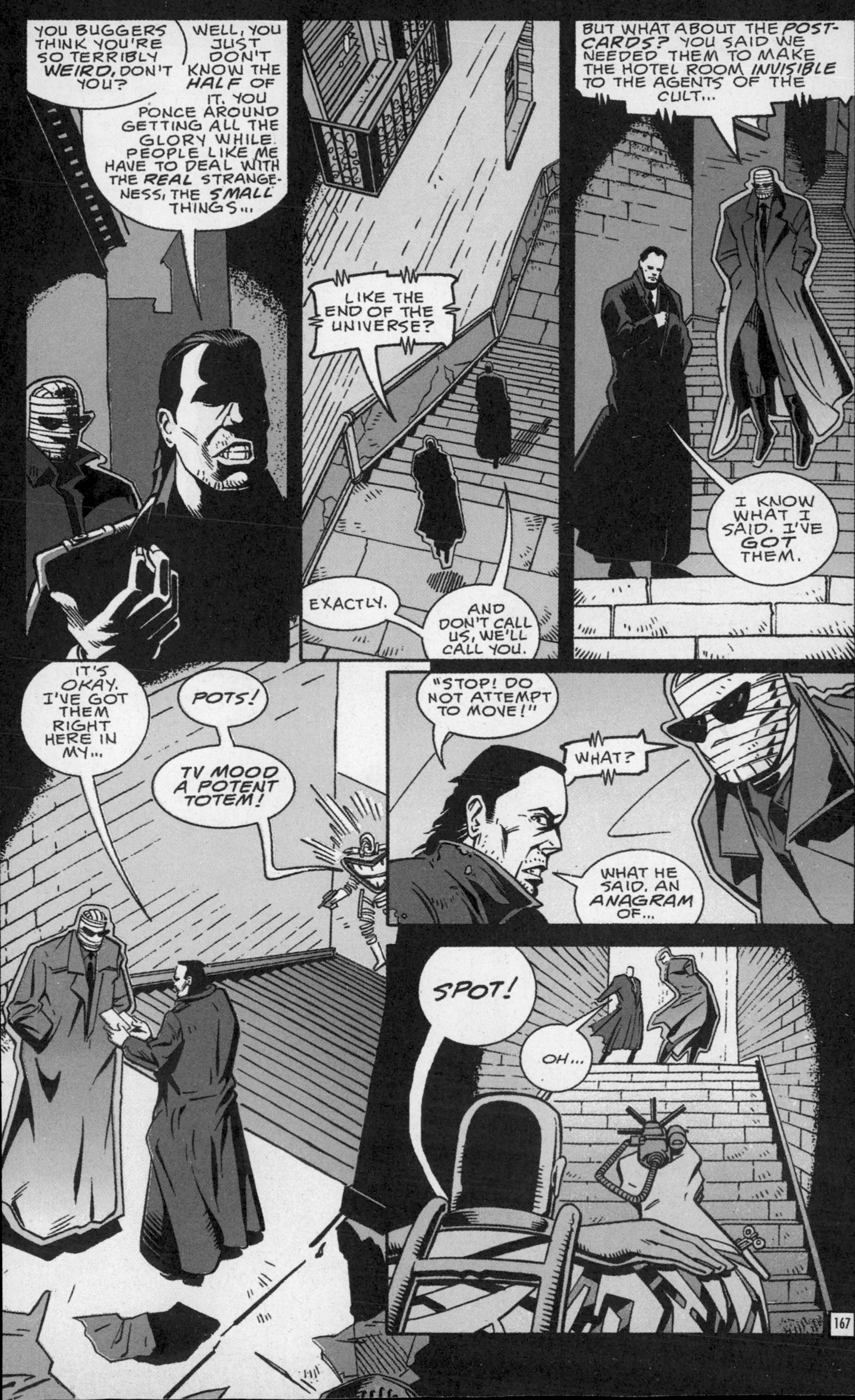
YOU BUGGERS THINK YOU'RE SO TERRIBLY WEIRD, DON'T YOU?
WELL, YOU JUST DON'T KNOW THE HALF OF IT. YOU PONCE AROUND GETTING ALL THE GLORY WHILE PEOPLE LIKE ME HAVE TO DEAL WITH THE REAL STRANGENESS, THE SMALL THINGS...
LIKE THE END OF THE UNIVERSE?
EXACTLY.
AND DON'T CALL US, WE'LL CALL YOU.
BUT WHAT ABOUT THE POSTCARDS? YOU SAID WE NEEDED THEM TO MAKE THE HOTEL ROOM INVISIBLE TO THE AGENTS OF THE CULT...
I KNOW WHAT I SAID. I'VE GOT THEM.
IT'S OKAY. I'VE GOT THEM RIGHT HERE IN MY...
POTS!
TV MOOD A POTENT TOTEM!
"STOP! DO NOT ATTEMPT TO MOVE!"
WHAT?
WHAT HE SAID. AN ANAGRAM OF...
SPOT!
OH...

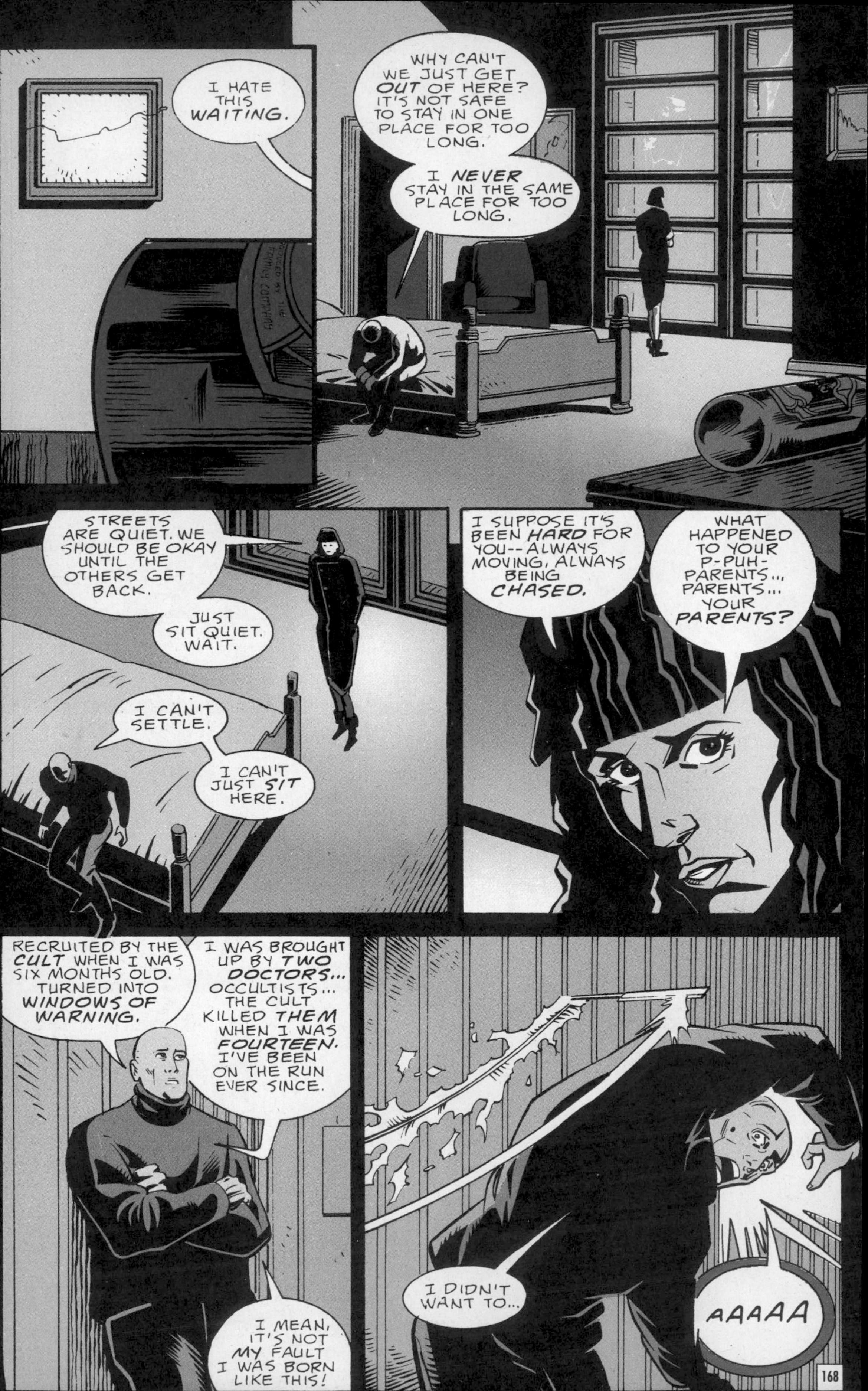
I HATE THIS WAITING.
WHY CAN'T WE JUST GET OUT OF HERE? IT'S NOT SAFE TO STAY IN ONE PLACE FOR TOO LONG.
I NEVER STAY IN THE SAME PLACE FOR TOO LONG.
STREETS ARE QUIET. WE SHOULD BE OKAY UNTIL THE OTHERS GET BACK.
JUST SIT QUIET. WAIT.
I CAN'T SETTLE.
I CAN'T JUST SIT HERE.
I SUPPOSE IT'S BEEN HARD FOR YOU-- ALWAYS MOVING, ALWAYS BEING CHASED.
WHAT HAPPENED TO YOUR P-PUH-PARENTS... PARENTS... YOUR PARENTS?
RECRUITED BY THE CULT WHEN I WAS SIX MONTHS OLD. TURNED INTO WINDOWS OF WARNING.
I WAS BROUGHT UP BY TWO DOCTORS... OCCULTISTS... THE CULT KILLED THEM WHEN I WAS FOURTEEN. I'VE BEEN ON THE RUN EVER SINCE.
I MEAN, IT'S NOT MY FAULT I WAS BORN LIKE THIS!
I DIDN'T WANT TO...
AAAAA

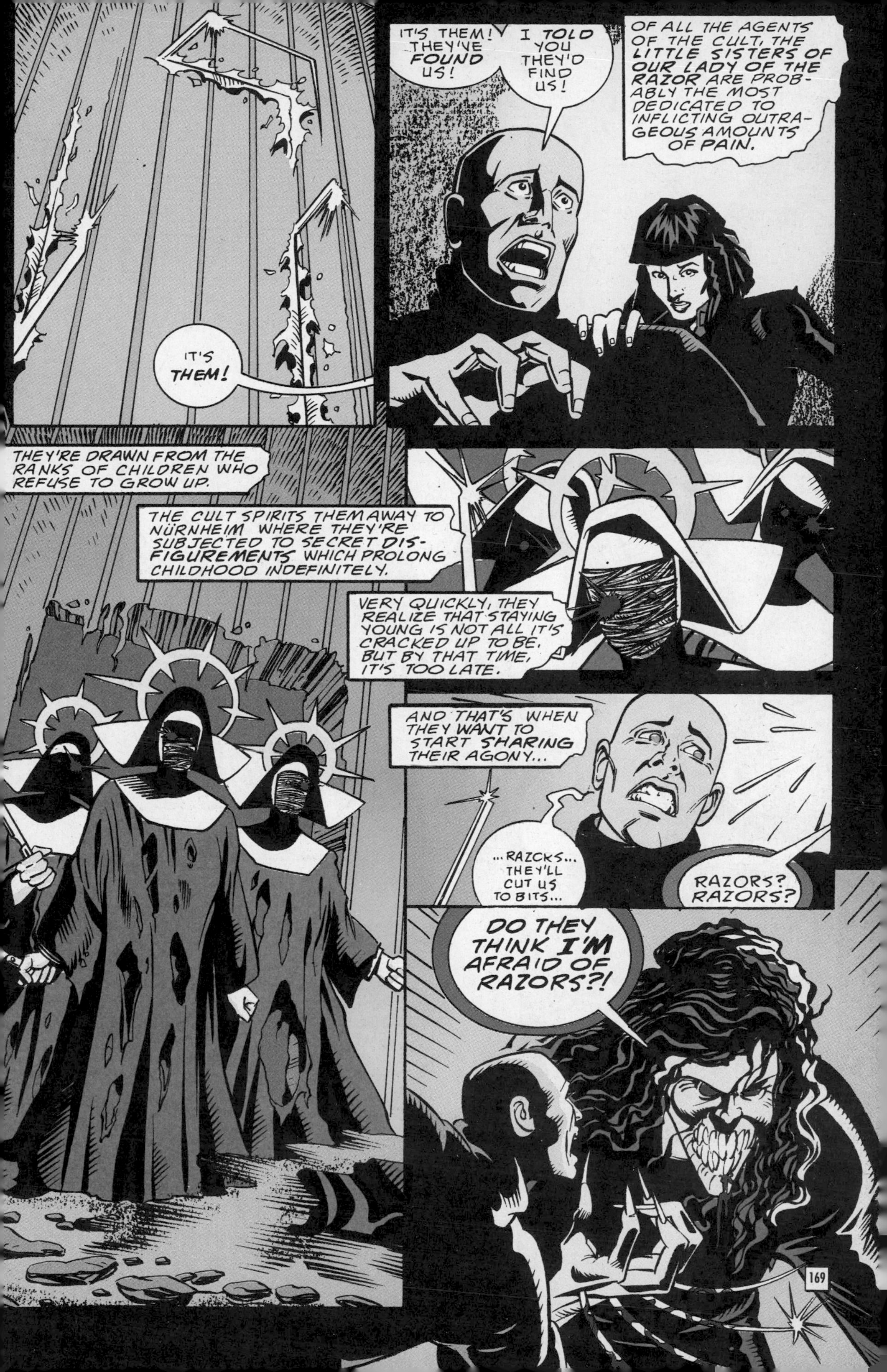
IT'S THEM!
IT'S THEM! THEY'VE FOUND US!
I TOLD YOU THEY'D FIND US!
OF ALL THE AGENTS OF THE CULT, THE LITTLE SISTERS OF OUR LADY OF THE RAZOR ARE PROBABLY THE MOST DEDICATED TO INFLICTING OUTRAGEOUS AMOUNTS OF PAIN.
THEY'RE DRAWN FROM THE RANKS OF CHILDREN WHO REFUSE TO GROW UP.
THE CULT SPIRITS THEM AWAY TO NÜRNHEIM WHERE THEY'RE SUBJECTED TO SECRET DISFIGUREMENTS WHICH PROLONG CHILDHOOD INDEFINITELY.
VERY QUICKLY, THEY REALIZE THAT STAYING YOUNG IS NOT ALL IT'S CRACKED UP TO BE. BUT BY THAT TIME, IT'S TOO LATE.
AND THAT'S WHEN THEY WANT TO START SHARING THEIR AGONY...
...RAZCKS... THEY'LL CUT US TO BITS...
RAZORS? RAZORS?
DO THEY THINK I'M AFRAID OF RAZORS?!

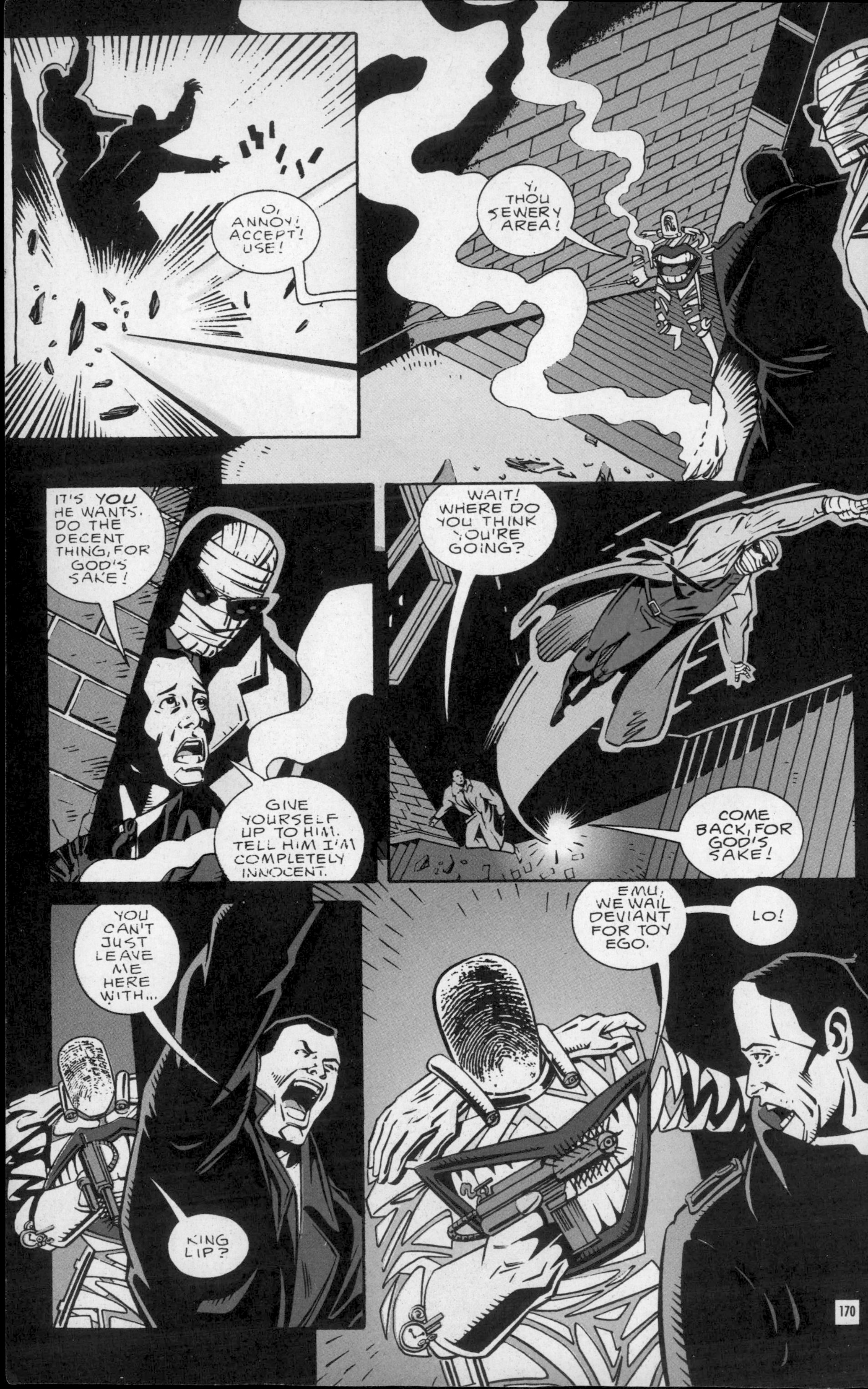
O, ANNOY! ACCEPT! USE!
Y, THOU SEWERY AREA!
IT'S YOU HE WANTS. DO THE DECENT THING, FOR GOD'S SAKE!
GIVE YOURSELF UP TO HIM. TELL HIM I'M COMPLETELY INNOCENT.
WAIT! WHERE DO YOU THINK YOU'RE GOING?
COME BACK, FOR GOD'S SAKE!
YOU CAN'T JUST LEAVE ME HERE WITH...
KING LIP?
EMU, WE WAIL DEVIANT FOR TOY EGO.
LO!

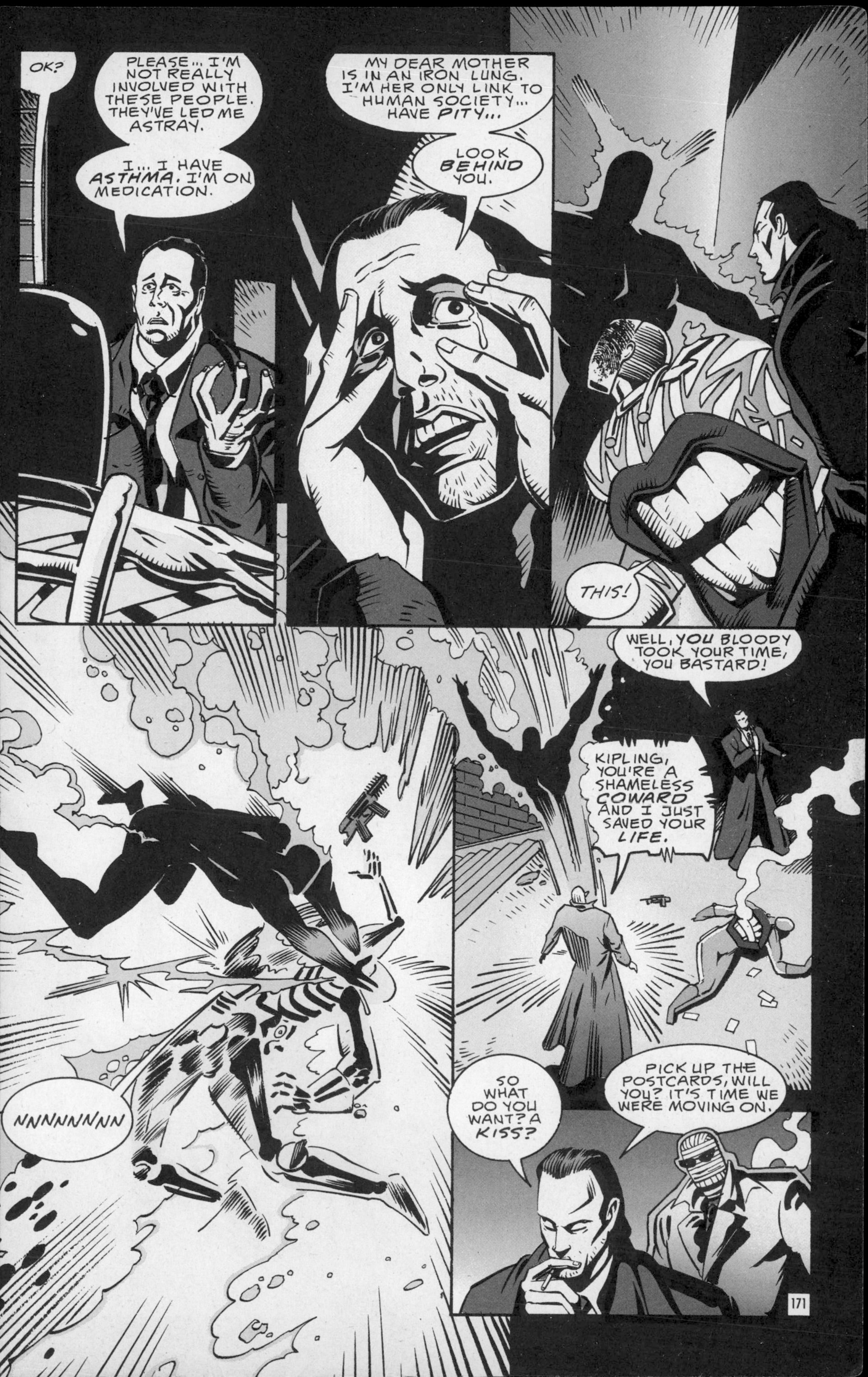
OK?
PLEASE... I'M NOT REALLY INVOLVED WITH THESE PEOPLE. THEY'VE LED ME ASTRAY.
I... I HAVE ASTHMA. I'M ON MEDICATION.
MY DEAR MOTHER IS IN AN IRON LUNG. I'M HER ONLY LINK TO HUMAN SOCIETY... HAVE PITY...
LOOK BEHIND YOU.
THIS!
NNNNNNNN
WELL, YOU BLOODY TOOK YOUR TIME, YOU BASTARD!
KIPLING, YOU'RE A SHAMELESS COWARD AND I JUST SAVED YOUR LIFE.
SO WHAT DO YOU WANT? A KISS?
PICK UP THE POSTCARDS, WILL YOU? IT'S TIME WE WERE MOVING ON.

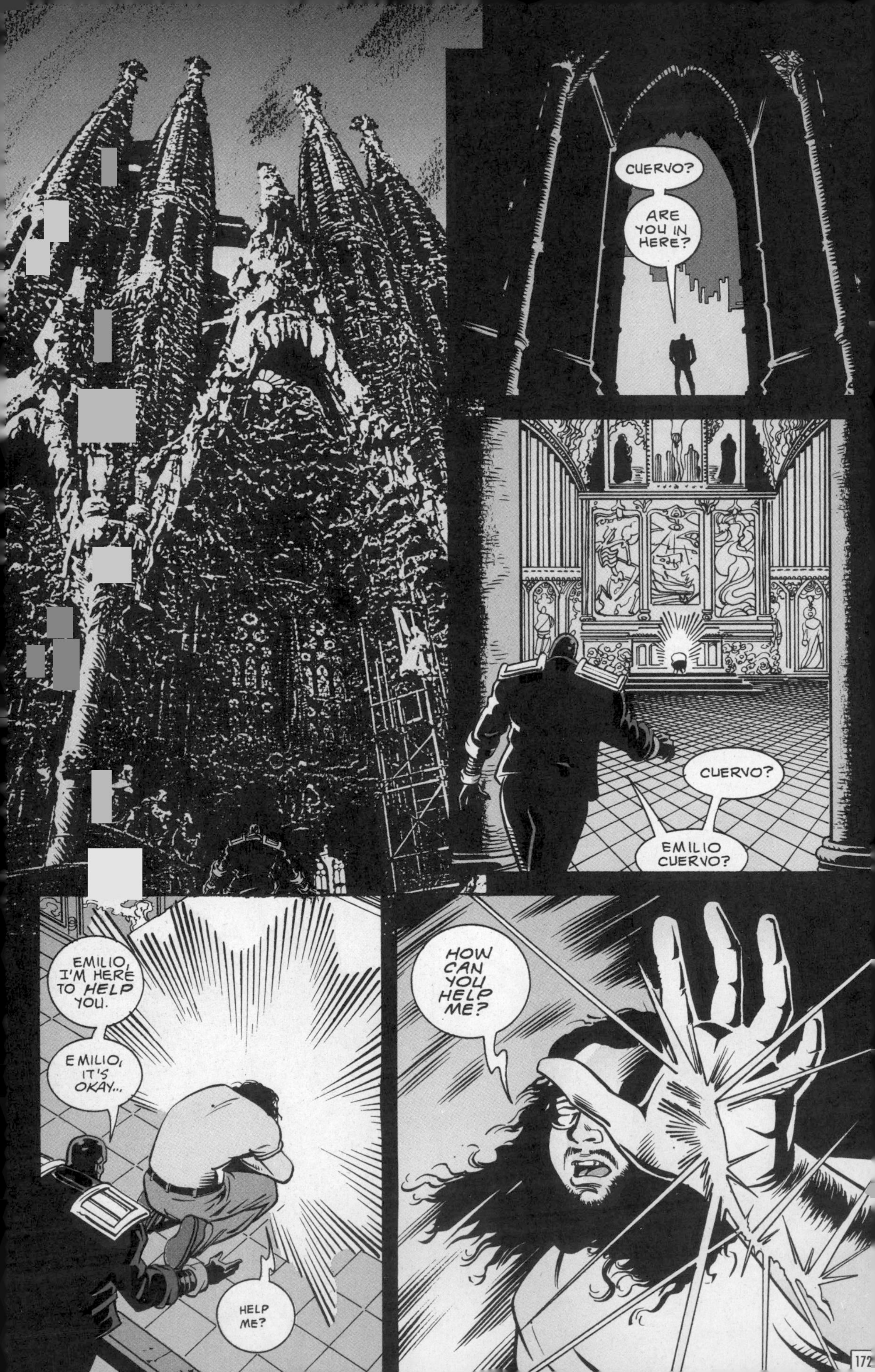
CUERVO?
ARE YOU IN HERE?
CUERVO?
EMILIO CUERVO?
EMILIO, I'M HERE TO HELP YOU.
EMILIO, IT'S OKAY...
HELP ME?
HOW CAN YOU HELP ME?

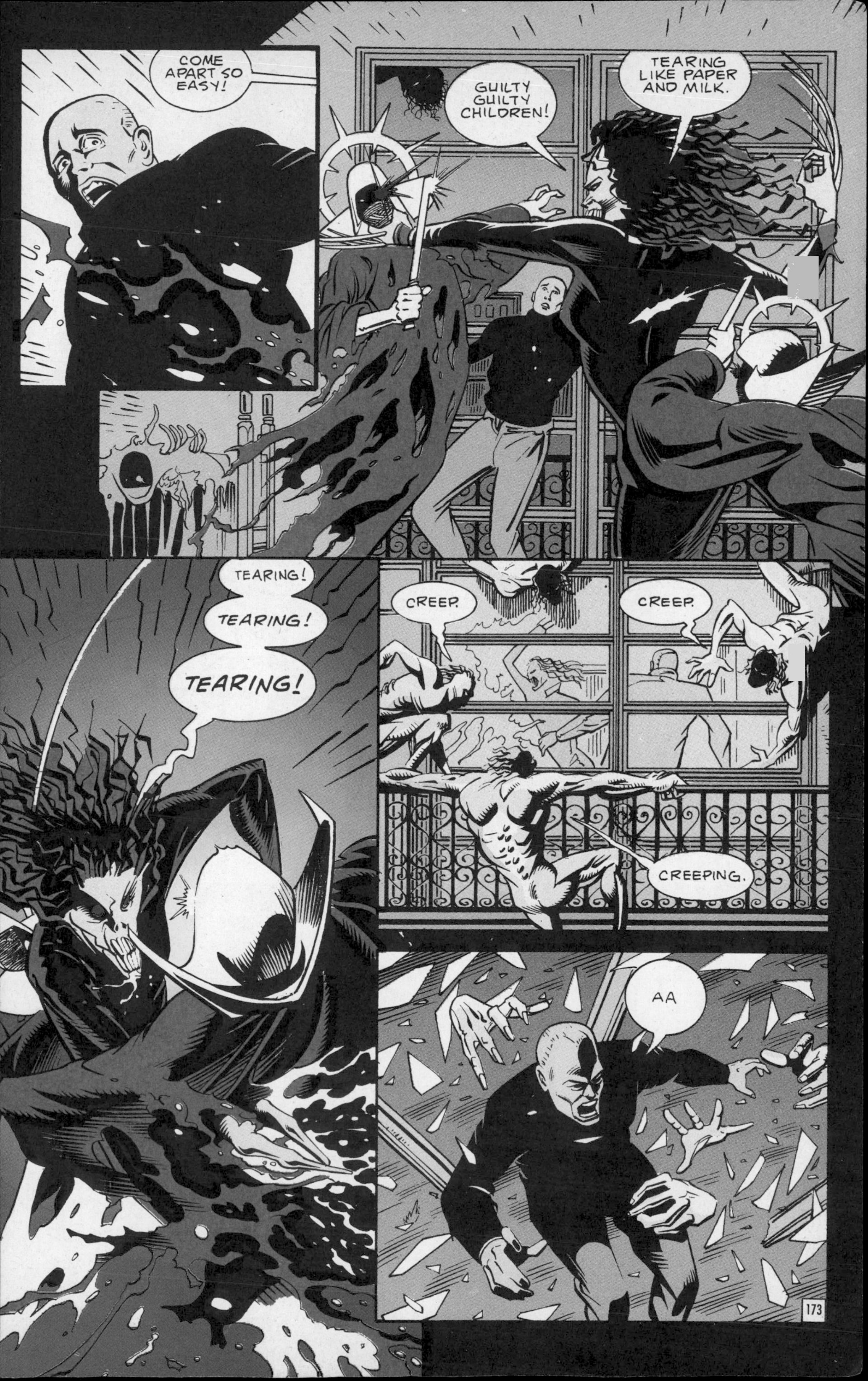
COME APART SO EASY!
GUILTY GUILTY CHILDREN!
TEARING LIKE PAPER AND MILK.
TEARING!
TEARING!
TEARING!
CREEP.
CREEP.
CREEPING.
AA

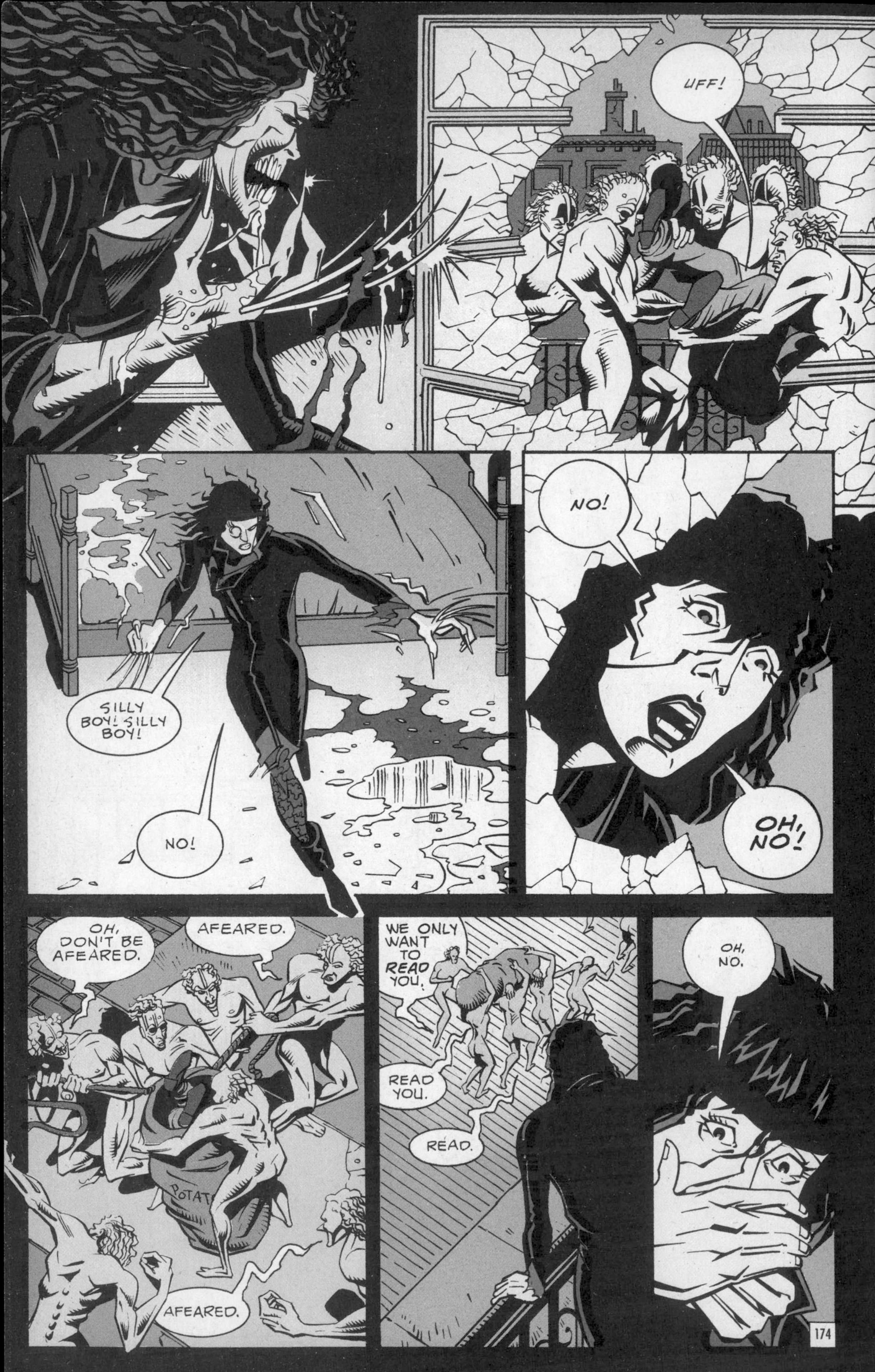
UFF!
SILLY BOY! SILLY BOY!
NO!
NO!
OH, NO!
OH, DON'T BE AFEARED.
AFEARED.
POTATO
AFEARED.
WE ONLY WANT TO *READ* YOU.
READ YOU.
READ.
OH, NO.

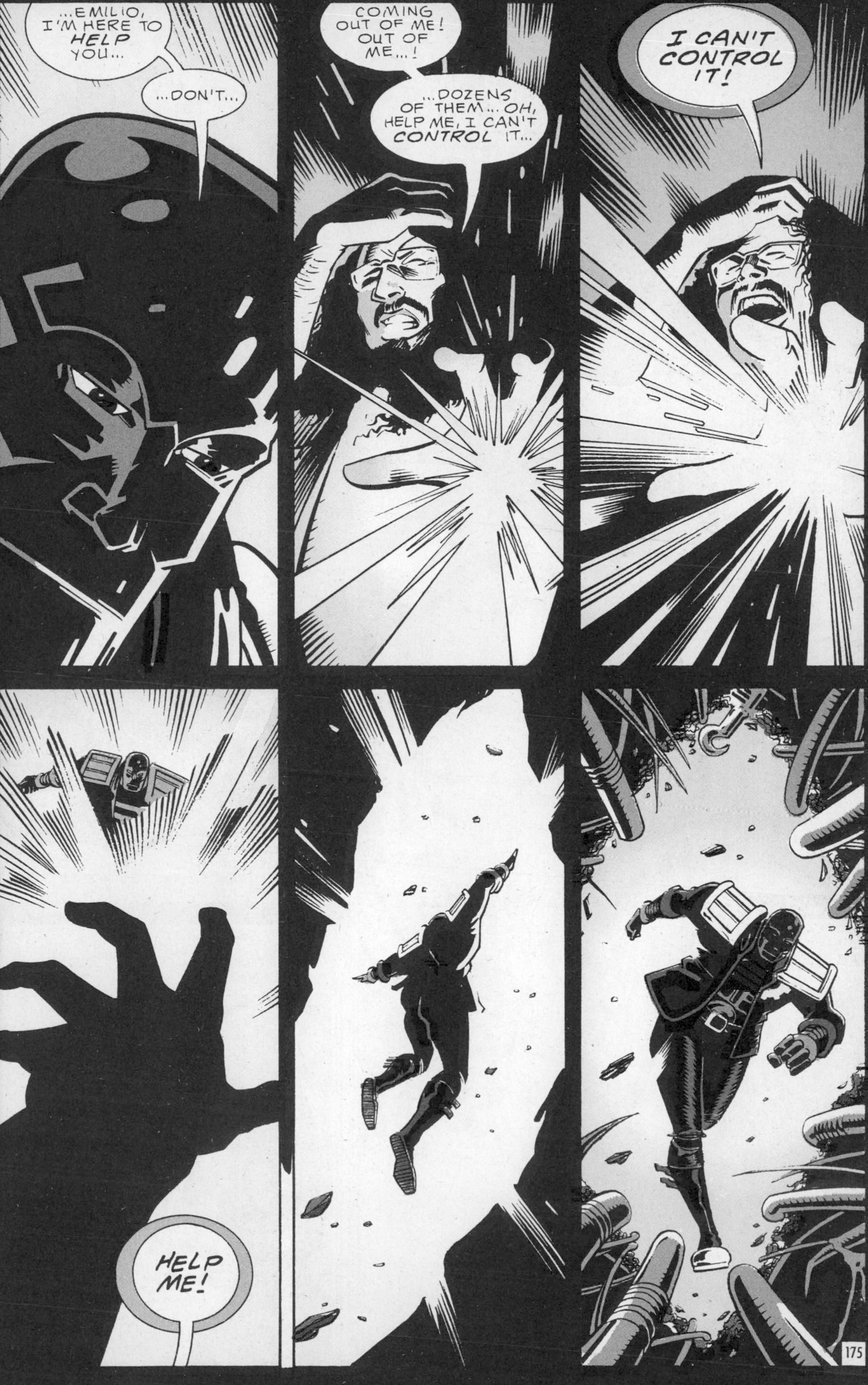
...EMILIO, I'M HERE TO HELP YOU...
...DON'T...
COMING OUT OF ME! OUT OF ME...!
...DOZENS OF THEM... OH, HELP ME, I CAN'T CONTROL IT...
I CAN'T CONTROL IT!
HELP ME!

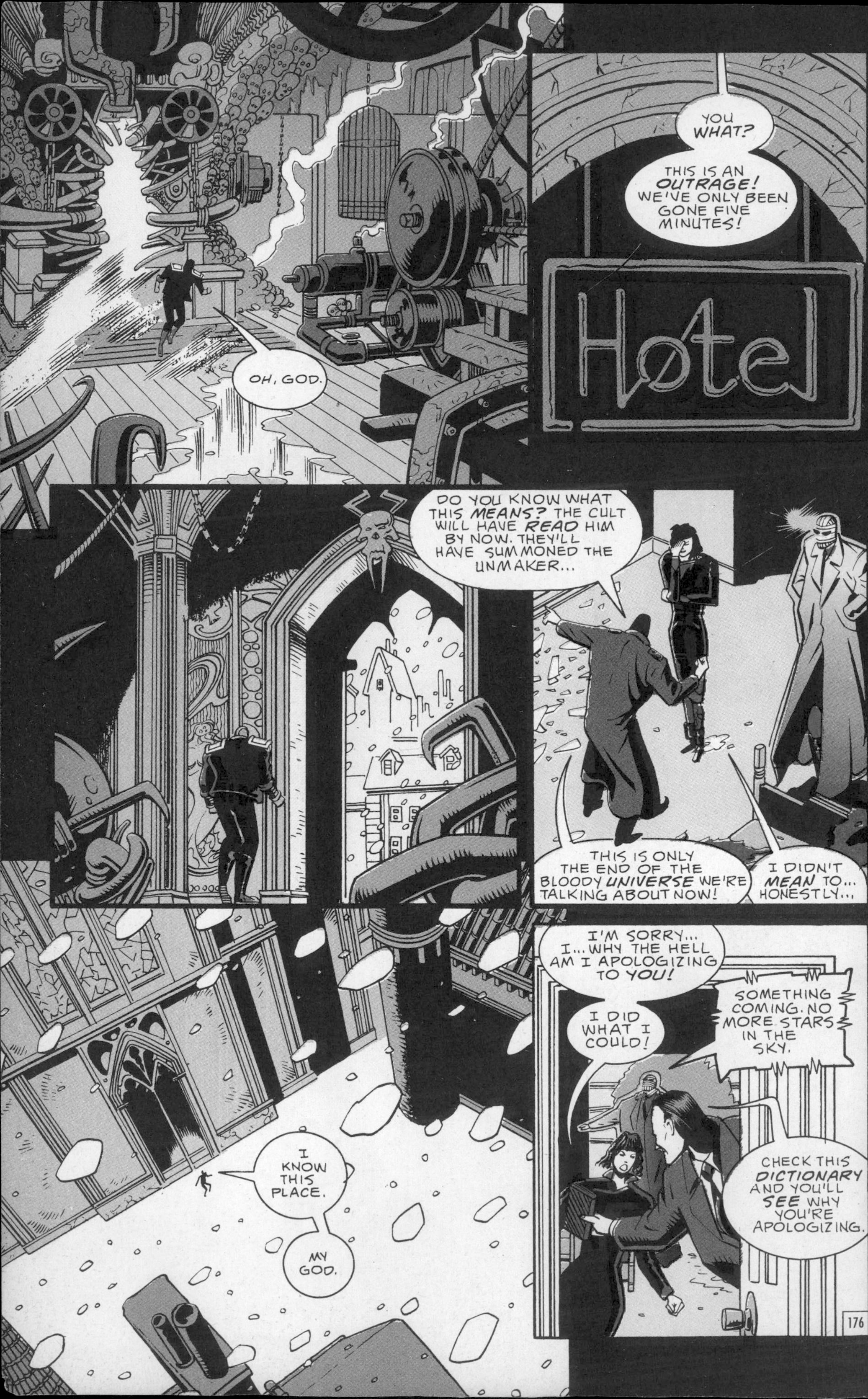
OH, GOD.
YOU WHAT?
THIS IS AN OUTRAGE! WE'VE ONLY BEEN GONE FIVE MINUTES!
Hotel
DO YOU KNOW WHAT THIS MEANS? THE CULT WILL HAVE READ HIM BY NOW. THEY'LL HAVE SUMMONED THE UNMAKER...
THIS IS ONLY THE END OF THE BLOODY UNIVERSE WE'RE TALKING ABOUT NOW!
I DIDN'T MEAN TO... HONESTLY...
I KNOW THIS PLACE.
MY GOD.
I'M SORRY... I... WHY THE HELL AM I APOLOGIZING TO YOU!
I DID WHAT I COULD!
SOMETHING COMING. NO MORE STARS IN THE SKY.
CHECK THIS DICTIONARY AND YOU'LL SEE WHY YOU'RE APOLOGIZING.

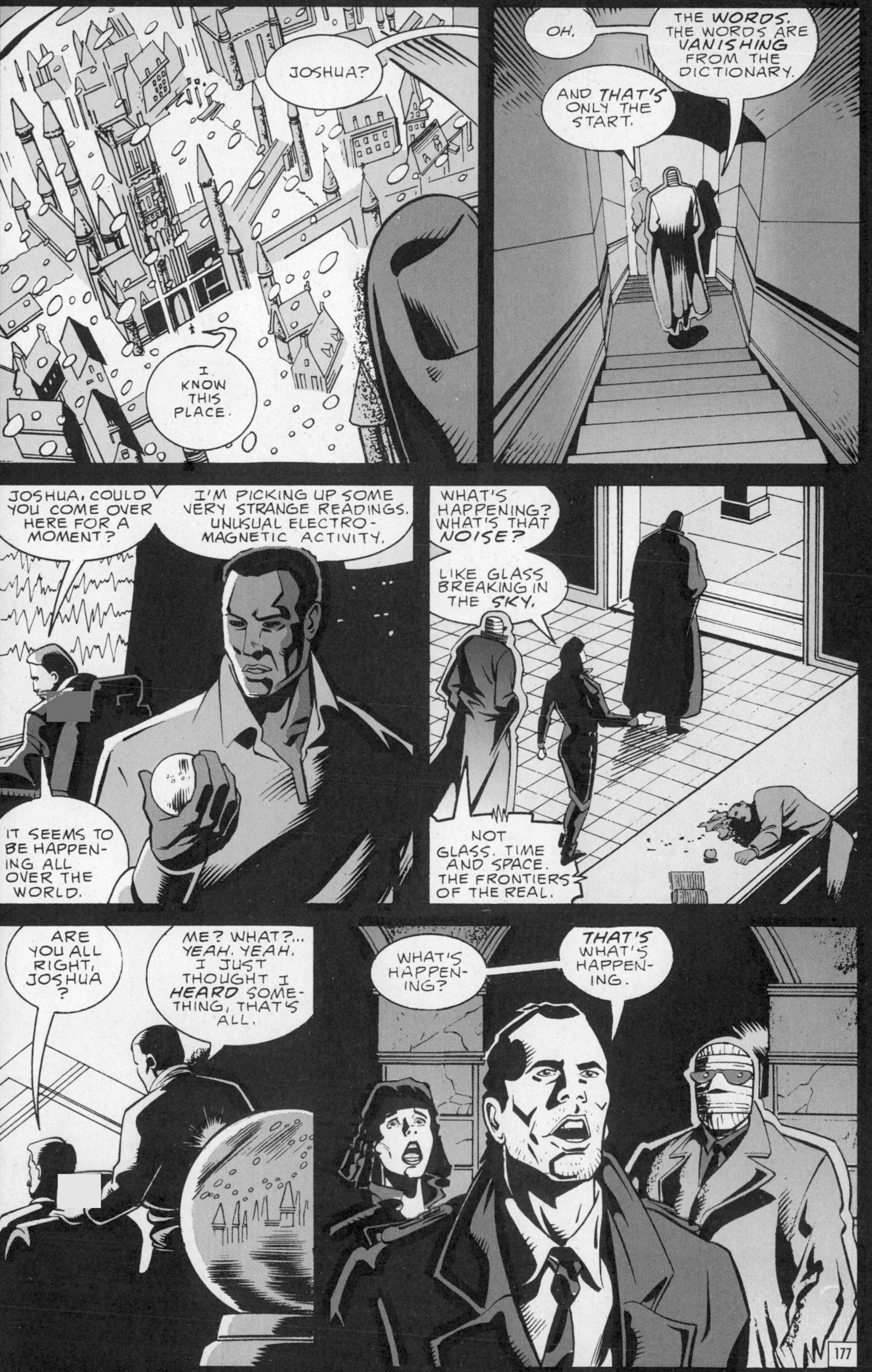
JOSHUA?
I KNOW THIS PLACE.
OH.
THE WORDS. THE WORDS ARE VANISHING FROM THE DICTIONARY.
AND THAT'S ONLY THE START.
JOSHUA, COULD YOU COME OVER HERE FOR A MOMENT?
I'M PICKING UP SOME VERY STRANGE READINGS. UNUSUAL ELECTRO-MAGNETIC ACTIVITY.
IT SEEMS TO BE HAPPENING ALL OVER THE WORLD.
WHAT'S HAPPENING? WHAT'S THAT NOISE?
LIKE GLASS BREAKING IN THE SKY.
NOT GLASS. TIME AND SPACE. THE FRONTIERS OF THE REAL.
ARE YOU ALL RIGHT, JOSHUA?
ME? WHAT?... YEAH. YEAH. I JUST THOUGHT I HEARD SOMETHING, THAT'S ALL.
WHAT'S HAPPENING?
THAT'S WHAT'S HAPPENING.

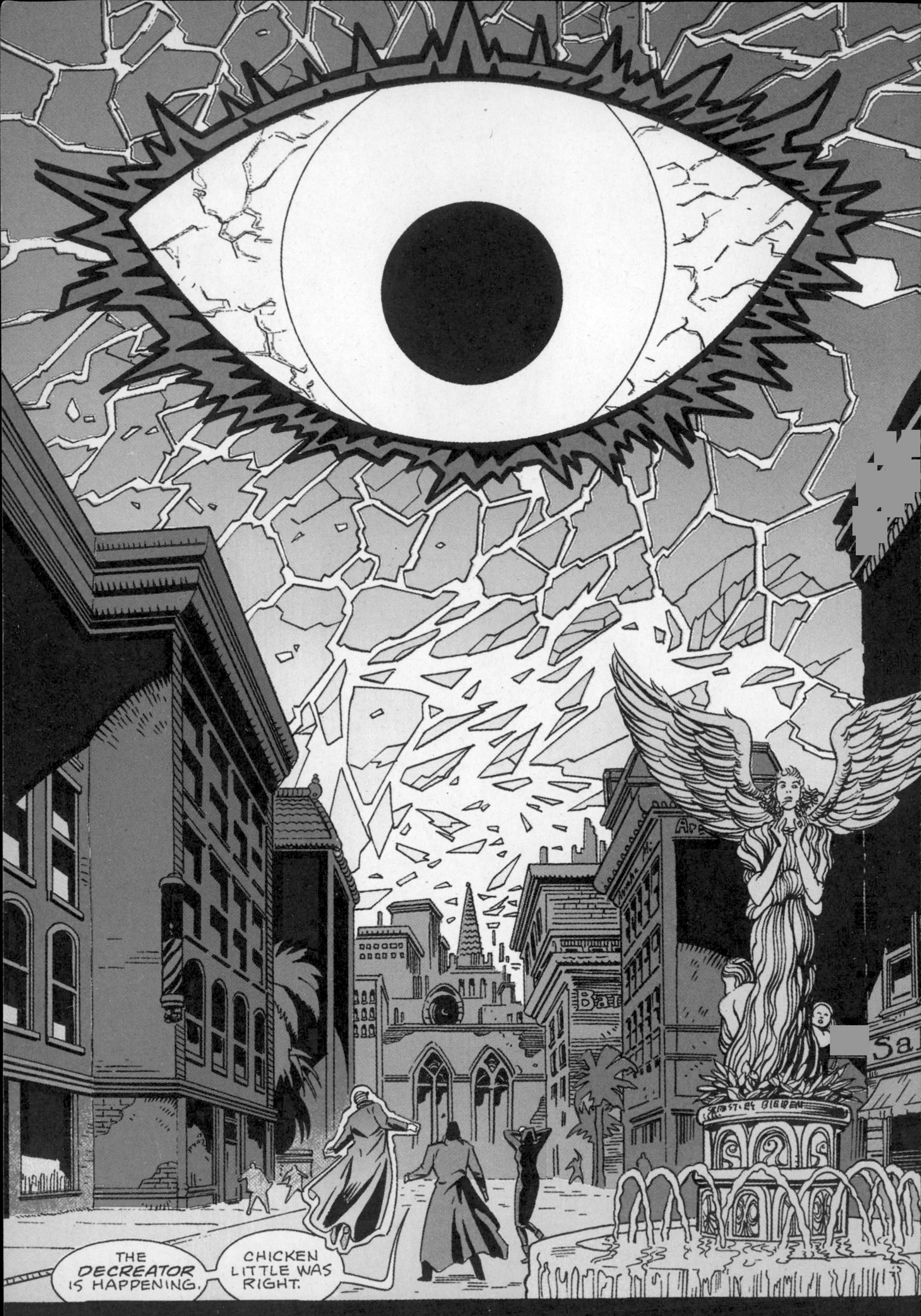
THE *DECREATOR* IS HAPPENING.
CHICKEN LITTLE WAS RIGHT.

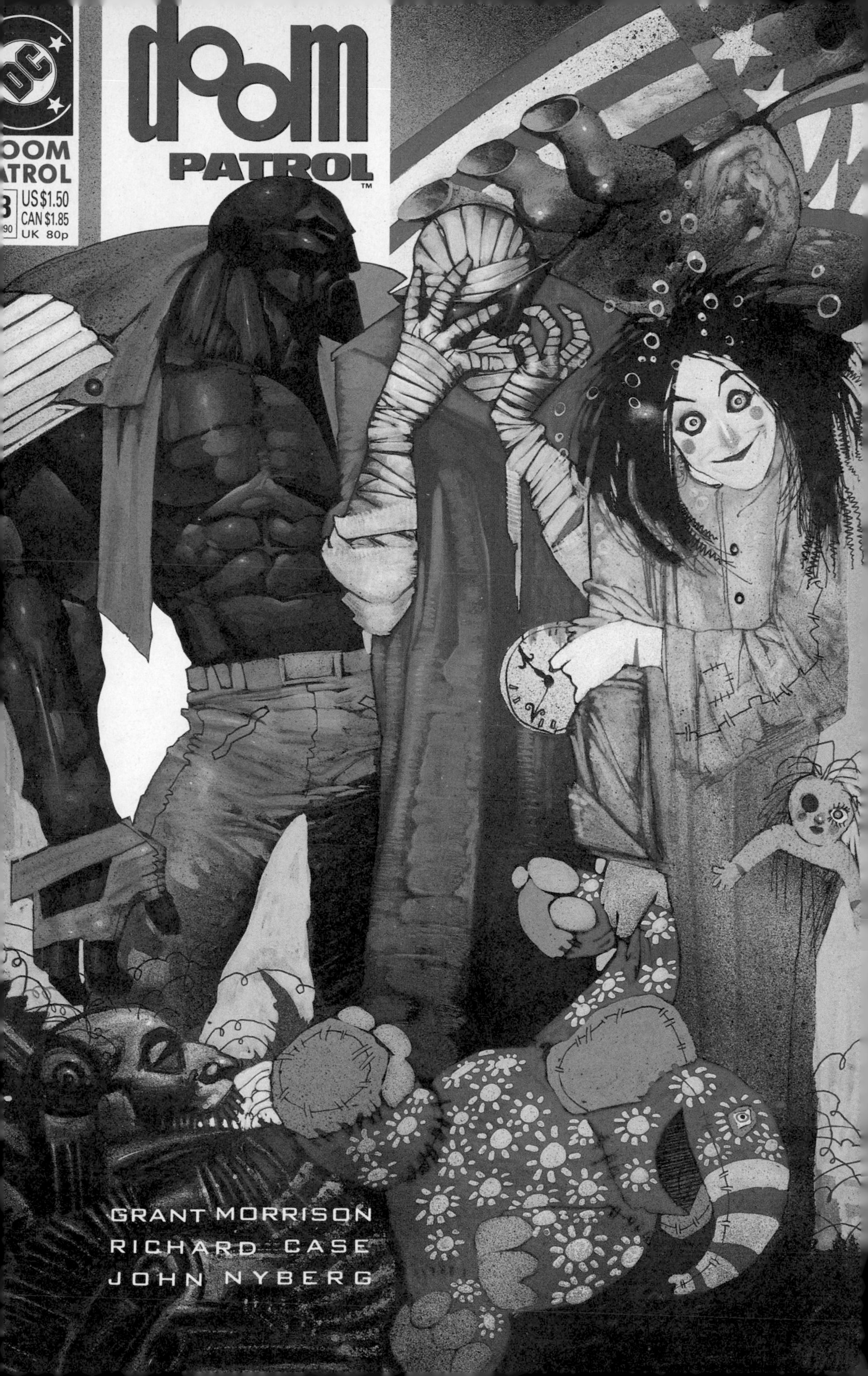
DC
doom
PATROL™
OOM
ATROL
US $1.50
CAN $1.85
UK 80p
GRANT MORRISON
RICHARD CASE
JOHN NYBERG

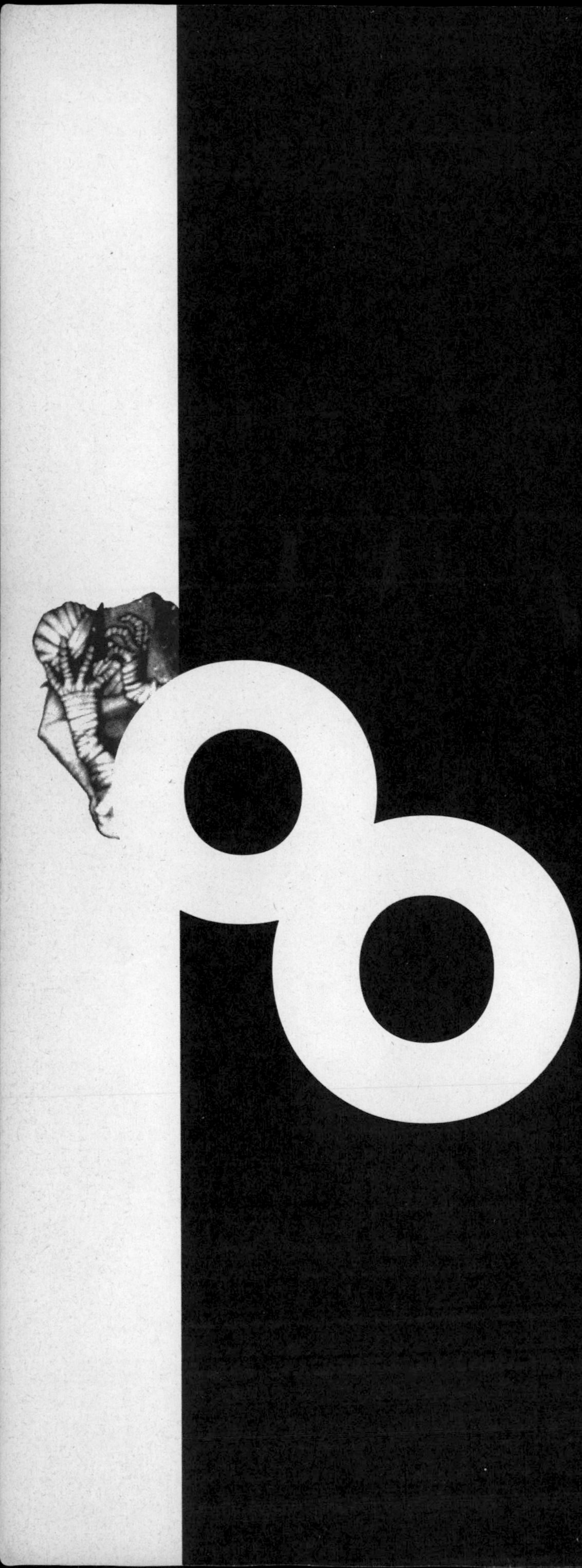
8

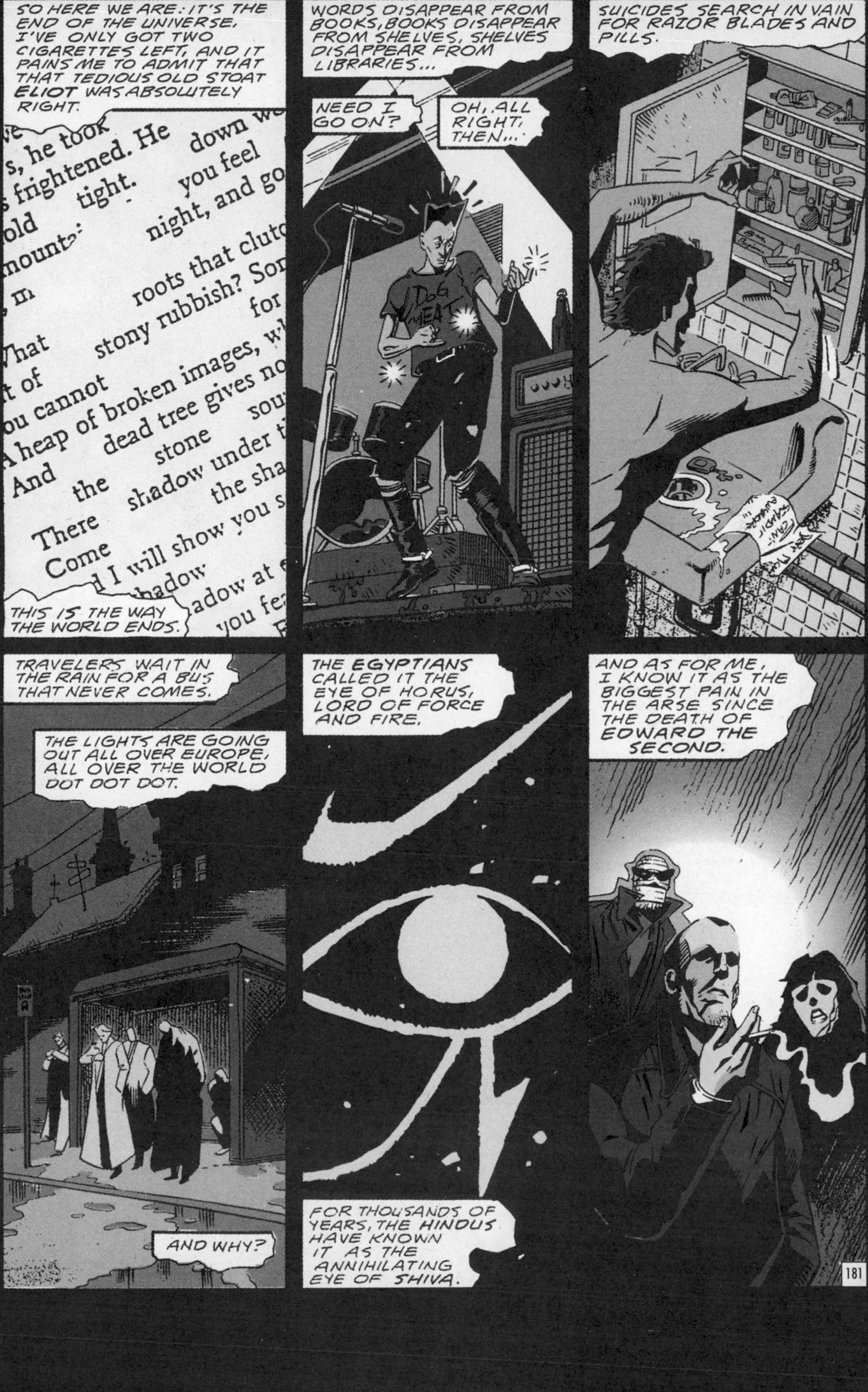
SO HERE WE ARE: IT'S THE END OF THE UNIVERSE. I'VE ONLY GOT TWO CIGARETTES LEFT, AND IT PAINS ME TO ADMIT THAT THAT TEDIOUS OLD STOAT ELIOT WAS ABSOLUTELY RIGHT.
s, he took
down
frightened. He
tight.
you feel
old
night, and go
mount
roots that clut
What
stony rubbish? Son
for
of
ou cannot
broken images, w
heap of
dead tree gives no
stone
sou
And
shadow under t
the
There
the sha
Come
I will show you s
hadow
adow at e
you fe
THIS IS THE WAY THE WORLD ENDS.
WORDS DISAPPEAR FROM BOOKS, BOOKS DISAPPEAR FROM SHELVES, SHELVES DISAPPEAR FROM LIBRARIES...
NEED I GO ON?
OH, ALL RIGHT, THEN...
DOG MEAT
SUICIDES SEARCH IN VAIN FOR RAZOR BLADES AND PILLS.
TRAVELERS WAIT IN THE RAIN FOR A BUS THAT NEVER COMES.
THE LIGHTS ARE GOING OUT ALL OVER EUROPE, ALL OVER THE WORLD DOT DOT DOT.
AND WHY?
THE EGYPTIANS CALLED IT THE EYE OF HORUS, LORD OF FORCE AND FIRE.
FOR THOUSANDS OF YEARS, THE HINDUS HAVE KNOWN IT AS THE ANNIHILATING EYE OF SHIVA.
AND AS FOR ME, I KNOW IT AS THE BIGGEST PAIN IN THE ARSE SINCE THE DEATH OF EDWARD THE SECOND.

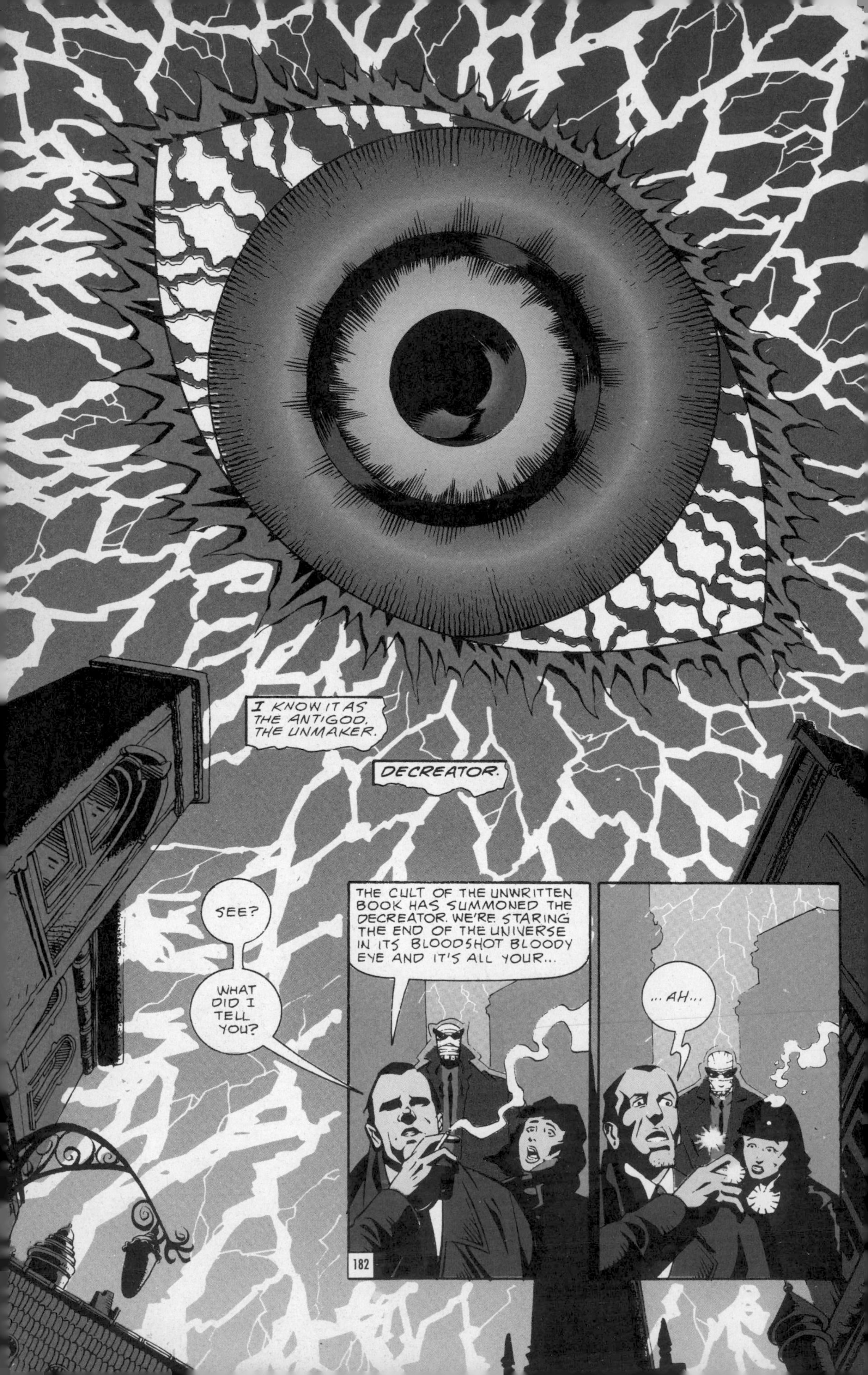

I KNOW IT AS THE ANTIGOD. THE UNMAKER.
DECREATOR.
SEE?
WHAT DID I TELL YOU?
THE CULT OF THE UNWRITTEN BOOK HAS SUMMONED THE DECREATOR. WE'RE STARING THE END OF THE UNIVERSE IN ITS BLOODSHOT BLOODY EYE AND IT'S ALL YOUR...
...AH...

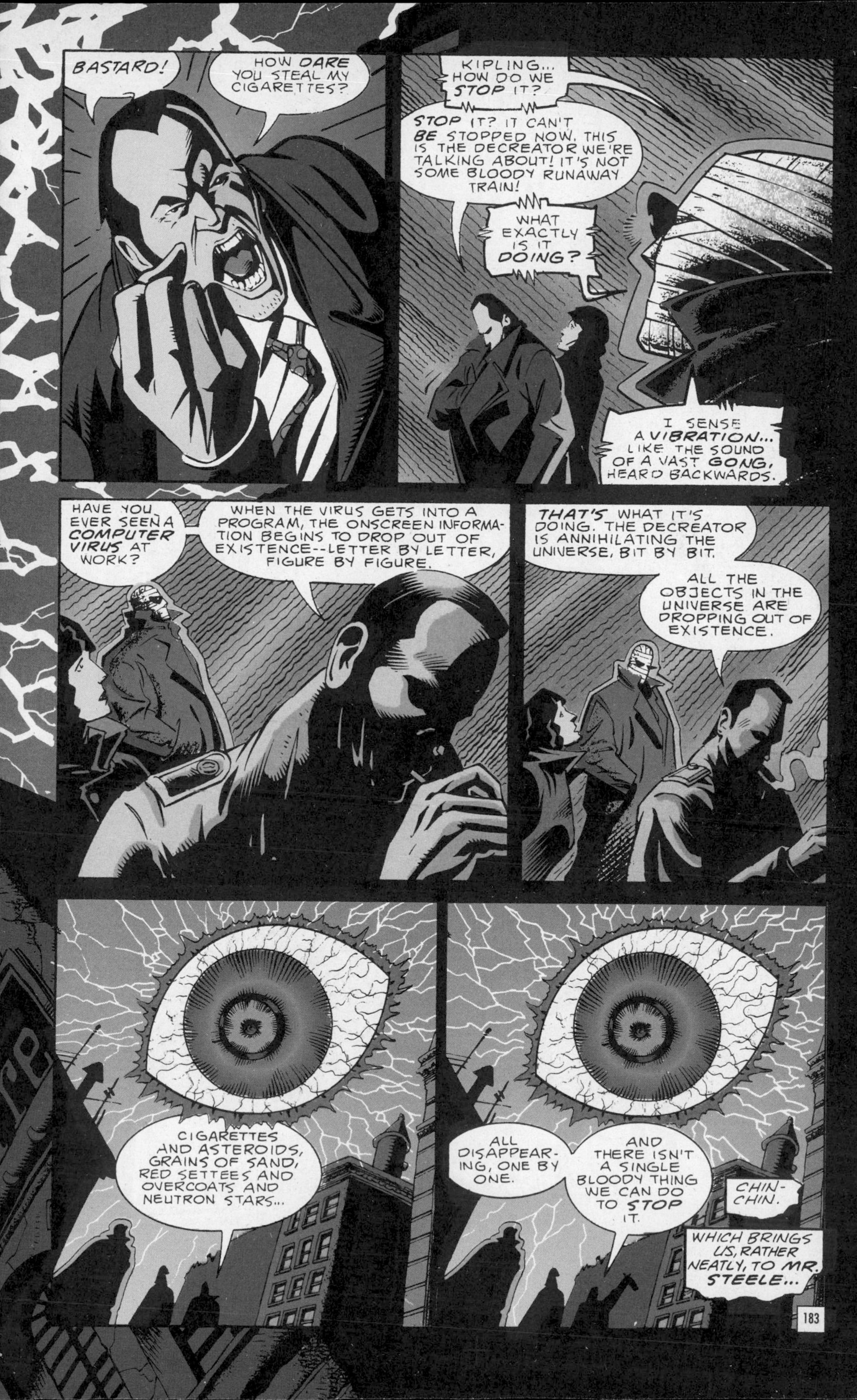
BASTARD!
HOW DARE YOU STEAL MY CIGARETTES?
KIPLING... HOW DO WE STOP IT?
STOP IT? IT CAN'T BE STOPPED NOW. THIS IS THE DECREATOR WE'RE TALKING ABOUT! IT'S NOT SOME BLOODY RUNAWAY TRAIN!
WHAT EXACTLY IS IT DOING?
I SENSE A VIBRATION... LIKE THE SOUND OF A VAST GONG, HEARD BACKWARDS.
HAVE YOU EVER SEEN A COMPUTER VIRUS AT WORK?
WHEN THE VIRUS GETS INTO A PROGRAM, THE ONSCREEN INFORMATION BEGINS TO DROP OUT OF EXISTENCE--LETTER BY LETTER, FIGURE BY FIGURE.
THAT'S WHAT IT'S DOING. THE DECREATOR IS ANNIHILATING THE UNIVERSE, BIT BY BIT.
ALL THE OBJECTS IN THE UNIVERSE ARE DROPPING OUT OF EXISTENCE.
CIGARETTES AND ASTEROIDS, GRAINS OF SAND, RED SETTEES AND OVERCOATS AND NEUTRON STARS...
ALL DISAPPEARING, ONE BY ONE.
AND THERE ISN'T A SINGLE BLOODY THING WE CAN DO TO STOP IT.
CHIN-CHIN.
WHICH BRINGS US, RATHER NEATLY, TO MR. STEELE...

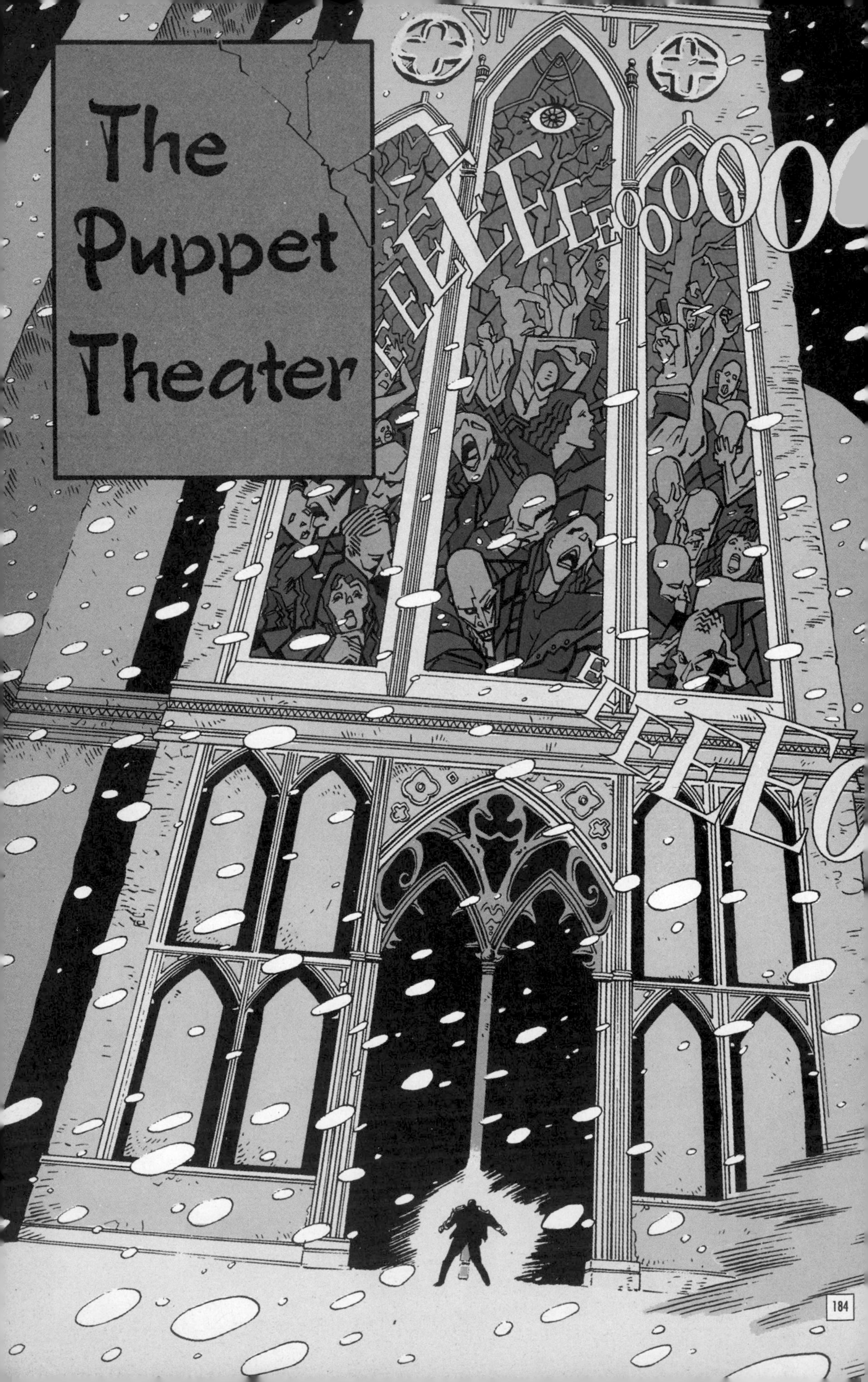
The Puppet Theater
EEEEEEEEEEOOOOOOOOO
EEEEEEEEO

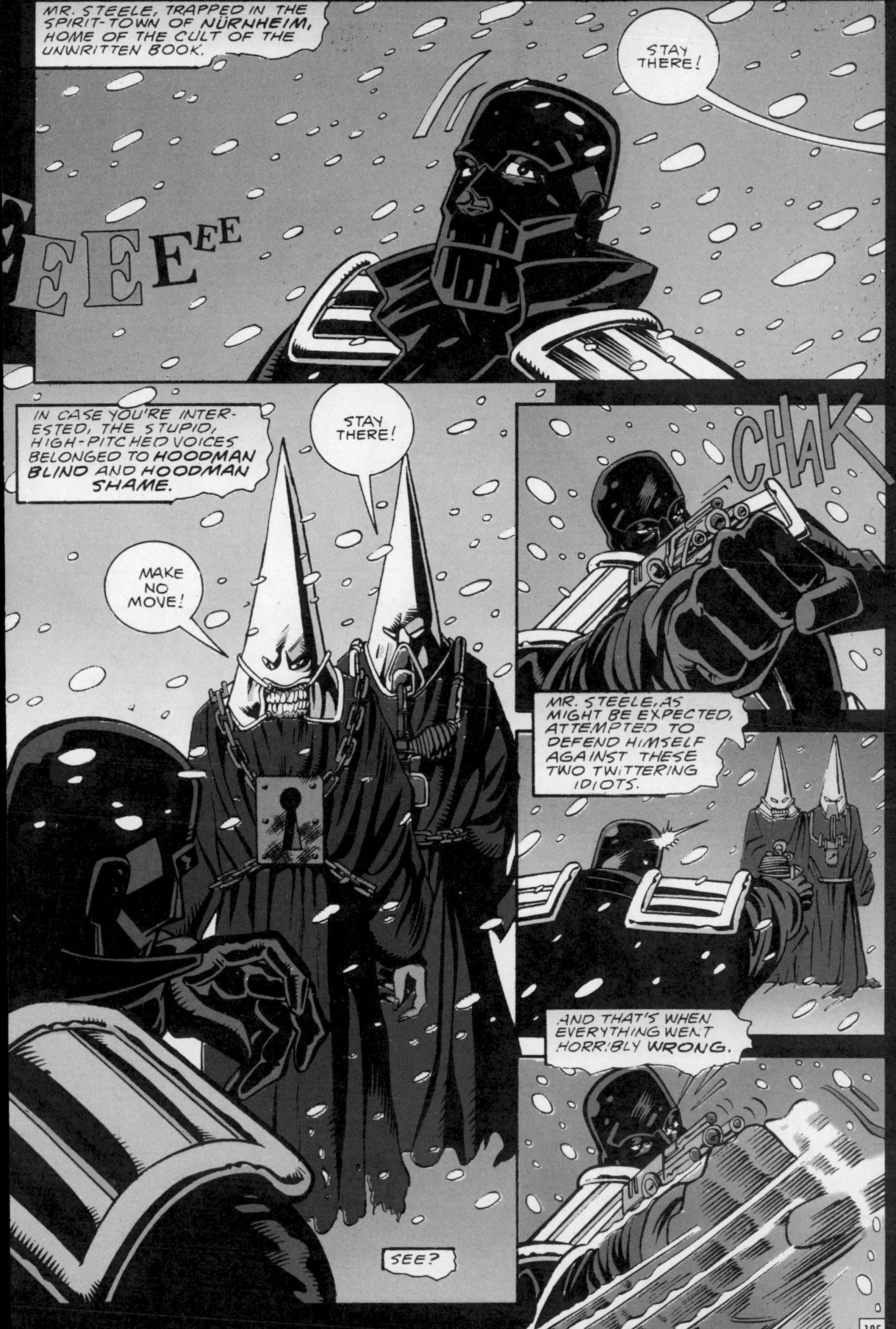
MR. STEELE, TRAPPED IN THE SPIRIT-TOWN OF NÜRNHEIM, HOME OF THE CULT OF THE UNWRITTEN BOOK.
STAY THERE!
EEEEEE
IN CASE YOU'RE INTERESTED, THE STUPID, HIGH-PITCHED VOICES BELONGED TO HOODMAN BLIND AND HOODMAN SHAME.
STAY THERE!
MAKE NO MOVE!
SEE?
CHAK
MR. STEELE, AS MIGHT BE EXPECTED, ATTEMPTED TO DEFEND HIMSELF AGAINST THESE TWO TWITTERING IDIOTS.
AND THAT'S WHEN EVERYTHING WENT HORRIBLY WRONG.

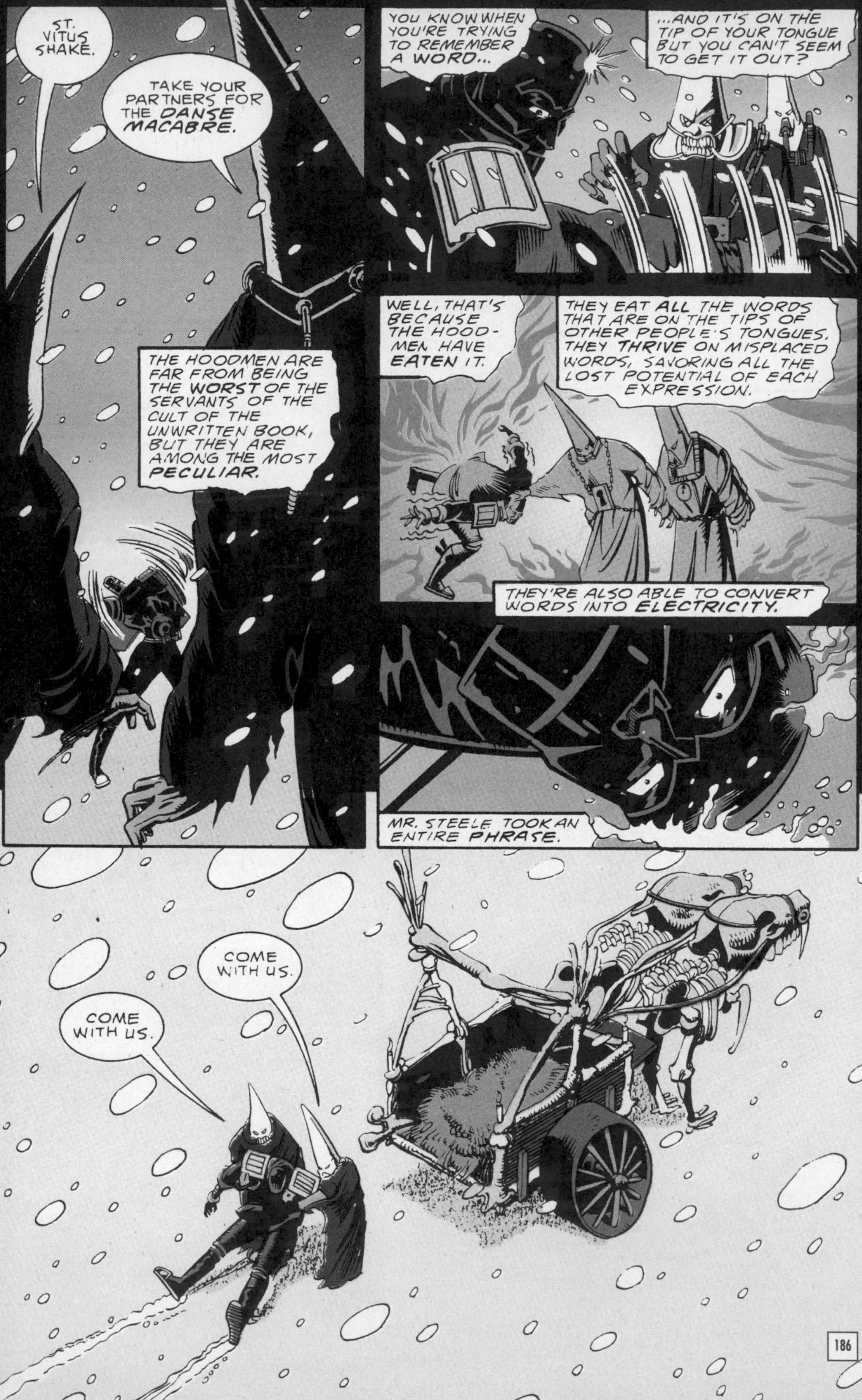

ST. VITUS SHAKE.
TAKE YOUR PARTNERS FOR THE DANSE MACABRE.
THE HOODMEN ARE FAR FROM BEING THE WORST OF THE SERVANTS OF THE CULT OF THE UNWRITTEN BOOK, BUT THEY ARE AMONG THE MOST PECULIAR.
YOU KNOW WHEN YOU'RE TRYING TO REMEMBER A WORD...
...AND IT'S ON THE TIP OF YOUR TONGUE BUT YOU CAN'T SEEM TO GET IT OUT?
WELL, THAT'S BECAUSE THE HOOD-MEN HAVE EATEN IT.
THEY EAT ALL THE WORDS THAT ARE ON THE TIPS OF OTHER PEOPLE'S TONGUES. THEY THRIVE ON MISPLACED WORDS, SAVORING ALL THE LOST POTENTIAL OF EACH EXPRESSION.
THEY'RE ALSO ABLE TO CONVERT WORDS INTO ELECTRICITY.
MR. STEELE TOOK AN ENTIRE PHRASE.
COME WITH US.
COME WITH US.

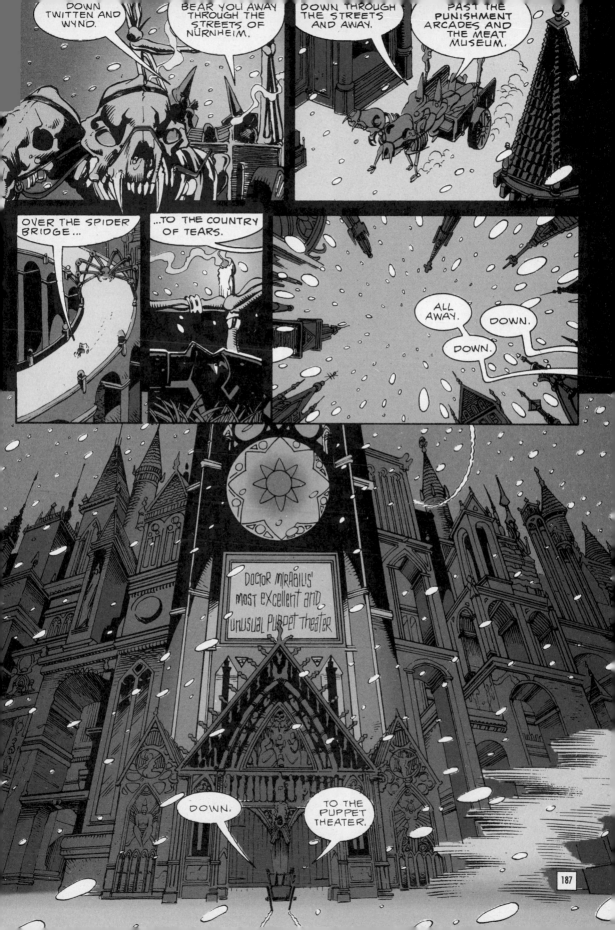

DOWN TWITTEN AND WYND.

BEAR YOU AWAY THROUGH THE STREETS OF NÜRNHEIM.

DOWN THROUGH THE STREETS AND AWAY.

PAST THE PUNISHMENT ARCADES AND THE MEAT MUSEUM.

OVER THE SPIDER BRIDGE...

...TO THE COUNTRY OF TEARS.

ALL AWAY.

DOWN.

DOWN.

DOCTOR MIRABILIS' MOST EXCELLENT AND UNUSUAL PUPPET THEATER

DOWN.

TO THE PUPPET THEATER.

187

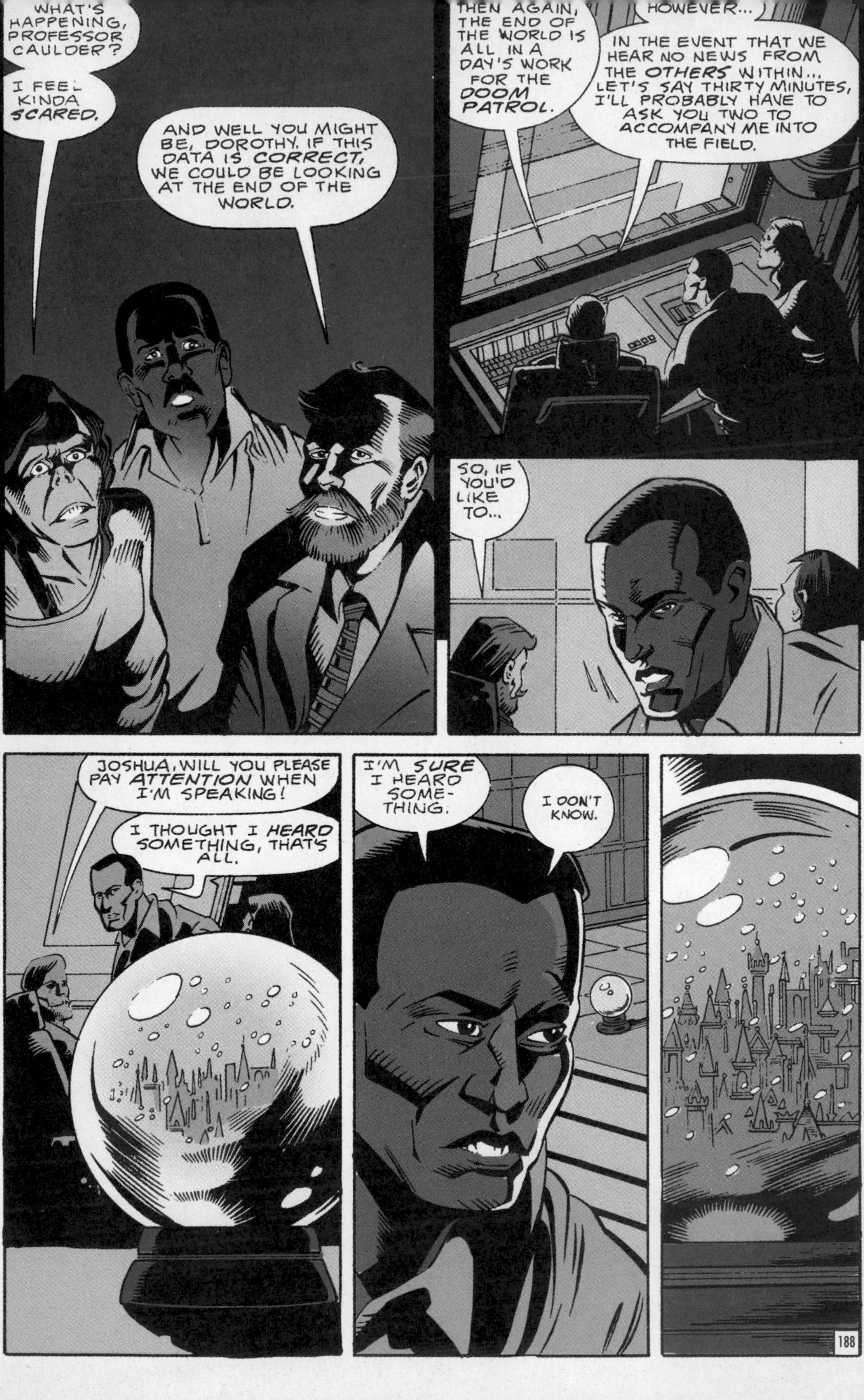

WHAT'S HAPPENING, PROFESSOR CAULDER?
I FEEL KINDA SCARED.
AND WELL YOU MIGHT BE, DOROTHY. IF THIS DATA IS CORRECT, WE COULD BE LOOKING AT THE END OF THE WORLD.
THEN AGAIN, THE END OF THE WORLD IS ALL IN A DAY'S WORK FOR THE DOOM PATROL.
HOWEVER...
IN THE EVENT THAT WE HEAR NO NEWS FROM THE OTHERS WITHIN... LET'S SAY THIRTY MINUTES, I'LL PROBABLY HAVE TO ASK YOU TWO TO ACCOMPANY ME INTO THE FIELD.
SO, IF YOU'D LIKE TO...
JOSHUA, WILL YOU PLEASE PAY ATTENTION WHEN I'M SPEAKING!
I THOUGHT I HEARD SOMETHING, THAT'S ALL.
I'M SURE I HEARD SOME-THING.
I DON'T KNOW.

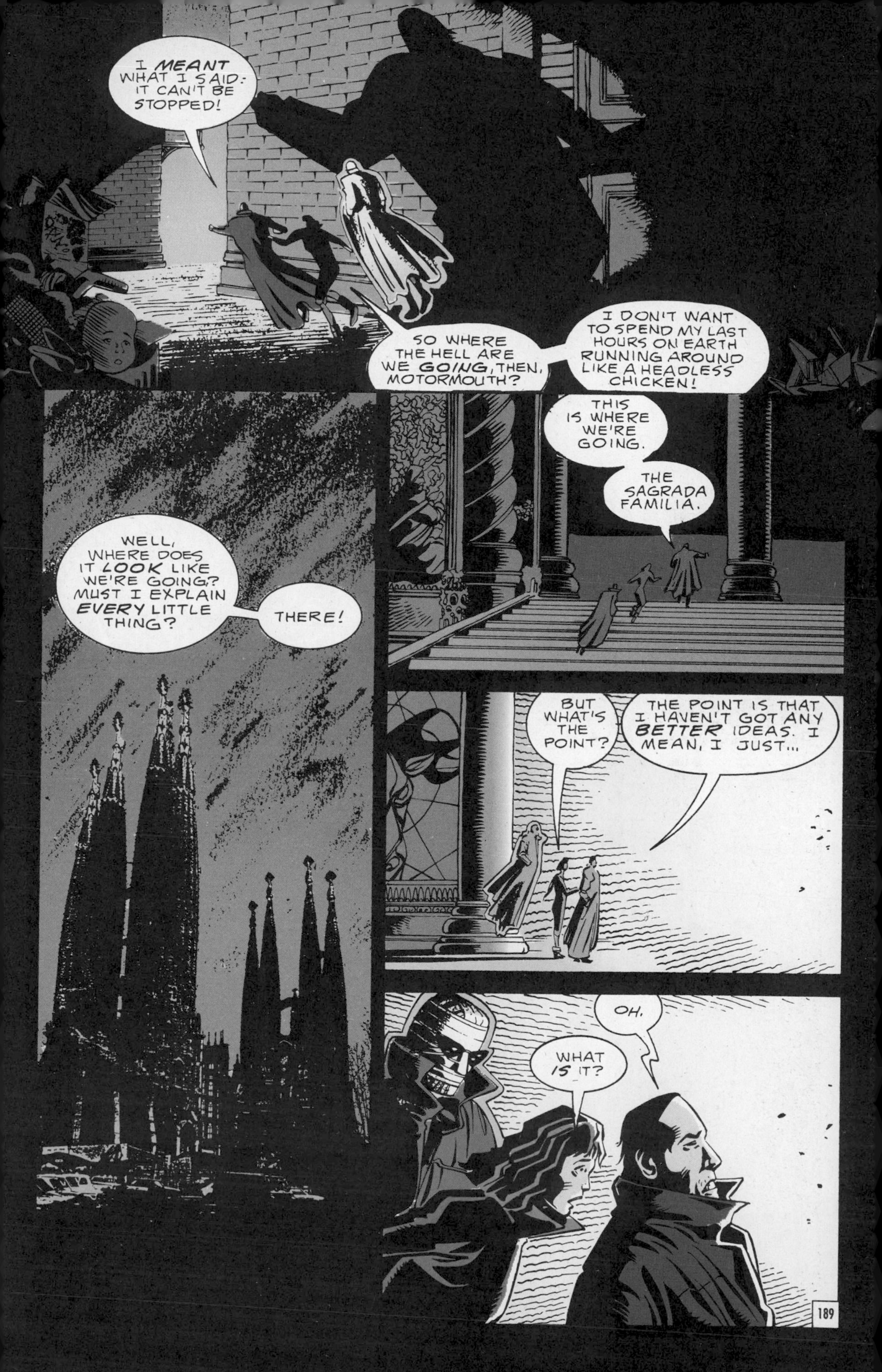
I MEANT WHAT I SAID: IT CAN'T BE STOPPED!
SO WHERE THE HELL ARE WE GOING, THEN, MOTORMOUTH?
I DON'T WANT TO SPEND MY LAST HOURS ON EARTH RUNNING AROUND LIKE A HEADLESS CHICKEN!
WELL, WHERE DOES IT LOOK LIKE WE'RE GOING? MUST I EXPLAIN EVERY LITTLE THING?
THERE!
THIS IS WHERE WE'RE GOING.
THE SAGRADA FAMILIA.
BUT WHAT'S THE POINT?
THE POINT IS THAT I HAVEN'T GOT ANY BETTER IDEAS. I MEAN, I JUST...
OH.
WHAT IS IT?

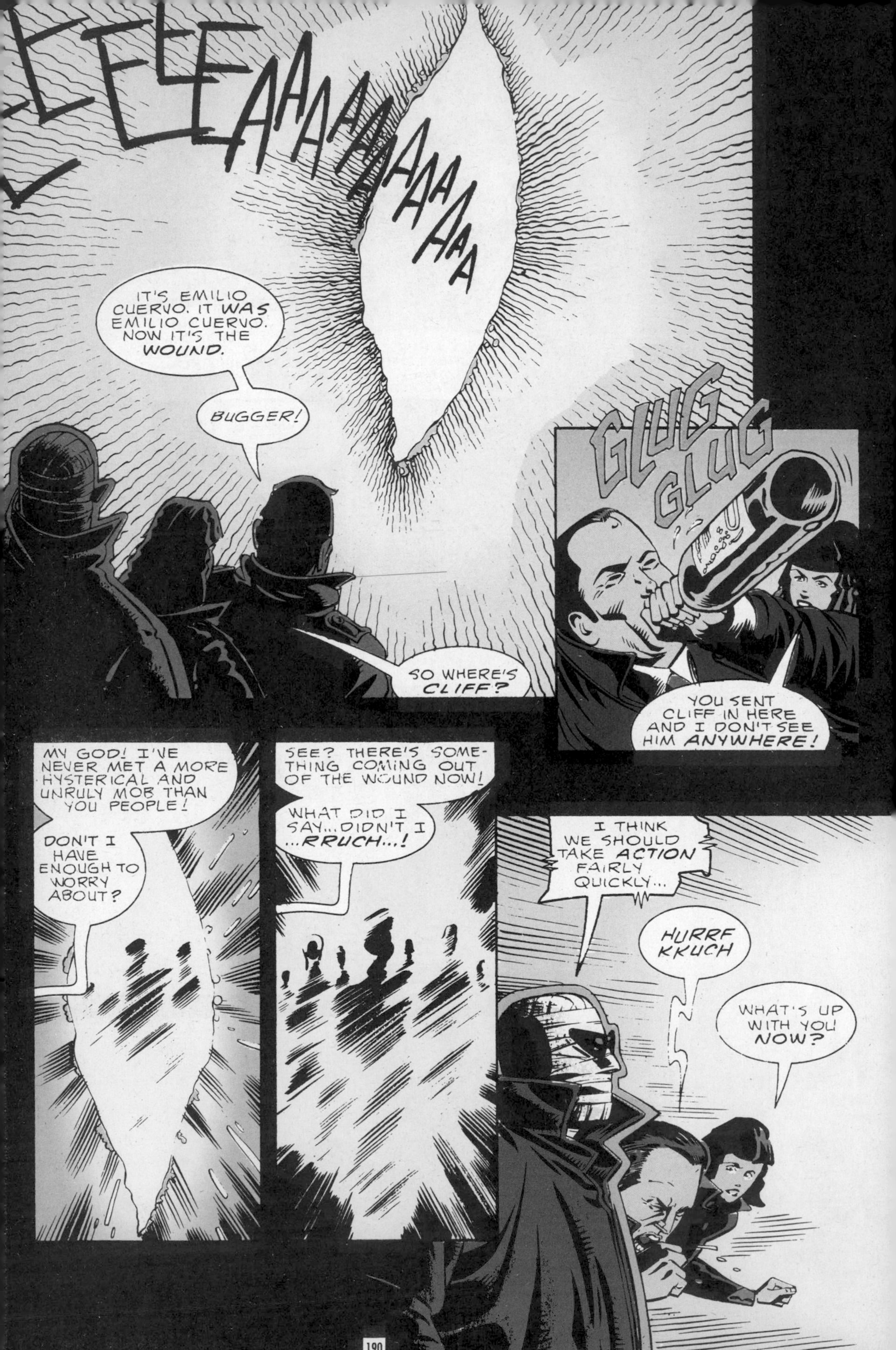
EEEEAAAAAAAAAAAAA
IT'S EMILIO CUERVO. IT WAS EMILIO CUERVO. NOW IT'S THE WOUND.
BUGGER!
SO WHERE'S CLIFF?
GLUG GLUG
YOU SENT CLIFF IN HERE AND I DON'T SEE HIM ANYWHERE!
MY GOD! I'VE NEVER MET A MORE HYSTERICAL AND UNRULY MOB THAN YOU PEOPLE!
DON'T I HAVE ENOUGH TO WORRY ABOUT?
SEE? THERE'S SOME-THING COMING OUT OF THE WOUND NOW!
WHAT DID I SAY...DIDN'T I ...RRUCH...!
I THINK WE SHOULD TAKE ACTION FAIRLY QUICKLY...
HURRF KKUCH
WHAT'S UP WITH YOU NOW?

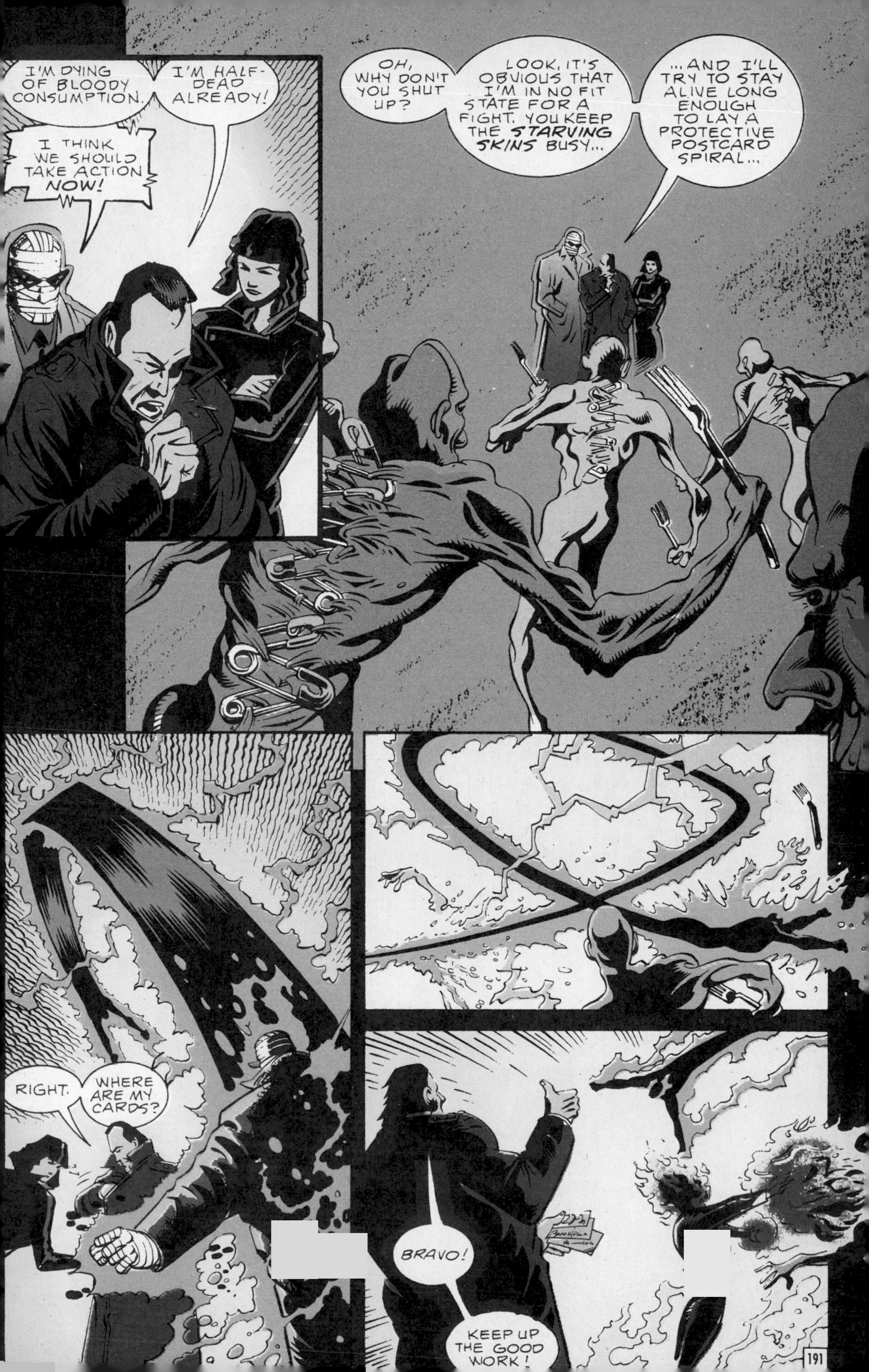

I'M DYING OF BLOODY CONSUMPTION.
I'M HALF-DEAD ALREADY!
I THINK WE SHOULD TAKE ACTION *NOW!*
OH, WHY DON'T YOU SHUT UP?
LOOK, IT'S OBVIOUS THAT I'M IN NO FIT STATE FOR A FIGHT. YOU KEEP THE ***STARVING SKINS*** BUSY...
...AND I'LL TRY TO STAY ALIVE LONG ENOUGH TO LAY A PROTECTIVE POSTCARD SPIRAL...
RIGHT.
WHERE ARE MY CARDS?
BRAVO!
KEEP UP THE GOOD WORK!

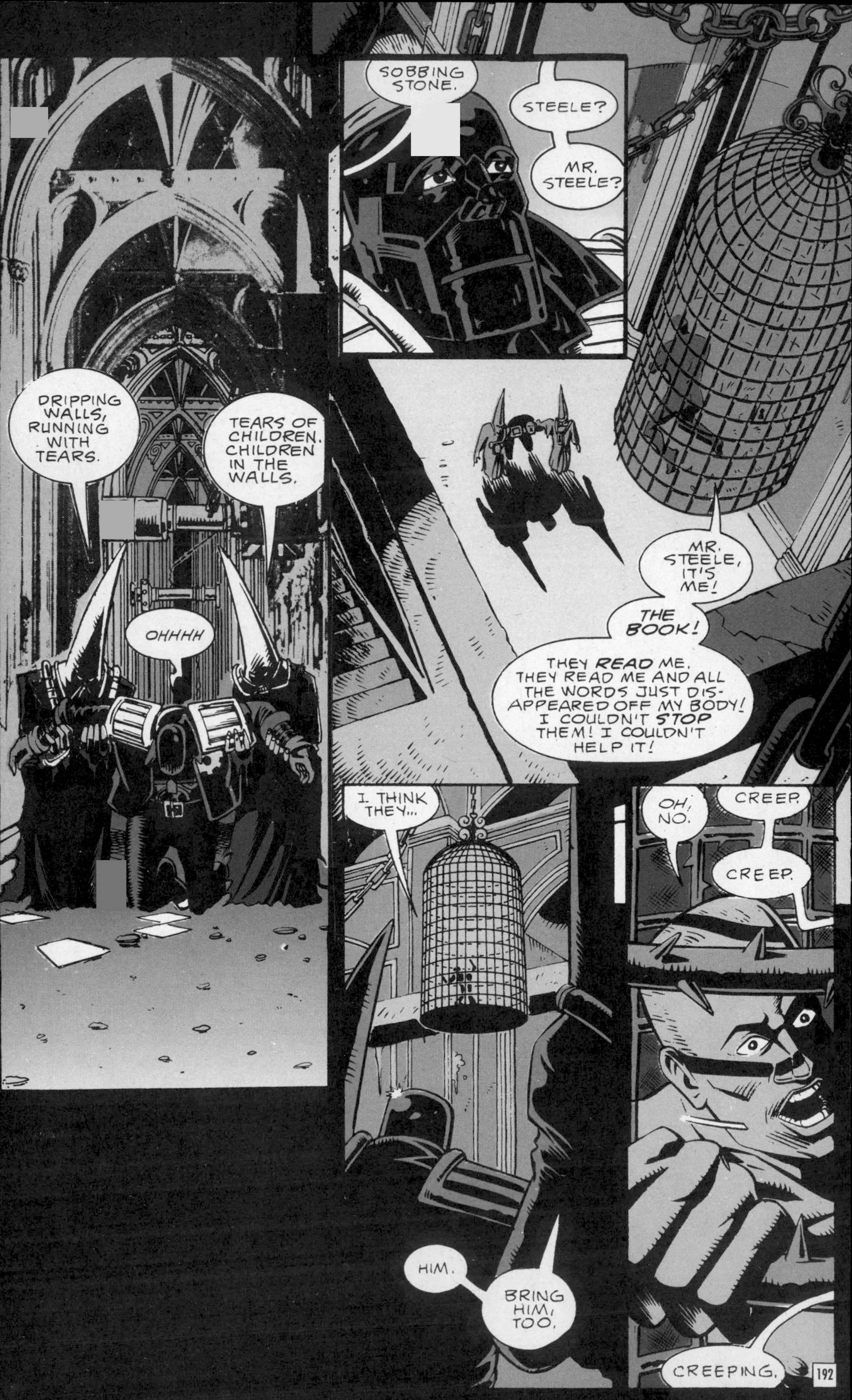
DRIPPING WALLS, RUNNING WITH TEARS.
TEARS OF CHILDREN. CHILDREN IN THE WALLS.
OHHHH
SOBBING STONE.
STEELE?
MR. STEELE?
MR. STEELE, IT'S ME!
THE BOOK!
THEY READ ME. THEY READ ME AND ALL THE WORDS JUST DIS-APPEARED OFF MY BODY! I COULDN'T STOP THEM! I COULDN'T HELP IT!
I THINK THEY...
HIM.
BRING HIM, TOO.
OH, NO.
CREEP.
CREEP.
CREEPING.

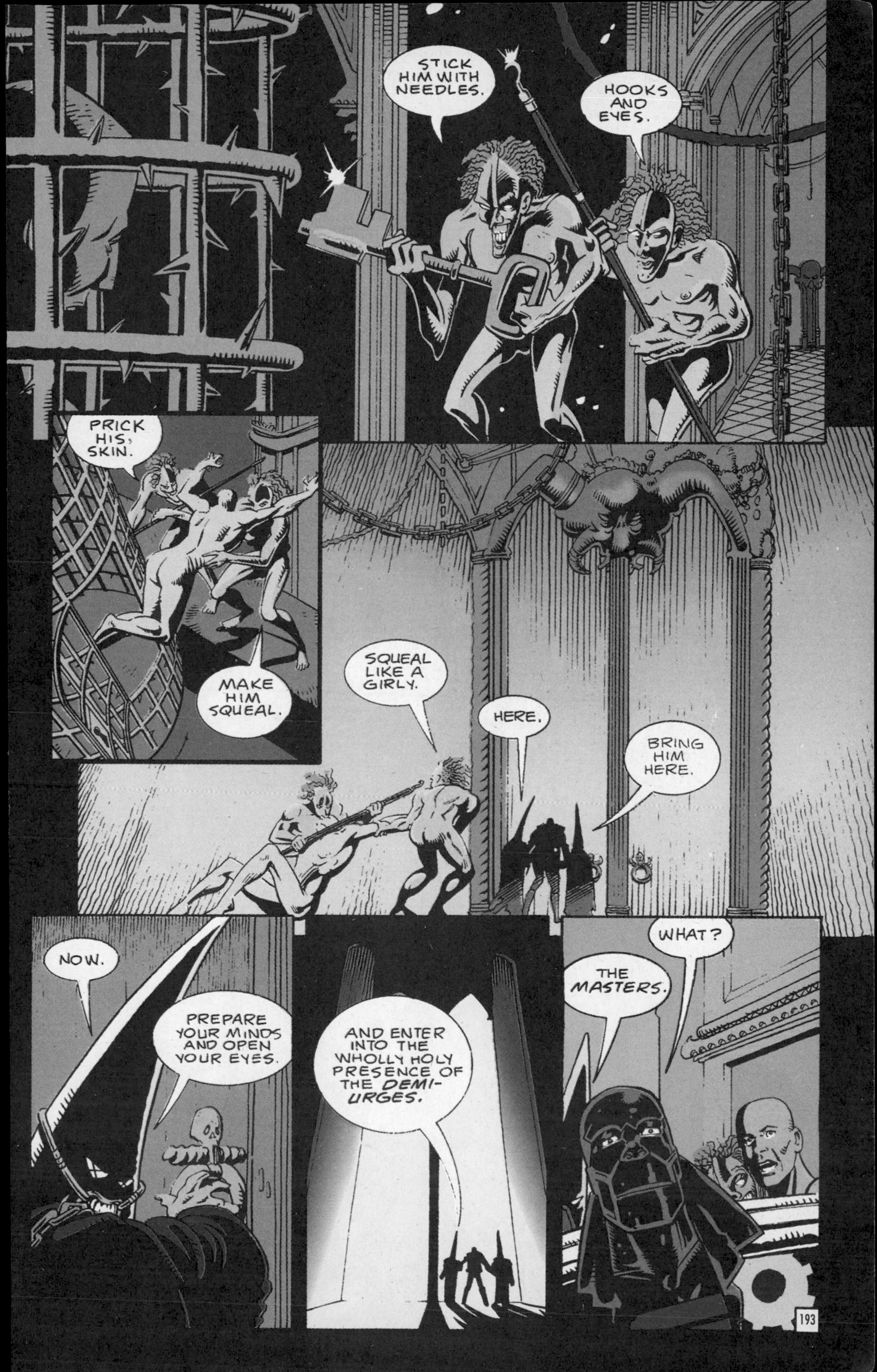
STICK HIM WITH NEEDLES.
HOOKS AND EYES.
PRICK HIS, SKIN.
MAKE HIM SQUEAL.
SQUEAL LIKE A GIRLY.
HERE.
BRING HIM HERE.
NOW.
PREPARE YOUR MINDS AND OPEN YOUR EYES.
AND ENTER INTO THE WHOLLY HOLY PRESENCE OF THE *DEMI-URGES.*
WHAT?
THE *MASTERS.*

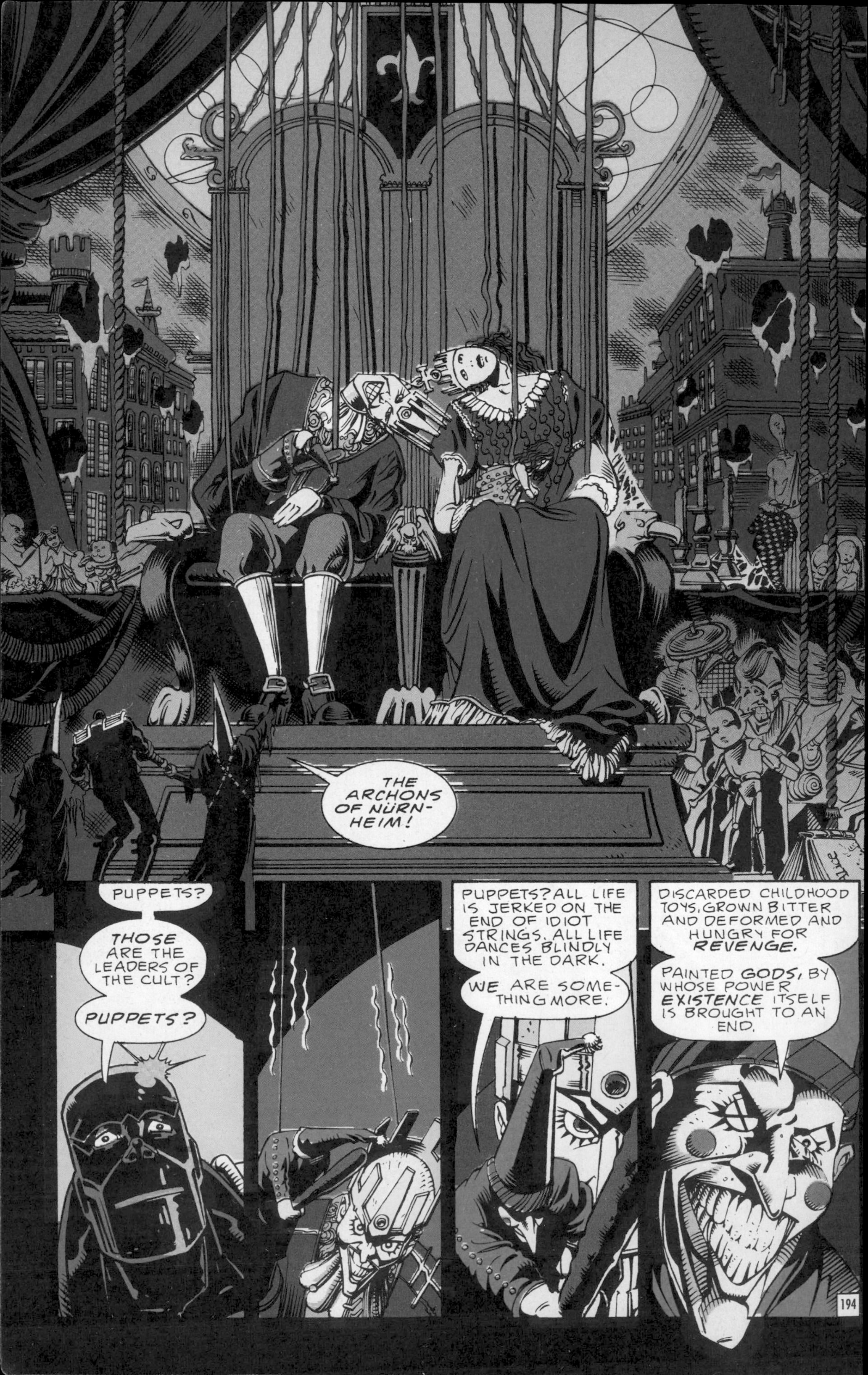
THE ARCHONS OF NÜRNHEIM!
PUPPETS?
THOSE ARE THE LEADERS OF THE CULT?
PUPPETS?
PUPPETS? ALL LIFE IS JERKED ON THE END OF IDIOT STRINGS. ALL LIFE DANCES BLINDLY IN THE DARK.
WE ARE SOMETHING MORE.
DISCARDED CHILDHOOD TOYS, GROWN BITTER AND DEFORMED AND HUNGRY FOR REVENGE.
PAINTED GODS, BY WHOSE POWER EXISTENCE ITSELF IS BROUGHT TO AN END.

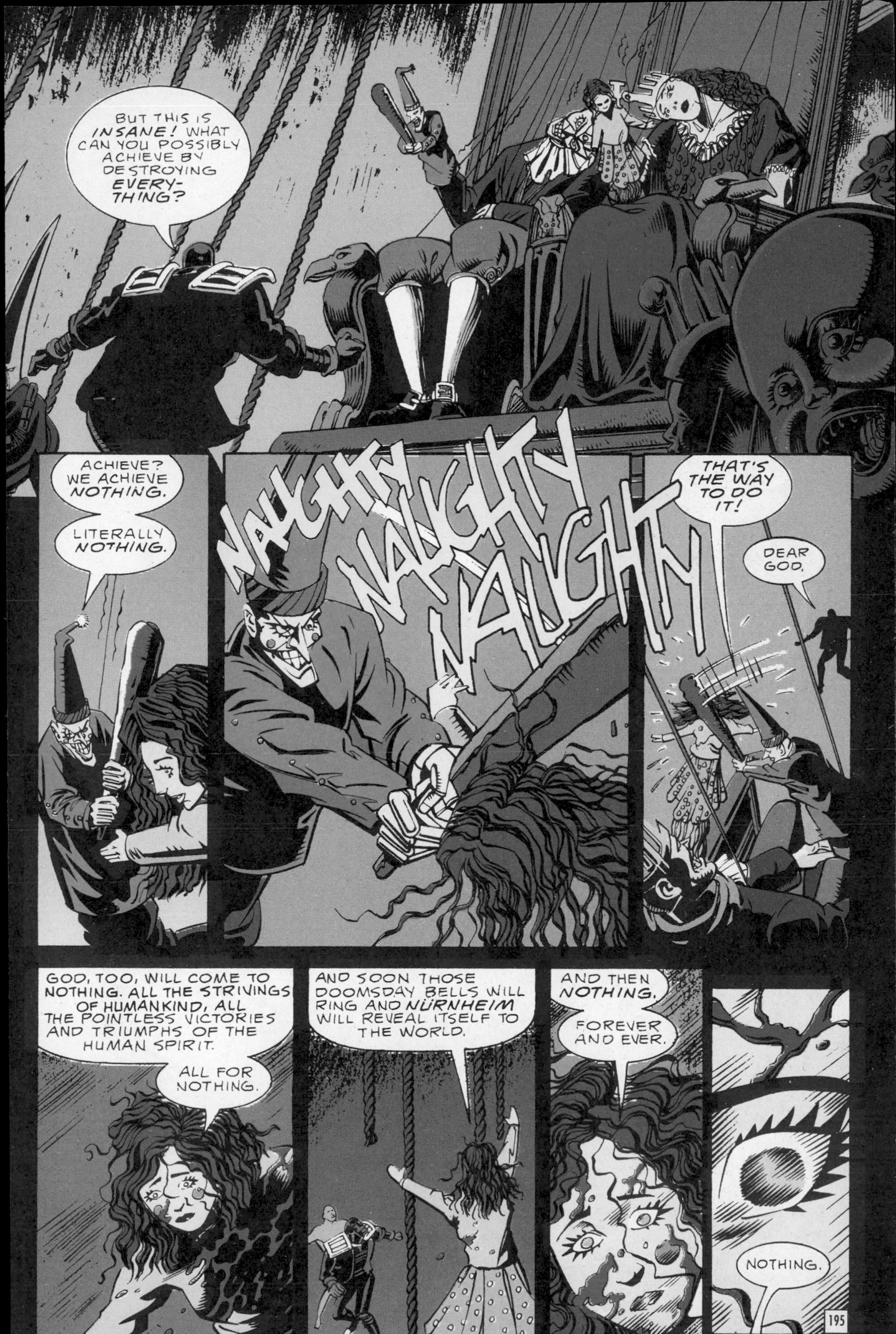
BUT THIS IS *INSANE!* WHAT CAN YOU POSSIBLY ACHIEVE BY DESTROYING *EVERY-THING?*
ACHIEVE? WE ACHIEVE *NOTHING.*
LITERALLY *NOTHING.*
NAUGHTY NAUGHTY NAUGHTY
THAT'S THE WAY TO DO IT!
DEAR GOD.
GOD, TOO, WILL COME TO NOTHING. ALL THE STRIVINGS OF HUMANKIND, ALL THE POINTLESS VICTORIES AND TRIUMPHS OF THE HUMAN SPIRIT.
ALL FOR NOTHING.
AND SOON THOSE DOOMSDAY BELLS WILL RING AND *NÜRNHEIM* WILL REVEAL ITSELF TO THE WORLD.
AND THEN *NOTHING.*
FOREVER AND EVER.
NOTHING.

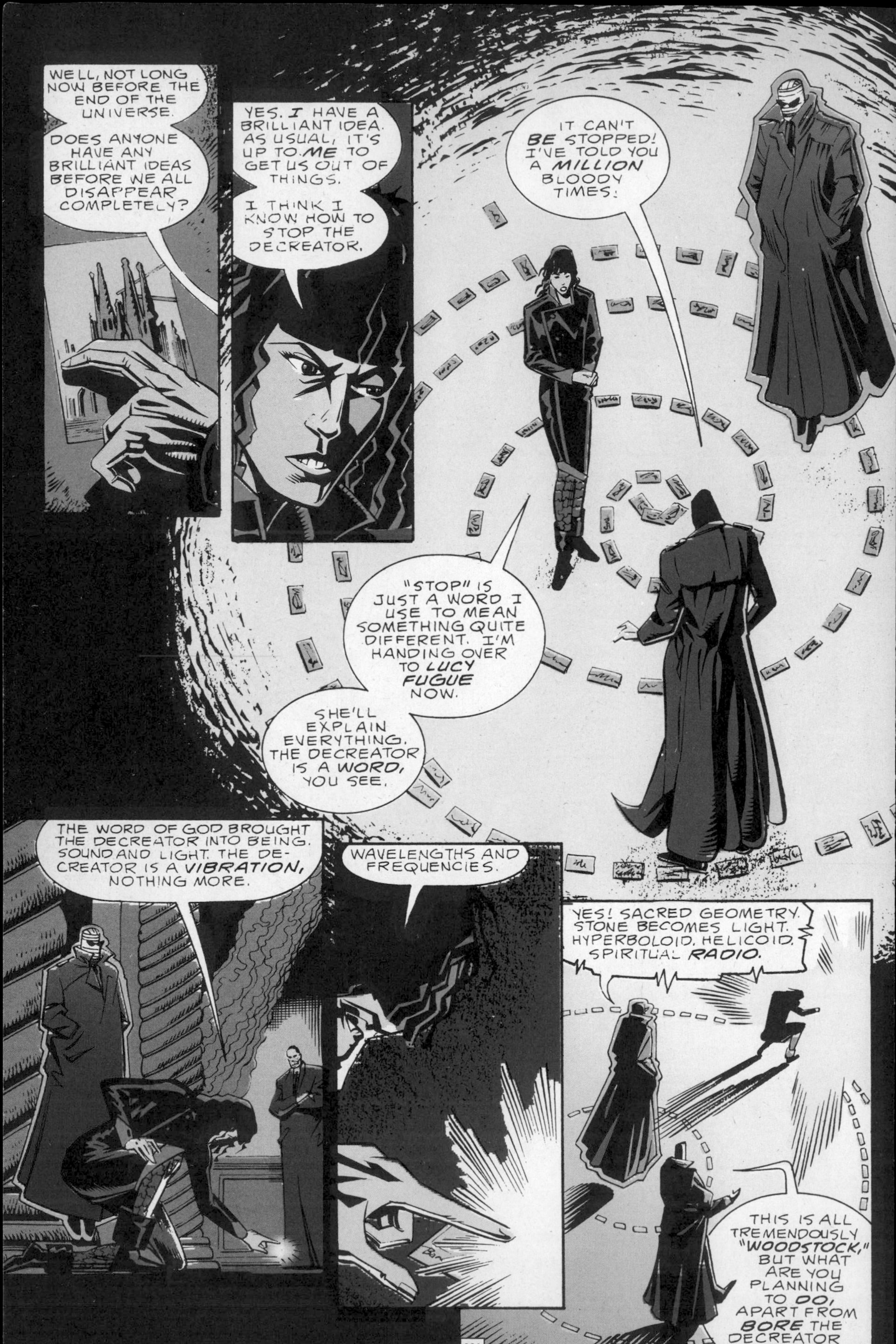
WELL, NOT LONG NOW BEFORE THE END OF THE UNIVERSE.
DOES ANYONE HAVE ANY BRILLIANT IDEAS BEFORE WE ALL DISAPPEAR COMPLETELY?
YES. I HAVE A BRILLIANT IDEA. AS USUAL, IT'S UP TO ME TO GET US OUT OF THINGS.
I THINK I KNOW HOW TO STOP THE DECREATOR.
IT CAN'T BE STOPPED! I'VE TOLD YOU A MILLION BLOODY TIMES!
"STOP" IS JUST A WORD I USE TO MEAN SOMETHING QUITE DIFFERENT. I'M HANDING OVER TO LUCY FUGUE NOW.
SHE'LL EXPLAIN EVERYTHING. THE DECREATOR IS A WORD, YOU SEE.
THE WORD OF GOD BROUGHT THE DECREATOR INTO BEING. SOUND AND LIGHT. THE DECREATOR IS A VIBRATION, NOTHING MORE.
WAVELENGTHS AND FREQUENCIES.
YES! SACRED GEOMETRY. STONE BECOMES LIGHT. HYPERBOLOID. HELICOID. SPIRITUAL RADIO.
THIS IS ALL TREMENDOUSLY "WOODSTOCK," BUT WHAT ARE YOU PLANNING TO DO, APART FROM BORE THE DECREATOR TO DEATH?

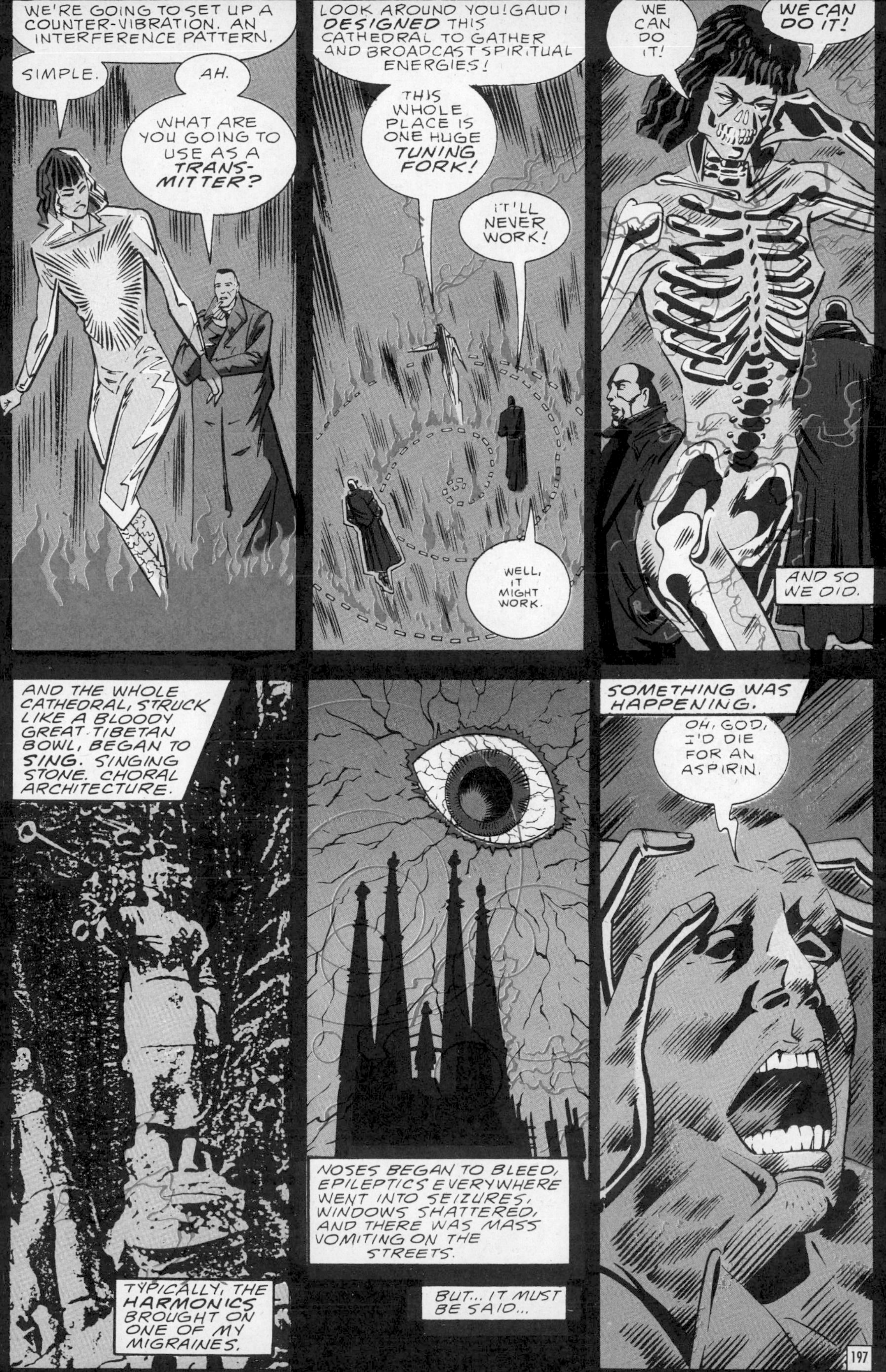

WE'RE GOING TO SET UP A COUNTER-VIBRATION. AN INTERFERENCE PATTERN.
SIMPLE.
AH.
WHAT ARE YOU GOING TO USE AS A TRANS-MITTER?
LOOK AROUND YOU! GAUDI DESIGNED THIS CATHEDRAL TO GATHER AND BROADCAST SPIRITUAL ENERGIES!
THIS WHOLE PLACE IS ONE HUGE TUNING FORK!
IT'LL NEVER WORK!
WELL, IT MIGHT WORK.
WE CAN DO IT!
WE CAN DO IT!
AND SO WE DID.
AND THE WHOLE CATHEDRAL, STRUCK LIKE A BLOODY GREAT TIBETAN BOWL, BEGAN TO SING. SINGING STONE. CHORAL ARCHITECTURE.
TYPICALLY, THE HARMONICS BROUGHT ON ONE OF MY MIGRAINES.
NOSES BEGAN TO BLEED, EPILEPTICS EVERYWHERE WENT INTO SEIZURES, WINDOWS SHATTERED, AND THERE WAS MASS VOMITING ON THE STREETS.
BUT... IT MUST BE SAID...
SOMETHING WAS HAPPENING.
OH, GOD, I'D DIE FOR AN ASPIRIN.

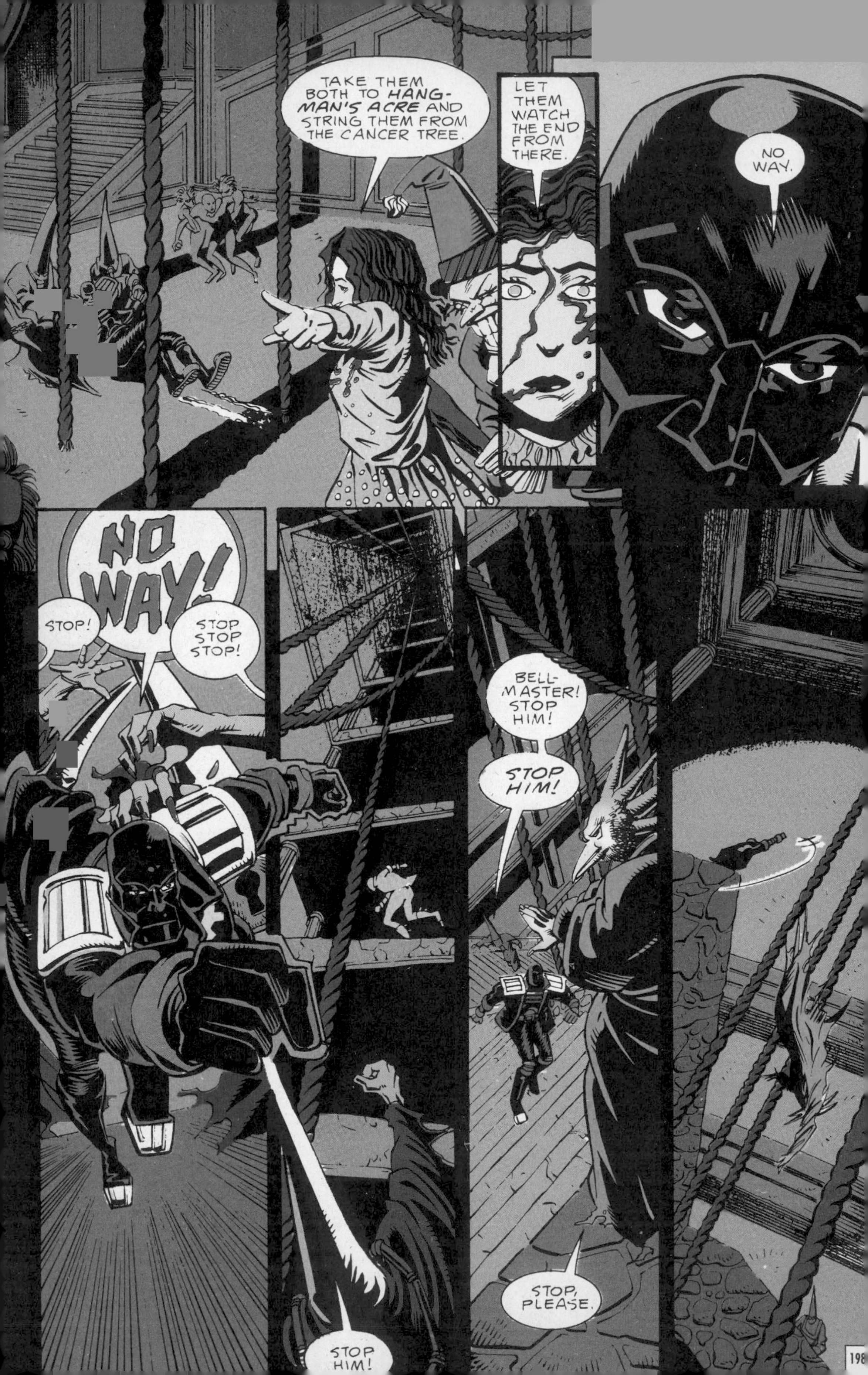
TAKE THEM BOTH TO *HANG-MAN'S ACRE* AND STRING THEM FROM THE *CANCER TREE.*
LET THEM WATCH THE END FROM THERE.
NO WAY.
NO WAY!
STOP!
STOP STOP STOP!
STOP HIM!
BELL-MASTER! STOP HIM!
STOP HIM!
STOP, PLEASE.

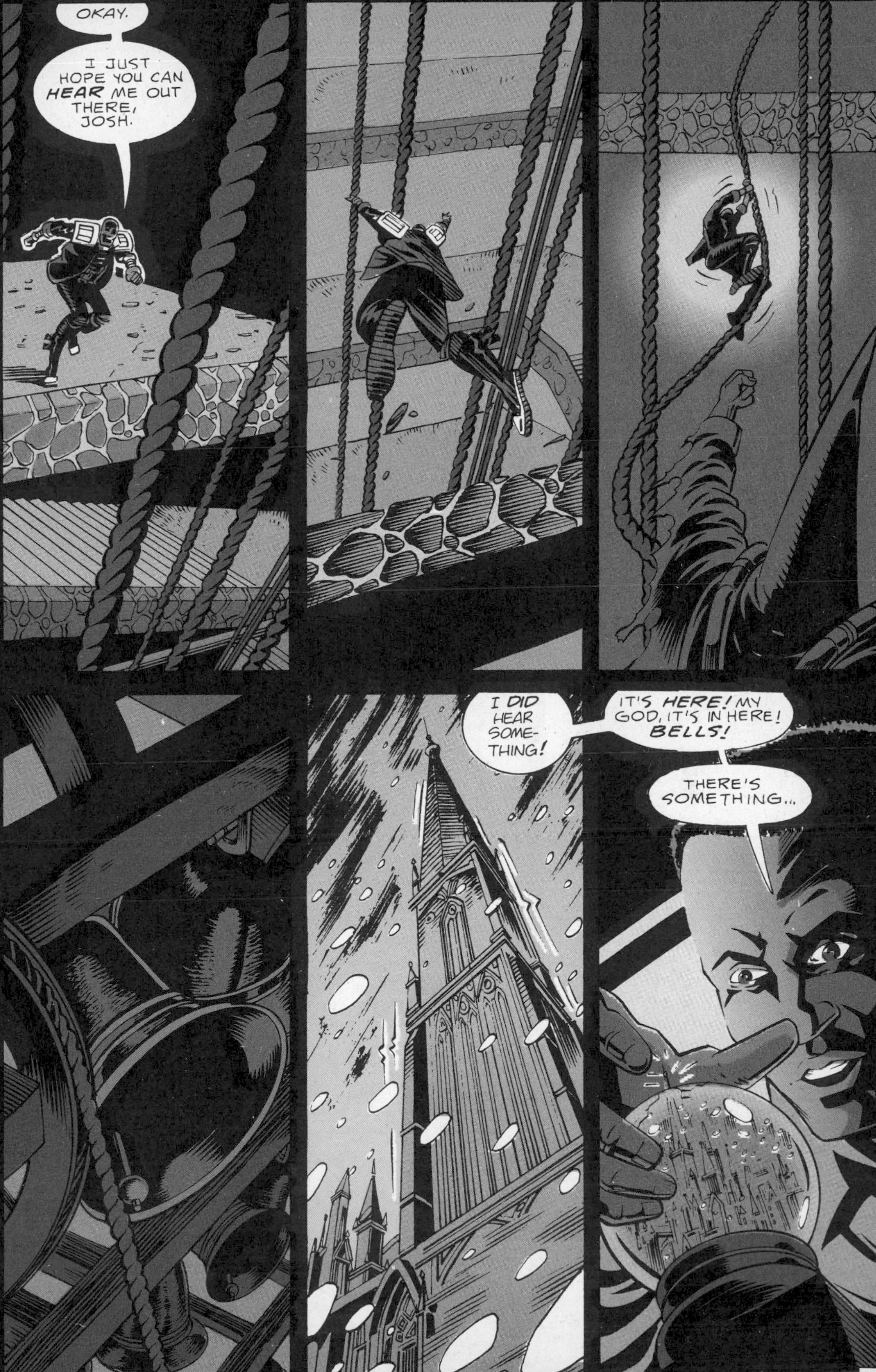
OKAY.
I JUST HOPE YOU CAN HEAR ME OUT THERE, JOSH.
I DID HEAR SOMETHING!
IT'S HERE! MY GOD, IT'S IN HERE! BELLS!
THERE'S SOMETHING...

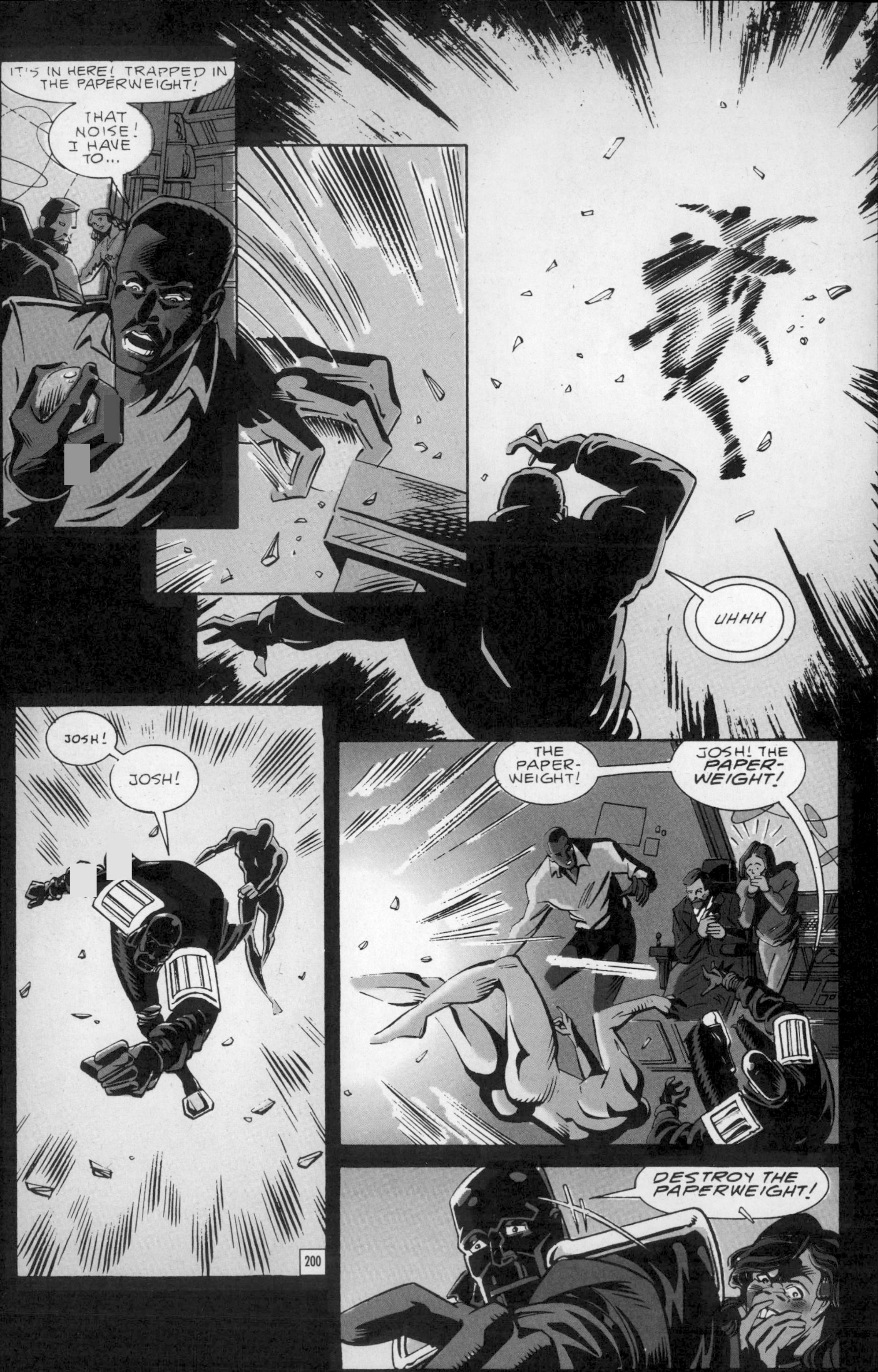
IT'S IN HERE! TRAPPED IN THE PAPERWEIGHT!
THAT NOISE! I HAVE TO...
UHHH
JOSH!
JOSH!
THE PAPER-WEIGHT!
JOSH! THE PAPER-WEIGHT!
DESTROY THE PAPERWEIGHT!

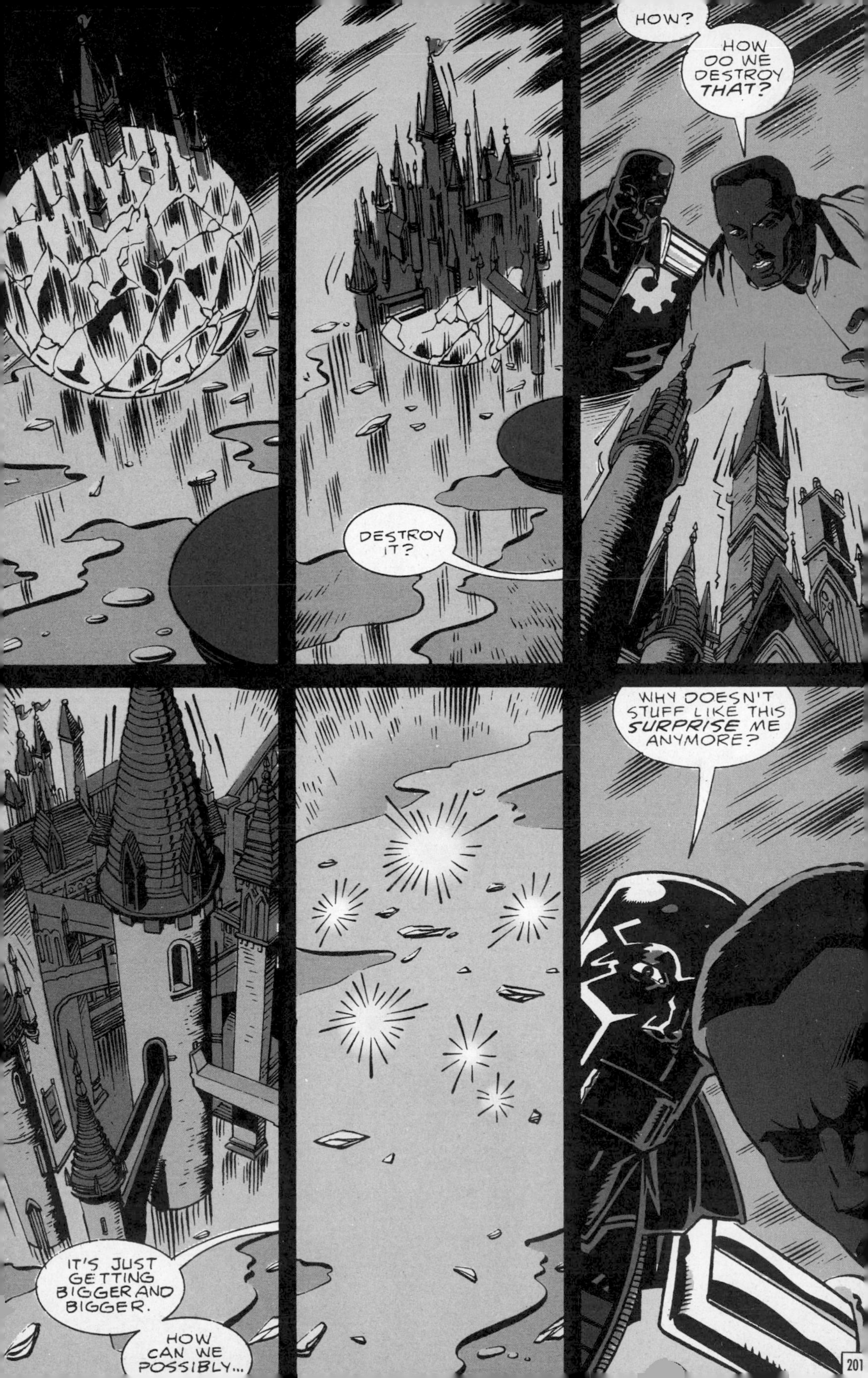
DESTROY IT?
HOW?
HOW DO WE DESTROY THAT?
IT'S JUST GETTING BIGGER AND BIGGER.
HOW CAN WE POSSIBLY...
WHY DOESN'T STUFF LIKE THIS SURPRISE ME ANYMORE?

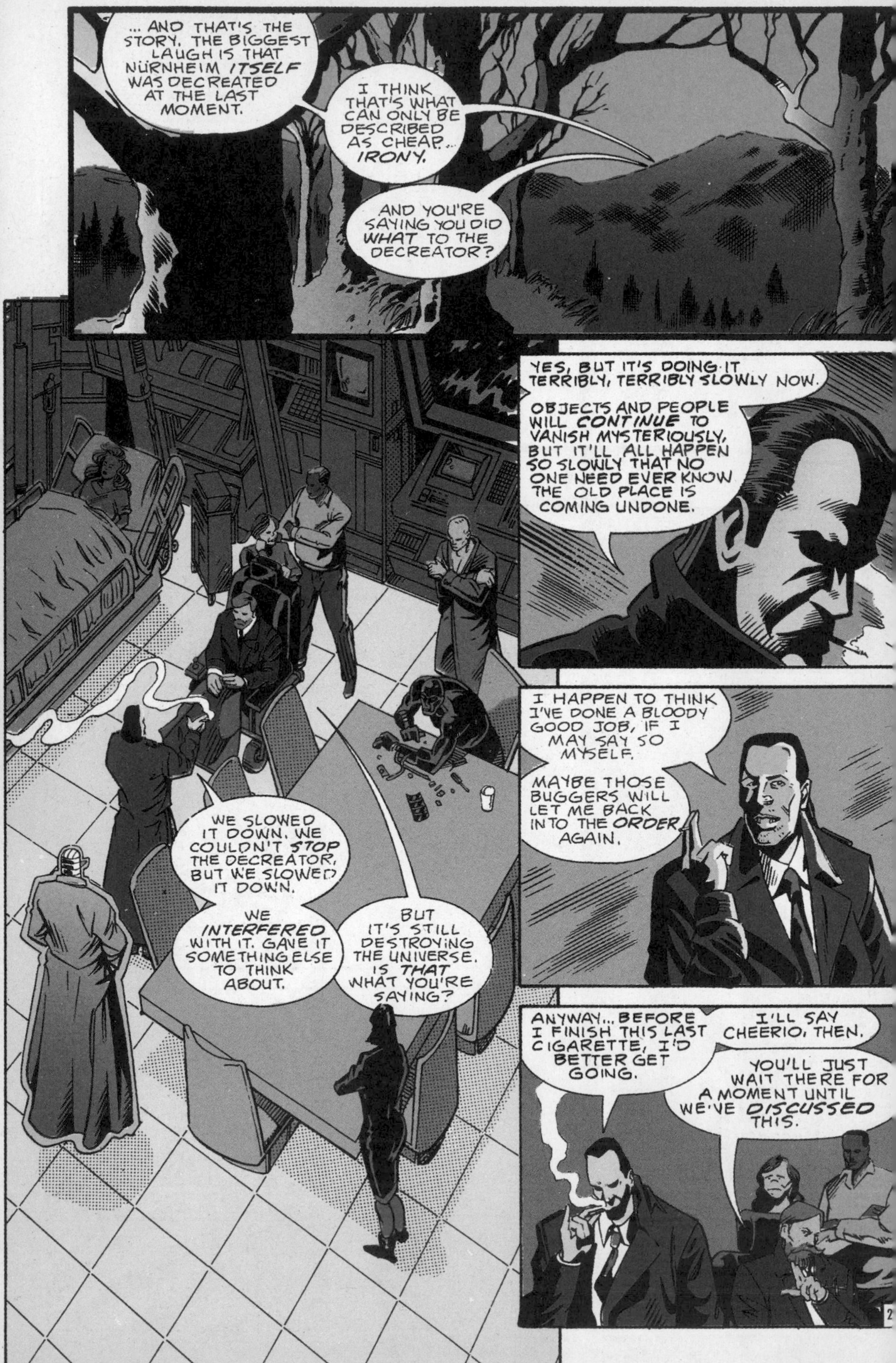
... AND THAT'S THE STORY. THE BIGGEST LAUGH IS THAT NÜRNHEIM ITSELF WAS DECREATED AT THE LAST MOMENT.
I THINK THAT'S WHAT CAN ONLY BE DESCRIBED AS CHEAP... IRONY.
AND YOU'RE SAYING YOU DID WHAT TO THE DECREATOR?
WE SLOWED IT DOWN. WE COULDN'T STOP THE DECREATOR, BUT WE SLOWED IT DOWN.
WE INTERFERED WITH IT. GAVE IT SOMETHING ELSE TO THINK ABOUT.
BUT IT'S STILL DESTROYING THE UNIVERSE. IS THAT WHAT YOU'RE SAYING?
YES, BUT IT'S DOING IT TERRIBLY, TERRIBLY SLOWLY NOW.
OBJECTS AND PEOPLE WILL CONTINUE TO VANISH MYSTERIOUSLY, BUT IT'LL ALL HAPPEN SO SLOWLY THAT NO ONE NEED EVER KNOW THE OLD PLACE IS COMING UNDONE.
I HAPPEN TO THINK I'VE DONE A BLOODY GOOD JOB, IF I MAY SAY SO MYSELF.
MAYBE THOSE BUGGERS WILL LET ME BACK INTO THE ORDER AGAIN.
ANYWAY... BEFORE I FINISH THIS LAST CIGARETTE, I'D BETTER GET GOING.
I'LL SAY CHEERIO, THEN.
YOU'LL JUST WAIT THERE FOR A MOMENT UNTIL WE'VE DISCUSSED THIS.

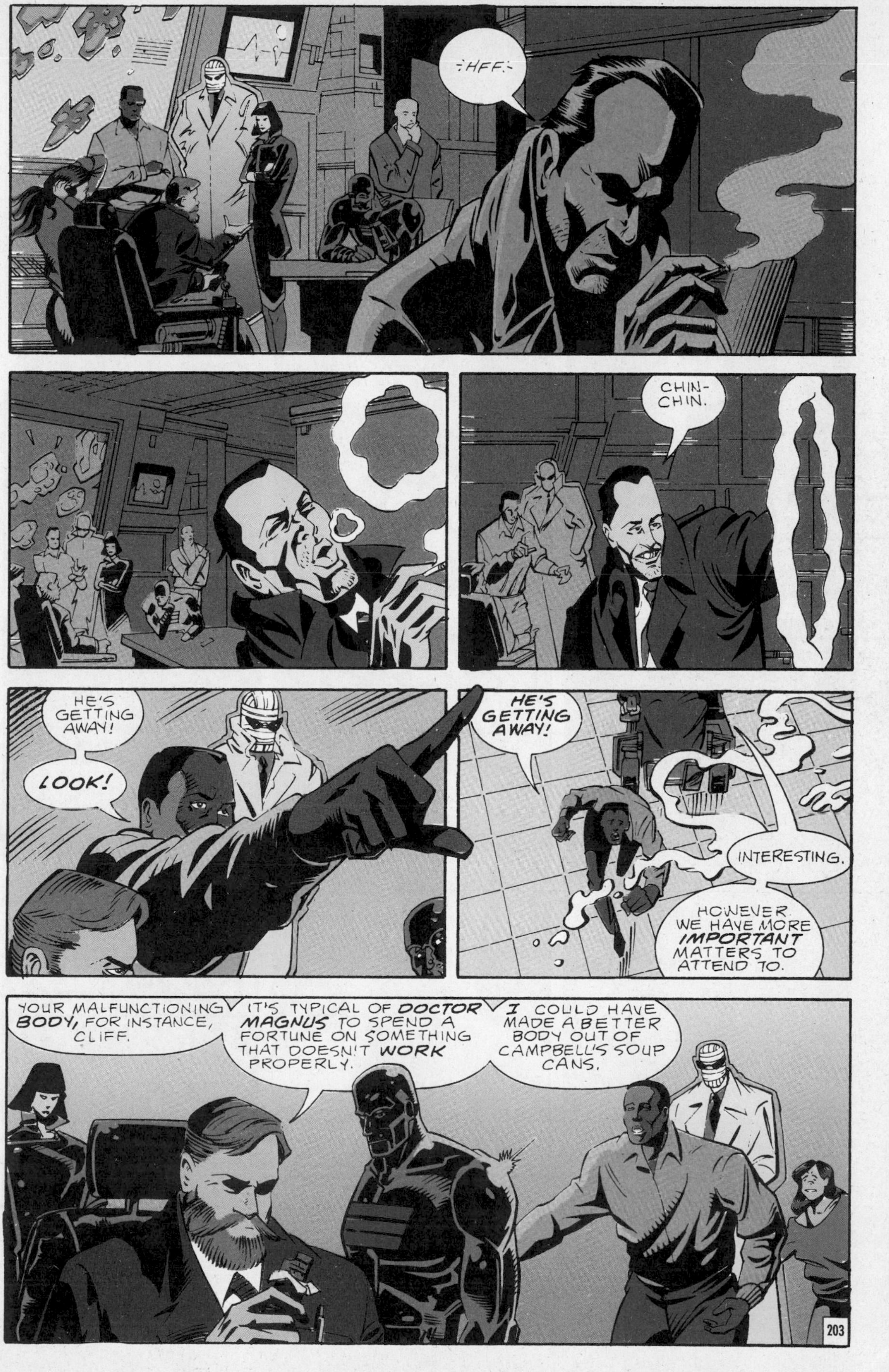

:HFF:
CHIN-CHIN.
HE'S GETTING AWAY!
LOOK!
HE'S GETTING AWAY!
INTERESTING.
HOWEVER WE HAVE MORE IMPORTANT MATTERS TO ATTEND TO.
YOUR MALFUNCTIONING BODY, FOR INSTANCE, CLIFF.
IT'S TYPICAL OF DOCTOR MAGNUS TO SPEND A FORTUNE ON SOMETHING THAT DOESN'T WORK PROPERLY.
I COULD HAVE MADE A BETTER BODY OUT OF CAMPBELL'S SOUP CANS.

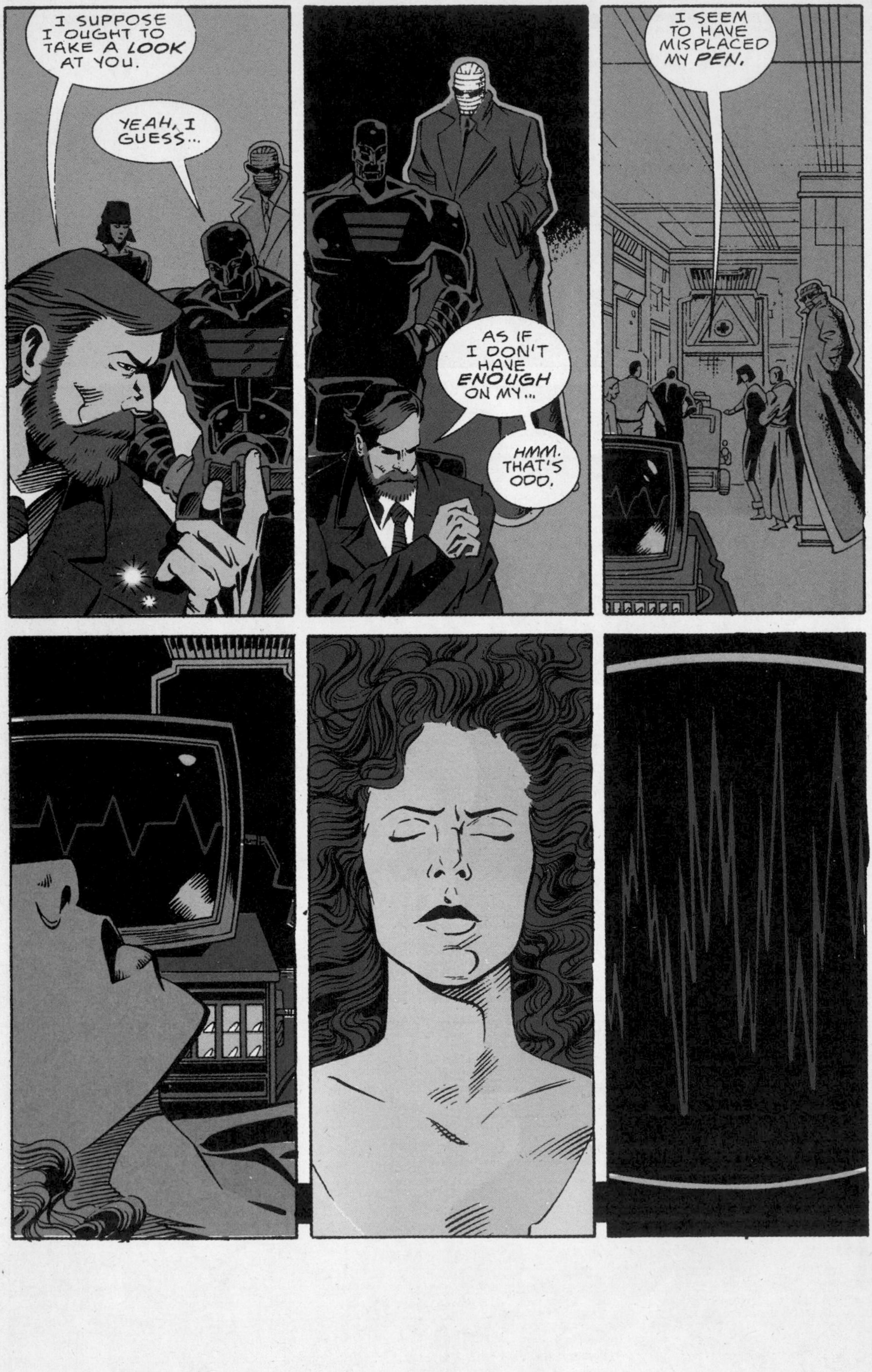
I SUPPOSE I OUGHT TO TAKE A *LOOK* AT YOU.
YEAH, I GUESS...
AS IF I DON'T HAVE *ENOUGH* ON MY...
HMM. *THAT'S ODD.*
I SEEM TO HAVE MISPLACED MY *PEN.*

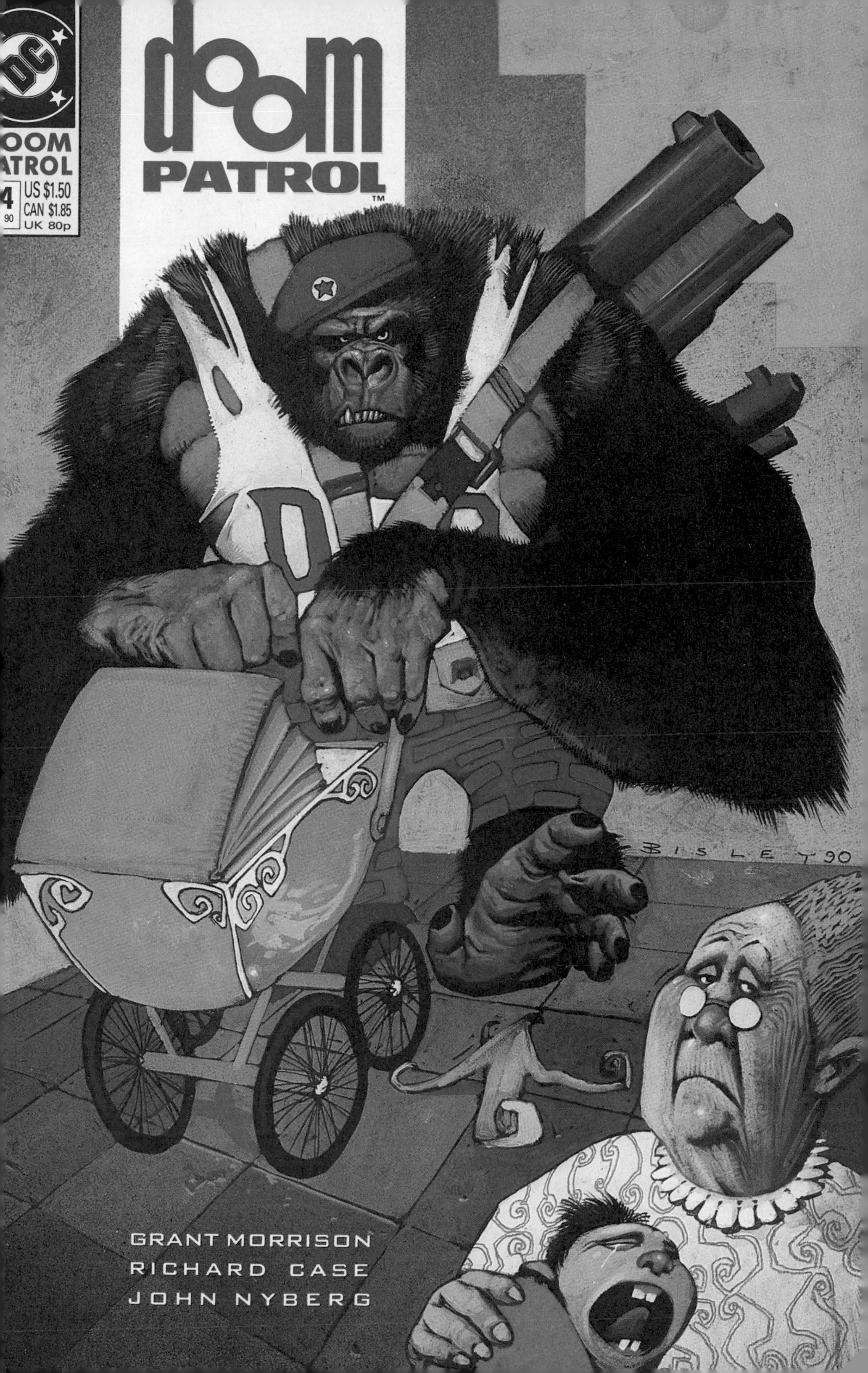
DC
OOM
ATROL
4
90
US $1.50
CAN $1.85
UK 80p
doom
PATROL
TM
BISLEY '90
GRANT MORRISON
RICHARD CASE
JOHN NYBERG

THE SOUL OF A NEW MACHINE

DOES THE BODY RULE THE MIND OR DOES THE MIND RULE THE BODY?

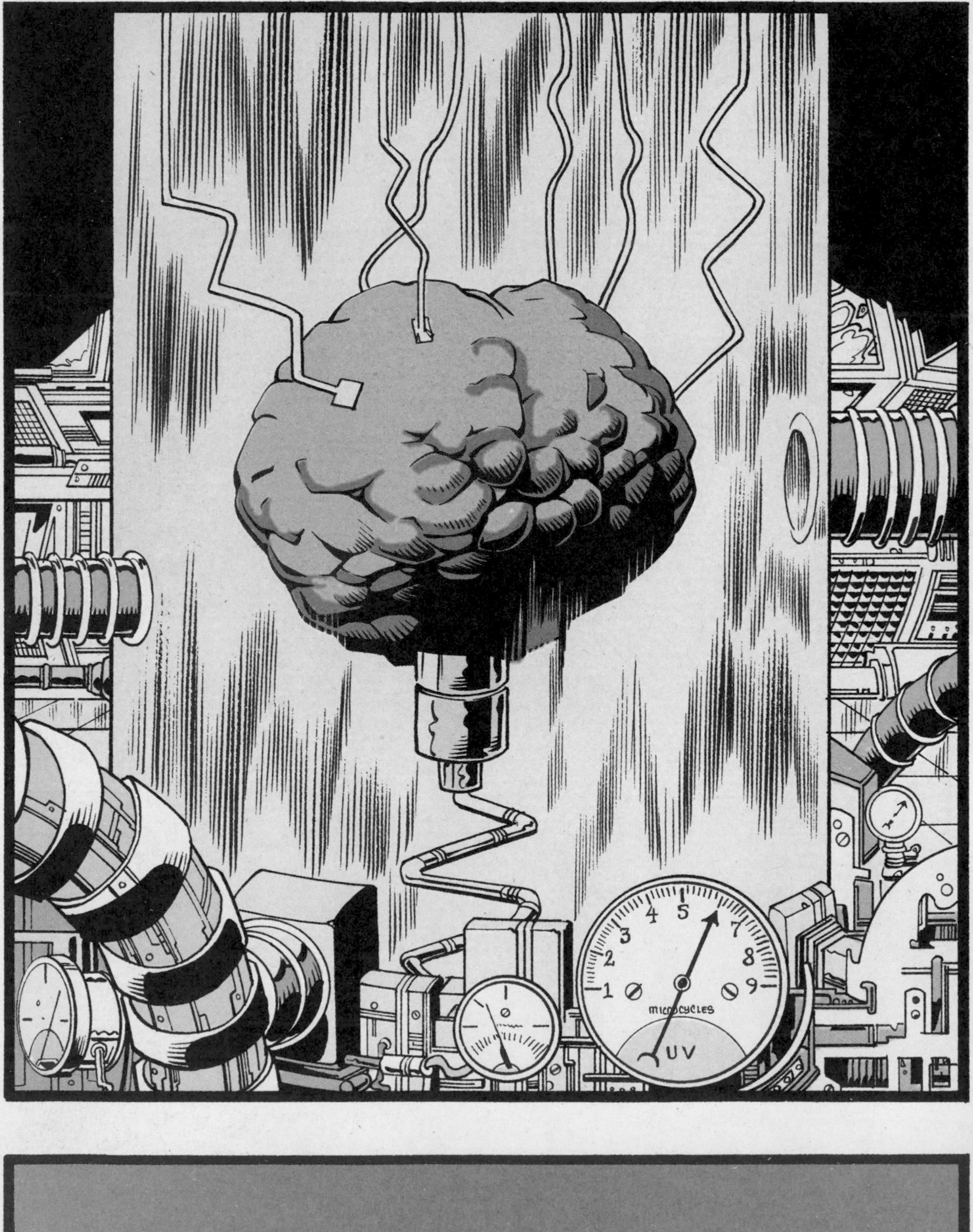
MICROCYCLES
UV

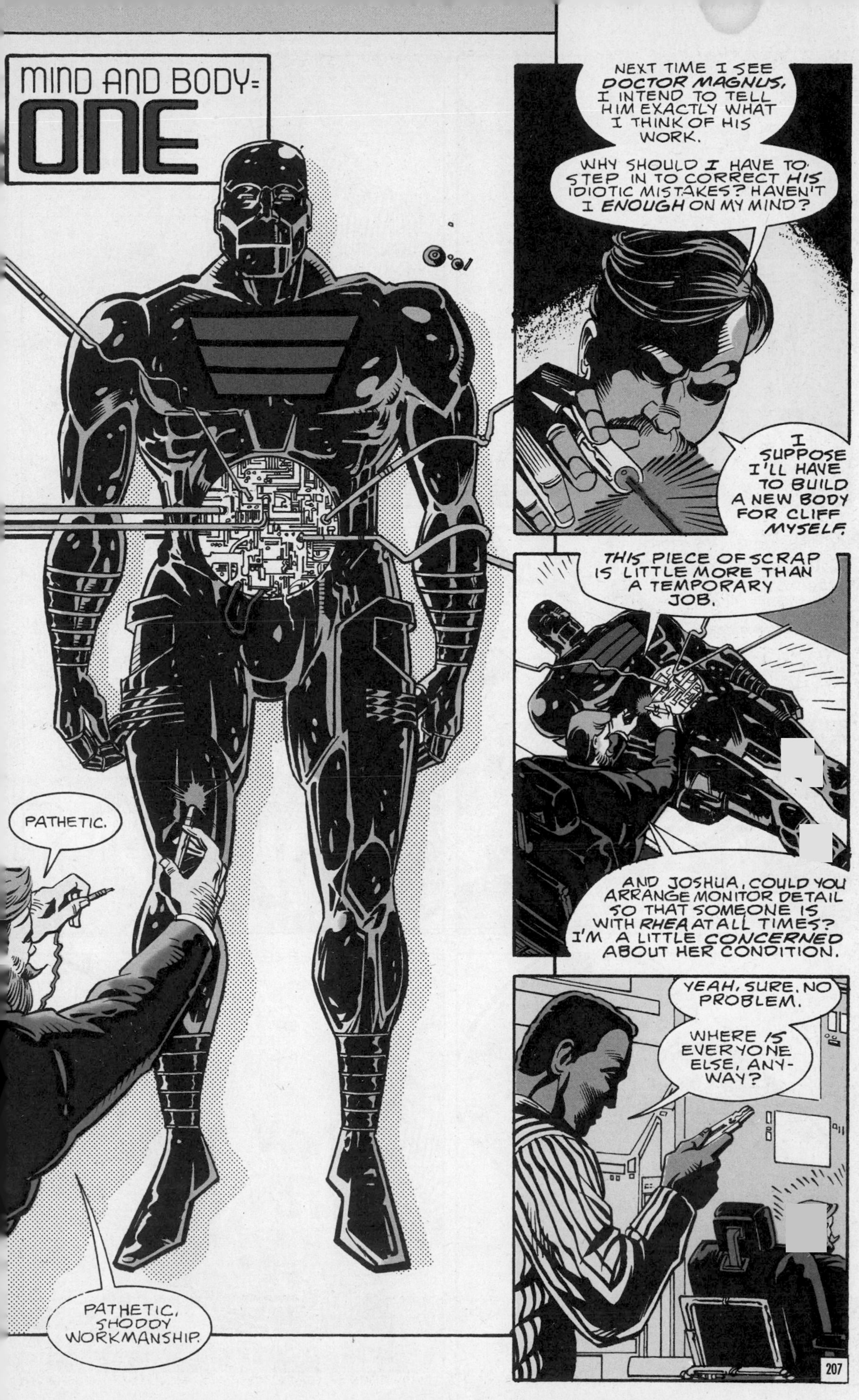
MIND AND BODY=
ONE
PATHETIC.
PATHETIC, SHODDY WORKMANSHIP.
NEXT TIME I SEE DOCTOR MAGNUS, I INTEND TO TELL HIM EXACTLY WHAT I THINK OF HIS WORK.
WHY SHOULD I HAVE TO STEP IN TO CORRECT HIS IDIOTIC MISTAKES? HAVEN'T I ENOUGH ON MY MIND?
I SUPPOSE I'LL HAVE TO BUILD A NEW BODY FOR CLIFF MYSELF.
THIS PIECE OF SCRAP IS LITTLE MORE THAN A TEMPORARY JOB.
AND JOSHUA, COULD YOU ARRANGE MONITOR DETAIL SO THAT SOMEONE IS WITH RHEA AT ALL TIMES? I'M A LITTLE CONCERNED ABOUT HER CONDITION.
YEAH, SURE. NO PROBLEM.
WHERE IS EVERYONE ELSE, ANYWAY?

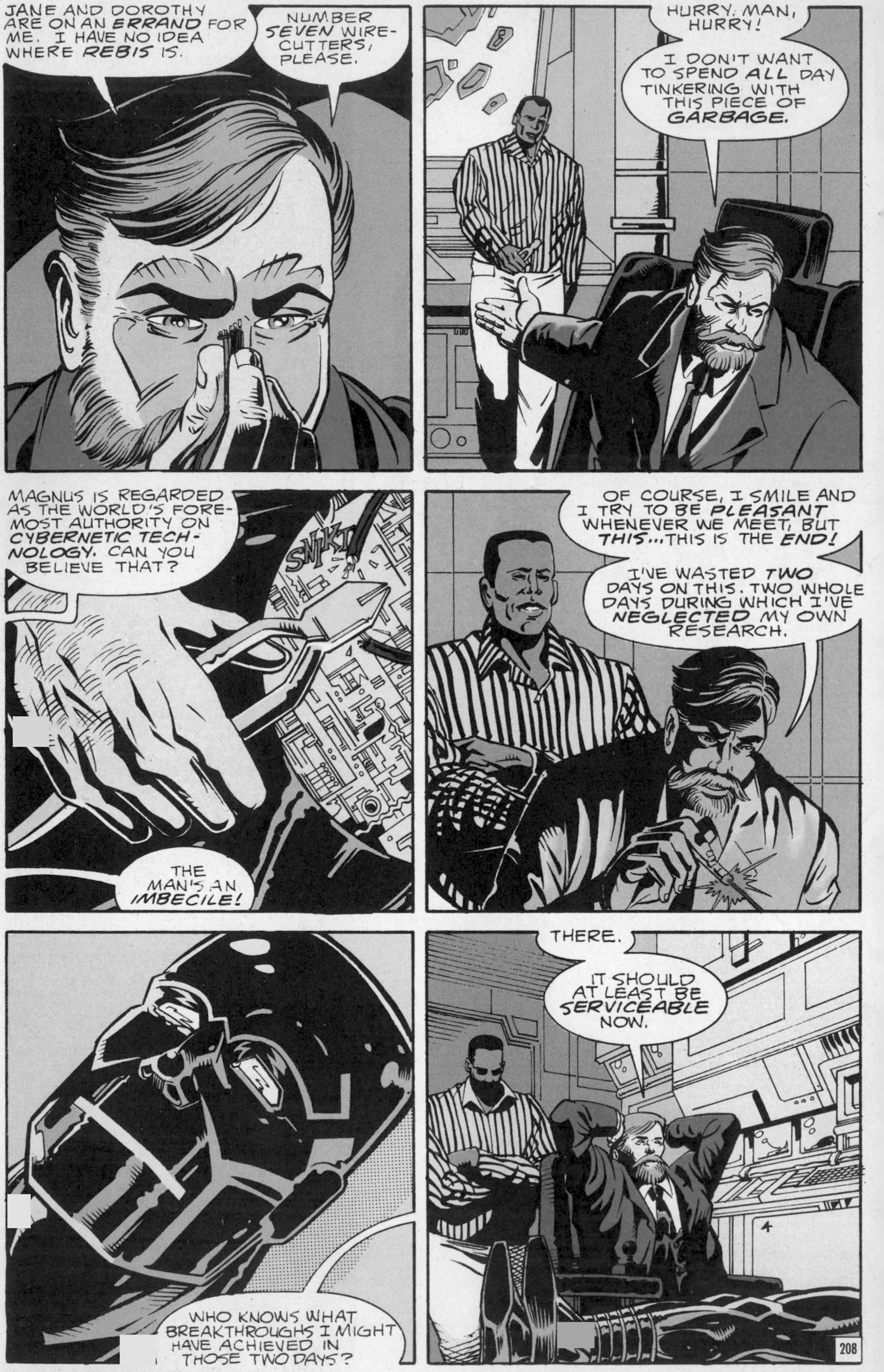

JANE AND DOROTHY ARE ON AN *ERRAND* FOR ME. I HAVE NO IDEA WHERE *REBIS* IS.
NUMBER *SEVEN* WIRE-CUTTERS, PLEASE.
HURRY, MAN, HURRY!
I DON'T WANT TO SPEND **ALL** DAY TINKERING WITH THIS PIECE OF **GARBAGE.**
MAGNUS IS REGARDED AS THE WORLD'S FORE-MOST AUTHORITY ON **CYBERNETIC TECH-NOLOGY.** CAN YOU BELIEVE THAT?
SNIKT
THE MAN'S AN *IMBECILE!*
OF COURSE, I SMILE AND I TRY TO BE **PLEASANT** WHENEVER WE MEET, BUT **THIS...** THIS IS THE **END!**
I'VE WASTED *TWO* DAYS ON THIS. TWO WHOLE DAYS DURING WHICH I'VE **NEGLECTED** MY OWN RESEARCH.
WHO KNOWS WHAT BREAKTHROUGHS I MIGHT HAVE ACHIEVED IN THOSE TWO DAYS?
THERE.
IT SHOULD AT LEAST BE **SERVICEABLE** NOW.

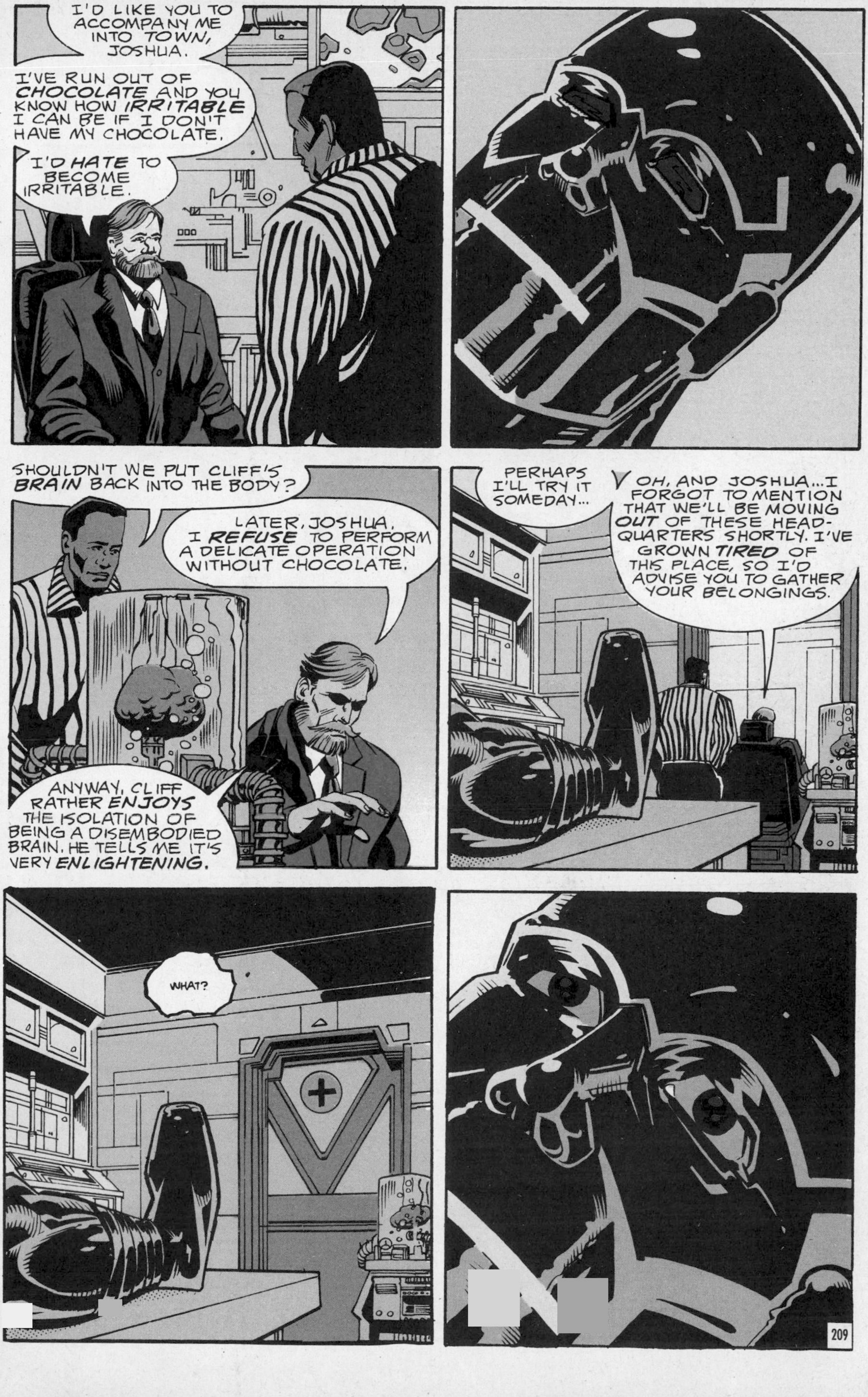
I'D LIKE YOU TO ACCOMPANY ME INTO TOWN, JOSHUA.
I'VE RUN OUT OF CHOCOLATE AND YOU KNOW HOW IRRITABLE I CAN BE IF I DON'T HAVE MY CHOCOLATE.
I'D HATE TO BECOME IRRITABLE.
SHOULDN'T WE PUT CLIFF'S BRAIN BACK INTO THE BODY?
LATER, JOSHUA. I REFUSE TO PERFORM A DELICATE OPERATION WITHOUT CHOCOLATE.
ANYWAY, CLIFF RATHER ENJOYS THE ISOLATION OF BEING A DISEMBODIED BRAIN. HE TELLS ME IT'S VERY ENLIGHTENING.
PERHAPS I'LL TRY IT SOMEDAY...
OH, AND JOSHUA... I FORGOT TO MENTION THAT WE'LL BE MOVING OUT OF THESE HEAD-QUARTERS SHORTLY. I'VE GROWN TIRED OF THIS PLACE, SO I'D ADVISE YOU TO GATHER YOUR BELONGINGS.
WHAT?

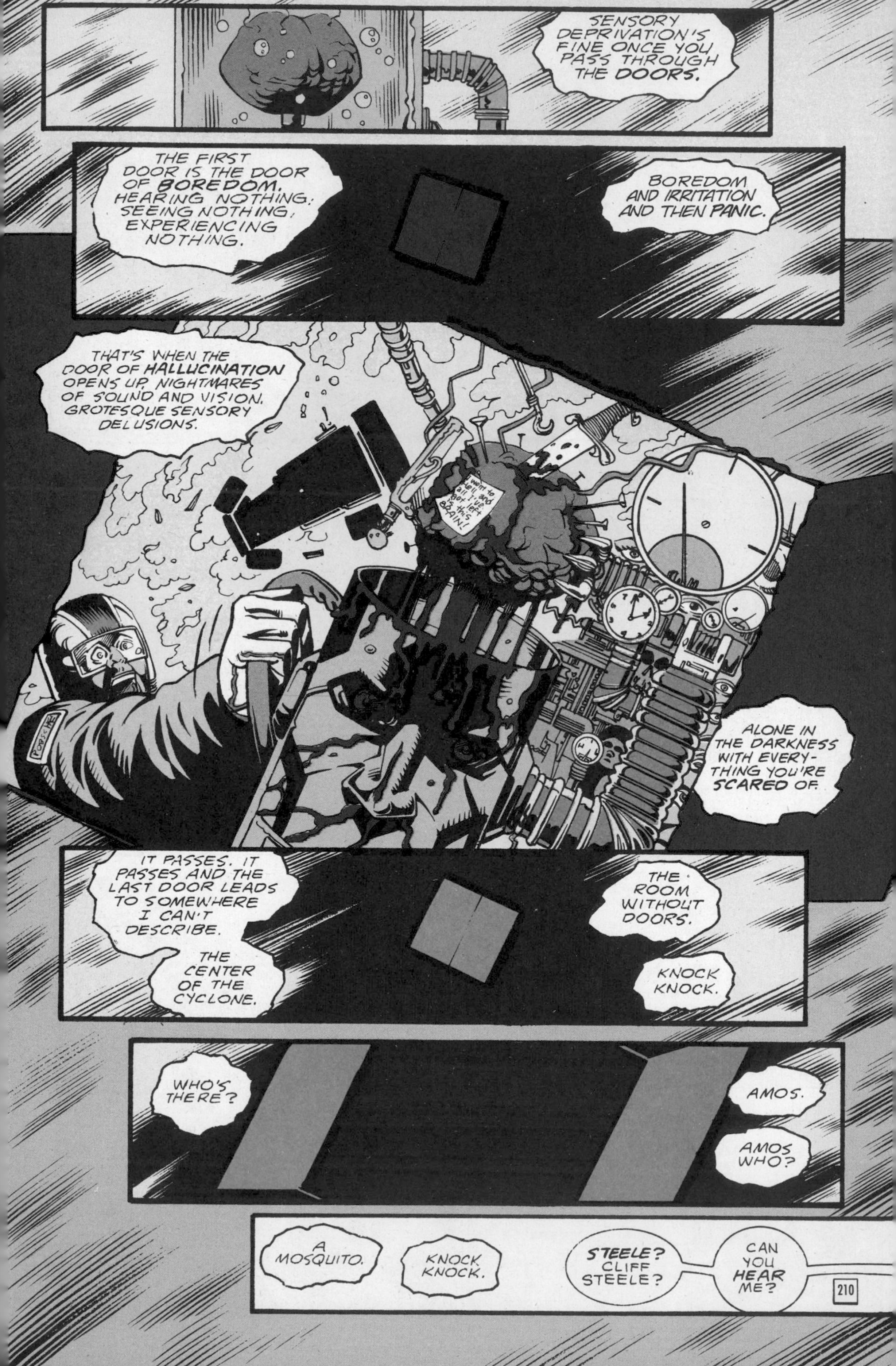
SENSORY DEPRIVATION'S FINE ONCE YOU PASS THROUGH THE **DOORS**.
THE FIRST DOOR IS THE DOOR OF **BOREDOM**. HEARING NOTHING; SEEING NOTHING; EXPERIENCING NOTHING.
BOREDOM AND IRRITATION AND THEN **PANIC**.
THAT'S WHEN THE DOOR OF **HALLUCINATION** OPENS UP. NIGHTMARES OF SOUND AND VISION. GROTESQUE SENSORY DELUSIONS.
I went to Hell and all I've got left is this BRAIN!
PORSCHE
ALONE IN THE DARKNESS WITH EVERY-THING YOU'RE **SCARED** OF.
IT PASSES. IT PASSES AND THE LAST DOOR LEADS TO SOMEWHERE I CAN'T DESCRIBE.
THE CENTER OF THE CYCLONE.
THE ROOM WITHOUT DOORS.
KNOCK KNOCK.
WHO'S THERE?
AMOS.
AMOS WHO?
A MOSQUITO.
KNOCK KNOCK.
STEELE? CLIFF STEELE?
CAN YOU **HEAR** ME?

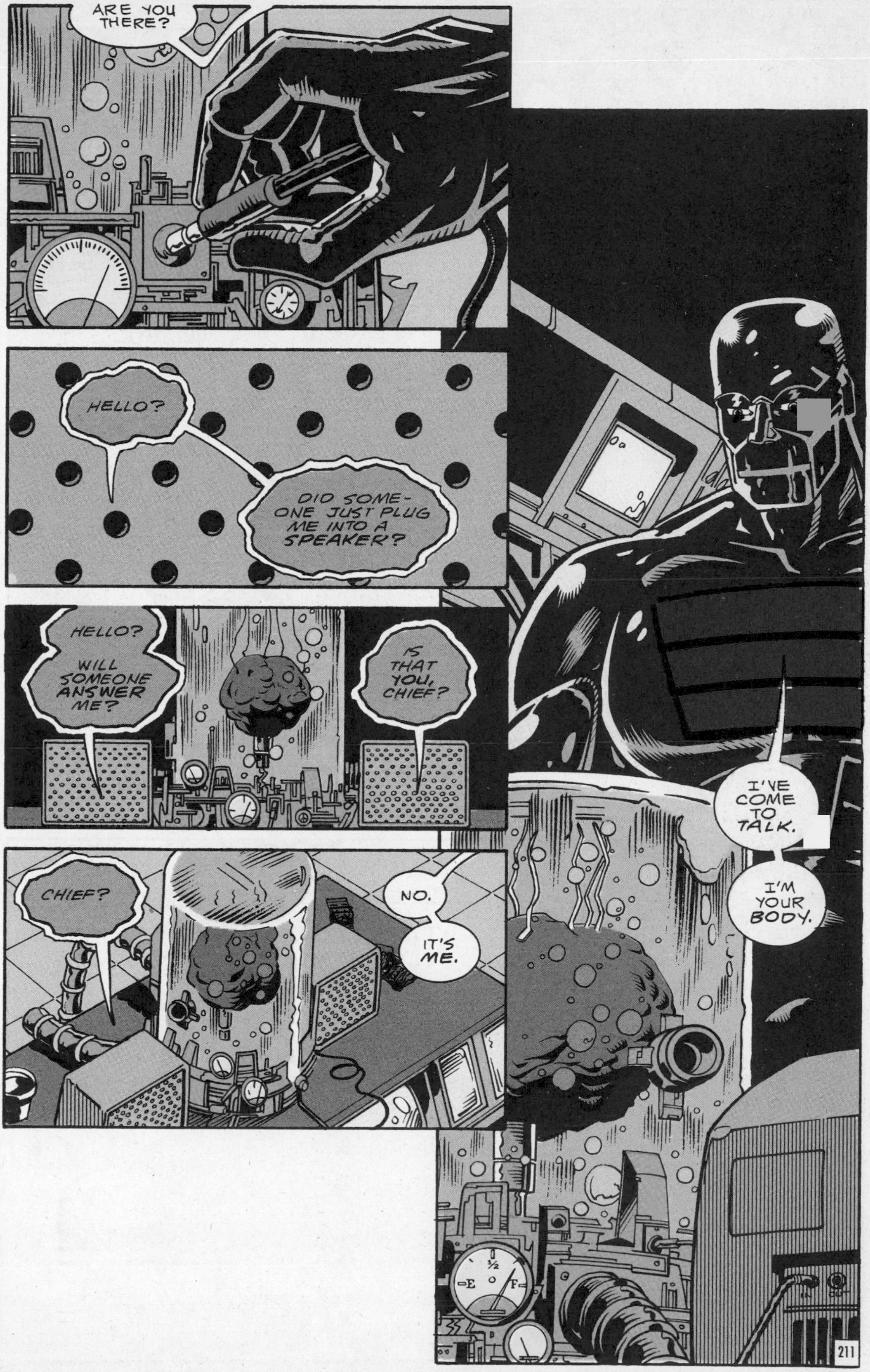
ARE YOU THERE?
HELLO?
DID SOME-ONE JUST PLUG ME INTO A SPEAKER?
HELLO? WILL SOMEONE ANSWER ME?
IS THAT YOU, CHIEF?
CHIEF?
NO.
IT'S ME.
I'VE COME TO TALK.
I'M YOUR BODY.

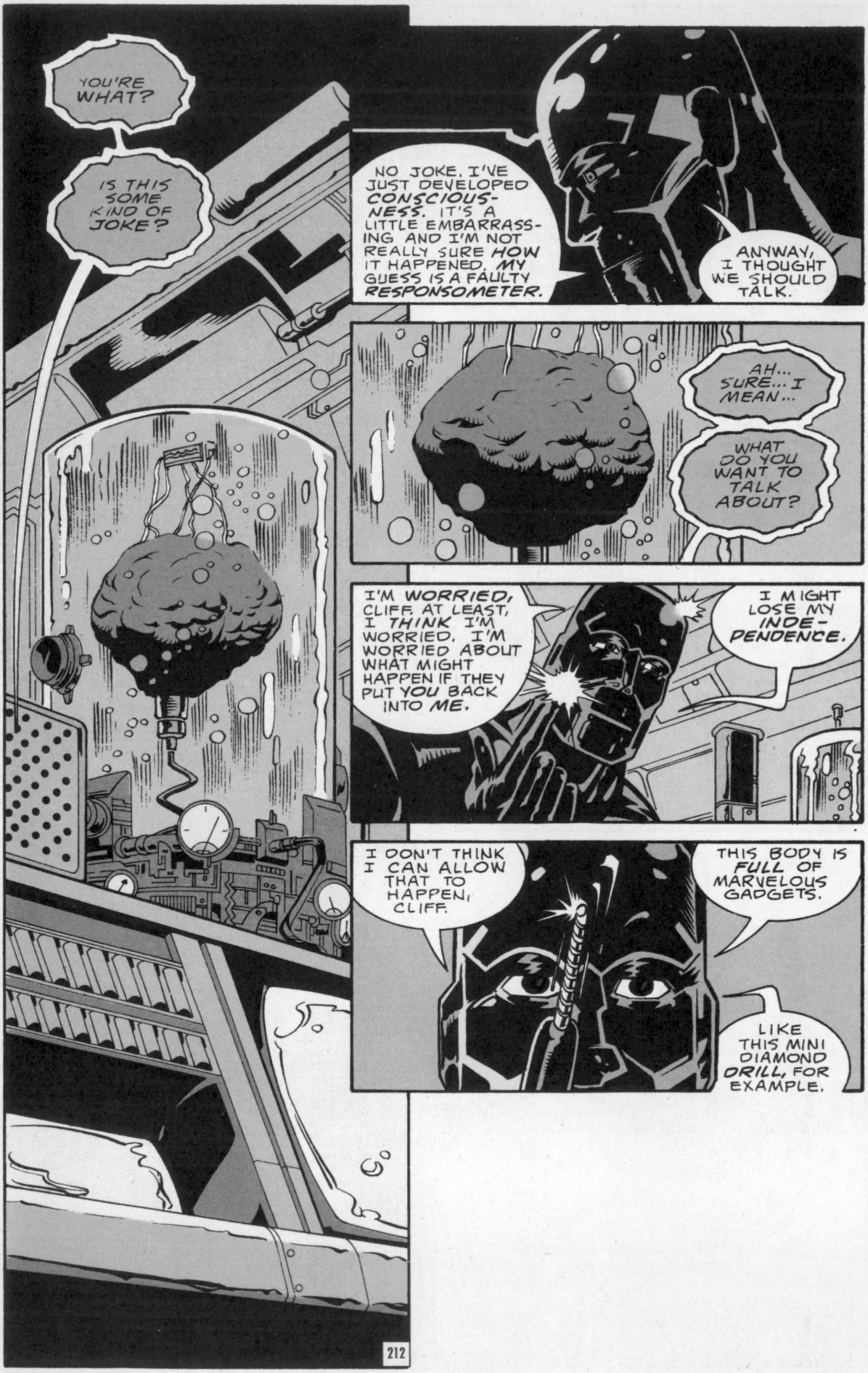
YOU'RE WHAT?
IS THIS SOME KIND OF JOKE?
NO JOKE. I'VE JUST DEVELOPED CONSCIOUSNESS. IT'S A LITTLE EMBARRASSING AND I'M NOT REALLY SURE HOW IT HAPPENED. MY GUESS IS A FAULTY RESPONSOMETER.
ANYWAY, I THOUGHT WE SHOULD TALK.
AH... SURE... I MEAN...
WHAT DO YOU WANT TO TALK ABOUT?
I'M WORRIED, CLIFF. AT LEAST, I THINK I'M WORRIED. I'M WORRIED ABOUT WHAT MIGHT HAPPEN IF THEY PUT YOU BACK INTO ME.
I MIGHT LOSE MY INDEPENDENCE.
I DON'T THINK I CAN ALLOW THAT TO HAPPEN, CLIFF.
THIS BODY IS FULL OF MARVELOUS GADGETS.
LIKE THIS MINI DIAMOND DRILL, FOR EXAMPLE.

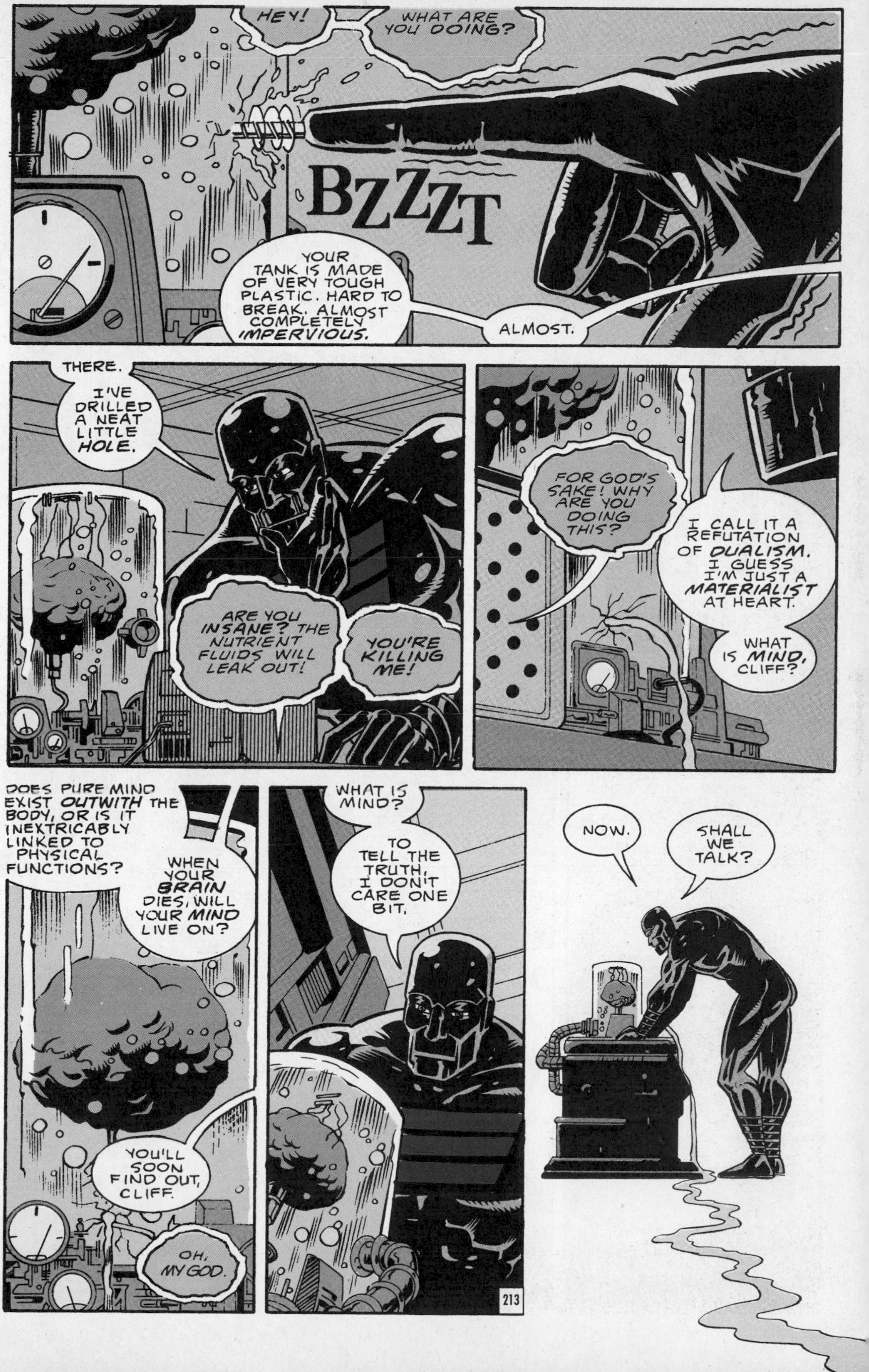
HEY!
WHAT ARE YOU DOING?
BZZZT
YOUR TANK IS MADE OF VERY TOUGH PLASTIC. HARD TO BREAK. ALMOST COMPLETELY IMPERVIOUS.
ALMOST.
THERE.
I'VE DRILLED A NEAT LITTLE HOLE.
ARE YOU INSANE? THE NUTRIENT FLUIDS WILL LEAK OUT!
YOU'RE KILLING ME!
FOR GOD'S SAKE! WHY ARE YOU DOING THIS?
I CALL IT A REFUTATION OF DUALISM. I GUESS I'M JUST A MATERIALIST AT HEART.
WHAT IS MIND, CLIFF?
DOES PURE MIND EXIST OUTWITH THE BODY, OR IS IT INEXTRICABLY LINKED TO PHYSICAL FUNCTIONS?
WHEN YOUR BRAIN DIES, WILL YOUR MIND LIVE ON?
YOU'LL SOON FIND OUT, CLIFF.
OH, MY GOD.
WHAT IS MIND?
TO TELL THE TRUTH, I DON'T CARE ONE BIT.
NOW.
SHALL WE TALK?

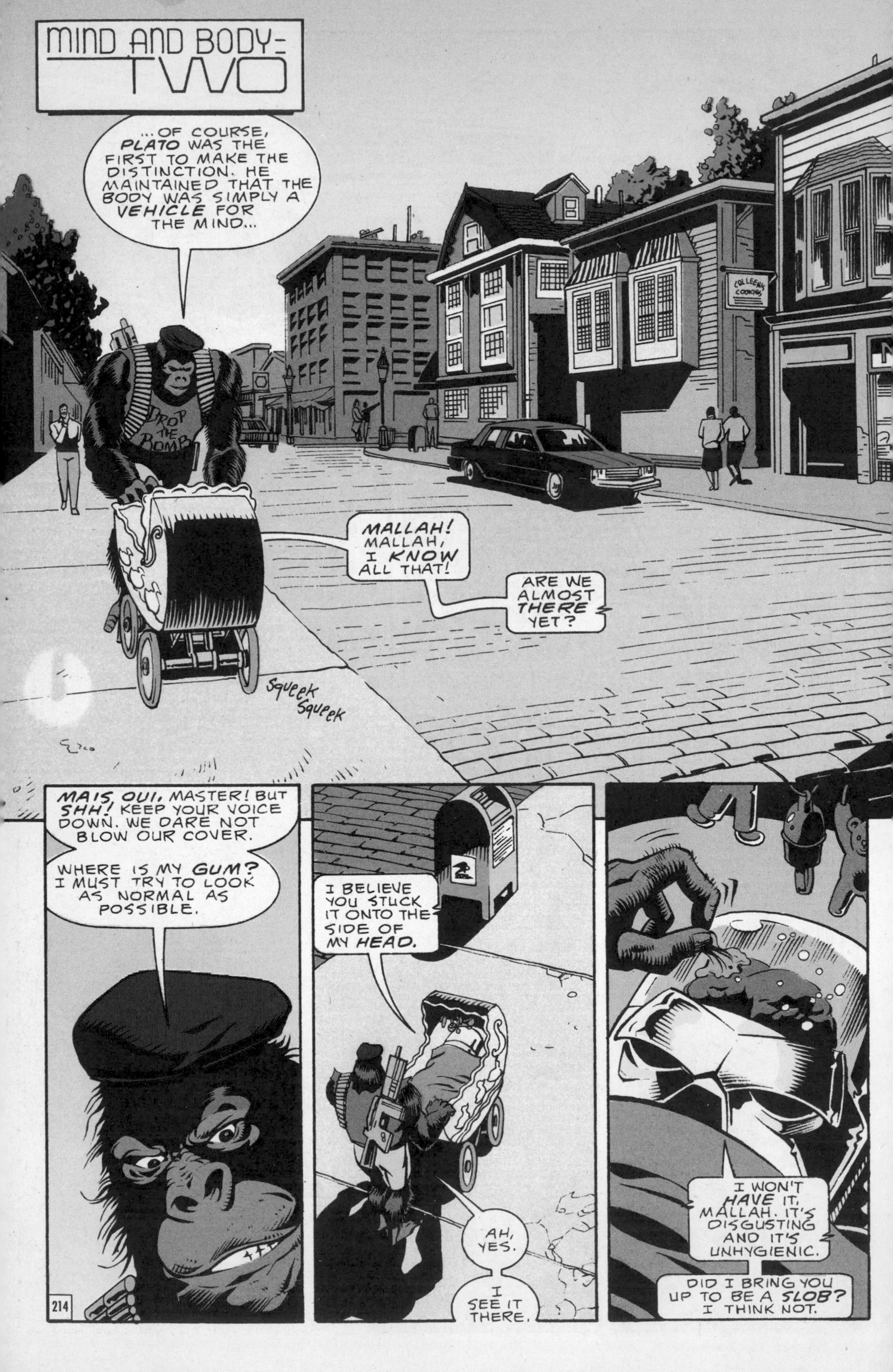
MIND AND BODY- TWO
...OF COURSE, PLATO WAS THE FIRST TO MAKE THE DISTINCTION. HE MAINTAINED THAT THE BODY WAS SIMPLY A VEHICLE FOR THE MIND...
DROP THE BOMB
MALLAH! MALLAH, I KNOW ALL THAT!
ARE WE ALMOST THERE YET?
SQUEEK SQUEEK
MAIS OUI, MASTER! BUT SHH! KEEP YOUR VOICE DOWN. WE DARE NOT BLOW OUR COVER.
WHERE IS MY GUM? I MUST TRY TO LOOK AS NORMAL AS POSSIBLE.
I BELIEVE YOU STUCK IT ONTO THE SIDE OF MY HEAD.
AH, YES.
I SEE IT THERE.
I WON'T HAVE IT, MALLAH. IT'S DISGUSTING AND IT'S UNHYGIENIC.
DID I BRING YOU UP TO BE A SLOB? I THINK NOT.

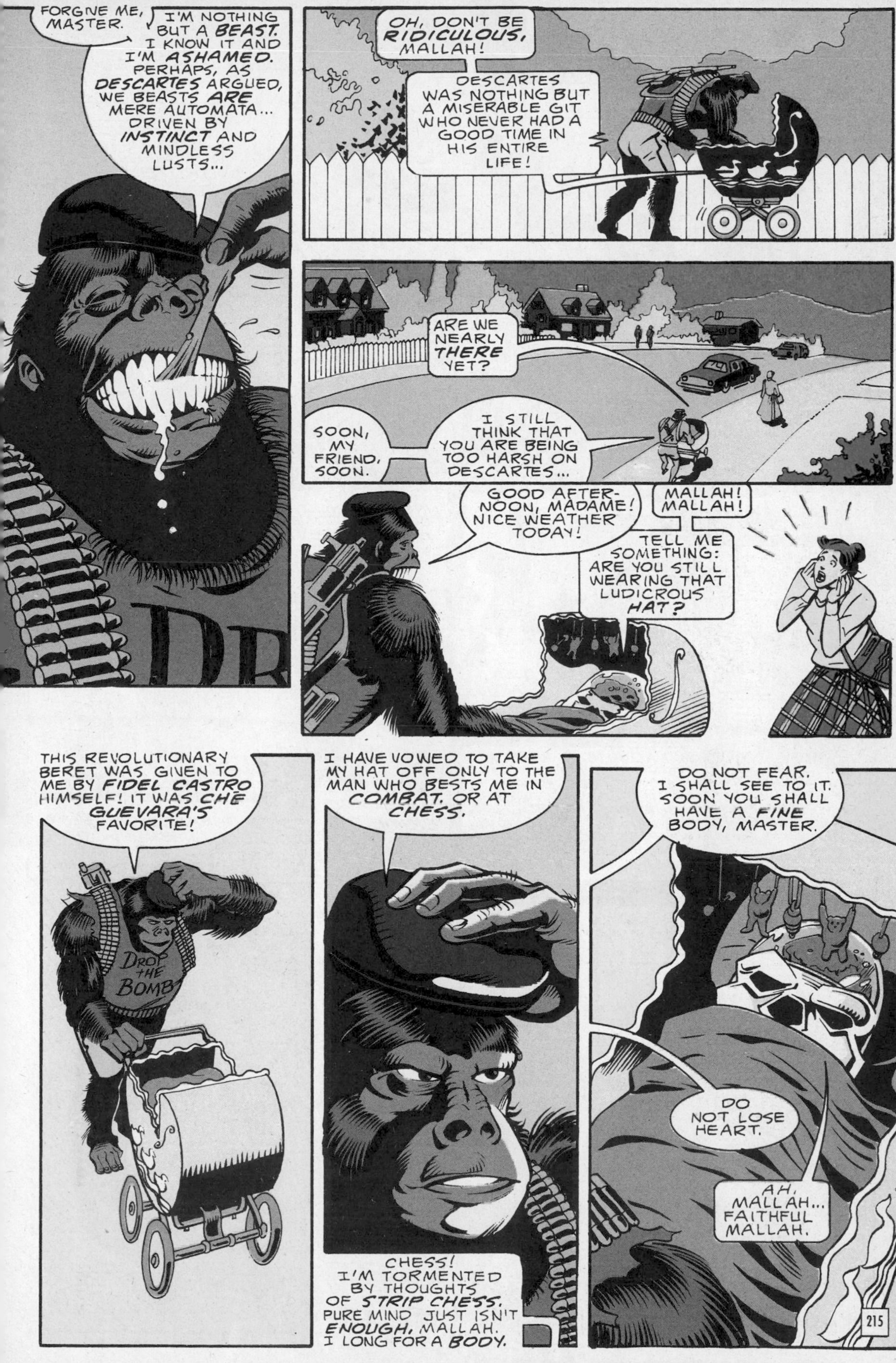
FORGIVE ME, MASTER.
I'M NOTHING BUT A BEAST. I KNOW IT AND I'M ASHAMED. PERHAPS, AS DESCARTES ARGUED, WE BEASTS ARE MERE AUTOMATA... DRIVEN BY INSTINCT AND MINDLESS LUSTS...
DR
OH, DON'T BE RIDICULOUS, MALLAH!
DESCARTES WAS NOTHING BUT A MISERABLE GIT WHO NEVER HAD A GOOD TIME IN HIS ENTIRE LIFE!
ARE WE NEARLY THERE YET?
SOON, MY FRIEND, SOON.
I STILL THINK THAT YOU ARE BEING TOO HARSH ON DESCARTES...
GOOD AFTER-NOON, MADAME! NICE WEATHER TODAY!
MALLAH! MALLAH!
TELL ME SOMETHING: ARE YOU STILL WEARING THAT LUDICROUS HAT?
THIS REVOLUTIONARY BERET WAS GIVEN TO ME BY FIDEL CASTRO HIMSELF! IT WAS CHÉ GUEVARA'S FAVORITE!
DROP THE BOMB
I HAVE VOWED TO TAKE MY HAT OFF ONLY TO THE MAN WHO BESTS ME IN COMBAT. OR AT CHESS.
CHESS! I'M TORMENTED BY THOUGHTS OF STRIP CHESS. PURE MIND JUST ISN'T ENOUGH, MALLAH. I LONG FOR A BODY.
DO NOT FEAR. I SHALL SEE TO IT. SOON YOU SHALL HAVE A FINE BODY, MASTER.
DO NOT LOSE HEART.
AH, MALLAH... FAITHFUL MALLAH.

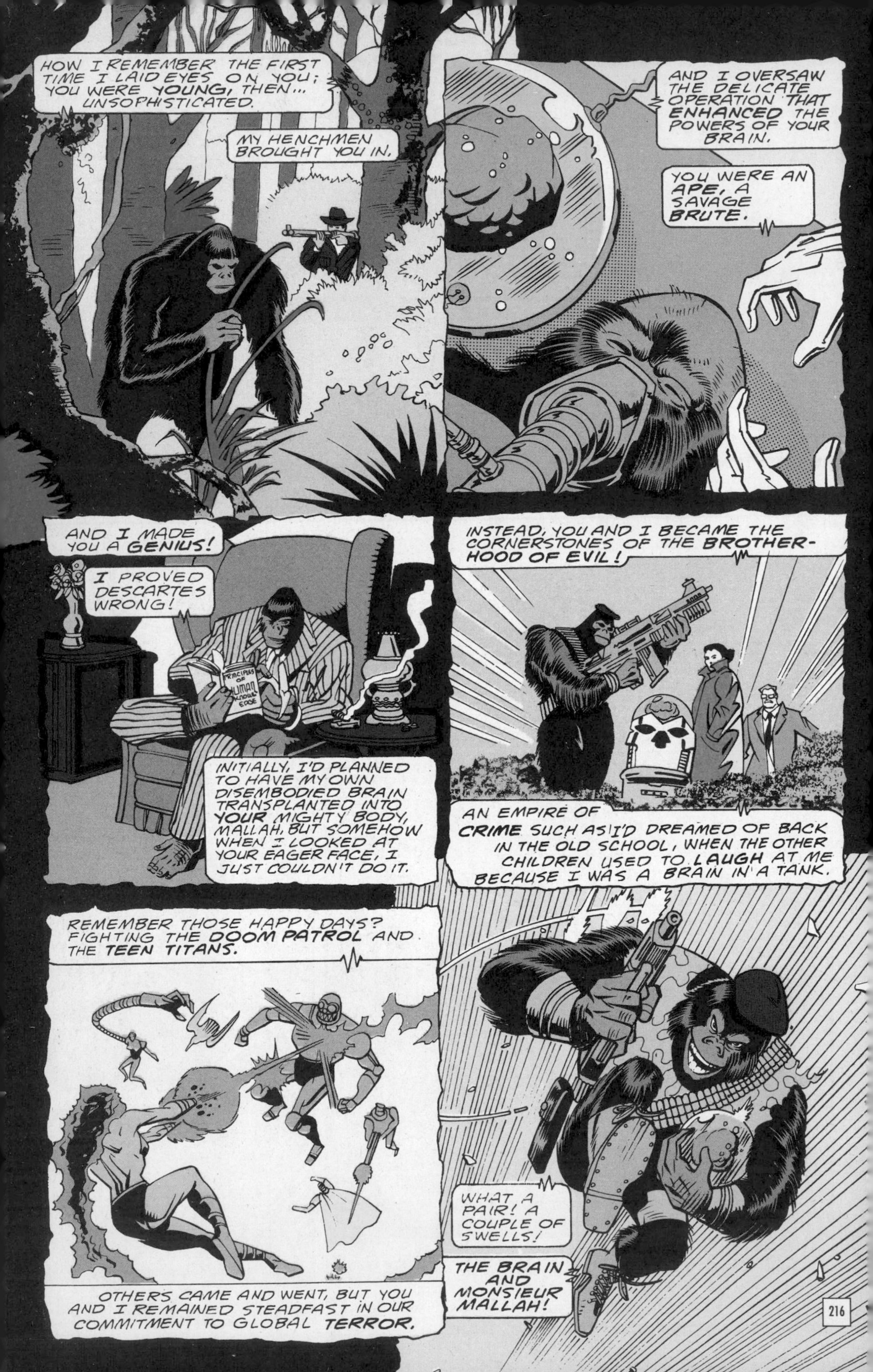
HOW I REMEMBER THE FIRST TIME I LAID EYES ON YOU; YOU WERE YOUNG, THEN... UNSOPHISTICATED.
MY HENCHMEN BROUGHT YOU IN.
AND I OVERSAW THE DELICATE OPERATION THAT ENHANCED THE POWERS OF YOUR BRAIN.
YOU WERE AN APE, A SAVAGE BRUTE.
AND I MADE YOU A GENIUS!
I PROVED DESCARTES WRONG!
PRINCIPLES OF HUMAN KNOWLEDGE
INITIALLY, I'D PLANNED TO HAVE MY OWN DISEMBODIED BRAIN TRANSPLANTED INTO YOUR MIGHTY BODY, MALLAH, BUT SOMEHOW WHEN I LOOKED AT YOUR EAGER FACE, I JUST COULDN'T DO IT.
INSTEAD, YOU AND I BECAME THE CORNERSTONES OF THE BROTHER-HOOD OF EVIL!
AN EMPIRE OF CRIME SUCH AS I'D DREAMED OF BACK IN THE OLD SCHOOL, WHEN THE OTHER CHILDREN USED TO LAUGH AT ME BECAUSE I WAS A BRAIN IN A TANK.
REMEMBER THOSE HAPPY DAYS? FIGHTING THE DOOM PATROL AND THE TEEN TITANS.
OTHERS CAME AND WENT, BUT YOU AND I REMAINED STEADFAST IN OUR COMMITMENT TO GLOBAL TERROR.
WHAT A PAIR! A COUPLE OF SWELLS!
THE BRAIN AND MONSIEUR MALLAH!

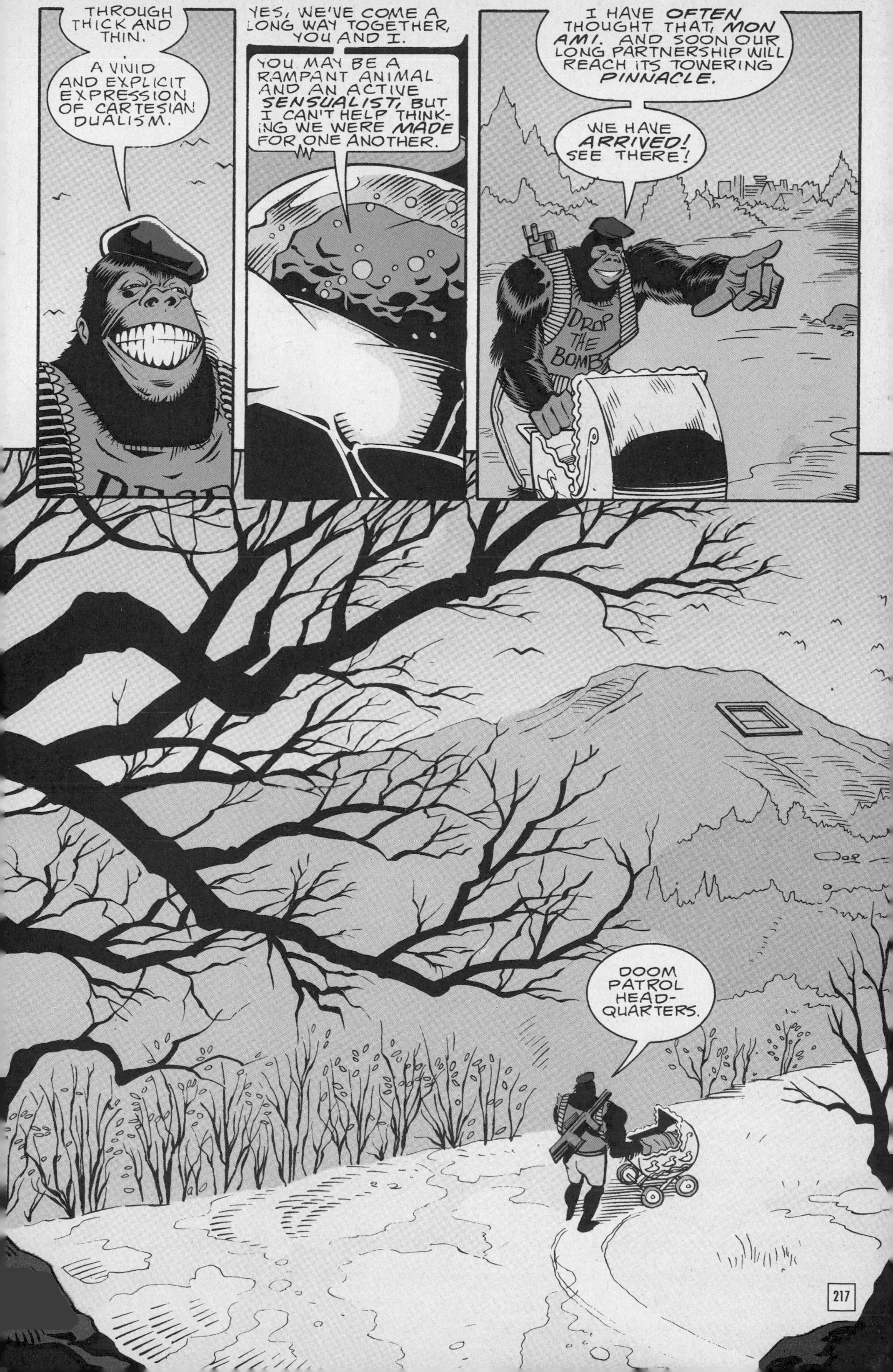

THROUGH THICK AND THIN.
A VIVID AND EXPLICIT EXPRESSION OF CARTESIAN DUALISM.
YES, WE'VE COME A LONG WAY TOGETHER, YOU AND I.
YOU MAY BE A RAMPANT ANIMAL AND AN ACTIVE SENSUALIST, BUT I CAN'T HELP THINKING WE WERE MADE FOR ONE ANOTHER.
I HAVE OFTEN THOUGHT THAT, MON AMI. AND SOON OUR LONG PARTNERSHIP WILL REACH ITS TOWERING PINNACLE.
WE HAVE ARRIVED! SEE THERE!
DROP THE BOMB
DOOM PATROL HEAD-QUARTERS.

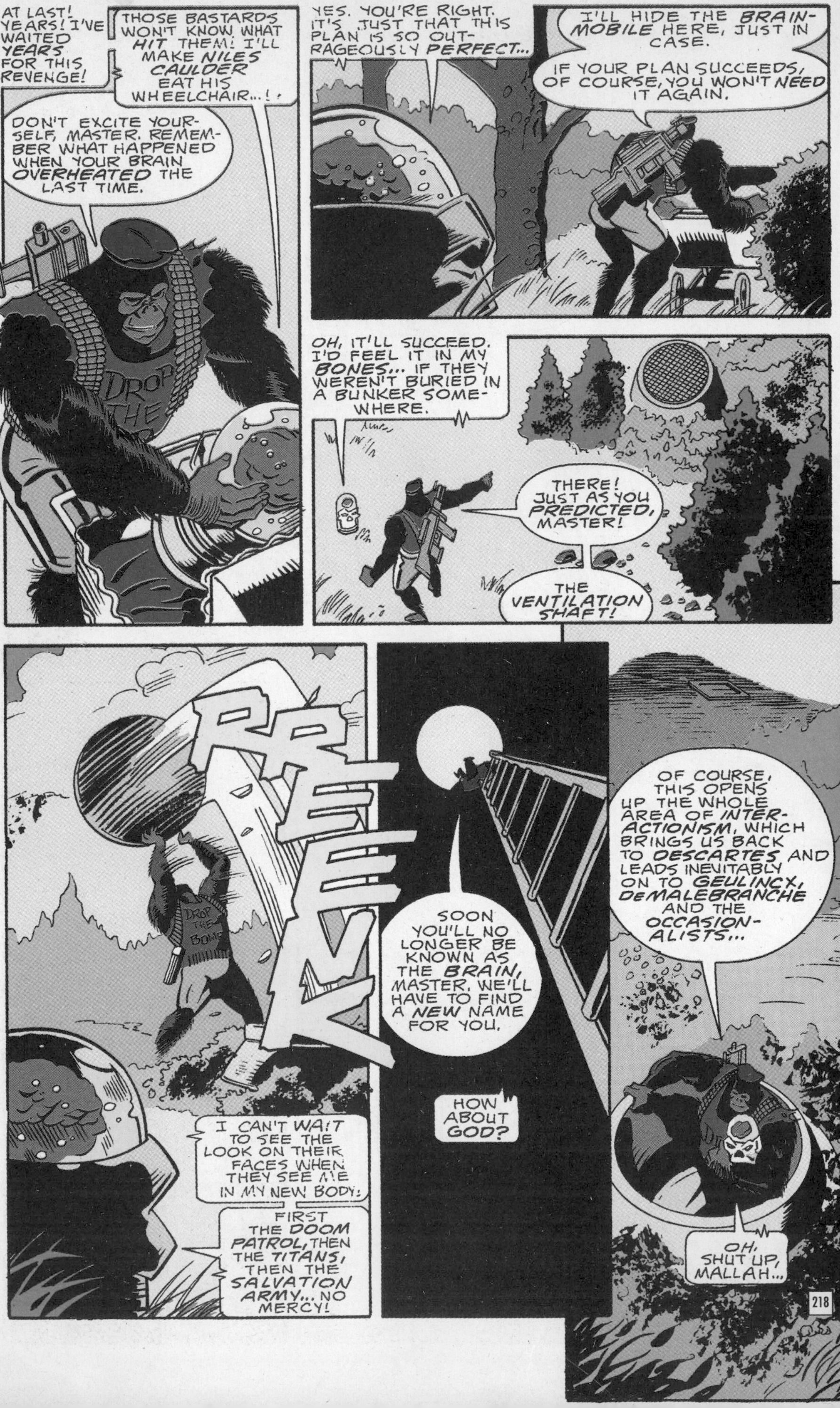
AT LAST! YEARS! I'VE WAITED YEARS FOR THIS REVENGE!
THOSE BASTARDS WON'T KNOW WHAT HIT THEM! I'LL MAKE NILES CAULDER EAT HIS WHEELCHAIR...!
DON'T EXCITE YOURSELF, MASTER. REMEMBER WHAT HAPPENED WHEN YOUR BRAIN OVERHEATED THE LAST TIME.
DROP THE
YES. YOU'RE RIGHT. IT'S JUST THAT THIS PLAN IS SO OUTRAGEOUSLY PERFECT...
I'LL HIDE THE BRAIN-MOBILE HERE, JUST IN CASE.
IF YOUR PLAN SUCCEEDS, OF COURSE, YOU WON'T NEED IT AGAIN.
OH, IT'LL SUCCEED. I'D FEEL IT IN MY BONES... IF THEY WEREN'T BURIED IN A BUNKER SOMEWHERE.
THERE! JUST AS YOU PREDICTED, MASTER!
THE VENTILATION SHAFT!
RRREEEV
DROP THE BOMB
I CAN'T WAIT TO SEE THE LOOK ON THEIR FACES WHEN THEY SEE ME IN MY NEW BODY!
FIRST THE DOOM PATROL, THEN THE TITANS, THEN THE SALVATION ARMY... NO MERCY!
SOON YOU'LL NO LONGER BE KNOWN AS THE BRAIN, MASTER. WE'LL HAVE TO FIND A NEW NAME FOR YOU.
HOW ABOUT GOD?
OF COURSE, THIS OPENS UP THE WHOLE AREA OF INTERACTIONISM, WHICH BRINGS US BACK TO DESCARTES AND LEADS INEVITABLY ON TO GEULINCX, DEMALEBRANCHE AND THE OCCASIONALISTS...
OH, SHUT UP, MALLAH...

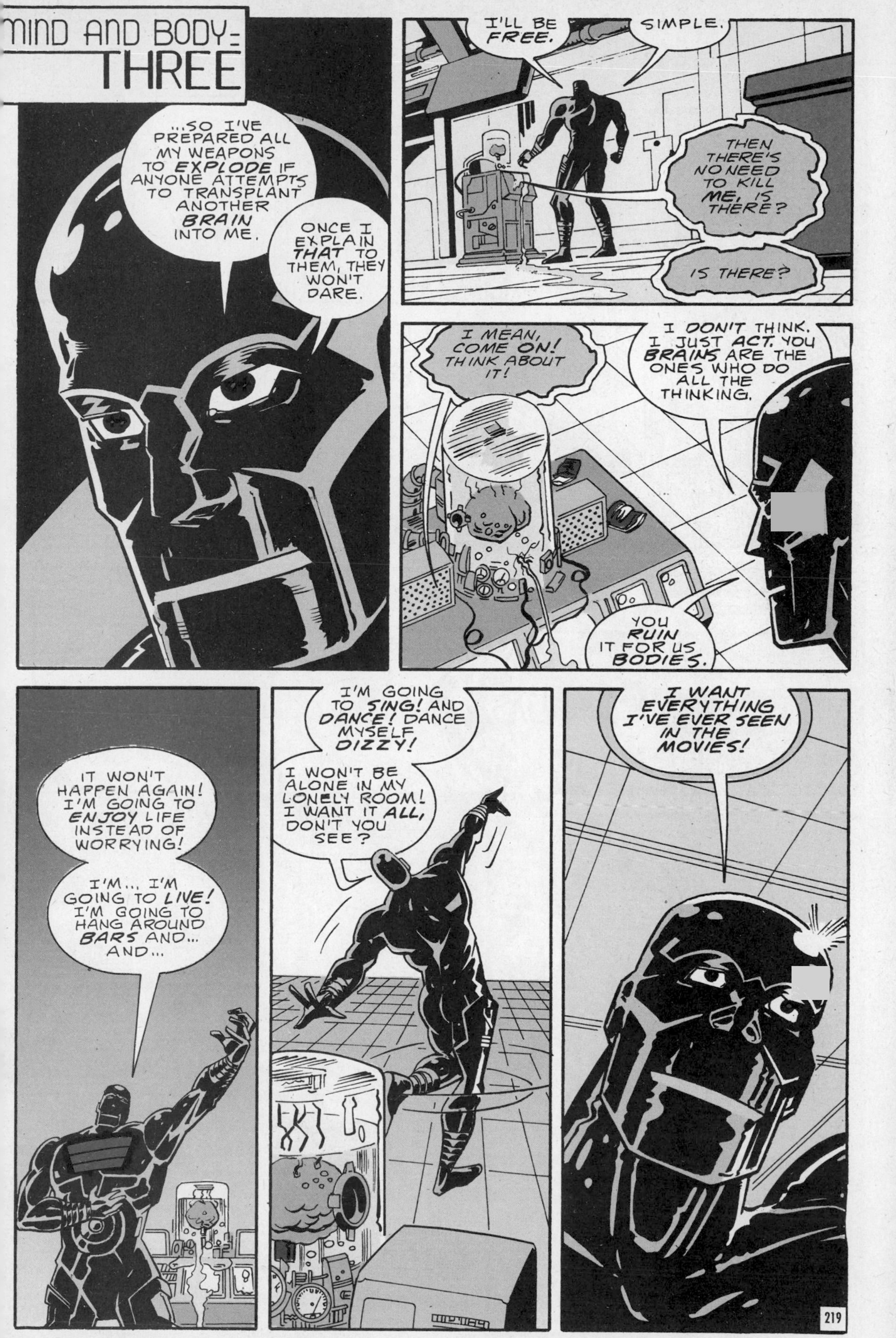
MIND AND BODY- THREE
...SO I'VE PREPARED ALL MY WEAPONS TO EXPLODE IF ANYONE ATTEMPTS TO TRANSPLANT ANOTHER BRAIN INTO ME.
ONCE I EXPLAIN THAT TO THEM, THEY WON'T DARE.
I'LL BE FREE.
SIMPLE.
THEN THERE'S NO NEED TO KILL ME, IS THERE?
IS THERE?
I MEAN, COME ON! THINK ABOUT IT!
I DON'T THINK. I JUST ACT. YOU BRAINS ARE THE ONES WHO DO ALL THE THINKING.
YOU RUIN IT FOR US BODIES.
IT WON'T HAPPEN AGAIN! I'M GOING TO ENJOY LIFE INSTEAD OF WORRYING!
I'M... I'M GOING TO LIVE! I'M GOING TO HANG AROUND BARS AND... AND...
I'M GOING TO SING! AND DANCE! DANCE MYSELF DIZZY!
I WON'T BE ALONE IN MY LONELY ROOM! I WANT IT ALL, DON'T YOU SEE?
I WANT EVERYTHING I'VE EVER SEEN IN THE MOVIES!

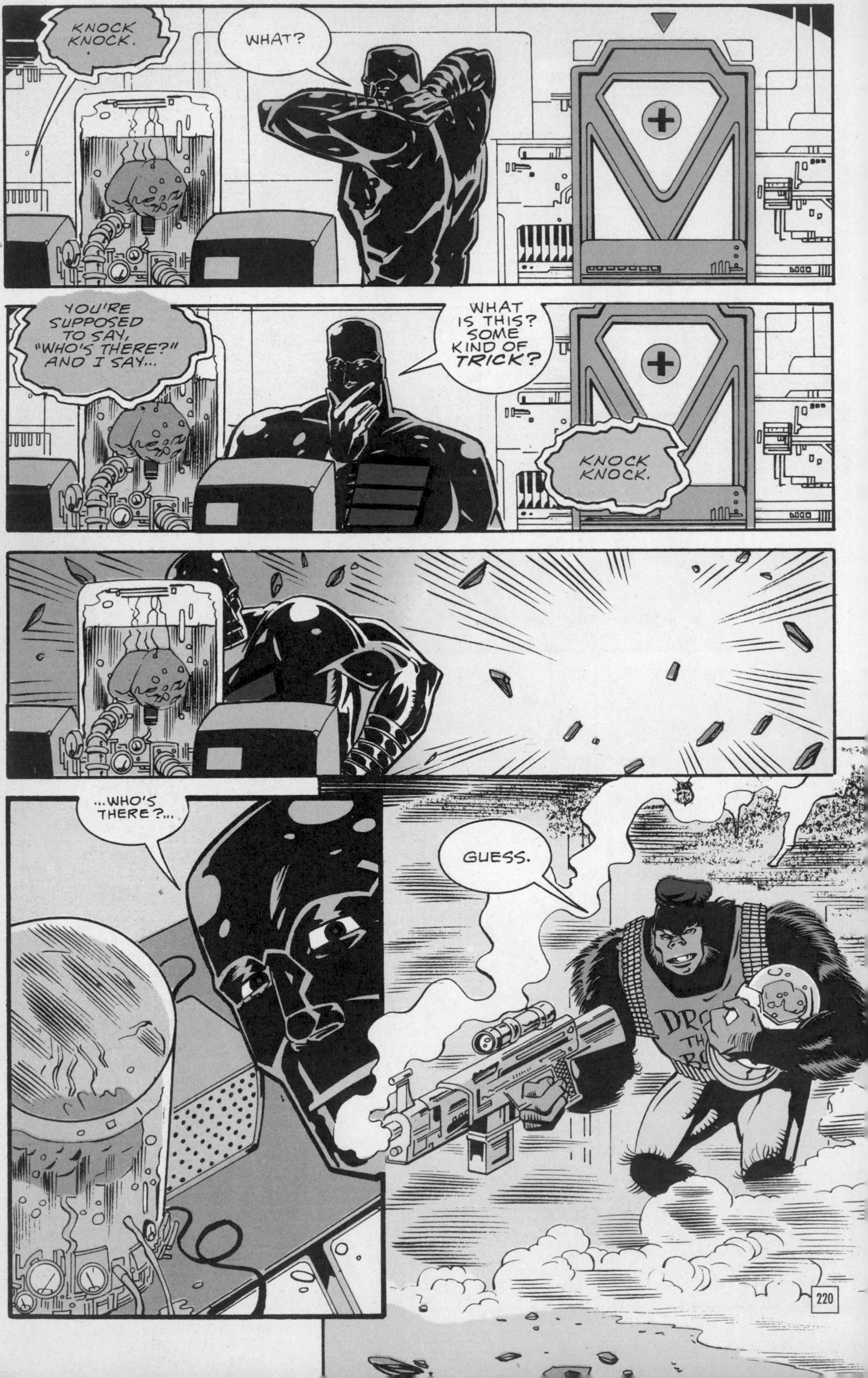
KNOCK KNOCK.
WHAT?
YOU'RE SUPPOSED TO SAY, "WHO'S THERE?" AND I SAY...
WHAT IS THIS? SOME KIND OF TRICK?
KNOCK KNOCK.
...WHO'S THERE?...
GUESS.

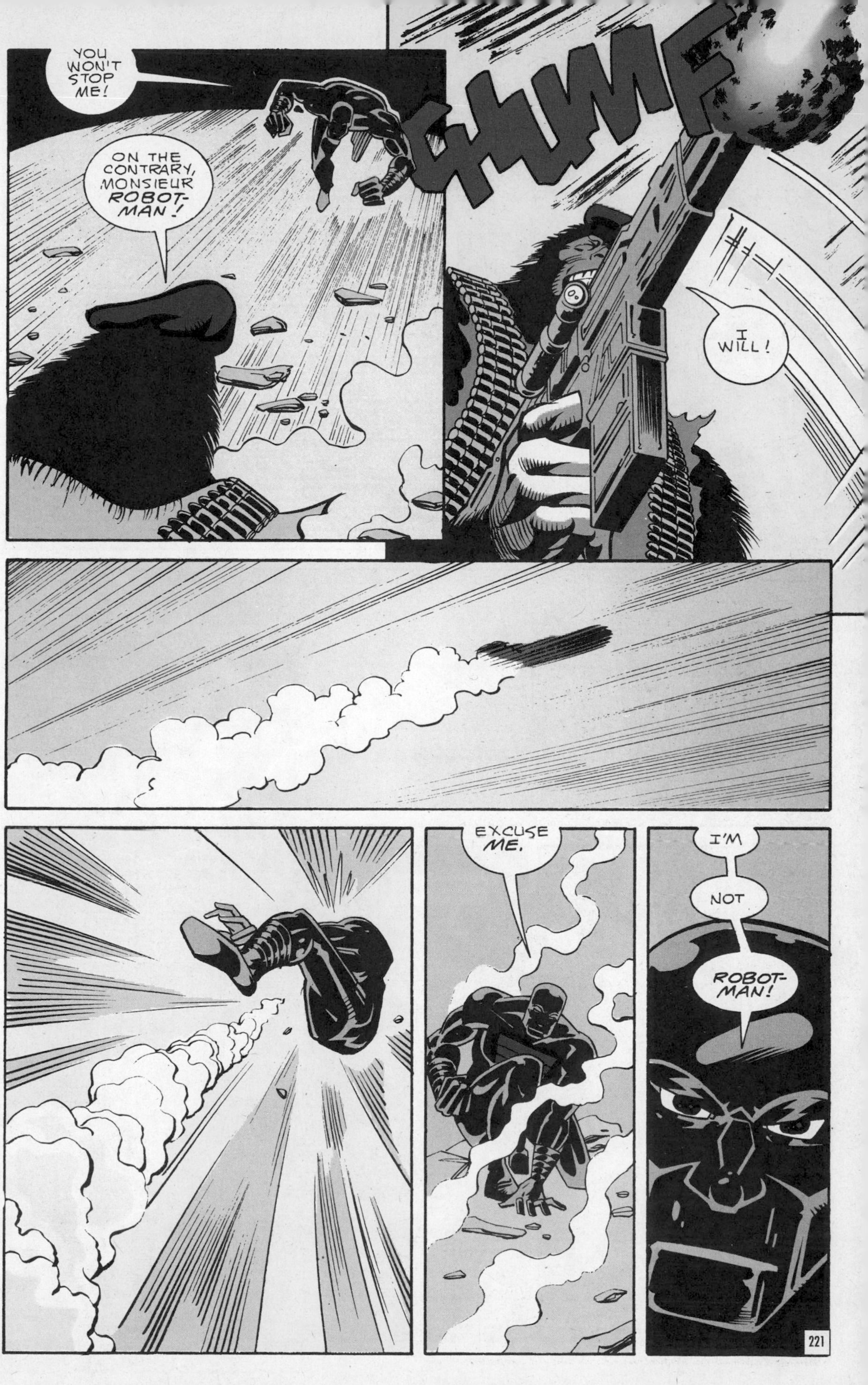
YOU WON'T STOP ME!
ON THE CONTRARY, MONSIEUR ROBOT-MAN!
CHUMF
I WILL!
EXCUSE ME.
I'M
NOT
ROBOT-MAN!

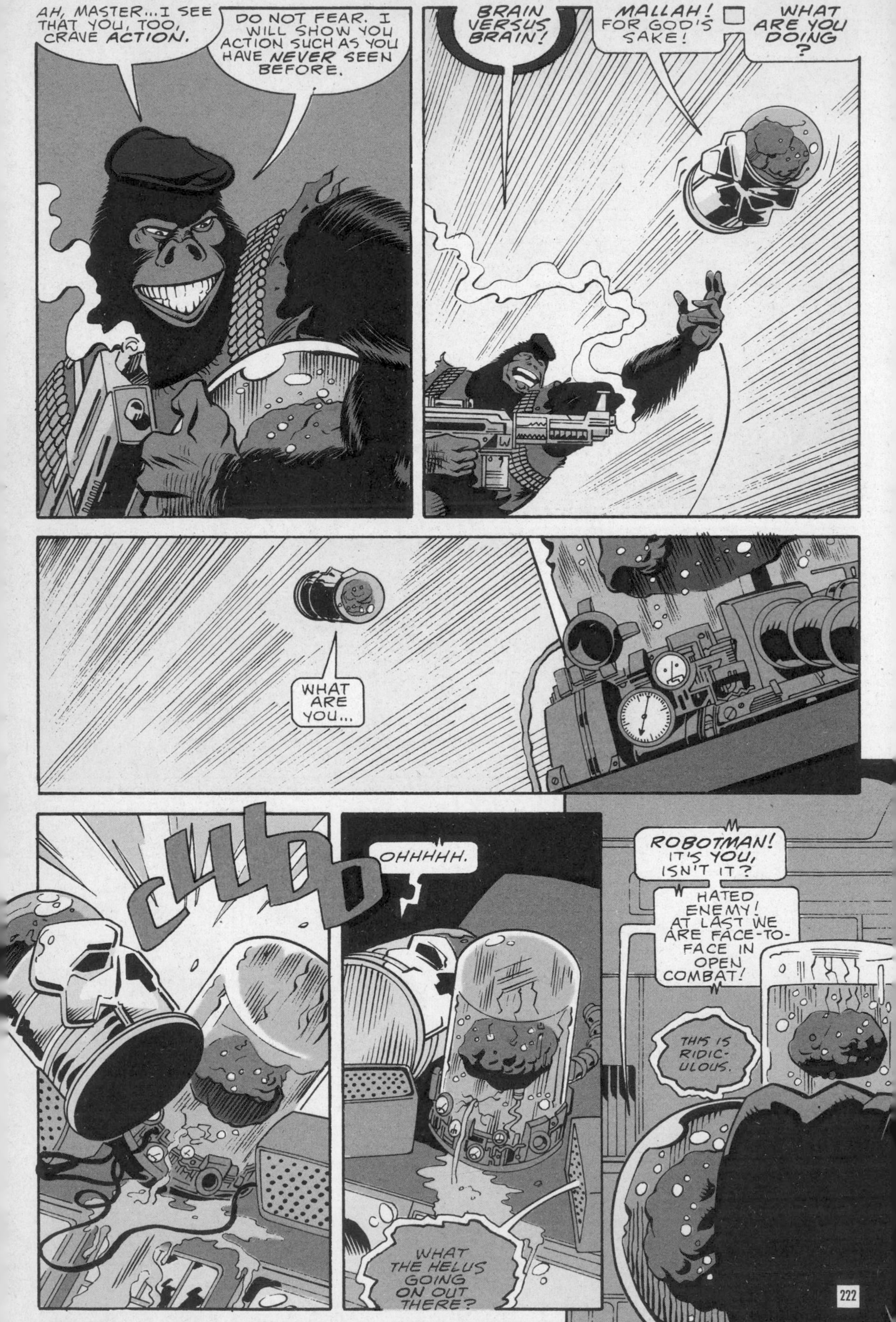
AH, MASTER...I SEE THAT YOU, TOO, CRAVE ACTION.
DO NOT FEAR. I WILL SHOW YOU ACTION SUCH AS YOU HAVE NEVER SEEN BEFORE.
BRAIN VERSUS BRAIN!
MALLAH! FOR GOD'S SAKE!
WHAT ARE YOU DOING?
WHAT ARE YOU...
CLUD
OHHHHH.
WHAT THE HELL IS GOING ON OUT THERE?
ROBOTMAN! IT'S YOU, ISN'T IT?
HATED ENEMY! AT LAST WE ARE FACE-TO-FACE IN OPEN COMBAT!
THIS IS RIDICULOUS.

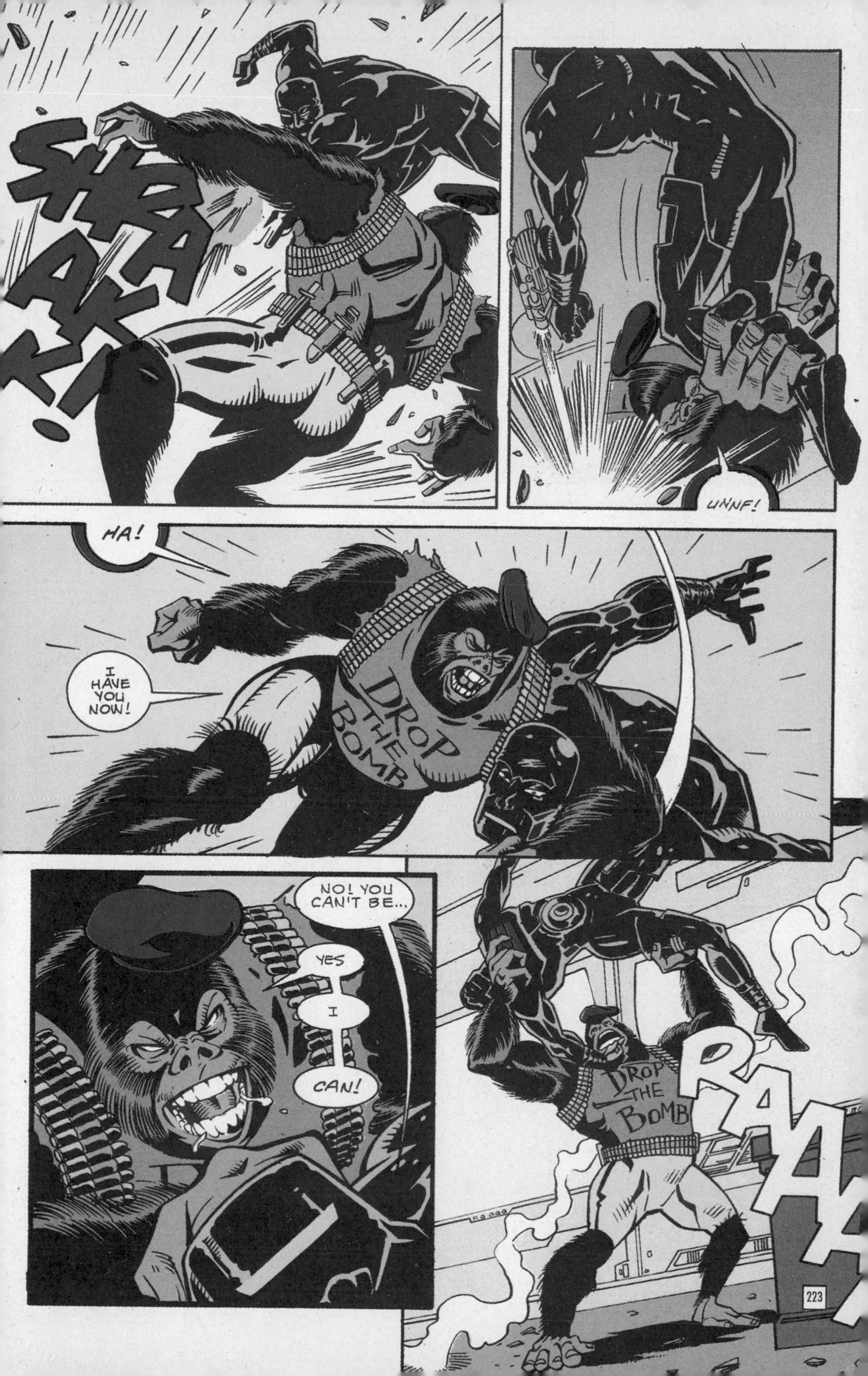
SHRAKK!
UNNF!
HA!
I HAVE YOU NOW!
DROP THE BOMB
NO! YOU CAN'T BE...
YES
I
CAN!
DROP THE BOMB
RA

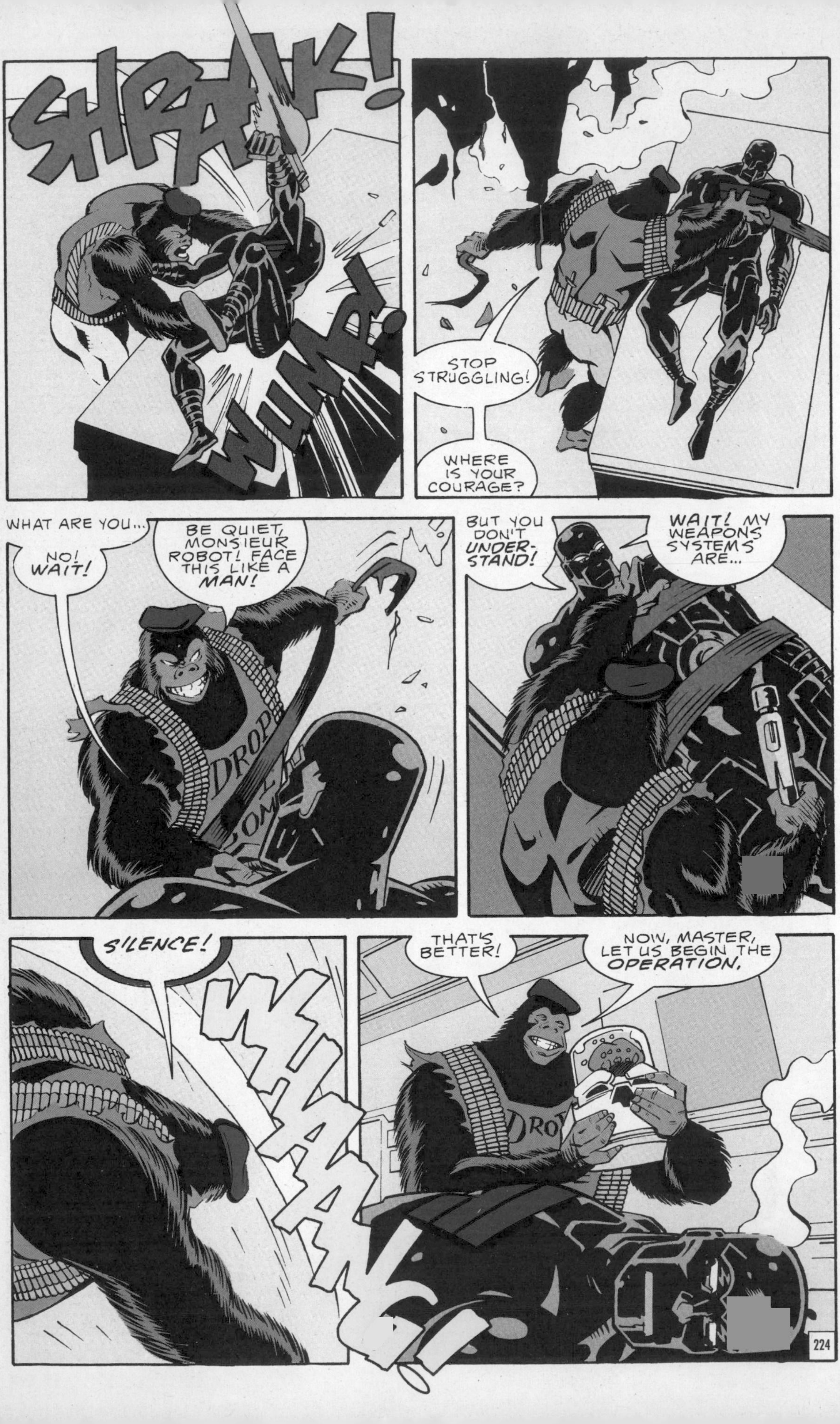
SHRAAK!
WUMP!
STOP STRUGGLING!
WHERE IS YOUR COURAGE?
WHAT ARE YOU...
NO! WAIT!
BE QUIET, MONSIEUR ROBOT! FACE THIS LIKE A MAN!
BUT YOU DON'T UNDER-STAND!
WAIT! MY WEAPONS SYSTEMS ARE...
SILENCE!
THAT'S BETTER!
NOW, MASTER, LET US BEGIN THE OPERATION.

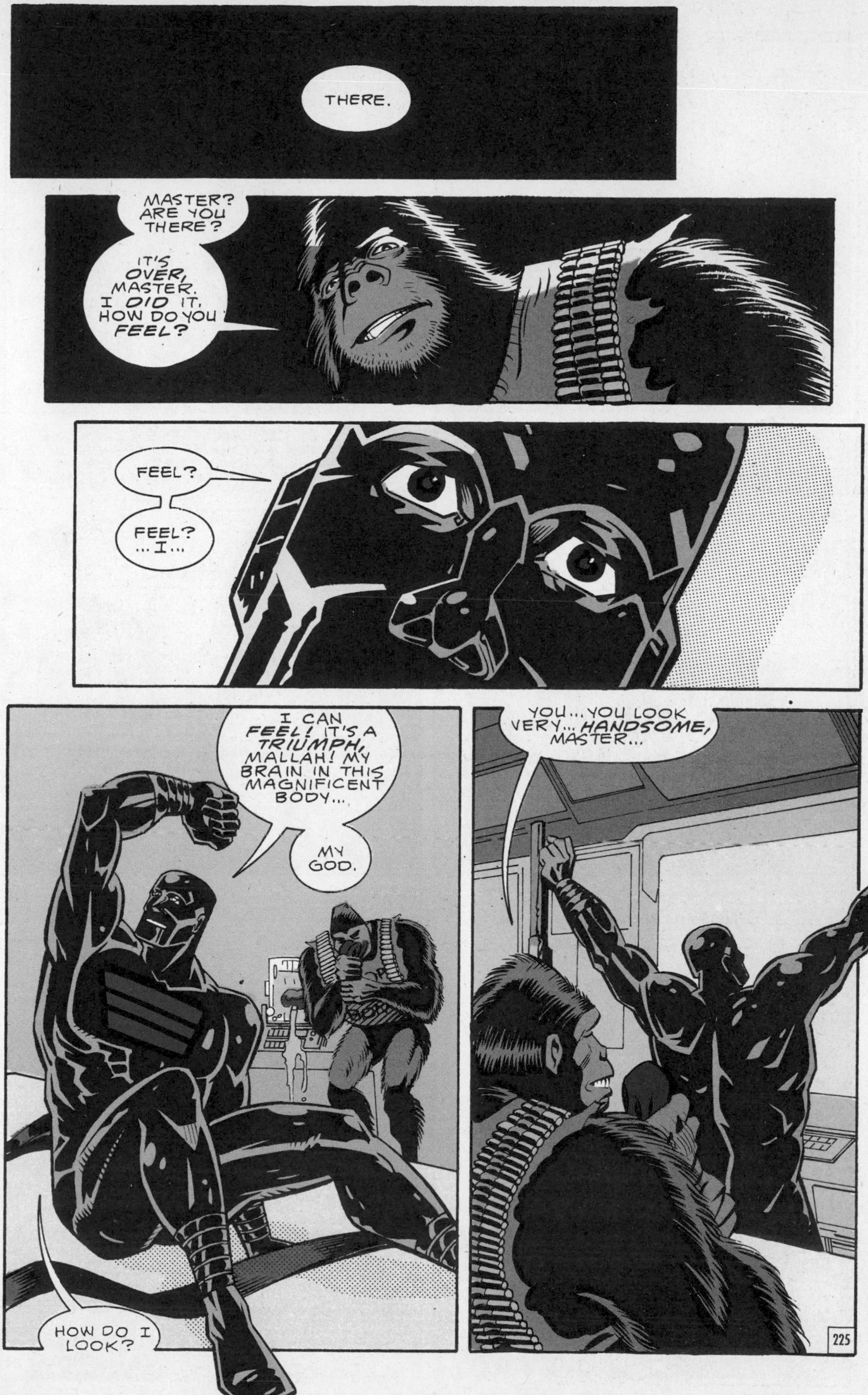
THERE.
MASTER? ARE YOU THERE?
IT'S OVER, MASTER. I DID IT. HOW DO YOU FEEL?
FEEL?
FEEL? ...I...
I CAN FEEL! IT'S A TRIUMPH, MALLAH! MY BRAIN IN THIS MAGNIFICENT BODY...
MY GOD.
HOW DO I LOOK?
YOU...YOU LOOK VERY... HANDSOME, MASTER...

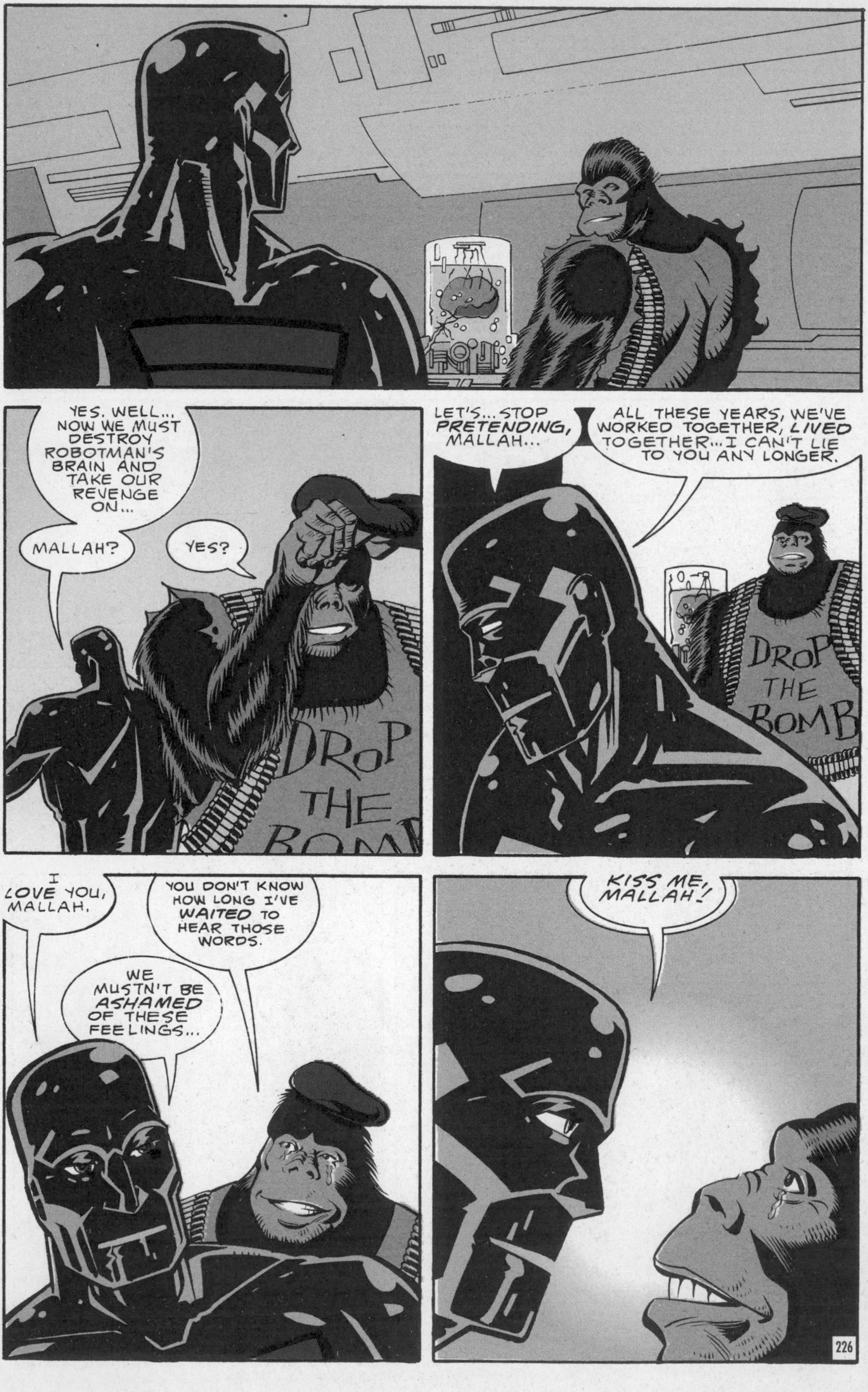
YES. WELL... NOW WE MUST DESTROY ROBOTMAN'S BRAIN AND TAKE OUR REVENGE ON...
MALLAH?
YES?
DROP THE BOMB
LET'S... STOP PRETENDING, MALLAH...
ALL THESE YEARS, WE'VE WORKED TOGETHER, LIVED TOGETHER... I CAN'T LIE TO YOU ANY LONGER.
DROP THE BOMB
I LOVE YOU, MALLAH.
YOU DON'T KNOW HOW LONG I'VE WAITED TO HEAR THOSE WORDS.
WE MUSTN'T BE ASHAMED OF THESE FEELINGS...
KISS ME, MALLAH!

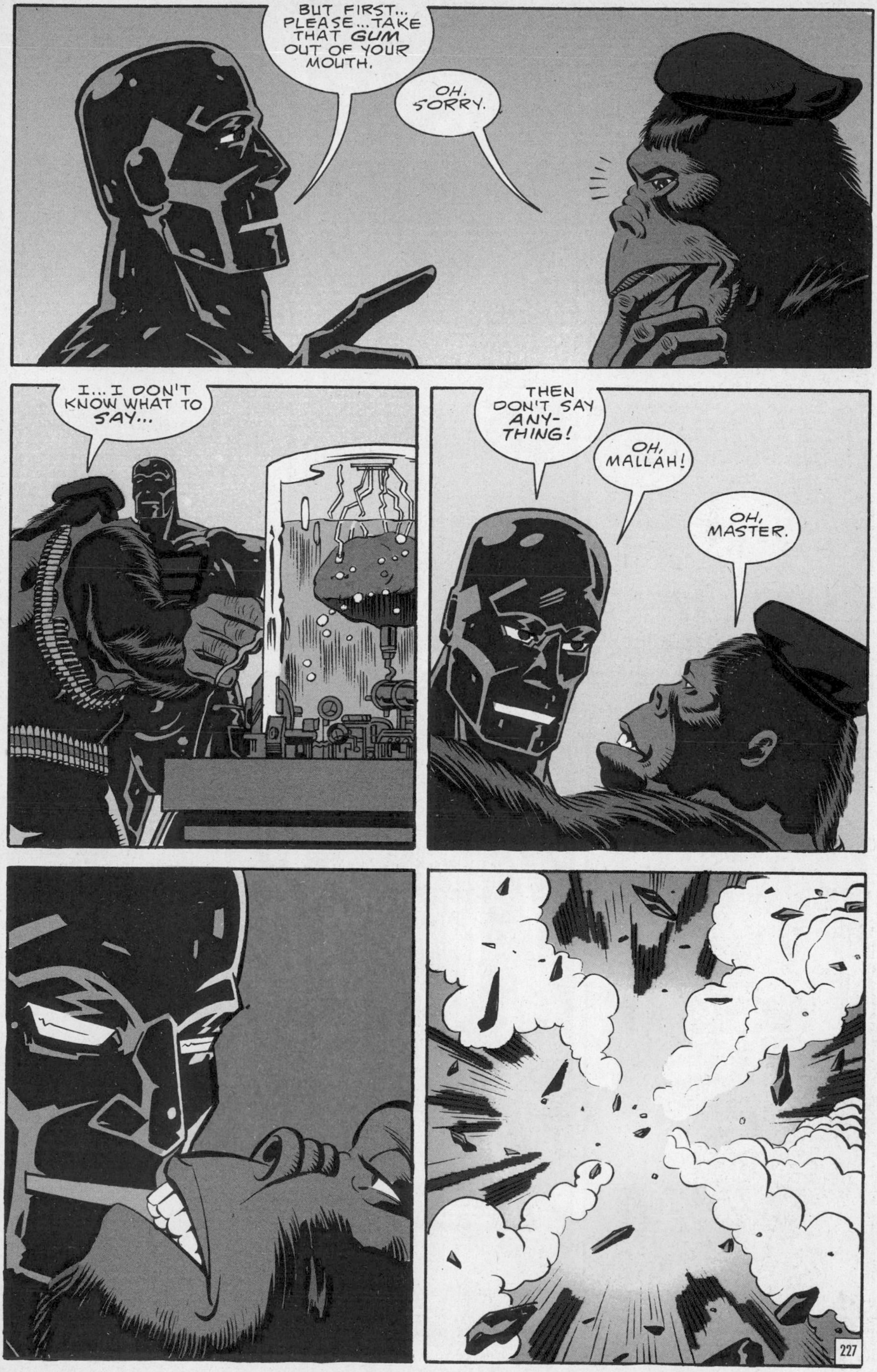

BUT FIRST... PLEASE... TAKE THAT GUM OUT OF YOUR MOUTH.
OH. SORRY.
I... I DON'T KNOW WHAT TO SAY...
THEN DON'T SAY ANY-THING!
OH, MALLAH!
OH, MASTER.

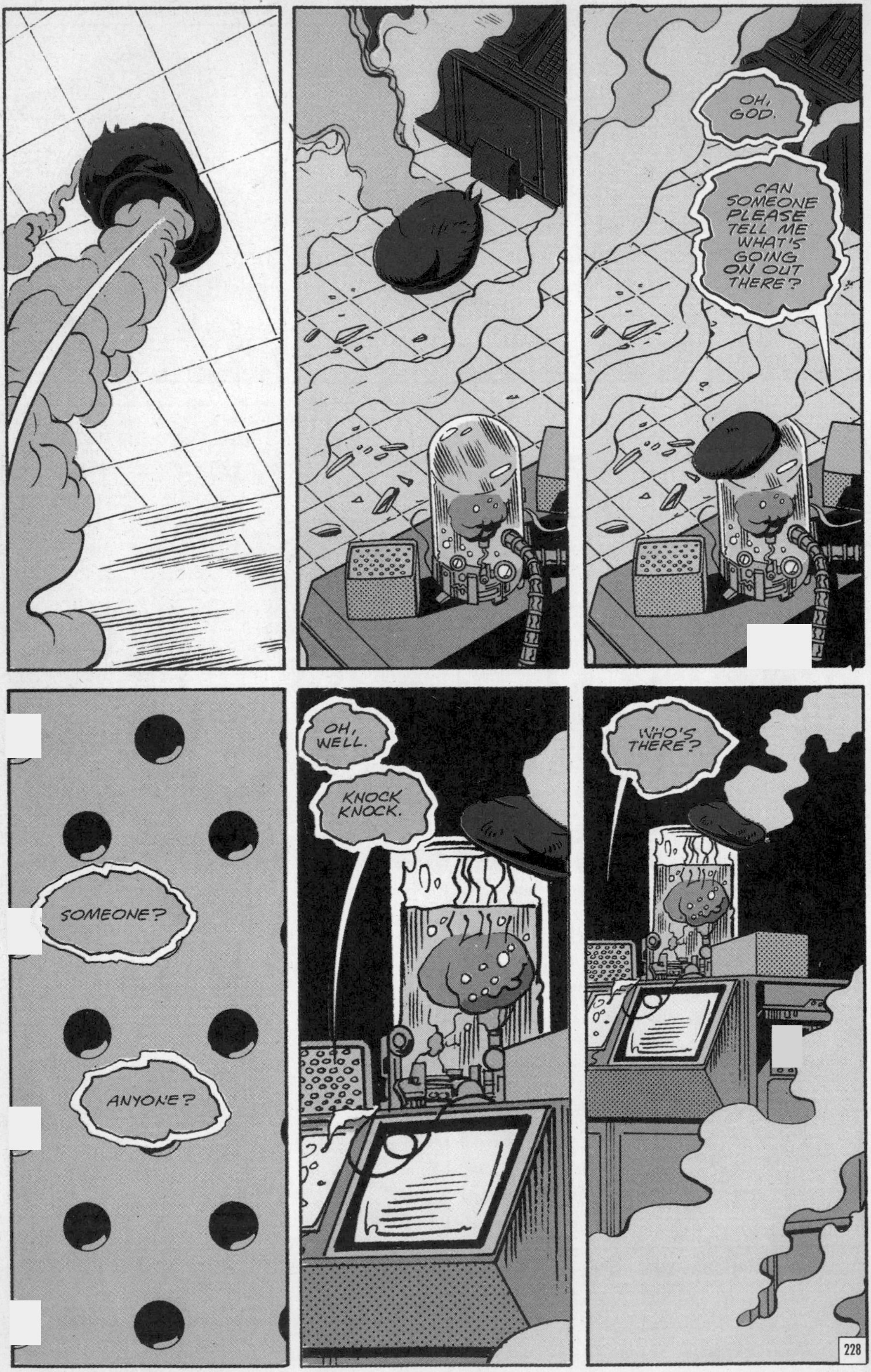
OH, GOD.
CAN SOMEONE PLEASE TELL ME WHAT'S GOING ON OUT THERE?
SOMEONE?
ANYONE?
OH, WELL.
KNOCK KNOCK.
WHO'S THERE?

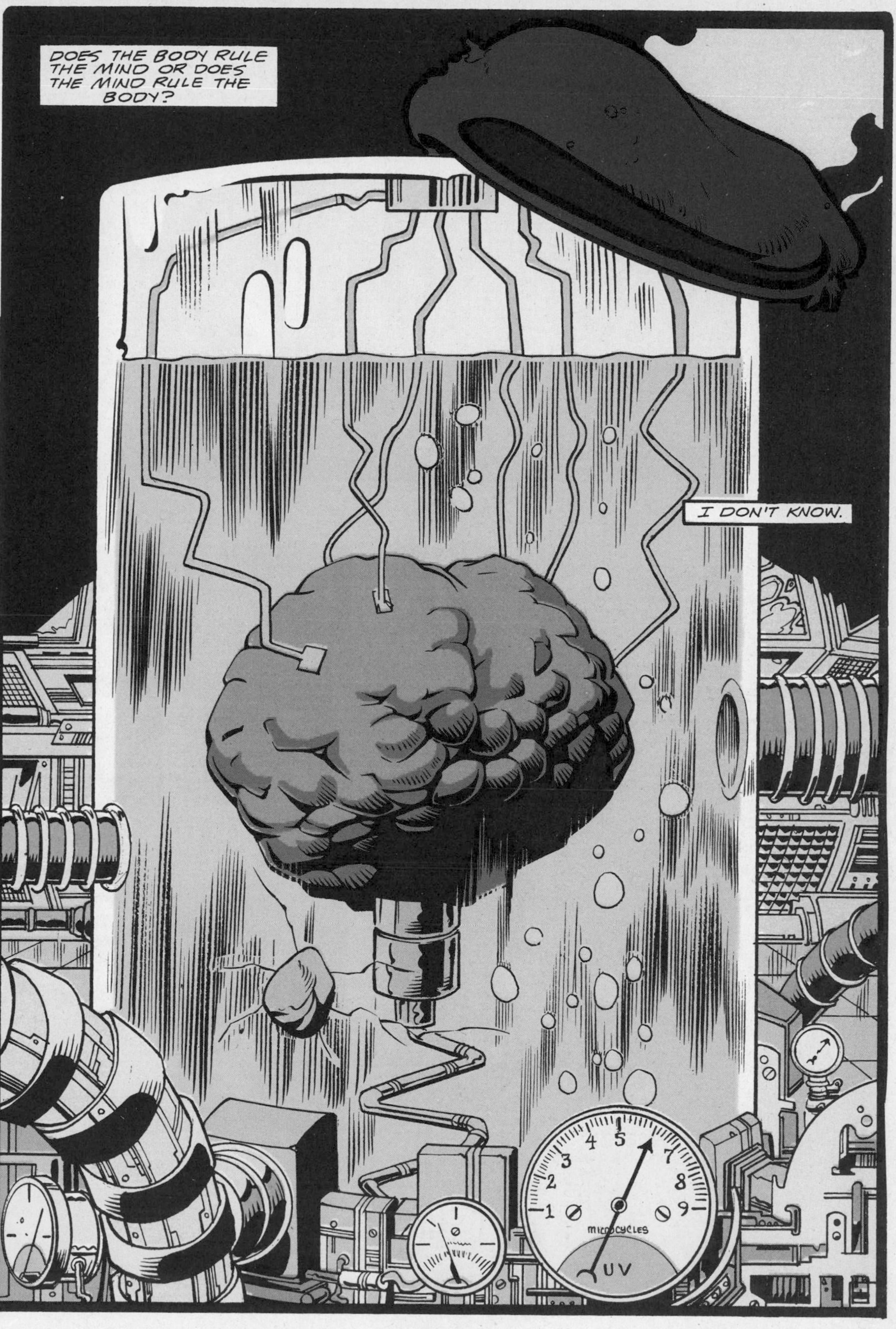
DOES THE BODY RULE THE MIND OR DOES THE MIND RULE THE BODY?
I DON'T KNOW.
MICROCYCLES
UV

THE GRANT MORRISON LIBRARY

ANIMAL MAN

A minor super-hero's consciousness is raised higher and higher until he becomes aware of his own fictitious nature in this revolutionary and existential series.

Volume 1: ANIMAL MAN
With Chas Truog, Doug Hazlewood and Tom Grummett

Volume 2: ORIGIN OF THE SPECIES
With Chas Truog, Doug Hazlewood and Tom Grummett

Volume 3: DEUS EX MACHINA
With Chas Truog, Doug Hazlewood and various

THE INVISIBLES

The saga of a terrifying conspiracy and the resistance movement combatting it — a secret underground of ultra-cool guerrilla cells trained in ontological and physical anarchy.

Volume 1: SAY YOU WANT A REVOLUTION
With Steve Yeowell and Jill Thompson

Volume 2: APOCALIPSTICK
With Jill Thompson, Chris Weston and various

Volume 3: ENTROPY IN THE U.K.
With Phil Jimenez, John Stokes and various

Volume 4: BLOODY HELL IN AMERICA
With Phil Jimenez and John Stokes

Volume 5: COUNTING TO NONE
With Phil Jimenez and John Stokes

Volume 6: KISSING MR. QUIMPER
With Chris Weston and various

Volume 7: THE INVISIBLE KINGDOM
With Philip Bond, Sean Phillips and various

DOOM PATROL
The World's Strangest Heroes are reimagined even stranger and more otherworldly in this groundbreaking series exploring the mysteries of identity and madness.

Volume 1:
CRAWLING FROM THE WRECKAGE
With Richard Case, Doug Braithwaite, Scott Hanna, Carlos Garzon and John Nyberg

Volume 2:
THE PAINTING THAT ATE PARIS
With Richard Case and John Nyberg

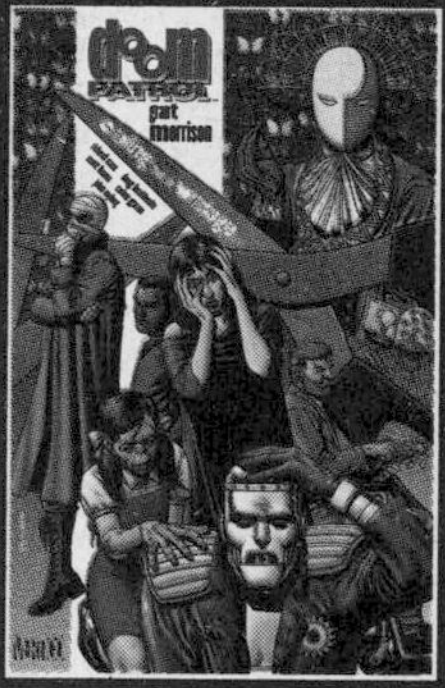
doom PATROL
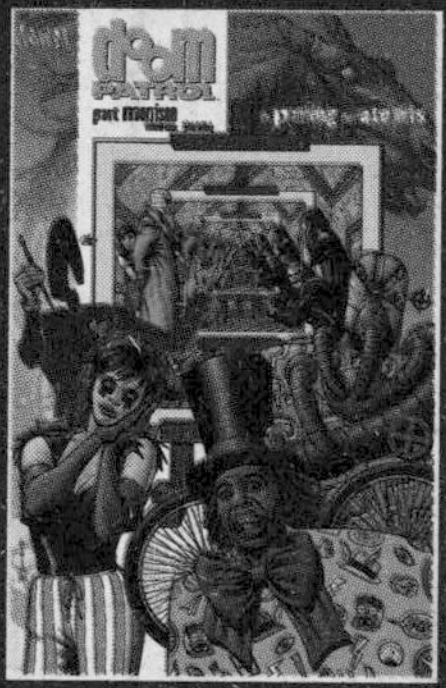
doom PATROL

THE FILTH
With Chris Weston and Gary Erskine

MYSTERY PLAY
With Jon J Muth

SEBASTIAN O
With Steve Yeowell

From VERTIGO
Suggested for mature readers.

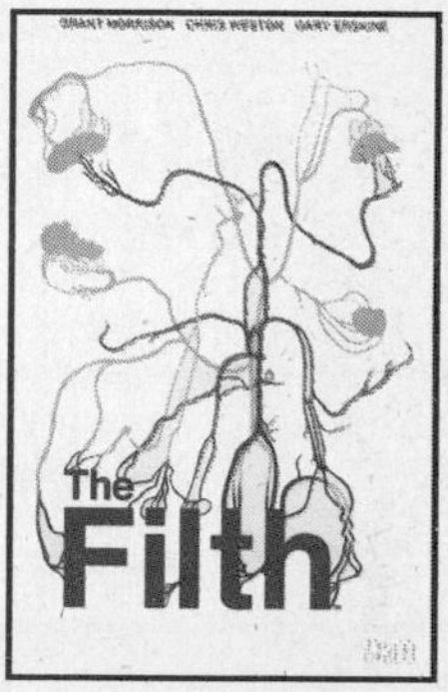
The Filth
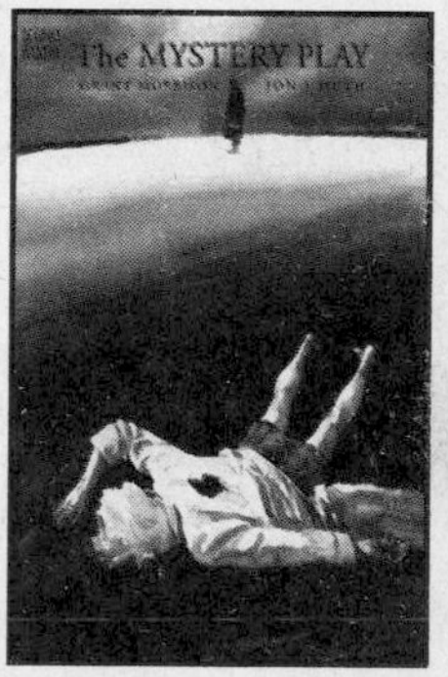
The MYSTERY PLAY
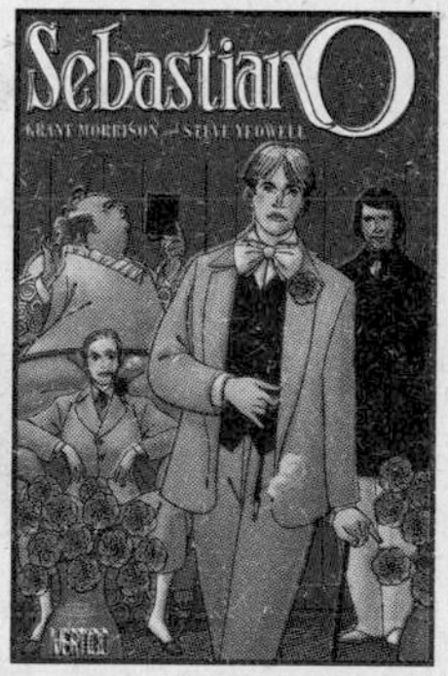
Sebastian O

From DC COMICS

BATMAN: ARKHAM ASYLUM
With Dave McKean

JLA: EARTH 2
With Frank Quitely

JLA: NEW WORLD ORDER
With Howard Porter and John Dell

JLA: AMERICAN DREAMS
With Howard Porter, John Dell and various

JLA: ROCK OF AGES
With Howard Porter, John Dell and various

JLA: ONE MILLION
With Val Semeiks, Prentis Rollins and various

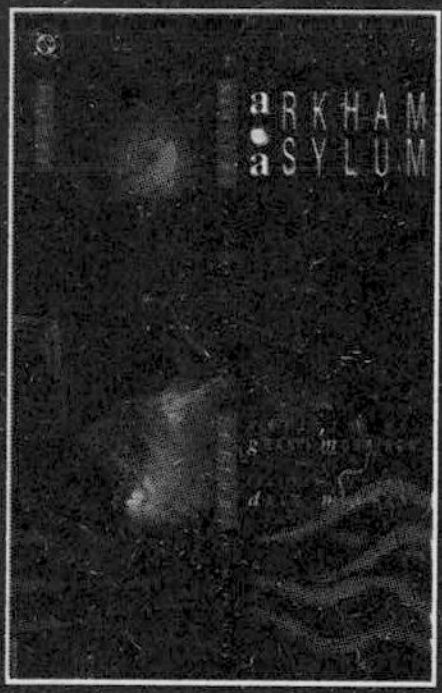
aRKHAM aSYLUM
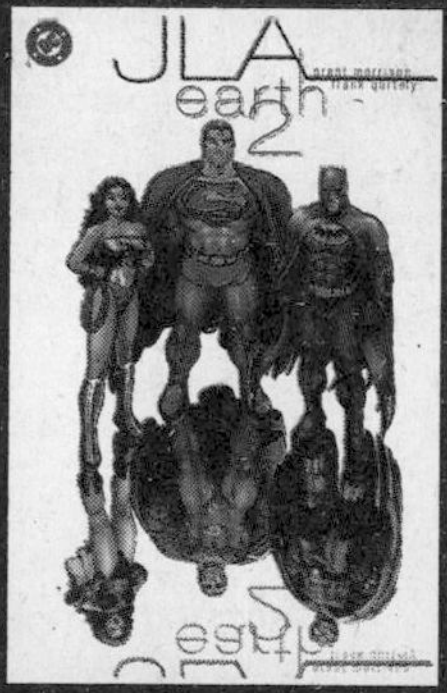
JLA earth 2
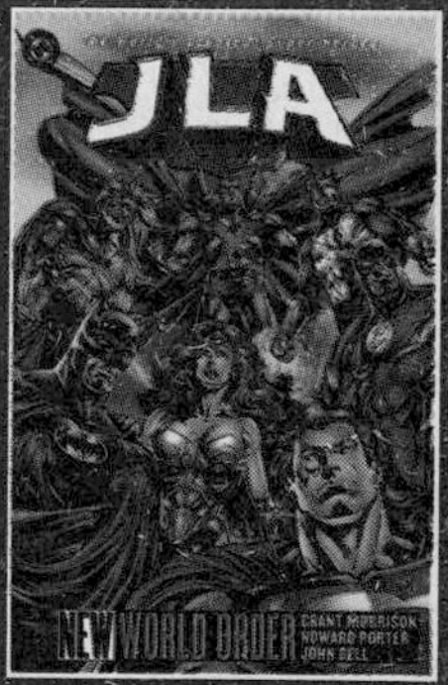
JLA
NEW WORLD ORDER
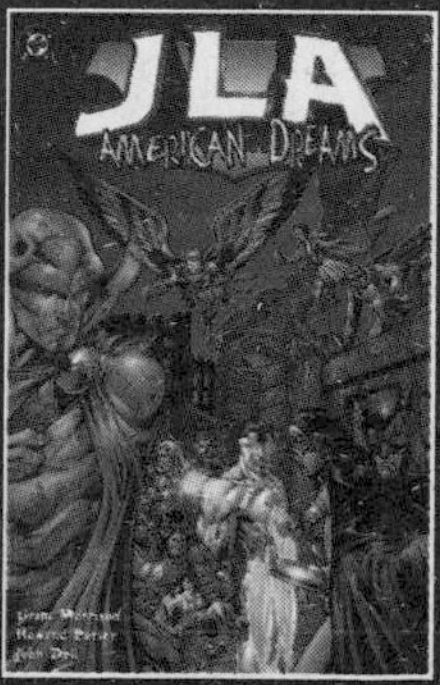
JLA
AMERICAN DREAMS
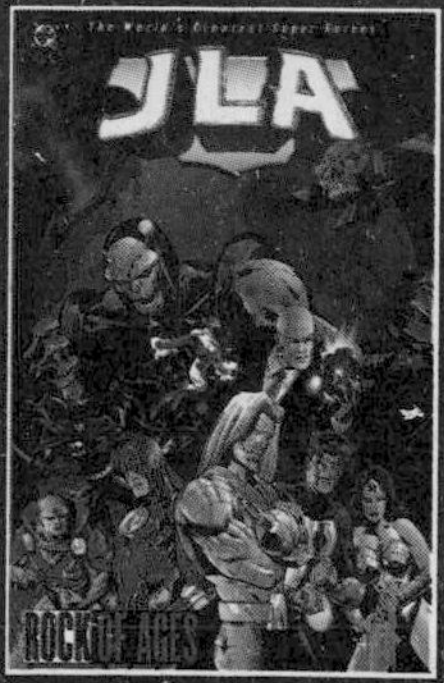
JLA
ROCK OF AGES
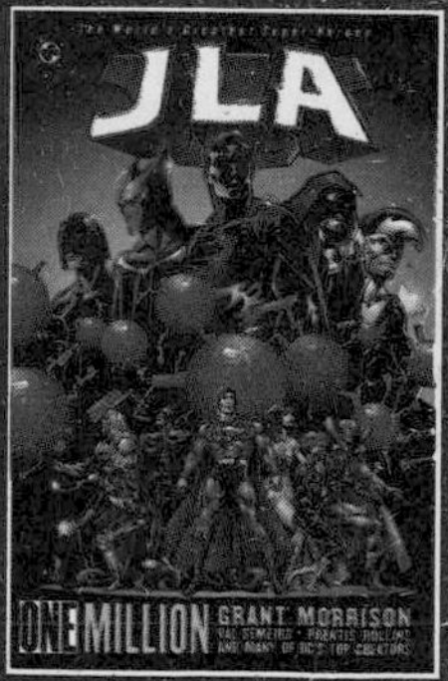
JLA
ONE MILLION GRANT MORRISON